Michael Eldred
Social Ontology of Whoness

Michael Eldred

Social Ontology of Whoness

Rethinking Core Phenomena of Political Philosophy

DE GRUYTER

ISBN 978-3-11-061681-1
e-ISBN (PDF) 978-3-11-061750-4
e-ISBN (EPUB) 978-3-11-061663-7

Library of Congress Control Number: 2018958301

Bibliographic information published by the Deutsche Nationalbibliothek
The Deutsche Nationalbibliothek lists this publication in the Deutsche Nationalbibliografie;
detailed bibliographic data are available on the Internet at http://dnb.dnb.de.

Printing and binding: CPI books, Leck
Cover image: Mutsumi Okada *Crystal Cucumber* 2005 oil on canvas 40 x 40 cm.

www.degruyter.com

For A.
ὃς κάλλιστος ἐν οὐρανῷ ἵσταται ἀστήρ
That fairest star set in heaven
 Homer *Iliad* 22.318

Content

Foreword —— 1

1   By way of introduction: Precious little —— 8

2   Loosening the ground:
     Thinking about society, thinking society —— 21
2.1   Society, needs and wants, language —— 22
2.2   What is λόγος? —— 23
2.3   Opinion: Holding things and each other to be (whatness and
         whoness) —— 25
2.4   Showing oneself off as somewho —— 26
2.5   The openness of three-dimensional time as the enabling dimension
         within which society is situated —— 29
2.6   Living well and being somewho – The need to interrogate the
         tradition —— 32

3   Further outline of the phenomenon of whoness —— 35
3.1   Bearing a name and standing in estimation in the community
         through valuing interplay —— 36
3.2   Human social being as self-presentation and showing-off in the 3D-
         temporal clearing in an interplay of estimable reputability
         (politeness, pride, vulnerability, arrogance, conceit) —— 40
3.3   Further exemplary phenomena of standing and not standing as
         somewho (flattery, manliness) — The existential possibility of
         coming to one's very own, genuine stand as self —— 44
3.3.1   Digression: Dialectic of self and other – Wrestling with Plato,
         Hegel, Heidegger —— 49
3.3.1.1 Preliminary considerations when approaching Plato's and Hegel's
         dialectical thinking —— 49
3.3.1.2 Approaching an existential dialectic of self and other through an
         interpretation of a passage from Plato's *Parmenides* —— 56
3.3.1.3 The Hegelian dialectic of the concept, primal splitting and closing
         together —— 66
3.3.1.4 Heideggerian selfhood as a "shining-back" from
         being-in-the-world —— 72
3.3.1.5 Interpreting the dialectic of primal splitting and closing together
         with regard to selfhood —— 80

4   The satisfaction of wants and the striving to have more — 91
4.1   Economics and chrematistics — 92
4.2   Weber's conception of economic activity — 99
4.3   The Cartesian cast of economics — 104
4.4   Schumpeter's equilibrium theory — 107
4.5   Aristotle on money and exchange — Money as a medium practically
            unifying social usages — 111
4.6   Endless money-making? — 117

5   Ontology of exchange — 122
5.1   Commodity exchange and the necessity of rethinking Aristotelean
            δύναμις — 123
5.2   Productive know-how, acquisitive know-how? — 126
5.3   Commodity exchange not guided
            by the insight of know-how — 129
5.4   Two complementary, reciprocal pairs of δυνάμεις: Reified value and
            desire — 134
5.5   Recapitulation and the coming together of goods in
            commerce — 142
5.5.1   A side-glance at Hegel's treatment of actuality, possibility,
            contingency, necessity and freedom — 145
5.6   Exchange as core phenomenon of social intercourse: Interchange
            and interplay — 153
5.6.1   Reciprocally showing off who one is in the interplay of mutual
            estimation — 158
5.6.2   The interplay of powers of self-presentation – engendering
            trust — 162
5.6.3   Mutual estimation: Personhood, esteem and respect, the power
            play over who-standing and the possible intimacy between
            you-and-me — 166

6   Justice — 170
6.1   Justice as a fundamental social phenomenon of having one's fair
            share (Aristotle) – Strauss' misconception of ontological origins –
            The goods of living: valuable things and esteem – Ongoing
            competitive interplay estimating each other's abilities — 170
6.2   Distributive and commutative justice — 178
6.3   Marxist critiques of capitalist social relations as unjust — 183

6.3.1 The untenability of the labour theory of value as a theory of just exchange masking exploitation —— 183
6.3.2 Groundlessness of sociating interplay —— 192
6.3.3 The untenability of the theory of surplus value as a theory of capitalist exploitation —— 196
6.3.4 Injustice of capitalist wage-labour per se? —— 198
6.4 The just distribution of the goods of living —— 205
6.5 Redistributive social justice, the welfare state and the alleviation of poverty —— 209
6.6 Esteem, honour and fame in social life with a focus on Aristotle and Schopenhauer —— 215
6.7 A just distribution of honour and fame in society? – The (non-)fame of creative recasters of an historical world —— 226
6.8 The gainful game among competitive players —— 230
6.9 Recent debates on justice in Anglophone moral philosophy and the disappearance of commutative justice —— 236
6.9.1 Walzer's plurality of distribution systems —— 239
6.9.2 Conceptions of distributive justice and the welfare state —— 241
6.10 Critical appraisal of Nozickian libertarianism —— 244
6.10.1 The legitimate founding of a state —— 244
6.10.2 The original appropriation of (landed) property —— 247
6.10.3 An attack on libertarian freedom conceived as individual caprice —— 249
6.11 A closer look at Rawls —— 252
6.11.1 The "original position" —— 252
6.11.2 Property-owning democracy —— 257
6.12 Anomalies in the gainful game and the political power play —— 261

7 Interlude and recapitulation with some intermediate conclusions: Everyday living of finite human beings – Security and insecurity —— 267
7.1 Securing the polity of civil society – An initial determination of government (Schmitt, Locke, Kant) – The rule of law —— 267
7.2 Exchange as the starting-point of social living (Plato, Hegel) —— 271
7.3 The reliability of things (Heidegger) —— 273
7.4 Exchange essentially unreliable —— 275

7.5   Free market exchange as both an unreliable and reliable form of
           sociation —— 277
7.6   Money-mediated exchange abstract and reified (Marx) —— 279
7.7   Risky enterprise and secure jobs —— 282

8   **The short reach of Cartesian certainty and Leibniz' principle of reason
           into the social science of economics —— 285**
8.1   Leibniz' principle of reason
           as a general "grand principle" —— 285
8.1.1   Digression: The principle of reason further considered —— 286
8.1.1.1   Leibniz —— 286
8.1.1.2   Hegel —— 289
8.1.1.3   Nietzsche —— 291
8.1.1.4   Heidegger —— 293
8.1.1.5   Anaximander and the fairness of interplay —— 296
8.1.1.6   Deepening the interpretation of Anaximander —— 302
8.2   "The economic law of motion of modern society" (Marx) —— 311
8.3   Adam Smith's notion of labour-value —— 313
8.4   Economics as a quantitative empirical science
           (Aristotle, Hayek) —— 316
8.5   The disclosive truth of markets —— 320
8.6   Stock market estimations of the future —— 323
8.7   Market irrationality, sentiment and psychology as phenomena of
           mood —— 326

9   **Sociation via reified interplay, the invisible and the visible
           hand —— 330**
9.1   Social democracy, reified sociating interplay and caring-for in a
           capitalist economy – Caring for one's own world and indifference to
           others (Heidegger's *Being and Time*) —— 330
9.2   Self-interest and mutual caring-for in exchange interplay —— 340
9.3   Reified sociating interplay and purportedly 'inhuman' alienation of
           human being —— 347
9.4   The wage-labour relation and caring-for – Co-operation and
           conflict – Hierarchy and reified discipline – Economic democracy
           and total economic control —— 353
9.5   The invisible hand and the ontological possibility of a caring
           capitalism – Unlimited economic growth through caring for each
           other —— 359

9.6 The set-up and the endless cycle of self-augmentation of reified value (Marx, Heidegger) – The historical possibility of the side-step into endless mutual caring-for —— 368

9.6.1 The gainful game —— 369

9.6.2 The set-up —— 376

9.7 State intervention in the economic interplay of civil society —— 384

9.8 Uncertainty of income-earning – The 'law' of social inertia and the tendency toward conservation of a way of life – Openness to the future vs. risk-aversion – The ensconcing of particular interests behind protectionist barriers —— 389

9.9 The manifestation of the visible hand in the shape of bureaucracy —— 398

9.10 State intervention as a visible helping hand for the invisible hand – An asserted unconditional right to be cared for – Caring-for that "leaps in" vs. caring-for that "leaps ahead" (Heidegger) —— 399

9.11 The paternalistic 'all-caring' state – Taxation and its tendentially asphyxiating hold on civil society —— 405

10 Social power and government —— 411

10.1 Ontology of social power —— 411

10.1.1 Recapitulation: Various kinds of social power —— 423

10.1.2 Aristotle on social and political power —— 427

10.2 Two related social powers: Rhetoric and the political power of government – Legitimacy, punishment, terror —— 431

10.3 Legitimacy of government further considered – Acceptance and affirmation of government —— 439

10.4 The "restlesse desire of Power after power" and the necessity of the Leviathan – Straussian "vanity" and the inevitable ongoing mutual estimating of who-status and individual powers – The modern individual subject as the foundation and starting-point for deriving the Leviathan —— 445

10.5 Legitimacy of the Leviathan – An arbiter in the "Competition of Riches, Honour, Command, or other power" – The predicament that "nothing is more easily broken than a mans word" —— 453

10.6 The individualization of the truth of being (Protagoras, Heidegger) – The ultimate socio-ontological source of strife – The finite process of resolving differences among individual perspectival views —— 459

10.7   Ontological powerlessness of the metaphysical, productive
        conception of power – The ultimate impotence of both political
        power and rhetoric – Ineluctably sharing an hermeneutic cast of
        the truth of beings in an historical age – Embeddedness of
        individual truth in a shared, historically cast truth – The Geist-Zeit
        and the enpropriation of human being to the clearing of 3D-time –
        Powerlessly free, mutually estimating power interplay, pluralism
        and benign indifference – Fairness as the ethereal ethos of a free
        society —— 470

11   **The socio-ontological constitution of 'we ourselves'** —— 477
11.1   Dialectical movement from the sensuous givenness of world to the
        identity of ego and world – The dialectic of recognition – "*Ego* that
        is *we* and *we* that is *ego*" (Hegel's *Phenomenology*) —— **477**
11.2   Universal self-consciousness and irrepressible, questioning,
        singular individuality – The ever-broken mediation between
        singularity and universality concretely realized in ethical
        life —— **487**
11.3   The question of who: Selfhood, my self, you-and-I (Heidegger's
        1934 lectures and *Being and Time*) —— **494**
11.4   How do we ourselves come about? – Belonging together in a
        situation —— **508**
11.5   Constitution of an historical people – Heidegger's authoritarian,
        anti-liberal casting of "we the people" – The historical decision to
        open up to the future – "We are the coming about of time
        itself" —— **511**
11.6   We the people and singular, rare individuals – The ethos of open-
        mindedness – Abstract personhood, interplay through a reified
        medium and the historical possibility of the free individual –
        The impossible mediation between universality and singularity –
        Singularity's shelter in the abstract rights of particularity –
        Heidegger's conjuring of a "fundamental attunement" among the
        people to support the work of a rare, singular individual —— **520**
11.7   The socio-ontological critique of liberalism – Contract as the
        abstractly universal shell-form for the metabolism of civil society –
        The possibility and ethos of a liberal We in free and fair
        interplay —— **530**

12   Government and the state —— 537
12.1   Recapitulation via Locke: The liberal conception of government, its critique and socio-ontological grounding in the power interplay of civil society —— 537
12.2   The totalitarian state as a counter-casting to liberalism – The yearning for a totally controlled "organic construction" at the pinnacle of productionist metaphysics (Ernst Jünger) —— 547
12.2.1   Heidegger's anti-liberal interpretation of the German tradition in 1933 (W. v. Humboldt, Kant, Hegel) —— 560
12.3   The forever contradictory, moving realization of freedom in civil society and state as power play (Hegel's *Rechtsphilosophie*) —— 569
12.3.1   Diremption of particularity from the universal in civil society and their mediation —— 569
12.3.2   The police and civic corporation as supplements to the interplay of civil society —— 574
12.3.3   A problematic transition from civil society to the state – 'Infinite', singular affirmation of the concept of freedom through an ethos of free and fair interplay – The chimæra of a final resolution of the power play —— 578
12.3.4   The inner constitution of the state and the singularity that remains plural – The endlessly contentious issue of taxation – Never-ending controversy over concrete conceptions of the universal good – The two-way power-mediation between civil society and state - The media and freedom of speech —— 588
12.3.5   Division of powers within the state in accord with the concept of freedom – Hereditary monarchy "outside human freedom" true to the hermeneutic cast of productionist metaphysics – The concept of freedom does not come to a unified closure – The people's (mis-)trust of the state —— 594
12.3.6   The transition from civil society to state reconsidered: The power play over sociating estimation and identity in belonging to a political whole — Constitutional rules of play for the ongoing political power struggle —— 599
12.3.7   The reality of freedom as the shared, ethical social living of a people and its fracturing, through which free societies remain in flux —— 602
12.3.8   Hegel's critique of the liberal conception of state – Kant's "idea of the original contract" —— 604

12.3.9   Pre-ontological ethical 'second nature' and ontological insight into the political realm —— **607**
12.3.10   The dispensability of the philosopher king and the precipitation of socio-ontological structures in historically lived, ethical usages —— **611**

13   Democracy —— 617
13.1   Democracy, competitive electoral struggle and majority will vs. individual freedom —— **617**
13.1.1   The political power struggle for estimation as a worthy politician – The government's power to enact concrete policy and its mirroring in democratic public debate – The infection of the universal good with particular interests – Protectionism —— **617**
13.1.2   The tendential danger of the dissolution of freedom in merely democratically mediated, state-posited will – The erosion of the freedom of interplay through the sham universal of redistributive social justice – Constitutional law as a bulwark against merely positive law —— **624**
13.1.3   Schumpeter's competition theory of democracy – The democratic We not merely a summation of individual wills – The legitimacy of democratically elected government – The vacillating vagaries of democratic electoral power struggles – The necessary universality of the democratic vote —— **628**
13.1.4   The socio-ontological isomorphism between the competitive gainful game and the competitive democratic struggle for political power more closely considered – The democratic constitution of a people as We with its customary way of life – Democracy's wavering course between an appetite for freedom and a craving for security —— **636**
13.1.5   Carl Schmitt's critique of the "parliamentary law-making state"– The contradiction between formal law-making procedures and substantial rights – Direct plebiscitary democracy —— **645**
13.2   Democracy, freedom and justice: A recapitulation —— **658**

14   Global whoness and global power plays —— 666
14.1   Whoness of a people —— **666**
14.2   The state as the universal that remains particular in the interplay among foreign powers —— **671**
14.3   Brute international power interplays —— **673**

14.4   Nationalism, protectionism and free, estimative power interplay
          among peoples —— 675

15   Bibliography —— 677

16   Index —— 684

Foreword

This new edition of my social ontology, first published in 2008, appears with a new title and subtitle: *Social Ontology of Whoness: Rethinking core phenomena of political philosophy*. The new title is meant to demarcate the distinctive character of this social ontology from the social ontology that has recently emerged as an interest in mainstream analytic philosophy and social science. Whoness names a socio-ontological concept of human being itself in society. It cannot be defined in a couple of sentences, but has to be unfolded in a conceptual development, starting from the inconspicuous and apparently trivial distinction between who and what, which are not merely linguistic features, but phenomena that show themselves in their own right. Recent mainstream social ontology should be properly named a social ontology of intersubjectivity, for it tacitly presupposes as unquestionably given that human being itself is to be understood *as* the subjectivity of the conscious subject with its intentionality. This conscious subject remains a what, a *res cogitans* or 'cogitating thing', even when it is given a psychological identity. Intentionality itself is the directedness of the subject's consciousness toward its object that is represented in consciousness. The social character of this subjectivity is then supposed to be captured by the collective or group nature of this intentionality: a shared directness of the intentions of subjective consciousness in the plural.[1]

As far as I can see, there is no attempt whatsoever made to conceptually develop and ground this conception of social human being. It remains simply one of the argumentative -ism positions within analytic philosophy, viz. "ontological individualism".[2] Nor is there any attempt to deal with the anomalies of an ontology of intersubjectivity embedded in presumably the most serious attempt at such an ontology, to wit, that of Edmund Husserl. There is no grappling with the question of the 'inter' in intersubjectivity,[3] but rather an ontologically naive

---

[1] Not only the sharedness of intentionality remains a crucial philosophical problem, but already the nature of intentionality itself, which presents a challenge to phenomenological thinking, albeit that analytic philosophy ignores it. Heidegger puts it thus in 1925: "What it means to say that what is intended is part of what belongs to the intention is obscure." ([...] was die Mitgehörigkeit des Intentum zur Intentio besagt, ist dunkel. *GA*20:63) Richard Rorty mistranslates this as the philosophical task of clearing up "the togetherness of *intentum* and *intentio*" (*Essays on Heidegger and Others* 1991 p. 61).

[2] Cf. Epstein, B. 'A Framework for Social Ontology' *Philosophy of the Social Sciences* 2016, Vol. 46(2) pp. 147–167.

[3] Cf. Eldred, M. 'Husserls Krisis: Fragen an die transzendentale Phänomenologie' 2017.

https://doi.org/10.1515/9783110617504-202

presupposing that this 'inter' is obvious and needs no interrogating. The individual is assumed as an individual subject without any attempt to explicate the subjectivity of this subject, its individuality or the sociality of this presupposed subjectivity as intersubjectivity.[4] Thus this new mainstream social ontology (one could say: shamelessly) skips over its most crucial foundational questions. This leads to the new subtitle of the present treatise.

The "rethinking" in the subtitle indicates this inquiry's character as a work demanding of the reader a willingness to think through in a connected, conceptual way the phenomena that are presented consecutively. This way of proceeding stands in stark contrast to scholarly works or social-scientific studies in which concepts are quickly introduced in brief definitions that presuppose that they are 'always already' understood without further ado, so that the phenomena in question are merely talked *about* rather than being thought *through*. Conventional studies do not demand a rethinking and re-vising enabling the social phenomena to present *themselves* differently from their initial, preconceived looks, namely, as phenomena pertaining to the *whoness of sociating human being*.

This deficiency is related to the naive preconception of ontology itself, in which there is no appreciation whatsoever of the *ontological difference* that characterizes all ontology (albeit of whatness: essence, quidditas) since its inception in Aristotle's *Metaphysics* as the investigation of τὸ ὂν ᾗ ὄν, i.e. of beings qua beings, of beings simply insofar *as* they are beings. The ᾗ ('as' or 'qua') in this classic formulation of the ontological difference is the *apophantic as* sayable in propositions because Aristotle locates truth in the λόγος, i.e. in propositions,[5] which can be either true or false. The *hermeneutic as*, by contrast, derives from the disclosive truth in understanding of the phenomenon in view itself, which is per se pre-linguistic, although articul*able* in language. The apophantic As is at work already in Plato's determination of language as λέγειν τὶ κατὰ τινός, i.e. saying something *about* something, addressing it *as* such-and-such. Correspondingly, the hermeneutic As names the circumstance that we humans always already understand all phenomena, even the most apparently

---

4 This criticism applies also to all kinds of pragmatism (e.g. William James, John Dewey, Charles Sanders Peirce, Robert Brandom, Richard Rorty, Richard J. Bernstein). Rorty, for instance, claims that "the search for objective truth is [...] a search for the widest possible intersubjective agreement." (*Truth and Progress* 1998 p. 63).

5 This continues to hold for mainstream philosophy up to the present day, despite its being philosophically challenged for well-nigh a century by the disclosive truth of the phenomena themselves which, in turn, is tied intimately to the hermeneutic As. Cf. Heidegger, M. *Sein und Zeit* (1927) and also his earlier lectures.

trivial, that come into view *as* such-and-such, even prior[6] to articulating this understanding in language, i.e. in propositions of any kind. Such understanding may well be also a misunderstanding, but it must be kept in mind that every *mis*understanding is also a mis*understanding*. The phenomena themselves can also show themselves *deceptively*, i.e. without full disclosure.

With Aristotle, the leading determination of the being of a being *as* such is its οὐσία, meaning literally 'beingness', but traditionally translated as 'substance' or 'essence' (quidditas, Wassein, whatness). The ontological difference is that between beings grasped in their ostensibly naked, 'ontic' facticity — as all modern natural and social science, in its entrenched ontological naivety, self-deludingly presupposes it does — and beings understood explicitly in their mode of being, that is, in the way they present themselves to the human mind *as* the beings they are, to be understood *as* such. The *as* is italicized to underscore its character as hermeneutic, interpretive. Beings are 'always already' understood, i.e. interpreted, in their beingness *as* such-and-such, and this interpretation is always historical within a given age. This hermeneutic *as* interposes itself between beings and their beingness, i.e. in the ontological difference that is everywhere denied and suppressed by all modern, positivist science, both natural and social) as well as by its hand-maiden, analytic philosophy.

The denial of the ontological difference with its hermeneutic *as* leads to recent mainstream social ontology's naively presupposing the validity of its own implicit unexamined pre-ontological preconceptions and prejudices. This is not a matter of an innocent oversight, nor is it a conspiracy, but is the outcome of the consummation of Western history in modern scientific knowledge, both natural and social, that is fixated on controlling movement and change of every conceivable kind. For this scientific way of thinking, history has already reached its end-point and has ostensibly closed in closing off the philosophical questioning still possible *as long as the ontological difference remains historically open*. For it is only within and from the ontological difference that the historical (re)casting of an alternative hermeneutic As can be even conceived and thus undertaken.

In the present historical time of the modern age, the interpretation of thingly beings (whats) is unquestionably and self-evidently *as* objects, the very opposite of their interpretation in Greek philosophy *as* ὑποκείμενα, i.e. *as* subjects. Their beingness in the modern age is their objectivity vis-à-vis subjective con-

---

6 The 'priority' here is not merely chronological, but ontological. Kant would call it transcendental a priori.

sciousness within which they re-present themselves *as* objects. With Descartes and Kant as the most famous representatives of subject/object metaphysics, we have inherited explicitly developed and minutely thought-through ontologies of the objectivity of objects as essential parts of their respective metaphysics of the subjectivity of the subject. The beingness of beings, the objectivity of objects, the subjectivity of subjects all emerge from the ontological difference which they interrogate and which has since been forgotten and repressed by modern mainstream philosophy. The other part of metaphysics, from its inception on, has always been the 'theological' investigation of the supreme being, no matter whether this supreme being is conceived as a god, or God, or the idea of the good (Plato), the idea of the fair (Aristotle), the highest good (Kant), the Absolute (Hegel), the will to power (Nietzsche), or whatever, whereby the beingness of beings (as idea or οὐσία) is often conflated with, and regarded simply as, a being (τὸ ὄν). All metaphysical thinking is thus bipartitely onto-theological, and the two parts are often confused.

A representative of recent analytic social ontology may now well say that this is all very interesting for the history of ideas, but is hardly pertinent to social ontology in the context of modern science, both natural and social, which has cut all theological ties. But is this really so? Even, and especially, when analytic philosophy and science eschew any consideration of the ontological difference, even when superficially readopting the term 'ontology' as long lost metaphysical child, they are both deeply embedded — whether they know it or not and whether they like it or not — in the ontology of subjectivity. They both also have a tacit 'theological' orientation, namely, toward the absolute will to effective power over all kinds of movement and change, both natural and social, which relies on the beingness of beings being pre-ontologically conceived *as* whatness. This hidden god of modern science, the will to effective power that has been covertly at work in all ontology since Plato and Aristotle, is all the more effective and its hold is all the more insidious for its being covert, for then it remains conveniently beyond questioning. Therefore it comes as no surprise that both analytic philosophy and modern science vehemently ward off with all available means any attempt to reopen the ontological difference, finally closed off through the rise of positivism, to reveal the hermeneutic *as* through which all beings are interpreted and understood in their modes of being in the present age. The hegemony of the modern scientific way of thinking has established its hold ubiquitously. For instance, why is it that average, everyday understanding will accept everywhere, even in the media, mention of space-time curvature as a proven 'fact' of mathematized physics, whereas reference to the ontological difference is met everywhere with stares of blank incomprehension?

Recent analytic social ontology baldly posits collective (or group) intention of will as its starting-point, thus revealing obliquely its commitment to the will to effective power, for this collective, willed intention aims at some kind of realization, i.e. a change, in the world proceeding precisely from this collective will. The "building blocks" (Epstein 2016) of the social ontology are said to be collective, willed intentions, whether it be the intention to achieve an intended goal or the collective intention to set up a given social institution such as a university, or the collective intention expressed in an agreement to set up the norm of a certain social convention. For instance, money itself is purported to be instituted by such a collective willed intention. The building blocks of the social world are thus conceived *as* proceeding from the individual will of individual subjects of consciousness collected in some way into a collectivity of conscious will. The ontological intentionality of these collective intentions is not explicated, unfolded or grounded, but taken for granted 'as read'. Given that each individual consciousness is purportedly enclosed somehow in a subjective interior, how is a collectivity of will at all possible? The question is not even posed by recent mainstrean social ontology.

Nor is even the subjectivity of the individual subject explicitly unfolded, but taken as a given obviousness. Indeed, recent social ontology is content to muse over such "social facts" (Epstein 2016) of group intention, etc. and their relation to other given facts, invariably expressed in propositions, i.e. statements (λόγοι), resulting ostensibly in explanations "about the way the social world is built" (Epstein 2016). For this recent analytic social ontology, a social fact asserted in a proposition is grounded ontologically in terms of other facts explaining why the social fact asserted actually *exists*. Ontology is thus reduced to grounded statements of existence, without ever asking what existence itself means nor about differing modes of existence, such as that between *who* and *what*, or between the individuality and collectivity of subjects.

All these questions would require reopening the *ontological difference* that is held so tightly closed in the present age, one could say, 'for dear life'. Instead of sticking with a social phenomenon to closely look at, i.e. intuit, it itself, it is replaced by a proposition asserting such-and-such, whose existential validity is then explained in terms of other propositions expressing other facts. In this way, the gaze is averted persistently and consistently from the phenomenon in question itself, ostensibly with ontological intent. This is hardly what counts as ontology in the long and rich tradition of Western thinking since Plato and Aristotle. To talk of "collective intentions" in any genuinely socio-ontological sense requires at the very least an ontology of intentionality itself as an aspect of the ontology of subjective will which, in turn, is an aspect of conscious subjectivity.

Such ontology of subjectivity and objectivity has to be explicitly laid on the table for close scrutiny. It is woefully inadequate to simply assume the factual existence of "individuals" as conscious subjects and argue for a position of "individualism". What mode of social being is an individual in modern society? What mode of social being is collectivity in modern society? The individual is not a bare social fact, but itself a certain historical kind of what I call 'sociation'. This socio-ontological interrogation as to the individuality of the individual is expressly taken up and unfolded stepwise in the body of this inquiry, along with the question of 'collectivity', i.e. the sociating of a We. Such interrogation is only possible because the present inquiry is not oblivious to the ontological difference and does not blithely skip over the crucial, simple, but fundamental questions.

Let us now set out on our way (for those of you wanting to come with me) to make way, thinking through a phenomenology of whoness in order to see anew, reinterpret and thus recast core phenomena of political philosophy, including critical social theory and the critique of capitalism. I regard this hermeneutic recasting of socio-ontological phenomena as a crucial task of philosophical thinking in our age for the sake of the next historical age in which philosophy has relearned to see the ontological difference and, prior to that, has learned to see the 3D-temporal clearing that enables the ontological difference. The present age is that of the consummation of Western metaphysical thinking which has culminated in positivist modern science, both natural and social, that is (not without motivation) wilfully oblivious to its own ontological underpinnings. Analytic philosophy's raison d'être is to serve faithfully as ancillary to modern scientific thinking. Its covert mission, more or less unbeknowns to itself, is to keep the lid on the ontological difference to prevent any hermeneutic interrogation of the beingness of beings in our own time. This is very different from the historical situation during the transition from the medieval to the modern age when the crucial philosophical task was liberation of the mind from the grasp of Christian theological thinking, for which philosophy was *ancilla theologiae*, to establish the modern metaphysics of willed, conscious subjectivity with its intentionality, starting with Descartes, who posited the self-certain ego as the ontological bedrock that continues to serve unquestioned, albeit tacitly, as such for all modern science. This Cartesian positing has cast us moderns into a certain, seemingly unshakeable and immutable, hermeneutic cast of mind that has long since become blind dogma, just as Christian theological thinking was the dogma of the medieval age.

The other prong of the transition from the middle ages to the modern age is that from feudal to bourgeois-capitalist society, which was accompanied by the political philosophies announcing and positing the free individual subject and the entire problematic of social and political freedom that has come powerfully to the fore in recent centuries. These influential original political philosophies (say, those of Hobbes and Locke), however, lack solid socio-ontological underpinnings, remaining mired in an ontological naivity. The free modern subject was somehow assumed to be the conscious ego-subject posited by Descartes, but its social nature has to date never been laid out in an explicit social ontology. The present work undertakes to do just that. Whether this message (Capurro) will one day get through? The core of this social ontology is one of sociating movement, a kind of movement sui generis I call *mutually estimative interplay* to be strictly distinguished from the sole kind of movement whose ontology has hitherto been worked out (originally by Aristotle), which is one of effective causal movement tied down to one-dimensional linear time, i.e. productive kinesis. For all its talk and analysis of political power and political power plays, political philosophy has never thought through an alternative ontology of *sociating* movement adequate to the phenomenality of social power, nor has it even ever felt to need to do so.

Interplay is therefore a crucial concept in the present inquiry, in a way the equivalent to the concept of value in Marx's dialectical theory of capitalism in *Das Kapital* (which will turn out to be intimately related to the ontology of sociating movement). On the basis of the concept of interplay, the phenomenon of *freedom* can be approached as a characteristic of the sociating movement of interplay thus showing, among other things, that all freedom, if it is anything at all, is social freedom and also that all freedom, for better or for worse, is a *power* interplay. Of which, much more later in this study.

> You must not forsake the ship in a tempest because you cannot rule and keep down the winds. No, nor you must not labour to drive into their heads new and strange information which you know well shall be nothing regarded with them that be of clean contrary minds. But you must with a crafty wile and a subtle train study and endeavour yourself, as much as in you lieth, to handle the matter wittily and handsomely for the purpose; ... Howbeit, this communication of mine, though peradventure it may seem unpleasant to them, but can I not see why it should seem strange or foolishly newfangled.
>
> Thomas More *Utopia* Book I

ME, Cologne, June 2018

1 By way of introduction: Precious little

Singularity hyperborean
Throbbing crystal
Precious little

καὶ περιττὰ μὲν καὶ θαυμαστὰ καὶ χαλεπὰ καὶ δαιμόνια εἰδέναι αὐτοὺς φάσιν, ἄχρηστα δ᾽,
ὅτι οὐ τὰ ἀνθρώπινα ἀγαθὰ ζητοῦσιν.

Aristotle Eth. Nic. Z 7 1141b7ff

> And while people say that they [thinkers such as Anaxagoras and Thales] understand
> things that are extraordinary, astounding, difficult and even superhuman, they neverthe-
> less claim that they are useless because they do not seek what is good for human beings.

Philosophical knowledge is useless, although common opinion may concede it
to be, as Aristotle puts it, "extraordinary, astounding, difficult and even super-
human". This knowledge does not embody practical reason directly applicable
to the practices of human living, but is theoretical speculation to be indulged in
only by those with the leisure to extricate themselves from involvement in
pragmatic affairs and escape to rarified climes supposedly divorced from the so-
called 'real world'.[7]

Abstract speculation seems to characterize philosophy in its more esoteric
mode and serves as a justification for why it can be put to one side by normal
mortals. Abstraction from what is palpably present to the senses or can be imagined in concrete terms with some reference to experience is difficult and strenuous for the unpractised mind to perform, and only in the case of mathematics,
whose abstractness is at least justified in the end to common sense by its practical application in technological feats such as suspension bridges, space travel
or genetic editing, does this abstractness appear to be worth the effort of mas-

---

7 "One can call philosophy a kind of luxury insofar as luxury designates those enjoyments and
preoccupations that do not belong to external necessity as such. Insofar, philosophy is certainly dispensable. However, the crucial point is what is to be called necessary. From the aspect of
mind and spirit, philosophy can be posited precisely as that which is most necessary." (Die
Philosophie kann man [...] eine Art von Luxus nennen, eben insofern Luxus diejenigen Genüsse und Beschäftigungen bezeichnet, die nicht der äußeren Notwendigkeit als solcher angehö-
ren. Insofern ist die Philosophie allerdings entbehrlich. Es kommt aber darauf an, was man
notwendig nennt. Von seiten des Geistes kann man die Philosophie gerade als das Notwendigs-
te setzen. G.W.F. Hegel *Vorlesungen über die Geschichte der Philosophie I* Werke Band 18 Suhrkamp, Frankfurt/M. S. 70) All translations from German are my own. Those from the Greek are
at least modified by me.

https://doi.org/10.1515/9783110617504-001

tering. Common sense is only prepared to more or less mistrustfully concede abstract thinking a place if it can ultimately prove its worth in practical life. Abstract algebra, for instance, can justify its existence by providing the mathematical theory that allows unbreakable encryption codes for electronic banking to be generated. When philosophy claims that there would not even be any such thing as electronics and digital technology, nor even electric power, without the thinking done at the heart of philosophy, this claim is greeted with boundless skepticism, since it seems patently otherwise, namely, that scientists, mathematicians and engineers worked for generations to develop such technologies and also their abstract theoretical foundations. To trace a line back to philosophy itself as the birthplace of technological knowledge would require thinking philosophically, and it is precisely this enterprise that seems to be less than worthwhile, not only for ordinary lay persons, but also for the highly educated. At best, such a tracing is apparently of interest only for a scholarly history of ideas in which initial, crude notions purportedly have evolved and been scientifically refined over the centuries. This perspective allows modern science to look back condescendingly on these putatively crude first beginnings of science. But what if this ancient Greek thinking were superior to modern scientific thinking?

It seems, even and especially to the highly educated today, that one can talk reasonably about the deepest secrets of the universe, such as the nature of time or life or thinking, without having to bother about philosophical, 'metaphysical' notions and 'speculations' that purportedly have long since been discredited and dispensed with by science with its experimental method. Indeed, philosophical speculations about time or life or thinking today, it is claimed, have been superseded by more reliable, empirically based, scientific knowledge. Einsteinian relativity theory is said to have theoretically captured the nature of time with its mathematical construction of 4D-space-time.

Even the mere word 'speculation' (Gr. θεωρεῖν, θεωρία) today has a pejorative ring, whereas in earlier times it was an honourable title for philosophical thinking itself. This inversion in status should give us pause. Experiments with light can be set up to test the notion of time in relativity theory. Life is the object of knowledge in modern, experimental biology with its diverse branches, including molecular biology and the digital decoding of the human genome, all of which tacitly assume that the secret of life itself will eventually be revealed in efficient-causal terms, say, by studying simple life-forms such as yeast. The nature of human thinking itself can be investigated in neurophysiology and modelled in computers, under the unexamined preconception that thinking itself is a function of the material brain, so that science can pronounce that it is an excusable delusion to believe that you yourself think; rather that it is your brain that thinks whilst simultaneously generating the illusion that you are thinking yourself. What need is there still in these areas for philosophy, which can provide no empirical evidence apart from apparently naive, trivial, general statements? Instead, don't data need to be collected, and treated and filtered by sophisticated statistical methods which have only been available for around a century? Doesn't our knowledge have to be based on verifiable and verified hard facts? Isn't truth a matter of fact?

Even the world's most prestigious universities today subscribe to the view that philosophy has outlived its usefulness for the deepest questions confronting humanity today, which is reflected in the granting of research funds to universities and institutes. Philosophy is preserved as a kind of venerable artefact of the West's cultural heritage, commemorating its historical beginnings and immured in ivory tower humanities departments where scholars spend their days, while the really crucial, 'relevant' thinking, the thinking that ultimately makes a difference to how we live today, gets done in institutes of natural and social science. The distinction popular today among the educated between 'soft' and 'hard' science or knowledge reflects entrenched prejudices of mind. 'Soft' knowledge is regarded as a kind of cultural embellishment to living that relies on 'fuzzy' concepts about things like humankind's 'humanity', its 'soul', etc. 'Hard' science, by contrast, is unquestioningly taken to be where the important, decisive thinking with 'real' effects in the world and 'real' implications for humankind, gets done.

So it has to be asked whether the opinion commonly held by popular understanding, the media and educated elites regarding the dispensability of philosophy in this age overlooks something. This something must have to do with the specific business of philosophy, which is thinking itself, i.e. learning through long effort and practice to think, and not the history of ideas. In the Foreword I have even named one crucial, necessary, but not exhaustive, characteristic of philosophical thinking, viz. that it must not overlook the ontological difference (nor, eventually, the challenge to philosophical thinking to also step back from the ontological difference, which is not a topice of the present work). It is hard to learn to think and practise many-faced ontological difference in thinking, just as learning to play a musical instrument well demands long years of diligent practice. Both common sense and the scientific way of thinking, along with its ancillary in analytic philosophy, are missing something that genuine philosophical thinking unearths.

This sounds like an arrogant assertion that could only increase the contempt for philosophy. It's easy for any of us to admit that they are ignorant of medicine if they are not a trained doctor, or that they cannot play a musical instrument if they haven't learned to play one, but there is nothing self-evident about philosophy covering an area of knowledge which someone could easily admit is not covered by any other endeavour, especially since medicine at least can restore health and music can give pleasure, whereas philosophy, to all intents and purposes, seems useless. Rather, thinking is taken to be the hallmark of humankind in general and not the domain of a specific endeavour. Employing the questionable taxonomy of genus (descent) and species ('look') inherited from the ancient Greeks, our very species is called homo sapiens, i.e. wise, knowing man, hence philosophical. Every instance of the species is a more or less thinking, knowing, understanding being. This capacity for knowledge, it is presumed, has developed over the aeons of human evolution to modern-day science, which is said to represent the culmination and pinnacle of human knowledge. Moreover, since it is the hallmark of human beings to think, and every single human being thinks it thinks, and takes its own thinking to be the yardstick for truth, it seems impudent to claim that, at first and for the most part, we think only deficiently and dwell outside the bounds of thinking that truly matters. Such a claim also seems impossible, for how could an individual's very thinking, through which it holds the world to be as it is, itself be put into question for something so alien as philosophical thinking?

And yet, it has been said that common sense and scientific knowledge, both natural and social, have not learned to think and do not even notice the deficit. On the contrary, science has been basking complacently for several centuries in an unquestioned superiority over philosophical knowing, which has ostensibly long since outlived its day. Philosophy's claim to a special, unique, general status is weakened by the facticity of diverse, specialized philosophical and scientific endeavours today and in the past. How is genuine philosophical thinking to be picked out from among the facticity of countless philosophical specializations and the plethora of philosophical authors? There are as many philosophies as there are philosophers, even when one reduces the number by concentrating on the great names in philosophy. The living philosophers recognized and acclaimed today in both the public domain and the learned institutions do not make preposterous, arrogant claims concerning the uniqueness of philosophical thinking and they take care not to insult people in this democratic age by claiming that they have yet to learn to think. This indicates that there is a tension in the very term, 'established philosophy', an immanent friction arising from philosophical thinking chafing under its bridling by a status quo that has, from the start, demarcated the zone within which philosophers are called on to say something.

The predicament is confounding: truth passes, and has to pass, through each individual *individually*, and this applies most of all to philosophical truth, i.e. to what philosophical thinking discloses, in the first place, the beingness of beings, and not merely their facticity and efficient-causal relations. Truth accepted on authority is not truth, but an adopted opinion based on trust or faith in another. For the truth to be appropriated, it must be disclosure to an *individual*, learning self. Isn't this statement tantamount to saying that each human individual has its own individual, 'subjective', ultimately opinionated truth or that each philosopher has his or her own particular, purportedly arcane knowledge, or system of 'beliefs', beyond the reach of most mortals and beyond the realm of 'objective' knowledge established by empirical, scientific method? Do philosophers only present views they believe in which others may find interesting? How then is a philosopher to be distinguished from a crackpot? Or are philosophers, if they are genuine philosophers, all crackpots, situated beyond the verifiability of 'hard' science? How to decide? Who is to decide? Each thinking individual has to decide for her- or himself, which however does not mean that truth is a matter of merely individual, 'subjective' opinion, because the vexing questions of philosophy are not just made up by individuals, but rather, each has its own tradition and pedigree which has to be taken on and grappled with in argumentation and questioning open also for others to follow. The individual is thus embedded in a greater whole of questions — starting perhaps with the universal question concerning the nature of human being and the 'human predicament' as such — that have always already, in one way or another, shaped the way all of us think and thus also our way of life, but which at the same time are kept alive and open ultimately only by questioning individuals, and not, say, by ethics commissions or theologies that start with preconceptions about the 'existence' of a supreme being called God.

If the endeavour of philosophical thinking is to uncover what is most hidden and most difficult to see, then the philosopher risks a lonely, hyperborean, perilous path of discovery. Who can follow the philosopher on the hazardous path of thinking? Who wants to bother? Only a rare few will ever find the courage and perseverance, will be unsettled and torn enough, and be enticed to see where a philosopher's thinking will lead them. The situation is different for the pursuit of scientific knowledge. It may be very difficult to acquire it, and only the most able minds are called to scientific endeavour, especially foundational research, but it is relatively easy even for the lay-person to gain at least a vague notion of what a given natural or social science is about. Scientific theories can even be successfully popularized. Not so with philosophy. It is not clear what philosophy is about, what it aims to uncover, and in truth, it only ever uncovers what each of us already understands implicitly. It seems to be all smoke and mirrors and vain speculation. Popularizations of philosophy are always at one remove, rough outlines, poor imitations — at best, useful signposts pointing into an abyss — that necessarily remain outside the movement of thinking itself because what philosophy is called on to think is absolutely incomparable, unique, demanding that each individual think, and learn to think, for her- or himself. Does this amount to an extreme form of elitism that surpasses even the social selection of the highly intelligent to join the ranks of scientific research at elite institutions? An elitism that, from the outset, can thrive only in specific rare individuals who find some sort of niche inside or outside the learned institutions to speculate? This rarity is expressed, for instance, in the relatively few names making up the set of important philosophers in world history; philosophers' names seem to have the longest half-life of all. Each of these great philosophers has been open to receiving an hermeneutic message about casting the very beingness of beings.

The situation is both dire and paradoxical. It is dire because philosophy endeavours to think what is most hidden and which therefore seems for the uninitiated to be nothing at all: plain self-evidence and gross triviality. It is paradoxical because philosophy deals with what everybody already knows, understands and is entirely familiar with, even and especially in the most mundane of everyday lives. Philosophy does not investigate — pace Platonist or popularized readings of Plato — some transcendent beyond or the farthest reaches of the universe, the dimmest dawnings in time nor the innermost secrets of sub-atomic matter, but rather what is necessarily known, intimately familiar and therefore closest to every human being, while at the same time being what is most unknown to human being, most overlooked.

Every human being is familiar with, knows and understands the world. This is taken for granted without question in every human existence. What philosophy is called on to think is the granting of world itself. This granting does not mean creation or a coming into existence, i.e. a becoming or ontogenesis, either through divine agency or through some natural process or other referred to as evolution. Philosophy questions the granting of world in how world opens up *as* world, in how beings open up and manifest themselves *as* beings, in how humans open up and show themselves *as* human beings. The questionable granting concerns the opening up of the hermeneutic 'as' and the dimension or 'between' beingness and their beingness within which this opening takes place. The 'as' or 'qua' which enables world to show up *as* world, beings to show up *as* beings and humans to show off *as* human beings to themselves and each other is the so-called *hermeneutic as* or hermeneutic qua. This understanding of beings simply as the beings they present themselves to be can also be said in statements or propositions about them that show what or who they are. This is the *apophantic as* showing beings linguistically in their being (or better: beingness). Such linguistic utterence is itself derivative of the hermeneutic as, for the understanding of beings in their being is prior to its articulation in language. The hermeneutic as and the entire granting of world, beings and human being are and can be and, in a sense, must be taken for granted by both common sense and scientific understanding, both natural and social. They balk at the task of thinking, ignore it, pass over it, skip over it, and fail to see it in their carefree oblivion.

An established world and way of shared social life depends on certain questions *not* being asked, so there must be a kind of uneasiness that provokes their being asked nevertheless. Moved by this uneasiness, the task of philosophy is to think the very granting itself in its manifold modes. This task requires learning to think slowly, being not too hasty to draw conclusions from apparently self-evident premisses, as rational, logical understanding is wont to do. Prior to logical argumentation there is the mute hermeneutic understanding of beings *as* beings. Instead of closing premisses together in a logical conclusion, thinking has to learn to open them up, allowing them to hover in questionability. This must be a very special kind of thinking, and this requirement appears strange to both common sense and sophisticated scientific thinking, for it seems to be the birthright of being human that each of us can naturally think and make sense of the world and the human condition. Philosophy demands a thinking of the simple, most hidden and apparently most self-evident that is the most subtle of all kinds of thinking to learn, surpassing in its simplicity even the difficulty of the most abstract mathematics or the complexity of the deepest secrets of matter as investigated by modern physics.

In view of all there is to know about the world and its intricacies and complexities on all levels, and in view of all the more or less urgent practical and political concerns facing humankind, it does not seem like much to try to think through the scarcely perceptible, scarcely comprehensible and apparently chimerical dimension of world-granting in its manifoldedness. It seems like *precious little*. It not only seems like precious little but it is precious little. The littleness of this precious little means that it makes no pretence to superiority or to usurping or displacing the importance of other forms of knowledge, wisdom and insight. Nevertheless, this little is genuinely precious, glowing softly, throbbing enigmatically. It cannot be dispensed with. And yet, for the most part, the kind of questioning thinking which Western philosophy in its best moments has embodied in its deepest thinkers, *is* dispensed with.[8] Why? Not only because it is hard to see the point of simple, questioning thinking, but because philosophical thinking provides no ground to stand on and therefore represents a disturbance, even an undermining for, in truth, it opens up the possibility of hermeneutically recasting an historical world.

Each historical world is built on a deeply impregnated cast of thought. Western societies today, for instance, are said to be built on firmly held values. Such values are taken to be and are firmly held to be, unquestioningly so. They are defended, especially in politics and universal declarations of human rights. To attempt to go behind values, in which all beings show themselves in a certain light of worth and worthiness, puts a world into question. But what is value itself? Such a putting-into-question could be an historical prelude to a recasting of world in an other cast of thought. This kind of endeavour is regarded as unhealthy by most, especially by those conservatively inclined, but they can easily put their anxious minds at ease because the sense of questioning simply is not understood by most anyway. The direction of the questioning remains unclear and seems pointless, leading nowhere, a mere mind-game. It seems to turn on esoteric minutae and to concern itself with the self-evident and trivial. How is the most self-evident and trivial to be interrogated? How to get a toehold? And there is seemingly endless strife, an endless back-and-forth, among the philosophers themselves over philosophical truth. Neither practical usefulness nor an explanation of the world overall, a worldview, is on offer in questioning thinking. Nevertheless, questioning thinking that engages with fathomlessness is a kind of tele-casting that casts far (Gr.: τῆλε) into the future, thus enabling future possibilities to take shape in thoughtful language and perhaps arrive as an hermeneutic message in the present at some future time.

The precious little on offer from questioning thinking today, after the firm establishment of the modern sciences has long since been achieved, does not lead to any ground. It does not provide a ground from which the world as a whole or even its principal aspects could be explained. It leaves the questions

---

8 Cf. e.g. Hegel "The treasure of Aristotle is more or less completely unknown now for centuries." (Der Schatz des Aristoteles ist seit Jahrhunderten so gut wie unbekannt, *Werke* Bd. 19 VGPII:198). And Heidegger writes with reference to a single short sentence in Aristotle, "With it [this short sentence], the greatest philosophical knowledge of antiquity is expressed, a knowledge which to the present day has remained unevaluated and not understood in philosophy". (Mit ihm ist die größte philosophische Erkenntnis der Antike ausgesprochen, eine Erkenntnis, die bis heute in der Philosophie unausgewertet und unverstanden geblieben ist. *GA*33:219 referring to Aristotle, *Metaphysics* 1047a24–26).

with which the sciences are concerned open. In truth, it not only leaves such scientific questions open, but it opens a line of questioning where the sciences, natural or social, do not see any question at all. Instead of a progress of knowledge, questioning thinking is a kind of learning that goes back into abyssal groundlessness — first of all, into that of the ontological difference —, for questioning loosens the ground and makes the supposed ground on which self-evidence thrives seismic. For most, this ground-breaking quality of philosophical questioning is unnerving and is therefore dismissed, as if there were no question worth asking with regard to apparent self-evidences. If the truth be known (it is not known), we can say, appropriating T.S. Eliot's words, that "human kind cannot bear very much reality" (Burnt Norton I, *Four Quartets*). "Reality" is understood here as truth in the sense of disclosedness, the disclosedness of what is so close to us that it is taken for granted in its manifold granting and to which we hold unquestioningly in understanding the world *as* world, the totality of beings *as* beings.

Questioning thinking, by questioning, not only leads into groundlessness, but discloses. What does it disclose? The manifold dimensions of world-granting itself along with the hermeneutic cast of the beings that present themselves in this world. This unheard-of and unforeseen eventuality of world-granting is by its nature groundless, but nevertheless it provides the ground upon which everything else stands. Questioning thinking, if it is well learnt, discloses the truth of groundlessness, the chasm that gapes beneath all that appears to stand unquestionably on solid ground. Above all, it is human understanding that loses the ground beneath its feet; it no longer stands so unquestioningly, so securely, so unshakenly. In view of the abysmal truth of world-granting, human understanding loses its unquestioned, firm stance and looks into the abysm whence it is granted whenever an historical world shapes up and is erected and recast in a way of thinking.

A word of warning to those inclined to treat these references to groundlessness, chasms, etc. as mere rhetorical metaphor: Metaphors exist only in a kind of thinking for which there are firmly given and named literal meanings for sensuously palpable, present things and facts whose names can be carried over (meta-phorein, μεταφορεῖν) or transferred to name something else that is given only by analogy, merely to the 'mind's eye' in a literary flourish. But if the self-evident reference to given, present beings *as* they show themselves itself becomes questionable, and thinking finds a way of putting what is literally given itself into question, then the comfortable and complacent use of the term 'metaphor' comes to show how comfortable and complacent its user is. Then language can start to speak in surprisingly other, revealing ways that are not tied down by supposedly 'concrete', 'rock-solid', sensuously plain meanings and statements of bald fact. It is in language itself, and through the mind's eye, that world takes shape for human being.

In raising questions, thinking seems irksome, undesirable. It awakens no desire on the part of those who are looking for answers, for 'meaning'. For them, questions are only the interlude leading as quickly as possible to the satisfaction of an answer which provides a ground to stand on again. Thinking then gives back, or renders, the ground under one's feet and reveals everything in its worthiness or unworthiness. Questioning thinking that opens the abyss, by contrast, does not echo with answers. It is therefore often accused of subversive ir-responsibility or nihilism. It leads rather into perplexity and overwhelms the questioner with a withdrawal of ground that recedes beyond the reach of a finite human lifetime. Nevertheless, such a questioning, sparking the passions in precious few, could be the prelude for recasting our historical world in ways hitherto unforeseen by uncovering what has been overlooked, but not entirely, or implicitly very well understood and even constantly addressed throughout the entire tradition of philosophical thinking without ever having been cast into its proper ontological concept.

The major question that will be posed and investigated in the present study is the question of *whoness*, which is a way of approaching the question concerning human being itself. This question represents a *side-step* in the history of metaphysics that complements the famous "step back" proposed by Heidegger to the question as to the meaning of being itself, without reference to beings. For all metaphysical thinking hitherto has concerned itself with the beingness of beings *as* whats, providing answers in terms of essence, i.e. *quidditas*, whatness. Has the question of whoness, the Werfrage, as an explicit fundamental philosophical question been overlooked in the history of philosophy? Not entirely. One could point to the tradition of dialogical philosophy and theology that had its heyday in Germany in the 1920s and was associated with names like Max Scheler and Karl Löwith[9] as well as many others[10] and which goes back

---

9 In his affirmative referee's report for Karl Löwith's habilitation dissertation *Das Individuum in der Rolle des Mitmenschen* (1928) Martin Heidegger writes, "Thus the task is, with regard to an unambiguous interpretation of the relation between the one and the other, to break the traditional dominance of reified concepts." (Es gilt somit, mit Rücksicht auf eine eindeutige Interpretation des Verhältnisses des Einen zum Anderen die traditionelle Vorherrschaft der Dingbegriffe zu brechen. In Karl Löwith *Sämtliche Schriften* Bd. 1 S. 471). Here, at least, Heidegger unequivocally supports Löwith's attempts at a phenomenology of relations between you and I, i.e. dialogical philosophy. The best parts of Löwith's Habilitationsschrift clearly bear Heidegger's phenomenological signature.

within the German tradition to Ludwig Feuerbach, and, implicitly, further to Hegel's dialectic of recognition between self-consciousnesses in the famous section of his *Phenomenology of Mind*. Despite these rich attempts at approaching the question of whoness, it could still be asked whether the question has been posed and pursued with the intensity, clarity and simplicity with which its parallel question, the question of what, the Wasfrage, has been posed and pursued since the first explicit formulation of metaphysics by Aristotle: the investigation of "beings insofar as they are beings", τὸ ὂν ᾗ ὄν, which opened up the vista on *what* a being is, with *whatness*, τὸ τί, being pronounced to be the first and primary sense of the beingness of a being, the whatness of a what. The mere fact that the problematic of dialogical philosophy is unquestioningly regarded as a question within the so-called theory of intersubjectivity — and thus still as a question amenable to the ontology of whatness — may be regarded as an indication of just how far we are still removed from even seeing and appreciating philosophically the question, Who are you?

The essence of a thing is its whatness, its quidditas. Even though we find in Plato's dialogues and Aristotle's ethical, political and rhetorical writings abundant food for thought on the question of whoness or *quissity*,[11] as distinct from the question of whatness, their investigations of social and political life never brought the phenomena of whoness to their concepts (in a social *ontology*) with the same decisiveness, clarity and explicitness as the phenomenality of whatness was cast into metaphysical concepts such as ἰδέα and οὐσία, i.e. idea and essentia, to name just two such fundamental concepts. The phenomenon of whoness is implicit in the ancient Greek — so-called ethical — philosophical texts, as indeed it is ubiquitously in all texts, including those of literature and drama, but still awaits its ontological explication in adequate concepts. Nor can it be said that the dialogical tradition in German philosophy went back to the Greek beginnings to unearth and recast the deepest, simple roots of Western philosophy in such a way that the question of whoness could be given its philosophical due. The attempts at dialogical philosophy in the nineteenth and twentieth centuries have therefore not gone deep enough, which would require engaging the Greek roots of the question. These roots, including the bifurcation

---

10 Further names include Martin Buber, Eugen Rosenstock-Huessy, Ferdinand Ebner, Eberhard Grisebach, Karl Heim, Gabriel Marcel, Friedrich Gogarten, Helmut Plessner, Adolf Reinach, Dietrich von Hildebrand, Wilhelm Schapp, Alfred Schütz, Ludwig Binswanger, Hermann Levin Goldschmidt. Cf. Michael Theunissen *Der Andere: Studien zur Sozialontologie der Gegenwart* 2nd ed. W. de Gruyter, Berlin/New York 1977 for a comprehensive overview.

11 Formed from the Latin for 'who', 'quis', rather than quiddity or whatness, which is formed from the Latin 'quid' for 'what'.

into whatness and whoness, should come to light in following sections of the present inquiry.[12] Whereas Heidegger's "step back" from metaphysical thinking is initiated by the famous question in his *Being and Time*, namely, the question concerning the meaning of being itself, without regard to beings, which leads to answering it in terms of a concept of originary time,[13] thus breaking with the Greek tradition of investigating the being of beings in their whatness, the side-step is inaugurated by trenchantly asking not just "Who am I?", but "Who are you?" and "How do we come about?", and all that with regard to the whoness of these whos in their different, apparently innocuous grammatical declinations.

The implications of the as yet not insistently asked question of whoness — a lack whose want is still not felt even today — are far-reaching. For how can the long and venerable Western traditions of ethics, political and social philosophy be said to have ever gained conceptual clarity about their simplest, elementary phenomena without having explored and conceptually grasped what it means to be somewho[14]? How can we ask who we are without adequate ontological concepts of whoness? Even the philosophical language for this phenomenality is lacking. Any social or political philosophy must tacitly presuppose that it knows whom it is talking about: us human beings. The traditional answers to the question are answers to the question, What is the human being? and not, Who is the human being?, or, even more directly, Who are you? How are you and I *as* somewho possible? The various philosophical formulations of the human essence indicate unwittingly just how strongly philosophical questioning has remained captive to and has been side-lined by the self-evidence of whatness and thinking in the third person, thus missing the very ontological dimension of the second person in which whoness originarily comes about. And yet the failure, to the present day, including and especially in the academy, to take the question of whoness seriously as preceding any subsequent questions of ethics (How should I act?), or social or political philosophy, and to skip over the phenomenon of who as distinct from what, and to ask for its mode of being, i.e. its way of presenting itself *as* such to understanding, as a pedantic quibble, a banal triviality and obviousness must be regarded as a scandal for philosophy, whose deepest calling, after all, has always been to question the most simple, elementary and apparently self-evident phenomena.

---

12 Starting in Chapter 2 and the whole of Chapter 3, and then interwoven throughout the following chapters.

13 Cf M. Eldred *A Question of Time: An alternative cast of mind* CreateSpace, North Charleston 2015

14 Oxford English Dictionary: "somewho, archaic: some one; somebody."

Such questioning of the phenomenality of who, that is complementary to insistingly interrogating the phenomenality of what, brings to light the hermeneutic cast of whoness, in parallel to that of whatness, as two parallel, intertwined ontologies. Uncovering *as* who we are cast in the present age goes hand in hand with uncovering *as* what things are hermeneutically cast in a given historical age, especially our own, both with a view to reviewing and thus also recasting on the basis of deeper insight. Especially with respect to whoness, casting is to be understood here in the threefold sense of i) casting into a role like a player on the stage, ii) casting in the sense of moulding and shaping and iii) projecting into the historical future.

2   Loosening the ground: Thinking about society, thinking society

There is a long tradition of Western thinking about society. Even a superficial browse through an encyclopaedia reveals that. Starting with Plato's purported 'Utopia' in his *Republic* and Aristotle's lectures on *Politics*, through to the present day, where social science comprises many different branches of inquiry such as economics, political science, cultural anthropology, sociology, social psychology, social statistics and social geography, one could be inclined to maintain that the rudimentary beginnings found in Plato and Aristotle have been differentiated and elaborated into more reliable, empirically well-founded knowledge about society. Similarly, the strand of Western thought known under the rubric of political philosophy and also first conceived in Plato's and Aristotle's writings, is in our own time still concerned with the questions of how 'men' can live together under just laws and a form of government most reconcilable with human freedom. One could say that we have a rich and deep tradition of political and social thought in the West and that this tradition informs, mostly via subterranean routes, political action, social policy, social, ethical and political issues, and a myriad other practices in today's modern societies.

But there is a difference between thinking about society and thinking society. It is questionable whether the Western tradition in thinking has ever thought the phenomenon of society in itself, its sociation (Vergesellschaftung) through a kind (εἶδος) of *movement* sui generis with its own peculiar ontology, namely, a social, *sociating* ontology. A preposterous claim that can be comfortably dismissed out of hand from a securely superior, more knowledgeable position such as that of empirically-based social science? Or a challenge that we (or I, at least) must first learn to even countenance the ontological question concerning sociation and thus to think society *as such* as a mode of being, and a somewhat presumptuous claim that political philosophy and social science per se do not think the very element in which their thinking moves? Although, paradoxically, nevertheless understanding it implicitly very well!

What does it mean to think society as such? Hasn't the tradition of Western philosophy already thought society as a sociation of human beings living together in communities? Don't other species of animals and even plants also form societies or sociations? What is the specific nature of human society? What is sociation as a mode of being? In Aristotle's *Politics* we read that "man is by nature a social animal", a ζῷον πολιτικόν. The social or political animal congregates around the pole of the πόλις, living together in communities. This famous

https://doi.org/10.1515/9783110617504-002

Aristotelean definition of humankind's essence, of what it means to *be* a human being as a *social* animal, is closely linked with that other essential definition of man as τὸ ζῷον λόγον ἔχον, the animal that has the λόγος, or language, through which it reasons. Accordingly, humankind would be sociated first and foremost by virtue of having the power of speech as a means of communication.

The sociation of human community in the first place would be linguistic in nature or essence through the practice of humans' talking with one another. Human community would thus be founded fundamentally on language employed to communicate in a context of common, shared living-practices, with language itself having arisen evolutionarily as enhancing survival chances of the human species. These basic definitions of human society seem to be hardly controversial statements and would presumably be accepted by both political philosophy and social science as rudimentary, essential, definitional characteristics of social human being that modern science operationalizes as a matter of course in the many branches of its empirical research (such as studying the 'language' of certain apes and its closeness or otherwise to human language). However, their apparent self-evidence is itself problematic for any socio-ontological questioning that takes neither human being nor sociating human being for granted, but rather patiently interrogates their meaning as modes of being. The run-of-the-mill way of thinking human being as the human species (εἶδος, 'look') subsumed under the genus (γένος, genesis, descent) of animals so well-established in scientific anthropology is one example of how superficially Greek thinking has been adopted and put to use, without the least inkling remaining of the ontological depths of thinking in which such terms εἶδος and γένος were first employed. There are good reasons to regard modern scientific thinking as the residual left-overs of Greek ontology unwittingly adopted which has long since covertly established its as-yet-unchallenged hegemony, whilst at the same attempting to extirpate the last remaining vestiges of the ability to think ontologically. Modern scientific thinking as degenerate and degenerating generation by generation?

2.1 Society, needs and wants, language

In Aristotle's *Politics* (Πολιτικῶν) or Plato's *Republic* (Πολιτεία), the founding texts of political philosophy, we (or I, at least) can read further that human society emerged historically, i.e. chronologically, ontogenetically, on the basis of human needs and wants. The manifold "necessaries and conveniencies of life", as one of the fathers of Political Economy, Adam Smith, will call them in a later age, are provided by various kinds of labour performed in a division of labour, which in turn, with the multiplication and diversification of means of "subsistence, conveniencies and amusements" (Smith), engenders the practices of trading, both within a community and without, i.e. with other communities. Human being itself is thus conceived as, in the first place, needy, and society would thus be based on the satisfaction of need as a kind of large scale household or οἶκος, albeit that this 'household' is not a single unit under a unified organization, but consists of a web of enterprises or 'households' connected by exchange according to certain customary rules.

Thus we have in Plato and Aristotle already an economic explanation of human society and its genesis which dovetails neatly with sociation based on language as a means of communication dedicated in the first place to enabling and facilitating the acquisition of what is necessary and convenient for living, starting with those putative anthropological constants, food, clothing and shelter, and conveniences relegated to second place to be had only once needs have been satisfied. It would seem that language in an elaborate form, embedded in the vital practices of exchange, specifies the human species as a social animal that employs language, in the first place, to satisfy need and thus survive. For common sense, for anthropological and evolutionary theories, and even for empirically based philosophy, we thus have, apparently, a cogent and 'reasonable', even 'indisputable' 'explanation' of society and man as a needy 'social animal'.

2.2   What is λόγος?

But what is language, what is λόγος? Can it be thought as a means of communication? Of course it can, but is this the essence of language, i.e. what it is? What does it mean for human beings to have the λόγος?

The λόγος as speech enables beings to be addressed and thus called to presence, presenting themselves in their 'looks' (εἴδη) to the understanding mind. Beings present themselves *as such* to human awareness, and humans, in turn, can address beings in their self-showing (as in 'the sun shows itself from behind the clouds') through language. Such self-showing as phenomena and addressing by language are intrinsically prior to any communication among humans that may take place and constitutes its very precondition of possibility. The more originary phenomenal meaning of λόγος, as Heidegger often points out, comes from λέγειν, meaning 'to gather', 'to glean'. In order to be beings and show themselves *as such*, beings gather or collect themselves into the defining outline of the view or look they offer of themselves for the sake of human awareness in which they come to stand in understanding to be understood *as* such. Beings' self-showing and human understanding of them *as* beings belong together, i.e. they depend upon each other and are in that sense the same, equivalent, identical.[15] They are of one ilk.[16] The sight or look or view of beings is a self-collecting gathering into a standing presence by virtue of which the being's well-defined outline *as* or *qua* a being can be understood and then also be addressed by speech. Understanding is prior to speech. Since Plato and Aristotle, *as* what beings show themselves *as* beings, i.e. ontologically, is called their ἰδέα or εἶδος (both words derived from the Greek verb ἰδεῖν meaning 'to see'), their view that is open to view, their look and looks that human beings can see by virtue of the mind's understanding. To break up this belonging-together of beings *as* such and human understanding is sheer folly, but this is precisely what the modern mind does.

How things in the broadest sense show themselves is how they are or at least seem to be, both of which are modes of being, self-presentation. The self-showing of beings of themselves *as* themselves (as the Greeks say, their ἀπόφανσις) is what and how they are in *truth*. Truth lies primarily in the self-showing of phenomena, and only secondarily in the λόγοι or propositions about this self-showing. But this self-showing can also be distorted, deceptive, obscured or even totally occluded for human awareness, which means that then things are not in truth what they seem to be. Their shining is deceptive. There is then a difference between things as they are in their truth, i.e. their full unconcealedness, as they show themselves of themselves *as* themselves, on the one hand, and illusion, on the other, in which the self-showing is obscured. In showing themselves illusorily, things are playing tricks on and mocking human awareness (from L. illudere: 'to mock, trick, deceive'). Things can even pretend that they are not there at all. They are then out of sight, invisible or forgotten, in oblivion. Or they can show themselves as that which they are not, i.e. as something else, thus pretending, under false pretences, to be something else. Or they can show themselves only partially, incompletely, deceptively, obscuring the view of other important aspects. For modern subjectivist thinking it is strange, at least in English, to speak of things showing themselves, but this is merely the prejudice of an entire age whose thinking proceeds foolishly from the 'self-

---

15 Identity and sameness are a belonging-together. The ancient English word 'same' has an Indo-Germanic root *somo-, whence Skr. samá level, equal, same, Gr. ὁμός same (cf. ὁμαλός level), and ablaut variants of this root in Greek include εἷς one, and ἅμα together. (Source: OED) Being and human being are thus 'level' with one another. And they can only be identical because they are different, i.e. carried apart from one another, διαφέρειν.

16 OED "Ilk 1 Same, identical; the (this, that) ilk, the same, the identical, the very same person, thing, etc....".

evident' preconception that it is always under-lying (i.e. sub-jective), internal, subjective consciousness that directs itself intentionally toward external objects.

2.3 Opinion: Holding things and each other to be (whatness and whoness)

Human beings, in being open to the self-showing of beings, hold them to be such-and-such. They hold an opinion or view about things according to how they seem to be to human understanding. In expressing an opinion or a view and thus in addressing things and calling them to presence, i.e. to mind, for oneself or others, human beings can either be deceived by appearances and express the view in accordance with the illusion, or they can express a view that diverges even from how things seem to them. This latter is the phenomenon of *lying*. Lying, to be sure, is one kind of communication first enabled by the self-showing of beings *as such* to human awareness. Things are then addressed not even as they seem to be to the speaker, but are re-presented to an other as something else.

The Greek word for 'opinion' and 'view', but also 'illusion' and 'appearance', is δόξα. Δόξα (from Gk. δοκεῖν 'to seem') is thus not only the appearance, view, sight or look which things present of themselves in their self-showing, nor is it only how things seem to be for human awareness, but it is also how things are held to be by human views or opinions (Dafürhalten). There is thus a double view or perspective: beings offer views of themselves *as* beings, on the one hand, and, on the other, they are held to be such-and-such in the view of human awareness, whether individual or collective, such views' being capable of sharing.

There is a further meaning of the Greek word, δόξα, which is not merely another lexicographical association, but indicates an interconnection among the phenomena themselves. This signification is 'reputation' or 'fame'. For, it not only holds true that things show themselves of themselves and as themselves to human awareness, but that human beings, too, willy-nilly put themselves on view to each other's view in sharing a world. Human beings show up as such for each other, presenting a view of themselves to each other. Whereas things show themselves to human awareness *as what* and *how* they are in their whatness, humans show, display and present themselves to each other's view *as who* they are and *how* they are in their *whoness*.

Whereas traditional ontology investigates the beingness of beings focused on things, thus on the whatness of whats, social ontology is called on to think through the whoness of whos, and not merely the subjectivity of subjects (conceived *as* a kind of whats), as all ontology in the modern age, starting with Descartes, has done, and as all modern science, in its simple-minded ontological naivety, implicitly continues to do. As human *beings*, humans *are* always somewho[17] and not merely some-what or something. This is a phenomenon and mode of being sui generis constituting the proper dimension of human sociation, and demanding its own socio-ontological concepts and phenomenological thinking-through, as will be slowly unfolded in the following chapters.

In being somewho or other, humans also present themselves to each other in a certain definite appearance, look and view. Showing themselves off *as* who they are is what humans do in presenting a face or mask to themselves and others which makes them a person (from persona and πρόσωπον for 'face', 'visage', 'mask', 'outward appearance'). They pretend, and must pretend, to be who they are. The view is never describable merely in terms of something resembling a physical appearance, but indicates *who* the person is in the community in question, i.e. in the ontological dimension of sociation. Pretending to be who I am to myself must also not be confused with the self-consciousness of a subjective consciousness that (not who) in being conscience of any object is simultaneously conscious (i.e. literally: co-knowing) of its self's being conscious of the object, hence a doubling of consciousness or co-knowing. Who someone is shows itself as *reputation* or *standing* in the broadest sense, which covers also all deficient and negative modes such as the 'invisible view' of anonymity and obscurity. Whoness as a mode of being is therefore always already social, involving others in their opinionated holding you to be who you are.

2.4 Showing oneself off as somewho

Fame, which is a certain, pronounced, highly visible, form of reputation, comes from the Greek φάναι 'to speak'. Fame is how people speak about another as somewho, thus defining who they are by power of word-of-mouth. This speaking about somebody is only possible because each person shows off who they are in view of others' perceptive and cognitive awareness. The being of a human is a who-being, a whoness, i.e. "that which makes a person who he is"[18], which is how somewho puts him- or herself on show. Human being as social being is essentially showing-off, self-display, self-presentation, including pretence.

---

17 OED: "somewho, archaic: some one; somebody."
18 OED: "whoness: a) That which makes a person who he is."

Whoness is therefore from scratch a *relational* mode of being between and among whos, lacking the substance of the lead ontological concept of whatness, viz. oὐσία, substance, essence. And how does the whoness of somewho present itself to view at first and for the most part? It shows itself at first and for the most part as what people are customarily occupied with and take care of in their daily lives, in how they habitually lead their lives, i.e. as an *occupation* or *vocation*. The view which persons offer of themselves is first and foremost their occupation which others understand, i.e. they show themselves as what they do habitually in the intermeshed, diversified network of activities in a division of labour that contributes to the fulfilment of needs and desires in the community in question. Thus, the view of a stockbroker, a newspaper seller, a bus driver, a builder's labourer or a housewife is offered to the view of others — and also to themselves, as a self-understanding, self-image or identity that is an average understanding and self-understanding of who one is in a general, third-person averageness of where one belongs in social standing, even one's 'social station'. One identifies one's self as belonging to a certain occupation on offer in one's world.

The view offered is not and cannot be conceived as a view open merely to sensuous perception, since whoness is not originarily a sensuous category, but is embedded in an understanding of human being itself as whoness per se within a shared, social world. Furthermore, self-identity is always a matter of how someone habitually lives, and is not a merely psychological self-image represented within consciousness, i.e. within an 'interior' representational imagining of who one is. Such self-identity is always a reflection of oneself in the mirror of how I live in the world, understanding the practices I habitually practise, i.e. identify with, as my own. Such identity with oneself is therefore always a reflection in a basic sense of the word, 'reflection', as a 'shining-back'. The view or look of an occupation is how the who in question comes to stand and show themself, at first and for the most part, in a standing within the community and, accordingly, how they are spoken about in the view of others. In this stand they are held to be who they are — in a δόξα. The δόξα is on the one hand the defined, definite view into which they are gathered and offer of themselves and, on the other, it is who they are held to be in the view or opinion of others in a reputation whose element is the medium of the spoken λόγος for a speaking-about, including a gossiping-about.

It is therefore not only things that show themselves in their being to human beings in their whatness that can thus be addressed, but also human beings themselves, who show themselves off and present themselves reciprocally and mirroringly to each other in their whoness, and that, as has been shown, at first and for the most part, through their quotidian occupations. This self-showing, self-display, or presentation of a view to view, is indicated also in the medium or middle voice of the Greek verb ἀποφαίνεσθαι, which means not only 'to pronounce a judgement or provide an account', 'to speak, to judge', but also 'to show something of oneself', 'to present oneself with one's abilities to view', 'to show off' (Benseler). The active mood of the same verb, ἀποφαίνειν, means 'to bring something to light or into view, to disclose, announce, present', 'to declare to be' or 'to appoint as'. The verb is thus both phenomenal and phenomenological, i.e. it signifies firstly bringing something to light or showing oneself off in a certain light (φῶς, φαίνειν) or view (ἰδέα), and secondly it indicates that the bringing to light also takes place in the medium of the λόγος, of speech uttered in sentences about somewho.

The Greek experience of the being of beings is that of their being gathered into a delineated stand or 'look' and showing themselves *as* beings in the light of human awareness that is bound to these sights in understanding, which are thus addressable by speech. Awareness (the Da, the mind, the psyche in the Greek sense) is the open clearing[19] in which beings can come to light as such.

---

19 'Clearing' is the translation of German 'Lichtung', which is one of the key concepts in Heidegger's phenomenology. The thinking-through of human being (Dasein) as the open clearing (Da) for the truth of being, the dis-covery of this clearing originally experienced and presupposed by the Greeks as ἀλήθεια, but not explicitly thought through by them, is at the heart of Heidegger's thinking. For the purposes of this inquiry, since it is not an exposition of Heidegger's thinking, it has to be assumed that the reader has read Heidegger, starting with *Being and Time* (1927). Cf. on the Lichtung e.g. in *Sein und Zeit* §28 S. 133 or the later study on the 'Origin of the Work of Art', "In the midst of beings as a whole, an open place holds sway. There is a clearing. [...] A being can only be as a being if it stands out into the cleared/lighted space (Gelichtete) of this clearing. Only this clearing grants and guarantees for us human beings a passage to those beings that we are not ourselves and access to those beings that we are ourselves. Thanks to this clearing, beings are unconcealed in certain and changing degrees. But a being can also be *hidden* only in the room for play for what is cleared/illuminated (im Spielraum des Gelichteten). Every being which or whom we encounter observes this strange opposition to presencing by at the same time always holding itself back in a hiddenness. The clearing out into which beings stand is in itself at the same time a hiding." 'Der Ursprung des Kunstwerkes' (1935/36) in *Holzwege* Klostermann, Frankfurt/Main 1950 S. 41f. Here I merely note the major controversial issue over Heidegger's confusing and conflating the three-dimensional, originary time that he unearths as the explicated meaning of being implicitly assumed by Greek thinking (what I call the time-clearing) with the clearing conceived as the openness for the disclosure or hiding of beings as such showing or concealing themselves, in short, the confusion of originary temporality with truth. Hence, for example, in the above-quoted passage, Heidegger puts presencing into opposition to hiding, thus presupposing that

The clearing is the open, *three-dimensional temporal clearing* in which beings presence and absence, occurring as occurrents and occurrences, and into which the categories of beings as such — as thought through in the long tradition of ontology from Plato and Aristotle through to Hegel's *Logik* — are inscribed, thus allowing a world to shape up and define itself for understanding. Humans share this temporal opening with each other and therefore can address for each other the self-showing of beings' looks. This is what is commonly called communication, which is a communication or exchange of views on beings' looks. Communication is therefore not an originary phenomenon, but is only an essential consequence of the ontological self-showing of beings *qua* beings; communication is a sharing with each other of the views which beings, human and otherwise, present of themselves *as* who and what they are. In particular, humans too show themselves and show themselves off in the light of awareness to each other in their whoness. This sharing of awareness of beings in their being and the mutual showing-off of humans to each other in their stands as some-who or other is the fundamental enabling dimension of human sociation within which all kinds of practical dealings with one another can take place. *Human sociation is enabled first of all by the openness of being itself, i.e. the 3D-time-clearing, within which beings can show themselves as something and human beings can show themselves off as somewho.* Since this openness is a 3D-temporal one, the showing and showing-off are a presencing and absencing in the temporal clearing that is not tied to a linearity or successiveness, but can be, and usually is, the mind's hopping-about freely hither and thither through its three dimensions.

2.5 The openness of three-dimensional time as the enabling dimension within which society is situated

This answer to the question concerning the sociation of human beings in society differs from the traditional answers, which nevertheless implicitly presuppose and take for granted the open dimension of being itself, which turns out to be the open clearing of originary 3D-time itself (cf. previous section), as a given. To think society as such as a mode of being rather than to think about society means in the first place, to think the originary enabling dimension(s) within which what we call society and sociation is at all possible. Traditional explana-

---

presencing itself is equivalent to disclosing. But this is phenomenally not the case. For details cf. my *A Question of Time* 2015.

tory, ontogenetic answers, in terms of beings, to the question concerning the fundamental nature of society refer to the need for humans to congregate and band together to fulfil their needs and wants, the primary ones being food, clothing and shelter, followed by the need to ward off dangers emanating from nature and hostile outsiders. The traditional answer runs, first of all, in terms of needy humans needing each other to fulfil their needs, and is thus given in terms of necessity and cause, in order to survive as merely living beings. Humans thus come, caused by need, to congregate around a pole where they can labour and exchange the fruits of their labour and also find protection against danger of attack from the outside by keeping what is harmful at bay or by warding it off. This is a plausible ontic explanation led by the categories of necessity and cause. But such neediness and the fulfilment of need (which apply also to animals in their struggle for survival) are both situated and are only possible *as such* within the enabling openness of being (the time-clearing), including its disclosive truth, within which a world comes about and shows up. Need and desire are what they are for human being only by virtue of its existential (literally: out-standing) exposure to being in its 3D-temporality, understanding the world in a certain way, living life within the practices of certain historically established customs and habits, and being affected by the moods of the quivering of the time-clearing.[20]

To take the apparently self-evident, ontic considerations with which political philosophy has almost exclusively operated in reflecting on the constitution of society and state back into the ground of the enabling dimension of being itself is to *ontologize* the question of human social being in a way that hitherto has not been attempted. Why? Because to date an ontology of whoness as a phenomenon enabled to presence by the open, manifold dimensionality of 3D-temporality has not been explicitly unfolded, nor even come vaguely into view. It has remained philosophically mute, although inevitably quietly present. Ontology as the investigation of the beingness of beings has hitherto not considered the whoness of human beings as sociating whos. Ontology as we know it has been preoccupied exclusively with beings in their whatness, i.e. in the third person,[21] i.e. with things and with humans considered as some sort of thing (e.g.

---

20 Cf. my *Thinking of Music* 2015.

21 "The definite and singular verbal form 'is', the *third person of the singular in indicative present tense*, has precedence here [in the Greek experience and interpretation of being]. We understand 'being' not with regard to 'you are', 'you all are', 'I am' or 'they would be', which all and just as well as 'is' are verbal modifications of 'being'." (Die bestimmte und einzelne Verbalform 'ist', die *dritte Person des Singular im Indikativ des Praesens*, hat hier [in der griechischen Erfahrung und Auslegung des Seins] einen Vorrang. Wir verstehen das 'Sein' nicht im Hinblick

as a being with a body, soul and mind). As we shall see, put in traditional grammatical terms, a phenomenological ontology of whoness will demand that human beings *as who they are* be conceived in the first place through the *interplay* between first and second person. These grammatical categories are *socio-ontologically* more originary than the relation of first person to third person within which human being has invariably been thought throughout the philosophical tradition. The dimensions of first-and-second-person and first-and-third-person name a fold, a *twofold* within the temporal clearing for being's play of truth, i.e. of disclosing and hiding.

Human labour itself is only possible on the basis of human awareness, i.e. human openness and enpropriatedness to the open dimension of 3D-time itself. How so? Because, to be adequate to the phenomena, labour has to be thought in a Greek way, as ποίησις, as the bringing forth of products into presence through human activity. But don't other animals also bring forth 'products', such as birds bringing forth bird's-nests and bees bringing forth honey? Yes, but in another sense. The specific nature of human labour is that it is activity under the guidance of the fore-seeing, fore-knowing, gathering λόγος. Humans have the know-how of how to bring forth a product which is foreknowingly envisaged before it is pro-duced, i.e. guided forth into presence as something present and hence ready to hand. This know-how is a *power* or *potential* residing in knowledgeable human awareness that consists in foreseeing and fore-casting, and in this sense pre-casting, the final product to be brought forth and knowing what transformative steps are required to achieve this end, and what steps and actions have to be avoided and kept in abeyance and absence. Such foreseeing presupposes that human understanding sees both the present and the future 'simultaneously', i.e. that the human mind has temporally 'double vision', an impossible conception for modern science, since it is fixated on sensuously present data. All potential, all potency, all power, whether reliably, efficiently productive or not, is a 'simultaneous' presencing and absencing, where the absencing refers to a future that may come to presence in the present. What is absent is still futural, lacking presence in the present, but nevertheless present *as* this lack (which Aristotle calls στέρησις). If the past (beenness, yesterness) is also taken into account, then the mind can be seen to be endowed even with temporally triple vision that sees into all three temporal dimensions *all at once*, and that this triple vision is the precondition for the mind's seeing move-

---

auf das 'du bist', 'ihr seid', 'ich bin', oder 'sie wären', die alle doch auch und ebenso gut verbale Abwandlungen des 'Seins' darstellen wie das 'ist'. M. Heidegger *Einführung in die Metaphysik* 1953 S. 70)

ment/change *as such* at all. With the insight into the 3D-temporal clearing, all movement and change, including social movement of sociation, is conceived hermeneutically *as* presencing and absencing, instead in the traditional hermeneutic cast in which (1D-linear) time is merely a parameter lifted off movement. This amounts to a radical turn in Western thinking.

An artisan's or other labourer's skills consist in being able to perform the various necessary steps of production under the guidance of the foreknowing foresight of the end-product, and to correct the mistakes that occur, so that the initial raw materials and auxiliary materials are finally (τέλος) transformed into the desired product in a finished presence. Plato and Aristotle were the first thinkers to think production in its being as a power or force (δύναμις), i.e. a human ability, guided by the fore-casting foresight of the λόγος.[22] Since the λόγος is insight into the gathering of beings into the sight or look (εἶδος) of their defining stand and is thus also the ratio or relationship of human being to being, it can be seen that labour as the labour of human *beings* depends essentially on humans' having always already been gathered definingly into the openness to being as beings with an understanding of being.

2.6 Living well and being somewho – The need to interrogate the tradition

To return to the initial question regarding what it means to think society in itself in its mode of sociation rather than to think about society: to think society *as such* means to think first of all the open, enabling, empowering dimension within which humans can be human beings as somewho or other and, as such who-beings, can enter into intercourse with one another to satisfy their communal needs, strive to fulfil their desires and share the practices that constitute their customary way of living together. The satisfaction of needs and wants, an economic end, is only one aspect of what Aristotle calls "living well" (εὖ ζῆν), and needs and wants have to be conceived in the broadest sense of all that contributes to a possibility of living well. Society is for the sake of its members living well (which in the fundamental, socio-ontological sense encompasses also all

---

22 Cf. e.g. Plato *Rep.* Book X 596b: "[...] the maker of each of these useful items, in viewing the sight, one brings forth bedsteads, the other tables [...]" (ὁ δημιουργὸς ἑκατέρου τοῦ σκεύους πρὸς τὴν ἰδέαν βλέπων οὕτω ποιεῖ ὁ μὲν τὰς κλίνας, ὁ δὲ τὰς τραπέζας) or Aristotle *Metaphysics* Book Theta (Θ).

the deficient or opposite modes of living poorly to cover the full spectrum of the phenomenon in question).

Although both Plato and Aristotle thought about society as a way of living together to fulfil needs and wants, and although both spoke copiously *about* phenomena of being somewho (but not of whoness itself), such as having a reputation and occupation, being esteemed and honoured, striving for esteem, and enjoying an acknowledged social standing (τιμή), and that even as a good of social living, neither explicitly thought through the phenomena of reputation or the love of esteem (φιλοτιμία) *as* modes of being in a social ontology (which would have meant shifting the ontological focus in a *side-step* from an ontology of the whatness of beings to that of the whoness of human beings). Nor did they explicitly "step back" (Heidegger) to think through the open dimension of being itself as the open clearing which primordially enables a being to presence *as* something and a human being to presence *as* somewho. Needless to say, the long ontological tradition following Plato and Aristotle, too, has nothing to say about the open, three-dimensional temporality of being itself nor did it take on the challenge of an ontology of whoness (but only of whatness: quidditas, es-sentia, substance). This applies even to the present day in philosophy and also in modern-day social science, which thrives on having banned any question of the ontological difference (cf. the Foreword).

Only Heidegger's thinking makes the backward leap into asking for the meaning of being itself, thus interrogating for the first time what Western phi-losophy has always obliviously taken for granted as a blinding obviousness. Hence his thinking opens future perspectives for history by re-opening ancient questions. But even Heidegger's thinking does not bring the ontological struc-ture of social relations into focus, since it is focused instead on working out and deconstructing the 'vertical' ontotheological structure of all metaphysical think-ing to uncover the sight of the simple clearing of originary 3D-time which is also the playground for the play of ἀλήθεια, i.e. of disclosing and hiding. Although Heidegger's thinking provides an indispensable, fundamental ground-plan for the structure of humans' sharing of the world (Mitsein, Mitdasein), the task of thinking through an ontology of social relations, of sociating movement, in the dimension of whoness in which you-and-I and we can *be*, presenting them-selves to each other *as* whos, is nevertheless left to us, no matter how much we still need to learn from the tradition, profiting from its many implicit clues and cues. There is a need to follow up, for instance, on Heidegger's distinction be-tween the Wasfrage and the Werfrage, i.e. the question of what and the question of who, present already in *Being and Time* and ask more insistently than Heidegger ever does what it means to be somewho in society. To think the sociating movement between and among human beings, the whoness of human beings — of us and you-and-me and them — must be explicitly worked out in ontological concepts so that they are not assimilated, by sleight of hand, to the ontology of mere things, i.e. to whatness, as the modern metaphysics of subjectivity still does.

To pursue the traditional question of how human beings could live well with one another requires, as a fundamental preliminary question, asking *who* we *are* as human beings, i.e. whoness as our mode of being — and precisely *not* the Kantian question, "What is the human being?"[23] that puts thinking on the wrong track from the outset. The question of whoness — the whoness of whos as distinct from the traditional whatness of whats — precedes all consideration of *why* humans sociate or *how* we *should* act in social intercourse with one another. The long Western tradition of ethics and moral philosophy has consistently skipped over the ontology of whoness, even though key phenomena such as honour, esteem and social standing (τιμή) or vanity and vainglory (Eitelkeit) have been preontologically clearly in view and a constant theme. But it is the very ontological dimension of whoness that first *enables* a social standing or vanity, and within which any consideration of striving for individual excellence or of submission to moral imperatives must be situated. We — or, at least, I — need to learn to see what it means to stand as who in the open 3D-temporal clearing for being's revealing and concealing truth, and to explicitly work out the socio-ontological structure of whoness, in order to even *envisage* our historical possibilities. This may contribute one day to our "living well" with each other on the Earth.

---

23 'Was ist der Mensch?' I. Kant *Logik* Wissenschaftliche Buchgesellschaft, Darmstadt 1983 Band III S. 448, A26.

3 Further outline of the phenomenon of whoness

Die Frage, wer der Mensch ist [...] läßt sich im Bereich der überlieferten Metaphysik, die wesentlich ‚Physik' bleibt, nicht zureichend fragen.

Martin Heidegger
Einführung in die Metaphysik S. 107

The question concerning who the human being is [...] cannot be adequately asked within the domain of traditional metaphysics, which remains essentially 'physics'.

A first, very rudimentary outline of the phenomenon of whoness[24] has already been sketched in the preceding chapter. Human beings show themselves off at first and for the most part in the look of their usual occupations *as* which they present themselves to each other within the openness of being. This outline now has to be fleshed out successively as we go along with the phenomenal content of what it means to be somewho. To participate in whoness means in the first place to show oneself off within the 3D-temporal clearing for presencing and absencing. To be somewho is to present a view or look[25] manifest to one's own and others' gaze and regard. The core of my look as somewho is not a visual phenomenon, but an aural one, but not aural in a merely sensuous sense. My very own, singular look is given first of all in my proper name by which I am called, through which my presence is communicated throughout the community and which I also call my self. This core of my whoness, my singular *proper name*, is associated with what is heard and said about me, i.e. with my *reputation* (see preceding chapter).

---

24 Cf. my *Der Mann: Geschlechterontologischer Auslegungsversuch der phallologischen Ständigkeit* Haag + Herchen, Frankfurt/M. 1989, *Phänomenologie der Männlichkeit: kaum ständig noch* Verlag Dr. Josef H. Röll, Dettelbach 1999, my Contributions to a Phenomenology of Manliness, a series of internet lectures first delivered to the Heidegger forum www.mitdasein.com between January and June 2003 and also 'Was heißt Männlichkeit' 2013–15 at URL www.artefact.org/untpltcl/wshstmnl.html. All these works could also bear the title Phenomenology of Whoness. Cf. also my collection *Entständigung* CreateSpace, North Charleston 2015.

25 Or 'regard' in the sense of 'habit or manner of looking' OED; notice also that in English the words 'view' and 'look' both have a Janus-faced status between object and subject, as if the phenomenon itself were interposed in the middle. Thus the view presents itself to the view of the viewers who view it, and the look presents itself to on-lookers to look at. This middle is in truth the ontological difference in which the hermeneutic As is situated.

https://doi.org/10.1515/9783110617504-003

This look of reputation was experienced by the Greeks as δόξα, which means also manifestation, or view in the sense of opinion. My singularity as this unique human being is first of all signalled or signposted by my unique proper name, which situates it, against the grain, within the universal element of language. I am therefore at heart a contradiction, for I am identified with what I am not, viz. a proper name. To say 'I am Michael Eldred' is to say a contradiction; in Hegelian language, it is to formulate an identity of identity and difference. Furthermore, my identity is elaborated in language in articulating my reputation, my standing in the view of others, by identifying my proper name with actions, abilities, attitudes, behaviours, views, etc. attributed to me. My unique singularity is always already exposed to the universal element of language via the particularities mediating between my singularity and universality. Through language, who I am becomes sayable and manipulable by others as merely a particular human being, no longer singular, but marked beneath the universal of human beings by specific differences, namely, the properties or qualities that, as predicates of my proper name, serve to characterize me. This contradiction will occupy us again in a later subsection of this chapter (3.3.1).

3.1 Bearing a name and standing in estimation in the community through valuing interplay

...und Hoffnungen nennt man in der Republik der Geister die Republikaner, das sind jene Menschen, die sich einbilden, man dürfe seine ganze Kraft der Sache widmen, statt einen großen Teil von ihr auf das äußere Vorwärtskommen zu verwenden; sie vergessen, daß die Leistung des Einzelnen gering, das Vorwärtskommen dagegen ein Wunsch aller ist, und vernachlässigen die soziale Pflicht des Strebens...

Robert Musil
Der Mann ohne Eigenschaften I Tl. 1 Kap. 13

...and promising individuals in the republic of intellectuals are called republicans, who are those persons that flatter themselves that one may devote one's entire energy to the substantial issue instead of expending a great deal of it on getting ahead; they forget that the individual's achievement is small, but getting ahead is everyone's desire, and neglect the social duty to strive...

In my everyday life, I am concerned not only with pragmatically taking care of what needs to be done for the sake of living, but also with the stand I assume as somewho in the community, i.e. in the mirroring view of others. My being-in-the-world is essentially immersed in the socio-ontological dimension of whoness, including even a possible deficient view of me in which I figure as merely one among many, or as a piece of data. My proper name is associated, as underlying subject, with all the acts I undertake in daily life and the quality of my life; how I can live, depends on the regard in which I am held by both others and myself. Regard and esteem, self-regard and self-esteem inhere essentially in the dimension within which I assume a stand *as* somewho (just as the self-showing of things is always also a self-showing not only of what they are in terms of physical properties, but also of what they are good for and thus what they are worth). My manifestation as who is thus not simply the revelation of a fact, but involves the showing of estimable worthiness or otherwise and is in this sense a *showing-off*, where this term is not to be understood in any pejorative or derogatory sense. In the view of others I always stand in their estimation, and they always stand in mine. We estimate each other in every encounter in a kind of *mirroring interplay* of who we are in our respective who-standings. This mirroring is a kind of mutual recognition and includes the entire gamut from awe and praise through utter indifference to negative modi such as hatred, condescension and disdain. Estimation means placing a value upon, as worthy or otherwise. Human being in its self-showing cannot escape this dimension of estimation of who-status. Phenomena such as fame or calumny cannot be thought as modes of being (presencing-*as*...) without the prior dimension of whoness as the site where they are ontologically situated.

A who is always viewed or regarded within the dimension of esteem. My reputational standing as somewho is essentially situated in a vertical dimension with above and below; in the view of others I am always held in high or low regard and esteem or somewhere in between, including, at first and for the most part, at the mid-point of indifference or averageness. Being somewho is thus always a being *valued* somehow or other *as* a who of such-and-such a reputational standing, even if this standing be average or neutral or indifferent. Just as things in their being, as encountered in everyday life, are always regarded *as* good or unsuitable for some application or other, so too are people in their whoness always regarded or esteemed highly or lowly or somewhere in between. Such valuing of each other is not a matter of mutually 'subjective' value judgements as distinct from some 'objective' valuation or other (e.g. that could be measured by collecting empirical data), but of the mirroring interplay *in between* in which individual qualities, above all abilities, come to be reflected in each other's estimation, and is thus subjective-objective, situated in the connecting hyphen (from Gk. ὑφέν 'together' 'in one' f. ὑφ', ὑπό under + ἕν one.). Status as who within the dimension of whoness therefore is constituted in the between and is prior to or undercuts any distinction between a subject and an objectivity standing over against it.

Without having explicitly seen the 3D-temporal clearing for being itself as the openness for presencing and absencing, nor having thought through the ontological phenomenon of whoness as a dimension sui generis within in the folds of being, Aristotle nevertheless associates the susceptibility to good and bad (ἀγαθοῦ καὶ κακοῦ *Pol.* 1253a18) with the essential determination of human being as τὸ ζῷον λόγον ἔχον (1253a10). This susceptibility and openness to understanding good and bad is not to be thought in the first place as a moral category, but rather pragmatically as the openness to seeing what is good in the sense of beneficial and suitable, and bad in the sense of what is harmful or useless (τὸ συμφέρον καὶ τὸ βλαβερόν 1253a15). The openness to being itself is not objective or neutral, but is essentially value-laden, 'coloured' with a valency. In other words, τὸ ἀγαθόν (the good) is another name for τὸ εἶναι (being itself), not only with regard to the self-showing of things themselves *as* what they are good for, but also and especially with regard to the self-showing and showing-off of human beings *as* who they are and how they are to be estimated and esteemed.

My proper name is the seed crystal of who I am that marks my singularity, my Jemeinigkeit in language, thus, paradoxically and painfully, making my singularity universal. To be a who means to bear a proper name and to bear the contradiction between singularity and universality. This means that *proper-named-ness* is an essential aspect or phenomenal-ontological moment of whoness. To this seed crystal of my proper name adhere all the practices and usages of everyday life I perform (ably or poorly) in which not only I understand myself, but through which also others view and regard me *as* who I am. My way of living is not only visible both to myself and others, but it is, as attributable to the underlying proper name which I bear, that for which I also bear *responsibility*. How I live is attributable to me as an individual human being leading my life, and shaping, casting my individual existence. My way of living is, on the one hand, the expression of my self-understanding with which I identify through self-reflection, i.e. my self-*identity*, that mirror-reflection which *belongs* to me *as* who I am. Self-reflection is to be understood here in the etymologically primal sense of a bending back on myself, which is the ontological structure of all self-identity. For others, on the other hand, my way of living is visible not only in having to do with me, but above all in what they hear about me. What they hear about me is my *reputation*, or in German, *Ruf* or 'call' or 'renown'. My reputation presents a view of me to the world which informs the views of others regarding how and whom they hold me to be.

Being held to be somewho in the view of others is also being held to be responsible for who I am and what I do. Who I am is always being estimated, both by myself and others. In my self-estimation resides the *call of conscience* (lit. co-knowing of my self, genitivus subjectivus) that estimates through self-reflection who I am and what I have done and how well I have done it. Being who thus means continually striving to stand in esteem and self-esteem, for the view of who I am is always subject to estimation, i.e. valuation. The striving to stand in esteem or honour is what Plato calls φιλοτιμία, literally, the 'love of esteem' or 'striving for esteem', and it is a phenomenon which plays a major role throughout Plato's thinking, in particular, in his *Republic* (Πολιτεία), although, it must be underscored, there is no ontology of whoness to be found in either Plato or Aristotle. This circumstance has given rise to the fateful *disjunction between ontology and ethics*. The striving to stand in esteem, i.e. to be validated in one's self-stand by others, is synonymous with the striving to be a human being with a standing in a community.

For human being, the world opens up not only in understanding things and states of affairs in their various interconnections, but also in estimating things, states of affairs and other persons in their goodness or badness in the amoral sense of whether they are good for something or good for nothing. Such goodness or badness is estimated in terms of whether the thing, state of affairs or person in question is beneficial or deleterious, suitable or unsuitable, applicable or inapplicable, relevant or irrelevant. Such estimating does not consist in sticking values onto so-called value-free facts, as if the facts were 'objectively' there first and the values were superadded later by a 'subjective' act, but rather, the world opens up from the outset, i.e. a priori, in what the situation, the thing, state of affairs or someone is good for. Their value is in their being, i.e. their mode of presencing, itself.

Whereas the being of something shows itself as *good for* or suitable for some application of other, the being of somewho is disclosed first of all in a *reputation* and *regard* which disclose what the person concerned is good for, thus being worthy of esteem. The goodness of a person does not mean in the first place that the person is morally good, but rather competent and able, excellent in some respect. Said negatively: the old Greek saying, οἱ πολλοὶ κακοί, does not mean that most people are morally bad, but that most people are good for nothing, or 'useless', 'worthless', which goes against today's democratic grain. Sharing the openness of 3D-temporal being as a social, sociating being means in its essence striving (through to the privative mode of failing to strive) to achieve and maintain a standing in reputation and regard that provides a good view of oneself, thus occasioning others to hold one in high regard as a worthy person.

One strives to present oneself in a good light and to show off that one is good for something or other with respect to the fulfilment of communal usages or what is appreciated and recognized by the community, however this community may be defined, be it a clique, a subculture, a peer group, a township, an electorate, or whatever. Such disclosure in a reputation, of course, does not have to correspond to how the individual concerned shows itself of itself as itself, but may be only partial or even totally deceptive, distortive and deluding. Furthermore, there may a great and painful disjuncture between how I regard my self and how I am regarded by others or by you. (The phenomena of recognition and you-and-I as modes of mutually mirroring and casting who each of us is will be investigated more closely in later chapters; cf. especially Chapter 5.6)

3.2 Human social being as self-presentation and showing-off in the 3D-temporal clearing in an interplay of estimable reputability (politeness, pride, vulnerability, arrogance, conceit)

Social intercourse and encounter, as I have said, take place in the ontological dimension or element of estimated and esteemed whoness, which enables and requires that the human beings encountering and entering into intercourse with one another regard and acknowledge each other a priori *as* worthy persons, where worthiness is regarded as an all-encompassing dimension covering also privative and neutral modes of estimation such as denigration, derogation, depreciation and indifference. This mutual regard (including one-sided disregard) applies even when the reputation of the other is hardly known, so that mutual acknowledgement becomes a matter of formal politeness. *Politeness* is the mode of conduct which pays formal regard to the estimable views or masks which the social actors present of themselves and show off as persons in general, daily social intercourse. As such, by formalizing the paying of regard, politeness allows social life to revolve around its pole without unnecessary friction. This lubrication is necessary only because human beings *are* somewho. *Impoliteness* too, of course, is situated within the dimension of estimated whoness as a deficiency in or privation of politeness, and can be characterized as the refusal to pay formal regard to, i.e. to disregard the worthiness of somewho as a person, which is a formal character mask, a *persona*. The worthiness to which politeness pays regard does not have the specific reputation of the individual concerned in view, but rather, politeness is a formal acknowledging of the status of estimable whoness in general. The other is formally and abstractly regarded as a worthy person, regardless of, and perhaps even despite, their particularity.

To be a *person* means to wear a mask of self-presentation to others, to present a look of who one is to others, and the polite intercourse among persons consists in the first place of calling each other by name. Impoliteness consists in overstepping the bounds of customary formal regard for the other as a person and may consist even in failing to address the other person by his or her proper name, the bearing of a proper name or *proper-namedness* being a hallmark and nub of whoness. The formal character of personhood means that the showing-off of oneself in social encounter and intercourse resembles the presentation of a mask through which the person pretends to be who they are. This mask is the form, i.e. εἶδος or look, that is presented to view. This pretence does not mean necessarily that there is anything false in the self-presentation, but merely that there is something schematic and even standardized about the view which an individual presents in the public open as a person.

One could ask why we are bothering with a phenomenon as banal, trivial and innocuous as politeness, a subject apparently more suitable for a sociology of manners. Why this concern with a mundane phenomenon of everyday life in a context concerned with the question of society as such? Would it not be more appropriate to discuss higher phenomena such as purportedly inalienable human rights and the dignity of the human person? Isn't it such noble, elevated ethical principles which should be the focus of our attention when discussing what it means to be a human being? However, are such principles of human dignity to be simply posited as celestial ideals, or rather, must it be asked how such principles can be grounded on Earth in view of the simple quotidian phenomena themselves that are first encountered? Is it not the case that the dignity of human being has its roots, and must have its roots in daily life if it is to be more than just some dreamt-up, concocted Utopian ideal or posited dogmatically as a birthright, putatively innate? How is the origin of human dignity (and indignity) to be located if not in social intercourse and encounter as they are lived everyday? One could perhaps offer an anthropological, evolutionary quasi-causal explanation in terms of the development of homo erectus, or a social history of mores, but such evolutionary arguments and social narratives are ultimately vacuous because, like all the sciences, they do not and cannot, as science, think through carefully and simply the phenomena themselves in their ontological structure, but instead necessarily implicitly presuppose them. Human being as such has to be thought as being's having laid claim on humans, appropriating them *as* human *beings* to the 3D-temporal clearing.

This has to be brought to light in the very first place. It is being itself which brings humans to stand as human beings in their being enpropriated to being, and it is the open temporal clearing for presencing and absencing as well as the truth of being that enables and empowers human beings to shows themselves off as *who* they are. Whoness is a phenomenon of being sui generis. It is being (the 3D-time-clearing) itself that in the first place enables and brings humans to stand as who by situating them in the clearing in a *sociating interplay of estimable reputability*. From such esteem and estimation springs not only the phenomenon of formal politeness, but also phenomena such as pride and vulnerability. *Pride* is the offensive showing-off of one's standing as who, whereas *vulnerability* arises from each who's being inevitably exposed to estimation by others, which includes the possibility of derogation and denigration.

Whoness is *the* essential, core, originally-enabling, social phenomenon of showing off to each other as human beings, and one's standing as somewho out there in the open is not just a neutral or 'objective' self-showing, but a showing-off which craves estimation and acknowledgement that can well be denied by others. To be human means to be concerned with and to care about one's standing in being estimated in the regard of others as somewho. This is an essential moment of the care of being human as the care of self, Selbstsorge. Human beings not only come to stand in being claimed and overwhelmed by being, thus being exposed to an understanding of being in an attunedness to it, but they also come to stand and be estimated in a look by each other in social interplay. The dimension of social interplay in sociative intercourse contains the folds of being into the first and second person, the phenomena of I myself, you yourself, we ourselves, you-and-I — phenomena that we will have to think through more closely in this investigation.

The circumstance that the whoness of whos is constituted through an interplay between and among whos implies that it is a thoroughly *relative* (πρός τι) phenomenon lacking the traditional substance (οὐσία) and also the very opposite of anything absolute, thus autonomous, self-contained, infinite. The relativity of whoness signifies the finitude and vulnerability of human being itself in its social, sociating nature. The vertical dimension of metaphysics is absent here; there is no longer any transcendent orientation toward a supreme being, whether it be God, the Absolute, the highest values or whatever.

Politeness is the mode of public social intercourse in which each person's standing as who in general is left uncontested and is formally acknowledged and respected, regardless of their specific merits or otherwise. Such formal respect for the other as a person (which is a kind of mask, a certain 'look') in everyday life must be regarded as the germ of general human dignity: the abstract, formal dignity of the person in its who-standing. Such possibility of standing as who is granted to humans in the first place by the openness of being's truth itself for revealing and concealing; insofar, a person's standing as who is not of their own making. From the outset, each human is cast into a standing as somewho. One may be proud, perhaps overweeningly so, of the standing one has achieved in one's social milieu, but the dimension of whoness which opens up the possibility of such a standing in the first place is not human-made and, in its mysterious grantedness, is not to be taken for granted and overlooked. The natural human dignity of a person as the mask-bearer of whoness is thus granted by being (the 3D-temporal clearing) itself in an ontological precasting; in other words, nature has to be understood in the early Greek sense as φύσις, i.e. as a name for being, meaning the emergence of beings into the open where they assume a stand *as* beings with their 'looks'.

The striving of human beings to stand as high as possible as somewho, may assume, for instance, the form of appearance of *arrogance* and *conceit*. In the phenomenon of arrogance, one claims too prominent a status for oneself in one's showing-off as who; one arrogates too much regard to oneself, similar to the phenomenon of conceitedness in which one narcissistically nurtures an overweening opinion of oneself and overestimates one's own qualities and worth. Originally, 'conceit' meant simply 'conception' or 'opinion' or 'view' and is thus related phenomenologically to Greek δόξα. Such self-conceit is, in the first place, the view one holds of oneself, one's self-image in a self-mirroring (but not in any 'inner', psychological sense). Such self-mirroring is enabled by the who's bending back (re-flecting) on its self. Such a view may correspond to how one is in truth but, in view of the striving for self-esteem, one's conceit of oneself tends to be, at first and for the most part, an over-estimation.[26] There is a striving, a reaching, an ὄρεξις on the part of every who to stand as high as possible in the interplay of whoness, and this leads inevitably to an over-estimation of oneself and a showing-off of oneself in order to stand as high as possible and thus to *be* more, higher, greater. This striving for a high standing as who could be termed the *phallic* germ of *phallocracy*. Another term would be *vanity*, which consists in holding a high opinion of oneself (a holding of oneself to be, to presence highly in the clearing for presencing), one that exceeds one's genuine abilities and merits and perhaps even covers up an intrinsic worthlessness. Social life is therefore not only ineluctably a showing-off of who one is, but for the most part is a parade of showing-off of standing and status and a *display of untruth* in the sense that humans as social beings tend to show themselves off as

---

26 As Hume remarks ontically, "Most men have an overwhelming conceit of themselves;" David Hume 'Of National Characters' Essay XXI, Part I in *Essays Moral, Political, and Literary* Part II 1752, reprinted Liberty Fund, Indianapolis 1985 p. 200.

more than who they are based on their genuine abilities, merits and achievements.

One could object that the above discussion of personhood, proper-namedness, politeness, the wearing of masks of self-presentation properly belongs to a sociology of social roles. But this would be superficial, for it would miss the point that all who-interplay of mutual estimation played out around the nub of the kernel of whoness consisting in my own proper name requires as stage not merely the world shared with others, but, prior to that, the open 3D-temporal clearing of being itself. My own proper name is the publicly visible side of my self. Selfhood has long since been an important subject in the modern ontology of consciousness, the nugget of self accompanying, as Kant says, all experience of the world. Once the phenomenality of whoness comes into view, however, it can be seen that the self bears masks of self-presentation to the world shared with others in mutually estimative games. I constitute my very self through such games of estimation, and that in a temporally three-dimensional way, because my self is not merely in the present moment, now, but itself temporal stretched into all three temporal dimensions. I am also who I once was and how this yester-self shows itself to me today. I am also who I may one day become, which may even be palpably visible to me in my ambitions, career-plans, etc. My polite comportment may be considered in the present situation, but has also its temporal correspondences in yesterness[27] and future. My impoliteness in the past, for instance, may well carry over to today in spoiling my reputation in the interplay with others who have heard rumours. Or my practising the locution of my speech may be part of *as* who I aim to present my self in the future. The theme of selfhood will recur in the following. It should be kept in mind that the playground for constitution of the self is ultimately the 3D-temporal clearing.

3.3 Further exemplary phenomena of standing and not standing as somewho (flattery, manliness) — The existential possibility of coming to one's very own, genuine stand as self

The complement to the phenomena of arrogance and conceitedness is that of *flattery*. Flattery is a comportment toward the other which mirrors to this other an unjustifiably aggrandized view of their standing as who. Flattery tickles the

---

27 From 'yester' "Of or belonging to yesterday" OED.

other's conceit and panders to their vanity in order to curry favour with the other. As such, flattery is a form of untruth of the who in the sense of a distorted self-showing that allows the other to wallow in vainglory and self-exaltation, either loudly and overtly or quietly and covertly. The flatterer presents in words and gestures a mirroring view of the flattered one which unjustifiably aggrandizes their standing and qualities. The flatterer does not reflect in words the view which the who presents of themself as themself, but rather reflects a distorted and exaggerated view of the flattered one. To exist as somewho means inevitably and essentially to be exposed in showing-off to the dangers of the falsity of both self-conceit and flattery in social intercourse. As far as oneself is concerned, at first and for the most part, one tends to over-estimate oneself and is thus in untruth with regard to oneself (*vanity*). Because of this tendency to over-estimate oneself, one is also prone to fall for the flattery in the manipulative mirrors which others hold up to magnify one's standing in order to achieve their own ends. Later (Chap. 5) we will see that this mirroring interplay is a power play among whos.

As a phenomenon of reflection of who one is and how tall one stands in the hierarchy of who-status, flattery is a (deficient) kind of *recognition*. The phenomenon of recognition, in turn, concerns how one comes to stand as one's own self, and thus with esteem and self-esteem, which will also be explored in more depth later on (cf. Chapter 5.6, Chapter 6.6 and the discussion of Hegel's "process of recognition" in Chapter 11.1).

Plato brings the phenomenon of flattery (κολακεία) into play very often in his dialogues, including the *Republic*, the *Laws*, *Symposium*, *Alcibiades*, *Phaidros*, and the *Sophist*[28]. It plays its most prominent role, however, in *Gorgias*, where rhetoric is classified as a merely empirical skill for flattering the souls of others with the aim of getting one's way with them (a kind of social power). The characterization of manliness in the first book of the *Laws*, however, provides perhaps one of the deepest insights into the essential nature of flattery as a vice and device that endangers the stand which an individual has won for itself in its existence. There we read:

ΑΘ. Τὴν ἀνδρείαν δέ, φέρε, τί θῶμεν; πότερον ἁπλῶς οὕτως εἶναι πρὸς φόβους καὶ λύπας διαμάχην μόνον, ἢ καὶ πρὸς πόθους τε καὶ ἡδονὰς καί τινας δεινὰς θωπείας κολακικάς, αἳ

---

28 "The sophistic λόγος, which serves a life [striving for] success at any price, pursues a κολακικὴ τέχνη (*Sophistes* 222e)." (Der sophistische λόγος, der dem um jeden Preis erfolgreichen Leben dient, verfolgt eine κολακικὴ τέχνη (*Sophistes* 222e). Peter Trawny *Sokrates oder Die Geburt der Politischen Philosophie* 2007 S. 30)

καὶ τῶν σεμνῶν οἰομένων εἶναι τοὺς θυμοὺς ποιοῦσιν κηρίνους. ΜΕ. Οἶμαι μὲν οὕτω· πρὸς ταῦτα σύμπαντα. (633d)

> Athenian: And, tell me, as what are we to define manliness? Whether simply as the struggle against fear and pain alone, or also against desires and pleasures and such powerful flattering enticements which make the heart as soft as wax, even of those who regard themselves as being above such things. Megillos: In my view, against both of these.

Manliness (ἀνδρεία), which is the abstract noun from ἀνήρ (man) and usually rendered in English as 'bravery', 'courageousness' or suchlike, is one of the four cardinal virtues, i.e. abilities and excellences, that recur again and again in Plato's and Aristotle's ethical discussions without ever gaining socio-ontological underpinnings as modes of being. As the above quotation, along with many others, shows, manliness is experienced by the Greeks as a steadfastness in the face of both physical and psychic danger. Above all, the psychic dangers, which consist in coaxing, cajoling, enticing, wheedling and flattering the soul with false esteem and the prospect of pleasures and the fulfilment of desire, have to be guarded against by assuming and upholding a firm stand. Such a sober, firm, well-defined manly stand stands like a bulwark in the way of succumbing to ἀκολασία, which means 'loss or lack of control', 'unbridledness', 'dissoluteness'. To be a human being means for the Greeks first and foremost to keep one's desires, i.e. the motive forces of the psyche that reach out (ὀρέγεσθαι), bridled and also to hold one's ground against phsycial dangers such as attack by an enemy or the terrors of natural forces.

Two typical ways in which loss of self-control takes place with respect to the body are gluttony and sexual indulgence. With respect to the soul or psyche, the principle of self-movement, to assume a manly, self-controlled stand means to exist as someone of good reputation who can regard themself in their self-presentation with self-esteem and can be regarded by others in high estimation. The prospect of pleasure or the satisfaction of desire with respect to both body and soul tends to cloud the view and to seduce the person concerned into a surrender of the control which upholds a commendable stand. In particular, in the case of flattery, the flattered one is enticed into surrendering their well-measured view of themself in favour of a grander view offered by the flatterer's charming, ensnaring words and actions, which are in themselves a pleasure to hear and enjoy. Such flattery could consist, for instance, in being invited to a sumptuous dinner with the most expensive wines.

The phenomena of love of esteem, flattery, manliness, etc. so prominent in the texts of Plato and Aristotle should not be viewed merely as admixtures, embellishments and ornamentation to the more serious, 'proper' concerns in their thinking, but instead should be interpreted in relation to how the Greeks experienced being and human being and human social being as presencing, as presentation and self-presentation, as self-showing and showing-off. The phenomenon of being 'who' is a phenomenon sui generis not to be thrown together undifferentiatedly with how Plato and Aristotle think through the being of beings in general as ἰδέα, εἶδος and in the κατηγορίαι (including δύναμις and ἐνέργεια). Rather, the phenomenon of 'whoness' should be put by us emphatically into relation with the more explicitly ontological concepts that capture the Greek experience of beings qua thingly beings in order to develop a *social* ontology with its own, specially fashioned and *differing* concepts.

Such a phenomenology of whoness brings to light a multifaceted ontological structure within a clearing, namely, the clearing of 3D-time in which human beings present themselves as who they are. As situated within the temporal clearing for presencing and absencing, the dimension of whoness is a clearing of *possibilities* for self-presentation as who in all three temporal dimensions, and the corresponding phenomenology is of modes of being, i.e. modes of presencing and absencing crossed with modes of revealing and concealing in the time-clearing,[29] and not merely an ontic typology. The open 3D-time-clearing for presencing and absencing offers a manifold of possibilities for self-presentation, both to oneself and to the others, which, in a German book.[30] I have called the *Gewer*. The prefix 'Ge-' in this context signifies a gathering into a manifold, whereas 'wer' means 'who'. Some of the existential possibilities held open by this manifold of whoness have been discussed above. They are above all possibilities of defining one's self both in one's understanding of oneself, so to speak, in one's self-image, and also for the others, in the look one presents of oneself.

At first, who I am is defined by how the others, or you, reflect back to me who I am. My self-understanding depends on who the others and you hold me to be, and I fashion my self-presentation in the shared openness of 3D-time accordingly. The cast I give to my as-yet-absent self in casting into the temporal dimension of the future is, at first and for the most part, borrowed from the others and you. By contrast, how I am held to be by others in their opinion is my reputation that is shaped largely from what they have heard about who I have been in the temporal dimension of absence. I continue to be also who I no longer am, my now absent who is also who I am, just as much as how I cast my self to be in a still absent future also constitutes an aspect of my whoness (e.g. my ambition), along with the present in which I present my self to myself and oth-

---

29 Such crossing implies a critique of Heidegger; cf. Eldred, M. *A Question of Time* 2015.

30 Cf. my *Phänomenologie der Männlichkeit: kaum ständig noch* 1999 and earlier: *Der Mann: Geschlechterontologischer Auslegungsversuch der phallologischen Ständigkeit* 1989.

ers. Whoness therefore is itself a temporally three-dimensional phenomenon of was, is and could be, all three of which are open to interpretation.

Your self-esteem is gleaned from the esteem in which others or I hold you to be at present based on your wasness as who. Coming to your very own, individual self-casting as a shaping of your own self-stand in existence is attained to a degree, if at all, only in freeing yourself from the approving or disapproving self-definitions and reflections held in stock by others. You come to your very own self-stand as who only in discovering and uncovering how your own world could be shaped in grasping your best existential possibilities, that is, your highest potentials. These potentials as powers residing in your individual freedom of self-movement in the world first have to be uncovered and nurtured into abilities. Only then can they be set to work as an energy, an ἐνέργεια, literally, an in-work-ness, and your self-presentation in the world then becomes the showing-off of your genuine inherent potentials and developed abilities, and does not remain merely the adaptation to the mirror images of how others, and be it ever so subtly, hold you to be.

This existential possibility of coming to your or my genuine, individual self-casting is only granted within the open dimension sui generis of the manifold of possibilities for being somewho. The manifold, itself a fold of being, must be granted a priori. Since my self-esteem, i.e. my estimation of who I am myself, is always intermingled with how I am held in esteem by others in the ongoing interplay, there is no autarkic self-definition entirely devoid of dependence on a shared world, no self-image that were not also a reflection from others. The standing in my self that I attain is thus always inclined, more or less, toward the others and you, and I gain my very own, genuine self-standing only through a differentiating process of estimation with certain others who mirror who I am to be. "Me in his eyes."[31]

So much for now on unfolding the phenomenon of whoness which will continue in later chapters. The phenomenon itself is present explicitly or implicitly throughout our *entire* inquiry into social being. Why? Because all social phenomena, as phenomena of sociating movement among the inevitable plurality of human beings, are of the estimative interplay of whos that is enabled in the first place by the open clearing of 3D-time for presencing and absencing.

---

31 James Joyce *Ulysses* Penguin, Harmondsworth 1968 p. 90.

3.3.1 Digression: Dialectic of self and other – Wrestling with Plato, Hegel, Heidegger

3.3.1.1 Preliminary considerations when approaching Plato's and Hegel's dialectical thinking

> Etwas Rätselhaftes, daß etwas ist als das, was es zugleich nicht ist.
>
> Martin Heidegger *Platon:Sophistes GA*19:580

> Somewhat perplexing that something is as that which, at the same time, it is not.

Let us first make our intentions clear in approaching the phenomena of self and other within the context of Plato's, Hegel's and Heidegger's thinking, by discussing in general terms what it means to interpret, or reinterpret today, a dialectical text of Plato's. We stand in an historical relationship to such philosophical texts, where history does not mean merely what is past and long past, but, since Hegel and Heidegger, the happening and shaping, along with and through philosophical thinking, of the continually temporalizing clearing in which we humans exist *as* human beings. Insofar, what Plato's thinking thinks is a stage in the progressive unfolding of those contours of beings in their being that have come to be known to philosophical knowing (Hegel). Moreover, what lies latent as *unthought* in Plato's texts can speak to us not merely innocuously in the fashion of a scholarly history of ideas (that has to be clearly distinguished from an Hegelian historical development of the Idea), but, by being receptive to what is sent and bringing the as-yet unthought to thought, as a shaping force for our historical future which has yet to arrive (Heidegger).

For Hegel, Plato's *Parmenides* — "the most famous masterpiece of Platonic dialectic" (dem berühmtesten Meisterstück der Platonischen Dialektik., *VGPII* W19:79[32]) — is a site where we can watch dialectical thinking in action and learn from it.

> Was nun die spekulative Dialektik des Platon anbetrifft, so ist dies, was bei ihm anfängt, das Interessanteste, aber auch das Schwierigste in seinen Werken, – so daß man es gewöhnlich nicht kennenlernt, indem man Platonische Schriften studiert. [...] Platons Untersuchung versiert ganz im reinen Gedanken; und die reinen Gedanken an und für sich betrachten, heißt Dialektik. [...] Solche reine Gedanken sind: Sein und Nichtsein (τὸ ὄν, τὸ οὐκ ὄν), das Eine und Viele, das Unendliche (Unbegrenzte) und Begrenzte (Begrenzende). Dies sind die Gegenstände, die er für sich betrachtet, – also die rein logische, abstruseste

---

32 G.W.F. Hegel *Vorlesungen über die Geschichte der Philosophie* II *Werke* Suhrkamp, Frankfurt/M. 1971 Band 19 S. 79, cited hereafter in the abbreviated form VGPII W19:79.

Betrachtung; dies kontrastiert dann freilich sehr mit der Vorstellung von dem schönen, anmutigen, gemütlichen Inhalt des Platon. (W19:65, 67)

As far as Plato's speculative dialectic is concerned, this, which begins with him, is the most interesting, but also the most difficult aspect of his works, so that one usually does not get to know it when studying Platonic writings. [...] Plato's investigation turns entirely upon pure thoughts, and to contemplate the pure thoughts in and for themselves is dialectic. [...] Such pure thoughts include being and non-being (τὸ ὄν, τὸ οὐκ ὄν), the one and the many, the infinite (unlimited) and finite (limiting). These are objects he contemplates for themselves — thus the purely logical, most abstruse contemplation; this of course then contrasts starkly with the notion of the beautiful, graceful, pleasant content of Plato's thinking. (W19:65, 67)

It always was a dull-witted caricature, one still doing its pedestrian service today, to characterize Hegel's dialectic as the three-step movement from thesis to antithesis to synthesis. Dialectic means to think through the interrelations among ontological concepts. The "pure thoughts" to which Hegel refers are not merely subjective ideas, but ideas with the full, ontological weight of the word as the 'looks' or sights of the beingness of beings presenting themselves to the mind's view. Philosophical thinking is able to see these facets of being, to speculate on them, explicitly bringing them to light as such, by engaging in the dialectic as "objective dialectic (Heraclitus), change, transition of things through themselves, i.e. of the ideas, that is here, of their categories, not external changeability, but inner transition out of and through itself" (objektive Dialektik (Heraklit), Veränderung, Übergehen der Dinge an ihnen selbst, d. i. der Ideen, d. i. hier ihrer Kategorien, nicht die äußerliche Veränderlichkeit, sondern inneres Übergehen aus und durch sich selbst, W19:66). The use of the word "category" is already an oblique reference to Aristotelean categories, which are likewise 'looks' of being, making Aristotle insofar just as much an 'idealist' as Plato and Hegel.

The "objective dialectic" must not be understood in the sense of so-called external change or temporal, ontogenetic becoming, but of the transitions of the ideas themselves out of themselves which can be thought through in dialectical thinking and which can be also externalized in external change, including the external, temporal change of human history which, according to Hegel, is the externalization of the one idea itself, i.e. the absolute Idea which for him is synonymous with God. Such externalization presupposes an interior which, for Hegel's subject-object ontology, is subjective consciousness, a preconception that calls to be put into question.[33] Thus, for instance, Plato's speculative dialec-

---

33 Cf. 'Clichés in Thinking' in my *A Question of Time* 2015.

tic is epoch-making not only in the history of philosophy but also "some centuries later constitutes the basic element in the fermentation of world history and the new shaping of the spirited human mind" (einige Jahrhunderte später überhaupt das Grundelement in der Gärung der Weltgeschichte und der neuen Gestaltung des menschlichen Geistes ausmacht, W19:66).

The perplexing thing about the ideas and their dialectical transitions is that they turn into their opposites. Hegel summarizes the overall result of Plato's masterly dialectic in the *Parmenides* as follows:

> Dieser Dialog ist eigentlich die reine Ideenlehre Platons. Platon zeigt von dem Einen, daß [es], wenn es ist, ebensowohl als wenn es nicht ist, als sich selbst gleich und nicht sich selbst gleich, sowie als Bewegung wie auch als Ruhe, Entstehen und Vergehen ist und nicht ist, oder die Einheit ebensowohl wie alle diese reinen Ideen sowohl sind als nicht sind, das Eine ebensosehr Eines als Vieles ist. In dem Satze 'das Eine ist' liegt auch, 'das Eine ist nicht Eines, sondern Vieles'; und umgekehrt, 'das Viele ist' sagt zugleich, 'das Viele ist nicht Vieles, sondern Eines'. Sie zeigen sich dialektisch, sind wesentlich die Identität mit ihrem Anderen; und das ist das Wahrhafte. Ein Beispiel gibt das Werden: Im Werden ist Sein und Nichtsein; das Wahrhafte beider ist das Werden, es ist die Einheit beider als untrennbar und doch auch als Unterschiedener; denn Sein ist nicht Werden und Nichtsein auch nicht. (W19:81f)

> This dialogue is, properly speaking, Plato's pure theory of ideas. Plato shows of the one that, if it is, and likewise, if it is not, it is equal and not equal to itself, movement as well as rest, arising and fading away, or, the unity as well as all these pure ideas are and are not, the one is one as well as many. The proposition, 'the one is', implies also 'the one is not one, but many', and conversely, 'the many is' says at the same time, 'the many is not many, but one'. They show themselves to be dialectical, are essentially the identity with their other, and that is what is genuinely true. An example is provided by becoming: In becoming there is being and non-being; what is genuinely true of both is becoming, the unity of both as inseparable but nevertheless different, for being is not becoming, and neither is non-being. (W19:81f)

As a summary of the result, this is not the dialectical movement of thinking itself that traces the transitions of the simple, pure ideas of themselves into their opposites, but only a description extrinsic to such a movement which, for Hegel, is divine:

> Indessen sehen die Neuplatoniker, besonders Proklos, gerade diese Ausführung im *Parmenides* für die wahrhafte Theologie an, für die wahrhafte Enthüllung aller Mysterien des göttlichen Wesens. Und sie kann für nichts anderes genommen werden. [...] Denn unter Gott verstehen wir das absolute Wesen aller Dinge; dies absolute Wesen ist eben in seinem einfachen Begriffe die Einheit und Bewegung dieser reinen Wesenheiten, der Ideen des Einen und Vielen usf. Das göttliche Wesen ist die Idee überhaupt, wie sie entweder für das sinnliche Bewußtsein oder für den Verstand, für das Denken ist. (W19:82)

> However, the Neo-Platonists, particularly Proclus, regard this explication in the *Parmenides* as the true theology, as the true revelation of all the mysteries of the divine being. And it cannot be regarded as anything else, [...] for by God we understand the absolute essence of all things; this absolute essence is precisely in its simple concept the unity and movement of these pure essentialities, of the ideas of the one and the many, etc. The divine being is the idea par excellence, as it is either for sensuous consciousness or for understanding, for thinking. (W19:82)

The divine being for thinking is shown, i.e. explicated, unfolded, in the *Logik* in the progressive movement of the dialectic from the abstract beginning of being in its "indeterminate immediacy" (unbestimmte Unmittelbarkeit) through its determination as determinate being (Dasein), via being, which is the self-certain truth of being in its immediacy, and essence in its appearance in the sense of a closer approximation of the philosophical idea to concrete reality (and conversely), to being as concept (Begriff), where the idea finally emerges as "subject-object", the concept as realized, insightful freedom. As a divine movement culminating in the absolute idea, the *Logik* can be called a theology, but as the movement from the purest, most abstract ideas such as being, non-being and becoming, through progressively more concrete ideas, which are concrete in the sense that they are the result of a progressive, cumulative 'growing together' of more and more determinations along the way, the *Logik*, along with the *Phänomenologie des Geistes*, is ontology. Heidegger comments on these works in 1942/43:

> Die eine und die andere Theologie [d.h. *PhdG* und *Logik*, ME] ist Ontologie, ist weltlich. Sie denken die Weltlichkeit der Welt, insofern Welt hier bedeutet: das Seiende im Ganzen.[34]

> The one and the other theology [i.e. *Phenomenology of Spirit* and *Logic*, ME] is ontology, is worldly/secular. They think the worldliness of the world insofar as world here means beings as a whole.

For Heidegger in a later, 1957 paper, this justifies the characterization of metaphysics in general, and Hegel's *Logik* in particular, as "onto-theo-logic" (Onto-Theo-Logik[35]). The divine thus comes into the world and is prosaically close at hand *as* the worldliness of the world. Being so close at hand, the godliness of the world is unrecognizable for a religion that experiences the divine as situated in a transcendent beyond. Hegel is above all a thinker who shows that the Abso-

---

34 Martin Heidegger 'Hegels Begriff der Erfahrung (1942/43)' in *Holzwege* 1950 S.187.

35 Martin Heidegger 'Die onto-theo-logische Verfassung der Metaphysik' in *Identität und Differenz* Neske, Pfullingen 1957 S. 56. Abbreviated *OTL*.

lute is not situated in some transcendent beyond, but commingles with finite beings which, as touched by the Absolute, are at the same time infinite, a synonym in Hegel's language for the Absolute and divine. This is apparent already in Hegel's interpretation of the Platonic ideas, which he brings down to earth, "that this essence of things is the same as the divine being" (daß dies Wesen der Dinge dasselbe ist, was das göttliche Wesen, W19:84). Such an interpretation agrees entirely with Heidegger's. The difference between Hegel and Heidegger is one of viewing angle, with the former looking toward the divine absolute, the latter toward the worldly, but with both looking at beings in their being. Hegel remains metaphysical in his thinking with its double character of ontology and theology, whereas Heidegger's thinking seeks no anchoring in a supreme being such as the absolute is, but retains the focus on ontology. In contrast to Hegel, Heidegger notes in his paper on onto-theo-logy:

> Wer die Theologie, sowohl diejenige des christlichen Glaubens als auch diejenige der Philosophie, aus gewachsener Herkunft erfahren hat, zieht es heute vor, im Bereich des Denkens von Gott zu schweigen. (OTL:51)

> Those who have experienced theology, both that of Christian faith and that of philosophy, from an evolved tradition, today prefer to remain silent about God in the realm of thinking.

Where Hegel speaks of the Idea, the being of beings, as the divine Absolute, Heidegger prefers reticence, but this may amount to the same thing, for Hegel himself underscores many times that the Absolute, a placeholder for God, is itself merely a "senseless sound" (sinnloser Laut; *PhdG* W3:26) whose meaning is given only through what is predicated of it through the movement of speculative-dialectical thinking, and these predicates are precisely the ontological concepts for the beingness of beings and ultimately the worldliness of the world. For Heidegger, the reason for keeping silent about God is not "some kind of atheism" (auf Grund irgendeines Atheismus, OTL:51), but the "step back" (Schritt zurück, OTL:46, 61, 63) from the onto-theo-logical constitution of metaphysics into the as yet "*unthought* unity" (*ungedachte* Einheit, OTL:51) of these two essential, onto- und theo-logical strands of metaphysical thinking. Whereas for Hegel, the God of the Christian religion is lifted[36] or sublated in *thinking* the

---

36 'Lift' as a rendering of the Hegelian term 'aufheben' captures at least some of its polysemy. 'To lift' means both 'to elevate' and 'to cancel' or 'to suspend', as in 'to lift a ban'. The third signification of 'aufheben' as 'bewahren' is 'to preserve', 'to keep'. An alternative, rhyming rendering of 'aufheben' is 'to raise, waive and save'.

Absolute dialectically (and therefore beyond the reach of and indeed unrecognizable for religious experience as normally understood), for Heidegger, this metaphysical God is merely a supreme being, a summum ens, a Causa sui:

> [...] Causa sui. So lautet der sachgerechte Name für den Gott in der Philosophie. Zu diesem Gott kann der Mensch weder beten, noch kann er ihm opfern. Vor der Causa sui kann der Mensch weder aus Scheu ins Knie fallen, noch kann er vor diesem Gott musizieren und tanzen. (OTL:70)

> [...] Causa sui. This is the appropriate name for the God of philosophy. Human beings can neither pray nor sacrifice to this God. Before the Causa sui a human being can neither kneel out of awe nor dance and make music.

However, it also can be observed that you don't need a god, whether Causa sui or not, to dance and make music, and that you can also kneel before a loved one, all of these acts being 'divine'. Heidegger had insight into the non-religious nature of the metaphysical god already early on:

> Θεῖον bei Aristoteles ist nichts Religiöses: θεῖον als das eigentliche Sein des Immerseins.[37]

> Θεῖον in Aristotle is nothing religious: θεῖον as the proper being of being-always.

It is therefore not without justification, and not even contrary to Hegel, that we shall further follow Heidegger's worldly viewing angle on metaphysical thinking, which situates the divine very close to home, at home even in prosaic, quotidian life[38] and not at all transcendent, if transcendence means a beyond. Then Hegel's *Logik* and Plato's *Parmenides* are indeed dialectics of the worldly, but divine in their worldliness insofar as they demonstrate the unique strangeness of human being itself, exposed as it is to the 'infinite' realm of ideas, ungraspable by finite understanding. Hegel himself is not at all far from Heidegger's worldly point of view when, in discussing the Neo-Platonist, Proclus, he notes that,

> Μυστήριον hat aber bei den Alexandrinern nicht den Sinn, den wir darunter verstehen, sondern es heißt bei ihnen überhaupt spekulative Philosophie. (W19:467)

---

37 Martin Heidegger *Grundbegriffe der Aristotelischen Philosophie* SS 1924 ed. Mark Michalski, Klostermann, Frankfurt/M. 2002 *GA*18:243.

38 Cf. Eldred, M. 'Absolutely Divine Everyday: Tracing Heidegger's thinking on godliness' 2008–2014 URL www.arte-fact.org/untpltcl/absdvnev.html

For the Alexandrians, μυστήριον does not have the meaning that we understand by it, but rather, for them it means speculative philosophy in general. (W19:467)

which brings philosophical thinking and the divine very close together, so close in fact, that it is the philosophers who hearken to what the Idea as Weltgeist has to send to humankind, a conception again not far removed from Heidegger's thinking on the history of being and its historical sendings, even though Heidegger underscores the leaps and ruptures in these sendings from being in its uniqueness rather than a continuous unfolding:

Wie es, das Sein, sich gibt, bestimmt sich je selbst aus der Weise, wie es sich lichtet. Diese Weise ist jedoch eine geschickliche, eine je epochale Prägung [...] In die Nähe des Geschicklichen gelangen wir nur durch die Jähe des Augenblickes eines Andenkens. (OTL:65)

How being gives itself is determined each time by itself in the way it clears and reveals itself. This way, however, is a sent/destinal way, an epochal coining [...] We only come close to what is sent through the suddenness of the moment of a commemorating thinking-upon.

Hegel, on the other hand, emphasizes the development or unfolding of the one Idea as Weltgeist. For instance, according to Hegel, with the discovery of the trinity, the concrete unity of three in one, "the Alexandrians grasped the nature of spirited mind" (Die Alexandriner [...] haben die Natur des Geistes aufgefaßt. W19:488)

Dies ist nicht so ein Einfall der Philosophie, sondern ein Ruck des Menschengeistes, der Welt, des Weltgeistes. Die Offenbarung Gottes ist nicht als ihm von einem Fremden geschehen. Was wir so trocken, abstrakt hier betrachten, ist / konkret. Solches Zeug, sagt man, die Abstraktionen, die wir betrachten, wenn wir so in unserem Kabinett die Philosophen sich zanken und streiten lassen und es so oder so ausmachen, sind Wort-Abstraktionen. ─ Nein! Nein! Es sind Taten des Weltgeistes, meine Herren, und darum des Schicksals. Die Philosophen sind dabei dem Herrn näher, als die sich nähren von den Brosamen des Geistes; sie lesen oder schreiben diese Kabinettsordres gleich im Original: sie sind gehalten, diese mitzuschreiben. Die Philosophen sind die μύσται, die beim Ruck im innersten Heiligtum mit- und dabeigewesen; die anderen haben ihr besonderes Interesse: diese Herrschaft, diesen Reichtum, dies Mädchen. ─ Wozu der Weltgeist 100 und 1000 Jahre braucht, das machen wir schneller, weil wir den Vorteil haben, daß es eine Vergangenheit [ist] und in der Abstraktion geschieht. (W19:488f)

This is not just a strange notion of philosophy, but a jolt to the spirited human mind, the world, the Weltgeist. The revelation of God has not happened to him as if by a stranger. What we contemplate here so drily and abstractly is concrete. People say that such stuff, the abstractions we contemplate when we let the philosophers quarrel and argue with one another in our cabinet and come to some agreement or other, are word-abstractions. ─

No! No! They are deeds of the Weltgeist, gentlemen, and therefore of destiny. The philosophers are closer to the Lord than those who nourish themselves from the crumbs of spirited mind; they read or write these cabinet orders straight in the original: they are obliged to copy them down. The philosophers are the μύσται who went along and were present in the innermost sanctuary at the jolt; the others have their particular interests: this reign, these riches, this girl. — That for which the Weltgeist needs a hundred or a thousand years we do more quickly because we have the advantage that it is a past and takes place in abstraction. (W19:488f)

When a 'pagan' Neo-Platonist such as Proclus retraces the abstract dialectic in Plato's *Parmenides* and works out the structure of the trinity, this is of course not a revelation of the Christian God, nor even necessarily of a supreme, divine being, but of the divine nature of being itself. The philosophers have a head start on human history as it is played out in strife and struggle because, in thinking through their abstractions, they fore-see the shape of ideas to come as they gain contour in the temporal clearing of historical time while the fog lifts from the human mind. In the above passage, Hegel employs the language of absolutist rule (e.g "cabinet orders"), but we need not be put off by the more authoritarian language of another age. Even today, as long as philosophy is practised, philosophical thinkers can hearken to that hidden source whose sendings, with much exertion on the thinkers' part, gradually come to light for speculative thinking, i.e. for the thinking gaze that looks past the mere given onticity of beings and sees the openness of being itself in its manifold. These general, preliminary thoughts on speculative, dialectical thinking may set the scene for what is at stake in interpreting, or reinterpreting and retrieving today from thoughtless oblivion, Plato's or Hegel's dialectic.

3.3.1.2 Approaching an existential dialectic of self and other through an interpretation of a passage from Plato's *Parmenides*

As announced, the initial focus in this digression is to be a lengthy passage from the mid-point of Plato's *Parmenides* which, alongside *The Sophist* and *Philebos*, is one of his dialectical dialogues, and the most elaborate and involved one in which Plato has the famous philosopher from Elea unfold a dialectic of τὸ ἕν, the one. The particular passage chosen is a dialectic of the one (τὸ ἕν), the others (τὰ ἄλλα), the same/self (ταὐτον) and the other (τὸ ἕτερον) which has a most perplexing, contradictory result. The reason for this choice is that the very ambiguity in the term ταὐτον, meaning both 'the same' and 'the self', holds promise of an interpretative twist that would allow the apparently abstract dialectic of simple essentialities, Wesenheiten or Platonic ideas to gain a concreteness and worldliness that it otherwise does not seem to possess, and did not yet possess in the historical world of the Greeks, for it is only in the modern age since Descartes that the self as an individual human subject has become the focus for philosophical thinking. We will read the passage not with a view to providing a detailed commentary and interpretation of it, but with regard to a more concrete idea of τὸ ἕν 'the one' and ταὐτον 'the same/self', namely, as "das Selbst", the individual self, for, to start with, we note along with Hegel that "the self is the simplest form of the concrete, the self is without content; insofar as it is determined, it becomes concrete" (Das Selbst ist die einfachste Form des Konkreten, das Selbst ist inhaltslos; insofern es bestimmt ist, wird es konkret [...], Hegel *VGPII* W19:487).

We can pursue such a strategy of reading because a dialectical development of the abstract ideas takes place in thinking that is the unfolding of the Idea itself, or the looks of being, i.e. the sights that being grants to beings, from very few, simple determinations through to progressively more determinations that 'grow together' in concreteness. Abstract ideas are the ontological building blocks of the world in its worldliness. The dialectical movement of ideas is the way thinking can come to grips with the being of the world, its ontological worldliness, bringing the manifold of separate determinations in their confusing multiplicity into an order of thinking that shows, if not their given complex, countless, ontic, empirical, partly causal interconnections, then at least their essential, simple ontological form-structure and how they hang together as looks or sights of being whose givenness is no longer taken for granted but becomes mysterious in the genuine sense of philosophy.

This is what Hegel means by bringing the phenomena to their concepts. The concept is always the ontological concept. Hegel's dialectic brings the phenomena to their concepts in a connected way under the encompassing idea of the absolute, thus creating a system. Otherwise the phenomena remain "begrifflos", "without concept", as they do throughout today's natural and social sciences, buffeted back and forth by the arbitrary winds and breezes of opinion and understood only as ungrounded notions or empirically given facts, whose ontological origins remain not only unclarified but entirely hidden. For, with Plato's discovery of the ideas as the looks of being lent to beings, the mystery of the world in its worldliness becomes graspable for (speculative) thinking, the thinking of Reason as distinct from Understanding, insofar as thinking can pursue the dialectic of these ideas, their contradictory movement into their opposites and into each other. Hegel therefore writes:

> Wenn Platon vom Guten, Schönen spricht, so sind dies konkrete Ideen. Es ist aber nur *eine* Idee. Bis zu solchen konkreten Ideen hat es noch weit hin, wenn man von solchen Abstraktionen anfängt als Sein, Nichtsein, Einheit, Vielheit. Dieses hat Platon nicht geleistet:

diese abstrakten Gedanken fortzuführen zur Schönheit, Wahrheit, Sittlichkeit; diese Entwicklung, Verpilzung fehlt. Aber schon in der Erkenntnis jener abstrakten Bestimmungen
selbst liegt wenigstens das Kriterium, die Quelle für das Konkrete. [...] Die alten Philosophen wußten ganz wohl, was sie an solchen abstrakten Gedanken hatten für das Konkrete. Im atomistischen Prinzip der Einheit, Vielheit finden wir so die Quelle einer Konstruk-
tion des Staats; die letzte Gedankenbestimmung solcher Staatsprinzipien ist eben das
Logische. (W19:85)

When Plato speaks of the good, the beautiful, these are concrete ideas. However, there is
only one idea. It is still a long way to such concrete ideas when one starts with such abstractions as being, non-being, unity, plurality. Plato has not achieved this, to continue
these abstract thoughts to beauty, truth, ethical life; this development/unfolding, spawn-
ing is missing. But already in the knowledge of those abstract determinations themselves
lies at least the criterion, the source for the concrete. [...] The ancient philosophers knew
very well that such abstract thoughts were invaluable for the concrete. In the atomistic
principle of unity, plurality we thus find the source for a construction of the state; the ultimate thought-determination of such principles of state is precisely the logical dimension. (W19:85)

The "principles" are the starting-points which govern a movement of thought,
allowing the simple ontological structure of a concrete manifold to progressively come to light. The simplest, most abstract ideas, such as the one and the
many, are only abstract, but they are the "criterion", the "ultimate thought-
determination", the "source", i.e. the ἀρχή in the Greek sense as the point of
origination or 'whence' that governs what follows from that origin, bringing
order and light into the confusing jumble of the world as it is ontically, factically
given to experience. The most abstract of ideas serve as principle, and "the
principle must gain content" (das Prinzip soll Inhalt gewinnen, *VGPII* W19:488)
because, at first, it is "only implicitly concrete; it is not yet known as concrete"
(nur an sich konkret, er wird noch nicht als konkret gewußt, (*VGPII* W19:488).
At first and for the most part, the ideas are seen and understood implicitly, i.e.
folded in on themselves, *an sich*.

In the present case we are not concerned with the "principle of unity, plurality" as "the source for a construction of the state" but with the dialectic of
five highly abstract ideas or looks of being: the one (τὸ ἕν), the not-one (τὰ μὴ
ἕν), the others (τὰ ἄλλα, τἆλλα, τἆλλα), the same/self (ταὐτον, identity, selfhood) and the other (τὸ ἕτερον, otherness) inhabiting "the logical dimension"
i.e. the ontological dimension, as the supposed "source", "criterion" and "ultimate thought-determination" for the ontological relations also between the
individual human self and the others. Let us finally hear the passage:

καὶ μὴν ταὐτόν γε δεῖ εἶναι αὐτὸ ἑαυτῷ καὶ ἕτερον [**146b**] ἑαυτοῦ, καὶ τοῖς ἄλλοις ὡσαύτως ταὐτόν τε καὶ ἕτερον εἶναι, εἴπερ καὶ τὰ πρόσθεν πέπονθεν.ᵔπῶς; --πᾶν που πρὸς ἅπαν ὧδε ἔχει, ἢ ταὐτόν ἐστιν ἢ ἕτερον· ἢ ἐὰν μὴ ταὐτὸν ᾖ μηδ' ἕτερον, μέρος ἂν εἴη τούτου πρὸς ὃ οὕτως ἔχει, ἢ ὡς πρὸς μέρος ὅλον ἂν εἴη.ᵔφαίνεται.ᵔἆρ' οὖν τὸ ἓν αὐτὸ αὑτοῦ μέρος ἐστίν; -- οὐδαμῶς.ᵔοὐδ' ἄρα ὡς πρὸς μέρος αὐτὸ αὑτοῦ ὅλον ἂν εἴη, πρὸς ἑαυτὸ μέρος ὄν.ᵔοὐ γὰρ οἷόν [**146c**] τε.ᵔἀλλ' ἄρα ἕτερόν ἐστιν ἑνὸς τὸ ἕν; --οὐ δῆτα.ᵔοὐδ' ἄρα ἑαυτοῦ γε ἕτερον ἂν εἴη.ᵔοὐ μέντοι.ᵔεἰ οὖν μήτε ἕτερον μήτε ὅλον μήτε μέρος αὐτὸ πρὸς ἑαυτό ἐστιν, οὐκ ἀνάγκη ἤδη ταὐτὸν εἶναι αὐτὸ ἑαυτῷ; -- ἀνάγκη.ᵔτί δέ; τὸ ἑτέρωθι ὂν αὐτὸ ἑαυτοῦ ἐν τῷ αὐτῷ ὄντος ἑαυτῷ οὐκ ἀνάγκη αὐτὸ ἑαυτοῦ ἕτερον εἶναι, εἴπερ καὶ ἑτέρωθι ἔσται; --ἔμοιγε δοκεῖ.ᵔοὕτω μὴν ἐφάνη ἔχον τὸ ἕν, αὐτό τε ἐν ἑαυτῷ ὂν ἅμα καὶ ἐν ἑτέρῳ.ᵔἐφάνη γάρ.ᵔἕτερον ἄρα, ὡς ἔοικεν, [**146d**] εἴη ταύτῃ ἂν ἑαυτοῦ τὸ ἕν.ᵔἔοικεν.ᵔτί οὖν; εἴ τού τι ἕτερόν ἐστιν, οὐχ ἑτέρου ὄντος ἕτερον ἔσται; -- ἀνάγκη.ᵔοὐκοῦν ὅσα μὴ ἕν ἐστιν, ἅπανθ' ἕτερα τοῦ ἑνός, καὶ τὸ ἓν τῶν μὴ ἕν; --πῶς δ' οὔ; --ἕτερον ἄρα ἂν εἴη τὸ ἓν τῶν ἄλλων.ᵔἕτερον.ᵔὅρα δή· αὐτό τε ταὐτὸν καὶ τὸ ἕτερον ἆρ' οὐκ ἐναντία ἀλλήλοις; -- πῶς δ' οὔ; --- οὖν ἐθελήσει ταὐτὸν ἐν τῷ ἑτέρῳ ἢ τὸ ἕτερον ἐν ταὐτῷ ποτε εἶναι; -- οὐκ ἐθελήσει.ᵔεἰ ἄρα τὸ ἕτερον ἐν τῷ αὐτῷ μηδέποτε ἔσται, οὐδὲν ἔστι τῶν ὄντων ἐν ᾧ ἐστιν τὸ ἕτερον χρόνον οὐδένα· [**146e**] εἰ γὰρ ὁντινοῦν εἴη ἔν τῳ, ἐκεῖνον ἂν τὸν χρόνον ἐν ταὐτῷ εἴη τὸ ἕτερον. οὐχ οὕτως; --οὕτως.ᵔἐπειδὴ δ' οὐδέποτε ἐν τῷ αὐτῷ ἐστιν, οὐδέποτε ἐν τινι τῶν ὄντων ἂν εἴη τὸ ἕτερον.ᵔἀληθῆ.ᵔοὔτ' ἄρα ἐν τοῖς μὴ ἓν οὔτε ἐν τῷ ἑνὶ ἐνείη ἂν τὸ ἕτερον.ᵔοὐ γὰρ οὖν.ᵔοὐκ ἄρα τῷ ἑτέρῳ γ' ἂν εἴη τὸ ἓν τῶν μὴ ἓν οὐδὲ τὰ μὴ ἓν τοῦ ἑνὸς ἕτερα.ᵔοὐ γάρ.ᵔοὐδὲ μὴν ἑαυτοῖς γε ἕτερ' ἂν εἴη ἀλλήλων, μὴ μετέχοντα [**147a**] τοῦ

"And again, it must be the same with itself and other than itself, [**146b**] and likewise the same with all others and other than they, if the preceding [argument] has been received." "How is that?" "Everything stands to everything in one of the following relations: it is either the same or other; or if neither the same or other, its relation is that of a part to a whole or of a whole to a part." "Obviously." "Now is the one a part of itself?" "By no means." "Then it cannot, by being a part in relation to itself, be a whole in relation to itself, as a part of itself." "No, that is impossible." "Nor can it be other than itself." [**146c**] "Certainly not." "Then if it is neither other nor a part nor a whole in relation to itself, must it not therefore be the same with itself?" "Necessarily." "Well, is not a being that is in another place/time than itself—being in the same with itself—necessarily itself other than itself, if it is to be also in another place/at another time?" "It seems so to me." "Thus the one was revealed to behave, being in itself and in an other at the same time." "Yes, it was revealed to be so." "Therefore, as it appears, the one would be insofar other than itself." [**146d**] "So it appears." "Well then, if something is other than..., will it not be other than another being?" "Necessarily." "Are not all that is not one other than one, and the one other than the not one?" "How could they not be?" "Then the one would be other than the others." "Yes, it is other." "But look, are not the same itself (sameness) and the other (otherness) opposites of one another?" "How could they not be?" "Then will the same ever come to be in the other, or the other in the same?" "No." "Then if the other can never be in the same, there is no being [**146e**] in which the other is during any time; for if it were in any being during any time whatsoever, the other would be in the same, would it not?" "Yes, it would." "But since the other is never in the same, it can never be in any beings." "True." "Then the other can be neither in the not one nor in the one." "No, indeed, it cannot." "Then not through the other will the

ἑτέρου.ⁿπῶς γάρ; --εἰ δὲ μήτε αὐτοῖς
ἕτερά ἐστι μήτε τῷ ἑτέρῳ, οὐ πάντη ἤδη
ἂν ἐκφεύγοι τὸ μὴ ἕτερα εἶναι ἀλλήλων; --
ἐκφεύγοι.ⁿἀλλὰ μὴν οὐδὲ τοῦ ἑνός γε
μετέχει τὰ μὴ ἕν· οὐ γὰρ ἂν μὴ ἓν ἦν, ἀλλά
πη ἂν ἓν ἦν.ⁿἀληθῆ.ⁿοὐδ' ἂν ἀριθμὸς εἴη
ἄρα τὰ μὴ ἕν· οὐδὲ γὰρ ἂν οὕτω μὴ ἓν ἦν
παντάπασιν, ἀριθμόν γε ἔχοντα.ⁿοὐ γὰρ
οὖν.ⁿτί δέ; τὰ μὴ ἓν τοῦ ἑνὸς ἄρα μόριά
ἐστιν; ἢ κἂν οὕτω μετεῖχε τοῦ ἑνὸς τὰ μὴ
ἕν; --μετεῖχεν.ⁿεἰ ἄρα πάντη τὸ μὲν ἓν
ἐστι, [**147b**] τὰ δὲ μὴ ἕν, οὔτ' ἂν μόριον
τῶν μὴ ἓν τὸ ἓν εἴη οὔτε ὅλον ὡς μορίων·
οὔτε αὖ τὰ μὴ ἓν τοῦ ἑνὸς μόρια, οὔτε ὅλα
ὡς μορίῳ τῷ ἑνί.ⁿοὐ γάρ.ⁿἀλλὰ μὴν
ἔφαμεν τὰ μήτε μόρια μήτε ὅλα μήτε ἕτερα
ἀλλήλων ταὐτὰ ἔσεσθαι ἀλλήλοις.ⁿἔφαμεν
γάρ.ⁿφῶμεν ἄρα καὶ τὸ ἓν πρὸς τὰ μὴ ἓν
οὕτως ἔχον τὸ αὐτὸ εἶναι αὐτοῖς; --
φῶμεν.ⁿτὸ ἓν ἄρα, ὡς ἔοικεν, ἕτερόν τε
τῶν ἄλλων ἐστὶν καὶ ἑαυτοῦ καὶ ταὐτὸν
ἐκείνοις τε καὶ ἑαυτῷ. [**147c**] --κινδυνεύει
φαίνεσθαι ἔκ γε τοῦ λόγου.

one be other than the not one or the not one
other than the one." "No, indeed." "And
surely they cannot through themselves be
other than one another, if they do not partake
of the other." [**147a**] "How could they be?"
"If then neither through themselves nor
through the other are they other, will they
then not at all escape out of being not other
than one another?" "Quite impossible." "But
neither can the not one partake of the one;
for in that case they would not be not one, but
would be one." "True." "Nor can the not one
be a number; for then, thus having number,
they would not be entirely not one." "No,
they would not." "Well, then, are the not one
parts of the one? Or would the not one thus
also partake of the one?" "Yes, they would
partake of it." [**147b**] "If, then, entirely, on
the one hand there is one and on the other not
one, the one cannot be a part of the not one,
nor a whole of which the not one are parts,
nor are the not one parts of the one, nor a
whole of which the one is a part." "No, indeed." "But we said that things which are
neither parts nor wholes nor other than one
another, will be the same as one another."
"We said so indeed." "Shall we also say,
then, that since the one relates thus to the not
one, they are the same with themselves?"
"Let us say that." "The one, then, is, it appears, other than the others and than itself,
and is also the same as the others and as
itself." [**147c**] "This dares to show itself from
the argument." (Perseus 2.0, modified)

The result of the intermediate dialectic, we read, is that "The one, then, is, it
appears, other than the others and than itself, and is also the same as the others
and as itself." [147c], a most perplexing result which is now to be translated into
its more concrete meaning with regard to human beings in their being. The one
then becomes the individual, and the others are other human beings. According
to the dialectical result, the individual is the same as itself, other than itself,
other than the others, and also the same as the others. How is this possible?
How can such a result, which defies plain logic, be arrived at? Is Plato's dialectic here only "superficial" (äußerlich), as Hegel claims generally for certain of

the transitions in the *Parmenides*? First of all, it seems perfectly obvious that the individual is the same as itself, and this indeed is the first leg of the intermediate dialectic 146b-147c which is arrived at indirectly by excluding in turn that the one could be a part of itself, or the one could be a whole of which it itself is part, or that the one could be other than itself.

More light can be shed on the one being the same as itself from a formulation in *The Sophist* occurring in the famous dialectic of the five abstract "genera" (γένη): movement (κίνησις), standstill (στασις), being (τὸ ὄν), the same and the other with regard to the first three: Οὐκοῦν αὐτῶν ἕκαστον τοῖν μὲν δυῖν ἕτερον ἐστιν, αὐτὸ δ᾽ ἑαυτῷ ταὐτόν. (254d14) Heidegger translates, overlooking that not two, but three genera are involved, "Nun ist doch von ihnen jedes der beiden ein anderes, selber aber ihm selbst dasselbe"[39] My own rendering: "Is not each of them other than the other two, itself however the same with itself." The queer thing about Plato's formulation is the threefold occurrence of "the same" in nominative, accusative and dative. Heidegger interprets this third, dative occurrence "*as* the mediation with itself" (*als* die Vermittelung mit ihm selbst; *GA57*:116), so that the identity of a being with itself is not merely an obvious tautology, saying 'nothing', as plain-speaking logicians would like to have it, but an ontological insight that first gains its full status in German speculative idealism with "Fichte, Schelling and Hegel" (Fichte, Schelling und Hegel, *GA57*:116). Heidegger offers a phenomenological interpretation of the mediated nature of the principle of identity, which is a statement (Satz), by pointing out that, "The statement A is A lays A there as A." (Der Satz A ist A legt A als A dar. *GA57*:111). That is, like all sentences such as 'The road is long', the principle of identity brings to presence and lays before us A *as* itself, i.e. the principle says that A shows itself of itself *as* itself. The principle thus refers to the *possibility* of A disclosing itself *as* it is of itself, the possibility of truth as disclosedness: A presents itself *as* A. With regard to the human individual, this abstract principle posits the possibility of an individual's presenting itself to itself and others *as* itself, which is one characteristic of authenticity, as will be laid out further below.

The second leg of Plato's above-cited dialectic is to show that the one is other than itself, and this is because it can be "in another place/time" [ἐτέρωθι 146c] whilst remaining itself, the Greek word ἐτέρωθι having, ambiguously, both a spatial and temporal sense. Any being, not just a human individual,

---

39 'Grundsätze des Denkens Freiburger Vorträge 1957', III. Vortrag 'Der Satz der Identität' in *Bremer und Freiburger Vorträge* ed. Petra Jaeger *Gesamtausgabe* Band 79, Klostermann, Frankfurt *GA79*:116.

whilst being itself is other than itself, *insofar* (ταύτῃ, in this point) as it is also itself at an *other* place or time which, of course, presupposes movement, change. The third leg is very brief and consists of only two steps. The one is other than the not-one seems uncontroversial since only the negation is applied to the one. But, in being other than the not-one, the one is other than other *beings*, and the not-one as beings are the others (τἆλλα). In particular, this implies that the individual is other than the others. The fourth and final leg of the proof is the lengthiest and involves a detour through a dialectic of sameness and otherness, which are opposites to one another (ἐναντία ἀλλήλοις [146d]). Being opposites, they cannot partake in each other at all; they contradict each other. In particular, otherness cannot be in any being for any time at all because, if it were, it would be in the same for this time and therefore insofar partake of sameness. Therefore, the one and the others, if they are other than one another, cannot be so by virtue of otherness being in them, nor, plainly, can they be so by virtue of sameness being in them. Therefore, they cannot "escape out of" (ἐκφεύγοι [147a]) being not other than one another. Nor can the one be part of the others as whole, nor the others part of the one as whole. There remains, by exclusion, only the possibility that the one and the others are the same. That, concisely, is the dialectic of the one and the others in the middle of the *Parmenides*.

What could this mean with a view to the individual and the others? The individual human being is the same or identical with itself in a way quite different from the sameness with themselves of other beings, for the individual human being *is* itself a self. That this self is the same (ταὐτον) with itself is not a 'logical' triviality like A = A, but has phenomenological content, for the individual as self relates to itself, i.e. it is reflexive, bent back upon itself in being open to, knowing and understanding itself *as* itself along with understanding objects. Consciousness in modern metaphysics is therefore literally a co-knowing of self along with the object. This doubling is what is traditionally referred to as self-consciousness, by virtue of which, according to Kant, the human being is the unique being able to say 'I'.

But in *saying* 'I', the individual has already betrayed itself *as* a singular individual, for by so saying, it has called itself by a universal title, raising itself out of its unique *singularity* into *universality*. When the 'I' comes over the human, making it a human *being*, this 'I' is supposed to designate I myself in my singularity, but in truth does just the opposite, for every individual human being is an 'I', encroached upon (übergriffen, 'reached over') and covered by this universal designation. There is no way of pointing to individual singularity without already translating it over the gulf to universality. It can even be said that there *is* no singularity at all, insofar as unique singularity has always already been universalized by the gathering of the λόγος. Is there only *logical* access to being? In what sense of λόγος and logic? Apart from the self-reflexivity of the I, there is also its possibility, as pointed out above, of its showing itself off as itself, insofar being itself: I am I insofar as I show myself to myself and the world as myself.

To say 'I am' is to speak in the first person vis-à-vis the others who, for the most part, are in the third person: 'they'. There is a gulf between the first person and the third person, for the I is only itself and not the others. I is *other* (ἕτερον) than the others. But even this description in terms of first and third person does violence to the phenomenological situation here, because these titles are themselves universal, not individual and singular. Moreover, the others also say 'I' of themselves; insofar we are the same as each other. And yet, when I reflect on myself as myself, I am aware of the unbridgeable gulf between my self and the others. There is and cannot be any language of singularity, which remains not only mute, but ungatherably beyond or prior to the λόγος altogether. Singularity itself is a universal designation. In bending back upon itself as a self in self-consciousness, thus becoming a human being *as* (modern) subject, the singular individual is always already cast irrevocably into universality, is *part* of this universality and insofar a *particular*, not a unique singularity. Being the same as itself in being reflected back upon itself *as* a self, the individual subject has already left individuality in the sense of unique singularity, for this self-reflection through which it understands itself *as* self goes hand in hand with the human individual's being *aware* of and *understanding* the world which can be *articulated* in language as a totality of beings. The individual has 'transcended' or 'climbed over' (überstiegen) to the world.

The individual as a self can say, 'I am', and it can say this in one place or another, one time or another, remaining itself as a self in becoming other in time and space (ἑτέρωθι [146c]). This would correspond to Plato's dialectic as we have discussed it, and also to Fürsichsein or being-for-itself as thought in Hegel's *Logik*. Existing as it does in time and space understood in the traditional senses, the individual self is *other* (ἕτερον) than itself through being not just living movement, but living movement that is bent back on itself as self-reflection: I know myself *as* my identical self, remaining myself through (traditional) moving time, and this phenomenon of self-identity is richer, more concrete than the abstract identity demonstrated in Plato's dialectic or initially in Hegel's *Logik* in the so-called Seinslehre or Doctrine of Being.

Moreover — and this corresponds to the most round-about part of the dialectic in the passage cited from the *Parmenides* — since sameness and otherness (or identity and difference) are opposites (ἐναντία [146d]), i.e. contradictory, otherness cannot reside in me in my singularity, for *as* singular I am purely identical with myself, a pure, empty tautology beyond any grasp or gathering and prior to any self-showing of myself *as* myself. Similarly, otherness cannot reside in the others as singularities. Insofar, I am not other than the others by virtue of otherness residing either in me or in the others. Furthermore, I as this singularity am not the whole who contains the others, nor are the others the whole of whom I am part. There remains therefore only the possibility of I and the others being the same. But this is only an indirect, negative proof which is also rather formal, so let us attempt a more phenomenological, positive demonstration:

The individual does not merely say, 'I am', nor does it say merely, 'I am I', thus expressly saying its reflexive identity with itself in a superfluous tautology, but rather it knows itself to be and says that it is other than I by understanding itself *as* such-and-such, for instance, 'I am tired'. I am not tiredness itself, but I am it also in a certain way, for as tired I partake of tiredness; it belongs to me in the given situation and insofar I am the same as tiredness. 'I am tired' brings my tiredness to appearance in presence, first of all, for myself in my self-understanding. Beyond transitory situations, I also understand myself to be a reliable person or of a certain vocation, and being reliable or exercising a certain particular vocation, say, translator, car mechanic or fashion designer, I *identify* myself with and *am* insofar the *same* (ταὐτόν) as reliability and the vocation in question in comporting myself within certain habitual practices in the world, for selfhood is not a matter of a so-called inner identity, but of an identity as a way or ways of being in the world, of how I comport myself habitually in the life practices that constitute my world that my mind encompasses. I identify myself plainly with what I am *not* in understanding my self *as* a translator, car mechanic or fashion designer, perhaps even saying occasionally to myself, 'I am a translator'. Only by identifying myself with something other, i.e. with what I am not, do I escape the hollow, tautological, selfsame selfness of 'I am I' (the self-confirmation of the self-conscious ego for itself and thus the origin of modern subjecthood), for, to say 'I am...' is already to expect an otherness, a difference, and not merely the repetition of a tautological identity that says nothing. Hegel expresses this in his *Logik* with regard to *all* beings (which must have been overcome by being to *be* beings) as follows:

> Es liegt also in der *Form des Satzes*, in der die Identität ausgedrückt ist, *mehr* als die einfache, abstrakte Identität [A ist A, ME]; es liegt diese reine Bewegung der Reflexion darin, in der das Andere nur als Schein, als unmittelbares Verschwinden auftritt; *A ist*, ist ein Beginnen, dem ein Verschiedenes vorschwebt, zu dem hinausgegangen werde; aber es

kommt nicht zu dem Verschiedenen; *A ist – A*; die Verschiedenheit ist nur ein Verschwinden; die Bewegung geht in sich selbst zurück. – Die Form des Satzes kann als die verborgene Notwendigkeit angesehen werden, noch das Mehr jener Bewegung zu der abstrakten Identität hinzuzufügen.[40]

Hence there is in the *form of the proposition* in which the identity is expressed *more* than the simple, abstract identity [A is A, ME]; there is this pure movement of reflection in it in which the other appears only as the shining of an illusion, as an immediate vanishing; 'A is' is a beginning, in which something distinct/different is envisaged, toward which a movement is made; but it never arrives at something distinct; 'A is – A'; the distinctness is only a vanishing; the movement goes back into itself. – The form of the proposition can be regarded as the hidden necessity to add to the abstract identity the excess/surplus of that movement.

Insofar, with regard in particular to the first person at issue here, to be who I am, I identify myself, and must identify myself with what or who I am not, i.e. with the other, and this identity with the other is by no means negatively an *alienation* (othering or estranging) *from* myself, but such othering from myself is constitutive of my genuine *identity with* myself, my sameness. In identifying myself with the other, and thus insofar *being* the other, I am simultaneously myself and also positively alienated or othered from myself. Moreover, to *be* myself *as* a self in the world, I must be *other* than myself and insofar *self-alienated, self-othered*. To be my singular self, I must *be* universal, graspable *as* who I am only through universals such as "tiredness" or "car mechanic". 'I am I' then does not say merely tautological self-identity but 'I present my self *as* who I am — to both myself and others'.

I am therefore other than myself in being identical with myself, and in being so, I, this unique singularity, am universal, my opposite, thus, a *living contradiction*. I can only understand myself *as* self through the universals which shape the world into which I have been cast, by partaking of those universals as a *particular* instance and thus understanding myself and being understood by others in terms of such particularity, which forms the always *broken middle* or rickety, mediating bridge between singularity and universality. Others can also partake of this universal. E.g. if I am reliable or a translator or a fashion designer, others can also be reliable or translators or fashion designers. Insofar, I am the same as the others, and the others are the same as me. The mediation between me and the others is that we partake, albeit each of us in countless, idiosyncratic, combinatorial constellations, of the same universal(s), thus being insofar identical with each other *as particulars* by participating willy-nilly in

---

40 Hegel *Logik II, Werke* Bd. 6 W6:44.

universality. Universality, for its part, is thrown up by an historical world as a cast of being enabling certain masks for participating existentially in it. *Particularity* bridges, i.e. mediates, the gulf between singularity and universality, and thus also between singularity and singularity, insofar as it can be bridged at all. This bridging may be relatively smooth, firm and affirmative, or broken, tortured and tentative, depending upon the degree of fracturedness with which singularity in its reflexiveness is able to identify itself with the universals, i.e. the ideas or looks of being, that shape its historical world in a given age. As already stated, I as this singularity am not the whole who contains the others, nor are the others the whole of whom I am part; for me to be merely a participant in a whole defined by the others would be a totalitarian conception of the individual. To be the same as the others, we must be mediated with one another by something in the middle in partaking of the same universal(s), for I *as* this singularity cannot be the same as the others *as* the singular beings they are.

3.3.1.3 The Hegelian dialectic of the concept, primal splitting and closing together

The last part of the preceding section is a provisional, initial attempt at an existential interpretation of the structure of identity and otherness proceeding not only from the passage in Plato's *Parmenides*, but from a passage in Hegel's *Logik* that deals entirely abstractly with the identity of the Satz or proposition, albeit that in Hegel's grand attempt at ontologization, all the traditional logical categories now become speculative, i.e. ontological. The proposition has long since been the locus for logic and the λόγος, as well a truth itself, starting with Aristotle, but the German word for proposition, 'Satz', offers also another, surprising rendering when attention is paid to the ambiguity, or indeed polyvalent signification of the word, a semantic polyvalence exploited also by Heidegger in his 1951 lectures, *Der Satz vom Grund*. 'Satz', namely, can mean not only 'sentence' or 'proposition', but also 'jump' or 'leap'.

When viewed from this perspective, the speculative Satz can be seen to demand a leap to the other, thus breaking with the tautological jumping on the spot of merely abstract identity, A = A, which says nothing apart from a bending back on itself. For the proposition to say something rather than nothing, it must leap to bring its subject into identity with its other, the predicate, i.e. with what is predicated of the subject or with what the subject is 'accused' (κατηγορεύειν) of being as a being. That the proposition is in truth a leap cannot be seen within the strictures of formal logic to which all analytic philosophy is bound, precisely because of its analyticity that excludes syntheticity, for formal logic is finite understanding at work, endeavouring to keep distinctions clearly distinct and separate rather than seeing the infiniteness and dialectical movement of the proposition understood ontologically as a leap from subject to predicate that constitutes synthetically an identity between different termini.

Let us pursue this line of thought further on the abstract level of logic understood in the Hegelian way as ontological structure by delving into the dialectic of the poles constituting identity. By doing so, we will be practising dialectics in the sense of "contemplat[ing] the pure thoughts in and for themselves" (W19:67) and also continuing to follow up on Hegel's insight that "[t]he ancient philosophers knew very well that such abstract thoughts were invaluable for the concrete" (W19:85), an insight today clouded by analytic glaucoma. We need to infiltrate the text to live and breathe through its pores in order to shake off the impression propagated by Hegel's many detractors in our profoundly unphilosophical age that he is performing merely capricious dialectical acrobatics that can be written off as 'mystical' or 'speculative' nonsense. The pure thoughts of dialectical thinking are the abstract, ontological elements from which the world in its worldliness is built.

The identity and difference of subject and predicate is dealt with in the *Logik* as the theory of the judgement (das Urteil) which is itself the second chapter of the first section of three sections in the Doctrine of the Concept, which in turn forms the concluding third part of the *Logik* as a whole. The first section of this culminating part of the *Logik* bears the heading "Subjectivity" (Die Subjektivität), which is itself misleading because the three chapters it comprises, The Concept (Der Begriff), The Judgement (Das Urteil) and The Conclusion (Der Schluß), are by no means to be taken as merely aspects of the (subjective) thinking mind, but equally as ontological structures of reality itself. The concept itself "contains the three moments: *universality*, *particularity* and *singularity*" (enthält die drei Momente: *Allgemeinheit*, *Besonderheit* und *Einzelheit*, LII W6:273) that are held in unity by the concept that, as free "being-in-and-for-itself" (Anundfürsichsein, W6:273), posits each of its moments, each of which being "just as much the *whole concept* as *determinate concept* and as *a determination* by the concept" (sosehr *ganzer Begriff* als *bestimmter Begriff* und als *eine Bestimmung* des Begriffs, W6:273). The emphasis here is at first on the concept's unity that holds together and mediates its three moments, but, as "absolute negativity" (absolute Negativität, W6:272) and initially as "immediate" (unmittelbare, W6:272) concept, it "dirempts itself" (dirimiert [...] sich, W6:272) so that "the moments become *indifferent to each other* and each for itself" (die Momente *gleichgültig gegeneinander* und jedes für sich wird, W6:272) and "its unity in this *division* [as judgement] is only a merely extrinsic *relation*" (seine Einheit ist in dieser *Teilung* nur noch äußere *Beziehung*, W6:272) of "moments posited as *independent* and *indifferent*" (als *selbständig* und *gleichgültig* gesetzte(n) Momente, W6:272).

The "unity of the concept lost in its independent moments" (Einheit des in seine selbständigen Momente verlorenen Begriffs, W6:272) therefore has to be regained through the "dialectical movement of the judgement" (dialektische Bewegung des Urteils, W6:272) which culminates in the "conclusion" (Schluß, W6:272) in which "not only the moments [of the concept] as *independent* extremes are posited, but also their *mediating unity*" (ebensowohl die Momente desselben als *selbständige* Extreme wie auch deren *vermittelnde Einheit* gesetzt ist, W6:272). The task is thus set at the opening of the Doctrine of the Concept in its free "subjectivity" of going through the dialectical movement (a thinking-through) in which the concept at first loses and then regains the unity of its three moments, universality, particularity and singularity.

Hegel understands the judgement (Urteil) or, more naturally in English, the proposition not as a subjective act but, proceeding from the etymology of the German word that cannot be imitated in English, as "the *original division* of what is originally one" (die *ursprüngliche Teilung* des ursprünglich Einen, W6:304) which was previously referred to as the concept "dirempting itself" (dirimiert [...] sich, W6:272). The "*original division*" of the concept is here rendered as the *primal split* (or schism) of an original unity in the concept or Begriff, which likewise can be understood from its etymology as a 'grasping together' or 'com-prehending'. The dialectical task of the third chapter of the first part of the theory of the concept therefore has to be seen in overcoming the primal split of the judgement in the movement to the conclusion (Schluß) which, in turn, again has to be understood in its deeper ontological sense as a 'closing together' of precisely this primal split which is located, in the first place, in the "abstract proposition [...] 'the *singular* is the *universal*'" (abstrakte Urteil [...] 'das *Einzelne* ist das *Allgemeine*', EnzI §166 Note). Hegel does not make an explicit point of the etymology of the German word 'Schluß' (although he does say that in the conclusion the subject "is closed together with an *other* determination" (mit einer *anderen* Bestimmtheit zusammengeschlossen, EnzI §182)), presumably because its signification as 'closing' is already apparent in German from the word itself, whereas in English, the sensitivity to the etymology of 'conclusion' has been lost.

To underscore that judgement/proposition and conclusion are not merely formal logical categories employed by 'subjective reasoning' in investigating the possibilities of linking propositions through a mediation in syllogisms (a togetherness of λόγοι), but rather are ontological structures of phenomena themselves, Hegel says in the corresponding part of the *Enzyklopädie* that "*All things* are a judgement/proposition" (*alle Dinge sind ein Urteil, EnzI* §167) and "*Everything is a conclusion*" (*Alles ist ein Schluß, EnzI* §181 Note). By the former statement he means that "they are *singularities* which in themselves are a *universality* or an inner nature, or a *universal* that *is singularized/individualized*" (sie sind *Einzelne*, welche eine *Allgemeinheit* oder innere Natur in sich sind, oder ein *Allgemeines*, das *vereinzelt ist, EnzI* §167). The primal split thus refers in the first place to that between the individual, singular being in its reality and its universal essence, its "inner nature", its beingness as a being. By the latter statement concerning the conclusion he means that "everything is a *concept*, and its determinate existence is the difference of the concept's moments so that its *universal* nature gives itself outward reality through *particularity* and thereby, and as negative reflection-into-itself, makes itself into an *individual/singularity*" (Alles ist *Begriff*, und sein Dasein ist der Unterschied der Momente desselben, so daß seine *allgemeine* Natur durch die *Besonderheit* sich äußerliche Realität gibt und hierdurch und als negative Reflexion-in-sich sich zum *Einzelnen* macht, *EnzI* §181 Note). "The conclusion is therefore the *essential ground of everything true*" (Der Schluß ist deswegen der *wesentliche Grund alles Wahren, EnzI* §181 Note), "what is *reasonable* and *everything* reasonable" (das *Vernünftige* und *alles* Vernünftige, *EnzI* §181), where reason for Hegel is a synonym for the idea (*EnzI* §214) and truth for him means the correspondence (as opposed to the "contradiction"; cf. *EnzI* §24 Add.2) between reality and the concept (*EnzI* §213 Add.) for absolutely, self-certain knowing. A singular being is true by virtue of corresponding to its concept of its essence, i.e. its whatness.

What is dirempted in the primal split between singularity and universality is to be 'closed together' again and unified via mediation in the conclusion, and this is achieved in the first place by the "apodictic judgement/proposition" (apodiktisches Urteil, *EnzI* §181 Add.) whose schema is given as "*this* — the immediate singularity — *house* — genus —, *of such and such a quality* — particularity —, is good or bad" (*dieses* — die unmittelbare Einzelheit — *Haus* — Gattung —, *so und so beschaffen* — Besonderheit —, ist gut oder schlecht, *EnzI* §179), where, for Hegel, "good or bad" (for a certain purpose) is synonymous with 'true or untrue'.[41] Hegel paraphrases this schema of the apodictic judge-

---

41 "Thus, for instance, one speaks of a true friend and means by this someone whose way of acting accords with the concept of friendship; likewise, one speaks of a true art work. Untrue then amounts to meaning bad or not in accord with itself. In this sense, a bad state is an untrue state, and the bad and untrue in general consist in the contradiction that takes place between the determination/purpose or the concept and the existence of an object." (So spricht man z. B. von einem wahren Freund und versteht darunter einen solchen, dessen Handlungsweise dem Begriff der Freundschaft gemäß ist; ebenso spricht man von einem wahren Kunstwerk. Unwahr

ment as "*All things* are a *genus* (their determination and purpose) in a *singular* reality and of a *particular* quality, and their finiteness is that the particularity of the singular reality can conform with the universal or not" (*Alle Dinge* sind eine *Gattung* (ihre Bestimmung und Zweck) in einer *einzelnen* Wirklichkeit von einer *besonderen* Beschaffenheit; und ihre Endlichkeit ist, daß das Besondere derselben dem Allgemeinen gemäß sein kann oder auch nicht. *EnzI* §179). The particular is the hinge that in the "*immediate* conclusion" (*unmittelbare* Schluß, *EnzI* §182) is supposed to mediate, closing the individual thing in its singular reality together with the universal of its "determination and purpose". Because most things are finite, the mediation with their essential "nature" through their particular qualities goes awry, so that they are "untrue" and therefore must "perish" (zugrunde gehen, *EnzI* §24 Zus.2). This would mean that, for Hegel, the world as we humans experience it is for the most part untrue, diverging from its true concept that speculative thinking can bring to light as a complex, dialectically unfolding, total onto-logical structure. The world is not as it *should* or *ought to* be, but this Ought is no longer impotent as it is in the moralism of subjective idealism and all kinds of subjective ethics, but rather, the non-correspondence with its concept compels a thing to go under, showing that the ontological concept, that is accessible through dialectical-speculative thinking, is stronger than empirically given reality.

Let us leave aside for the moment the question of the closing together of the primal split in the conclusion and return to a consideration of the primal split or judgement/proposition itself. This accords with Plato's determination of language as λέγειν τὶ κατὰ τινός, i.e. saying something *about* something, addressing it *as* such-and-such. One of Hegel's standard examples for a judgement is the simple statement of sensuous perception, "This rose is red" (diese Rose ist rot, *EnzI* §166 Add.) which brings a singular thing, "this rose", into identity with what it is not, namely, the universal, "red". An even simpler example is 'This is a rose' or 'This is a glass' in which 'this' points to a singular, real thing, proclaiming that it *is* what it is *not*, namely, the universal, 'rose' or 'glass', thus lifting the unique, singular thing through the λόγος (without frictional loss?) to being in its universality. The even more abstract, simple example, 'This is something', also identifies a singular, real thing with what it is *not*, namely, the universal, 'something', where 'something' for Hegel is a category of immediate

---

heißt dann soviel als schlecht, in sich selbst unangemessen. In diesem Sinne ist ein schlechter Staat ein unwahrer Staat, und das Schlechte und Unwahre überhaupt besteht in den Widerspruch, der zwischen der Bestimmung oder dem Begriff und der Existenz eines Gegenstandes stattfindet. *EnzI* §24 Add.2)

being, viz. the reality of determinate being or Dasein. The primal split therefore is truly primal, affecting every being in its being by putting each singular being into a contradictory identity with what it is not simply by virtue of its being what it is. The primal split is *prior* to whether a being is true or untrue, i.e. whether, in its singular reality as an individual being, it corresponds with its universal concept or not, thus splitting both true and untrue beings alike.

The simple, not to say trivial, judgement, 'This is a glass', would normally not be spoken, but nevertheless understood on seeing a glass, and there can be no doubt that we continually *practise* this judgement in everyday living in identifying *practically* the things around us *as* what they are and distinguishing *practically* one thing from another, which, in turn, is an aspect of each finite being, that it has a demarcating border-line that marks it off negatively from what it is not. Moreover, not only do we practise this identifying, but the things around us also present themselves to us *as* what they are, marking themselves off from what they are *not* through their self-presentation *as* such-and-such (the hermenetic AS that need not be put into a statement addressing the being as such-and-such: the apophantic AS). Hence, Hegel says that each determinate being is a *negation*, defined *as* what it is only through its delimitation from what it is not. Our everyday understanding of the world in its very quotidian banality is already beset by the contradiction of the primal split that every singular being can only be what it is in an identity of identity and difference. 'This *is* a glass' (i.e. 'This shows itself as a glass.') expresses in the so-called copula unequivocally the identity of 'this' and 'glass', whereas '*This* is a *glass*' expresses a difference between 'this' and 'glass'. Here already resides the *mystery of being* insofar as it is beingness.

Although 'This is a glass' would normally not be spoken, a similarly simple judgement such as 'This is a wine glass' could be spoken in the context of distinguishing, perhaps for someone else's sake, a stemmed wine glass from a similarly stemmed, but smaller, water glass. For a waiter serving in a restaurant, for instance, making such a distinction among all the restaurant-things is important. Such a judgement introduces a further determining negation, namely, 'wine' as distinct from 'water', allowing a finer limit to be defined among things, but such finer distinctions obscure the primal split inherent already in every single being *as* a being, leading to its being missed in a phenomenological ontological investigation. By viewing the judgement in its simplest phenomenal form, it can be seen most unobstructedly that *everything is a contradiction*.

The trivial judgement or proposition, 'This is a glass', contains the so-called demonstrative pronoun, 'this' which demonstrates in the sense of 'pointing out' a singular being. Hegel says of a being, "but it is only *this* insofar as it is *mon-*

strated/pointed out. Monstration/pointing-out is the reflecting movement which collects itself into itself and posits immediacy, but as something external to it" (es ist aber nur *Dieses*, insofern es *monstriert* wird. Das Monstrieren ist die reflektierende Bewegung, welche sich in sich zusammennimmt und die Unmittelbarkeit setzt, aber als ein sich Äußerliches. W6:300). The singular thing, however, is more than this pointed-out, immediate thing because it is a moment of the concept and as such has a relation to its other moment, universality or the essence of the thing, its "inner nature" (*EnzI* §167) or whatness which, "climbs down" (heruntersteigt, W6:296) into singularity, so that "by resolving to become a *judgement*/by opening itself up to the *primal split* in singularity, it posits itself as something *real*" (indem er sich in der Einzelheit zum *Urteil* entschließt,[42] sich als *Reales* [...] setzt, W6:403), the moments of the concept being as they are initially "still enclosed within the concept" (noch in den Begriff eingeschlossen, W6:403). The moments of the concept have thus become "independent determinations" (selbständigen Bestimmungen, W6:301) and the concept has "lost itself" (sich verloren, W6:301) in the "original *division*" (ursprünglichen *Teilung*, W6:301) of the judgement or primal split. In this primal split, to see anything is to "see *double*, once in its singular reality, and once in its essential identity or in its concept: the singular being raised into its universality or, what is the same, the universal singularized/individualized into its reality" (*doppelt* sehen, das eine Mal in seiner einzelnen Wirklichkeit, das andere Mal in seiner wesentlichen Identität oder in seinem Begriffe: das Einzelne in seine Allgemeinheit erhoben oder, was dasselbe ist, das Allgemeine in seine Wirklichkeit vereinzelt. W6:311).

3.3.1.4 Heideggerian selfhood as a "shining-back" from being-in-the-world
What does this dialectic of the concept, the primal split and closing together have to do with the question concerning the dialectic of self and other and the ontological constitution of the self in its selfhood? Before hazarding an interpretation of the dialectic of the concept with a view to selfhood, we will prepare the ground by first considering Heidegger's rejection of Hegel's dialectic in the *Logik*, thus implicitly refusing Hegel's insight that the movement of "abstract thoughts [is] invaluable for the concrete" (W19:85). In his lectures in Summer

---

42 According to its standard dictionary signification, "Sich entschließen" means 'to decide, resolve', but more etymologically (and Hegel of course has the etymology in mind) it means 'to open oneself up'.

Semester 1927,[43] Heidegger devotes a long chapter to the problem of logic, namely, that logic has become a "special discipline within philosophy" (gesonderte[] Disziplin innerhalb der Philosophie, *GA*24:252) emptied of any ontological content and therefore divorced from "the central problems of philosophy" (den zentralen Problemen der Philosophie, *GA*24:252). The chapter in question therefore takes up *"the question concerning the connection of the 'is' as copula to fundamental ontological problems"* (*die Frage nach dem Zusammenhang des 'ist' als Kopula mit den ontologischen Grundproblemen, GA24:254* italics in the original).

Heidegger notes that this problem "will not budge until logic itself is taken back into ontology again, i.e. until Hegel is comprehended who, conversely, dissolved ontology into logic" (kommt solange nicht von der Stelle, als die Logik selbst nicht wieder in die Ontologie zurückgenommen wird, d.h. solange Hegel, der umgekehrt die Ontologie in Logik auflöste, begriffen ist, *GA*24:254). Heidegger therefore praises Hegel for breathing philosophical life back into the formal, abstract discipline of logic whilst at the same time finding fault with him for turning ontology into logic which, in Hegel's understanding, however, is the pure movement of dialectical thinking itself speculating on the *ontological* structure of the world.[44] The later Heidegger, for instance, in the 1957 Freiburg lectures cited above, no longer so rudely accuses Hegel of dissolving "ontology into logic" but claims instead, and once again questionably,[45] that "the [dialec-

---

43 Martin Heidegger *Die Grundprobleme der Phänomenologie* Marburger Vorlesung SS 1927 *Gesamtausgabe* Band 24 ed. Friedrich-Wilhelm von Herrmann, Klostermann, Frankfurt/M. 1975.

44 Hegel is explicit about conceiving his *Logik* as speculative ontology, e.g.: "...the science of logic constituting metaphysics or pure speculative philosophy proper, has hitherto been very much neglected." (...die logische Wissenschaft, welche die eigentliche Metaphysik oder reine spekulative Philosophie ausmacht, hat sich bisher noch sehr vernachlässigt gesehen." Preface to the first edition 1812, LI:16) and "If we take into consideration the last form of the elaboration of this science [metaphysics], then it is firstly ontology into whose place objective logic steps, — that part of metaphysics that is supposed to investigate the nature of the *ens* as such;" (Wenn wir auf die letzte Gestalt der Ausbildung dieser Wissenschaft [der Metaphysik] Rücksicht nehmen, so ist [es] erstens unmittelbar die Ontologie, an deren Stelle die objective Logik tritt, — der Teil jener Metaphysik, der die Natur des Ens überhaupt erforschen sollte; LI:61) The later Heidegger is much more careful with polemical broadsides against Hegel, obviously coming to a deeper appreciation of his thinking in the late 1930s and early 1940s. Cf. Heidegger's careful interpretation of Hegel's concept of experience in the Introduction to the *Phenomenology of Mind* from 1942, a first version of which is included in *GA*68, with a completely reworked version from 1942/43 published in *Holzwege*.

45 Cf. Eldred 2000/2015.

tical-speculative ME] system as 'the thought' is being itself that dissolves all beings within itself and thus outlines the preliminary form of that which comes to appearance as the essence of the technical world." (Das [dialektisch-spekulative ME] System ist als 'der Gedanke' das Sein selbst, das alles Seiende in sich auflöst und so die Vorform dessen abzeichnet, was jetzt als das Wesen der technischen Welt zum Vorschein kommt. *GA*79:140).

Significantly and surprisingly, although calling for the "overcoming of Hegel [as] the inner, necessary step for developing Western philosophy" (Überwindung Hegels [als] der innerlich notwendige Schritt in der Entwicklung der abendländischen Philosophie, *GA*24:254), Heidegger does not attempt a critical engagement with Hegel's dialectical-speculative logic in these lectures, but instead discusses Aristotle as the father of logic and then the later non-dialectical logicians, Hobbes, J.S. Mill as well as the post-Hegelian, Lotze. Following this discussion, Heidegger attempts, in the chapter in question, to re-translate the copula that couples subject and predicate in a logical proposition back into a way of being-in-the-world by showing that the simple proposition is embedded within the prior "uncoveredness" (Enthülltheit, *GA*24:311) of the world for Dasein, an attempt not dissimiliar to Hegel's phenomenological interpretations of logical categories speculatively, i.e. ontologically, in his system. This problem of the copula does not concern us here. Rather, what interests us is how, in the same lectures, Heidegger interprets *selfhood* as a way of being-in-the-world, for this may shed light on how Hegel's dialectical logic can be translated into a phenomenology of constitution of the self.

Heidegger in fact approaches the phenomenon of the constitution of the self through a concept that he explicitly borrows from Hegel, namely, the concept of "reflection". "Reflect means here to refract on something, to radiate back from there, i.e. to show oneself in the reflection/shining-back from something. In Hegel, this optical meaning of the term 'reflection' resonates at one point... (Reflektieren heißt hier: sich an etwas brechen, von da zurückstrahlen, d.h. von etwas her im Widerschein sich zeigen. Bei Hegel [...] klingt einmal diese optische Bedeutung des Terminus 'Reflexion' an..., *GA*24:226). Heidegger, translating the Latin-derived 'Reflektieren' into the German-rooted 'Widerschein' or 'shining-back', goes on to make a great deal phenomenologically out of this "show[ing] oneself in the reflection/shining-back from something".[46] This "opti-

---

46 In earlier lectures in Winter Semester 1921/22, Heidegger speaks of "relucence" (Reluzenz): "Life caring for itself in this relation [to itself ME] casts back light onto itself, develops in each situation the illumination of its surroundings for its next care-contexts" (Das Leben, in diesem Bezug sich sorgend, leuchtet auf sich selbst zurück, bildet aus die Umgebungserhellung für

cal" etymology of reflection serves Heidegger as an alternative to the well-known etymology of 'bending-back' as in the bending back of consciousness upon itself to become aware of itself *as* a self in self-reflective self-consciousness.

Instead, Heidegger thinks the self as reflected back from the world, and he is able to do so because human being is no longer thought as inner, self-reflective subjectivity vis-à-vis the external world in its objectivity, but rather as Dasein, as being always already involved with beings in the world. Dasein is therefore always already embedded in and exposed to the world. Strictly speaking, therefore, there is no such thing as introspection, for Dasein is willy-nilly always looking 'outward'. (And in truth, there is no inside and outside for Dasein, for the Da of its Dasein is itself the pre-spatial, all-encompassing 3D-temporal clearing for presencing and absencing within which world takes place.[47]) "[I]n immediate passionate surrender to the world, Dasein's own self shines [back ME] out of things themselves" ([I]n unmittelbarem leidenschaftlichen Ausgegebensein an die Welt selbst scheint das eigene Selbst des Daseins aus den Dingen selbst [zurück ME], *GA*24:227). Heidegger says it is remarkable "that at first and, in everyday life, for the most part, we encounter ourselves from things and are opened up to ourselves in our self in this way. [...] To be sure, the cobbler is not the shoe and yet he understands *himself* from his things, *himself*, his self" (daß wir uns zunächst und alltäglich zumeist aus den Dingen her begegnen und uns selbst in dieser Weise in unserem Selbst erschlossen sind. [...] Gewiß, der Schuster ist nicht der Schuh, und dennoch versteht er *sich* aus seinen Dingen, *sich*, sein Selbst, *GA*24:227, emphasis in the original). One could say that this is a truly speculative insight into the nature of selfhood on Heidegger's part: the cobbler can only see his self in a "mirroring-back" (Widerspiegelung, *GA*24:248) from the world. The cobbler's things, his workshop surroundings hang together in an interconnection of practical things (Zeugzusammenhang, *GA*24:231) that refer to each other and which is understood by the cobbler, constituting the ontological worldliness of his workshop-world.

"The self radiating back from things" (Das von den Dingen her widerscheinende Selbst, *GA*24:229) in Dasein's everyday involvement with them is "inauthentic" (uneigentlich, *GA*24:228) because "we have lost ourselves to things *and people* in the everydayness of existing" (wir uns selbst in der Alltäglichkeit des Existierens an die Dinge *und Menschen* verloren haben,

---

seine jeweilig nächsten Sorgenszusammenhänge [...]. *Phänomenologische Interpretationen zu Aristoteles: Einführung in die phänomenologische Forschung GA*61:119).

47 Cf. 'Clichés in Thinking' in my *A Question of Time* 2015.

GA24:228 italics ME), being unable to "understand ourselves [...] continually out of the ownmost/propermost and most extreme possibilities of our own existence" (verstehen uns [...] ständig aus den eigensten und äußersten Möglichkeiten unserer eigenen Existenz, GA24:228). This implies that, for Heidegger, the cobbler who understands his self *as* being-a-cobbler is casting his self only inauthentically and not from his "most extreme" possibilities of existing, for this is impossible on a daily basis. But why should the cobbler's "ownmost" possibility of existing not consist precisely in practising the vocation of cobbler? This would mean only that the most extreme possibility of casting one's self would coincide, or at least conform, with the casting of self resulting from the radiating back of the self out of the things constituting an individual Dasein's everyday world. It would seem that Heidegger denies that the choice of vocation can be an *authentic* choice from utmost existential possibilities, potentials and opportunities for a singular individual that sets the course for this individual's existence.

Furthermore, if Dasein does not cast its self out of a shining-back from the world, whence otherwise could it cast itself? Surely not out of the ego-point resulting from Dasein re-flecting or bending-back upon itself as self-consciousness, but always from the possibilities of existing radiating back from the world in which Dasein factically and practically exists.

Heidegger is at pains to comprehend "this enigmatic shining-back of the self out of things philosophically" (diesen rätselhaften Widerschein des Selbst aus den Dingen her philosophisch, GA24:229) by grounding it in a more originary, ontological "transcendence" (Transzendenz, GA24:230) to the world which he conceives as Dasein's a priori being-in-the-world with "practical things" (Zeug, GA24:232). "[T]his enigma, the world" ([D]ieses Rätselhafte, die Welt, GA24:236) is therefore conceived philosophically by Heidegger as a "totality of interrelated usefulness" (Bewandtnisganzheit, GA24:235) of *things* rather than *people*. Although Heidegger points out that this world structured by a totality of interrelated, useful things that is understood by everyday Dasein is a "shared world" (gemeinsamen Welt, GA24:234), this does not suffice to make the ontological structure of the world, i.e. its worldliness, comprehensible as a world inhabited by both things and people in ontological-existential interrelation. Moreover, this focus on the ontological worldliness of the world leaves out of account that both *Being and Time* and the contemporaneous lectures in GA24 are concerned to deepen the analysis of Dasein by showing how the ontological structure of the world is embedded ultimately in originary, three-dimensional temporality (Zeitlichkeit) itself. This has the consequence that the discussion of the self's constitution through a shining-back from the world is tacitly assumed to be a shining-back in the present, for the other two temporal dimensions go without mention.

This means firstly that Heidegger does not take up, but rather *skips over* the philosophical problem of how "we have lost ourselves to [...] *people* in the everydayness of existing" (wir uns selbst in der Alltäglichkeit des Existierens an die [...] *Menschen* verloren haben, *GA24*:228 italics ME). He touches on the problem without taking it up and explicating it, presumably because it is one more difficult than the worldliness constituted by the interconnections among things. If Dasein's self is constituted, at least "at first and for the most part", through a shining-back from things in the everyday world, why should it not be co-constituted 'equally primordially' by a shining-back from people, i.e. from other Dasein in the everyday world? Secondly, what does this shining-back look like when all three temporal dimensions are taken into view? What does it mean to say that "we have lost ourselves to [...] *people*" and how does this loss of self relate to the shining-back from the world through which the self is constituted ontologico-existentially? It does not suffice, as many scholars are wont to do, to refer merely to Heidegger's concepts of Mitsein and Mitdasein, Wersein and Mansein in *Sein und Zeit* and other of his writings, to 'prove' that Heidegger has not 'forgotten' the other, for a study of these writings shows precisely that the problem of the constitution of self remains, to put it mildly, underdetermined. This underdetermination results from Heidegger's primary focus, in *Sein und Zeit* and elsewhere, on the being of things in the world and the merely secondary or even derivative status of Mitdasein *understood via things*.

Let us consider Heidegger's own example of the cobbler to see what Heidegger leaves out of phenomenological account. Not only the shoe and all it hangs together with in the cobbler's workshop-world "shines back" at the cobbler in constituting his everyday self, but also and especially the cobbler's *customers* who encounter the cobbler *as* a cobbler not merely by knowing that there's a cobbler's shop in such-and-such a street, but above all by *recognizing* and *estimating* his work as cobbler, thus reflecting back the cobbler's self in *calling on* and *paying* for his service of repairing shoes competently. A cobbler who does not come to enjoy this validating shining-back from his customers *as* the cobbler-self he is, is no longer a cobbler. (In Hegelian language: He is a bad cobbler who does not correspond to the concept of cobbler.) Such shining-back of the cobbler's self resides in the cobbler's customers' comportment toward him, namely, in their *estimating* and *valuing* his services by paying for them. The cobbler-self is therefore a reflection from the others, a mirror-reflection in which the cobbler can see that he *is* a cobbler, i.e. that he can understand his self *as* a cobbler-self.

Who he is is not a result of tautologous self-re-flection, i.e. of his being bent back upon himself in an awareness of himself in a self-definition, but of a shining-back from the others in their estimating him *as* a cobbler. His *whoness* is at least equally a validating mirror-reflection from the others, not just a shining-back from things. The others estimate him to *be* a cobbler because he has the *ability* to mend shoes, and this estimation by the others assumes the palpable form of their paying for the actual exercise of his powers to repair shoes, thus confirming and valuing these powers and also enabling the cobbler to continue his existence *as* a cobbler who understands his self *as* 'cobbler'.

The self is a reflection, a shining-back from the world of things *and* others, and the worldliness of the world is not exhausted in the interrelations among useful, practical things, but encompasses also the *interplay* among people who mutually reflect who each other is by estimating 'at first and for the most part' each other's abilities, competencies. The so-called division of labour in society is itself structured as a mutual mirroring of who each other is by estimating and valuing each other's powers and abilities. The worldliness of the world therefore has a mirror-complexity that goes beyond that elaborated by Heidegger as the Bewandtnisganzheit of practically useful things whose ontological whatness resides in what they are practically good for.

In addition, we now have the others, who are also good for something or other through exercising their abilities, including deficient modes of being 'good for nothing'. Who they are is defined not only by what they are good at, i.e. by their possessing certain abilities, but by these abilities also being shone back by a world shared with others in an ongoing estimating play of mirror-reflection of who each other is. From this it can be seen that the *whatness* or *quidditas* of what something is has to be clearly distinguished from, and complemented with, the *whoness* or *quissity* of who somebody is, and this insisting on a distinction only furthers, and by no means repudiates or diminishes, Heidegger's grand effort to phenomenologically work out the peculiar ontological character of human being itself as Dasein, i.e. as being-in-the-world, thus breaking with the Cartesian tradition of an all-too-simple and inadequate distinction between res extensa and res cogitans.

In extending Heidegger's analyses and twisting them toward the others,[48] the question of the selfhood of Dasein becomes a matter of Dasein's understand-

---

48 Lévinas does not extend Heidegger but rather ethicizes ontology, claiming that ethics is prior to ontology (if this were at all possible). Lévinas' ethics of the other does nothing to deepen Heidegger's existential ontology of being-in-the-world by exploring the unheard-of possibil-

ing its self as radiating back from things *and* the others. For Heidegger, this conception of selfhood would still be inauthentic selfhood, indeed more so, because Dasein allows itself to be defined as *who* it is from the estimations shining back from the others, das Man. Thus, Dasein is more than ever "lost" to the others, a mere plaything of their mirror-reflections of how they estimate it to be as somewho.[49] But the shining-back does not have to operate so smoothly, without resistance and fractures. Is there not also the possibility that Dasein, as a free origin of its very own self-casting, is able to *differentiate* and to discover in this mirror-reflection from the others, and also nurture, its ownmost potential for being (Seinkönnen) in the world, finally exercising this potential as developed abilities? Could not, and must not, a critical, i.e. differentiating, Dasein choose its self at the extreme in choosing its ownmost potential and devoting itself to nurturing precisely this potential? Or is the potential factually nurtured only ever merely a reflection from the others (in the first place, one's parents reflecting a self from the temporal dimension of the past) who predefine who Dasein is to be?

To be sure, without the reflection from others, Dasein as being-in-the-world-with-others would be unable to choose itself at all, but this does not exclude that the self that Dasein, ultimately as an origin of free nothingness, does choose and fashion from the range of mirror-reflections could be its ownmost, authentic self. Nor does the mirror-character of selfhood mean that authentic selfhood could not and must not reside in critically developing and realizing one's ownmost potential discovered in the shining-back from the world, albeit that this potential could only be realized in a world shared with others in a definite historical time with its own temporal atmosphere, which implies essentially also that the others must in some way or other also estimate these abilities.

It is also important to emphasize that the shining-back of self from the world in its worldliness is a temporally triple reflection. First of all, I cast myself as a self by casting myself into the future guided by how I envisage myself in future possibilities of existing. This self-casting into the future is informed by who I have been and how others have reflected back to me my possibilities by estimating (right through to thoroughly downplaying and disparaging) my individual potentials.

---

ities nascent in a phenomenology of whoness. See my 1997/2010 essay *Worldsharing and Encounter: Heidegger's Ontology and Lévinas' Ethics* Ver. 3.0 2010.

49 And Aristotle, too, would say that Dasein (the individual) is lost in the play of τιμή, esteem, becoming dependent on the others; cf. *Eth. Nic.* I. v. 1095b 23–25.

Does this discussion of Heidegger's phenomenology of Dasein that has led to a more refined and phenomenally concrete understanding of selfhood as an aspect of whoness than Heidegger himself presents mean that a consideration of Hegel's dialectic is now superfluous? What does Hegel have to offer that Heidegger's groundbreaking phenomenology itself does not already provide? To decide this question, we must return to the discussion of the dialectic of the concept, primal splitting and closing together of the preceding section.

3.3.1.5 Interpreting the dialectic of primal splitting and closing together with regard to selfhood

At first sight it would seem that Hegel's *Logik* is of no use for the question of selfhood because the phenomenon of whoness does not appear explicitly on the horizon of Hegel's thinking. The example proposition we have discussed, 'This is a glass', is on a par with an example such as 'Socrates is mortal' about the singular human being, Socrates, formulated in the third person singular, the preferred grammatical person and number for metaphysical thinking as a whole, emanating from the simplest of statements 'S is P' taken already by Plato and Aristotle as the model for a λόγος. Already Aristotle observes that the simple proposition is a σύνθεσις νοημάτων (*De anima* 430a28), a synthesis of what is thought, and at the same time a διαίρεσις (*De anima* 430b3), a taking-apart or splitting, dividing. In Hegel's thinking, this unity of opposites is sharpened to a contradiction: a singular being *is* what it is *not*, namely, a universal, and this is the primal split of the ontological judgement.

Taking up Heidegger's example of the cobbler once again, the proposition, 'John Brown is a cobbler', is also a primal split between the singular, proper-named human being, John Brown, and the universal, 'cobbler' (which in turn is a particular, relative to the universal of human vocation defined by a specific difference, i.e. a difference in the 'look' of cobble vis-à-vis other occupations). As has been shown in the previous section, to *be* a cobbler, in turn, is to constitute one's self through a shining-back from the world of things and others in casting one's own existence. Thus, John Brown is his self only through, i.e. not without, the mirror-reflection from the things with which he is engaged daily and from the others who estimate and validate him *as* a cobbler. His identity is the mirror-reflection from what and who he is *not* by being in the world in a certain vocational way. The negation and contradictoriness in the constitution of self through a radiating back from the world is inadvertently expressed already by Heidegger when he writes, as already cited, "Reflect means here to refract/break on something (sich an etwas brechen), to radiate back from there" (*GA24*:226). The individual has to "break on something", namely, the world, especially the world of the others, to *be* a self, in a radiating-back from this refraction *as a universal*. Singularity has to be broken in (like a brumby or mustang) to take on the mask of universality in a primal split.

Other things are not constituted *as selves* through a shining-back from the world; selfhood is a prerogative of human being as being freely exposed to the clearing of three-dimensional time, within which the world itself is embedded, that permits a maximum of degrees of freedom for casting one's self. In a reflection back to himself, John Brown, understands *himself* as a cobbler and is absorbed by the world in being a cobbler by exercising his cobbler vocation, his cobbler business. This means that he adopts for himself the judgement of the primal split, 'I am a cobbler'. This is now a proposition in the *first* person, rather than the *third* person proposition, similarly a primal split, 'John Brown is a cobbler'. This third-person judgement is made from the standpoint of the others, for it is they who talk about John Brown, determining him *as* a cobbler, and conducting themselves toward him accordingly. For John Brown to be a cobbler, is it sufficient for the others to understand John Brown as a cobbler, in line with the third-person judgement expressing the phenomenon, 'John Brown is a cobbler'? Is there a discrepancy between the third-person proposition and the first-person proposition, 'I am a cobbler'? Can the others foist the identity of cobbler onto John Brown? To take the moment of self-reflection in the constitution of self: I am a cobbler not merely by being defined as such by the shining back from the others, but only if, in addition, I myself, on self-reflection, adopt the mask of cobbler *as* my own identity. There can be a discrepancy between the two, a painful contradiction, say, if I am forced by pecuniary circumstances to continue in an occupation that no longer interests me, for I would rather cast my self in an entirely different direction.

Or, to take another example, is there a discrepancy between the third-person proposition, 'Charles is heir to the throne', and the first-person proposition, 'I am heir to the throne'? This latter example makes the discrepancy abundantly apparent, because, to *be* heir to the throne, it matters little what I think about it and who I understand myself to be, because being heir to the throne is first and foremost a shining-back from the others who understand the heir to the throne as a socio-political role in accord with the practised traditions (if any) of monarchical lineage in the land. I may renounce my heirship to the throne by abdicating, thus breaking with the determination of my self by the others and making the discrepancy apparent, but I cannot cast my self out of my self as heir to the throne, for that would be only to make myself a laughing stock, again making the discrepancy between self-casting of the self and casting of one's self through the reflections from others apparent. Or, in case of doubt about succession to the throne, there could be a contest, a power play, between different pretenders to the throne that has first to be fought out until others come to recognize one pretending successor as successor. This example shows also that it is not self-evident that 'I am I' purely and simply, as a matter of formal logic, because presenting myself of myself *as* myself may not be possible in a world in which who I am is cast primarily by others. My self is always a self-identification with difference.

To cast my self as such-and-such an identity is to adopt a certain comportment toward, and thus an habituated stance in the world of things and others through which I show myself off (ἀποφαίνεσθαι) to myself (the self-reflective first person) and the others (third person) *as* who I am — the 'apophantic AS', now in the first person tacitly interpreted by others in an 'hermeneutic AS'. To cast my self as a cobbler means exercising my acquired abilities in a regular, habitual way, and in this sense it means putting on a certain *mask of identity* by identifying with what I am not, namely, the complex of practices constituting the vocation of cobbler. My self-casting is therefore an identity of identity and difference, because the practices constituting the vocation of cobbler are a universal in the sense of belonging to a given historical world, i.e. a cast of being in a given time. The moment of *difference* in this self-casting becomes apparent if I decide to cast myself in an alternative way, putting aside the mask of the vocation of cobbler, and adopting the mask of another vocation or perhaps another kind of mask altogether. The mask, conceived ontologically, is an existential possibility of identity through casting one's self as a way of comporting oneself habitually in the world, and is possible only because there is a *difference* in the constitution of self-*identity*. This implies already that it is delusory for me to opine that I have to set out on an existential search to discover my 'really true', unique identity 'inside' me or prefigured 'inside' my very body. The usual ontic understanding of mask in play-acting is derivative of this deeper ontological-existential concept of self-identity and is something interposed between an individual and the world in the difference between self and world that allows someone to show himself off as *who* he is.

My ontological-existential mask of self-identity as cobbler also has to be reflected back from the world in order for me to *be* a cobbler. It is not sufficient for me to simply say to myself, 'I am a cobbler', or to adopt the comportment of a cobbler by busying myself in a cobbler's workshop. In addition, the others have to *validate* this comportment by giving me cobbler's work to do. For the most part in everyday life, the validation of vocational identity takes place through being *paid* for the exercise of abilities, money being the universal, reified medium for valuing and thus recognizing and validating individual powers. So there must be some sort of congruity between the first-person judgement, 'I am a cobbler', and the third-person judgement, 'He is a cobbler', for me to have my self cast and defined *as* cobbler in the world into which I have always already been cast. The others with their third-person judgements therefore have a power over my own determination of self and I am partly dependent in my cobbler-being on having this identity as self reflected by the others.

The discrepancy between my own casting of self and how the others judge me to be from their third-person viewpoint is a constant feature of existing in the everyday world, since there is a fundamental difference ontologically between the first-person and the third-person perspective, each of which represents a fold in the manifold of being, i.e. modes of presencing. This fundamental difference arises from the nature of selfhood as being a constitution of self through a shining-back from the world, including especially the world of others. The discrepancy between first-person and third-person casting of an individual self may be experienced in the first person merely as the *pain* on hearing discrepant third-person opinions about oneself, or it can sharpen into an opposition and outright contradiction when the individual refuses or is unable to see its self in the identity reflected back from the world. The others can reflect back to me a self with which I cannot identify, a mirror of self-identification in which I, as this singular individual, cannot recognize myself.

My identity is then truly broken and refracted in the mirror of the others. I am then *alienated* from the world, finding in the reflections from the others only the *otherness* of the self-casting I have defined for myself. The struggle and pain to become one's own, self-cast self arise both out of the difference between self and world that is necessary for identity to be shone back (thus constituting a more or less tenuous identity of singularity and universality), and also out of the discrepancy between one's own self-understanding (constituted as just such an identity of singularity and universality) and the reflections received back from the others estimating me. The individual's singularity *must in any case break on the world* in assuming an identity by adopting a universal reflected back from the world, and this breaking on the world in a primal split is *ontologically prior to* and therefore deeper than the issue regarding a possible discrepancy or divergence between my own self-casting and a casting of self foisted upon me by the others.

This struggle and pain can be the process of finding one's own refracted reflection in the world in the sense of finding the mask of self-comportment that *truly fits* one's ownmost potentiality for being-in-the-world in a given sociohistorical time, i.e. one's own authentic self. I as the abstract identity of 'I am I' is an emptiness and nothingness, an "abstract negativity" demarcating me in my abstract, indeterminate freedom from the world, that can only be escaped by casting my self in the broken dialectic between my singularity and the universality of what the world shines back. Moreover, the struggle and pain can be *in addition* the process of striving to have one's self-chosen identity also reflected by the others, thus bringing one's first person exposure to the world into congruity with the third-person judgement and estimation of the world in its opinions that hold me to be who I am. The more singularly I cast my self as a way of self-comportment in the world, adopting my ownmost universal, the more likely it is that this singular self-casting will fail to find a reflection from the others. The greater degree of singularity results in a more brittle and broken mediation by singularity and an adopted universal offering itself in a given historical world in a given historical situation and time, and results also in a divergence between a self-chosen way of self-comportment and the standard set of masks of self-comportment offered by the world of the others, including those offered by the cultural traditions cultivated.

In one way or other, the individual is always confronted with having to find its self in a mediation between its singularity and the universal options it is surrounded by in the world, for singularity is always and essentially caught in the primal split of having to *break* and *be* other than it is, namely, a universal. The self is both the same as and different from the world that radiates back, thus echoing Plato's dialectical result, discussed in a previous section, that the one is both the same as and different from the other and the others.

The individual finding its self in the world in the first person requires a *mediation*, albeit broken and more or less brittle, between its unique singularity and universality considered here as the modes of comportment available in the world in which that individual exists. This mediation is a closing together of the primal split between singularity and universality in freely finding an identity as self in a "*self*-determination [...] to close itself together only with itself" (*Selbst*bestimmung [...], sich nur mit sich selbst zusammenzuschließen, *RPh.* § 7). Although any given way of comportment such as being a cobbler adopted by the singular individual as its self is a universal, any given way of comportment, when viewed from the perspective of the world, is only a *particular* way of existing in the world within the totality of ways of existing held open by an historical age. The particular way of existing in the world chosen by a singular individual in constituting its self-identity is to serve as the mediation that bridges the primal split between singularity and universality, allowing the individual to be part of its world. Nevertheless, despite this mediation, individual singularity can only *be* its self by *being* its other, namely, a (particular) way of existing in the world that shines back a universal as its identity. This is a 'closing together' of the individual with the world termed formally the "conclusion of determinate being" (Schluß des Daseins) in Hegel's *Logik*. This conclusion or 'closing together' has "an indeterminate set of mediating termini [...] so that it lies in[50] an extrinsic *arbitrariness* or an *external circumstance* and contingent determination with what kind of universal the subject of the conclusion is to be closed together" (eine unbestimmbare Menge von Mediis Terminis, [...] so daß es ganz in einer äußerlichen *Willkür* oder überhaupt in einem *äußerlichen Umstande* und zufälligen Bestimmung liegt, mit was für einen Allgemeinen das Subjekt des Schlusses zusammengeschlossen werden soll. *LII* W6:364). Even this formal description of the "conclusion of determinate being" has an existential-ontological interpretation when read in the present context of how the individual is to find its self in the world, since the individual is cast into the world, confronted with "external circumstance[s]" on which it is refracted and from which it chooses, sometimes in an arbitrary and capricious manner, thus allowing its identity to be dictated 'inauthentically' by these "external circumstance[s]".

The totality of possible ways of being in the world open to an individual comprises all the particular ways of existing from which the individual has to choose among its options into which it is thrown in its individual situation, and this choice 'breaks in' the individual's singularity, mediating it with a particular, factually chosen way of existing (such as its particular vocation) that shines back as its identity. This is a kind of 'disjunctive closing together' in which individual singularity is now mediated with a particular identity through the universal of the totality of possible ways of existing in an historical time. The individual *must* choose among the totality of its possibilities; its self is a *necessary* closing together with the world in one identity or other, no matter how impoverished, tenuous or brittle this identity may be. In the disjunctive conclusion, the culminating "conclusion of necessity" (Schluß der Notwendigkeit, W6:391) in Hegel's *Logik*, the mediating link is the "universal sphere which contains its total particularization" (allgemeine Sphäre, die ihre totale Besonderung enthält, W6:398), and it is this "universal sphere" as totality that confronts the singular individual as the world on which it is broken and from which it must choose its self.

But is there not yet another kind of mediation between the singular individual and the universal of the others through a particular other that could close together the primal split between the individual self and the world? So far we have considered the others in general or as a whole, who reflect the individual's

---

50 Cf. OED 'lie' v. 12 g. and h. "to lie in: to consist in, to have its ground or basis in".

self and its self-standing by esteeming and validating it in positive, neutral or negative modes. But, of these others, there is always also the *particular* other whom the individual encounters *face to face*. This particular other is a definite, particular other, a "bestimmte[s] Bestimmte" (W6:296), i.e. another *singular* real individual with whom the face-to-face encounter takes place in its *own dimension*, namely, the dimension *in-between* of the *first-and-second person*, as distinct from the usual first-and-third person relations with the world both of things and others. Hegel says that the singular is "determinacy relating to itself" (sich auf sich selbst beziehende Bestimmtheit, W6:288) through which the concept "steps into actuality" (tritt in Wirklichkeit, W6:299). In the present context this means that the singular individual encounters its self in breaking on and shining back from the other, actual individual whom it encounters face to face.

'At first and for the most part', however, such an encounter does not take place in everyday life, even when people meet in person, because the personal dealings with one another are mediated overwhelmingly by the matter at hand, such as giving the cobbler one's shoes to heel, paying the cashier at the supermarket check-out or arranging a bank loan with the bank employee. In such dealings, the person-to-person interchange is reduced to a ritualistic, conventional *politeness* that serves only to lubricate the exchange, and the recognition of each other is only the formal, schematic recognition as persons in general. The other in such dealings is only one among many, i.e. a *particular* specimen of a *general* class (a *universal*) such as 'customer' or 'patient'. In such general dealings with one another, the face of the other itself remains only a general schema particularized in this particular person, and does not attain the unique singularity of a definite, singular, individual other. For the most part, social intercourse is an interchange among particular persons, not singular individuals. Even social gatherings usually remain on the level of general, albeit particularized, exchanges in which one inquires about the other in the conventional manner in which one politely inquires about others in such social situations, for instance, a dinner party. The other's singularity remains for the most part hidden behind the mask of the particular persona.

The face-to-face encounter, by contrast, is a *mutual* mirroring of who each other is in which *individual singularity* shows itself — 'I am I' in a radical sense of self-presentation of myself *as* myself —, and this mirroring takes place through the way in which the individuals comport themselves *as* singular individuals toward each other, no matter how fleetingly and en passant. Such mutually reflecting comportment in which singularity shines through shows (ἀποφαίνειν) ineffably how the two individuals estimate and esteem each other *as* who they are in their singularity. Each individual has a status as somewho in the world, and the way the other individual comports itself toward the first individual makes it apparent whether this status as self is affirmed or whether its stand as self is depreciated through behaviour that shines back as slighting the individual in its whoness. Every encounter is therefore to a greater or lesser degree a test of self-standing in the world, and because this is so, minute attention must be paid to the *kindness* and *attentiveness* of comportment if the other is not to be offended by having its who-self slighted, no matter how slightly. If the other behaves coarsely and impolitely in the encounter, this can be brushed off by, in turn, estimating this person at a lower self-status. The mirror-play with such persons then has little weight in defining or affirming, through reflection, one's own self and its standing, and the encounter between individuals becomes instead a mere exchange between particular persons. 'Rude behaviour' as the negation of politeness does not touch the singular individual but offends only the conventional, general rules of interplay between persons for which singularity remains withdrawn into the background.

On the other hand, the individual also has truly face-to-face encounters with other, significant individuals, so that the shining-back from these others carries more weight in one's own self-definition. To be *close* to another individual in the existential-ontological dimension sui generis 'in-between' you-and-me means to mutually disclose (mostly mutely, atmospherically) in the mirror-play more of one's singular self in the sense of how one understands the world in more detail (since world-understanding is self-understanding) and to give weight to how this singular other reflects this self-definition of the self: appreciatingly or depreciatingly within an attuned *atmosphere* of encounter that enables mutual self-disclosure. This is the encounter in the moment or Augenblick in which gazes are exchanged. Such a close, face-to-face encounter has the intimacy of eye-to-eye, "My face in thine eye, thine in mine appeares" (John Donne *The good-morrow*). The gaze of the other that shines back can be either an affirmative, understanding, empathic look or a depreciating, destructive look to kill. Such close encounters with an intimate other, a confidant, are a mediation with the world that embed the individual more deeply in the world than the reflections of its self through average everyday dealings with others.

With those individuals to whom it is close in the sense of mutual self-disclosure, mutually supportive self-affirmation and also conflicts that touch each other's understanding of self, a singular individual shares its world by confiding its ownmost masks of identity (there is no maskless identity since identity is always and essentially identity with other). The *conflicts* between you and me are how we break and refract on each other, reflecting back to each other selves with which it is painful to identify. The dimension in-between of you-and-me can be the crucible in which we mutually cast and form each other's selves through conflicts over differences in which our respective singularities are refracted, moulded and remoulded in adopting hitherto unfamiliar universals radiated back through the respective other, sometimes with the burning sharpness of a laser beam. You and I may break apart through our mutual refractions on each other, or we may emerge from the crucible, each recast as selves and welded together in a mutual understanding and harmonious attunement borne by Eros.

The shared world of you-and-me provides the more or less fleeting existential shelter of *homeliness*. Such being-at-home in the world is possible only because in a close relationship of you-and-me an affirmative mutual mirroring of self in its singularity takes place, above all atmospherically in mood, thus providing both individuals with a firmer stance *as* selves borne in the world. Because the other individual, 'you', mediates me with the world in which I have to find myself in self-refraction and self-reflection, there is also the ontic possibility that you-and-me cut off from the world of the others, cocooning ourselves in a *symbiotic* relationship of mutually mirroring affirmation. The mediation with the world through the interstice of you-and-me thus fails. You as my significant other therefore have to maintain your self in your otherness from me as a mediating link with the world if I as this individual self am to be truly 'closed together' with the world and my primal split with the world alleviated through an impossible mediation.

As has been shown repeatedly, mediation is ultimately impossible because self-identity is an identity of identity and difference, i.e. a living, moving, phenomenal contradiction between singularity and universality in which there is friction and fracture to a greater or lesser degree. We have gained this insight into the *contradictory* nature of selfhood and therefore human existence as a whole ontological structure by asking what the Platonic, and then the Hegelian dialectic could have to do with the constitution of the self in a reflective, refractive interplay with the other in three guises: the thingly world, the others and the singular other of 'you'. It is not to be had solely from Heidegger's thinking, which only dimly illuminates the phenomenon of you-and-me and also eschews dialectical figures of thought, for which contradiction is the nub.

But, someone will object, isn't there a problem with the Hegelian dialectic's claim to achieve absolute knowledge in which the totality of the world's ontological structure is revealed in the blinding, infinite light of systematic dialectical reason? Isn't Heidegger's life-long struggle to open up an access to being prior to that of the λόγος conceived as proposition and reason pertinent above all with regard to the absolute claims of Hegel's *Logik* as "the highest summit" (der höchste Gipfel; *GA*79:150) of the Western λόγος? Does this circumstance not justify Heidegger's indictment of dialectical thinking? These objections are indeed worth making. First of all it must be noted that Hegel's thinking is metaphysical and as such onto-theological, i.e. composed of an ontological orientation toward dialectical thinking-through of the being of beings in their totality, on the one hand, which renders his system speculative, i.e. ontological, and, on the other, an orientation toward a supreme being which, for Hegel, is the absolute, which renders his system theological. The dialectic of the phenomena practised by Hegel reveals the being of beings even when the theological orientation toward the absolute is bracketed off. This holds true, say, also for Plato's dialectical thinking when his orientation to the supreme idea of the good is bracketed off. Metaphysics as onto-theology, whether it be Plato's, Aristotle's, Hegel's or some other thinker's in the Western philosophical tradition, is insightful also when interpreted solely as a phenomenological ontology. The baby does not have to be thrown out with the bath-water.

In the present specific context, moreover, it will be noticed that the dialectic of self and other presented above is a *broken* Hegelian dialectic that rests on the insight — *pace* Hegel — that existential singularity cannot be mediated, 'closed together' entirely smoothly with the universal via particularity, not even in absolute knowing that is supposed to attain an ultimate reconciliation of consciousness in its tornness ("Zerrissenheit" Hegel). There is a *refraction* through which the singular individual is broken on the world and raised to participate as a particular individual in the universal cast of a world. The contradiction between singularity and universality thus signifies here an existential pain of entry to the world. But what, more precisely, does this have to do with Heidegger's thinking? It has to do with Heidegger's more originary, more incipient (anfänglicher) conception of λόγος and λέγειν as a gathering laying-together that brings beings (Anwesendes) to present themselves in presence (Anwesen) *as* what they are (cf. *GA*79:143) in a 'timely' way. Hegel's insight into the contradiction that the identity of a being is an identity of identity and difference (e.g. 'This is a glass.'; cf. above) is aligned with Heidegger's insight into the prelogical hermeneutic *as* that interposes itself so that a being shows itself *as* what it is, an insight that depends on an hermeneutic-phenomenological interpretation of Aristotle's λέγειν τι κατά τινος (*Anal. Priora* I 24a14; cf. *GA*79:143) that does not amount simply to 'saying something about something', i.e. as not relating merely to statements but to the self-showing of beings in the open 3D-time-clearing of presence-and-absence. Insofar, Hegelian dialectic and Heideggerian phenomenology are not at loggerheads.

With respect to the first-person statement of identity, 'I am I', the phenomenological, existential interpretation yields something other than the self-positing of the modern ego-subject as fundamentum inconcussum, i.e. unshakeable foundation, as it does with Fichte. Rather, it yields an insight into the fragility and groundlessness of the individual human being in its singularity. How so? Above it was said that first-person self-identity enunciates "the possibility of an individual presenting itself to itself and others *as itself*". Such self-identity, however, viewed strictly, is impossible, or void if identity is understood as selfsame equality without difference, I = I. Why? Because the *as* inevitably introduces a difference in between I and I. 'I am I' demands a difference, for otherwise it remains an impotent, tautological, 'autistic' statement of singularity's existential nothingness, i.e. its inchoate freedom. A singular existence *must* proceed to identification with an other that shines back from the world; it *must* assume a mask in which it appears *as* who it is of itself. The issue is whether the mask it adopts as its own is it ownmost, utmost potential for existing in the world.

Similarly, *any* being's self-presentation of its identity with itself as itself, i.e. 'A is A' understood as A presenting itself *as* A, *must* proceed to difference in its identification with an appearance-*as*-... This hermeneutic *as*, however, is the scaffolding of an historical time that is always already interposed between beings and their self-presentation. The historical *as* that casts beings in their totality *as* resources whose movement and change are to be knowingly calculated and controlled is intermeshed with the historical *as* that casts beings in their totality *as* opportunities promising gain. These superposed ontological scaffoldings characterize our own times. The step back from the twofold constellation of being I call the "grasp"[51] to letting beings present themselves of themselves *as* they are, however, does not leave them in their naked truth, but allows them to show themselves in an alternative historical scaffolding sent by propriation *as* an *other*, simpler historical mode of human being in its plurality and being itself belonging together. In this alternative hermeneutic cast, human beings become more receptive to and appreciative of beings' and each other's self-presentations *as* granted in the open time-clearing in which the world is embedded.

---

51 Cf. my *Capital and Technology* 2000/2015 Ch. 7.2 .

4 The satisfaction of wants and the striving to have more

As laid out in the preceding, according to the tradition, society is in the first place a communal set-up based on the satisfaction of needs and wants for the sake of living well (εὖ ζῆν). Human beings lack what they need and want for daily life and are therefore concerned with appropriating what they lack in some way or other, whether it be through their own labour or through exchange. This entrenched thought is often expressed in economics by saying that it is 'the science of the distribution and use of scarce resources', a misleading formulation derived from the ontology of whatness that will not concern us further here. Today it is almost beneath the dignity of philosophers to engage with fundamental economic questions, posing emphatically ontological questions, which would be their proper task. Not only hidebound German professors today and in the past subscribe either implicitly or explicitly to Nietzsche's sentiment:

> Alle politischen und wirthschaftlichen Verhältnisse sind es nicht werth, dass gerade die begabtesten Geister sich mit ihnen befassen dürften und müssten: ein solcher Verbrauch des Geistes ist im Grunde schlimmer, als ein Nothstand. Es sind und bleiben Gebiete der Arbeit für die geringeren Köpfe, und andere als die geringen Köpfe sollten dieser Werkstätte nicht zu Diensten stehen:...[52]

> All the political and economic relations are not worth it that the most gifted minds, of all things, should be allowed to and should have to engage with them. Such an expenditure of mind is basically worse than a state of emergency. They are and will remain areas of work for lesser minds and anything other than small minds should not serve this workshop...

Nietzsche's pseudo-aristocratic hauteur and his low opinion of Aristotle, where economic thinking begins, are also well-known. Despite Nietzsche's disapprobation, we will return to these seminal Aristotelean writings, for here the germ is to be found for a reinterpretation that will eventually make their profound socio-ontological implications explicit, given sufficient patience.

---

[52] Friedrich Nietzsche *Morgenröthe* Drittes Buch 179. *Sämtliche Werke* Kritische Studienausgabe ed. Giorgio Colli and Mazzino Montinari Band 3 dtv/de Gruyter, Berlin 1980. Abbreviated KSA.

https://doi.org/10.1515/9783110617504-004

4.1 Economics and chrematistics

The first question is whether what humans lack for living well, the desiderata of existence, are finite or infinite. Do human needs and wants have a limit or are they are limitless? This is a question which concerned both Plato and Aristotle. As already discussed in Chapter 2, both posit the ontogenesis of human society on the satisfaction of an increasingly elaborate, diversified network of needs-cum-wants-cum-desires proceeding hand in hand with ongoing refinements in the division of labour. In the case of Plato, his *Politeia* describes how the ever-increasing complex of necessaries and conveniences of life leads ultimately to war among cities over resources for fulfilling the felt needs of their populaces when they "overstep the horizon of what is necessary and strive for limitless possession of goods" (ἐπὶ χρημάτων κτῆσιν ἄπειρον, ὑπερβάντες τὸν τῶν ἀναγκαίων ὅρον; *Rep.* 373d).

This overstepping of the bounds of what is necessary is echoed also in Aristotle. In his *Politics* he says with regard to "true wealth" (ἀληθινὸς πλοῦτος) that the "self-sufficiency of such property for good living is not limitless" (ἡ γὰρ τῆς τοιαύτης κτήσεως αὐτάρκεια πρὸς ἀγαθὴν ζωὴν οὐκ ἄπειρος ἐστιν; *Pol.* I iii 1256b31). Aristotle thus distinguishes between two different ways of acquiring wealth, one which is integrated within the management of a household and has its limits in the needs arising from maintaining the way of life of that household, and another art of acquiring wealth which is a striving to gain wealth for its own sake and is therefore without limit. Aristotle calls the art of household management οἰκονομική or 'economics' and the art of gaining wealth and property for its own sake χρηματιστική (1256a12), 'chrematistics'. Both these ways of acquiring property take place within the social interplay of exchange. A further way of acquiring apart from exchange which crops up in both Plato (*Rep.* 373d) and Aristotle (*Pol.* I iii 1256b27) is that of warfare (πόλεμος) which consists in appropriating the wealth of others through brute military force.

Two millennia later, Karl Marx takes up this Aristotelean distinction in his opus magnum when distinguishing between the simple circulation of commodities on the one hand, and the circulation of money as capital, on the other. The simple circulation of commodities has the formula C_1-M-C_2, or selling a certain commodity in order to buy another for the satisfaction of a felt lack. The circulation of money as capital, on the other hand, has the inverted formula M_1-C-M_2, where M_2 is greater than M_1, or buying commodities in order to make more money out of their subsequent sale.[53] In the simple circulation of commodities, on the one hand, it is supposedly the usefulness of the respective commodities and the modest acquisition of specific commodities for the fulfilment of needs which are at the focus of attention and the motivating end for the exchange. Money is only a means of exchange, i.e. a means for exchanging one commodity for the other for the sake of satisfying a need through the commodity's use-value. In the circulation of money as capital, on the other hand, the usefulness of the commodities is only a vehicle for money-making. The commodities are here only a means for the putatively ever-restless, endless end of the augmentation of money. Money is no longer a mere means of exchange but is the universal representation of wealth itself in a quantitative form with the potential and potency (δύναμις) to lay a claim on any goods at will.

There is thus an excessiveness lying at the heart of dealings with money, and this excessiveness is nothing other than human wanting to have more. Such wanting-to-have-more (πλεονεξία 359c) plays a role throughout Plato's discussion of *justice* in his *Politeia*. Such a desire for more goes beyond a more in order to satisfy a want, but is the desire for more *as such*. The human psyche is not merely finitely needy, as all socialist ideology would have it, but infinitely desirous. Even in the simple circulation of commodities mediated by money there is nothing to hinder modest need turning into blatantly immoderate desire for luxurious things. Nevertheless, with the circulation of money as capital, this desire for more, now abstracted or unhinged from the fulfilment of a specific need or want, is purely quantitative and finds its adequate object in money itself, which is the abstract, quantitative embodiment of wealth (even though the money be ultimately merely digital digits stored in an electronic bank account or block-chain). Desire itself has become abstractly quantitative, abstracted from the specific usefulness of goods, unhinged from the end of living modestly well along with the unhinging of the human psyche itself. This abstraction goes hand in hand with the inversion of the simple circulation of commodities into the circulation of capital, an endlessly self-augmenting principal sum.

The desire to have more is ultimately the desire for mere potential, potency and social power as embodied in money-capital as reified value-in-movement and, once achieved through one circuit of capital, can only repeat itself — over and over again, the pure ἐνέργεια or energy of money at work in self-augmentation. The self-augmentation of money as capital is endless, borne as it

---

53 Karl Marx *Das Kapital* Bd. I *Marx Engels Werke* Dietz , Berlin 1962 Band 23 S. 167 and passim; henceforth abbreviated MEW23:167.

is by an endlessly desirous will to have abstractly more: πλεονεξία. Since excessive wealth exceeds what can be used in the usages of life, it is had (ἔχειν) only as a potential and a possibility (δυνάμει), as a power and potency (δύναμις) which gives its possessor influence through being at work (ἐνεργείᾳ) in mere self-augmentation. There is no ἐντελέχεια of money-capital in the sense of a final, perfect presence in which the movement of self-augmentation has attained its end and come to rest and to which nothing further could be added; the movement can never have (ἔχειν) itself in its end (τέλος) in an attained, perfected presence, but rather, money-capital only attains its ἐντελέχεια in the endless movement itself; ἐνέργεια and ἐντελέχεια are one and the same in this case.

Are these references to the satisfaction of need and desire, and the acquisition of wealth in Plato, Aristotle and Marx merely the citation from doxographic sources in the history of ideas, or do they indicate something essential about historico-temporal human being itself? Is human being in its whoness characterized essentially by a limitless striving to have more? Is human being boundless in this regard? Is such a condition of boundlessness an historical, anthropological invariant, or could bounds be set to human acquisitiveness from within human who-being itself? Are there historical societies in which desirous greed was not a feature? For the West at least — and not only the West —, this question can be confidently denied. Aristotle points out that the limitless striving to accumulate wealth arises from "the striving for life, but not for the good life" (τὸ σπουδάζειν περὶ τὸ ζῆν ἀλλὰ μὴ τὸ εὖ ζῆν; 1257b 41). And what is this good life which could of itself set a limit? For Aristotle, the best way of life was the theoretical, philosophical life devoted to contemplating the beingness of beings, and thus a kind of frugal, self-sufficient existence, but this is hardly a proposal for living well in society as a whole. It is the exception.

Another answer is given perhaps by Sophocles' *Antigone* in which he provides an essential outline of human being itself. The famous chorus sketches the seemingly limitless scope of human enterprise which finds a way to overcome almost any obstacle. However, "From Hades alone will he not be granted any escape" (Ἄιδα μόνον φεῦξιν οὐκ ἐπάξεται; 360). Death is the ultimate limit and horizon for mortal human being in its whoness. The good life takes its measure and its stand in keeping death in view. The accumulation of wealth, too, can only find its limit in regarding the bounds of human existence which lie in the inevitability of death and the mortal time span which death stakes out for each individual existence striving to be somewho. But, says Aristotle, "since the longing of the heart for life is limitless, so too do people long in their hearts without limit for what makes for living" (εἰς ἄπειρον οὖν ἐκείνης τῆς ἐπιθυμίας οὔσης, καὶ τῶν ποιητικῶν ἀπείρων ἐπιθυμοῦσιν; 1258a1). This longing and urging of the heart (ἐπιθυμία) for life and to avoid death is expressed also in Sophocles' lines, but conversely, in formulating the inevitability of death, "From Hades alone will he not be granted any escape, Even having thought out a way to flee untreatable illnesses" (Ἅιδα μόνον φεῦξιν οὐκ ἐπάξεται· νόσων δ' ἀμηχάνων φυγὰς ξυμπέφρασται; 361). Human beings willingly postpone the thought of their own dying, and in this postponement and forgetting of their own mortality, they strive endlessly for riches as the means for living, as if they would live forever, perhaps dynastically through their children. They seek all possible means to overcome even apparently incurable illnesses, or they strive for an Ersatz-immortality in their offspring. Modern medicine, too, is driven by the will to stretch the limits of human mortality. The self-moving motivation of life — the striving and stretching and reaching out of appetite (ὄρεξις) and desire (ἐπιθυμία) for the ὀρεκτόν, the thing reached out for and striven for — in itself strives boundlessly, even without the entrance of self-augmenting capital that facilitates this endless striving. Capital per se is not to blame for unfulfillable human desiring.

The potential to gain access to all the possible means of living, whether they be means of enjoyment or means for prolonging life, is crystallized in money as the representation and embodiment of wealth and the universal reified power for acquiring any particular valuable, useful thing. There is thus an inherent ambivalence in money: firstly, as a means for living by providing the necessary access to the means of life and secondly, as an abstract end in itself whose possession provides the abstract potential of concretion in useful, valuable things and whose endless accumulation therefore becomes the motive for furthering the movement of self-augmentation of money as capital. The endless, circular, self-augmenting movement of money as capital would thus seem to be motivated on the side of human beings by an endless striving for immortality, or at least by an endless denial of mortality, as if the circle of human life could partake of the seemingly eternal circular movements of the stars, at least through the natural cycle of propagation of oneself in one's progeny. But it is not enough just to feel oneself a part of an endless natural cycle of progeneration; one's Ersatz-immortality can only be realized by passing on one's family name — that kernel of whoness — to one's own progeny who will continue to bear it down through the ages. When thought from the ontological dimension of whoness, immortality becomes an immortality of one's being *as* who as expressed in one's proper name that can have a more or less illustrious and long history of which its bearer is proud.

The possibility of Ersatz-immortality aside, what do people do as long as they are alive? They strive to have more, thus turning money from a means into a motivating end in itself, for wealth itself enhances one's own who-status and self-esteem. Is that necessarily a bad thing, measured against the yardstick of living well? The striving to have more is expressed above all in the gainful activity of wealth-making which Aristotle calls chrematistics (χρηματιστική). The Greek word, τὸ χρῆμα, means 'thing' in the broadest sense, including 'issue', 'undertaking', 'event', but also, in the plural, it signifies 'goods', 'money', 'wealth'. Chrematistics is contrasted with economics (οἰκονομική; 1257b20), which latter is the art of wealth-making in accordance with nature (κατὰ φύσιν; 1257b20) and has its end (τέλος) in living well or the good life (εὖ ζῆν or ἀγαθὴ ζωή; 1256b32). Aristotle says that this natural art of wealth-making has an end and a limit in which it comes to rest, "just as in the other arts" (ὥσπερ καὶ ταῖς ἄλλαις τέχναις; 1256b34).

The question is, however, whether economics or chrematistics, as arts of "making riches" (ποιητικὴ πλούτου; 1257b8) or arts of (limited or unlimited, respectively) "acquisition" (τέχνη κτητική 1256b38), are arts in the paradigmatic Greek sense as a knowledge for bringing forth a definite, foreseen end, for there is clearly a difference between the know-how involved in making a bedstead or a house and the know-how required to 'produce', i.e. gain, wealth or money. The difference resides in the essential double character of goods themselves which are, on the one hand, primarily good for a certain purpose or useful in a definite context of application within a certain customary practice of life and, on the other, are derivatively 'good' for gaining money by way of producing and trading. This double-sided or Janus-faced goodness of goods is referred to in political economy as use-value, on the one hand, and exchange-value, on the other (cf. Chapter 5 on the ontology of exchange for more details).

Whereas the use-value of goods can be reliably produced by a technically effective process of production in the proper sense, as a potential inherent in the product itself, whereby the use-value of means of production is employed according to well-defined knowledge of the production process, the exchange-value of goods cannot be produced reliably by a technical production process because exchange-value is only realized or put to work (ἐνεργείᾳ, 'energized') in the exchange for *other* goods or money. This otherness is not within the knowing, controlling reach of the potential of the goods in question to be exchanged. The production of exchange-value cannot be set up simply as a technical production process, since the production or bringing-forth of exchange-value is in truth a turning-out-to-be, i.e. exchange-value turns out to be what it is, both qualitatively (in being saleable at all) and quantitatively (in the amount of money, or price attained by the goods) in exchange on the market.[54] This simple, but crucial, insight holds true just as much for Aristotle's times as it does for our own, in which the capitalist mode of economic life, including both capitalist production *and* capitalist markets, prevails, despite all the conspicuous and deep differences in the *historical constellations* constituted by the socio-ontological elements in different places at different times.

The art of making money is an art sui generis whose knowledge is not reliable, but rather exposed to the contingency of markets. It is the merchant's art. This means that the art of making money is strictly speaking not a τέχνη (ποιητική) in Plato's sense, but rather merely an empirical skill (ἐμπειρία). Plato distinguishes between an art (τέχνη) and an empirical skill in that the latter "does not have any defining insight into what it brings to bear, what its nature is, and therefore does not have the cause of each [in its power] to say" (τέχνην δὲ οὔ φημι εἶναι ἀλλ' ἐμπειρίαν· ὅτι οὐκ ἔκει λόγον οὐδένα ᾧ προσφέρει ἃ προσφέρει ὁποῖ" ἄττα τὴν φύσιν ἐστίν, ὥστε τὴν αἰτίαν ἑκάστου μὴ ἔχειν εἰπεῖν, *Gorgias* 465a) and is "simply a retained memory of what usually happens" (μνήμην μόνον σῳζομένη τοῦ εἰωθότος γίγνεσθαι, *Gorgias* 501b). Because exchange-value cannot be produced like use-value, money-making or wealth-making is not an art based on insight into the causes which bring forth exchange-value, i.e. to which exchange-value is indebted (αἰτία), but is rather, in Plato's terminology, an empirical skill based on a retained memory of what usually happens, of observed regularities, especially in the market (even when today they may be modelled mathematically as stochastic processes or by learning-algorithms unleashed onto enormous quantities of merely empirical data). One can only say that, based on experience, a produced good is generally worth such-and-such and can be actively marketed at such-and-such a price, but such experiential knowledge of regularity is subject to contingency (κατὰ συμβεβηκός) and variation and is thus not only unreliable, but is essentially lacking genuine, controlling insight (λόγος) and foresight. Because economics in both the ancient and modern sense is essentially concerned inter alia with the exchange-value of goods in the broadest sense, including services, it cannot be a science in the proper (Aristotelean) sense as a knowledge of causes or first principles. Rather, it can only develop empirical methods (including, today, sophisticated mathematical statistical methods using supercomputers to uncover regularities in so-called 'big data') which provide pseudo-knowledge that

---

54 Cf. Eldred, M. 'Technology, Technique, Interplay: Questioning *Die Frage nach der Technik*' 2007–2014.

may or may not be reliable for the most part, i.e. as a rule, but which lacks essential insight into any final causes.[55]

In switching perspective to the capitalist market economies prevalent today, we can say that money-making in the guise of capitalist enterprise is indeed an enterprise subject to the uncertainties of the market-place where exchange-value is realized. Such uncertainty and contingency are essential to exchange-value, for exchange-value depends upon what others are prepared to give for certain goods of a given quality and quantity on the market at a specific point in time. No reliable knowable causes quantitatively determining exchange-value can be specified. All calculations of prices that can be realized on the market and all price functions that express price, say, as a function of demand quantity, have only relative, empirical reliability which may suddenly turn out to be completely off the mark. (This line of thought will be deepened, i.e. simplified, in Chapter 5, in which an ontology of exchange interplay in connection with the ontology of whoness will be presented. There it will be seen more clearly and deeply in what the essential lack of insight consists and how the valuing of whats is related to the valuing of whos.)

Apart from the question as to whether the art of making money can be a science or a genuine τέχνη ποιητική in the sense of a reliable, fore-knowing know-how, the point here in the first place is that money-making need not have an end in which it comes to rest, "just as in the other arts" (1256b34). To return to the above distinction between economics and chrematistics: Does the endless pursuit of money necessarily imply a denial of one's own mortality? Is there a measure to money-making residing in living well that dictates that the getting of money for its own sake is necessarily a perversion of human living? Can the endless cycle of making money simply be a form of social movement rather than an activity undertaken for a specific, finite end? Can one live beyond oneself in making money, not only, say, for the sake of one's children, but for the sake of how money-making lubricates, facilitates an economy as a whole and contributes to the well-being of the economy as a whole, i.e. to the well-being of other social players, by keeping the interplay of earning one's living going and enhancing the mode of play? Is the role of entrepreneurial capitalist as the mobilizer of money as capital a socially useful and commendable one that can be regarded as a valuable profession along with others, despite or precisely because it is the business of keeping capital augmenting in endless circuits? Can the entrepreneur dedicating his or her life to running a successful enterprise with continually growing profits be congruent with enhancing the well-being of

---

55 Cf. my *The Digital Cast of Being* 2009/2011 Chapter 5.

society, or is this incessant preoccupation with growing the enterprise and the accumulation of wealth a perversion of what economic life, both personally and on the social level, could or should be about? We will take up these questions again in later sections, starting with Chapter 4.6.

4.2   Weber's conception of economic activity

The Aristotelean distinction between household management and money-making is echoed not only in Karl Marx's thinking, but also in the modern positivist social sciences of economics and sociology. Thus, for example, we find in Max Weber's *Economy and Society*[56] the same distinction in social economic action between the orientation of a "household" toward the satisfaction of need (Bedarfsdeckung, WGII § 15 S. 64), on the one hand, and the orientation of an "enterprise" toward gain as such (Erwerb, WGII § 11 S. 48), on the other. Economic action itself is defined as *peaceful* social action oriented toward catering to the desire for useful benefits (Nutzleistungen, WGII § 1 S. 31). Useful benefits themselves are, "in becoming the object of caring and providing for oneself, what are assessed to be, by one or several economic actors, as the concrete, *individual* (real or presumed) chances of present or future use" (die von einem oder mehreren Wirtschaftenden als solche geschätzten konkreten *einzelnen* zum Gegenstand der Fürsorge werdenen (wirklichen oder vermeintlichen) Chancen gegenwärtiger oder künftiger Verwendungsmöglichkeiten, WGII § 2 S. 34) which, as potential means for the ends of the economic actors, become the orientation for the actors' activities. The final end of the economic actors is what they regard to be the enhancement of their existence, in Aristotelean language, "good living", or in modern parlance, the maintenance and improvement of their standard of living. Such useful benefits "can be the benefits provided by non-human (objective) things or the services of humans" (können Leistungen nicht menschlicher (sachlicher) Träger oder Leistungen von Menschen sein, WGII:34.).

The orientation of social action toward useful benefits in the context of taking care of one's own is thus an orientation toward *chances* (κατὰ συμβεβηκός) in the double sense of a potential (δύναμις) and opportunity, but one that is exposed to uncertainty or risk. The risk resides not only in failing to gain power of disposal, but also in the hoped-for useful benefits not being forthcoming.

---

56 Max Weber *Wirtschaft und Gesellschaft* J.C.B. Mohr, Tübingen, 5th. revised edition, 1980. Abbreviated as WG in citations.

Similarly, gainful activity is defined as "action oriented toward the chances of (once-only or regularly recurring: continual) gaining new power of disposal over goods" (ein an den Chancen der (einmaligen oder regelmäßig wiederkehrenden: kontinuierlichen) Gewinnung von neuer Verfügungsgewalt über Güter orientiertes Verhalten, WGII § 11 S. 48). The reference to "new" here means that gainful activity is oriented always toward an *augmentation* of power, toward a *more*, i.e. more potential for disposing over goods. Such a striving for more is essentially purely quantitative and can therefore be termed purely capitalist. Gainful activity, Weber says, is economic if it is oriented toward *peaceful* chances of such gain and it is *market* economic activity if it is oriented toward chances or opportunities provided by market situations (Marktlagen, WGII:48). The market situation of a commodity is said to be "the totality of chances or opportunities of exchange for money by purchase or sale *recognizable* in a given situation for those interested in exchange in their orientation toward the struggle over prices in competition" (die Gesamtheit der jeweils für Tauschreflektanten bei der Orientierung im Preis- und Konkurrenzkampf *erkennbaren* Aus- und Eintauschchancen desselben gegen Geld, WGII § 8 S. 43). The emphasis on "recognizable" shows that a market situation is defined by a certain openness and visibility of possibilities.

But what Weber blurs is that his term "economic gain" (wirtschaftliches Erwerben, WGII § 11 S.48) is, strictly speaking, self-contradictory, since gain is not economic, i.e. "provision for a desire for useful benefits". Or, if it is not self-contradictory, the concept of "useful benefit" (Nutzleistung) is. For, on the one hand, useful benefits are defined as "what are assessed to be, by one or several economic actors, as the concrete, individual... chances of present or future use" " (WGII § 2 S. 34) and thus as a *potential*, and, on the other, are exemplified by "the benefits provided by non-human (objective) things or the services of humans", i.e. by the *actualization* of a potential in the satisfaction of desire. If it is only a matter of gaining power over a potential, then the economic activity of a household would be essentially the same as an enterprise's striving to make money as the universal potential. But then, a household's objective would not be the satisfaction of need (Bedarfsdeckung, WGII § 15 S. 64). Weber, who can here be regarded as a representative of both the social sciences, sociology and economics, glosses over the inversion that takes place when money-making becomes an end in itself, thus subsuming the striving of modest mortals to satisfy their finite, mortal needs under the abstract augmentation of money as capital. We must turn rather to thinkers such as Aristotle and Marx to see the contradictoriness inherent in economic activity itself.

Competition in the market-place is the way in which the struggle over the power of disposal over "useful benefits" is carried out in a market economy. Weber in fact defines economic activity as the peaceful struggle over the power of disposal over useful benefits, which indicates that there is also the possibility of a non-peaceful struggle through war, piracy, plunder, banditry, etc. In any case, there is a struggle among people over the appropriation of useful benefits potentially provided by things and people which are not freely and limitlessly available, i.e. they are scarce. Since having power of disposal over given goods and services is mutually exclusionary among economic agents, there are essentially always *conflicts of interests* of many and various kinds among people in their desire to possess what is useful for living and therefore valuable. Thus there are not only differences in the views people hold about a situation or a general state of affairs, and thus a dispute about the *truth* of a matter, but there is also the difference of *conflicting interests* and opposed social powers based on mutually exclusionary claims to the power of disposal over useful benefits in not unlimited supply. That latter is an ontic insight; as representative of positivist sociology, Weber nowhere digs deeper into the ontology of social ontology, which is only possible with a clear view of ontological difference that sociology keeps adamantly closed off to view.

Differences in views and conflicting interests have to be distinguished conceptually from each other. The former are more fundamental because differences in views arise from the play of truth itself in revealing and concealing what and how the world is, whereas conflicts of interests derive, in addition, from the striving to gain power of disposal over limited useful benefits, i.e. over beings in the world. Such self-interests of course substantially colour the view which a given party holds about a given situation so that how it is revealed and held to be is biased in the direction of furthering the perceived self-interests of the given party. Having self-interests means that the view of a situation is *held* to be other than how it would reveal itself of itself, without distortion. For this reason, the search for truth has traditionally always been regarded as a matter of *disinterested* observation and contemplation (which does not mean, however, that truth becomes objective, since there is no truth at all without human being).

Economic activity is carried out on a formally rational basis, in Weber's terms, if it is calculable in numbers (WGII § 9 S. 44). The "consummate" (vollkommenste) means of economic calculation is money, which Weber describes, in his purportedly 'value-neutral', positivistic fashion, as "the formally most rational means of orientation for economic action" (das formal rationalste Mittel der Orientierung wirtschaftlichen Handelns, WGII § 10 S. 45). Such monetary calculability is the basis of capitalist gainful activity. "Capitalist calculation is the estimation and control of opportunities for gain and their success by comparing the estimated monetary amounts" of all the goods used in the gainful economic activity at the beginning and at the end of a period of reckoning (Kapitalrechnung ist die Schätzung und Kontrolle von Erwerbschancen und -erfolgen durch Vergleichung des Geldschätzungsbetrages einerseits der sämtlichen Erwerbsgüter (in Natur oder Geld) bei Beginn und andererseits der (noch vorhandenen und neu beschafften) Erwerbsgüter bei Abschluß des einzelnen Erwerbsunternehmens..., WGII § 11 S. 48). This calculation enables profit and loss and profitability of the enterprise to be quantitatively determined, but always in retrospect. Capitalist calculation is *quantitative* calculation based on relevant monetary quantities. This calculation presupposes ontologically the sociating medium of reified value (cf. Chapter 9). Profitability is the ultima ratio for the rational calculation of economic success and failure, whereas the success or otherwise of a household in meeting its needs has to be evaluated in a more qualitative way since needs and their satisfaction are not measurable simply in monetary quantities.

The advance calculation associated with economic activity is, in Weberian terms, always a calculation of the chances for gaining power of disposal over useful benefits. The terms 'chance', 'gain', 'power' in this statement all have to be ontologically investigated as ways of being, something which, needless to say, Weber as a sociologist does not undertake, but which presents itself to *us* as a philosophical task to be tackled in subsequent chapters. To continue for the moment in a preliminary, more ontic mode: Such chances for gain always involve uncertainty and risk, whether it be for a capitalist enterprise or a household. The orientation of economic activity is indeed toward a certain end (in Weberian terms, the end of achieving power of disposition over the embodiments of useful benefits either for consumption or for further augmentation), but the way to this end is not controllable by technical means, since 'technical' in its original sense always means having a foresightful knowledge of how to securely attain an end whilst keeping interfering contingent factors at bay. Τέχνη ποιητική in the Greek sense is ἀρχὴ μεταβολῆς and as such, more specifically, a δύναμις μετὰ λόγου i.e. a foreseeing, knowing point of origin governing a change. Such knowing, foreseeing, fore-casting control which governs an outcome in the temporal dimension of the future is lacking in economic activity because it necessarily involves social relations of exchange, i.e. an uncertain interplay. In economic activity there can only be an orientation toward probable, estimated outcomes of activity that is wagered and risked.

The essential sources of uncertainty for the opportunities offered for gainful activity reside in the market-places for purchasing and selling goods and services. As Weber himself says, the prices achieved on the market are always the result of a competitive struggle over price, i.e. of an *interplay* among social actors with various potentials, abilities. Whereas the use-value of a good or service is its potential to be used in providing a benefit in consumption or in production as a means of production, and this use-value potential can reliably and foreseeably be counted on to be realized when necessary, the exchange-value of a good or service is its potential to be exchanged for money on a market, and the realization of this potential depends upon the momentary market situation or predicament with all its contingencies. When exchange-value is realized on the market, the current market *predicament*, which is not precontrivable, precontrollable or *predictable*, defines or *predicates* how much the exchange-value *is* quantitatively. The exchange-value of a good or service can even vanish, momentarily or even permanently, into nothing. There may suddenly be no takers for a certain commodity on the market, even though the commodity's quality has not altered. The exchange-value depends *essentially* also on the *others*, not just on the economic actor who is out for gain.

Since uncertainty and risk are associated with all kinds of capitalist, market-oriented, gainful economic activity, the economic actors feel a need to compensate for this uncertainty by making provision for it. Such provision normally involves *saving*, especially in monetary and near-money form, for a buffer of money and saleable assets can be employed to gain control over useful benefits (in Weberian terminology) should the current income-earning activity (cash flow) be momentarily insufficient to cover needs. Saving itself is a peculiar phenomenon because it is a way of controlling the future by stocking up on money or near-money assets that function as a *store of value*, i.e. as an abstract, reified medium that gives its possessor the power to procure at will goods for living or for further production at any time now or in the future. Such a store of value is thus a buffer against unfavourable future events. Market-mediated economic activity essentially involves taking risk and thus also hedging against risk in case plans and precalculations go wrong. If, as Weber says, all economic action is oriented toward chances or opportunities, then all economic action is also projected toward the future, a future which is beset more or less with uncertainty. The management of risk and uncertainty in capitalist economic activity also has an economic solution, but at a price that must be deducted from an enterprise's gross gain. The risk of an unfavourable outcome of entrepreneurial activity can be spread by means of insurance policies, or the risk can be hedged by transferring it to another economic actor (a so-called speculator), say, by means of a futures contract which fixes a purchase or sale price at some definite date in the future.

The option of insurance is open also to households for the eventuality that income earned is insufficient to cover core needs. This spreading or transfer of risk is made possible ontologically by the sociating medium of reified value itself because in its 'look' as money, reified value as a quantified, reified social relation allows a price to be put even on something as abstract and intangible and futural as risk. A peculiarity of a capitalist market economy is that even outcomes in the future, because they can be monetarized, can themselves be traded on a futures market. This makes risk calculable for a given economic actor, but it does not make the risk itself precalculable or predictable, because the buyer of the risk, i.e. the insurance company or the futures trader, then bears the risk and then has to itself hedge or spread (reinsurance) the specific risk it has taken on. Risk is intimately related to the uncertainty of (social) movement, a topic to be resumed and deepened in Chapter 5.

4.3   The Cartesian cast of economics

Our purpose here, however, is not to discuss the practicalities of risk management. Rather, the insight into the essential uncertainty inherent in market-mediated economic activity has equally essential consequences for the social science of economics (cf. also Chapter 8). At the core of economics is always a theory of exchange and price couched in quantitative terms. Whether it be a labour theory of value, a theory of marginal utility, a theory of economic equilibrium or some other approach, economic theory as we know it is always concerned with writing equations for the exchange relations among goods in the broadest sense that have futural, predictive power. The qualitative phenomena of commodity, exchange, market, price and money necessarily play a part in any economic theory, but the phenomena themselves are not thought through and brought to their ontological concepts.

Instead, the focus is set singlemindedly at the outset upon seeking a ground in quantitative relations enabling precalculability, and the phenomena themselves are reduced to mere variables in equations. Why is it taken for granted from the outset that positivist economics, which arose out of moral philosophy, must be concerned with quantitative relations? It seems to be unquestioningly self-evident that, say, price is a phenomenon interesting only from a quantitative point of view. Therefore no deeper questions are asked by economists about what price is, i.e. its essence, its 'look' of whatness.

The orientation of economics toward uncovering quantitative causes or reasons preferably expressed in equations lies in the circumstance that economics willingly models itself on the mathematical natural sciences which served and continue to serve as the paradigm par excellence for scientificity. This means that economics as a social science is cast in the mould of Cartesian science, i.e. scientific knowledge and, above all, scientific *method* as understood in the modern age aiming at certain knowledge — and in particular, certain fore-knowledge — for the conscious subject posited *as* the fundament of self-certainty in Descartes' famous dictum, cogito ergo sum. Descartes was the first thinker to expressly formulate the requirement that scientific knowledge must assume a quantitative form. This goes beyond the Aristotelean concept of science, according to which all knowledge must be derivable from 'first principles' or 'first causes' or 'grounds'. According to Descartes, certain knowledge is attainable only through intuition (direct looking-at) and deduction (syllogistic reasoning), i.e. through the only reliable actions of understanding for finding the truth (*De Regulae* Rule 3). Descartes also laid down the "rule" in his *Regulae* according to which everything to do with beings has to be brought into the form of proportions and equations. And only that can be brought into the form of an equation "except by admitting a more or less, and indeed all this comprehended in terms of magnitude" (Rule 14.4 "nisi quod recipit majus et minus, atque illud omne per magnitudinis vocabulum comprehendi"[57]). The upshot, according to Descartes, is that "we no longer think of involving ourselves with this or that subject, but only in general with comparing certain quantities among themselves" (Rule 13.1 "non amplius cogitemus nos circa hoc vel illud subjectum versari, sed tantum in genere circa magnitudines quasdam inter se comparandas"). The import and consequences of this casting of the criteria for scientific knowledge in the modern age can scarcely be overestimated. In the case at hand, with regard to economics, it means that this science self-evidently and therefore unthinkingly takes for granted that it must conceive economic phenomena in quantitative terms amenable to mathematical calculation if it is to be a science at all. The very form of economic knowledge is thus already precast, unbeknowns to economists themselves, by an ontological preconception, the casting of the self-certain subject of consciousness that represents the objects to itself in knowing consciousness. The economic phenomena themselves in their

---

57 R. Descartes *Regulae ad Directionem Ingenii* in *Philosophische Schriften* Meiner, Hamburg, 1996 S. 120. For more on Cartesian rules in connection with digital being and the mathematization of scientific access to the world, see my *The Digital Cast of Being: Metaphysics, Mathematics, Cartesianism, Cybernetics, Capitalism, Communication* ontos, Frankfurt 2009/2011.

being do not call for thinking, or rather, the call of the phenomena themselves to be thought through in their own specific qualitative mode of being is not heard. Instead, it is demanded of economic science that it be useful, and such usefulness is automatically understood as quantitative calculability that provides certain results above all in the form of predictions and forecasts. And precalculability in the economic realm inevitably means ultimately precalculability in terms of money quantities. As we have seen (and will further investigate), however, the calculability of money quantities does not provide any basis for predictability akin to the laws of physics which provide a basis for precalculating future motion in the physical realm on the basis of relations of cause and effect. There are no such well-founded, axiomatic economic laws of motion, but only *a posteriori* calculations after the event or else projections and extrapolations from previous empirical data which are necessarily subject to revision and, depending on the assumptions made in the mathematized model, result in various 'scenarios'. There are no grounds or principles governing economic motion since exchange-value itself is inherently, i.e. essentially, contingent on others' actions and is thus an interplay. Thus no predictive calculations can be made with certainty but only on the basis of empirical regularity and envisaging a range of possible future scenarios. Economists therefore seek to discover patterns of regularity in what has been and to extrapolate these patterns into the future in order to make a forecast. This is a kind a knowledge based on what is the case 'for the most part' (Aristotle's ἐπὶ τὸ πολύ), i.e. on regularity, and highly sophisticated mathematical statistics has been developed in the modern age to squeeze out the regularities from masses of data on what has already been the case. But even these highly sophisticated, computer-assisted, number-crunching techniques employed in constructing models of what is presumed to be economic 'reality' cannot overcome the essential, insurmountable problem that economics as a *social* science lacks a single unifying, controlling principle from which economic outcomes could be derived.

Modern economic science is calculation with monetary quantities, especially predictive precalculation. We have already pointed out that deeper thinkers who concerned themselves with economic phenomena, namely Aristotle and Marx, very clearly discerned a distinction between economics as household management and the art of making or getting money (chrematistics, τέχνη κτητική). Further consideration of the phenomenon of money-making or entrepreneurship reveals that there cannot be an art of money-making in the strict sense as foreknowledge, but only an empirical skill (ἐμπειρία Plato cf. above), an *art of gainful interplay*.

Furthermore, the quantitative bias and indeed ground-plan and basic cast of modern economics, which unthinkingly skips over and necessarily takes for granted the qualitative, ontological aspects of the phenomena it must deal with (i.e. their very *being*), means that modern economics concerns itself basically only with chrematistics. Chrematistics, however, is concerned not with the satisfaction of need, but is a striving to have more, where this 'more' remains quantitatively indeterminate and therefore limitless. This is the source of tension between modern mathematical economics and political economy, which, having arisen originally out of moral philosophy, is concerned more with the moral predicament of how well and especially how badly people do in economic life. But political economy, too, overlooks the ontological questions that remain unasked in economics and resorts instead to an ultimately impotent moral standpoint merely of what *ought* to be.

The more modern name for chrematistics is capitalism or capitalist entrepreneurship. Under capitalism, the augmentation of money — or more nebulously, 'economic growth' — becomes an end in itself rather than money being the means to the end of living well. So along with the neglect of the phenomena themselves for the sake of quantitative (pseudo-)'scientific' understanding and precalculability, as (iron-)cast, by the Cartesian paradigm for what is to be regarded as knowledge at all, there is an inversion of means and ends in which the quantitative monetary moment becomes dominant as if by sleight of hand. The connection between economic growth as measured by growth in gross domestic product or some such macroeconomic indicator and people living well in an economy has to be considered more deeply from a philosophical perspective, and not just by putting hard numbers into relation with some measure or other of 'quality of life'. This will involve thinking through economic activity as an important mode of caring-for (cf. Chapter 9.3).

4.4 Schumpeter's equilibrium theory

Let us take as a further example besides the sociologist Max Weber, the work of one of the most famous economists of the twentieth century, Joseph Schumpeter, who is an adherent of the equilibrium theory which investigates the conditions of reproduction of the macroeconomic process, analogous to conservation laws in physics from which equations spring. An equilibrium theory or theory of the (initially simple) reproduction of an economy proceeds by building a model based first of all on very simple, counterfactual assumptions. A national economy is treated as a household which unchangingly reproduces the conditions of its own existence. These very strong assumptions mean, for example, that the "wages and rents — the only cost elements which exist here — are necessarily equal to the values of the consumer goods which the labour power and natural powers paid for by these wages and rents produce either directly or via the produced means of production or unfinished products".[58] Furthermore, "Here at least there is still no occasion to misuse the word capital which it would be best to expunge from our vocabulary and which for us is merely a monetary and in particular, although not exclusively, an accounting concept." (p. 116) It should be noted that this desired exclusion of the concept of capital, which applies to the entire chapter, occurs precisely in a chapter entitled "The Capitalist Economic Process". The model-building starts with assumptions that are so strong that the concepts of value, money and capital are trivialized with the consequence that "The Capitalist Economic Process" as such is not treated. The strategy of this theoretical approach is to start with a very simple model based on very strong, counterfactual assumptions, and then proceed to gradually relax those simplifying assumptions in order to progressively approximate economic reality by allowing a continual increase in complexity.

But underlying this entire approach is the conception that the value of commodities can be determined quantitatively by means of equations more or less complicated, formulating conditions of reproduction of an economy in the sense of a large and complex *household* (Aristotle's οἰκονομική cf. Chapter 4.1). "Since the monetary magnitudes and the monetary processes in the economy are given their sense by the magnitudes of goods and processes in the world of goods to which they correspond and therefore an understanding of the monetary processes presupposes an understanding of processes in the world of goods and cannot be determined independently of it, we thus have already with the considerations just made and the conceptual constructions resulting from these an initial point of approach for an analysis of the sphere of credit and money." (p. 119) The conditions of reproduction of the economy, no matter whether this be thought as simple reproduction or whether it means expanded reproduction (economic growth), provide the basis upon which value equations can be written to determine credit and money volumes. The stepwise incorporation of more and more complicated conditions of reproduction only modifies and complicates, but does not suspend, the initial assumptions that money is only a means mediating the reproduction of an economy conceived as a household — and thus its augmentation is never an end in itself, i.e. money as capital. This initial

---

58 Joseph A. Schumpeter *Das Wesen des Geldes* Vandenhoeck & Ruprecht, Göttingen 1970 p. 116; cf. *Das Wesen und der Hauptinhalt der theoretischen Nationalökonomie* 2. Aufl. Duncker & Humblot, Berlin 1970, unaltered reprint of the first edition from 1908.

assumption means that the magnitude of value is determined by something extrinsic, namely, reproduction (i.e. the *production* once again) of an economy, and thus has a ground which can be used to calculate value magnitudes. Such value magnitudes can be calculated because exchange, whether it be on the micro or a macro level, is conceived in some sense or other as an exchange of *equivalents* and this equivalence is thought as conditions of reproduction. But such a preconception, no matter in what guise, means that the economy is being thought of as a kind of household-machine and not genuinely as a capitalist economy in which the groundless exchange interplay is at play and the augmentation of exchange-value is the motivating principle (the principle of movement), but with uncertain outcome.

The existence of money, however, implies nothing other than that the value of economic entities in the broadest sense, i.e. what they are 'good for' as measured abstractly by the quantitative, reified sociating medium of money, has assumed a form (i.e. 'look') of existence independent of the goods, services, natural resources, etc. whose value is validated in money. It is only by virtue of having assumed such an independent, reified form of existence that the augmentation of money itself can become the simple driving force and motive of economic activity. But the augmentation of money as capital in the circulation of capital does not presuppose an exchange of equivalents, where equivalence is determined by the equality of some extrinsic factor. Rather, money itself is its own measure and therefore the augmentation of money as capital can only be measured by itself in a kind of 'self-reflection' back onto itself as an incremental difference, i.e. as a differential. The sense of a capitalist economy is to augment money as capital. Capital is thus a dynamic concept, a concept of movement measured by the differential increment of money-capital through its circuitous movement. Schumpeter, by contrast, posits with an appeal to self-evident common-sense that "the objective sense of economic activity [...] is of course the satisfaction of need." (p. 129) With this appeal to common-sense, he has circumvented all the fundamental questions concerning capitalist economy.

There is, however, an essential disjunction between money-making and the satisfaction of need, between chrematistics and household management, between capitalism and providing for individual and social needs that calls for thinking. And the seed crystal of this essential disjunction lies in the essence of money itself as an independent embodiment of value, as the quantitative reification of a qualitative relation among things themselves. Exchange-value, as Marx very clearly saw, is disjunct from use-value, although Marx also sought to preserve a quantitative, extrinsic substance of value residing in labour content which thus, in his conception, has a double nature as productive of both exchange-value and use-value. Here it has to be seen that exchange-value, with its own peculiar entity, money, is an independent social dimension that essentially corresponds to and ultimately *enables, in an interplay of powers, the striving to have more* (πλεονεξία) as a *possibility of human existence*. Once use-value is expressed universally, abstractly, quantitatively in exchange-value in its 'look' as money, it has become alienated from itself, i.e. it confronts itself with its other. We must, however, not be too quick to morally condemn this ontological alienation, as we shall investigate later on (Chapter 9.1).

The point here is that Joseph Schumpeter and other economists are far removed from an insight into the true nature of money, value and capital because they are loath to involve themselves with the socio-ontological issues slumbering in the foundations of their social science. Thus, for instance, as a positivist social scientist, Schumpeter writes in a review of the history of thinking about money, which begins with a few remarks on Plato and Aristotle, that "general remarks on the essence of money are of much less interest than believed to be by those who still regard our science as a conglomerate of philosophy and dogmas. For science it is only a matter of what is made out of such starting-points." (p. 41f) But everything is decided by the starting-point (ἀρχή), for the starting-point, with its fore-casting pre-conceptions of what knowledge is (a heritage from the Greek conception of ἐπιστήμη), has a hold over and governs all the thoughts and concepts which follow.

For Aristotle, knowledge (ἐπιστήμη) is characterized as knowing the starting-points (ἀρχαί) governing movement in the observed phenomena. This is not a matter of merely fanciful philosophical speculation. Far from it! The truly speculative insight into the simple essence of money as a crystallization of exchange-value serving as medium of social interplay is crucial for all thinking about economic phenomena, a circumstance that economists gladly obscure with their sophisticated, complicated economic models (today running their computations on computers with so-called learning algorithms fed with masses of empirical digital data) that pretend to 'scientifically' grasp the 'real economic world' and claim not to be beholden to 'abstract theories', but to the 'empirical facts' embodied in 'big data'. It is, however, precisely through this hard-headed empiricism that economics as a social science remains unbeknowns beholden to the quantitative Cartesian cast of being (see section 4.3 above). The socio-ontological understanding of value will concern us at length in following chapters.

4.5 Aristotle on money and exchange — Money as a medium practically unifying social usages

Where is the starting-point for thinking about the economy? The historical start-ing-point for Western thinking about money, woefully neglected as a starting-point also for *thinking* by economics, lies with Aristotle, in particular in his *Nicomachean Ethics*, Book V, Chapter 5, which deals with reciprocity in relation to justice. For both Plato and Aristotle, social life in the polis is based on a division of labour and the exchange of the products of labour for the satisfaction of need and provision of the "conveniencies of life", that are an essential component of living well, which in turn is the aim of living together in community. Here I do not take the polis to be simply the historical ancient Greek city-state, but read it as 'polity', i.e. "an organized society or community" with its "civil organization and civil order" and "form of government" (OED), having a meaning not only in an historical sense but for all forms of Western society. Aristotle points out that "in sociations of exchange, it is such justice which holds them together, recip-rocal justice on the basis of proportionality and not on the basis of equality." (ἐν μὲν ταῖς κοινωνίαις ταῖς ἀλλακτικαῖς συνέχει τὸ τοιοῦτον δίκαιον, τὸ ἀντιπεπονθός, κατ᾽ ἀναλογίαν καὶ μὴ κατ᾽ ἰσότητα. 1132b32) He continues that "through proportional reciprocity, namely, the polity remains together" (τῷ ἀντιποιεῖν γὰρ ἀναλογίαν συμμένει ἡ πόλις 1132b34). The reciprocal give and take of exchange is what constitutes society on the basis of everyday sociation, giving rise to men's "communication" (μετάδοσις 1133a2). Through it, men "re-main together" (συμμένουσιν 1133a2) in sociation. The exchange of useful things in civil society can only work as a sociating bond if they are exchanged in just proportions, and without them "there would be no exchange and no sociation" (οὐκ ἔσται ἀλλαγὴ οὐδὲ κοινωνία 1133a24). This link between the practice of exchange and the constitution of social community is reflected also in the Greek word, κοινωνία, rendered here as 'sociation', whose semantic field stretches from "dealings" and "sociability" through "association" to "community".

How is a just give and take between the owners or producers of different products to be achieved? "Nothing, namely, can prevent the product of one of the parties being better than that of the other, and in that case therefore they have to be equalized." (οὐθὲν γὰρ κωλύει κρεῖττον εἶναι τὸ θατέρου ἔργον ἢ τὸ θατέρου, δεῖ οὖν ταῦτα ἰσασθῆναι 1133a13) The exchange of useful products and services only makes sense if the products are different and are suitable for dif-ferent uses. Aristotle adduces the example of the exchange of a physician's services for a farmer's products which "have to be equalized" (δεῖ ἰσασθῆναι. 1133a18). "Thus everything must be comparable in some way if exchange is to be." (διὸ πάντα συμβλητὰ δεῖ πως εἶναι, ὧν ἐστιν ἀλλαγή. 1133a19) And how is this comparability achieved? Aristotle continues, "Money has resolved this and is a kind of middle term, for it measures everything and so also too much and too little and how many shoes are equal to a house or food." (ἐφ' ὃ τὸ νόμισμ' ἐλήλυθε, καὶ γίνεταί πως μέσον· πάντα γὰρ μετρεῖ, ὥστε καὶ τὴν ὑπεροχὴν καὶ τὴν ἔλλειψιν, πόσα ἄττα δὴ ὑποδήματ' ἴσον οἰκίᾳ ἢ τροφῇ. 1133a20)

Money is thus the solution in practical human social life for how qualitatively different things which are suitable for very different uses can be compared and measured in an abstractly quantitative medium, thus forming the basis for a just, proportional exchange of everything in which one value is exchanged for another, equal value. The justness is apparent in the mutual satisfaction of the exchangers themselves who have struck a deal on the proportions to be exchanged. Even though everything differs from each other in their respective uses and thus in their use-values, everything is also identical with each other and therefore comparable as being useful in abstracto. "So it is necessary for everything to be measured by some unity" (δεῖ ἄρα ἑνί τινι πάντα μετρεῖσθαι 1133a26) and this unity is "in truth, use, which holds everything together" (τοῦτο δ' ἐστὶ τῇ μὲν ἀληθείᾳ ἡ χρεία, ἣ πάντα συνέχει· 1133a28), for exchange is carried on in order to acquire the useful things which one lacks. "Thus as a kind of substitute for use, money has come about by agreement." (οἷον δ' ὑπάλλαγμα τῆς χρείας τὸ νόμισμα γέγονε κατὰ συνθήκην 1133a29)

Money is the universal representative for useful things in the broadest sense and is the medium or middle term which mediates their exchange with one another and thus the give and take of daily social intercourse. It arises as a practical solution from the context of the practice of exchange itself, enabling fair and just sociation in dealings with one another. "Thus, like a measure, money makes things measurable and creates an equality, for without exchange no community would be possible and without equality there would be no exchange, and without commensurability there would be no equality. In truth, however, it is impossible that things so different could become commensurable, but with respect to use this is sufficiently possible. Thus there must be a unity and this is so from what has been supposed." (τὸ δὴ νόμισμα ὥσπερ μέτρον σύμμετρα ποιῆσαν ἰσάζει· οὔτε γὰρ ἂν μὴ οὔσης ἀλλαγῆς κοινωνία ἦν, οὔτ' ἀλλαγὴ ἰσότητος μὴ οὔσης, οὔτ' ἰσότης μὴ οὔσης συμμετρίας. τῇ μὲν οὖν ἀληθείᾳ ἀδύνατον τὰ τοσοῦτον διαφέροντα σύμμετρα γενέσθαι, πρὸς δὲ τὴν χρείαν ἐνδέχεται ἱκανῶς. ἓν δή τι δεῖ εἶναι, τοῦτο δ' ἐξ ὑποθέσεως 1133b17)

The proof that very different things are commensurable is a practical, conventional one, for very different useful things are in practice exchanged on a basis of mutually agreeable agreement, thus equating their uses in some way. In mediating exchange, money proves itself to be the embodiment of universal use, for it can be used to purchase anything useful, but in being exchanged for money, the concrete, particular use of a specific thing is abstracted from or bracketed off. Money is thus the abstract, universal, unified representative of the uses of things, i.e. their value.

Each thing is useful and thus valuable or good-for-something in its own way, but through its potential exchange for money (its price) it becomes abstractly valuable and commensurable in value with everything else that is good for some application or other. Only this abstraction from all concrete, useful qualities to pure quantities allows a just exchange of goods because, according to Aristotle's treatment of exchange, a kind of proportionate equality has to be achieved in the exchange relation for it to be fair and equitable. Justice therefore entertains an intimate relation with arithmetic, for justice is concerned with fairness, and the Greek word for 'fair', ἴσος, is also the word for 'equal'. The reason for this is that justice in general is a phenomenon concerned with the relations, i.e. sociating movement, between *different* people and their goods, so that the relations require some sort of common ratio. These relations are the forms of sociation on which society is based and they must be such that fairness prevails and no one gains the better of the other. Where difference prevails, recourse to a kind of quantifiable equality that serves as a common ratio or denominator must be taken. The existence of markets shows that this kind of equalizing of all sorts of marketable goods takes place on a daily practical level. Even very different qualitative, non-commodity goods (including things like esteem, reputation, celebrity status, privacy, etc.) which come into relation with each other in social life (such as when one person slanders another) have to be quantified in some way if fairness and equity are to prevail (such as a penalty imposed on a slanderer to redress by means of monetary compensation the wrong done to the slandered person in depreciating the esteem and reputation in which that person is held). Money can thus serve the cause of justice even in the case of 'non-marketable' goods.

In the above citations of Aristotle, one of the pivotal words, ἡ χρεία, has been rendered as 'use'. In other translations the same word is rendered as 'demand' or 'need'. Depending upon the translation chosen, it is use, need or demand "which holds everything together", and money is conceived as having come about "as a kind of substitute for" either use, need or demand. Employing the word 'demand' in relation to the exchange of products would seem to be the most modern alternative for a translation, and thus an interpretation, because we are familiar today with conceiving exchange on the market as the interplay of supply and demand. However, the Greek word χρεία has nothing to do with economic demand but means lexically in its primary significations either 'need' or 'use'. But is it admissible to orient oneself towards dictionary meanings? Not per se, because it is the phenomena themselves to which Aristotle is pointing our thoughtful gaze which must decide what the most appropriate translation and consequent interpretation are. The Greek verb related to χρεία is χρῆσθαι, which means 'to use' or 'to need' and comes from the word for 'hand', ἡ χείρ. With regard to the goods involved in a reciprocal exchange it is the use to which these goods can be (potentially) put and enjoyed in the usages of daily life which forms the basis upon which they are needed and *not the other way round*.

A usage is an "habitual use, established custom or practice, customary mode of action, on the part of a number of persons; long-continued use or procedure; custom, habit." (OED) Only because certain goods are usually used are they needed, and these uses that are embedded in usages of an historical way of life of a people are historical discoveries and inventions based on human ingenuity that is in turn enabled by a given historical cast of mind. Neither do needs fall from the sky nor are they naturally inherent to the human being considered, say, as a species of animal, but are always situated within the historically variable gamut of practices of everyday life. There is a need for holy water, for instance, only in a society that practises certain religious rites, i.e. certain usages honouring a god or gods, and there is a need for oysters only in a society that practises the usage of eating oysters. The use of the goods also involves handling them by hand in such a way that the hand's handling is appropriate for realizing the usefulness of the thing used. Such a realization of usefulness is the enjoyment of a possibility of human existence disclosed and proffered by the thing used within the context of an historical constellation of usages. The (customary, usual) usages of daily life determine what things are useful and what are not for that usual, historical way of living. The uses of things are embedded in the usages of daily life and only in the context of such habitual usages do needs for things which may be lacking arise.

The widening of the motive and aim of the exchange of goods, in line with the well-considered phenomena themselves, beyond the 'satisfaction of need', which suggests some kind of mere subsistence or an 'objective', 'biological' or 'physiological' necessity, fits well with the inauguration of political economy in the eighteenth century. Adam Smith writes that, "Every man is rich or poor according to the degree in which he can afford to enjoy the necessaries, conveniences, and amusements of human life"[59], himself echoing Cantillon's definition

---

59 Adam Smith *The Wealth of Nations* 1776 Bk. I Ch. V edited with notes, marginal summary and enlarged index by Edwin Cannan, The Modern Library, New York 2000 p. 33.

of riches, "La richesse en elle-même n'est autre chose que la nourriture, les commodités et les agréments de la vie"[60]. The enjoyment of life, or εὖ ζῆν, and not merely the satisfaction of needs, lies at the base of the exchange of goods, and the enjoyment of life consists for the most part in practising the habitual usages which constitute an agreeable life in a given historical social milieu. Even the formulation, "merely the satisfaction of needs" is misleading because it is not a matter of pointing out an excess or surplus beyond need-fulfilment that would allow "agreeable" living, but of seeing the *derivative* nature of need compared to usage. Even the so-called 'basic need' of human beings to eat and drink is an abstraction because what is eaten and drunk is always highly particularized within given cultural usages. There is no need for pork, for example, in a society in which the usage of eating pork is not cultivated, and the religious usages prohibiting the eating of pork in such a society are therefore a more basic 'need' than the abstract 'basic need' to eat 'food', overriding any consideration of the scientifically established, 'objective' nutritional value of pork.

The context for the entire consideration of exchange as a — or indeed, the — paradigmatic form of reciprocal justice in Book V of the *Nicomachean Ethics* is social life in its habitual usages. Such usages for the benefit and sake of living well with each other in society is what Aristotle has in view when discussing χρεία, or use. This can be seen more clearly by considering money as a kind of "substitute" (ὑπάλλαγμα 1133a29) for use. The use of money is to mediate the procurement of what is used habitually in the usages of daily life. Money represents these uses and substitutes for them as a thing, a means, which can be used now or in the future to supply what is needed for use in the practices of daily living (1133b13). Aristotle says that through money being this conventional substitute, it "has the name νόμισμα (money, or usage, custom) because it exists not by nature but by customary usage (νόμῳ) and can be changed and made useless by us". (τοὔνομα ἔχει νόμισμα, ὅτι οὐ φύσει ἀλλὰ νόμῳ ἐστί, καὶ ἐφ' ἡμῖν μεταβαλεῖν καὶ ποιῆσαι ἄχρηστον. 1133a31) This passage is usually taken to mean blandly that Aristotle is a proponent of a 'conventional theory of money'. Money is said to exist only by convention. But there is another, deeper perspective on this passage. For how is money being spoken of here?

The entire passage reads: "So it is necessary for everything to be measured by some unity, as was said before. This unity is in truth use, which holds everything together. If namely nothing were needed or not in a similar way, either there would be no exchange or it would not be the same. Thus as a kind of substitute for use, money has come about by agreement." (δεῖ ἄρα ἑνί τινι πάντα

---

60 Cited in *The Wealth of Nations* Bk. I Ch. V p. 33.

μετρεῖσθαι, ὥσπερ ἐλέχθη πρότερον. τοῦτο δ' ἐστὶ τῇ μὲν ἀληθείᾳ ἡ χρεία, ἣ πάντα συνέχει· εἰ γὰρ μηθὲν δέοιντο ἢ μὴ ὁμοίως, ἢ οὐκ ἔσται ἀλλαγὴ ἢ οὐχ ἡ αὐτή· οἷον δ' ὑπάλλαγμα τῆς χρείας τὸ νόμισμα γέγονε κατὰ συνθήκην 1133a26ff) The problem is clearly that of unity, a unity which serves to hold everything together, i.e. to unify the social whole of living-together as sociating movement. The social whole, however, is constituted by a sharing of uses in various diverse usages. In order to be able to share uses, exchange is necessary, but if uses become self-sufficient or they change, then either exchange is obviated or the changing uses make reciprocally just exchange impossible. And if there is no exchange, there is no sociation and hence no society. Aristotle states this two lines before the passage quoted, "For without this [reciprocal proportion], there would be no exchange and no community (κοινωνία)" (1133a25). Money thus arises for the sake of *holding society together by sociation* and this means, on the level of everyday life, that money enables mediatingly a complex unity of the manifold usages in which things are used. This is the sense in which money has to be understood as customary, i.e. as *related to usages*, and not merely as a convention agreed upon out of the blue. As related to usages, the use of money is in itself a usage unifying the multifarious uses by enabling and facilitating the exchange of what is needed for these various uses. Since it is incorporated into the usage of exchange, and this is its raison d'être, money itself can be changed or taken out of use. This does not mean, of course, that the necessity for *some* kind of money as a substitute unifying all the various uses could be done away with. Therefore money is both customary and necessary.

This alternative understanding of Aristotle's thinking on money and exchange has implications also for how society itself in its sociating movement is to be thought. For can it be said that the basis of society is the satisfaction of need given that there is a division of labour, thus necessitating the exchange of the products of labour? Or is it rather the case that human beings always already share a world and that this essential world-sharing, as a disclosure and enabling of existential possibilities, precipitates a communal sharing of the practised usages *from which needs arise* which then have to be unified in some manner? How can such a question of priority be decided? Only by proceeding from what is most originary and elementary. And what is most originary and elementary here is human being itself as sharing exposure to the openness to being, not just as a matter of what humans hold to be true, but also practically in their shared and mutually understood, customary practices which themselves are a kind of movement now conceived hermeneutically *AS presencing and absencing in the 3D-time-clearing that being itself turns out to be*. Such a sharing of the openness to being can never be attained by proceeding merely from a notion of a division of labour and a consequent necessity to exchange the products of labour in order to satisfy need (food, clothing, shelter), for a division of labour is already a sharing of practices based on a shared understanding of the world, at least to the extent that the various uses of things in the various usages are understood as such.

Furthermore, there is no such thing as a need for food, clothing and shelter *in abstracto* because these latter generalities do not exist as such to be needed. Food, for instance, as a genus exists as a need only in its particularizations into flour, sugar, rice, ostrich meat, sweet potato, deer meat, witchetty grubs and so on endlessly, and whether these particular foods are needed depends entirely upon the culinary usages of the specific society in question. For example, there is a need for flour only in a society that practises the custom of eating specific food (e.g. bread) and dishes in which flour is an ingredient. The modern orthodox text-book definition of economics as "the social science that studies the methods by which individuals and societies organize production activities and allocate scarce resources to meet material wants and needs" is therefore thoughtless pseudo-science with pretensions to 'objectivity'.

Both Plato and Aristotle present their account of the genesis of society on the basis of such considerations of the gradual historical development of exchange between households and communities, and this account has its plausibility as an ontogenetic history. But ontogenesis should never be confused with the order which the phenomena themselves call for to be properly thought through ontologically in their *mode of being*. And here the issue is the social mode of being of human being itself in its sociating movement. The sociation of society is most fundamentally the sharing of human beings' 'mindful' openness to being, i.e. the shared exposure to the 3D-time-clearing, which first enables a communication with each other, a showing-off to each other as *who* each individual *is* in social exchanges and also a life-enhancing sharing of sociating practices in differentiated, particular usages which requires the exchange of all sorts of different goods both tangible and intangible. Exchange interplay mediated by money is a practical solution to the problem of how practical sociation can be constituted from diverse difference, so giving rise to a kind of unified social whole.

4.6 Endless money-making?

After having gained a new perspective on commodity exchange through money by considering more reflectively what usage, use and need mean, it is opportune to reconsider the Aristotelean distinction between economic household management and chrematistic money-making. It has already become question-able that society can be thought, even ontically, as based on the satisfaction of need, because what is primary for the constitution of society is not neediness but the sharing of usages, i.e. of shared, habitual practices of living. So it is worthwhile to take a closer look at Aristotelean οἰκονομική (economics). The word itself is composed of οἶκος, meaning house, home, homeland and an end-ing related to the noun νόμος, meaning what is allotted, customary usage, prin-ciple or law. The related verb is νέμειν, meaning firstly, to allot or distribute, secondly, to possess in the sense of control and administer, or build on, use, enjoy and therefore dwell on, or thirdly, to allot as pasture and thus to shepherd and allow to graze. The verb νέμειν is also related to German 'nehmen', mean-ing 'to take' (including 'to take into possession'). Another related verb is νομίζειν, one of whose meanings is to have in customary usage or to be used to. The words clustering around νέμειν stake out a semantic field that signifies a taking into possession, a taking into care and management for the sake of the enjoyment of life. Aristotelean οἰκονομική is therefore not simply household management, but has a far richer meaning as that which is related to *dwelling in the usages of one's home and homeland*. Managing a household in the mundane economic sense is only a partial aspect of οἰκονομική. The exchange of goods in connection with the usages of one's habitual way of dwelling has these usages and the enjoyment of this way of dwelling as its end or τέλος. And in fact, Aris-totle relates οἰκονομική explicitly to the usual way of dwelling in usages which he calls "living well" or εὖ ζῆν (1258a1).

The habitual usages of living well form the limits to the means needed for this end, whereas the limitless striving to accumulate more and more goods, i.e. chrematistics, is said to have lost sight of this end and has thus become end-less in a pernicious sense. Chrematistics is the striving to end-lessly acquire χρήματα, which means goods, property, the collectivity of what is useful, or money and assets, i.e. wealth. Aristotle says that chrematistics, which usually takes the form of the striving to accumulate money, is not in conformity with nature (παρὰ φύσιν 1257a29) in that the wealth required for living well has a limit. And yet, he points out, "all those involved in the accumulation of goods strive to augment money without limit" (πάντες γὰρ εἰς ἄπειρον αὔξουσιν οἱ χρηματιζόμενοι τὸ νόμισμα. 1275b34), so that "their entire way of life is a waste of time getting wealth" (πᾶσα ἡ διατριβὴ περὶ τὸν χρηματισμόν ἐστι 1258a5). But time is lifetime. Finite lifetime. With chrematistics an inversion of means and end takes place: one no longer makes money for the sake of living well, but rather lives for the sake of making money.

Is this inversion a perversion? Can money-making itself constitute the, or a, primary 'end' of life? Is money-making elevated to the status of an end in itself meaningless or morally reprehensible? Aristotle does not deal with chrematistics in terms of moral categories, but rather according to whether it accords with nature or not, i.e. with what comes to a stand in presence of itself, καθ' αὑτό. The nature which is of central importance here is human nature, i.e. human being itself, because we and Aristotle are dealing with sociated human living. Is it contrary to human nature to spend one's life primarily in making money? This question is to be distinguished from a moral condemnation of human nature as being essentially greedy and incessantly wanting to have more.

The endless end of making money has a momentum all its own, for it cannot cease. It is an end that surpasses even the finitude of an entire human life. But can money-making even be a circular end in itself? Even if an individual devotes him- or herself entirely to money-making, doesn't this activity have social consequences that willy-nilly go beyond the individual intention? If an entrepreneur (or any other participant in competitive market-economic life) has the skill of making money, why should the exercise of this skill not be the entrepreneur's purpose in life, not merely for the sake of accumulating riches, but because the activity itself of participating in the economic interplay is personally fulfilling, not least of all for the satisfaction it gives in providing income-earning employment to willing employees? Cannot an entrepreneur decide for him- or herself to continue a satisfying entrepreneurial activity, taking account of the finiteness of life and other aims he or she may have in life? Is it not possible for an individual, competing economic actor to take a step back from the endless end of making money and decide what is appropriate for his or her own mortal life? If this is the case, then money-making is no longer an end in itself, but a means for living one's finite, mortal life for one's own sake in sociation with others, perhaps many others. The entrepreneur per se could enjoy an enterprising life risking an undertaking for which having to turn a profit in the long run is only a boundary condition and not the end in sight. This is the individual perspective on money-making, which by no means must exclude continued money-making insofar as continuing to be a player in the economic interplay may well be beneficial both for oneself and other players. Entrepreneurial activity can be continued for the sake of keeping an enterprise running in which others work and from which they benefit, along with suppliers and customers.

At first glance it seems that the endless end of making money stands diametrically opposed to the aim of fulfilling one's needs through economic household management. This assumes that what is needed to live well is finite, so that needs can be satisfied and a modest way of life could or should be sufficient. Can a limit be found in the satisfaction of need (accepting for the moment that human being is needful rather than desiring)? Is there a limit at which one should or could 'naturally' cease to be a gainful economic player, say, when one has made 'enough' money, in order then to devote oneself to 'higher', more 'social' ends? Why should a successful economic player — taking the entrepreneur here as the personification of money-making — at some point necessarily want to cease to engage in the social usages surrounding the interplay called 'business'? As has been shown, need itself is embedded in and arises from the usages that make up a given historical way of social life. In any given time, these usages constitute an habitual way of life and could therefore be considered as providing a limit within which needs could be satisfied. But these usages are continually evolving, and people in a given society are continually inventing or adapting new ways of living in an ongoing interplay with inventions of all sorts that intermesh with new ways of living. There is therefore also an endlessness to discovering enhanced or, at least, different ways of living and hence also in the commodity goods and services that can contribute to living well defined in some fashion or other.

This limitlessness does not have to be regarded as a pernicious kind of infinity, say, as senseless consumerism, but could be considered as an aspect of the beneficial endlessness of human inventiveness and ingenuity in caring for each other in social intercourse. There is no inherent limit to the possibilities of human existing that can be discovered, nor, therefore, an inherent limit to the development of human abilities, nor an inherent limit to what human beings can do for each other in the mutually beneficial exercise of their abilities, i.e. there are no limits to economic growth properly understood, and, as well shall see, it is possible to regard even self-interested economic activity as a kind of reciprocal caring-for each other in a fundamental existential-ontological sense (cf. Chapter 9.2.5).

Herein lies an ontological connection in understanding money-making, for Aristotle's distinction between economics and chrematistics depends on an understanding of χρήματα, which, as already pointed out, means goods, property, the collectivity of what is useful, or money and assets. Chrematistics is thus understood as accumulating wealth in the form of property, of things which one owns, forming part of one's estate, with Aristotle pointing out that, beyond a certain limit, it is senseless to heap up possessions. The Greek word for 'estate', however, is οὐσία (G.: Anwesen) as the gathering of all that one owns and therefore lies readily available to hand for use. The word, in turn, is the substantive form of the feminine present participle for 'to be', εἶναι, namely οὖσα, and could thus sensibly be rendered also as 'beingness' in English, its appropriate rendering in the context of ontology. In the philosophical tradition, however, οὐσία has come to be translated as 'substance' or 'essence' which is synonymous with the Greek understanding of being itself as 'standing or lying there in presence', as standing presence or "ständige Anwesenheit" (Heidegger). This means that wealth itself in the Western tradition is tied to the fundamental understanding of being as standing presence, as substance, so that the acquisition of wealth is synonymous with the accumulation of substantial riches, of substance, of essential whatness. A man of wealth, for instance, is thus a man of substance, whose who-status and self as somewho is an identity mirrored back from an accumulation of acquired whats.

A mere heaping-up of whats in the form of wealth indeed provides the man of substance a mirror in which to reflect his self-standing that is a continually 'standing' presence, but this is antithetical to movement, change, becoming in which life itself consists, so that static riches hardly measure up to the Aristotelean standard of εὖ ζῆν, i.e. living well. If endless money-making is to justify itself as a possible mode of living well, it must do so as the movement of a way of living, as already outlined above. A man of substance's self-esteem, for instance, may be bolstered by his looking at the achievement of having accumulated considerable wealth. What is important, however, are not the χρήματα, i.e. mere things, but the χρείαι, i.e. the usages, in which they are used in the movement of life. I will return to the question of endless money-making in the guise of capitalist economy in later chapters (Chapter 9), but turn first to developing explicitly an ontology of exchange that is required to deepen the phenomenology of whoness.

5 Ontology of exchange

The father of ontology is without doubt Aristotle.[61] His *Metaphysics* itself is both ontological and theological in character, as discussed in the Foreword, so ontology is only one part of metaphysics, the part that is of interest here. Apart from the standard ontological categories or 'predicaments' (Augustinus) describing the situation of a being, truth itself as a mode of being and the distinction in modes of being between presencing of itself (καθ' αὐτό) or only contingently (κατὰ συμβεβηκός), the distinctive concepts of his ontology are δύναμις, ἐνέργεια and ἐντελέχεια, which are traditionally rendered in English variously as potentiality, actuality and perfected actuality, respectively. These three concepts are essential to Aristotle's endeavour to conceptualize the being of those beings that can move or be moved, which comprise all those beings which progenerate, grow and decay, change, or move, or be moved, from one place to another. This Aristotelean ontology of movement tacitly underlies all modern science, starting with Newtonian physics.[62] The main site for Aristotle's investigation of δύναμις and ἐνέργεια, his ontology of (productive, effective) movement, is *Metaphysics* Book Theta, a clear indication that all modern physics, despite violent denials, is metaphysical. There, the prime definition of δύναμις which guides the investigation is given as:

> πᾶσαι αρχαί τινές ἐισι, καὶ πρὸς πρώτην μίαν λέγονται, ἥ ἐστιν ἀρχὴ μεταβολῆς ἐν ἄλλῳ ἢ ἧ ἄλλο. (*Met.* Theta 1, 1046a9f)

> All are some sort of governing points of origin and are said with respect to one meaning which is: point of origin governing a change in something else or in the same being insofar as it is regarded as something else.

This primary definition of δύναμις: a source governing a change, could be regarded inter alia as the ontological source for the statement, 'Knowledge is power'. The standard illustrative example of this definition provided by Aristotle is that of the τέχνη ποιητική, i.e. productive art, of house-building, which is a δύναμις μετὰ λόγου, i.e. a potential or power guided by the knowing insight of understanding. This know-how is a point of origin, or starting-point residing in a builder (δύναμις) governing the change in wood, stone, tiles, etc. (ἐνέργεια) so

---

61 Cf. my study 'Heidegger's Restricted Interpretation of the Greek Conception of the Political' URL www.arte-fact.org/untpltcl/rstrpltc.html

62 Cf. Eldred, M. *The Digital Cast of Being* 2009/2011 Section 2.9. 'Time and movement in Aristotle's thinking' URL www.arte-fact.org/dgtlon_e.html#2.9

https://doi.org/10.1515/9783110617504-005

that in the end a finished house comes about (ἐντελέχεια). The know-how is not the change in wood, stone, etc. itself, but only the starting-point for such a change, albeit the starting-point governing such change.

The movement of change itself is the power (δύναμις) at work, i.e. its ἐνέργεια or energy to attain the end (τέλος) of a finished house in perfect presence (ἐντελέχεια). Insofar as the know-how of house-building resides in the house-builder as a being other than the wood, stones, etc., he is able to (potentially) bring forth houses. The "insofar" qualification built into the definition covers the case when a know-how residing in a being is applied not to another being but to itself, as in the case when a physician treats himself. In this case, the starting-point for bringing about the change consisting in a restoration of health does not reside in another being, a doctor, but in the patient himself, but not insofar as he is a sick person, but insofar as he is a doctor.

5.1 Commodity exchange and the necessity of rethinking Aristotelean δύναμις

I now want to consider first of all the phenomenon of exchange of goods on the market with regard to whether and how it can be seen in terms of δύναμις, this fundamental concept that permeates all of Aristotle's thinking on phenomena of κίνησις, μεταβολή, i.e. movement/change of all kinds. In a later section (5.6) I will return to consider the phenomenon of exchange as the paradigmatic onto-logical structure of sociating intercourse in general, covering both whats and whos. The exchange of goods in Greek is called ἀλλαγή, συναλλαγή or μεταβολή which is already an indication that it involves change (μεταβολή) in the sense of both alteration (ἀλλοίωσις) and interchanging one with another. Μεταβολή comes from the verb μεταβάλλειν, which means most literally 'to throw into another position' and thus also 'to change one with another, exchange, inter-change'. But is there an ἀρχή, i.e. a starting-point governing the exchange, in-volved here? One candidate for a starting-point governing the exchange is the owner of the goods. The owner of goods is able to exchange them for other goods (barter) or for money (sale). The exchange does not change the goods involved in the exchange themselves, but only 'changes one with another' in the sense of interchanging their ownership and possession between two parties. Exchange is a social relation (πρός τι, πρὸς ἕτερον) involving and sociating two exchangers. This ability to exchange could be called a δύναμις in the sense that the goods offered for sale have not only a use-value in use, but also an ex-change-value in getting something else. As Aristotle points out, goods (πράγματα) can be used in a double way, namely, not only in their use proper, but also for exchange (μεταβλητική, ἀλλαγή *Pol.* I iii 1257a10,14):

> ἑκάστου γὰρ κτήματος διττὴ ἡ χρῆσίς ἐστιν, ἀμφότεραι δὲ καθ' αὑτὸ μὲν ἀλλ' οὐχ ὁμοίως καθ' αὑτό, ἀλλ' ἡ μὲν οἰκεία ἡ δ' οὐκ οἰκεία τοῦ πράγματος, οἷον ὑποδήματος ἥ τε ὑπόδεσις καὶ ἡ μεταβλητική. ἀμφότεραι [10] γὰρ ὑποδήματος χρήσεις· καὶ γὰρ ὁ ἀλλαττόμενος τῷ δεομένῳ ὑποδήματος ἀντὶ νομίσματος ἢ τροφῆς χρῆται τῷ ὑποδήματι ᾗ ὑπόδημα, ἀλλ' οὐ τὴν οἰκείαν χρῆσιν· οὐ γὰρ ἀλλαγῆς ἕνεκεν γέγονε. τὸν αὐτὸν δὲ τρόπον ἔχει καὶ περὶ τῶν ἄλλων κτημάτων. ἔστι γὰρ ἡ [15] μεταβλητικὴ πάντων,... (*Pol.* I iii 1257a7–15)

With every article of acquired property there is a double way of using it; both uses are related to the article itself, but not related to it in the same manner—one is proper to the thing and the other is not proper to it. Take for example a shoe: there is its wearing as a shoe and there is its use by way of exchange; for both are uses of a shoe, and even he who exchanges a shoe with someone needing a shoe for money or food uses it *as* a shoe, but not in its proper use, since shoes have not come about for the sake of exchange. And it is the same also with other articles of acquired property; for there is exchange of all of them,...

But does the owner of goods govern the exchange in the sense of having control over it? In the first place, the potential or power to exchange (if it is a δύναμις at all[63]) resides primarily in the goods, which have an exchange-value, i.e. a δύναμις to exchange for some other good, and only secondarily in the owner of the goods, who enjoys such a power only by virtue of possessing the goods, just as in the case of the productive δύναμις of house-building, where the house-builder has the power to change stone and wood into a house only by virtue of possessing the know-how of house-building.

But even granting that the δύναμις or power to exchange resides first of all in the goods themselves by virtue of their 'usefulness' in exchange as possessing exchange-value, and not primarily in the owners of the goods, the answer to the question as to whether the owner of the goods governs the exchange of goods has to be 'no' because, in the first place, it takes *two* to make an exchange, and two already *destroys the unity of a single point of origin*. An exchange can only come about if two parties agree to exchange goods for goods (barter) or goods for money (sale). The ownership of goods or money does provide the owner with the potential or δύναμις for making an exchange, but this ownership is not potent enough to make it the ἀρχή, i.e. *the* governing starting-point, of exchange. One could say that in the case of exchange, there are two

---

63 One meaning of δύναμις is 'the value of goods or money', from δύνασθαι, 'to be able, powerful' and thus, with respect to goods and money, 'to be worth' in the sense of being 'exchangeable for'.

starting-points, two ἀρχαί which, however, have to coincide and reciprocate for any exchange to come about. The two ἀρχαί are the two goods in the quality as possessing exchange-value, a kind of power.

In the second place, consider the phenomena of money and value. Money and goods are said to have value or, more specifically, exchange-value. The owner of money is able to buy goods on the market to the value of the money he possesses. The goods are offered for sale on the market at more or less definite prices quantitatively expressing their value, and the owner of money can decide at will to buy this or that, depending on how much money he has. The purchase of goods, as distinct from the exchange of goods, would thus seem to be conceivable as the exercise of a potential or potency or δύναμις residing in money, its value potency, which allows its possessor to purchase goods to a certain value. This means that the potent starting-point for the purchase lies in the first place not in the owner of money, but in the money itself. A phenomenal proof of this is that, if the money is stolen, its new possessor, the thief, can spend it just as well as the original legitimate owner. The use-value of money is, in the first place, its exchange-value, which can be exercised at any time, and thus also, secondly, held at the ready as a store of exchange-value. In its simple, perfect presence (ἐντελέχεια), money has the δύναμις of exchanging universally with any goods of a given value. Only the quantitative relations of price can shift. In itself, money refers to all the other commodities available on the myriad markets with which it can potentially exchange.

The owner of goods, by contrast, does not seem to be in such a happy position as the owner of money. Even though goods, too, have a double value in both use and exchange, and the exchange-value can be regarded as a kind of δύναμις, the realization of this value in exchange, i.e. in sale, depends on the momentary market conditions. The current situation on the market may preclude sale altogether at the moment (e.g. real estate), or it may dictate unusually low prices. Thus in both cases, namely, the purchase of goods with money and the sale of goods for money, if not a specific second party, then at least the market or markets or momentary market situation co-determine whether and in what quantitative proportions an exchange can come about. Insofar, the starting-point of exchange (sale or even purchase) may be said to reside neither solely in the owner of the goods or the owner of money respectively nor solely in the goods themselves nor solely in the money itself. The very exchange-value of goods or money is relational (πρός τι), depending on two double poles, the buyer and the seller, on the one hand, and the goods and money, on the other, which meet together on the market or markets which in turn comprise many buyers and sellers, and many exchange-values. The phenomenon of exchange is, after all, a social relation involving sociation of at least two and, in general, of many.

But more than that, it is crucial not to overlook that the two poles of even the simple exchange relation cannot be regarded as an actor on the one hand and another suffering the action on the other, as in the case of building a house, i.e. transforming wood and bricks, which have the passive power of allowing themselves to be changed into a finished building. Rather, the purchaser of goods has to have the 'active' consent of the seller for the exchange to take place; the seller does not simply passively suffer (πάσχειν) to have his goods sold. This would only be the case if the seller were under some sort of coercion to sell and therefore could not be regarded as the starting-point of a sales trans-action. The exchange would then not be free, which is not the usual situation for commodity exchange.

5.2   Productive know-how, acquisitive know-how?

Consider again the exchange of goods for money, i.e. a case of sale, with regard to whether it can in some way be considered as an instance of δύναμις. A change (μεταβολή) is to be brought about in the goods in the possession of the owner. In this case, the change is an ex-change (ἀλλαγή, μεταβολή). Is there something resembling a know-how (τέχνη ποιητική) residing in another being, in this case, the owner, which serves as starting-point for the change? This is thought in parallel to ποίησις as the τέχνη of bringing-forth. The τέχνη in this case would be a τέχνη κτητική, the know-how or art of acquiring, of getting. The goods, whether they be bananas or television sets, would suffer themselves to be changed into money under the direction of mercantile or commercial know-how. Aristotle indeed points out that the mode of being of δύναμις always in-volves the unity of two δυνάμεις, an active force and a passive force (δύναμις τοῦ ποιεῖν καὶ πάσχειν 1046a19ff). The passive force in this case would reside in the goods themselves which suffer themselves to be exchanged, and would have to be called the (exchange-)value of the goods. The goods' exchange-value is expressed in money, in quantitative prices, as if there were a potential or tendency or readiness within the goods themselves to change into money in some ratio or other. The active force or power in this case would be the commer-cial know-how which has knowledge of the markets, of how to find a buyer, perhaps through means such as *advertising*, and (interplayfully) *effect* a sale, i.e. to transform the 'commercial matter' into the value-form of money. Advertis-ing itself is the art of adverting, i.e. of turning the attention of others, prospec-tive buyers, to the good for sale.

The analogy of commercial know-how with productive know-how is imperfect, however, because the former is not a simple governing starting-point for effecting a change, an interchange. There are (at least) four poles involved and not just two. The other two poles are the purchaser and his money (or even: two multiple poles comprising the market of potential purchasers and their money). The purchaser embodies an active force for acquiring goods (which could be called desire or appetite or ὄρεξις, the striving of reaching out for something), and the money has the passive δύναμις to suffer itself to be transformed into goods at the behest of the purchaser. Is this an adequate characterization of the phenomenon? It seems not to be because the power of acquiring goods resides in the money, not in the purchaser. The money has an inherent power of self-transformation into goods and the purchaser as possessor of money merely employs this power. Similarly, the owner of goods himself does not have the active power of transforming the goods into money, but rather, the goods themselves, because they are useful, have an exchange-value which expresses itself in the current prices on the market. The owner of the goods only realizes this apparently inherent value in transforming his goods into money. Use-value is also only apparently inherent because it depends on the usages in the society in which the goods could potentially be used and is thus relative. Commercial know-how only facilitates this transformation of the value of the goods into money; it does not create the exchange-value of the goods, which depends essentially on the value of the goods in use.

But what does it mean to 'create' exchange-value? Doesn't a skilful salesperson 'create', bring forth — and not merely 'facilitate' — exchange-value by arousing and stimulating the desire of the prospective customer and finally bringing the transaction to a close? Isn't there an analogy here with the skilful house-builder who knows how to create, to produce, to bring forth houses, but nevertheless still requires building materials to do so? To put these questions aside for the time being, it can still be said that in any case the potential for exchange, the exchange-value, does not reside in the respective owners of money and goods, but reified in the money and goods themselves, respectively, i.e. in *both*, and both are required in reciprocation for an exchange to come about.

Let us examine this more closely with regard to Aristotle's ever-deepening investigation of δύναμις in *Metaphysics* Book Theta.[64] In Chapter 2 he is con-

---

64 The account provided here draws heavily on Heidegger's lectures on Aristotle's *Metaphysics* Theta 1–3 in Summer Semester 1931 published as *Aristoteles, Metaphysik Theta 1–3: Von Wesen und Wirklichkeit der Kraft* Freiburger Vorlesung SS 1931 *Gesamtausgabe* Band 33 ed. Heinrich Hüni 1981, pp.136ff in which Heidegger provides detailed onto-phenomeno-logical

cerned with investigating not just the lead or prime meaning of δύναμις as δύναμις κατὰ κίνησιν but more particularly, δύναμις μετὰ λόγου, ability guided by the λόγος, for which the paradigm is ἐπιστήμη ποιητική, the knowledge or know-how of producing, of bringing forth. Productive knowledge is guided by the sight or look of what is to be produced, the εἶδος (which is standardly trans-lated in traditional metaphysics as 'idea', 'species', 'form' or 'kind'). This sight or look is seen in advance, from the start, before any productive activity has commenced at all, and it determines how the productive activity is to proceed, its sequence, the materials chosen, the tools, the materials for the tools, the correction of mistakes, etc. With respect to the definition of the leading or guid-ing sight provided in the εἶδος, the materials are without any form or limits; they are ἄπειρον, whereas the εἶδος, the defined, delimited look, is μορφή, form, shape, Gestalt. The materials only assume a form during productive activ-ity under the guiding pre-view and consideration (διαλέγεσθαι) of the sight of the εἶδος, which is seen from the start through the knowing fore-sight of the know-how. Heidegger elaborates further in his interpretation of *Met.* Theta, after having characterized the role of εἶδος:

> Beim Herstellen steht das Herzustellende — obzwar noch nicht fertig, ja nicht einmal an-gefangen — notwendig im Vorblick; es ist im eigentlichen Sinne nur erst vor-gestellt, aber / noch nicht als Vorhandenes bei- und her-gestellt. Dieses vorblickende Vor-stellen des ἔργον in seinem εἶδος, ist gerade der eigentliche Anfang des Herstellens, nicht etwa erst die Verfertigung im engeren Sinne des Handanlegens. Dieses In-den-Blick-nehmen des Aussehens ist in sich das Bilden eines Anblicks, das Bilden des Vorbildes. Damit aber wird etwas kund: Dieses Bilden des Vorbildes kann nur geschehen als Umgrenzen dessen, was zu ihm gehört; es ist ein Auslesen, ein auslesendes Sammeln des Zusammengehörigen, ein λέγειν. Das εἶδος ist ein so zusammengelesenes Ausgelesenes, ein λεγόμενον, es ist λόγος. Und das εἶδος ist τέλος — das be-endende Ende, τέλιον — das Vollkommene, das Vollendete, Erlesene, Auserlesene; τέλος ist seinem Wesen nach immer ausgelesen: λόγος. (*GA*33:141f)

> When producing, although it is not yet finished, and not even started, what is to be pro-duced must necessarily stand in pre-view, in fore-sight [as what is envisaged]; in the proper sense it is first only fore-seen or pre-conceived, but not yet brought forth as some-thing present at hand. This foreseeing pre-conceiving of the ἔργον [work] in its εἶδος [look] is precisely the proper starting-point for producing, and not the manufacturing in the nar-rower sense of handling materials. This taking-into-view of the look is in itself the forming of a sight, the building of the pre-image. But in doing so, something becomes known. This

---

interpretations of δύναμις and ἐνέργεια, the two key concepts in Aristotle's ontology of move-ment. Heidegger's translations of passages from Book Theta alone are well worth studying carefully.

forming and building of the pre-image can only happen as a defining of what belongs to it; it is a selecting, a selective gathering of what belongs together, a λέγειν. The εἶδος is something which is selected out and gathered together, a λεγόμενον, it is λόγος. And the εἶδος is τέλος — the end which brings to an end, τέλιον — the perfect, completed, selected, chosen; τέλος is in its essence always selected and gathered: λόγος.

This passage provides a concentrated view of how the λόγος which guides production, ποίησις, is to be seen onto-phenomeno-logically as a gathering into a defined view. The guiding λόγος is the defined foreseen sight seen by the knowing look which allows the knowing producer to make step-by-step what is to be produced. The materials are selected and formed under the guiding pre-view and consideration of the εἶδος seen by the λόγος, thus allowing continual corrections to be made during the making to the as yet undefined and unformed materials to gain form and assume the final shape and look of the product. Δύναμις μετὰ λόγου — as knowing foresight of the defined, standing εἶδος according to which μορφή is to be shaped into the materials — knows how to effectively bring forth if only the chosen materials, each with its δύναμις παθητική (*Met.* 1021a15), are available.

5.3 Commodity exchange not guided by the insight of know-how

The phenomenon of exchange, by contrast, is entirely different in the ontological structure of its specific kinesis. The εἶδος of the goods or money to be acquired through purchase or sale respectively which serves as the immediate τέλος that will complete the envisaged action can indeed be seen and fore-seen, but this is not a knowing look that provides step-by-step guidance for how to effectively bring about the transformation of goods into money or money into goods. Why not? Because there are two starting-points which must coincide, concur and reciprocate if a transformation is to come about in a mutually agreed transaction. Moreover, what drives exchange is not so much know-how but rather the *desire* for something. Namely, even with regard to ποίησις Aristotle grants that what first moves or motivates the act of production as its starting-point is something desired and striven for, an ὀρεκτόν (*De Anima* Gamma 10 433a28; cf. *GA*33:150ff) because the movement of what is living is "always for the sake of something" (ἀεὶ ἕνεκά τινος 432b15), namely the matter for action, the πρακτόν. "So that there is something else more powerful that motivates making in accordance with knowledge, and not knowledge itself" (ὡς ἕτερον τινὸς κυρίου ὄντος τοῦ ποιεῖν κατὰ τὴν ἐπιστήμην, ἀλλ' οὐ τῆς ἐπιστήμης

433a5f), which converts the finished product itself from a τέλος into a means on the way to attaining the true τέλος of fulfilling a desire. For the act of making itself, the finished product in pre-view is then the εἶδος as eidetic cause of movement.

The true motivator for the making is desire (ἐπιθυμία 433a3), and appetite (ὄρεξις 433a7), which in turn are subordinated to follow reason in those who have strength in themselves (οἱ γὰρ ἐγκρατεῖς ὀρεγόμενοι καὶ ἐπιθυμοῦντες οὐ πράττουσιν ὧν ἔχουσι τὴν ὄρεξιν, ἀλλ᾽ ἀκολουθοῦσι τῷ νῷ. 433a7ff). With regard to trade and exchange, a kinesis sui generis, it can at least be seen that desire is a motivating factor for the act of purchase or sale, the desire to gain certain goods or money (for the sake of some existential purpose or other, whether 'reasonable' or 'unreasonable'), and that, for an act of exchange to take place, there must be reciprocal, complementary desire on the part of both purchaser and seller for the transaction (a kind of μεταβολή) to come about. Trade and exchange are not a realm of knowledge (ἐπιστήμη) and know-how (τέχνη ποιητική), but a realm of sociating action, i.e. *inter*action (πρᾶξις),[65] in which desire and appetite hold sway as motivating causes, i.e. as ἀρχαί, whether under the ultimate governance of (practical) reason (νοῦς, φρόνησις) or not. Under the motivation of desire, the exchange relation does not require in addition any know-how, no knowing pre-view of what is to be brought forth, even though what is desired is certainly envisaged, and what is to be exchanged must have been, or must be, produced.

This is illustrated by the historical example of the barter (as opposed to appropriation by sheer force) carried on several centuries ago between European world explorers and primitive natives in far-off regions of the Earth. The kind of τέχνη which comes into play in the case of such social interaction is something resembling rhetoric, which is the technique of 'knowing how' to skilfully sway somebody's (singular or plural) mood and thus persuade them. But the technique of rhetoric, too, cannot be regarded as a τέχνη ποιητική, because the rhetor's audience is not simply a passive material that is knowingly worked on by the skilful rhetor.[66] The 'know-how' of rhetoric is thus not a knowledge in the strict sense of a knowing starting-point for governing a change in some *thing*

---

65 As will become apparent, there is good reason to avoid altogether the terms 'action' and 'interaction' in the context of social ontology in order not to create a confusion between two fundamentally different ontologies of movement, i) that of *productive, effective movement* inherited from Aristotle which provides the tacit ontological foundation of all modern science, and ii) that of *sociating interplay* developed in the present study; cf. section vi) below.

66 Cf. my study *Assessing How Heidegger Thinks Power Through the History of Being* 2004 URL www.arte-fact.org/untpltcl/pwrrhtrc.html

else, but a *social skill* and *social power* (cf. Chapter 10) in talking others around, in engendering trust, in persuading others in an interchange in a given mooded situation, which may or may not be successful. The rhetor who is skilful in 'reading' the mood of his audience and swinging it is someone "with a real power of disposing men's feelings to his wish" and even with the "power to hold men's minds, and to direct their courses into the willing quietness of eventual obedience", a power that often depends decisively on *who* the orator is. The who-status may be derived, for instance, from an authority acknowledged "thanks to the revered descent from the Prophet".[67]

For the sake of clarity, it is therefore advisable not to speak of rhetoric as a kind of knowledge or a know-how but as a social power, a power that is not simply a power over others, but a power that comes to 'effect' only in an inter-play[68] between and among free ἀρχαί that have the power of freedom of move-ment, including interchange, and that not merely as a reciprocation between an active power and a passive power. Namely, it is crucial to see that rhetoric, along with all other phenomena of social interchange, including the exchange of goods, breaks the mould of the schema of δύναμις as worked out in Book Theta of Aristotle's *Metaphysics* and cannot be captured by the distinction be-tween active and passive powers. Aristotle characterizes the being of a passive power as "the one [kind of power] namely is a power of suffering, a starting-point in the suffering thing itself for change by an other or insofar as it is an other" (ἡ μὲν γὰρ τοῦ παθεῖν ἐστὶ δύναμις, ἡ ἐν αὐτῷ τῷ πάσχοντι ἀρχὴ μεταβολῆς παθητικῆς ὑπ' ἄλλου ἢ ᾗ ἄλλο, *Met.* IX 1046a21–23) The audience or whoever else is on the other side of a sociative interchange, however, is not merely a passive power that has the power to suffer a change (or even to resist such suffering) by an other, active power (a rhetor or whoever), but is itself a starting-point, an ἀρχή of free self-movement in actively listening, exchanging, desiring, etc., and these different ἀρχαί have to intermesh in an interplay. The Aristotelean distinction between active and passive δύναμις, by contrast, ap-plies to a dovetail fit between an active transformative power and its suitable passive material.

The social power of rhetoric is not restricted to the situation of an orator speaking to an audience or to a deliberative situation in which a group is com-ing to a decision, but comes into play more or less in all situations of social interchange, including that of the exchange of goods, especially where trust

---

67 Last three quotes from T.E. Lawrence *Seven Pillars of Wisdom* Penguin Modern Classics, Harmondsworth 1962 pp. 100, 102.
68 The concept of interplay will be explicitly developed in section vi) below.

needs to be engendered. In essentially breaking the ontological mould of productive δύναμις, and hence the ontology of productive movement, cast in Aristotle's *Metaphysics*,[69] rhetoric could never become a technology for manipulating others (which would be the dream of modern social science in its Cartesian cast, e.g. by means of learning algorithms fed with huge amounts of digital data for the purpose of advertising), but remains an art of (always reciprocal) persuasion that is an essential component of the technique of getting along with one another. This latter technique is perhaps one of the hardest for humankind to learn, requiring lifelong practice.

Rhetoric, especially in the form of advertising, has a close connection with commercial exchange and is an indispensable part of the art of acquiring, for others have to be talked round, persuaded. Here an ambiguity in the phenomenon and concept of calculation becomes apparent, an ambiguity also present in Greek λογισμός. This ambiguity arises from the essential ambiguity of the term μεταβολή in the Aristotelean definition of the ontological essence of δύναμις, an ambiguity with historical consequences that can scarcely be overestimated. Calculation can be poietically calculating in working out, often with mind-boggling sophisticated technical skill, how to bring something forth in some kind of production process. Such calculation (including arithmetic and mathematical calculation, or deliberation and reasoning) presupposes that there is a passive material that can be worked upon to bring about the envisaged result or τέλος.

But when what is to be worked upon is not merely passive material, but rather a free other or others, each of whom is a free origin of self-movement, as in any rhetorical situation (in court, parliament, meetings of any kind, in the market-place), including any commercial situation of exchange, the kind of calculation employed is the kind of cleverness that can turn a situation with an other or others to (what one envisages as) one's own advantage. This is also the meaning of Greek λογισμός as 'cold calculation' (cf. Benseler). Paradoxically, such cold calculation works at enkindling the warmth of trust to bring others round and always has an eye as to how a situation can be exploited for one's own advantage. This eye is a kind of envisaging of a τέλος, but it is a one-sided view of a two- or many-sided situation in which two, several or many are involved. Cold calculation is already a perversion of the situation of sociative interchange in which free ἀρχαί come into interplay with one another and have the freedom not

---

69 On breaking the ontological mould of productive δύναμις and the Aristotelean ontology of productive movement as well as the side-step into quissity see my 'Technology, Technique, Interplay: Questioning *Die Frage nach der Technik*' 2007–2013.

only of gaining an advantage at the expense of the other or others, but also of reaching a mutually beneficial and satisfying result. Calculation in this sociating sense of interchange does not have to be cold; one shade of meaning of Greek λογίζεσθαι, apart from 'to calculate, count, think, consider, view, conclude' is namely 'to hope'.

To return to the question of desire and acquiring: In the case of trade, the motivating factor of desire for something, either money or specific goods, does not directly motivate a production process under the guidance of the foreseeing, knowing λόγος which has gathered the sight of the goods to be brought forth into the fore-sight of the εἶδος, but rather it immediately motivates an exchange transaction, a purchase or a sale. This transaction presupposes that the money or goods in the possession of the desiring person *can be* exchanged, i.e. that they have a reified δύναμις, a potential and potency, for exchange, an exchange-value, within themselves (καθ' αὐτό), for it is not the mere desire of the owners of goods or money which enables the desired thing to be acquired, but rather what the desiring person can give in return for acquiring what is desired, and what is given must have a potential, potency or δύναμις which, in turn, makes it desirable for someone else to acquire, for any reciprocal, complementary exchange to eventuate at all. There is thus a disjunction between the desire of the desiring person and the potential for exchange, or *exchange-value*, which resides reified in goods and money insofar as goods or money can be exchanged by whoever possesses them, even a thief, regardless of the desire motivating any exchange.

The δύναμις of exchange-value which resides reified in goods or money is thus essentially, i.e. ontologically, different from the δύναμις μετὰ λόγου of ἐπιστήμη ποιητική which resides firmly in the knowing producer by virtue of having been learned. Indeed, one meaning of the verb δύνασθαι is simply 'to be worth', as in 'five pairs of shoes are worth one table'. The δύναμις of exchange-value in the case of goods is their potential to be exchanged, but this potential to be exchanged is only derivative of their primary potential to be put to use in the usages for which they are suitable. The δύναμις of exchange-value in the case of money is simply its ready potential to purchase anything offered for sale on a market. Neither of these potentials as such has to do with the power of knowledge or know-how to bring forth.

Sociating interplay in its *fathomlessness* is a fundamental hallmark of the sociating 'process' of exchange of commodities, whether they be produced things or services provided. The products themselves are pro-duced, i.e. brought forth knowingly through the exercise or actualization of powers, namely, labour power, natural powers and the powers of already produced means of production. These powers working together as ἐνέργεια — in the literal Aristotelean sense of 'being-at-work' — on the raw materials, which themselves possess passive powers to suffer being worked upon, constitute the labour process, whose product is then validated abstractly on the market as being valuable, thus validating not only the labour power producing them as valuable, but also the powers of nature and means of production that have been employed in the labour process. To have value (German: Wert) is itself a power in the sense that these goods and services command a certain price and thus can be exchanged for something else.

The original sense of value derives from L. valere which, apart from meaning 'to be able-bodied, strong, powerful, influential, to prevail' can also mean 'to be worth something in exchange for something else, to have monetary value'. Etymologically, 'valere' is related (via an Indo-European root *ual-; cf. Duden) to German 'walten' which means 'to prevail', again from L. prævalere 'to be very able', 'to have greater power or worth', 'to prevail' and thus itself a comparative or enhanced form of possessing power. L. valere, in turn, is the standard Latin translation of δύνασθαι, so that the connection to the Greek word for power, δύναμις, in all its phenomenal senses, is secured. This is not merely a scholarly matter to excite philologists and lexicographers, since it points not only to power as a fundamental experience of human being in the world, but also to the multi-dimensional layers of the phenomenon of power. In particular, the productive powers that bring forth products of all kinds must be distinguished clearly on a fundamental ontological level from the 'exchange powers', i.e. the exchange-values, of those products in being worth something in interchange on the markets where they are validated as *actually* (ἐνεργείᾳ), and not merely *potentially* (δυνάμει), being valuable. Since this interchange is an interplay of powers, it is a game in the strict, i.e. not merely playful, sense that defies the specification of any unified, single power, such as the labour power of the labourers producing one of the products in the exchange process, as prevailing over the others, thus determining the product's exchange-value independently of the fathomless interplay of powers itself.

5.4 Two complementary, reciprocal pairs of δυνάμεις: Reified value and desire

Goods and money can be referred to collectively for the sake of convenience as *assets*, i.e. as the *estate* or *effects* in someone's possession which are sufficient (from the French legal phrase *aver assetz*, 'to have sufficient') for settling that person's debts arising through exchange transactions. Assets have the δύναμις (social power) of exchange-value capable of 'effecting', i.e. providing, satisfaction in exchange transactions. The δύναμις of value residing reified in assets is that they themselves are desirable in the eyes of others and therefore attract the attention and arouse the desire of others willing to acquire them. Valuable assets show themselves off as desirable for others and this gives them the reified, i.e. thingly, power of exercising exchange-value in an exchange transaction which brings about a change of money into goods and, simultaneously and reciprocally, goods into money, depending on which perspective is assumed. In an exchange transaction, the reified exchange-value potentials of both goods and money — that is, of *whats* — are put to work to bring about the exchange; they are complementary, reciprocal powers or δυνάμεις both largely disjunct from the respective non-reified, living, motivating desires of the exchangers — that is, of *whos* — (i.e. apart from any 'powers of persuasion' which may come to bear to make apparent the good uses of the goods on offer), since the exchangeable, valuable assets owned by any one person are a matter of accident and the vicissitudes of fortune in life.

Goods that are put on display in some way or other on the market show themselves off as being desirable in one respect or another in the sense that they are capable of fulfilling the desire of a prospective purchaser in some existential use or other. The goods potentially (δυνάμει) suffer themselves (πάσχειν) to be used in a usage and hence possess a *passive power*. This capability of passively fulfilling some desire or other in use, or use-value, is also a δύναμις residing reified in the goods which discloses itself and can be perceived (αἰσθάνεσθαι) by prospective purchasers who thus have the *active power* (δύναμις) of perception (αἴσθησις) to disclose (ἀληθεύειν) the goods in their desirability *as* use-values. The two δυνάμεις of being passively perceptible as valuable for fulfilling a desire and the active perception of things in their suitability for satisfying desire are complementary passive and active powers of disclosure. Such powers play out in the open 3D-time-clearing that enables the presencing — and thereby also the disclosive self-presenting — of beings, both whats and whos, to the understanding human mind. This openness of time-mind or Zeit-Geist, whose investigation will not be further undertaken in this study but is constantly assumed,[70] is the *a priori enabling three-dimensional temporal playground for the play of all social powers*.

The perception involved here is namely not merely sense perception but a kind of understanding of the goods in their suitability for satisfying certain desires in use, i.e. the αἴσθησις is αἴσθησις μετὰ λόγου, perception guided by the

---

70 Cf. Eldred, M. *A Question of Time* 2015.

λόγος, which gathers the sight put on view into an understanding of existential usefulness (a mode of being). This perception of the goods as desirable can motivate the prospective purchaser to acquire them by giving money in exchange for them. Money will only be accepted in exchange because it, in turn, has the reified universal δύναμις of being able to purchase any goods offered on the market up to a total price equal to the amount of money involved. As universal means of payment, money is the reified universal δύναμις, potential, power or potency for acquiring commodity goods and is therefore, in turn, itself desirable as being universally valuable for the purpose of acquiring goods of all kinds. In other words, the use-value of money is its exchange-value.

There are thus, to start with, three pairs of δυνάμεις involved in exchange: i) the reified δύναμις of goods being exchangeable for money, which in turn has the complementary reified δύναμις of being able to acquire any goods offered for sale on the market; ii) the active and passive δυνάμεις of perceiving goods *as* being valuable for use in their self-display and therefore *as* being *desirable*, thus potentially motivating a purchase; and iii) the active and passive δυνάμεις of perceiving money as being valuable in its self-display and therefore *desirable*, thus potentially motivating its acquisition. The latter two pairs are alaethic or disclosive powers relying on the self-disclosure of beings in their being and human understanding of beings in their being in conjunction with human desiring itself. If the active and passive pairs of δυνάμεις are counted only as one (because all δυνάμεις involve complementary active and passive forces or potencies, capabilities or potentials), then there are two complementary, reciprocal pairs of δυνάμεις: i) the reified power of goods and money to exchange for each other (whereby money has a peculiar use as universal means of purchase and thus embodies pure exchange-value) and ii) the reciprocal powers of buyer and seller to perceive in their understanding the use-value of goods and money as something desirable.

When the goods offered, the money available, the respective desires of purchaser and seller, and the perception of the goods and money to fulfil desire all coincide and complement each other, then an exchange transaction will *actually* come about, i.e. presence (always at some quantitatively definite price). There must therefore be a coincidence, alignment and reciprocity of various potentials or δυνάμεις for the potentials of exchange-value to be exercised in realizing an exchange. The prime motivating starting-points (ἀρχαί) are the coincident, complementary *desires* of prospective buyer and seller. Such coincidence happens κατὰ συμβεβηκός, i.e. at happenstance, contingently, and does not, in turn, fall under a superior governing starting-point or ἀρχή that makes it happen. Advertising, for instance, is only a rhetorical way of *encouraging* the coincidence of buyer and seller, not of knowingly and surely bringing it about (more on this below).

Desire is always desire to acquire what one does not possess. Desire derives from lack, absence, στέρησις motivating the overcoming of lack by bringing what is lacking into presence by some method of acquisition, of reaching out (ὀρέγεσθαι) and getting (κτᾶσθαι). Desire must therefore be endowed, like all understanding, with the *double temporal vision* of seeing the *present* state of lack and also 'simultaneously' a *future* in which the lack is remedied by the presencing of the goods hitherto lacking or *temporally withheld*. This presupposes that what is lacking, i.e. absent, is *mentally* present in its absence *as* something lacking. Its absence is felt and seen by the mind which in turn, is motiviated or driven by desire. Desire therefore motivates movement, a movement of sociation with the end of getting from another. Trade is a practice of mutual, reciprocal acquisition motivated, i..e. set in motion, by mutual desire which constitutes a sociating relation, i.e. an interplay sociating two or more people with each other. The sociating interplay is constituted for the sake of two goods (ἀγαθόν), namely, realizing an existential end in each of the exchange partners' lives. Something valuable is given away in return for something else of value. The motivation of desire can only come about because the goods are put on display in some way or other and reveal themselves, i.e. show themselves off as reified whats being useful for satisfying certain existential desires. This is the function of a market or an exchange: to put goods for sale on display.

The exchange of goods for money must be motivated by desire (ἐπιθυμία), especially the desire of the prospective buyer, who must be *motivated* to exercise the exchange-value potential inherent in his money. Such motivation presupposes an understanding of the goods on offer as having the potential to quench desire in some respect or another, i.e. the perceived use-value of the goods on offer is a necessary element in motivating a purchase as part of the movement of factical everyday life. The purchaser's motivation residing in his desire is thus also a decisive starting-point or ἀρχή for an exchange.

Merely putting goods (including services) on display either directly (say, in a display window) or indirectly (via advertising or listing on a market) discloses them to prospective buyers whose desires are aroused (or not) for something they lack, but potentially could acquire through exercising the power of money, i.e. its reified, universal exchange-value. With the arousal of desire for something lacking, buyers *suffer* themselves (i.e. passively) to have them aroused in response to the *active* potential of advertised goods on offer to arouse them. Here we have yet another complementary pair of δυνάμεις: the *passive power* of prospective buyers to suffer the arousal of their desires in response to the *active power* of goods on display to arouse them. (On the other side, the sellers of goods are motivated by their desire to gain money-income in general, which is why they are in business in the first place, suffering themselves to willingly become players in the gainful game, as will be explicated in Chapter 6.8 below.)

The disclosure of goods can and often does take the form of desire-stimulating *advertising*, which puts up signs in the public domain adverting, turning the attention of all and sundry to goods offered for sale. The goods are then not displayed directly and physically on a market-place, but indirectly through the means of advertising in its attention-drawing, referential sign-function. Such signs have to be understood by prospective buyers. (All practical dealings with the world are in an elementary way μετὰ λόγου, i.e. guided by the basic perspectives uncovered by understanding, including the categories,[71] but not μετὰ λόγου in the sense of amounting to pro-ductive knowledge.) Advertising endeavours to present the goods in their self-display in such a way as to stimulate prospective buyers' desires to acquire them. Advertising is thus motivating in the sense of an active δύναμις, or power, of persuasion which aims at bringing about a decision on the part of prospective buyers to suffer their desire to be aroused to the point of actually (ἐνεργείᾳ) purchasing, thus bringing about a change of hands (μεταβολή), a sociating movement, so that, after the hand-over, what is present-to-hand for the purchaser in full and final presence

---

71 Cf. "Rather, the situation is thus, that all λέγειν already moves and is guided within certain categories. They do not signify some bunch of forms which I can put into a system, nor principles for dividing up sentences, but, as their name already says, they have to be understood from what the λόγος itself is in its distinctive way: *constituting the discoveredness of world in such a way that this discoveredness shows the world in its basic respects/senses.* If we have a more or less lively understanding for the existence of the world, we will be careful not to stipulate a definite number of categories. [...] And indeed, the categories are ways of addressing and showing up beings understood as the beings in the surrounding world as the world is in ζωὴ πρακτική (practical living). The ζωὴ πρακτική is μετὰ λόγου. In this μετὰ λόγου reside the distinctive λόγοι, the categories." (Vielmehr liegt der Tatbestand so, daß alles λέγειν schon bewegt und geführt ist in bestimmten Kategorien. Sie bedeuten nicht irgendwelche Formen, die ich in ein System bringen kann, auch nicht Einteilungsprinzipien der Sätze, sondern sie müssen nach dem, was ihr Name besagt, verstanden werden aus dem, was der λόγος selbst in seiner ausgezeichneten Weise ist: *das Entdecktsein der Welt ausmachend, so, daß diese Entdecktheit die Welt in ihren Grundhinsichten zeigt.* Wenn man ein einigermaßen lebendiges Verständnis für das Dasein der Welt hat, wird man vorsichtig darin sein, auf eine bestimmte Zahl von Kategorien sich festzulegen. [...] Und zwar sind die Kategorien Weisen des ansprechenden Aufzeigens des Seienden, verstanden als das Seiende der Umwelt, so wie die Welt ist in der ζωὴ πρακτική. Die ζωὴ πρακτική ist μετὰ λόγου. In diesem μετὰ λόγου liegen die ausgezeichneten λόγοι, die Kategorien. M. Heidegger *Grundbegriffe der Aristotelischen Philosophie* ed. M. Michalski *GA*18:303, 304f.)

(ἐντελέχεια) is the commodity good in the stead of money and what is present-to-hand for the seller in full and final presence (ἐντελέχεια) is the money in the stead of the commodity good. In disclosing goods in their potential usefulness, advertising can also obscure this potential usefulness or present it falsely, or arouse potential buyers' desires which cannot truly be fulfilled by the goods in question. This is false advertising which arises when the advertising signs indicate not how the advertised goods show themselves of themselves but rather misleadingly and enticingly indicate that certain consumer desires can be fulfilled by them.

There is a peculiar and essential intertwining of the δυνάμεις of reified use-value and exchange-value. The potential or δύναμις of use-value resides in goods (they *are* potentially useful), which potential can be perceived and understood by human beings owing ultimately to the identity of 3D-time and mind. The potential is only exercised in use itself; the potential is then at work in the goods being used. This being-at-work of the potential is what Aristotle calls ἐνέργεια, en-erg-y. The second potential or δύναμις residing in goods is their exchange-value. This potential is put to work or realized only in the act of exchange, i.e. in the interaction, or rather interplay, of sale for money. Goods only have exchange-value by virtue of having a use-value. Said negatively, goods which are useless or no good (lacking in ἀγαθόν) for any practice in human living in the widest possible sense do not have any exchange-value either. Why not? Because for goods to arouse the desire of prospective buyers to acquire them in an exchange transaction, they have to offer something in their self-display by way of being useful, i.e. good, for some practice or other. The δύναμις of exchange-value is also the potential residing reified in goods to effect an actual (ἐνεργείᾳ) social interchange between buyer and seller. When exchange-value is exercised and thus at work in a state of ἐνέργεια, a sociating interplay between people is being realized, presencing. Such being-at-work of exchange-value brings about a movement of social life, which consists, among other things, of a multitude of exchange transactions in which goods and money change places in a kind of μεταβολή, i.e. change as ex-change, inter-change. The end of this movement is the final and complete presence of money and goods in changed hands; the δυνάμεις of the exchange-values have achieved ἐντελέχεια.

With regard to money as distinct from goods, it can be said that the two δυνάμεις of use-value and exchange-value coincide or intermesh, since the usefulness of money lies precisely in its being exchangeable universally for commodity goods offered on the market. The use-value of money is exercised in the movement of exchange itself and not subsequently in a further practice of (individual or productive) consumption. The function of money as reified *store of value*, too, is simply due to its potential consisting in exchange-value, which is retained over time. This potential, exchange-value, may, of course, be impaired by the passage of time through a general rise in prices (price inflation), but this quantitative change does not entirely negate the function of money as store of value. The only requirement is that the money itself does not deteriorate so that it will still be recognized by others *as* money. Such longevity can be assured by a metal such as gold, or today simply by binary digits in an electromagnetic medium kept secure in a bank or similar.

The function of money as store of value is entirely secondary to understanding the modes of being pertaining to goods and money with regard to the sociating practice of exchange. Insofar as goods and money possess exchange-value within themselves they are δυνάμεις in the sense of ἀρχὴ μεταβολῆς, i.e. starting-point for a change or interchange, but this sense of ἀρχὴ μεταβολῆς is neither the sense of productive know-how which resides in something other than what changes, nor is it the sense of natural change or movement according to which a living being changes itself through growth and decay, natural alteration, locomotion or progeneration. In the case of productive know-how, the governing starting-point brings about a change in something else, whereas in the case of living physical beings, the starting-point (the psyche in the Greek sense) governs a change initiated by the being itself. The phenomenon of exchange-value as δύναμις does not accord with either of these senses of starting-point. Once more, why not?

Consider the potential of exchange-value residing in money. The money has reified in itself — by virtue of the social usage of commodity exchange — the power to purchase something else. The ἀρχή therefore resides reified in the money (and, by virtue of owning money, derivatively in the money-owner), but the change brought about is neither of the money itself (φύσις) nor of something else such as the goods that are purchased (ποίησις). Rather, the change which the money brings about in being exercised as exchange-value at work is its own change of place (μεταβολή) for something else, so that both itself and something else (the goods purchased) are affected by the change. This change of place (τόπος) is not a physical locomotion (κίνησις κατὰ τόπον), but a change of social place or ownership: goods and money swap ownership places and re-place each other. The change that is brought about through the exercise of exchange-value is a *social* change of position or re-placement directly constituting a sociation and involving social relations, viz. the sociating interplay between buyer and seller and their respective ownership relations (for ownership, as rightful possession, is a phenomenon to be distinguished from possession as such).

A further peculiarity of the δύναμις of reified exchange-value as a starting-point, as already noted, is that for an exchange to be effected, *two* reciprocal starting-points (two δυνάμεις) must be exercised (ἐνέργεια) complementarily and coincidentally, i.e. the exchange-value residing in the money and the exchange-value residing in the goods must be exercised (contractually, whether written or not) simultaneously and reciprocally to effect the re-placement interchange (ἐντελέχεια), which is an ownership swap in which money and goods interchange their ownership and possession status. A change of ownership and possession is a change only within the social dimension of whoness and makes sense only within this dimension. A change in possession, which could be regarded as a physical change in the sense of who has control over an article of property, is not necessarily a change of ownership, as is apparent in the case of theft. Here, however, it is the phenomena of exchange-value as reified δύναμις and the social practice of exchange which are at the focus of investigation. *Neither a poiaetic nor a physical understanding of δύναμις suffices to account ontologically for the sociating phenomenon of exchange of goods against money, as banal and self-evident as this phenomenon may seem.*

An entirely different ontology of movement is demanded, an ontology of social-sociating movement. For the sake of conceptual clarity and of avoiding a confusion firmly entrenched in the onto-theological tradition itself, we would be well advised to keep exchange and production, Austausch und Herstellen, κτῆσις and ποίησις quite distinct. At long last 'we' — that is, we few left, still able to think the phenomena from the ontological difference despite the progressive *wilful* degeneration of mind in the end-game of modern times perpetrated by the institutions of higher learning themselves — must become sharply aware that there is an ambivalence in the term μεταβολή that lies at the very heart of Aristotle's key concept of δύναμις, namely, μεταβολή can mean both 'change' and 'exchange'.[72] In its meaning as 'change', μεταβολή points to beings in the way of φύσις (self-movement) or ποίησις (productive power over things), but in its signification as 'exchange', μεταβολή points to sociating interchange and interplay involving at least two starting-points or ἀρχαί.

The seller of desirable goods will, or may, *attempt* to gain control over the one starting-point for an exchange by stimulating the prospective customer's desire, and that not just by extolling the virtues (i.e. use-value) of the goods on

---

72 Cf. Eldred, M. 'Technology, Technique, Interplay: Questioning *Die Frage nach der Technik*' 2007–2014.

offer, but by persuading the prospective customer in any way possible, which includes also engendering trust (because exchange relations would be altogether impossible if trust, πίστις, were completely lacking) and making the purchase seem as easy as possible (say, by way of easily available, low-interest credit). Insofar as the seller has a know-how or technique of how to motivate and stimulate the desire of prospective buyers and gain their trust, this could be termed a psychological or rhetorical know-how or τέχνη ῥητορική through which the bipolarity or bilaterality of the exchange interplay, consisting of two ἀρχαί, would be reduced by subordination to one ἀρχή, namely, that of the seller's manipulative desire for money, albeit that a necessary precondition remains of having goods to sell at all.

If it were possible to subsume the other manipulatively as an ἀρχή under one's own ἀρχή, that would indeed be an uncanny power (as discussed in Plato's *Gorgias*). Such a psychological (in the modern sense) or rhetorical know-how is a knowledge, or at least a skill, a knack, of how to deal with people, how to gain their trust and persuade them of the fine qualities of a product offered for sale. Dealing with people with an eye to persuading them, gaining their trust and arousing their desire for purchase, however, (and despite the turn of phrase saying that a charismatic speaker is able to 'make' his listeners into 'putty in his hands') is not the same thing as knowingly and surely impressing the form of a finished product step by step on passive materials under the guiding fore-sight of the εἶδος, as in the case of τέχνη ποιητική, since the other, as a living being guided in its actions by understanding, is itself an origin of action, its own ἀρχή, i.e. it is a *free* source of its own movement. The other's *freedom of movement* is therefore the ontological limit to any rhetorical or psychological know-how, no matter how insidiously manipulative, employed as a technique of persuasion in order to bring about a sale. This bringing-about must be distinguished ontologically from bringing-forth under the guidance of a reliable, fore-seeing knowledge, i.e. from ποίησις as a δύναμις μετὰ λόγου.

5.5 Recapitulation and the coming together of goods in commerce

By way of recapitulation, what has been gained so far through this investigation of the ontology of exchange proceeding from the basis of the three crucial concepts in the Aristotelean ontology of productive, effective movement? As has been laid out in the preceding section, the ontology of exchange differs essentially from the ontology of ποίησις or production on which Aristotelean (and all of Western) ontotheology is based, including the onto-theological investigation of the unmoved mover as the supreme producer, the divine maker. Despite all misguided attempts to force a square peg into a round hole, starting with Aristotle himself in his study on *Rhetoric*, the simple ontological structure of the phenomenon of exchange-movement does not admit a reduction to a single ἀρχή but instead is irreducibly an interplay between, at least, the one and the other in which there are four ἀρχαί and four δυνάμεις (namely, two principal, 'wilful' ἀρχαί residing in the desirous, understanding buyer and seller, and two reified ἀρχαί residing in the things — goods and money — to be exchanged, namely, their respective exchange-values as powers). The unity of the productive ἀρχή amenable to efficient, linear causality disintegrates into the fathomless, uncontrollable, polyarchic interplay among many ἀρχαί. Despite the exercise of powers of persuasion, the free other is not subsumed under the governing control of a starting-point, but rather, one thing is "changed away" (μεταβάλλειν) for another, one thing is "given, relinquished whilst receiving something else in return" (OED), and therefore exchange-movements are unpredictable in the strict sense of being inherently outside the certain, calculating reach of a τέχνη ποιητική proceeding from a single governing origin.

The interplayful relationship is bilateral in the case of an exchange transaction between two individuals or multilateral, if a market as a whole is considered. In accordance with Heidegger's thesis that the original sense of being for the Greeks is Hergestelltsein,[73] the social interplay of exchange can also be thought (misleadingly) in the *broadest* sense *as* a Herstellung conceived as a bringing-to-presence to stand in the defined outline of a self-presentation in the 3D-temporal clearing. Exchange is then thought of *as a Herstellung* in the sense of a (reciprocal) bringing-forth into presence through the (reciprocal, intermeshing) exercise of two reified exchange-value potentials so that another being stands respectively present-to-hand for the exchangers (buyer and seller) but, as shown in detail in the preceding section, such *Herstellung* is not only ontically, but ontologically distinct from ποίησις, i.e. production. Such exchange-Herstellung is indeed a movement of practical life, but its ontological structure conforms neither with the ontological analysis of movement (κίνησις) constituting physical being (φύσις) which Aristotle carries out in the *Physics*, nor with the ontological analysis of the movement of production (δύναμις μετὰ λόγου) in Book Theta of the *Metaphysics*.

73 "Denn der Sinn für Sein ist ursprünglich Hergestelltsein." M. Heidegger 'Phänomenologische Interpretationen zu Aristoteles (Anzeige der hermeneutischen Situation)' *Dilthey-Jahrbuch* Bd. 6 MS:50. Cf. the first section of this chapter.

Analogously to the paradigm of artisanal production for developing the Aristotelean ontology of productive movement, exchange is the simple paradigm for a genuinely social kinesis sociating people in the interplay of practical life which can be called *commerce*. These two paradigms are not merely epistemological paradigms such as those invoked frequently and facilely since Thomas Kuhn introduced the term but, much more deeply and far-reachingly, two different ontological paradigms for interpreting movement capable of overturning the as-yet unchallenged hegemony of modern science's theological absolute will to effective power over movement/change of all kinds.

The 'com-' in commerce means 'together', whereas the 'merce' comes from 'merx' for 'good' or 'ware'. Commerce is the social practice of goods coming together, reflecting, estimating and validating their value in each other, sociating and changing places. Mediated through the goods, people come together and sociate. The social relation of exchange can therefore be termed *reified*, i.e. mediated by things. The prefix 'com-' or 'together' implies a horizontal, at least bipolar relation which cannot be hierarchized under a single, dominating, governing ἀρχή. The coming together of goods on the market, their trafficking and trade, is a fundamental, elementary practice of sociation constituting society on an everyday, lived plane. Plato's and Aristotle's insight that society is constituted practically in the first place through trading in merchandise seems to be a genuine phenomenological insight requiring explicit explication onto-hermeneutically *as* the basic ontological structure of sociating movement and social being. The exchange of goods on the market, in which the potential exchange-value of goods is exercised, is the common, rudimentary practice constituting social life.

Etymologically, the word 'common' comes most probably from 'com-' 'together' and '-munis' 'bound, under obligation' (cf. OED). In the present context, this etymology, when interpreted with a view to the phenomena themselves, implies that trade is the bond which, at first and for the most part, brings people bindingly into sociation with one another. This bond obliges them to exchange, to give and take and, for the purposes of exchange, also to *trust* each other. In giving and taking goods through the mediation of money, humans individually practise the bond which sociates them in society. The giving and taking imply that this is not a relation of domination of one over the other, but one of equal intercourse between free individuals as free origins of their own life-movements in which each constitutes an independent starting-point for diverse, renewable, potential transactions. In striving to fulfil their individual desires, people in their generality bring about and maintain the social bond forming the fabric of practical quotidian life and share to a greater or lesser extent in the wealth produced by the whole.

Exchange as an elementary form of movement of sociating life depending on myriad transactions resulting from individual decisions to reciprocally exercise the exchange-value potential latent in goods and money, of course, does not and cannot bring about an equal distribution of social wealth. This is an immediate corollary of the contingent nature of the exchange interplay that will be taken up again later when investigating (redistributive) social justice in Chapter 6.

5.5.1 A side-glance at Hegel's treatment of actuality, possibility, contingency, necessity and freedom

Further light may be shed on the ontological structure of exchange as a paradigmatic form of fathomlessly sociating interplay through the prism of the Hegelian dialectic of actuality, possibility, contingency, necessity and freedom as unfolded in the *Logik* as the third and concluding part of the Doctrine of Essence. This Doctrine of Essence, in turn, forms the transition to the Doctrine of the Concept as the ontology of freedom. The corresponding part in the *Enzyklopädie*, C. Die Wirklichkeit (Actuality), covers §§ 142–159. I shall show that the interplay is groundless in the strict Hegelian sense.

Actuality for Hegel is "the unity of essence and existence, or of the inner and the outer that has become immediate" (die unmittelbar gewordene Einheit des Wesens und der Existenz oder des Inneren und des Äußeren, *Enz.* § 142). At first, however, this unity is in the 'loose' mode of mere formal possibility and mere contingency because the essence is merely the "identity" of "reflection into itself" (Reflexion-in-sich, § 143) as *"abstract* and *inessential essentiality"* (*abstrakte* und *unwesentliche Wesentlichkeit,* § 143), whereas the "outer" is actual in its "difference from possibility [as] the *inessential* immediate" (Unterschiede von der Möglichkeit [als] das *unwesentliche* Unmittelbare, § 144). This inessential, immediate existence, divorced from essence, is *contingent* (*ein Zufälliges,* § 144). The contingent, however, in turn, in its "immediate existence" (unmittelbares Dasein, § 145), can be "the possibility of another being" (die Möglichkeit eines Anderen, § 145) and as such a "condition" (Bedingung, § 145). Outer existence, thus unfolded into a circle of actual, contingent conditions that are mediated with the inner possibility, becomes the "real possibility" which entails that the possibility also becomes *actual.* The inside and the outside in their tight mediation with one another have become the "totality" (Totalität,

§ 147) which moves as the "actuation of the matter" (Betätigung der Sache, § 147) as no longer mere, formal possibility, but as "the *real* ground" (der *reale* Grund, § 147 case modified ME) so that "when *all* the conditions are given, the matter *must* become actual" (wenn *alle* Bedingungen vorhanden sind, *muß* die Sache wirklich werden, § 147).

This now tight unity of the inner essence (the matter at hand) with the outer, real, contingently given conditions is *necessity* (*Notwendigkeit*, § 147). The matter 'uses up' the pre-posited, contingent, "*complete circle of conditions*" (*vollständiger Kreis von Bedingungen*, § 148) to become actual. Necessity thus has three moments: the condition, the matter at hand and the *activity* (*Tätigkeit*, § 148), the last-mentioned firstly "existing independently" (selbständig existierend, § 148) e.g. as a human being, and secondly, being "the movement of translating the conditions into the matter, and the matter into the conditions as into the side of existence" (die Bewegung, die Bedingungen in die Sache, diese in jene als in die Seite des Existenz zu übersetzen, § 148). *Freedom*, finally, arises when the *hidden* "band of necessity" (Band der Notwendigkeit, § 157) loses its blindness and becomes "*revealed*" (*enthüllt*, § 157). As embodying revealed necessity, actual beings become independent, acting in self-awareness in accordance with insight into the essence's actualization. Such free, independent beings are subjects such as reason-endowed human beings and, for Hegel, the Christian God. The transition from necessity to freedom is therefore simultaneously the transition from the objective logic to the subjective logic, or from the ontology of essence to that of the concept as "*free* as the *substantial power existing for itself*, and [...] *totality*" (das *Freie*, als die *für sich seiende substantielle Macht*, und [...] *Totalität*, § 160).

What does this dense review of actuality, possibility, necessity and freedom according to Hegel's speculative dialectic mean with regard to the paradigm of commodity exchange we have been considering? The essence to be considered in this case in its unity with existence is exchange-value, which can be contrasted instructively with use-value. A useful thing has the potential of being used in a certain concrete way, and this constitutes its essence: to be good for a certain use. A use-value is therefore more than a merely formal possibility, but rather a potential. This usefulness, however, cannot be realized if the contingently given conditions are not right. For instance, it is no good trying to use an adhesive on a wet surface, because the adhesive's essential potential, viz. adhesiveness, cannot be translated into existence under such conditions. If, however, all the appropriate conditions are given, such as the right kind of surfaces to be glued, at the right temperature, humidity, etc., then the glue will 'use up' these conditions, under the appropriate activity of a user, to actually translate the glue's essential potential into actually stuck surfaces, such as a mended cup handle.

To take the example of an adhesive further, but with regard to the adhesive's exchange-value, we see that the situation is entirely different. Because the adhesive is potentially useful, as we have seen from the discussion of Aristotle in 5 i), it also has the derived potential of being exchangeable for some other use-value. This potential is also more than a merely formal possibility, just as the adhesive's usefulness is also more than a merely formal possibility, i.e. in Hegel's sense, merely conceivable as non-self-contradictory. Nevertheless, the conditions and above all the activity required to translate the adhesive's exchange-value into actuality differ essentially from the conditions and the activity required to translate the adhesive's use-value into actuality, because now the former activity does *not* have "its possibility solely in the conditions and the matter at hand" (ihre Möglichkeit allein an den Bedingungen und an der Sache, § 148), but depends also on the activity of an *other* who has a demanding desire for the adhesive. The activity of realization has split into *two* independent activities. Moreover, this other's demanding desire for the adhesive depends not only upon whether this other has a use for it, but also upon what and how much has to be given in exchange. Exchange-value always has *essentially* a quantitative aspect, namely the exchange ratio, but the quantity of exchange-value does not reside solely in the adhesive itself but only *in relation to* that for which it is exchanged which simultaneously actualizes *its* exchange-value. The actual, quantitative realization of exchange-value is therefore the result of an interplay between the (at least) two exchange-values and also the activities of the (at least) two exchangers who must each decide, but mutually, at what exchange ratio, or range of exchange ratios, they are prepared to actually exchange. There are no contingently given conditions as pre-posited, pre-supposed (Vorausgesetztes, § 146) that could guarantee that "the matter [here: the adhesive's exchange-value ME] must become actual" (§ 147).

Even if the other's demand for the adhesive at an exchange ratio (or price) of x is included among the pre-posited conditions that are supposed to make the actualization of exchange-value a necessity, and the exchange concluded on those terms, this implies that the actualization of the adhesive's exchange-value is not the necessary actualization of an essence inherent in the adhesive itself, but is conditional upon, i.e. merely *contingent* upon, not only an offer made by another, which itself is merely contingent and has no necessity, but also upon whether this offer is accepted (there is no necessity to accept the offer and no inherent, essential, quantitative exchange-value that would dictate the acceptance of a certain offer). Conversely, even if a fixed exchange ratio (or price) of x is set (ultimately: arbitrarily) for the adhesive, whether this quantitatively fixed exchange-value is actually realized then depends on the *contingent* decision of another (the 'buyer'), having nothing essential to do with the adhesive's inner essence, to *actually* exchange at that set asking rate (or price). The higgling over exchange ratios in the market-place is a contingent interplay whose 'post-posited' outcome is determined with necessity neither by the commodities exchanged in themselves nor by the actors in themselves.

There is no actualization of an essence inherent in the commodity taking place when it is actually exchanged, but rather the coming about of an outcome of a *dyadic interplay* in which the exchange-value first comes to be what it actually, but contingently, is as a certain definite quantitative exchange ratio. Because of the dyadic or split structure of interplay, there is no unified "*totality of form* for itself, the immediate self-translation of the inner [essence] into outer [reality] and of the outer into the inner" (*Totalität der Form* für sich, das unmittelbare Sichübersetzen des Inneren ins Äußere und des Äußeren ins Innere, § 147). Hegel says that "this self-movement of the form is *activity*, activation of the matter [= content, ME] as the *real* ground that lifts itself up to actuality, and activation of contingent actuality, of the conditions" ([d]ies Sichbewegen der Form ist *Tätigkeit*, Betätigung der Sache [= Inhalt, ME], als des *realen* Grundes, der sich zur Wirklichkeit aufhebt, und Betätigung der zufälligen Wirklichkeit, der Bedingungen, § 147) In the present context of dyadic interplay, however, there can be no "self-movement" because there is no single self, but at least two selves, each with its freedom of movement. Furthermore, the matter here is the exchange-value (the essence) which cannot lift *itself* up into actuality, even if pre-posited conditions are given.

The dyadic interplay (and even more the polyarchic interplay of markets) is therefore *groundless*, and this *groundlessness* is of the essence of interplay. Strictly speaking, the dyadic ontological structure of exchange interplay is itself doubled because each exchange-value has its bearer, who as a free self is a groundless origin of decision. This *doubledness of dyadic exchange interplay* makes it a *quadratic interplay* in which each player is *empowered* by the *exponent* of an exchange-value with its inherent potency to exchange.

The *dyadic* ontological structure of exchange interplay must not be confused with a *binary* structure since the options of the free other in the interplay are not restricted to the binary choice between 1 and 0. Such a binary logic would again make the interplay calculable and therefore controllable. The other as free origin of movement can play in a contingent way, choosing a countermove that is between 0 and 1, 'no' and 'yes', or outside a merely quantitative option altogether. The exchange situation in itself cannot be grasped quantitatively; only its outcome of a certain quantitatively determinate exchange ratio is quantitative, and this is because the practice of (ultimately universal) exchange is an abstracting one that abstracts from the qualities of the goods being exchanged, thus reducing them to quantity. The moves and countermoves of the two (or more) exchange players may change the complexion of the exchange situation altogether, vitiating any prospect of necessity. The dyadic interplay is not ruled by necessity at all, but is in itself already the outbreak of freedom, making the *pretensions to power of the one over the other* nugatory.

The generalized or universal dyadic exchange interplay is the market interplay that entwines all the market players and their goods within itself, constituting a moving unity that attains the palpable, reified, singular form of the universal equivalent or money as mediator of exchange in which exchange-value is universally actualized as price. This practically achieved unity in commerce, i.e. in the meeting of the goods for living well, however, does not do away with the differences among the goods, nor does it bind them into a necessary actualization of an inherent exchange-value, but rather allows the free play of the many differences to play itself out in the interplay. The unity of exchange-value as a sociating web of interchanges is hence the *unity of unity and difference* or of the *one* and the *many*. The many are not absorbed in the unity of the one; on the contrary, their free play is enabled precisely by the looseness of the sociating interplay which nonetheless achieves a dynamic, pliable, constantly changing unity.

In the case of exchange-value, therefore, actuality does not proceed beyond contingency to become necessity as the actualization of an essence, and this is so because of the dyadic ontological structure of the exchange situation in which *freedom meets freedom*. The difference (Unterschied, § 144) between the inner essence or matter and the outer, contingent reality of conditions is not brought together in a *ground* that would guarantee *necessity*. Even both players acting in accordance with 'reason' or 'rationally', whatever that might mean (the fictional rational economic actors posited quaintly by economic theory?), would not guarantee with necessity the actualization of an essential exchange-value inherent in the commodities exchanged. It is entirely 'reasonable' for the players to exchange at the rate freely und mutually agreed upon as the (non-pre-determined) *outcome* of their interplay, where 'reason' in this (social) context means only 'in accord with the (dyadic) ontological structure of the exchange situation'. It would also be entirely 'reasonable' for the players to mutually refrain from the exchange if agreement cannot be reached.

Moreover, on the one hand, the players are *not* free in the Hegelian sense of acting with the knowing awareness of an insight into a necessity *insofar* as there is no quantitatively definite exchange-value inhering in the commodities that could be actualized in exchange as a quantitatively definite exchange ratio or price. Their freedom is therefore from this perspective that which Hegel maligns as mere arbitrariness. Then again, however, the players *are* indeed free in the Hegelian sense *insofar* as they act with insight into the dyadic ontological structure of the playful exchange situation, which precisely does not necessitate that a quantitatively definite, inherently predetermined exchange ratio nor even that an actual exchange at all come about, but rather 'necessitates' only that the players play freely with one another, validating each other's freedom of movement, with each player having, from its individual viewpoint, insight only into the *conditions* pertaining to the currently concrete situation of play, which may *necessitate* one strategy of play as being more favourable for that player rather than another. Whether an exchange *actually* takes place nevertheless remains an open contingency depending upon the interplay of freedom with freedom, whose outcome is not necessitated by pre-posited conditions, and whose ostensible arbitrariness and caprice are, in truth, the *truth of interplay* in the Hegelian sense, i.e. the correspondence of the reality of interplay with its ontological concept. What seem to be mere arbitrariness and caprice, because unnecessary, are in truth well-considered moves in the interplay. The ontology of interplay breaks the mould of tight, productionist necessity.

Because the interplay of exchange remains open and does not close together in a necessity, it also cannot be characterized further as a relation of substance (§ 150, in this context: the purported "value-substance" (Wertsubstanz, Marx, MEW23:49) of exchange-value) manifesting itself in its accidents. Such a 'value-substance', if it existed, would be, as Hegel claims for "substance", an *"absolute power"* (*absolute Macht*, § 151), but the unity of such a power is broken already in its originary dyadic ontological structure, and exchange-value is therefore only ever a *relative* power at play with other powers, viz. the potencies of other exchange-values. Nor can this (non-)substance of exchange-value be determined as an "originary matter" or "cause" (Ursache, ursprüngliche Sache, § 153), actively effecting an effect (Wirkung, § 153) as the actuality (Wirklichkeit, § 153) of an actual exchange, because the other exchange-value never merely passively 'suffers' itself to be exchanged. Nor can the Hegelian ontology be saved by positing the interplay of exchange as a relation of *reciprocity* or reciprocal action and reaction (Wechselwirkung, § 155) between two exchange-value substances in which each acts on and reacts to the other, because the action of one exchange-value on another cannot be characterized as one of cause and effect in the first place. Instead we are left with the hitherto untackled task of thinking the *unfathomability of interplay itself* in all its facets.

This has consequences in particular for the ontological concept of (exchange-)value as *the* fundamental concept for Marx's theory of capitalism. Such a concept, in Hegelian terms, would have to be a *"totality* in that *each* of the moments is *the whole* that the *concept* is and is posited as an unseparated unity with the concept" (*Totalität*, indem *jedes* der Momente *das Ganze* ist, das *er* ist, und als ungetrennte Einheit mit ihm gesetzt ist, § 160). These moments of the concept are universality, particularity and singularity. As a free totality, there is no rupture in the unity of the concept.

But what about the concept of exchange-value? One could say, perhaps, that there is a totality of exchange-values, namely, the commodities. The universality of the concept of exchange-value would be particularized into a totality of different, particular, real commodities, each of which being merely a determination of the universal or a "determination of the concept" (Bestimmtheit des Begriffs, *LII* W6:283). This totality of many commodities as exchange-values would again come to the unity of universality and particularity in the singularity of money which embodies value in its universality in a single, real thing which, in turn, mediates between the particularity of particular commodities and their universality as exchange-values. This mediation takes the form of the commodities having a *price* for which they would have to be sold. The pure universality of the concept of exchange-value would thus have "climbed down" to the singular reality of money as the embodiment of exchange-value in a single thing. The Marxian concept of value would thus be shown to be truly of Hegelian provenance, and value could go on to assume the status of an absolute subject, since the Doctrine of the Concept is the domain of free subjectivity, not subject to blind necessity, that culminates in the absolute idea.[74]

Alternatively, the universality of pure value could be differentiated into the totality of particular kinds of commodities, and these kinds of commodities further determined as the singularity of the individual commodities. In the opposite direction, according to the formal con-clusion of the apodictic judgement, each individual commodity, having such-and-such a particular quality (qualifying it as a use-value), would be part of the totality of commodities and therefore also a value. This assumes that being a genuine use-value guarantees a commodity's status also as exchange-value.

But, no matter which of the two schemata of universality, particularity and singularity is applied in this case, such a purported unity and transparency of

---

74 Cf. the work of Christopher J. Arthur on the homologies between the Hegelian *Logik* and the 'logic' of capital. Published to date: *The New Dialectic and Marx's Capital* Brill, Leiden/Cologne/Boston, 2002 hb. 2004 pb. esp. Chapter 5.

the concept of value has to be examined more closely to prevent a precipitous entrance into the inexorable dialectical movement toward the totalizing absolute idea. To this purpose, let us reconsider the simple exchange situation. Already here, the incipient concept of value must be present. The owners or, more neutrally, the 'bearers' of commodities A and B are bargaining over an exchange of their commodity use-values. Or even more primordially, the persons A and B themselves are bargaining over mutually exercising their abilities for each other's benefit. A and B are each interested in the use-value of what the other has to offer, either in 'coagulated' objective form or in the 'liquid' form of live, labouring activity, and the exchange-value of each use-value is its power to exchange for the other use-value. A pair of shoes may be worth ten loaves of bread, or eleven, or twenty. Or A may offer B, I'll make you a pair of shoes if you make me ten loaves of bread. There is nothing inherent in the shoes or the bread themselves, no inherent value, that would necessitate a factual exchange, but rather, A's exchange-value *is* nothing other than xB *if* a transaction comes about at exchange ratio x. If it doesn't come about because, say, B does not really like the shoes, they are then, for the moment, worthless relative to B. A will have to try to bring his shoes (or his shoe-making abilities) into play in another way to have success in the interplay of exchange. If he makes the wrong particular kind of shoes for the prevailing fashion, he may have very little success in the exchange game, and his shoe-making activity, even though it is the exercise of genuine abilities for making perfectly usable shoes, may gain little or no estimation and validation by others in exchange.

If, now, money acts as medium of exchange, this singular thing may be regarded as the universal of value incarnate having the power to exchange, again relatively, for anything offered on the market at such-and-such a price, but such mediation does not obviate the particular use-values from having to be brought into play to actually become exchange-values, and the problem of exchange-value being actualized only in an exchange transaction would only be displaced from another commodity to money. It is therefore wrong to conceive the pure concept of value as being particularized in the totality of commodities of various kinds, because this totality is still only a totality of use-values which may, indeed, be related to each other as representing a division of labour that 'adds up' to an organically differentiated and interconnected totality of use-values of some kind or other.

But a totality of differentiated products or a totality of differentiated labouring abilities still only *becomes* exchange-value within the interplay of exchange itself wherein it *turns out* what each particular commodity product or ability is worth, either in other commodity use-values or monetary price, and the configuration of exchange-values that thus arises is infinitely variable depending upon how the multitude of exchange-players plays, i.e. on how the exchange interplay plays out. Each individual commodity, (or each individual ability), has to *negotiate* its very existence as an exchange-value through its interchange with an *other* commodity (or exercised ability). Prior to the exchange transaction, its exchange-value is merely a possibility depending upon the contingency of its use-value being recognized and esteemed by another. The essence of exchange-value thus revealed in its relativity rather than substantial absoluteness by considering the very simple and primitive exchange situation is not altered when many transactions on myriad markets and mass production are considered. Such complexity only obscures the view of the simple, groundless, 'playful' essence of exchange-value.

5.6   Exchange as core phenomenon of social intercourse: Interchange and interplay

Up until now I have been examining only the exchange of commodity goods with the aim of uncovering its ontological structure as a kind of movement sui generis. In singling out the phenomenon of the exchange of goods, I am not merely following in the footsteps of the tradition starting with Plato and Aristotle of regarding exchange as the elementary kind of social intercourse that sociates human beings. A direct consideration of how we have dealings with each other in taking care of our daily affairs shows just as well that exchange is indeed one of the elementary acts of social intercourse that makes up the complexion of daily life. This observation in itself justifies putting the phenomenon of exchange (barter, bargaining, buying and selling, hiring, trade, commerce) at the centre of attention for initiating the investigation of the ontology of the movement that is sociating life. In the early days of political economy, exchange was even exaggeratedly accorded a quasi-absolute status in the constitution of society, e.g. "Society is purely and solely a continual series of exchanges. [...] *Commerce is the whole of society.*"[75]

This contrasts with a political opinion commonly heard today, according to which society, or 'living', begins only where commerce ends. Nevertheless, I claim to have uncovered a paradigm for *social* ontology that has to be clearly distinguished from production as the paradigm for all of ontological thinking on

---

75 A.L.C. Destutt de Tracy *A Treatise on Political Economy* Georgetown 1817 pp. 6ff, cited in Hayek *LLL2*:186.

movement from its beginnings up to the present day (cf. sections 5.4 and 5.5 above). The ontological structure of exchange, although simple, is more complex ontologically than the phenomenon of production that has ruled onto-theological thinking from its inception. This ontological complexity has as yet untold and unthought consequences for all philosophical and modern scientific thinking, for it brings into play the *mutually estimating interplay* between human beings in their whoness as an as-yet-unaddressed issue for ontological thinking and not merely, as has been the case hitherto, as a topic for philosophical ethics. Traditional ethics itself has lacked a proper grounding in an ontology of sociating movement.

Social ontology investigates the whoness (quissity) of whos in the mutually estimative, sociating movement of social life, in contrast to the traditional ontology of movement applicable to the physical and productive movement of whats in their whatness (quidditas, essence), thereby providing an ontological basis for thinking through social life itself, which has always been the concern of ethics. *Social ontology based on an ontology of mutually estimative sociating movement supersedes ethics in its traditional sense, starting with Aristotle.* It is as if thinking had always skirted arounded the simple, and therefore difficult, questions of social ontology with the characteristic features of its necessary ontology of peculiarly *social* movement, in favour of merely pronouncing (ethically, morally) what should be or criticizing social reality with a view to changing and improving it, whilst leaving the prevailing ontology of productive movement unchallenged and intact, as well as avoiding the ontological questions of whoness vis-à-vis the long established and entrenched ontology of whatness. The bipolar and multipolar essence of exchange, its bi-archy or polyarchy,[76] breaks the mono-archic ontological cast of "productionist metaphysics" (Michael E. Zimmerman[77]) and reopens the realm of future historical possibility on the basis of a social ontology that rests on the alternative paradigm of *exchange* or, employing terms derived from the Greek, *katallaxy*,[78] *allagae* or *synallagae*.

---

76 The signification of 'polyarchy' here differs from its standard dictionary meaning as "The government of a state or city by many: contrasted with monarchy" (OED). The realm of human society, including its polity, is that of a multitude of free, governing starting-points, ἀρχαί, and therefore an interplay and interchange among these many individual sources of free social movement.

77 Michael E. Zimmerman *Heidegger's Confrontation with Modernity: Technology, Politics, Art* Indiana University Press, Bloomington 1990 pp. xv and passim.

78 On the term 'katallaxy' cf. the footnote in Chapter 9.5.

The phenomenon of exchange is richer and more multifaceted than the mere exchange of goods, i.e. the practices of barter, trade, commerce, etc., and indeed it can and must be interpreted *from within the ontological dimension of whoness* as the paradigm of social intercourse pure and simple. For, not only goods (reified whats) are exchanged among people, thus sociating them in social relations in which they effectively serve each other, but people (desiring whos) sociate and maintain social intercourse with one another by exchanging also greetings, smiles, waves, glances, simpers, views, opinions, news, compliments, insults, blows, kindnesses, gifts, sexual favours, etc., etc. They do this in sociating interchanges (μεταβολαί) whose ontological structure for the movement of whos is homologous to that of commodity exchange, a movement of whats. Exchange and interchange are the metabolism of social life, and they are the soil for the freedom of movement of many individual human ἀρχαί.

As Hegel puts it in the language of subject-object metaphysics, "This relationship of will to will is the characteristic and genuine soil in which freedom has *determinate being*" (Diese Beziehung von Willen auf Willen ist der eigentümliche und wahrhafte Boden, in welchem die Freiheit *Dasein* hat. *RPh.* § 71 *Übergang vom Eigentum zum Vertrage*). All social relationships are interchanges of some kind, and the interchange is always, i.e. essentially, embedded in a *mutual estimation of the value* of each other as *who* one is and *what* one has. Such mutual estimation as an existential-ontological structure, of course, includes also deficient and negative forms of estimation such as indifference, derogation and disparagement. The interchange that forms the moving fabric of economic social life, in particular, is a mutual estimation of the value of each other *as who* one is and *what* one has, and that with a view to mutual benefit in the sense of the use-value of what one has to offer each other in the broadest sense, and be it merely interesting conversation.

With regard to the presentation in the preceding sections of this chapter, even the paradigm of the exchange of commodity goods chosen for an exposition of the peculiar ontological structure of interchange and interplay, although well established in traditional socio-political thinking and thoroughly familiar from everyday life, is not the most originary paradigm that could have been chosen. As shown in 5 iv), the exchange of goods involves two pairs of δυνάμεις, or the four terms of commodities-whats, A and B, and their respective desiring who-bearers. The use-values exchanged are embodied, reified in the commodity products, and that they have been produced is presupposed. More elementary and primitive is the exchange simply between two individual whos of their *useful abilities*, their *powers*, in the sense of what each can do for the other by way of exercising their (labour) powers mutually for each other's benefit in providing services for each other. Such a simplification allows it to be seen without obstruction that "what holds everything together" in society on an everyday basis are interchanges in which people *do things for each other.*

Services in the sense of the exercise (ἐνέργεια) of individual powers are more elementary than products, which are the independent end or ἐντελέχεια of the exercise of such powers; the independent, separate (χωριστός) existence of the product as a what is not essential to an economic exchange. Indeed, the exchange of commodity products is *derivative* of the exchange of powers because the products are the object-ive results of the expenditures of individuals' abilities, i.e. their labour powers. Social interchanges thus take the form in the most elementary socio-ontological situation — which could perhaps be called the (ontological, and not merely ontogenetic, historical, chronological) *primal scene of sociation* — of *mutual estimation* of each other's individual *powers* with a view to exercising these powers for each other's benefit. This interplay of mutual estimation and validation also makes the ontological structure of social interchange as a *power play* transparent already on the economic level. What people, i.e. whos, (offer to) do for each other is the simplest manifestation of the power play as an interplay of (the mutual estimation of) powers that has been latently present already from the start in the present investigation of the ontology of whoness, and which forthwith will thematically accompany, either in the foreground or in the background, this socio-ontological inquiry throughout. But to continue with a consideration of interchange in general:

'Interchange' (συναλλαγή) here is a bland, general term for human sociation and intercourse on the level of myriads of interwoven everyday practices. There is always a reciprocity in our interchanges. We do not just meet, but we meet *each other* or *one another*, and that *as who* we are. This 'each other' or 'one another' expresses the reciprocity that is necessarily a part of sociating interchange, and this reciprocity is itself a kind of exchange based on our conducting ourselves toward each other that is always also a *mutually mirroring recognition and estimation* of each other *as whos.* In my conducting myself toward you, I am from the outset *attuned* to how you, in return, conduct yourself toward me, i.e. my conduct toward you is always already reflected in an anticipated reciprocal conduct of you toward me.[79] I can conduct myself toward things, i.e. whats, but a thing cannot conduct itself toward me, and there is no reciprocity

---

79 On Sichverhalten (conducting oneself, comporting oneself), the "Verhältnismäßigkeit der Verhältnisse" (S. 93) among people and other phenomena of Mitsein, cf. Karl Löwith *Das Individuum in der Rolle des Mitmenschen* (1928) reprinted in *Sämtliche Schriften* Bd. 1 ed. K. Stichweh, Metzler, Stuttgart 1981.

of conduct in my relations with things. I also do not expect anything from a thing by way of reciprocity. I can also conduct myself toward animals which in some way or rather behave, sometimes even seeming to behave themselves toward me, but it is moot whether animals have selves at all which would be the presuppostion for their behaving them*selves*.

But my relations with people (whos) are all based on a reciprocity of our conducting ourselves toward each other, even when that conduct is deficient (e.g. impolite or deranged) or displays indifference. The very lack of response on your part when you conduct yourself indifferently toward me, ignoring my very presence, is precisely the deficient reciprocity of your conduct in this case. In my relations with things, by contrast, there can be no indifference on the part of the things I use, because a thing cannot conduct itself toward me or respond to me at all. This difference between my relations with things and my relations with others rests on the fundamental twofold in being between *whatness* and *whoness*, between *quiddity* and *quissity*. From the very start, all relations between human beings must be considered as (sociating) relations between whos, not whats. This simple observation has far-reaching ramifications, as we have already begun to see.

Interchanges can also be,and frequently are, asymmetrical and may even be deficient in lacking reciprocity (e.g. being snubbed). Giving and receiving a gift or assistance is an asymmetrical interchange, but — *pace* Derrida — it is still reciprocal because a gift or assistance offered still has to be *accepted* and can also well be refused. There is an interplay of offering and accepting, and such a reciprocal interplay can be very subtle and delicate, depending on the who-status of each player in the interplay. By contrast, the non-reciprocal interchange of one-sidedly insulting or assaulting someone out of the blue where the one insulted or assaulted has no chance of responding is a deficient mode of interplay which shows, through the absence of reciprocity, just how essentially interchange is based on reciprocity. Being insulted by a stranger suddenly in a public place may be so outside the context of any interchange and so lacking in reciprocity and mutual estimation that it does not even amount to an insult, but only to the ranting some disturbed person *who* need not be taken seriously. Physical assault by a stranger where the one assaulted defends himself is a kind of reciprocal interchange, albeit an involuntary and deficient one aimed at physical negation of the other who through the exercise of physical power that, in this case, is sociating, albeit that the whos are in a sense thus degraded to whats.

Even prior to the reciprocity of our conducting ourselves toward each other, my own conduct is always essentially reflexive, i.e. I conduct *myself*. This self-conduct is always a presentation of myself as somewho, a self-presentation in which I show myself off to my self, in bending back reflectively on myself, and also to others *as* who I am and have cast my self to be (cf. Chapter 3.3.1.5). In conducting myself I am always at the same time mirroring myself reflexively as who I am in my self-understanding, i.e. in the ἰδέα or 'look' of my self. My ways of conducting myself are therefore an ensemble of masks of self-presentation of my self to myself and also to the world of others; they are modes of self-comportment in which I comport myself *with* (com-portare, literally, 'to carry with') the masks of self-presentation that show off who I am. The term 'comportment' will be employed in preference to 'conduct' to emphasize the bearing of masks that define and show off who I am *as* somewho (and not as something). I bear my who-masks with me in all my self-comportment. I cannot comport myself at all without presenting myself in the mask of somewho or other.

Thus even in the most rudimentary interchange there is at the very least a reciprocal exchange of the most formal and non-descript masks in which we present ourselves in how we conduct and comport and bear our selves toward each other. Since I always comport my*self*, no matter how self-alienated and conformist this self-casting may be, this self always has a mode of self-presentation in my comportment, and the same applies to you and everywho else. Our social intercourse is therefore always a reciprocal interplay of mask-presentations that are nothing other than the ways in which we comport ourselves and thus present our selves and show ourselves off as *who* each of us *is*. This showing-off, as set out in Chapter 2, is one side of the ambivalent ἀπόφανσις in its middle voice as ἀποφαίνεσθαι: not only do beings show themselves *as what* they are, but each of us human beings shows off him- or herself *as who* he or she is.

5.6.1 Reciprocally showing off who one is in the interplay of mutual estimation

The reciprocal showing-off of ourselves *as* somewho takes place in all interchange, including even the impersonal or anonymous exchange of things on the market in commercial transactions. Even the buyer and the seller present themselves *as* buyer and seller from within a certain understanding of themselves in their specific occupational who-roles in the exchange. At first and for the most part, occupational roles are the masks of self-presentation in daily life. The seller may be a professional seller whose occupation as somewho is designated as merchant or salesperson or middleman or cashier, etc., and in the exchange relation the seller presents him- or herself *as* a seller, i.e. in the role of seller that defines their whoness in the outline of a certain understood 'look'. Likewise the buyer. This showing-off of who each is in the transaction is an abstract showing-off insofar as only the general roles of buyer and seller, particularized perhaps according to the particular market, occupation, etc. come into view within the transaction, which is usually carried out anonymously, i.e. without addressing each other by proper names. Where the transacting exchange partners give their proper names, these signs of individual singularity function in this context merely formally, as singular designations only, say, for registration purposes or to deliver the goods or to be polite. Singularity itself has no place in a formal, abstract exchange transaction that requires only general roles of self-presentation as somewho. Nevertheless, calling each other by one's proper name is part of the ritual of acknowledging each other *as* somewhos, although in some contexts a 'Good day' or simply a nod or a wave may suffice to politely acknowledge the other's presence.

As shown in preceding chapters, insofar as in all social interchange there is a reciprocal showing-off of who one is, all social intercourse is marked by conducting oneself toward the other *as* somewho or other and vice versa. This means that there is necessarily a reciprocal *estimation*[80] of each other as somewho, no matter how privative, depreciating or indifferent this estimation may be. Any mode of comportment toward others presupposes some kind of estimation of the other, because I have always already presented myself to the other *as* somewho in masks of self-presentation, and any response at all (including even no response) to this self-presentation is a mirror of recognition and estimation. Merely being always-already cast into the world, which is always also a social, shared world, casts me into the mould of whoness and also into the mould of understanding the others as presenting themselves similarly from within the ontological-existential casting of whoness. In any interchange at all, we have a priori *understood* each other as somewho or other and *comported* ourselves toward each other as somewho or other and thus also willy-nilly estimated each other as somewho or other. Thus all sociating interchange is a reciprocal mirroring estimation of who we are in the double sense of both esteeming each other and also sizing each other up in respective who-status. It is not possible to evade the cast of whoness so long as we are human beings cast into the world.

---

80 "Estimation' throughout always in the double sense of "estimating or esteeming" OED. "The action of appraising, assessing, or valuing; statement of price or value; valuation" and "appreciation, valuation in respect of excellence or merit; esteem considered as a sentiment. Phrase, to have or hold in estimation" OED.

Every encounter is a reciprocal acknowledgement of each other expressed merely by a nod or some kind of salute, calling each other by name through to calling
each other names.

At first and for the most part, estimation is in the mode of indifference or the
mere abstract formality of estimation of personhood expressed by comporting
ourselves politely toward each other, which signals *respect* for or at least *distance* from the other as a free human being. This formal recognition in *politeness* is a kind of reciprocal acknowledgement of each other as who that lubricates everyday social intercourse when conducting the business of daily life.
Politeness is the formal mode of recognition of the other as a free human being
in civil society. Behind the mask of politeness there may be hidden a deep indifference toward the other or a mere instrumentalization of the other for the purpose of achieving one's own end (which is the case especially in commercial
transactions), but the formal politeness and friendliness is adequate to lubricate
the intercourse of everyday living, rendering it pleasant enough. Viewed the
other way around, the formal, abstract nature of estimation in commercial
transactions, i.e. the exchange of goods and services, dispenses the parties to
the transaction from having to make any more elaborate or impressive self-
presentations. It is the goods and services and money involved in the transaction that 'do the talking' in the sense that each party is interested in acquiring
what the other has on offer, and is hardly interested in with *whom* the transaction is to be carried out.

An extreme, deficient possibility of mutual mirroring as who in the interplay of estimation is provided by the phenomenon of *narcissism*. This phenomenon is so striking because, although it is derived from the myth of Narcissus
falling in love with his own image in a pool of water, this implies precisely a
lack of mirroring in interchange with a narcissist. In interchange with a narcissist, namely, there is no mutual, reciprocal mirroring play of estimation, because you are the mirror for the narcissist, but he is no mirror for you. He is a
black hole that absorbs all reflected radiation of estimation. The play of showing off who one is becomes unidirectional, instead of being a mutual interplay.

Because all social interchange comes about through individuals' comporting themselves, it is based on human *freedom of movement*, for each of us is free
to comport him or herself in a variety of ways for which bearing we also ineluctably bear *responsibility*, i.e. for which we have to answer. This implies that we
choose the masks and roles of self-presentation in choosing how we comport
ourselves toward others, and that we have the *power* (δύναμις) of choosing such
self-presentations. All comporting-myself presupposes my self as distinct from,
and aware of, the comportment itself. The power of freely being able (Seinkön-

nen, ἀρετή) to choose my masks of self-presentation implies that there is a distance between my self as the governing starting-point (ἀρχή) of choice and my self as the ensemble of who-masks of self-presentation understood as embodied ways of comporting myself. Such a self-reflective distance enables not only the possibility of belonging to my masks of self-comportment, thus shaping my *identity* as the ensemble of self-masks that genuinely belong to me, but also the possibility of presenting my self through bearing masks of self-comportment that do not properly belong to me and therefore fit ill and alienate me from my self in masks adopted from the other (alius) or even in masks that present me distortedly as someone who I am *not* (deception, imposture).

The power of each of us being able freely to choose his or her self-presentation as somewho or other is neither a natural power of self-movement in the Aristotelean sense, nor is it a poiaetic, productive power, again in the Aristotelean sense. Why not? Because the power of self-presentation to others, of choosing the masks in which we show ourselves off *as who* we are, is a self-reflexive (i.e. bent-back-on-the-self) *social* act of sociating interchange embedded in the movement of willy-nilly estimation, but for the most part, as least in today's Western societies, it does not demonstrate power *over* the other, i.e. my self-presentation to others certainly induces estimation on the part of others, no matter how deficient or indifferent or negative (e.g. derogatory) that estimation may be, but because the others in turn are likewise *free* human beings who comport themselves as somewho in showing themselves off as who they are, they are free to respond to my self-presentation in a variety of ways of self-comportment which I am *not able* to control. I can in-duce some kind of estimation in showing myself off, but I cannot pro-duce a desired, intended mode of estimation.

My power of self-presentation does not reach so far as to rule how others respond, in turn, in their self-comportment toward my self-presentation. Others' responses lie outside the ambit of the ἀρχή of my being able to choose my self-presentation masks. The interplay of estimation in mutual self-presentation *as* somewho is thus an interplay of powers that is ontologically isomorphic with the simple bi-archic ontological structure of commercial exchange relations investigated in preceding sections, albeit that it is no longer mediated by reified whats. Whereas in the case of commercial exchange it is essentially the goods, i.e. the whats, that are presented, and the roles assumed and shown off are merely the formal roles of buyer and seller, in the case of other social interchanges, the masks of self-presentation *as* somewho exchanged and mutually estimated are more elaborate, more concrete, more particular and even individual, singular, idiosyncratic. These masks also carry more weight in the mutual estimation.

5.6.2   The interplay of powers of self-presentation – engendering trust

Even in exercising the power to present oneself as somewho in *impressive* ways of comporting oneself, these impressive masks of self-comportment aimed at making an impression on others are only ever an attempt at impressing the others in the desired, intended way. The will to power can indeed assume the form of the will to impress with one's own showing-off. This will to power has the structure of being the starting-point for a change in the other, namely, to leave a desired *impression* as a somewho on the other. Such an impression is a kind of change (μεταβολή) in the other, that will be reflected more or less openly in the other's response, in the way the other comports him- or herself in response to the impressive self-presentation of who-standing. For the most part, it is sufficient that the other give some small sign that one's own impressive self-presentation has been noticed at all, and thus estimated. But there is no guarantee that my will to an impressive self-presentation in choosing my masks for showing myself off as an impressive who will in fact bring forth the desired impression in the other or the others, say, in the form of positive comments of admiration or simply in talking about me. My attempt to impress may not even be noticed at all.

This interplay of social powers of self-presentation is indeed a *power game*, but the game allows no certain, precalculable strategy for winning because the interactors are all free human beings as sources of power of their own self-movement who choose their modes of self-comportment and thus how they respond to others showing themselves off as who they are. This is to be contrasted ontologically, i.e. in essence, with the power of production, i.e. of knowing surely how to causally bring forth a fore-seen, envisaged change in something else and thus an end-product, a topic already investigated in some detail in the preceding sections. The phenomenon of sociating interplay among human beings as essentially (i.e. in their fundamental ontological structure) a power play or, perhaps said best of all, a *power interplay* will be investigated more closely in Chapter 10.

Quite apart from the reciprocal estimation of each other as somewho that is ineluctable in all sociating interchange, there are those practical interchanges in which the interchange concerns *something practical*. In practical everyday life, this something is either the goods involved in an exchange or an issue on which agreement is to be reached in an exchange of views. The former is the paradigm of commercial exchange; the latter is the rhetorical situation of deliberation with a view to action. Since each of the parties to an exchange of goods or views is a free starting-point of action with the power to act one way or the other, agreeing on a common course of action, whether it be a commercial transaction or some other practical project, depends on elevating the individual standpoints of the various parties as free starting-points of action into some kind of intermeshed unity in which goods and money can actually be exchanged or a common course of concerted action can be agreed on the basis of a shared view of how the issue is to be practically approached.

The very freedom of each of the parties as individual ἀρχαί means that agreement does not involve the exercise of power of one over the other but is only possible on the basis of *trust* that an agreement will be kept to. There is an essential element of trust in all practically sociating interchange. Therefore, for an agreement to come about at all, mutual trust must be won and proven through *reliability*. Each of the parties must give *credence* to the other (or others) and *believe* that what has been agreed will actually be performed. In commercial transactions, this credence is called *credit* and the one giving credit in monetary terms is the creditor, i.e. the one who believes in good faith that the other will pay the agreed amount on the agreed date in the future. But the purchaser, too, gives credence in the sense that he or she has good faith that the seller will actually provide the goods (including services) at the agreed time, to the agreed amount, of the agreed quality, etc.

In a deliberative exchange of views on a practical issue, the various views presented must be brought to some kind of consensus through an altercation, through having-it-out with one another in such a way that a common decision can be reached. The altercation itself is an exchange of differing views (δόξαι) on the issue supported by arguments pro and contra, by persuasive πίστεις (proofs) aimed at engendering πίστις, i.e. trust and confidence. Such an engendering of trust in each other is necessary because social intercourse is an interplay of free starting-points each of whom remains in its freedom essentially incalculable for the other. The other becomes calculable only insofar as trust is placed in his binding himself to his word. This is the deliberative rhetorical situation described by Aristotle which is oriented toward the future, as opposed to the judgemental rhetorical situation that is oriented toward assessing actions in the past as just or unjust or the eulogical rhetorical situation that is oriented toward appraising as praiseworthy or blameworthy someone who or something that is present.

In the interchange of a deliberative rhetorical situation (which may relate to a common political, social or business project), the other has to be won over to one's own view through a process of persuasion in which each of the views involved remains fluid. Reaching a consensus view on the issue is not merely a matter of attaining a common truth on the matter but above all of gaining each other's trust and confidence, and reaching a compromise, so that a common will to concerted action can be formed. Each of us must have faith that the other or others are genuinely involved in and committed to the issue and will also keep to the consensus reached. All agreement in a practical situation is based on trust and faith, and practical situations of interchange can only succeed if faith is not broken and each of the parties is reliable. This *reliability*, when demonstrated, in turn forms a further basis of trust, so that trust can be seen as the very element and lubricant of social interchange which also *grows* or can be destroyed and *decay*. In contrast to the *dependability* of things that dependably perform the use to which they are applicable, the *reliability* of other people depends on their fulfilling the faith that has been placed in them by freely acting according to what they have committed themselves to.

Whereas trust plays no part in automated productive movements in which things are subjected to a purely technical process set up to run efficiently, the trust necessary for practical interchanges between human beings is the obverse of the abyssal circumstance that all social interplay among whos is *dangerous* and *risky* in the sense of incalculable, unpredictable and uncertain, because each human who is and remains a free starting-point, a free ἀρχή of its own self-movement or, to cite Kant characterizing freedom as "spontaneity" (Spontaneität), each human being as free has the power, "to begin of itself a state of affairs".[81] To take a felicitous phrase from Adam Smith, "...in the great chessboard of human society, every single piece has a principle of motion of its own...."[82][83]

---

81 "einen Zustand von selbst anzufangen" (KdrV B561), cited in M. Theunissen *Sein und Schein: Die kritische Funktion der Hegelschen Logik* 1980 S. 201.
82 Adam Smith *The Theory of Moral Sentiments* (1759) Part VI, Section II Chapter II, penultimate paragraph p. 343.
83 In his thought-provoking "new statement of the liberal principles of justice and political economy" (sub-title) in the tradition of British moral philosophy, Friedrich A. Hayek misrecognizes the socio-ontological source of the incalculability of social movement that resides in its polyarchic ontological structure. Instead, he attributes this incalculability to an (ontic) ignorance of facts that is made a fundamental tenet of his entire study: "What we must ask the reader to keep constantly in mind throughout this book [...] is the fact of the necessary and irremediable ignorance on everyone's part of most of the particular facts which determine the

The interplay among free powers in the practical situations of everyday life, if it is to be more than merely a chaotic interplay, has to be based on trust and confidence in each other. For practical purposes, whether it be the exchange of goods or the exchange of views in coming to agreement on a course of concerted action, we must have faith and place trust in each other. Such faith as a dimension of human beings' sharing a world comprises the entire gamut of good faith and bad faith and the thoughtless indifference in between. Bad faith is where a show is made of commitment, a promise is made but without the intention of sticking to the commitment or promise.

In all practical interchanges oriented toward future action, whether commercial exchange or united action (as in political deliberative situations), the word given by each of the parties must bridge the gap between the present and the future. This word is a *promise*, the sending-forth (L. pro-mittere) of a word that announces and gives hope to the other or others of the performance of a future action. Whether a word given as bond is a rickety bridge and the consequences thereof will be considered later, in Chapter 10.5, when discussing Hobbes' *Leviathan*. In coming to an agreement in which a future interaction or concerted action is resolved, we must have mutual trust and faith that promises will be kept. Keeping one's word in a defined future is where human reliability lies. The mutual giving of promises is thus a significant part of sociating inter-

---

actions of all the several members of human society. [...] There exists [...] a great temptation, as a first approximation, to begin with the assumption that we know everything needed for full explanation and control" (Hayek *LLL*1:12) A fact, however, is, quite literally 'a thing done or performed' (OED). A fact refers to what has already come into presence and is established as having been actualized. Even knowing all the particular facts (of what has already come into presence) could never allow "the actions of all the several members of human society" to be determined. Why? Because each of these "several members" "has a principle of motion of its own" (Adam Smith), i.e. each is an ἀρχή, and social intercourse is an interplay of free ἀρχαί that is not explicable or determinable in terms of what has been, but is a polyarchic starting-point for reciprocally or mutually or collectively shaping the future in a groundless game arising from polyarchic human freedom. Knowing all the particular facts does not allow future, free action and its results in its polyarchic interplay to be precalculated. Insofar, despite his clear view of the issue of individual freedom, Hayek remains captive to the rationalist paradigm of productivist ontology that he is trying to overcome. He remains so because, like other social scientists, he does not delve into the question concerning the ontology of social 'interaction', which can never be conceived of as the interaction of forces in some quasi-Newtonian manner whose resultant could be computed, but must be seen as the free interplay of mutual estimation and the building of trust among free, human agents as origins of movement through which social intercourse and interaction shapes, unpre-calculably, what comes about in social living, arriving from the future without being the pro-ductive, causal bringing forth by a positing will, individual or collective, autocratic or democratic, or otherwise.

change, and such promises are embedded in the dimension of trust and faith that opens up a bridge enabling the world to be shared among free human beings, each of whom has the power to freely act one way or another, but nevertheless find they also have to act in concert in any common project, or reciprocally in commercial and economic exchange. Without the bridge of faith and trust in its positive modi, individual practical human freedom could not be unified into a common action and practical social interchange would be impossible. A free society characterized by individual freedom of movement thus has as one of its indispensable conditions of possibility established usages of social trust.

5.6.3 Mutual estimation: Personhood, esteem and respect, the power play over who-standing and the possible intimacy between you-and-me

To return to the phenomenon of estimation: The will to power exemplified by the attempt to impress others with one's own self-presentations and the embeddedness of existence in the sociating interchanges of daily life show that existence as who essentially involves self-presentation to others and thus the mirroring of one's own standing as who in the estimation necessarily given by others. All my self-comportment in daily life is more or less a self-comportment also in the eyes of others and is therefore always also a mirroring of my self-stand as who in and through the others, near and far. This circumstance indicates some kind of dependence on how the others mirror who I am in my self-presentation. My very own self-understanding depends in some way on the responsive reflections of estimation from others, and in particular on the estimation by certain 'significant' others. These certain others are those whom I respect, i.e. whom I, in turn, estimate positively with high estimation in the inevitably *mutual* process of estimation. Those whom I estimate highly have more weight in mirroring who I am or can be. Their estimation and recognition of who I am matters most for my stand as self, for my self-esteem. Both with regard to these certain others and in general, entirely privative or indifferent modes of estimation undermine my self-standing, for I am not so independent and autarkic that I could do entirely without affirmative, uplifting estimation of who I am.

The stand I assume as who can be encouraged and firmed by others' estimation; it can be boosted through affirmative reflection in the mirror of the other, just as it can be shaken by derogatory ways of estimating me as somewho that detract from my stand and drag me down, perhaps into depression, by putting me down. My self, my standing as self is therefore co-constituted by the others in sociating interchange, and it is not possible to entirely insulate one's self-stand as who against the mirroring reflected by others' estimation in all its various positive, negative and neutral variants (cf. Chapter 3.3.1). In fact I become who I am *also* in learning how others mirror who I am. This is a possible interpretation of Pindar's famous line in the context of the mirroring interchange of recognition: "Become, learning who you are." (γένοι᾽, οἷος ἐσσι μαθών. 2nd Pythian Ode, line 72).

This ineluctable openness and exposure to estimation by others in the double sense of esteeming and sizing me up makes itself felt above all in my mood, in my attunement as a whole with how I find myself in the world, especially the shared, social world which, in turn, is embedded in the 3D-temporal clearing. As a self, I always already *feel* some way about my *self*, either uplifted or downcast. This self-feeling is not just a self-reflexive feeling concerning myself as some kind of ego-point or inner self-consciousness, but the globalized, totalized feeling of how I currently am and find myself resonated in the world. The degree of dependency of my feeling about myself on others' estimation does indeed, in turn, depend on my self-confidence, on the strength of my self-standing, and the resonant sensitivity to estimation by others is expressed by saying that I am thin-skinned or thick-skinned, i.e. that I am more or less permeable to the mirroring of others' estimation. Feeling good or bad about oneself is ontically one of those entirely banal, ubiquitous and familiar phenomena of everyday living, but its ontological underpinnings in whoness (a sui generis mode of being) have hitherto remained invisible in the blinding light of obviousness. My self as somewho vibrates moodfully with the time-clearing of world, whereas whats lack ontologically such vibrant temporal sensitivity.

In the general sociating interchanges of daily life, estimation usually takes the form of abstractly formal recognition of each other as persons, whose importance for sharing a world with each in civility is not to be under-estimated. We comport ourselves toward each other politely, i.e. respecting the social forms of the polity, which means, in particular, that we do not in general attack or undermine each other's self-standing in our dealings with each other. In commercial transactions in particular, which are based on some kind of mutual satisfaction and gain to be achieved by the transaction, the mode of mutual estimation is for the most part friendly and polite, for this kind of formal, affirmative estimation lubricates everyday intercourse and the mutual satisfaction of what we want from each other. This formal politeness and friendliness themselves indicate just how much the self-standing as who of the actors in everyday life depends on the mirroring in the inevitable estimation given and taken in everyday social intercourse.

For the most part, we do not *touch* each other in our self-stands in our daily intercourse. Our encounters for the most part preserve a distance guaranteed by the formal estimation of each other as persons. But there are also closer encounters in which the interplay of estimation touches us and affects us in our self-standing *against our will*. Such an encounter may be merely an exchange of glances. Such a momentary glance is a mode of estimation, of estimating mirroring the other. The glance can have erotic import, thus boosting my self-stand in an uplifting feeling, or the glance can be a 'look to kill' that tendentially undermines my self-esteem and may even trigger some downcast mood. The exposure to the interplay of estimation in some mode or other that constitutes one essential aspect of sharing the world with others within the cast of whoness is the basis on which familiar, banal phenomena such as the striving for honour or fame or celebrity-status at first become ontologically comprehensible. Only by explicitly understanding the whoness of human beings in contradistinction to the whatness of things can we begin to understand the peculiar interplay of human sociating interchanges (μεταβολαί). The ineluctable daily game of estimation in relations with others and the inevitable exposure to how I am mirrored by others opens the possibility of my being touched in my interplay with an other. The other touches me in my self-standing often in a scarcely present, fleeting in-between. Even the exchange of words or glances with a stranger can touch me in a fleeting moment in which the other becomes a momentary 'you'.[84]

As somewhos we human beings are continually casting ourselves into the future, thus defining who we are or could be and one day may be. The situation in which we find ourselves, into which each of us has been individually cast, is always the starting-point for such self-casting. The self-definition achieved in casting yourself into the future can never amount to a substantial, standing presence, even though to *be* somewho means to be constantly engaged in coming to a stand as who you are by showing yourself off above all through your abilities, i.e. your individual powers, in how your can cast and mould yourself through future actions. Each of us remains an ongoing, insubstantial self-casting that has always already been cast and, as such an open clearing for the presencing of world in striving to show ourselves off and define who we are through mutually estimating interplay, we remain essentially substanceless, lacking enduring stand, almost nothing at all. In other words, the presence of individualized human being in its self-presentation is a moment in the conjunc-

84 Cf. my *Worldsharing and Encounter* 1997/2010 and *Phänomenologie der Männlichkeit: kaum ständig noch* 1999, noting that kaum ständig noch means "barely still standing".

ture of beenness (yesterness[85]) and future, striving to gain a momentary self-stand (cf. Heidegger *GA*22:270) as who.

Furthermore, the self-casting each of us necessarily continually engages in takes place in the interplay of estimation with others. Only in such mutually mirroring interplay does each of us come to define a *self* as somewho. Our encounters with each other are always an interplayful joint presencing in nothingness in which each of us seeks moving self-definition in the mirror of the other in which each of us comes momentarily to a stand that is experienced above all moodfully. Our standing presence as selves is always a who-stand on recall that is dissolving from one moment to the next and is thus being continually temporally generated in an ongoing striving, alleviated only by the standing presence of esteemed works and achievements that our able actions may bring forth, thus affording some degree of permanence to our reputational stance.

A lasting relationship between you and me is constituted only within a continually regenerated, refreshed positive mode of mutual estimation of each other in our respective standings as who and, on the whole, a sheer, uplifting enjoyment of each other's presence. Such a relationship must be borne by a mutual *respect* and *esteem* for each other, especially each other's *abilities*, and a mutual *attentiveness* to each other's world predicament. Such respect, esteem and attentiveness enable a closeness that for the most part has no place in everyday social life. Mirroring each other by way of esteem, i.e. by valuing highly who the other is in his or her self-standing, is the precondition for our coming close in a relationship of you-and-me in which interplay assumes a very different hue and warmth. Indifference and derogatory modes of estimation destroy the possibility of you-and-me. In general social intercourse, one is on one's guard and maintains a distance to protect one's own self-standing against the unkindnesses of those who would bring one down. For the power to show off who one is, to impress the others with one's own self-stand and to stand as high as possible is more often than not expressed in the striving to put others down in order to stand higher oneself. Since all standing as somewho is social, it is also relative, and therefore a higher who-status can be achieved in many situations by putting others down. This struggle over the altitude of one's own who-standing arises out of the vertical structure of the dimension of whoness itself, inducing a self-defensiveness and distance in everyday sociating interchanges.

---

85 From 'yester' "Of or belonging to yesterday" OED.

6   Justice

6.1   Justice as a fundamental social phenomenon of having one's fair share (Aristotle) – Strauss' misconception of ontological origins – The goods of living: valuable things and esteem – Ongoing competitive interplay estimating each other's abilities

I take up Aristotle once again for a treatment of justice as a crucial aspect of social intercourse, not simply because this is one of the points of departure for all Western thinking on justice, but above all because Aristotle treats the phenomenon in a very direct, clear and simple way in Book V of the *Nicomachean Ethics*, the very same book in which his thinking-through of money and exchange is to be found. For Aristotle, justice is concerned with human practice and action, and the habitual acquired dispositions (ἕξεις) which give rise to action, *always considered in relation to others* (πρὸς ἕτερον V i. 1129b27, 1130a3, 8, 13), i.e.. justice is concerned with interaction, interchange, interplay among individuals, with "operationes quae sunt ad alterum".[86] It should therefore be underscored at the outset, that justice is a social phenomenon applicable to the sociation of people living together in a community sharing a world, including the interplay between individuals living in different communities (in particular, trade and commerce).

There are two closely related (σύνεγγυς 1129a27) senses of justice and injustice which Aristotle examines: acting outside the law (παράνομος 1129a33) and taking more than one's fair share (πλεονέκτης καὶ ἄνισος 1129a34). Injustice in this second, more particular sense, Aristotle writes, is motivated by the "pleasure of gain" (ἡδονὴν τὴν ἀπὸ τοῦ κέρδους 1130b4) and is directed toward gaining "esteem or goods or safety" (τιμὴν ἢ χρήματα ἢ σωτηρίαν 1130b2). Conversely, justice is concerned with the fair and equitable allotment of goods in the context of striving to gain what is good for one's life in social interplay with others, on the one hand, and striving to avert what is deleterious for one's life, on the other. Such a twofold striving of attraction and repulsion could be called the striving to win in the game of life, and human being itself could be characterized as the striving to be a *winner*. But what is good for one's own life — in so-

---

[86] "For the use of this term by the late Spanish schoolmen see C. von Kaltenborn *Die Vorläufer des Hugo Grotius* Leipzig 1848 p. 146. The conception of justice being confined to action toward others however, goes back at least to Aristotle, *Nicomachean Ethics* V i." Hayek *LLL*1:101, 170.

https://doi.org/10.1515/9783110617504-006

called win-lose situations — may be gained at the cost of curtailing or harming what is good for another person's life or the life of the community, and conversely, averting what is damaging to one's own way of living may be achieved at the cost of harming someone else or the community as a whole. So all justice in Aristotle's conception has to do with the allotment, one way or another, of what is beneficial or deleterious for a good life among those living with one another in a polity. The allotment of what is beneficial and deleterious, in order to be just, must be equitable and fair (ἴσος 1129a35).

Along with abidance by the law which upholds customary usage (νόμιμος 1129a34), the fairness or equitableness of allotment of the beneficial and the deleterious, the goods and bads of living, thus lies at the core of Aristotle's conception of justice. Anyone who strives to have more than their fair share of the good at the expense of others, or who strives to take less of the bad to the detriment of others, is unfair and thus unjust. The unjust person gains an advantage (πλεονεξία 1129b9) at the expense of another or others and so gets more (πλεονεκτεῖν) unfairly. The unjust member of the polity is an unfair winner motivated by the will to have more (πλέον ἔχειν, πλεονεξία 1129b9) than their fair and equitable share. To be just in this sense is to practise what is "simply always good" (ἁπλῶς ἀεὶ"ἀγαθά 1129b3) and not what is good for "someone" (τινὶ 1129b3), i.e. for oneself. In this conception of injustice as striving to have more than one's fair share, Aristotle echoes Plato's thoughts on the tendency for men to be unjust "because of the striving to have more which every being by its nature pursues as a good, whereas by the force of law it is led aside to esteeming what is fair." (διὰ τὴν πλεονεξίαν, ὃ πᾶσα φύσις διώκειν πέφυκεν ὡς ἀγαθόν, νόμῳ δὲ βίᾳ παράγεται ἐπὶ τὴν τοῦ ἴσου τιμήν. Plat. *Rep.* 2.359c).

The other, closely related and more general meaning of justice is action in accordance with the law (νόμος), law, however, not being posited arbitrarily by the legislature, but itself in accordance with "what brings forth and guards happiness and the parts thereof in the political community" (τὰ ποιητικὰ καὶ φυλακτικὰ τῆς εὐδαιμονίας καὶ τῶν μορίων αὐτῆς τῇ πολιτικῇ κοινωνίᾳ 1129b19). And what is good for the polity is what has also become custom and habitual usage in that community such as not running away in battle, not committing adultery and not speaking badly about other people (cf. 1129b21ff), so it can be seen that for Aristotle, the justness of acting in conformity with the laws is based more deeply on practice in conformity with virtuous, excellent, able (ἀρετή 1129b26) action towards others as established by custom and usage. Therefore the deeper meaning of law (νόμος) is custom and usage (also a signification of νόμος) practised habitually for the sake of the happiness of the political community as a whole or, as we could also put it, for the sake of sharing the world with one another fairly, beautifully.

To *habitually practise such usages in the interplay with others* is to be *ethical* in the originary sense of the word. Usages are practices rooted in tradition, in what has been passed down from ancestors, and which are regarded as good, valuable, useful in the first place because they continue tradition, i.e. a traditionally good way of life that has proven itself over time. The underlying sense of justice, however, remains throughout: acting fairly within the bounds of what does not harm others and is good for the whole community, and not simply to one's own advantage, as is shown by the example of the law forbidding a man to run away in battle, for desertion amounts to taking less than one's fair share of what is detrimental to life at the cost of the community as a whole.

There nevertheless remains a tension between injustice regarded as breaking the law and custom, and having an inequitable share of the goods and harmful things of life, which Leo Strauss has investigated under another title in his book *Natural Right and History*.[87] According to Strauss, philosophy arises as the discovery of nature ("The discovery of nature is the work of philosophy" p. 81), and political philosophy emerges as the discovery of natural right in which justice is sought in an investigation and questioning of human nature, as opposed to the "primeval identification of the good with the ancestral" (p. 86). Justice conceived of as conformity to law and custom is based on an acceptance of authority, especially, originally, divine authority, which must remain unquestioned if law and custom as handed down by tradition are to be experienced as just. But philosophical questioning "will prove to be the quest for what is good by nature as distinguished from what is good merely by convention" (p. 86), i.e. good merely through conformity with traditional usage.

Strauss does not make any clear conceptual distinction between right, good, justice in his book, but uses the terms synonymously in various contexts. He characterizes the philosophical quest for natural right as the "quest for the 'principles' of all things and this means primarily the quest for the 'beginnings' of all things or for 'the first things'" (p. 82), where these "first things" are (mis)understood *exclusively* in a chronological or ontogenetic sense "for, when speaking of nature, the first philosophers meant the first things, i.e. the oldest things; philosophy appeals from the ancestral to something older than the ancestral" (p. 91f). In interpreting "principles" (ἀρχαί) in an exclusively chronological sense of linear, successive time, Strauss overlooks the more fundamental, philosophical sense of ἀρχή effective in philosophical thinking and explicated

---

87 Leo Strauss *Natural Right and History* University of Chicago Press, 1953, abbreviated *NRH*.

by Aristotle as "whence something is first known" (ὅθεν γνωστὸν τὸ πρᾶγμα πρῶτον *Met.* Delta 1 1013a14), for, philosophy is concerned with knowing things as derived from their governing 'first principles' in the *ontological* sense and not merely as descended from chronological origins in an ontic, ontogenetic sense. In understanding the quest for the "first things" of natural right in a chronological sense throughout his investigation, Strauss, like so many others, displays his ignorance of the ontological difference, considering only chronological beginnings of human nature, not only when discussing the modern natural right tradition starting with Hobbes, which does indeed proceed from some 'state of nature' for humankind understood as chronologically prior, but also in his exposition of the Greeks.

> In order to arrive at a clear distinction between the natural and the conventional, we have to go back to the period in the life of the individual or of the race which antedates convention. We have to go back to the origins. With a view to the connection between right and civil society, the question of the origin of right transforms itself into the question of the origin of civil society or of society in general. This question leads to the question of the origin of the human race. (p. 95)

It should be noted that this passage occurs in the chapter entitled "Origin of the Idea of Natural Right" dealing with the ancient Greeks. Strauss even explicitly rejects a non-chronological, ontological understanding of the quest for the ἀρχή in referring to § 258 Note of Hegel's *Rechtsphilosophie*: "What is important, we have been told, is 'the idea of the state' and in no way 'the historical origin of the state'" (p. 96), claiming that "this modern view is a consequence of the rejection of nature as the standard" (p. 96). But then everything hangs on how "nature" is understood. Strauss obviously understands nature in an ontic-chronological way as that which is oldest:

> The philosophic quest for the first things presupposes [...] that the first things are always and that things which are always or are imperishable are more truly beings than the things which are not always. (p. 89)

He thus does not ponder that Greek φύσις is another name for being, and that being, or more precisely, the beingness of beings (which is not a being, an entity) is called idea in both Plato's and Hegel's philosophies. The idea, in turn, can only be seen by the mind's regarding the ontological difference. Being itself cannot be comprehended merely ontically as the "oldest things" and therefore, natural right too, as the philosophical concept of right, cannot be regarded as knowable through the investigation of chronological human origins. With regard to the question of justice, this means that Strauss indeed rightly draws attention to the tension between justice understood as conformity to convention as handed down from venerable ancestors and the questioning of that tradition set in train by philosophical thinking that is not content to simply accept tradition on authority, but rather poses the ontological *question* concerning justice, as in Plato's *Republic*. This tension corresponds to the distinction in Aristotle between justice conceived as conformity to law and custom on the one hand, and 'having one's fair share' on the other, but the philosophical conception of justice as fair apportionment is not derived from any consideration of the chronological origins of humankind, as Strauss would like to have it. Rather, as Hegel puts it in the passage from which Strauss himself cites, "philosophical contemplation is concerned only with the *thought concept*" (Die philosophische Betrachtung hat es nur mit [...] dem *gedachten Begriffe* zu tun. *RPh.* § 258 Note), and this thought conceives the beingness of the thing thought, in this case, justice, which resides in the phenomenon of interplay among human beings sharing life with one another.

Strauss, like almost all others today, confuses ontology with ontogenesis, or rather, again like most others today, he is entirely oblivious to the ontological difference vital to genuine philosophical thinking. One could even say, more pointedly, that Strauss — like countless others, including the so-called cutting-edge thinkers of our time, not to mention social scientists and historians — misuses the all-purpose conception of linear, successive time counted off movement like a washing-line to hang his narrative on it. Today's philosophy is light years removed from posing the question concerning time itself or even feeling ever so slightly the need to do so. To do so would require not only seeing the ontological difference between beings and their beingness, but gaining insight into being itself *as* the open clearing of 3D-time.

Hegel's approach applies just as much to Aristotle's investigation of justice in the *Nicomachean Ethics*. Both thinkers have the lived phenomenon of justice itself in view for theorization, contemplation. The concept of justice as the fair apportionment of what is good for or detrimental to living has to be seen as arising from a consideration of men living together in society for the sake of living well. This living together is interplay, either directly or indirectly, with one another, i.e. a mode of kinetic being of human beings, and as such depends on how human nature, i.e. human being itself, is conceived. Human being itself has to be conceived inter alia as a practical relation to the goods of life (where 'goods' should be conceived so broadly as to include even what is bad for human living). These goods are in the first place χρήματα, i.e. what is useful for living, but also what enhances living in being appreciated and esteemed and honoured by others (τιμή) in the course of practical, everyday interplay. Esteem is a good whose being depends essentially on human beings' living together, i.e. it is a good of shared human living itself, and that it can be a good at all says something about human being itself as a desire for *estimation* by others. Such estimation makes sense only if human being itself is seen as *whoness*. To say that human being is 'by nature' a ζῷον πολιτικόν is to say, inter alia, that human being is a striving for estimation by others in *being* somewho, as investigated in Chapter 5.6, not merely a so-called 'political animal', which is one standard rendering of Aristotle's famous definition. Through the mirror of estimation in ongoing interplay with others, human beings come to stand *as who* they are. Such a philosophical insight into τιμή as a mode of human sociating being has nothing at all to do with a consideration of chronological historical origins. Rather, to adequately conceptualize esteem and honour as a good for living well requires explicitly working out an ontology of whoness to complement the ontology of whatness within which the 'goodness' of the material goods of life is situated. Strauss' ontic-chronological approach to "natural right" is not up to posing the pertinent socio-ontological questions concerning justice. The phenomenon of "natural right" itself does not come conceptually into sight throughout his treatise.

The fair allotment of the goods (and bads) of life can be broken down, as has been shown, into *what* human beings *have* (ἔχειν) and enjoy by way of material goods (χρήματα) and the estimation (τιμή, esteem, being valued, social standing, reputation, honour, public office, etc.) of *who* they *are*. Justice therefore concerns the *relation* to, i.e. the interplay with, things and others and is never reducible simply to the moral rightness of action where this action proceeds from a subject in itself as the bearer of that action, nor to the compliance with commandments, nor to the ostensible interiority of conscience. To understand justice as such an interplay with things and others, in turn, requires that the ontology of whatness (what things are) and whoness (who people are) be clearly distinguished. The being of things is what they are good for, and the being of people is, in the first place, their goodness in the sense of ability of some kind (a good artisan, a good statesman, a good entrepreneur, a good mediator, a good host, etc.) as exercised in their interplay with others.

The goodness of things is understood in their being valued, estimated, just as the goodness of human beings is understood and estimated in their being esteemed. The value of things therefore depends on their being understood by human understanding in their usefulness in the broadest sense, whereas the value of people residing in their abilities depends on how these abilities are understood and estimated. Because the 'thing' valued in the latter case is a human being and therefore also a self, there is always a relation between self-esteem and how one is estimated and esteemed by others, even though this relation may be entirely a misrelation, and even though one's self-esteem can require that one stems one's self-stand steadfastly against the estimation given or refused by others. Because human beings are selves reflected back on themselves and also from the world, and social relations are always the interplay of mirroring, mutual estimation, the ontology of whoness is situated, grammatically speaking, primarily in the interplay of first and second persons, whereas the traditional ontology of whatness is situated, grammatically speaking, in the third person.

Since material goods are generally valued by way of the market through their reified, monetary value, and the provision of material goods on the market could be regarded as the provision of a service to those who will finally use the goods by all those who have contributed in some way to producing the good in question, one could say that the value placed on material goods in the market place is, indirectly, in large part (apart from the valuing of the Earth) a value-estimation of the services or labours provided by others to furnish those goods. Insofar, the valuation of material goods through the market could also be regarded indirectly as an estimation and valuing of the labouring abilities of those providing the goods and thus as a form of social estimation in which others are esteemed in a down-to-earth utilitarian sense of having provided something useful and valuable for daily living. If justice is understood in a primary sense as the fair allotment of the goods of life, then all justice must be seen in the light of the process of estimation of each other in sociating interplay and above all in how the abilities of people are mutually esteemed. Even something so banal as acquiring, owning and enjoying a loaf of bread is, indirectly, an act of valuing and esteeming not only the baker's able labour which has provided the service of bread-baking but also, in part, the able labour of all those who have contributed to providing the service of oven-making, etc.

The Greek phenomenon and concept of τιμή applies not just to people, but also to things. Τιμή has a whole range of meanings: esteem, honour, public office, recognition, dignity, magistracy, reward, estimate, value. The basic trait of τιμή is valuing, of being esteemed as having a value. Both material goods and persons can have τιμή. This means nothing other than that they are both valued as goods of living. This observation enables a deeper phenomenological insight into the essential connection between the economic exchange of goods and the interchange of estimation and thus into the ontological ties between whatness and whoness. The linch-pin is that both goods and human beings are values and are valued, esteemed in the interchanges of daily life, of sociating kinesis.

The exchange of goods is a mutual valuing and estimating of what the other possesses, and these estimations are brought into equivalence and realized when an exchange is practically carried out. But, as shown above, all estimation of the value of goods on the market can be regarded as an indirect estimating in large part (i.e. leaving aside nature's contribution valued as ground-rent and finance capital's contribution valued as interest; cf. viii) below) of the labouring abilities of all those who have contributed in some way — including the production-line worker, the truck driver, the sales manager, the store manager, the advertising staff, the executive management of the various companies involved, etc. — to making the product available on the market. What is given in exchange for material goods (usually money of some kind) is in a literal sense a *token of esteem* for the abilities of all those whose labouring activities contributed in some way to providing the commodity product.

If we now bracket off this mediation, it becomes apparent that the basic form of esteem that goes on in daily interchanges is the mutual estimation of each other's *abilities* which are ultimately 'honoured' in money being paid for them or in something else of value being given in exchange for their use in being actually exercised. This is everyday ἀγάπη or charity, Latin caritas, meaning 'love founded on esteem' (OED), being one of the translations of Biblical ἀγάπη, but this ἀγάπη is a mutual esteeming based on mutual benefit, not the traditional 'one-way' understanding of charity. Seen from the perspective of whonness and who-status, this means that the basic way we come to stand with self-esteem as somewho in social life is in having our *abilities* estimated and esteemed. This is charity in a genuine sense.[88] Our abilities, as powers or δυνάμεις to perform a valuable service or to bring forth something valuable in use, are the core of our 'goodness', and this goodness becomes manifest in the sociating interplay of mutual estimation.

The prosaic way in which this estimation takes place for the most part is that we are paid for hiring out our abilities, whatever they may be, in the service of others. Economic activity, which consists in large part of market exchanges, is thus the primary 'charitable' theatre in which people come to stand as who they are in having their abilities esteemed by receiving remuneration for them. Conversely, the failure to have one's abilities estimated and esteemed in the prosaic form of monetary payment for them is a blow to one's stand as somewho. The refusal of estimation (e.g. unemployment) is also a kind of estimation, namely, a deficient kind, and this interplay undermines self-esteem. The self has to have attained a more or less independent self-stand in order not to be

---

88 This understanding of charity is compatible with the ideas of Muhammad Yunus.

entirely dependent upon esteem from others and to maintain self-esteem in one's own abilities despite refusal of their estimation.

Even apart from remuneration, having one's abilities esteemed in the interplay of social life constitutes the core movement in the *worldplay of whoness*, and this esteem of one's abilities mostly assumes the form of having the actions performed or the products brought forth by one's abilities esteemed, not necessarily in money, but, say, in the form of public or private praise. The whatness of valuable things is thus taken back into the whoness of valuable human beings with valued abilities, and social living, including economic life, can then be seen for what it is: *an ongoing interplay of estimating and esteeming each other's abilities*.

Furthermore, since there is a *multiplicity* of human beings involved in this ongoing interplay of sociating kinesis, the striving to have one's abilities esteemed by others is always also *competitive*. One strives to have one's abilities esteemed *more highly* than others. This may take the prosaic form of striving to have one's abilities more highly *remunerated* than others. One's who-status is in any case always a standing higher or lower than others' who-stands, i.e. it is comparative. The interplay of everyday social life thus reveals itself to be a competitive power struggle in which individuals show themselves off in their abilities that are estimated and esteemed in a *contest* of social estimation.

This insight into the phenomenal connection between estimated valuable goods and esteemed valuable abilities will be important when further considering the concept of justice.

6.2 Distributive and commutative justice

Apart from the general understanding of justice as habitually practising interplay with others in conformity with the law and custom, Aristotle has basically two kinds or 'looks' (εἶδος 1130b31) of justice related to not having more than one's fair share (πλεονέκτης 1130a27) relative to others (πρὸς ἕτερον), namely, *distributive justice* (ἐν ταῖς διανομαῖς 1130b31), and *corrective justice* (also called *commutative* justice cf. OED) in sociating interchanges (τό ἐν τοῖς συναλλάγμασι διορθωτικόν δίκαιον 1131a1), especially contractual transactions. Corrective justice is concerned with correcting injustice or unfairness arising in the συναλλάγματα, i.e. commutations or interchanges, between people. These interchanges may be a business transaction, i.e. a contract for the exchange of material goods, or the interchange may be an exchange of insults in which social who-status is attacked and injured. A third candidate for a type of justice is reciprocity, i.e. retaliation or 'suffering in turn' (τὸ ἀντιπεπονθὸς 1132b21) which, however, is only a hybrid of distributive and corrective justice because it involves a proportionality (as in distributive justice) rather than an equality in an interchange (as in commutative justice; see below).

The primary type, kind or 'look' (εἶδος 1130b31) of justice in the narrower sense that presents itself to view is distributive justice which lies "in the distributions of esteem, goods and other divisible goods to those sociated [i.e. citizens] in the polity" (ἐν ταῖς διανομαῖς τιμῆς ἢ χρημάτων ἢ τῶν ἄλλων ὅσα μεριστὰ τοῖς κοινωνοῦσι τῆς πολιτείας 1130b31). To be just, this distribution (or apportionment, allotment) must be fair and equitable. Fair distribution, according to Aristotle, does not mean that each person gains an equal share, but that the distribution is according to the worth (κατ' ἀξίαν 1131a24) of each citizen. The criteria for personal worth are specified as free birth, wealth, nobility of birth and ability/excellence (ἐλευθερία, πλοῦτος, εὐγενεία, ἀρετή 1131a27ff). Just distribution is thus distribution proportionate to the worth of each person. The first criterion, free birth, can refer only to a potential for freedom bestowed on those born free, because individual freedom itself can only be played out in the game of life itself, which is necessarily an interplay with others. The last criterion, personal worth, ἀρετή, i.e. ability and excellence or attained accomplishment, is explicitly related to aristocrats (ἀριστοκρατικοί 1131a28), but this is aristocracy in the ancient Greek sense of the rule of the best, and these best are worthy on the basis of merit, i.e. worth based on individual excellence. The word 'merit' itself is of Greek origin: μέρος, 'share', thus 'just desert'. The individual of merit, being of greater worth, would thus also justly deserve a greater share of the goods of life, which is an interpretation that also makes sense in the modern age insofar as individual merit is esteemed and rewarded. Aristocracy hence really means meritocracy.

The four dimensions of personal worth are thus laid out as simply having been born free, which in the democratic modern age applies to every human being (the age of Here Comes Everybody, cf. the Universal Declaration of Human Rights); wealth, which depends on the outcome of economic striving (in which also luck plays a role); nobility of birth or well-bornness, which depends only upon the family lineage into which an individual has been cast; and individual excellence and merit, which could be regarded as a quintessence in which the first three criteria may conspire to bring forth an outstanding human being who has worth and merit in him- or herself and therefore also justly deserves high estimation.

The just distribution of the goods of social life, notably esteem and wealth, for Aristotle, therefore depends on both the worth of the goods and that of the persons and thus involves "at least four terms" (ἐν τέτταρσιν ἐλαχίστοις

1131a19, 32, 1131b10) among which a proportionality and thus a kind of equality must prevail if the distribution is to be just. The worth of the goods "possessed by and allotted to" (ἔχωσι καὶ νέμωνται 1131a24) A in proportion to A's worth measured by some yardstick such as free birth, wealth, noble birth or merit must be equal to the worth of the goods "possessed by and allotted to" B in proportion to B's worth as measured by the same yardstick. Or more concisely, the goods of life are justly apportioned according to merit. The appearance of this quadruple in Aristotle's discussion of justice signifies that social relations have a more complex ontological structure than that of τέχνη ποιητική, which can be grasped ontologically as a single δύναμις and ἀρχή residing in a maker in relation to something to be made, i.e. as a unidirectional, bipolar, power relation involving only two terms. This has been shown in Chapter 5 with regard to both commodity exchange relations and social interchange in general, which are kinds of sociating intercourse among members of society in contradistinction to an holistic social distribution organized according to the particularization of a whole into an organic totality.

Moreover, the way in which both things (χρήματα) and persons manifest themselves of themselves in the sociating interplay must be in terms of their value and worth (ἀξία), for otherwise it would not be possible to form a proportion. Ontologically, the whoness of whos is hence tacitly presupposed and understood alongside the whatness of whats. In the Greek experience of things and men there is no split between some such thing as an 'objectively neutral view' and a 'subjectively coloured', 'valued-laden view', but rather, in daily life, things show up and persons show themselves off *as* what they are good for and thus *as* what they are worth. In considering the just distribution of the goods of life it is thus insufficient to consider only the valuableness of the goods themselves, i.e. their beingness as whats. The beingness of whos of the members of society among whom the goods of life are distributed must also be explicitly laid out, a task and challenge hitherto neglected. Hence, in connection with the phenomena of justice, too, this calls for an ontology of sociated being, i.e. of whoness, to explicitly conceptualize the standing of sociated human beings in their who-status. The above four Aristotelean criteria can be regarded as four possible measures of social standing in the dimension of whoness with the first — the equality of being born (potentially) free — and the fourth — individual ability, excellence and merit — being the criteria 'self-evidently' most applicable to our own times.

In the case of the remaining principal kind of justice, *corrective* justice (διορθωτικόν V iv 1131b25), which operates in sociating interchange, i.e. in transactions or commutations with one another (ἐν τοῖς συναλλάγμασι 1131b25), the fairness, and thus the justness, of the dealing does not depend on the worth of the persons involved in the intercourse (they are all of equal worth; the playing field is level), but simply upon whether one of the parties has inflicted an injury such as fraud, theft, calumny or adultery on the other. The parties involved are themselves regarded as equal (ὡς ἴσοις 1132a6), i.e. abstractly equal as persons. A just allotment of the goods involved does not follow from a 'geometrical' equality of the proportions of the value of the goods to each person's individual worth, but depends only on the 'arithmetical' equality of the values involved in the interchange, with neither party in the interchange having harmed the other through an unfair exchange, where exchange here includes such one-sided and deficient acts as theft, vandalism, slander, public insult, etc. in which one party is only a victim and not an active participant in a transaction, as is the case in the phenomenon of fraud. Justice here involves rectifying by means of restitution the injury through which the other party has made a gain (κέρδος 1132a13) and the other has suffered a loss (ζημία 1132a14), thus correcting this imbalance by reinstituting equality of values.

The judge mediates this correction by dividing up the 'goods' in question once again in an equitable way. This is a kind of finding of the mean through dividing into halves (δίχα 1132a31), for which reason Aristotle provides an etymology of what is just (δίκαιον 1132a31) from halving, and relates the judge (δικαστής 1132a32) to the 'halver' (διχαστής 1132a33) in his activity of redividing the shares so as to rectify and re-establish equality in which parties in interchange with one another "have their own" (ἔχειν τὰ αὑτῶν 1132a28, 1132b18). Thus, in both distributive and corrective justice, justice consists in the fair and equitable allotment of goods in the broadest sense of what is good for living so that the members of society each enjoy "their own", i.e. what is rightly due to them, what they deserve.

A modification of corrective justice are exchange transactions for material goods and services in which a proportionate reciprocity has to prevail if the exchange is to be fair and thus just. Reciprocal justice, or fair give and take, has already been discussed above (Chapter 4.5) in connection with exchange and money. Simple reciprocity involves *retaliation, retribution* or giving back an injury just as one has suffered it in an interchange with someone, and Aristotle will not allow that this simple 'paying back' is just, because the gravity of an injury depends on (the status of) who performed it or whether the injury was done deliberately or by mistake, etc. (1132b28ff). So a kind of proportionality comes into play in weighing up just retribution and wrack.

There is also a kind of proportionate reciprocity at play in exchanges of goods. The exchange of goods has a relation to the worth of the goods involved, this worth being their usefulness in the usages of everyday life, but in exchange it is the momentary relative worth of the goods for the exchangers which is customarily measured abstractly by money as a 'fair' price in the current market situation. The exchange-value of goods and services is not correlated with the quality and quantity of the labour which produces them, so that the product of a house-builder would be worth more than that of a shoemaker on the basis of labour content, as in labour theories of commodity value starting with Adam Smith (cf. 1133a7ff and the next section). Nor is the exchange-value of the goods exchanged proportionate merely to the social who-status of their respective owners. Rather, money itself assumes the role of a kind of "middle term" (μέσον 1133a21) which customarily uniformly measures the value of diverse goods and services, thus mediating and enabling their exchange. Nevertheless, money as this middle term, in measuring the value of the goods, also indirectly measures and estimates the value of all the various services, i.e. labours and abilities, required to provide those goods.

The exchange of goods is reciprocal and fair if it takes place at fair prices. The fairness of price, however, cannot be taken from usefulness in general because this latter has no unified, quantitative measure in itself. Instead, the fairness of price must be measured against the prices currently prevailing on the market, i.e. the current state of market interplay, and is in this sense customary and not intrinsic, relative and not absolute. The market is a complex whole, a network of continual interchanges which undertakes the valuation of the multifarious goods and 'arbitrates' a kind of varying overall measurement against which the fair price for a transaction can be ascertained at any given time. Goods exchange at fair prices if and only if the competitive market interplay generating such prices is fair. *Commutative justice* is that of fair interchanges, whereas *corrective* justice is its converse side, its determinate negation. In correcting an unfair exchange, corrective justice has to take into account the proportionate values of the goods exchanged which amounts to assessing the fair monetary value of the goods exchanged as an outcome of fair market interplay. Fraud, for instance, consists in presenting goods for purchase as more valuable than they are in truth, i.e. there is some hidden defect in the goods, some hidden catch in the service provided, or suchlike, so that the buyer is hoodwinked, blind-sided. Likewise, monopoly and oligopoly prices are intrinsically unfair through one supplier or few suppliers, respectively, having a stranglehold on the supply of a certain commodity which allows them to more or less dictate prices.

6.3 Marxist critiques of capitalist social relations as unjust

6.3.1 The untenability of the labour theory of value as a theory of just exchange masking exploitation

Two millennia after Aristotle, the branch of moral philosophy called political economy arose, which is associated most famously with the names of Adam Smith and David Ricardo (to whom I shall return), among others. These first economists proposed that there was indeed a measure for the fairness of the exchange of goods apart from fair price and that this measure resided in the amount of labour embodied in the things exchanged (cf. the discussion of Adam Smith's conception of commodity value in Chapter 8.3). The question of justice was thus posed in a new guise that blurred the distinction between distributive and commutative justice. The labour theory of value was adopted also by Karl Marx in the nineteenth century, although he went further and deeper than his predecessors in investigating philosophically, i.e. ontologically, how the abstract labour whose magnitude purportedly determined exchange-value ultimately assumed the form of price and money under generalized commodity production and exchange. His theory of value therefore is beset by an ambiguity. Under the name of dialectic of the value-form, he offered an ontology of that unique sociating thing, money.[89]

For Marx, too, the just and equitable exchange of goods was based on the exchange of equal labour-times embodied in those goods. Marx not only sees the phenomenon that the practice of the generalized exchange of the products of labour as commodities practically effects a kind of equalization or Gleichsetzung (MEW23:65, 74; cf. Aristotle ἰσασθῆναι *Eth. Nic.* V 1133a13) of diverse kinds of concrete labour and thus the constitution of what can rightly be termed 'abstract labour', but he goes further and pronounces abstract labour to be the "value-building substance" (wertbildende Substanz, MEW23:53) which constitutes an *intrinsic* exchange-value and also quantitatively determines its magnitude. To take this additional step and obtain a value-substance (Wertsubstanz, MEW23:49), Marx must introduce an ambiguity or, even more than that, a confused and confusing polysemy, into the concept of abstract labour. It cannot be i) simply commodity-producing labour in its quality as being universally practi-

---

89 For a reconstruction of Marx's socio-ontology of the forms of commodity value that avoids the pitfalls of the labour theory of value, see the Appendix *A Value-Form Analytic Reconstruction of 'Capital'* co-authored with Marnie Hanlon, Lucia Kleiber & Mike Roth in Eldred 1984/2015.

cally equated on the market with all other kinds of labour, but it must have ii) an intrinsic existence *independent* of the practice of commodity exchange (which is a *relation* (πρός τι), not a substance, οὐσία cf. Aristotle's categories) if it is to serve as a 'value-substance' and measure capable of quantitative determination of the magnitude of value.

To serve as substance, abstract labour is therefore determined iii) to be physically, pre-sociated "productive expenditure of human brains, muscles, nerves, hands, etc." (produktive Verausgabung von menschlichem Hirn, Muskel, Nerv, Hand usw., MEW23:58), i.e. "expenditure of human labour power in the physiological sense" (Verausgabung menschlicher Arbeitskraft im physiologischen Sinn, MEW23:61), and the phenomenally visible, socially practical abstraction corresponding to this is iv) that "in our capitalist society, depending upon the changing direction of demand for labour, a given portion of human labour is supplied alternately in the form of tailoring or weaving" (MEW23:58), i.e. the ability to deploy labour 'abstractly' in different industries in a social division of labour, depending on demand is said to be the practice underlying the abstraction of abstract labour, as distinct from the abstracting practice of generalized commodity exchange that abstractly equalizes all the very different concrete commodity goods in the market-place.

Marx argued further on the basis of these *third* and *fourth* understandings of abstract labour as value-substance that the peculiar commodity, labour power, has the characteristic of creating in the production process more labour-value than it is itself worth on the market. Labour power is a peculiar commodity first of all because it is the *potential* to labour residing in the labourer and not itself already the perfect presence of a congealed objectification of labour in a finished commodity good. Second of all, labour power is not sold outright (which would amount to the slavery of indentured labour), but hired out by the labourer embodying the labour power. For these reasons, its value, according to Marx, has to be determined both *qualitatively* and *quantitatively* indirectly by the exchange-value of the goods consumed in maintaining and reproducing that labour power. On the basis of assuming that both the fair and factual exchange of goods are determined by magnitudes of ("socially necessary") labour-time measuring abstract labour as value-substance, whilst simultaneously excluding the possibility that entrepreneurial labour could play a part in determining the value of the commodity product, Marx develops the concept of surplus value which purportedly demonstrates that the labourers give more value to the capitalists than they receive in wages and are thus quantitatively exploited of a portion of the exchange-value they produce through the expenditure of their labour power during working hours.

Without postulating a quantitatively determinate value-substance residing in a kind of pre-sociated abstract labour, Marx would not have been able to develop the theory of surplus value as a quantitative theory of class exploitation which is perhaps *the* foundation of so-called "scientific socialism" from which Marxism historically drew much of its persuasive strength and above all, its moral justification based on a putative proof that workers are systematically and 'objectively' ripped off by the 'capitalist system' under the mere guise of fair exchange that feeds working-class resentment which, in turn, became a powerful motive force in the socialist political movement. The labour theory of value as the foundation for the theory of surplus value serves as a purported proof of capitalism's essential social injustice. The putative *essentially* 'unfair' exchange between the wage-labourer and the capitalist entrepreneur, independently of any agreement at all made between them (commutative injustice claimed at the heart of the hire contract for labour power), serves to expand into a critique of the 'capitalist system' as socially unjust in toto (*distributive* injustice between capitalist and working classes suffered systemically, via systematic *commutative* injustice in the labour-power markets, under capitalist relations of production).

In his opus magnum, *Das Kapital* Marx, explicitly refers to Aristotle's treatment of reciprocal justice, which is a variant of commutative justice concerning mainly proportionately fair exchange at value, in Book V v of the *Nicomachean Ethics* and claims that Aristotle was unable to discover abstract labour as the "value-building substance" and labour-time as the quantitative measure of this substance regulating fair exchange because he lived in a society based on slave labour. Marx writes:

> Daß aber in der Form der Warenwerte alle Arbeiten als gleiche menschliche Arbeit und daher als gleichgeltend ausgedrückt sind, konnte Aristoteles nicht aus der Wertform selbst herauslesen, weil die griechische Gesellschaft auf der Sklavenarbeit beruhte, daher die Ungleichheit der Menschen und ihrer Arbeitskräfte zur Naturbasis hatte. Das Geheimnis des Wertausdrucks, die Gleichheit und gleiche Gültigkeit aller Arbeiten, weil und insofern sie menschliche Arbeit überhaupt sind, kann nur entziffert werden, sobald der Begriff der menschlichen Gleichheit bereits die Festigkeit eines Volksvorurteils besitzt. Das ist aber erst möglich in einer Gesellschaft, worin die Warenform die allgemeine Form des Arbeitsprodukts, also auch das Verhältnis der Menschen zueinander als Warenbesitzer das herrschende gesellschaftliche Verhältnis. Das Genie des Aristoteles glänzt grade darin, daß er im Wertausdruck der Waren ein Gleichheitsverhältnis entdeckt. Nur die historische Schranke der Gesellschaft, worin er lebte, verhindert ihn herauszufinden, worin denn 'in Wahrheit' dies Gleichheitsverhältnis besteht.
>
> (*Das Kapital* Vol. 1 MEW23:74)

That however in the form of commodity values all labours are expressed as equal human labour and therefore as of equal worth could not be read by Aristotle out of the form of value because Greek society was based on slave labour and therefore had as its natural basis the inequality of people and their labour powers. The secret of the expression of value, the equality and equal validity of all labours because and insofar as they are human labour in general, can only be deciphered once the concept of human equality has the firmness of a popular prejudice. This, however, is only possible in a society in which the commodity form is the general form of the product of labour and therefore also the relation of people to each other as commodity owners is the predominant social relation. Aristotle's genius shines precisely in the fact that he discovers in the expression of value of commodities a relationship of equality. Only the historical limit of the society in which he lived prevented him from finding out in what this relation of equality consisted 'in truth'.

But, it must be countered, by keeping the phenomenon at hand clearly in view, Aristotle does indeed find out in what this relation of equality consists "in truth", a phrase which is in fact a quote from the relevant passage in Aristotle. It has already been shown in Chapter 4.5 that use or utility (χρεία) is "in truth" the unity "which holds everything together" (1133a28). And this unity consisting of diverse, qualitatively different commodities requires a quantitative measure for exchange to equalize the products exchanged, which is provided by money. Money thus arises from the usage of exchange itself and becomes the unified, visible, palpable, practical, reified measure which, while divorced or abstracted from use, which it measures, nevertheless precisely by virtue of this separation (abstractly and quantitatively[90]) measures the inherent unity of use upon which all exchange of goods is based. For goods are exchanged — to underscore it once more — only because they are useful in the usages of daily life and this nexus is the first, rudimentary, sociating bond constituting society, the sociation of human beings both locally and with foreigners, i.e. domestically and abroad. The differing commodities exchanged are different precisely because of a division of labour.

One of Marx's first and most clear-sighted critics took the so-called "law of value" (Wertgesetz) to task as the theoretical foundation of *Das Kapital* shortly

---

90 Note that Marx's great teacher, Hegel, is in the background here with his ontological insight into quantity: "Die *Quantität* ist das reine Sein, an dem die Bestimmtheit nicht mehr als eins mit dem Sein selbst, sondern als *aufgehoben* oder *gleichgültig* gesetzt ist." ("Quantity is pure being in which determinacy is no longer posited as one with being itself, but as *suspended/cancelled-and-preserved* or *indifferent*.", Hegel *Enz. I Werke* Bd. 8 § 99). Whereas the abstraction from all determinacy, i.e. quality, occurs for Hegel in pure thinking in the transition from quality (determinate being or Dasein) to quantity, for Marx, the value-form of universal exchange relations achieves this abstraction and indifference practically, through sociating interplay itself and "behind the backs" of the social players.

after Engels finally edited and published the third volume of this momentous work in 1894. Eugen von Böhm-Bawerk had already published a critique of the labour theory of value twelve years before he published his *Zum Abschluß des Marxschen Systems* (On the Close, or Completion, of the Marxian System) in 1896 in which he attempts to show up the irreconcilability of the contradiction between the "law of value" and the theory of prices of production at which capitals sell their commodity products to reap an average rate of profit. This is the so-called transformation problem that has been with economics since the 1880s and which has drawn the attention of illustrious names in this social science who have invariably overlooked, and continue to overlook, the issue of the social ontology of the value-form, i.e. the socio-ontological 'look' of value. The transformation problem is confronted with the contradiction between two different quantitative determinations of commodity prices, namely, by quantities of abstract labour time, on the one hand, and by costs plus average profit, on the other. This mathematized transformation problem can be formulated as a system of simultaneous equations, which many economists have since done over the last century in various ways.

But Böhm-Bawerk does not concentrate his intellectual fire-power exclusively on this quantitative, mathematized problem, but returns even to the ontologically prior, simple grounding of the concept of value itself in *Kapital* Vol. I. He notices perspicaciously that Marx had already borrowed "from old Aristotle the thought that 'exchange cannot be/exist without equality, and equality not without commensurability'" (Marx hat schon beim alten Aristoteles den Gedanken gefunden, daß 'der Austausch nicht sein kann ohne die Gleichheit, die Gleichheit aber nicht ohne die Kommensurabilität'[91]).

It is to Aristotle, the father of ontology, that thinkers return when approaching the simple phenomenon of exchange and value, but perhaps even Marx did not listen closely enough to Aristotle and follow what he had in view. Böhm-Bawerk points out the fallacy in Marx's reasoning in deducing abstract human labour as the value-substance which putatively makes exchange commensurable. Contrary to Marx, he claims that, in considering what is "common" (gemeinsam) when two different commodities are equated in exchange, one could just as well conclude that it is abstract use-value:

---

91 Eugen von Böhm-Bawerk 'Zum Abschluß des Marxschen Systems' in Friedrich Eberle (ed.) *Aspekte der Marxschen Theorie 1: Zur methodischen Bedeutung des 3. Bandes des 'Kapital'* Suhrkamp Verlag, Frankfurt/M. 1973 p. 81 citing MEW23:73f.

Wenn Marx zufällig die Reihenfolge der Untersuchung verkehrt hätte, so hätte er mit genau demselben Schlußapparat, mit welchem er den Gebrauchswert ausgeschlossen hat, die Arbeit ausschließen und dann wiederum mit demselben Schlußapparat, mit welchem er die Arbeit gekrönt hat, den Gebrauchswert als die allein übrig gebliebene und also gesuchte gemeinsame Eigenschaft proklamieren und den Wert als eine 'Gebrauchswert-Gallerte' erklären können.

Böhm-Bawerk 1973 p. 89

If Marx had accidentally reversed the sequence of the investigation, with precisely the same deductive apparatus with which he had excluded use-value, he could have excluded labour and then, once again, with the same deductive apparatus with which he had crowned labour, he could have proclaimed use-value to be the sole remaining and thus the sought-for common property and explained value as a 'jelly of use-value'.[92]

This would have been in line with Aristotle and also would have been truer to the phenomenon of exchange itself, not through a string of deductions, but by carefully looking at and contemplating the phenomena themselves. Since use-values are universally equated in the sociating practice of generalized commodity exchange, they are indeed abstracted from, and this practical abstraction could very well be termed abstract use-value, just as Aristotle says that it is "use which holds everything together" (cf. Chapter 4.5). But being true to the phe-

---

92 Hegel, another intensive student of Aristotle, has a similar insight in his *Rechtsphilosophie* § 63, where he sees that the universality (Allgemeinheit) of a useful thing is *"need in general"* (*Bedürfnis überhaupt*). Abstracting from the particular usefulness of a thing results in "the *value* of a thing" (der *Wert* einer Sache; italics in the original). In the addition to § 63 we read, "The qualitative being disappears here in the form of something quantitative. [...] In property, the quantitative determinacy which steps forth from the qualitative determinacy is *value*. [...] The value of a thing can be very diverse in relation to need; but when one wants to express not the specific being, but the abstract being of value, this abstract being is *money*." (Das Qualitative verschwindet hier in der Form des Quantitativen. [...] Im Eigentum ist die quantitative Bestimmtheit, die aus der qualitativen hervortritt, der *Wert*. [...] Der Wert einer Sache kann sehr verschiedenartig sein in Beziehung auf das Bedürfnis; wenn man aber nicht das Spezifische, sondern das Abstrakte des Wertes ausdrücken will, so ist dieses das *Geld*.) Hegel as a genuine phenomenologist sees no need to recur to a value substance residing in labour, but sticks with the phenomenon to uncover value as abstract usefulness. In his notes to the *Rechtsphilosophie*, Hegel even writes that "What money is can only be understood when one knows what *value* is — A lot becomes clear — when one has the firm determination/definition of what value is." (Was Geld ist, kann nur verstanden werden, wenn man weiß, was Wert ist — Es wird vieles klar, — wenn man die feste Bestimmung dessen hat, was Wert ist.) Value results from an abstraction from usefulness or use-value, and this abstraction is carried out *practically* by the all-encompassing, i.e. universal, exchange interplay in which one use-value is set equivalent to all others. Unfortunately, modern economics has not learned this lesson from Hegel; it still does not know "what value is".

nomenon of commodity exchange and not asking too much of the phenomena and thus abstracting abstract use-value would also be the end of the matter, for abstract use-value does not offer any obvious intrinsic quantitative measure (such as clock-time, whose ontology itself should be regarded as a problem and not thoughtlessly taken for granted) which could then be postulated as the extrinsic determinant of the exchange proportions, nor any obvious intrinsic substance.

This is where the labour theory of value goes awry and does violence to the phenomena. Although it is perfectly admissible to point out that the social practice of generalized commodity exchange abstracts from the concrete labours producing specific concrete use-values, thus giving rise to something which could rightly be called abstract labour, this in no way justifies concluding that labour under this determination constitutes a value-substance which quantitatively — in the dimension of quantified, counted clock-time — measures the magnitude of value and determines the exchange proportions.

Once this fallacy is seen, the entire transformation problem becomes secondary and in fact entirely irrelevant and vacuous — something which Böhm-Bawerk, along with most modern economists, does not see. The transformation problem misses, or rather, skips over the more elementary and far more crucial point. The problem is that the quasi-science of economics has no quantitative law at its foundation with which it could compete with modern (Cartesian) mathematical natural science and emulate its success in postulating quantitative, precalculative and therefore predictive 'laws of motion' (cf. Chapter 8). There can be no social science of economics establishing mathematized laws on firm grounds, but there could be a phenomenology of katallactics that investigated the fathomlessness of sociating interplay on the basis of an ontology of whoness.

The postulation of abstract labour-content as the substance for the intrinsic measure of equitable exchange does not stand up to the test of a closer look at the phenomena themselves, for labours, too, are qualitatively different and diverse, being the exercise of diverse labouring *powers* or *abilities* in combination with more or less productive powers (produced and natural means of production). Moreover, the phenomenon of the mobility of labour power between different branches of industry within the social division of labour must be clearly distinguished from the beneficial levelling practice of generalized commodity exchange of the products of labour and the role of money in this exchange. The postulation seems motivated by an ideal of abstract, formal human equality valid in other social spheres, viz. one person-one vote, democratic government and abstract equality of persons before the law, and is directed initially toward justifying private property ownership claims according to how much labour is put into property. 'Sweat' should be fairly rewarded.

It was John Locke who famously justified private property ownership by mankind through labour: "Whatsoever then he removes out of the State that Nature hath provided, and left it in, he hath mixed his *Labour* with, and joyned to it something that is his own, and thereby makes it his Property. It being by him removed from the common state Nature placed it in, hath by this *labour* something annexed to it, that excludes the common right of other Men."[93] This is a germ of the labour theory of value which, under the influence of the Newtonian-Cartesian spirit of mathematized science, is amenable to reformulation as a quantitative theory of relative prices, thus providing a foundation for a pseudo-mathematical science of economics that is today awarded Nobel Prizes. Note, however, that labour postulated as a justification for private property in itself says nothing about the quantitative exchange-value of that property.

Marx himself has to admit the qualitative difference between labours and between labour powers, just as Aristotle does, and has to base his investigation of quantitative labour values on the simplifying and falsifying assumption of presentation that "every kind of labour power is regarded directly as simple labour power, whereby only the trouble of a reduction is made superfluous" (Der Vereinfachung halber gilt uns im Folgenden jede Art Arbeitskraft unmittelbar für einfache Arbeitskraft, wodurch nur die Mühe der Reduktion erspart wird. MEW23:59). First of all, qualitatively different kinds of labour and of labour power are transformed into merely various forms of "complicated labour" (komplizierte Arbeit, MEW23:59), the first step in a quantitative reduction of difference by introducing a scalar factor. But by what measure can "complicated labour" regarded quantitatively as "*multiplied* simple labour" (*multiplizierte* einfache Arbeit, MEW23:59) be reduced? Marx himself admits plainly that this reduction only takes place "by a social process behind the backs of the producers" (durch einen gesellschaftlichen Prozeß hinter dem Rücken der Produzenten, MEW23:59), to wit, through the exchange of the products of labour themselves on the market in which the "*value* [of a commodity product of the most complicated labour] equalizes it [the commodity ME] with the product of simple labour" (Eine Ware mag das Produkt der kompliziertesten Arbeit sein, ihr *Wert* setzt sie dem Produkt einfacher Arbeit gleich und stellt daher selbst nur ein bestimmtes Quantum einfacher Arbeit dar. MEW23:59), thereby reducing his

---

93 John Locke *Second Treatise of Government* in Locke *Two Treatises of Government* 1965 § 27; italics in the original. The first and second *Treatises* are henceforth abbreviated as *1TG.* and *2TG.* respectively.

postulate of labour content as the *independent* or *intrinsic* measure for exchange to vicious circularity.[94]

It is to be emphasized that these criticisms are aimed at the much discredited *quantitative*, pseudo-mathematized labour theory of value as a theory enabling the exchange ratios between commodities to be determined in terms of a quantitatively measurable "value-substance" (Wertsubstanz, MEW23:49), and not at Marx's socio-ontological analyses of the form or 'look' of value as the abstract universal 'look' of sociation of labour in societies dominated by generalized commodity production. In Chapter 5 I have offered an alternative, more far-reaching ontology of exchange in which the value-form is transformed into the fundamental interplay of estimation and validation of human abilities, thus making explicit the link between the value of whats and the value of whos. A vicious circularity pertains only as long as one is aiming at a quantitative, law-like theory of relative price in which relative prices are determined theoretically by some independent measure, whether this be labour-content measured by labour-time, marginal utility, or something else. As shown in Chapter 5, the biarchic or polyarchic ontological structure of exchange — in contrast to the mono-archic ontological structure of τέχνη ποιητική on which natural science is based — rules out on the deepest, ontological level the possibility of emulating modern mathematized natural science that modern social science has been chasing after for centuries. Fathomless, multipolar, sociating interplay refuses phenomenologically to be cast into the mould of mathematical laws. Rather, the fathomlessness of sociating interplay itself demands to be thought through *as such*, and this poses almost insuperable problems for the scientistic habits and prejudices of thinking in our own age.

---

94 Christopher J. Arthur (2002) futilely tries to virtuously break this circularity by switching sites from commodity exchange to show that "'socially necessary exploitation time' in the capitalist production process determines the magnitude of value" (p. 41). Abstract labour thus gains a double determination, already present in Marx's texts: firstly, the abstraction from concrete labours achieved in commodity exchange, and secondly, the abstractness of labour that capital achieves by abstractly exploiting labour *sans phrase* in the production process, manifest in phenomena such as Taylorism. This does nothing to ground an intrinsic measure for exchange-value, especially since the abstraction from use-values achieved through universal market exchange is of a different kind from the more or less indifferent deployment of labour powers 'abstractly' in highly mechanized or automated production processes that, in any case, are not the universal mode of capitalist production since it still requires differentiated labour powers.

6.3.2 Groundlessness of sociating interplay

The envious fixation on mathematized natural science with its productionist ontology as the paradigm for social science depends in part on forgetting a distinction made in Aristotle's thinking between those movements (κίνησις) and states of affairs that always are as they are and those movements and states of affairs that "admit having it otherwise" (ἐνδεχόμενον ἄλλως ἔχειν *Nic. Eth.* 1140a23 and passim), i.e. are not *necessary*, in particular, not *causally* necessary. That which "admits having it otherwise" is further subdivided into what happens "in most cases" (ἐπὶ τὸ πολύ, as a rule, for the most part) and what happens accidentally out of the blue, simply 'coming by' (κατὰ συμβεβηκός *Met.* 1027a.32). Modern-day science also no longer knows, i.e. is wilfully ignorant, that Aristotle's thinking has a category for thinking groundlessness, namely, τὸ συμβεβηκός, contingency, that which simply 'comes along' (συμβαίνειν, 'to go along with'), i.e. simply presences in the 3D-temporal clearing. There can only be a science (ἐπιστήμη) of those movements and states of affairs that do not admit having it otherwise, so that the movements can be derived reliably from first principles (ἀρχαί) that govern the movement. "Because what simply comes along [τὸ συμβεβηκός] cannot be gathered [into the limits of the λόγος], and does not fit into the limits of a rule, it cannot be learnt or taught; it lies next to the rule and comes about one way and then another."[95] Both art (τέχνη) and skill (ἐμπειρία) are concerned with those realms of human affairs that admit having it otherwise but still have regularity. Whereas τέχνη in Aristotle's ontology is exclusively concerned with making or at least bringing-forth (ποιητική 1140a23) in which a fore-knowing ἀρχή, as a single starting-point, reliably governs the movement of bringing-forth in manipulating things and humans regarded as things, in the realm of sociative interchange, such as exchange on the market, there is no single governing ἀρχή that with gathered, composed, knowing fore-sight (μετὰ λόγου 1140a23) reliably governs the outcome of sociating interplay. Sociative interchange, being without fore-sight, admits what happens suddenly or unversehens (unexpectedly).[96] Aristotle's exclusion of contingency from his *Metaphysics* as a phenomenon for investigation is intimately related to

---

95 "Weil das Beiläufige das Unsammelbare ist, das in die Grenzen einer Regel nicht hinein-paßt, ist es auch das Unlernbare und Unlehrbare, es liegt neben der Regel und ereignet sich einmal so, einmal anders." Michael Eldred 'Vom Wesen der Polis und vom Unwesen des Bei-läufigen' in *prima philosophia* Bd. 2 Heft 2 April 1989: pp. 185–216, here p. 204, included in my *Entständigung* 2015.

96 The German word for 'suddenly', 'unversehens', meaning etymologically 'ohne Vorah-nung', 'ahnungslos', 'un-fore-seen'.

his restriction of movement to productive, effective movement in his ontology (cf. *Met.* VI (E) Chaps. 2 and 3). Only such movement is 'knowable' in his terms.

Even supply and demand regarded as 'variables' remain in fathomless interplay, *pace* Marx, who at times, like many political economists, relates demand to need rather than customary usage and treats need as an independent factor that can account for market prices. By explicitly excluding τὸ συμβεβηκός from consideration in his onto-theological *Metaphysics*,[97] Aristotle's thinking never comes to ontological grips with the phenomenality of sociative interplay, which, as I have shown in Chapter 5, should not be confused with physical interaction. *The genuinely social realm of interchange and interplay not only admits having it otherwise, but it refuses a single ἀρχή whence any social movement, i.e. any social interchange, could be determined with pre-calculable, knowing foresight.* To requote a congenial phrase from Adam Smith in this connection, "...in the great chess-board of human society, every single piece has a principle of motion of its own..."[98]

Since each individual is its own free ἀρχή of self-movement, all social intercourse sociating these individuals is an interplay, i.e. a play in the midst of the 'inter-' in which individuals participate as players. As already often noted in preceding chapters, this 'inter-' is the open clearing of 3D-time itself. It is therefore misleading to think of social intercourse as interaction, as has become usual, because interaction is still determined by the action of the individual forces acting along with the reaction of other individual forces, and therefore a resultant force results from the interaction. There is no open *midst* among the forces at work because the time of efficient causality necessary for modern science is linear and events eventuate along a line, so that the result can be fore-seen and

---

97 Cf. Aristotle *Met.* VI 1026b2–5: πρῶτον περὶ τοῦ κατὰ συμβεβηκος λεκτέον, ὅτι οὐδεμία ἐστὶ περὶ αὐτὸ θεωρία. σημεῖον δέ· οὐδεμιᾷ γὰρ ἐπιστήμη ἐπιμελὲς [5] περὶ αὐτοῦ οὔτε πρακτικῇ οὔτε ποιητικῇ οὔτε θεωρητικῇ. "it must first be said of what simply comes along, that there can be no speculation about it. This is indicated by the fact that no science, whether practical, productive or speculative, concerns itself with it." Some years ago I commented, albeit inadequately, "This means with regard to the exclusion of contingency from metaphysics that the contingent itself in its way of presencing somehow does not presence, but rather holds itself back so that its way of presencing itself cannot be understood." (Das heißt hinsichtlich des Ausschlusses des Beiläufigen aus der Metaphysik, daß das Beiläufige selbst in *seiner Art der Anwesung* irgendwie doch nicht anwest, sondern vielmehr sich an sich hält, so daß seine Art der Anwesung selbst sich nicht verstehen läßt. Eldred, M. 'Vom Wesen der Polis und vom Unwesen des Beiläufigen' in: *prima philosophia* Bd. 2 Heft 2 April 1989: pp. 185–216, here p. 199)
98 Adam Smith *The Theory of Moral Sentiments* (1759) Prometheus Books, New York 2000 Part VI, Section II Chapter II, penultimate paragraph p. 343.

fore-cast, as it is in Newtonian physics in which resultant forces can be calculated mathematically by vector addition. Not so in the case of interplay, because the midst among the players is the openness of three-dimensional time itself for the oft capricious play of what just comes along by accident, i.e. κατὰ συμβεβηκός. The fundamental concepts of the Aristotelean ontology of movement, δύναμις, ἐνέργεια and ἐντελέχεια depend upon there being no gap, no midst between the δύναμις (force), its being-at-work, i.e. its ἐνέργεια, and the outcome. The δύναμις is in this case a power as a point of origin (ἀρχή) that governs and determines an outcome, an ἐντελέχεια. The δύναμις has its end already within itself and only has to be put to work to actually (ἐντελεχείᾳ) attain and to have (ἔχειν) this end. This is the onto-theological origin of the Western will to power, for the ontology of productive movement is transferred also to the supreme being, whether it be God or the will to power.

In the interplay among individuals, by contrast, each individual as ἀρχή does not act upon the other as a passive object that suffers itself to be acted upon, but rather, each individual player plays with the possibilities of the open situation in the midst among the various players. The moves of the other players still leave room to move in the midst, a room for play in which each individual player is still a genuine point of origin of its move *responding*, and not merely *reacting*, to other moves, so that the connection between the moves of individual players and the outcome remains loose. Even though each player may attempt to anticipate the moves of the other players (as in complex combinatorial games like chess or go, whose moves remain finitely countable, albeit enormous in number), and may do so successfully some or even much of the time, there remains nevertheless uncountably infinite room for play in the midst for a surprising outcome which just 'comes along'. There is *slippage*. The temporal midst as the room for play of contingency is that which had to be excluded by Aristotle from ontology from the outset.

There is an *ontological looseness* or *slippage* in the sociative interplay among individuals that can never be brought under control by a single ἀρχή (principle, prince, despot, government, state, controlling instance, scientific principle). Even when the countermoves of the other players are anticipated as a finite set of alternative responses (scenarios), and contingency plans are put in place for each of the contingencies that may fall into the midst, there remains incalculable room for play among the various contingencies. Δύναμις as a force that determines an outcome (ἐντελέχεια) retreats to δύναμις as a mere possibility in the room for play amidst the players. The reality (ἐντελέχεια) of what comes about through the interplay is then merely a contingent reality that could just as well be as not be, i.e. presence as not presence.

The open temporal midst of the interplay pulls the ground from under the powers and forces that strive to determine a certain, predictable outcome, so that sociating interplay is *ontologically groundless*. Each individual player as a point of origin for movement is free to think in 3D-time according to its level of insight into, or interpretation of, what was, what is and what may be, to opine according to how it holds the world to be or how it may possibly become or have been, to act according to its own individual will striving for some goal, and any attempt by others to influence the player's moves, to motivate it, say, by persuasion, cajoling, threats, etc., falls into, or incides upon the room for play of freedom that each player *is*. Each individual player as free gives itself its own ground provisionally by deciding on a purpose, an end, and acting accordingly to realize its purpose. When individual players come into interplay with one another, however, a groundlessness in the midst of the players makes itself felt that can be controlled by none, which thwarts merely individual purposes and makes outcomes unpredictable and uncertain. Individual goals may well remain unattained and replaced by other surprising outcomes, both good and bad.

Since it measures itself against the paradigm of mathematized physics ushered in by Newton and formulated as the paradigm for all knowledge by Descartes in his *Regulae*, all modern economic theory is fixated upon preferably quantitative laws as the acme of scientificity and derides so-called metaphysical speculation (in truth: ontological theorizing) on the simple, foundational phenomena of economics themselves (such as exchange and money) which seem to be and *are* the most 'obvious'. It is precisely obviousness that always has to be made questionable in any deeper philosophical inquiry. Thus, for instance, Schumpeter (mis)characterizes Marx's labour theory of value as having been adopted holus-bolus from Ricardo. "His theory of value is the Ricardian one. [...] Marx's arguments are merely less polite, more prolix and more 'philosophical' in the worst sense of this word."[99] Schumpeter's aversion and hostility to philosophy are apparent not only here. They lead him, along with colleagues throughout the social sciences, to shy away from philosophy as mere "speculation" in favour of empirical social-scientific research and analysis.

But it is precisely the step back to an ontological consideration of the simple phenomena themselves that can provide the way forward for liberating Marx's philosophical, ontological insights from the strictures of a Ricardian or Smithian labour theory of value in particular and from the self-evident, standard,

---

99 Joseph A. Schumpeter *Capitalism, Socialism and Democracy* Harper & Row, New York, 3rd edition 1950, paperback edition 1975 p. 23; hereafter abbreviated as *CSD*.

quantitative, precalculative concerns of economic theory in general, including even general, secular economic laws of motion, in order to gain ontological insight into the essence of money and exchange relations and ultimately into the enabling dimension of human sociation itself and the essential nature of human interchange.

6.3.3 The untenability of the theory of surplus value as a theory of capitalist exploitation

If the quantitative labour theory of value is untenable as a pseudo-Newtonian foundation for a quantitatively, mathematically conceived science of economics, then, as I have shown, so is the theory of surplus value as a theory of the systematic quantitative capitalist exploitation of the working class through the appropriation of surplus labour and *therefore* surplus value. The critique of capitalism as a system of social injustice based on the exploitation of the working class through the extraction of surplus value therefore collapses. Neither is the — oft antagonistic — relationship between capital and labour unjust in the sense of straight out fraud or robbery (as long as the rules of contractual intercourse are adhered to or enforced under the rule of law) and thus the wage deal is not an instance of injustice falling under the rubric of corrective justice. One does not need an — anyway flawed — labour theory of value to conceptualize the opposed interests of, and struggle between capitalists and workers in the carving up of the money-value proceeds from the sale of the product of the capitalist production process.

Value 'creation' cannot be attributed, even in retrospect, solely to labour power, since what is produced cannot be attributed solely to labour power as the effective cause on which the production of the product can be 'blamed' (cf. the Greek for 'cause', αἴτιος, which means 'that on which something can be blamed'). Nor even can value 'creation' be attributed to labour power in conjunction with the other factors of production (produced means of production and nature) whose active combination is the labour process proper, since value is not 'created', not produced at all, but *comes about* as an interplay of estimation among *all* the powers exercised to make the product available in free interchanges on the market.[100] (There is an essential ambiguity in the term 'labour'

---

100 This estimative interplay is a movement of *validation* (from L. validus) of the concrete labour performed in the sense that this performed concrete labour has the power (L. valere,

regarded on the one hand as the exercise of labour power pure and simple, and on the other as the realization of the powers residing in labourers, means of production and natural forces all working in combination in a labour process. For the sake of clarity, the latter should be called a production process.) The corollary is that there is no surplus value 'creation' attributable to surplus labour.

There is also no intrinsic, independent measure for the monetary exchange relationship between capital and labour, but only the price relations, i.e. wage levels, factually established in the market-place. This market-place, of course, is also a place of competitive struggle over the price of labour power (the potential to labour) — i.e. wages, the price for hiring labour power — and also over working conditions in which the interplay, or rather power play, of supply and demand decides. Traditionally this struggle has been viewed as that between the capitalist and working classes. Supply and demand in this case include the organization of workers in labour unions, the organization of capitalists in employers' associations, tactical moves in the competitive power struggle such as strikes and lock-outs, the mobility of capital and labourers regionally and globally, the level of education and training of the workforce, and many other such factors. These factors, or rather, strategies of play, do not 'make' (L. facere) the price of labour power, however, but flow into an interplay of social powers that, because it *is* an interplay, is groundless and continually shifting. There is also no reason to restrict the view of the power struggle over wages and working conditions to the traditionally connoted working class vis-à-vis a capitalist class, for it encompasses all employees in all industries.

The power struggle over wages and working conditions must be seen as fundamentally an estimative interplay between the contracting parties, albeit perhaps a grudging kind of estimation (cf. Chapter 5.6). The fairness or otherwise of the struggle thus depends on customary social conditions and cannot be said to be inherently and systematically unfair and unjust. The class antagonism between capital and labour over the determination of wages and working conditions, although as a conflict of interests remaining a perpetual struggle, may lead to a fair and just outcome in the Aristotelean sense of reciprocal exchange and commutative justice if the metabolism of free market interchange is allowed to hold sway without undue monopoly influence on either side. Just as often, it may lead to an unfair and therefore unjust outcome, depending on the continually shifting power balance between the two sides in various industries,

---

validus, Gk. δύνατος) of commanding an equivalent in exchange on the market and thus has a value (L. valere, Gk. δύναμις).

in various countries and at different conjunctures in the economic cycle. Periods of prosperity for workers and other employees may deteriorate into periods of austerity in living standards, and vice versa. Apart from the economic struggle, political power struggles also affect economic power plays, and vice versa. As yet, however, I have not considered the ontology of political power, which is reserved to Chapter 10.

6.3.4 Injustice of capitalist wage-labour per se?

A further possibility for injustice in the relationship between capital and labour is the famous "double freedom" (Marx) of the labourer, namely, "that as a free person he has disposal over his labour power as his commodity, and on the other hand that he does not have any other commodities to sell, that he is well and truly free of all the things necessary to realize his labour power" (...frei in dem Doppelsinn, daß er als freie Person über seine Arbeitskraft als seine Ware verfügt, daß er andrerseits andre Waren nicht zu verkaufen hat, los und ledig, frei ist von allen zur Verwirklichung seiner Arbeitskraft nötigen Sachen. MEW23:183). In short, the working class is excluded from ownership of the means of production and is forced to sell labour power in order to live. The labourer's freedom is said to be only formal, i.e. only in sight, because under the conditions of the free exchange of commodities between formally free and equal persons, the capitalist as the wealthier owner of the conditions of production has the upper hand in dictating the terms of the wage contract since his wealth makes him more independent in wage bargaining.

It has been observed not only by Marx, but also by the 'bourgeois sociologist', Max Weber, that "the formal right of a worker to enter a labour contract of any content whatsoever with any entrepreneur whatsoever does not practically signify for someone looking for work the least freedom in shaping his own working conditions and does not guarantee him in itself any influence whatsoever on these working conditions". (Das formale Recht eines Arbeiters, einen Arbeitsvertrag jeden beliebigen Inhalts mit jedem beliebigen Unternehmer einzugehen, bedeutet für den Arbeitsuchenden praktisch nicht die mindeste Freiheit in der eigenen Gestaltung der Arbeitsbedingungen und garantiert ihm an sich auch keinerlei Einfluß darauf.[101])

---

101 'Freiheit und Zwang in der Rechtsgemeinschaft' in Max Weber *Soziologie Universalgeschichtliche Analysen Politik* Kröner Verlag, Stuttgart 1973 p. 76f.

From the outset it must be kept clearly in view that the question concerning the justice or injustice of the capitalist wage-labour relation as a socio-ontological question is not, and cannot be, the question concerning the injustice of factual relations in the world that are conceived *as* unjust within the hermeneutic cast of an historical age. The socio-ontological question must be a one concerning the essence of the capitalist wage-labour relation, not the question concerning whether reality corresponds to its essence. The *fact* that there are endless injustices in the world only shows that an understanding of what justice and injustice are enables factual injustice to be visible for understanding in the first place and therefore also on all levels contestable. When, for example, Marx graphically points out and depicts with copious empirical documentation the "despotic" (despotisch, MEW23:351) nature of the nineteenth century English factory system and its cruel conditions of work, this is understood by the reader *as* injustice only because the reader already has an understanding of what justice, what fairness is, an understanding itself cast in the forge of historical struggle over ideas.

The socio-ontological question, therefore, is whether the capitalist wage-labour relation is inherently, i.e. *essentially* unjust in the whatness of what it is. Such a question cannot be answered by empirical investigation. If it were *essentially* unjust measured against an adequate socio-ontological concept, as developed in this study, then social revolution to overthrow capitalist relations of private ownership and production would be justified and necessary. The relation between capital and wage-labour is a sociation between whos, not whats, because both the capitalist employer(s) and the waged employee(s) are whos who perforce engage in an interplay of estimation with each other. Such mutual estimation has many aspects, including the employer's appreciation of the employee's powers and abilities, the employee's appreciation of the employer's offer of wages and working conditions, the sizing-up, i.e. estimating, on both sides of their respective bargaining positions in the current market situation in the economy, the employee's assessment of the employer's offer for enhancing the employee's skills, the employer's assessment of the power of the employee's trade union or professional association, the employee's estimate of alternative opportunities for employment by other employers, etc. etc.

The interplay of mutual estimation between capitalist employer and employee is therefore two-sidedly a reciprocal appreciation of each other's potentials, on the one hand, and, on the other, a reciprocal sizing-up of each other's bargaining power over remuneration and working conditions. The latter renders the interplay as a power struggle that has the potential to turn antagonistic. Conversely, an agreement can be reached on either an individual or collective basis about conditions of employment with which both sides are satisfied. In this case, the interchange between capital and wage-labour is fair and equitable and commutative justice is satisfied. There is nothing inherent in, i.e. essential to, the interplay between capital and wage-labour on a collective basis that necessarily prevents fairness and equitability being achieved in the bargain struck, even when fierce power struggles precede resolution of the dispute. Such power struggles are part of that social movement called bargaining process in which each side flexes its muscles, i.e. exercises its respective powers, demonstrably, thus enabling each side to estimate the power of the other to assert its demands.

In particular, the struggle to improve working conditions, and so lessen the purported 'despotism' of the capitalist employer over the wage labourers, is only possible because those working conditions are measured against acceptable, just, fair working conditions, i.e. the phenomenon of working conditions is viewed against the *conception* of commutative justice of the power interplay between capital and wage-labour. Such commutative justice that shows itself as an *idea* to the social actors is the socio-ontological beingness of the interplay, i.e. its hermeneutic interpretation *as* the mode of being of the phenomenon of sociating interplay. Pointing out the factual existence, say, of miserable sweat-shops can readily be admitted to be unjust in *view of the idea* of commutative justice and is no argument against capitalist wage-labour *per se*, but only a forceful argument in the context of ongoing power plays that these sweat-shop conditions be changed for the better under the guidance of an understanding of what constitutes just, fair working conditions. Reality is then brought to approximate its socio-ontological concept.

Insofar as fair conditions of employment can be struggled for within existing capitalist employment relations and attained historically without overthrowing capitalism, it shows that the socio-ontological *concept* of the power interplay between capital and wage-labour is congruent with the socio-ontological *concept* of commutative justice. Ongoing struggles over the enhancement of conditions of employment show that the power plays between capital and wage-labour never come to a final resolution in some kind of social ἐντελέχεια. Even gains made in establishing good employment conditions can also be subsequently lost. These ongoing struggles, however, are always conceived against the yardstick of commutative justice. The capitalist side of the employers, too, can appeal to this yardstick in struggles with, say, powerful trade unions whose power, through bloody-mindedness, can even destroy a capitalist employer or an entire industry. In this sense, commutative justice as a guiding socio-ontological idea or 'sight' kept continually in view by the struggling parties (as well as the public in general) cuts both ways. Hence, for instance, 'propaganda wars' may be fought out in the media over the justness or otherwise of workers' or employers' demands.

But is the capitalist wage-labour unjust in other respects according to a socio-ontological *concept* of justice as an interplay among whos? Is accepting a job and its conditions of employment *per se* an injustice? Is it an injustice *per se* that I subordinate my will to a capitalist employer, or is it an injustice only under certain *factual* conditions of employment that I can more or less adequately specify which constitute a commutative injustice? What constitutes an injustice in this context, of course, is not merely a matter of whether a practice is legal or illegal measured against statutes of legislation. As Marx and countless others have copiously pointed out, the 'bourgeois' legal system has historically ridden roughshod over workers' legitimate rights, and it is easy also today to point to factual instances of the abuse of legitimate workers' rights. Legality and legitimacy, legislation and right, factual injustice and essential injustice, however, must not be confused with one another. Here is not the place to discuss unjust legislation, because as yet we have no socio-ontological concept of government and state power, which will be developed in later chapters.

At present it is to be considered whether it is an injustice *per se* under a concept of justice other than that of commutative justice that the individual worker has to hire out his or her labour power to some company or other to earn a living and is not in a position to dictate just how he or she would like to work? Or is it a (commutative) injustice only if the factual working conditions themselves are grossly unacceptable, i.e. unfair and unjust? If factual working conditions are unjust in the sense that they contravene the law, then the judiciary can correct this injustice, but this does not concern us for the moment. If factual working conditions are unjust in the sense that they do violence to an understanding of commutative justice whilst at the same time being in compliance with the state's positive law, then it is positive law itself that does not correspond to the concept of justice, and this law can be changed, most often through some kind of socio-political struggle to have that law changed. Through this movement of power play, reality comes closer to the socio-ontological concept of justice, which itself serves as yardstick.

Hence I return to the question whether it is an injustice *per se* for a worker to have to earn a living by hiring out his or her ability to labour to a capitalist entrepreneur and having to accept 'alien' working conditions which that worker is not able to posit him or herself, or only to a limited extent, in the preceding bargaining interplay over the employment contract? Since the working conditions are posited by another, namely, the company or its managing entrepreneur, the working conditions themselves are in this neutral sense 'alien', i.e. largely imposed by another, so there is justification in talking of an *essential* alienation, i.e. exposure to the otherness of another's will, in the capitalist wage-labour relation owing to the whatness of what it is.[102] For in accepting employment and hiring out my power to labour I am subject to the will of the capitalist employer within a more or less heirarchically structured organization. But is this alienation pernicious? Does it amount to an *essential* injustice that contravenes the socio-ontological concept of commutative or some other kind of justice? Or is it part of social human being itself to have to accept conditions of earning a living that one has not posited through one's own free will?

It has been shown in preceding chapters that social being itself in sociating interplays among whos is itself a metabolism of myriad power plays among the many actors. This implies that the individual will that wills one life-movement or another is never an *absolute* positing, but always *relative* to the others who likewise will their own self-movements in leading their respective lives. The individual as always already sociated can never be autonomous. Even an absolute, despotic ruler does not have absolute power to subjugate all and sundry to his will, despite all the show that is made of the exercise of despotic power. An apparently absolute, despotic ruler is most often an entirely suspicious, paranoid ruler, for he knows that, despite all measures taken to nip subversion, from whatever quarter, in the bud, the absoluteness of his ostensible absolute power is ultimately a sham. For members of society in general it therefore cannot be the case that having to subordinate oneself to the will of another to a greater or lesser extent is a violation of the justness of the movement of sociating interplay. Only the total surrender to another as his or her property entirely negates and subordinates the will of an individual as the slave of another who is his or her master. Such total subjugation is indeed unjust when viewed against the idea or 'look' of justice conceived *as* the power interplay between and among players, each of whom is a free starting-point for his or her own life-movements. Therefore, endangering the lives of employees or impairing their health are unjust because commutative power interplays among human beings who are the sources of their own freedom of movement presupposes and requires in the name of justice that their very life and limb are not endangered by the capitalist

---

102 "The system of their labours therefore confronts them ideally as a plan, practically as the capitalist's authority over them, as the power of an alien will which subjugates their actions to his purpose." ("Der Zusammenhang ihrer Arbeiten tritt ihnen daher ideell als Plan, praktisch als Autorität des Kapitalisten gegenüber, als Macht eines fremden Willens, der ihr Tun seinem Zweck unterwirft." MEW23:351).

employer. The fundamental concept of justice is therefore that of commutative justice, i.e. of fair play.

If, then, it is untenable to hold that every individual has the 'inalienable' right to determine its own working conditions without being interfered with by 'alien' influences, i.e. by others, then the question becomes, under what conditions alien working conditions are unjust. Are they essentially unjust if the worker does not have a 'say' in determining his or her own working conditions or mode of working? Is this 'say' sufficient merely through the fact that, as a free person, the worker is able to choose among the jobs on offer or negotiate with the potential employer on working conditions to some extent? After all, the prevailing labour market conditions at any given time allow a greater or lesser degree of leeway when striking a bargain over the conditions of employment. Or does this 'say' have to extend to co-determination of working conditions in some kind of internal company set-up in which the employees collectively, through their representatives, are able to shape working conditions in ongoing negotiations with the employers? Or is this possibility, historically realized above all by German social democracy, optional with regard to the question of commutative justice? Conceptions of fair and equitable conditions of employment are highly malleable historically and are themselves shaped by historical power struggles, but they are not arbitrary. Conversely, historical power struggles themselves are waged only in the light of conceptions, i.e. ideas, 'looks', of fair and equitable conditions of employment.

That competitive economic life is a struggle, a continual power play and does not guarantee success for all participants, but on the contrary produces also losers, does not speak for its injustice *per se*. Power interplays on the employment market that are rigged by prejudicial attitudes against certain social groups *do* merit being branded unjust because such attitudes are a refusal to properly estimate and esteem the powers of individuals with certain social characteristics as equally free players. Prejudice makes blind and offends the concept of commutative justice insofar as the players in the power play of mutual estimation are prejudicially underestimated and underesteemed. Furthermore, those who are unable to fend for themselves in the competitive economy, either temporarily or permanently, and for whatever reason, need help and charity from others. Charity itself, however, is not a matter of justice, and there is no right to charitable assistance. The issue of support for those who cannot help themselves will be discussed in connection with the social welfare state (Chapter 6.5).[103]

A further twist in trying to discover an essential injustice in capitalist wage-labour is to point to the capitalist's 'privilege' in being at all in a position to hire employees. Why should some be in a position to do so while the 'masses' are forced to sell their hides? Apart from the *envy* that is blatantly apparent in such a claim, it amounts ultimately to an abolition of the right to hire employees altogether for, if everyone is in a position to hire employees and exercises this power, where are employees to be found at all? If everyone is potentially and potently a capitalist employer of wage-labour, then no one is. However, considering that free individuals of their own free volition shun the option of becoming an enterpreneuer, are perfectly willing to work for someone else, and can even find such paid employment entirely rewarding in all senses of the word, it is hard to see how the capitalist employment relation could be essentially unjust coming about as it does through a mutual estimation of powers. Rather, this kind of critique of capitalism is a lazy one driven by envy and the conviction that one has been badly treated by life; in short, it is driven by *resentment*. Moreover, the role of the entrepreneurial capitalist is itself a kind of occupation with its own not inconsiderable skills, effort, responsibilities and especially risks that is not for everyone and which deserves its own reward. The entrepreneurial role in a capitalist economy is one deserving its own estimation and appreciation.

Hence on all scores it cannot be maintained that the power interplay between capitalist and waged employee is essentially unjust. It is not based on an essential exploitation of the workers' labour power through the extraction of surplus-value; nor is it unjust *per se* for workers to have to submit to the alien command of the capitalist to earn a living; nor is it unjust because some (the entrepreneurs) are able and willing to employ workers while others are not. On the contrary, the abstract social relations of capitalism are so Protean that even satisfying, rewarding working conditions can be achieved in general for the working class along with wages supporting even a comfortable standard of living. Since the multifarious power plays in a capitalist economy, including those over wages and conditions of employment, are ongoing, a comfortable standard of living attained can also be eroded, but this does not put into question the socio-ontological conception of commutative justice itself. And it must be kept in mind that worker satisfaction and the general standard of living are

---

103 Cf. also my essay, 'Why social justice is a specious idea' 2005 at www.artefact.org/untpltcl/scljstsp.html

not the touchstone when considering the justice or injustice *per se* of wage-labour in capitalist sociative interplay.

I now leave the Marxian context of the justice or otherwise of so-called 'capitalist relations of production' assessed against the foil of a conception of commutative justice based on the socio-ontology of mutually estimating power interplay to consider the seminal Aristotelean concept of distributive justice. This will enable us to see whether today's still very popular and pervasive idea and ideal of social justice in its European, social-democratic, redistributive sense, makes sense or whether its apparent self-evidence in many quarters needs to be shaken thoroughly by socio-ontological interrogation.

6.4   The just distribution of the goods of living

I return (cf. section 6.2 above) to consider more deeply that second kind of Aristotelean justice, viz. distributive justice, concerned with the apportionment of the goods (and bads) of living in accordance with just desert. Whereas the socio-ontological character of commutative justice *as* fair play can be read off the sociating interplay of mutual estimation between whos (the basic sociating movement of society itself), the social movement of distributing goods according to desert has another mode of being altogether *as* another kind of social power interplay among whos — including the whoness of a superior instance of power — with different criteria of estimation. Distribution (allotment, apportionment) of the goods of living, whether material or immaterial) requires an apportioning instance that distributes according to a criterion or criteria of worthiness. Here I will consider first only the apportionment of material goods, leaving the consideration of that other major good of living, esteem itself, to a later section (cf. 6.7).

In the case of a small group such as a family, the pater- or materfamilias may be the superior apportioning instance who allots goods to the family's children on the basis of a criterion of equality. Each child is to be treated even-handedly without favouring one over the other in order, especially, not to generate envy among siblings. This kind of parental 'distributive justice' may well work well for a family composed of children who are not yet able to freely lead their own lives, but becomes problematic for any larger group or a whole society of free individuals.

First of all it has to be considered *who* is to be the superior apportioning instance. If the group's general meeting is to have this role, then it must continually deliberate and decide on just distribution to individuals in the group. If this meeting's resolutions are not to be arbitrary and capricious, varying from meeting to meeting, certain criteria for distribution must serve to decide apportionment. In larger groups or a whole society, the superior apportioning instance must be some kind of standing executive or government that is recognized *as* such a *legitimate* superior instance, usually by virtue of having been elected by the group's or society's members or, in yesteryear, by virtue of an hereditary line of descent. The phenomenon of legitimacy in connection with government will be considered later in Chapter 10. Here it is only important to see *that* distributive justice requires some kind of superior instance with the *power* to exercise over the social movement of apportioning to individuals (or groups thereof) on the basis of some criterion or criteria. Each individual has to be estimated by the superior instance of social power as to his or her deservedness for an allotment of goods. Conversely, the individual whos estimate the superior apportioning power *as* legitimate.

Hence, in the case of distributive justice, the horizontal power interplays between and among the players in mutually estimating each other no longer suffices, as it does in the case of commutative justice, for conceptualizing its mode of social being. Whereas commutative justice derives from the mutual estimating interplay among formal equals itself being fair and equitable, requiring correction by a superior judge only in the case of an infringement of fair play, in the situation of distributive justice, a 'vertically' superior instance of power is required from the outset to estimate apportionment and direct distribution according to certain criteria. If the apportionment is to be estimated *as* just, the criterion or criteria must not be arbitrary or capricious. This would be the case, for instance, with a despotic ruler whose hold on power were apparently so firm that he could ride roughshod with impunity over his subjects without regard to whether they esteemed him as legitimate ruler.

The originary sociating power interplays between and among the members of society estimating each other as whos according to their individual powers and abilities are now complemented by a power interplay between the members of society and its superior apportioning instance whose exercise of power is the actual social movement of distribution. Let us call this superior apportioning instance for the sake of convenience the *state*. The estimating power interplay between state and the members of society who are the state's subjects, involving as it does mutual estimation, requires a socio-ontology of whoness to bring to light the beingness of this peculiar being, viz. the estimating power interplay itself, itself a kind of social movement.

The next question concerns the criterion or criteria for just distribution. The four criteria named by Aristotle, namely, free birth, wealth, nobility of birth and ability/excellence (cf. section 6.2 above) must be supplemented by a fourth from modern times: that of neediness. First of all it must be noted that these criteria are incompatible with each other and therefore incoherent.[104] Nobility of birth contradicts the equality of free birth (as a potential) and is therefore inapplicable in our modern democratic times of so-called universal human rights. Similarly, wealth as a criterion offends the equality of human beings, each of whom is the source of his or her own freedom of movement in casting and shaping a life. The criterion of ability and excellence already comes into play with the power interplays of mutual estimation among the members of society themselves and therefore the justness of these interplays can be decided already according to the criterion of commutative justice, which is fair play. There remain only two modern criteria: equality and neediness.

Equality itself is a problematic criterion, for it is ambiguous. Does the equality refer to each individual who *as* a (potential) power-*source* of its own freedom of movement, or to the *outcomes* of such freely exercised movements in the power interplays of mutual estimation with others? This is the socio-ontological difference between power (δύναμις) and its final presence (ἐντελέχεια). If the criterion of equality applies to the outcome of fair power interplays, then this amounts to the abolition of commutative justice altogether, for, as has been shown, the outcomes of power interplays among many whos are uncertain and unpredictable, so that an outcome of equality (say, of income earned) is merely fortuitous and not the rule. This would offend the criterion of realized equality if it is to be the criterion for distributive justice with the upshot that the outcomes of free and fair power interplays would have to be continually revised, i.e. levelled, by the state. (The modern welfare state actually does practise such continual revision of the outcomes of interplay; cf. the next section.) This would thoroughly dampen, if not extinguish, the incentive to engage in the power interplay of mutual estimation to earn income at all on the basis of the esteeming of one's own powers and abilities by their being estimated in the universal

---

104 The questionableness of distributive justice in an attempt to set up a just social order is voiced by Bertrand de Jouvenel who also fundamentally questions the notion of (re)distributive social justice: "No proposition is likelier to scandalise our contemporaries than this one: it is impossible to establish a just social order. Yet it flows logically from the very idea of justice, on which we have, not without difficulty, thrown light. To do justice is to apply, when making a share-out, the relevant serial order. But it is impossible for the human intelligence to establish a relevant serial order for all resources in all respects. Men have needs to satisfy, merits to reward, possibilities to actualize; even if we consider these three aspects only and assume that — what is not the case — there are precise *indicia* which we can apply to these aspects, we still could not weight correctly among themselves the three sets of *indicia* adopted." Bertrand de Jouvenel *Sovereignty* London 1957 p. 164 cited in Hayek *LLL2*:177.

reified measure of value, i.e. money, that mediates the interplay. Moreover, it would turn freedom as freedom of movement, that is, the movement of mutually estimating power interplays, into a sham.

Therefore, if at all, only a criterion of equality of starting-points, of potentials can be considered as candidate for a criterion for distributive justice. Accordingly, the state would have to ensure equality of opportunity for each member of society by enabling each individual to first develop his or her full potential for the power interplays of society. Such a conception of distributive justice is known under another name: the *justice of equality of opportunity*, and this is in line with conceiving freedom socio-ontologically originarily *as* the freedom of each individual to be the starting-point for his or her own freely decided life-movements without, however, guaranteeing successful realization. In this conception, freedom is conceived as it is, namely, as a characteristic of the individual potential or power that can initiate sociating movement. By contrast, it quickly becomes plain that to conceive freedom *as* a characteristic of realized outcomes is socio-ontologically incoherent, especially when this freedom is supposed to consist of equal outcomes.

Since the *justice of equality of opportunity* is not known under the name of distributive justice, I will leave it out of further consideration. Such justice implies the necessity that the superior power instance of the state apportion the wealth of society in such a way that each member of society has equal opportunity in starting to cast and shape his or her life. This applies first and foremost to the state's providing a good education to each and every child, each of whom is an as-yet inchoate starting-point for leading and shaping a life. Such a right in the name of justice is uncontroversial today in the West, and also in other parts of the world, although its realization has by no means been achieved. And given the enormous individual differences and the differences in social situation within any society, it is plain that equality of opportunity is unattainable. Nevertheless, the 'look' of equality of opportunity is today firmly established for the mind *as* just and as such serves to guide the sociating movement, especially the political power struggles, in society. This is expressed, for instance, in saying that it is just to 'give everybody a fair go' or 'a fair crack of the whip'. Such equality of opportunity is often conceived as the 'look' of a level playing field, an image adopted from sport where its meaning is plain. The justness of a competitive game of sport is seen to lie in equal starting-conditions of play for both sides, so that the game's final score can be extremely uneven and yet is accepted as entirely fair. The competitive struggle of the play, too, may be extremely tough and relentless without impairing the game's being perceived *as* fair. Such perceptions are not merely 'subjective' vis-à-vis some criterion of 'objective fairness' because fairness itself is only ever an hermeneutic conceiving-as... A subject/object split makes no sense whatever socio-ontologically.

Accordingly, the outcomes of the competitive power plays of economic life are not subject to a criterion of justice so long as starting-conditions, i.e. the opportunities, are fair and equitable. Potentiality is given precedence of final actuality, as it must in any consideration of freedom. The power interplay of economic life does indeed result in a factual distribution of social wealth and total social income, and in general this factual distribution will be far from equal. Great discrepancies in the factual distribution of income and wealth within a society become problematic when those on the lower rungs have to struggle to make ends meet. They then do not see that they are 'living well' and become resentful against the very wealthy, in particular, whose lives with regard to income-earning, at least, are carefree. Moreover, the wealthy have more reified social power (cf. section 6.7 below) to throw around. This is not a question of distributive justice but of the political prudence of engendering a social whole in which each member, through exertion of his or her own powers, is able to lead a more or less satisfying life outside a state of destitution.

6.5   Redistributive social justice, the welfare state and the alleviation of poverty

This leaves the sole remaining candidate for a criterion of distributive justice, *neediness*, to be considered. Accordingly, the needy poor are said to be deserving of a distribution of goods from the state which must estimate these needy *as* needy and therefore deserving. Such a state is called a *social welfare state* and distributive justice is renamed (i.e. misnamed) *redistributive social justice*. This is then no longer a power interplay of mutual estimation between equals, but a submission of the needy to estimation by a superior instance of power *as* needy. The needy subject has to be assessed by the state as needy in the state's estimation according to criteria of neediness that are laid down in multiple regulations intended to define a neediness profile. To be able to do this, the state first requires the wealth resources to allot to the needy, which it must raise by taxation (or levies, which is taxation under another name) in order to *redistribute* the wealth of society. Hence such distributive justice is, strictly speaking, *re*distributive justice. Secondly, the state requires a bureaucracy to carry out the work of assessing the needy as to their (level of) neediness and allotting welfare benefits.

In modern Western societies, social welfare is provided by a state apparatus run by a bureaucracy according to government policy, administrative law and myriad regulations. The bureaucracy is an organized, organizational will of the state. As such a concrete realization of a purported (redistributive) social justice that is set up to deliver social benefits, the social welfare system is firstly subject to the criterion of its effectivity in achieving the envisaged just redistribution of wealth. Secondly, it is itself by no means immune to unjust actions perpetrated either by itself or its clients. In contrast to contractually based economic intercourse which is splintered into myriads of individual transactions, a bureaucratic apparatus is an organization run according to a plan and a policy laid down by government and legislation. The apparatus is supposed to function like an entire, unified organism with the will of the government and the legislature as its controlling head and many hierarchically organized bureaucrats constituting its executive administrative organs.

A complexly articulated organizational will is inevitably retarded in its execution by its multiple articulations through the wills of a multiplicity of bureaucrats acting according to countless regulations laid down by administrative law. This could be called the *bureaucratic retardation* in the realization of a practical conception of redistributive social justice as envisaged by government and legislature. Such bureaucratic retardation is the first appearance in this study of the phenomenon of the *inertia* of *social movement* (about which more later; cf. Chapter 7.9 and Chapter 9.8) which is to be discovered everywhere in social life. In the case of the practical institution and realization of a conception of (re)distributive social justice through the state's social welfare apparatus, the lack of efficiency may be so great as to invert such purported social justice practically into absurd injustice such as self-contradictory 'catch 22' regulations or the capriciousness of bureaucrats. The inertia and inefficiency of this organized state will calls for comparision with sociation via the commutations in civil society mediated by reified value in its various forms, its principal one being money. But this is a secondary issue compared with that of the purported justness per se of redistributive social justice (see below).

As shown in Chapter 4.5, need itself is not originary but arises only from the usages within which the members of society customarily live their lives. Since there are many customary usages, those usages must be posited and defined which are deemed to give rise to socially acknowledged needs for which a needy person can apply for welfare benefits. This itself is a politically contentious issue giving rise to political power struggles within the state over which needs are to be estimated as deserving over against those estimated to be undeserving of being acknowledged as falling under the criterion of neediness. According to the criterion of state-defined neediness, redistributive justice is to apportion goods, generally in the form of monetary welfare benefit. A multitude of needs arising from very disparate usages must therefore compete for acknowledgement *as* needs within the profile of neediness defined bureaucratically by the state. In states where there is democratic government (cf. Chapter 13), there are interminable political struggles over the definition of neediness in the name of redistributive social justice in which there are no clear criteria but only political convictions and electoral weightings. What defines neediness therefore becomes more or less arbitrary and along with it the very justness of redistributive social justice. The socio-ontological concept of distributive justice therefore remains vague, since the goal of redistribution of income for the sake of satisfying need also remains nebulous. Neediness itself defies clear definition and along with it, the satisfaction of need as well, which turns out to be insatiability itself that continually pushes the social welfare apparatus to the limits. The nebulousness of need has led to some critics of redistributive social justice calling it simply a "mirage".[105]

It is perhaps because of this nebulousness that Thomas Hobbes altogether restricts the notion of justice to free interchanges between persons, viz. "That men perform their Covenants made"[106]. The notion of an in-jointness of the social whole in its distribution of the goods of living (including, negatively, the distribution of the unavoidable adversities of living) goes back at least to Plato who, in his *Politeia*, describes the just polis as a polis in which its various main parts consisting of the rulers, the guardians and the commoners are in joint, i.e. are in the proper, balanced relation to each other in that each part fulfils its proper function in the functioning of the whole of society. Society is conceived as an organism, a conception which feeds down through the tradition to understanding society as a kind of organization organized for ends executed by organs functionally designed for that purpose. This leaves no room for the metabolism of civil society as a free — and therefore unpredictable — interplay among many players not under supreme control by a superior instance, whether it be a despot or some kind of totalitarian or all-caring social-democratic state. There is therefore an essential socio-ontological difference in the *kinds of social movement* (roughly: horizontal interplay vs. vertical, heirarchically controlled movement) in a state that lays down by law the rules of play for free commutations among free players, on the one hand, from one, on the other, that surveils

---

105 Friedrich A. Hayek *Law, Legislation and Liberty* Vol. 2 The Mirage of Social Justice, Chicago U.P. 1976. *LLL2.*
106 Thomas Hobbes *Leviathan* eds. Richard E. Flathman and David Johnston, Norton, New York/London, abbreviated *Lev.* p. 71.. Page references to *Leviathan* are consistently to the Head edition of 1651.

and intervenes in these commutations to impose its own aims, in particular, according its self-posited conception of redistributive social justice.[107]

The very aim of satisfying need through redistribution is in truth a delusion insofar as need is always outflanked by the endlessness of human desire for more and more for the sake of living well (cf. Chapter 4.1). The satisfaction of need assumes on the contrary that neediness is finite and therefore somehow definable. This delusion regarding the satisfaction of need is entrenched, in particular, in all socialist and communist thinking, which has long seeped also into social-democratic political thinking widespread in so-called liberal-democratic Western societies today. Insofar as neediness and its alleviation become a matter of (redistributive) social justice, the fulfilment of needs itself becomes a *right* that citizens can then 'rightly' claim as an entitlement. These claims then 'naturally' grow under the impetus of endless human desire masked as need. And because this right putatively applies to everybody, it is then seen in the 'look', i.e. the idea, of a universal human right.

Since, however, the superior instances of power administering such redistributive social justice are *nation* states, the universal claim to the status of human right is pruned to that of the right of each citizen of a given nation state to be cared for by that particular state — to the exclusion of foreigners who are not estimated and esteemed to be legitimately needy in the name of social justice, but are deemed to be 'social welfare refugees' by those citizens feeling threatened by the claims of outsiders. Such fears can be fanned by skilful political demagogues. The definition of neediness in this sense, too, i.e. whether redistributive social justice is national or universal, thus remains an issue for endless political contestation.

---

107 Listen to Plato on state surveillance of its citizens commutations: "It is necessary for the law-giver to keep a watch on the acquisitions and spending of the citizens, how they come about, and to examine the sociations they have with one another, and the dissolutions thereof, whether they be voluntary or involuntary and with regard to what kind each of these sociating dealings is which they practise with one another, whether justice is in them or not, and in which it is lacking, [...]." (ἀνάγκη τὸν νομοθέτην τὰς κτήσεις τῶν πολιτῶν καὶ τὰ ἀναλώματα φυλάττειν ὄντιν' ἂν γίγνηται τρόπον, καὶ τὰς πρὸς ἀλλήλους πᾶσιν τούτοις κοινωνίας καὶ διαλύσεις ἑκοῦσίν τε καὶ ἄκουσιν καθ᾽ ὁποῖον ἂν ἕκαστον πράττωσιν τῶν τοιούτων πρὸς ἀλλήλους ἐπισκοπεῖν, τό τε δίκαιον καὶ μὴ ἐν οἷς ἐστιν τε καὶ ἐν οἷς ἐλλείπει, Plato *Laws* 632b). In the (money-mediated) dealings among citizens lies already the germ of the modern free individual as a practised form of sociation with many degrees of freedom of movement, and also the core of commutative justice *as* the fairness correcting the possibly unfair ugliness of these interchanges. But Plato aims also at surveilling and controlling the commutations in society in line with keeping them in line with a conception of the polis *as* an organic whole.

The very name, social justice, is itself a usurpation and a pleonasm,[108] for all justice is per se social, since it concerns how people live together in society and, in this context, the primary meaning of justice is commutative, i.e. that the commutations between individual whos in the sense of sociating power interplays of mutual estimation be fair and equitable.

Proclaiming so-called 'freedom from want' as a right in the name of social justice is itself politically motivated to lend weight to the claims of the needy in one sense or another to get more from the state. Poverty in a society is indeed a problem whose causes are complex and manifold, and its alleviation remains a continual challenge, for social living as a whole suffers when a significant minority is chronically unable to take care of itself. State welfare benefits can be important in tiding those over who are temporarily unable to fend for themselves, but a genuine alleviation of poverty depends on enabling the poor to gain a foothold in the income-earning interplay of mutual estimation itself. This is a tall order, but in this way they come to stand on their own feet and do not have to rely on state hand-outs. Such welfare benefits on the whole are in any case *demeaning*, for they demand that the prospective welfare recipient first subject him- or herself to the state's bureaucratic estimation as to whether that individual fulfils the state's definition of needy.

Far from encouraging the needy to take heart and learn to stand on their own feet in the power interplay of a capitalist economy, state welfare tends to further a dependency of its clients on the welfare state.[109] This constitutes a major contradiction for civil society and the state, ubiquitously felt in political life: on the one hand, to keep the stimulus of individual self-interest sharp in

---

108 "In this sense justice clearly is a social phenomenon and the addition of 'social' to the noun a pleonasm such as if we spoke of 'social language'" Hayek *LLL2:78*.

109 Hegel puts it this way: "If the immediate means existed in [...] public property [...] to maintain the mass tending to poverty on the level of their orderly way of life, the subsistence of the needy would be secured without being mediated by labour, which would go against the principle of civil society and the feeling of its individuals for their own independence/self-reliance and honour." (...oder es wären in anderem öffentlichen Eigentum [...] die direkten Mittel vorhanden, die der Armut zugehende Masse auf dem Stande ihrer ordentlichen Lebensweise zu erhalten, so würde die Subsistenz der Bedürftigen gesichert, ohne durch die Arbeit vermittelt zu sein, was gegen das Prinzip der bürgerlichen Gesellschaft und des Gefühls ihrer Individuen von ihrer Selbständigkeit und Ehre wäre. Hegel *Grundlinien der Philosophie des Rechts, Werke* Bd. 7 Suhrkamp, Frankfurt/M. 1970 § 245.) Nietzsche is harsher: "one does not have any right, either to work or to exist, not to mention a right to 'happiness'; the individual human being's situation is the same as that of the lowest worm" (man hat kein Recht, weder auf Dasein, noch auf Arbeit, noch gar auf 'Glück'; es steht mit dem einzelnen Menschen nicht anders als mit dem niedersten Wurm, 11 [259] KSA13:98; cf. KSA13:95, 100).

giving incentive for independent, self-reliant individuals to provide for themselves through their own efforts, by developing and exercising their own abilities, thus building self-esteem, and, on the other, to care for the unsuccessful or unwilling players in the often tough and unpleasant competitive game, thus removing the motivation to care for themselves.

This tendency to encourage dependency is all the more the case when state welfare is seen *as* a right in the name of social justice. The 'look' of (redistributive) social justice as a socio-ontological idea is therefore itself thoroughly deceptive, although attractive to many, like a mirage in the desert. This 'look' is also antithetical to freedom, for freedom consists in the first place in each individual who being a starting-point freely deciding on his or her own moves in the sociating interplay. As Aristotle puts it, a free society consists in "free and equal persons sharing their lives in order to be independent selves" (κοινωνῶν βίου πρὸς τὸ εἶναι αὐτάρκειαν, ἐλευθέρων καὶ ἴσων *Eth. Nic.* V 1134a27)

The state's helping the needy to get out of poverty is thoroughly in line with a socio-ontological conception of freedom as free and fair power interplay. The alleviation of poverty itself, however, is not a question of 'social justice' but of improving the social whole through enabling the poor to gain independence and thus also self-esteem. Charity, too, conceived as caring for one's neighbour, is a good of living as a helping hand, but not a right that can be claimed in the name of so-called social justice.

Another perspective on poverty resulting from the uncertainties of the competitive interplay in economic life is that of *insuring* against unwanted events such as unemployment or sickness via the medium of reified value. Insurance works by spreading the risk of certain unforeseen events happening. The insurance premia paid to an insurance company by an individual can be a viable alternative to having ever to rely on the state to acknowledge one's own neediness at a given juncture. Likewise, individual 'rainy-day' saving along with financial nouse and prudence in handling one's own financial affairs serves as a buffer to the vicissitudes of income-earning. Both are aspects of a free individual's responsibility to take care of him- or herself. Both these alternatives are also superior to the state's doling out welfare benefits insofar as they do not demand submission to a superior instance to ascertain and acknowledge neediness, but require only that the individual conclude suitable insurance contracts or make suitable investments in advance for a rainy day.

6.6 Esteem, honour and fame in social life with a focus on Aristotle and Schopenhauer

Groß ist nun, was für groß gilt; allein das heißt, daß letzten Endes auch das groß ist, was durch tüchtige Reklame dafür ausgeschrien wird, und es ist nicht jedermann gegeben, diesen innersten Kern der Zeit ohne Beschwernis zu schlucken ...

Robert Musil
Der Mann ohne Eigenschaften I Tl. 2 Kap. 96

Now great is what is held to be great, but this means that ultimately also that is great which is cried out to be such by competent advertising, and not everyone is able to swallow this innermost core of the times without trouble ...

By way of contrast, how do things stand with that other exemplary good to be socially distributed, namely esteem and honour, reputation and regard, social standing, public office and prestige, and the justice of such distribution? That such things are goods of living at all indicates that estimation by others *as who* one *is* constitutes part of living well in society. In fact, as has been shown in Chapter 6.1, the mutual esteeming of each other's abilities is at the centre of the interplay called social being, i.e. the movement sui generis of sociation. The Greek name for these 'values' is τιμή or εὐδοξία.

Aristotle says already in the first book of the *Nicomachean Ethics* that the esteem in which one is held by others cannot be regarded as the good life and as the end of living together in community, "for it seems to reside more in the ones esteeming than in the one esteemed, whereas we inkle that the good is something inherent and cannot be taken away. Furthermore, they [men in practical life] seem to pursue estimation in order to assure themselves of their own good merit." (οἱ δὲ χαρίεντες καὶ πρακτικοὶ τιμήν· τοῦ γὰρ πολιτικοῦ βίου σχεδὸν τοῦτο τέλος. φαίνεται δ' ἐπιπολαιότερον εἶναι τοῦ ζητουμένου· δοκεῖ γὰρ ἐν τοῖς τιμῶσι μᾶλλον εἶναι ἢ ἐν τῷ τιμωμένῳ, τἀγαθὸν δὲ οἰκεῖόν τι καὶ δυσαφαίρετον εἶναι μαντευόμεθα. ἔτι δ' ἐοίκασι τὴν τιμὴν διώκειν ἵνα πιστεύσωσιν ἑαυτοὺς ἀγαθοὺς εἶναι· I v. 1095b25) Since men are esteemed because of their ability (ἀρετή), and not conversely, Aristotle concludes that "one can assume that ability or excellence is the end of life in the polity rather than honour" (ἄν τις τέλος τοῦ πολιτικοῦ βίου ταύτην ὑπολάβοι 1095b31). Life in the polity for Aristotle revolves around the pole of having (ἔχειν, ἕξις) excellent ability, i.e. of habitually practised good usages that one has acquired and has, rather than honour and esteem, which is a (mere?) reflection from others in their estimation.

Accordingly, the issue of the just distribution of standing in high estimation among the members of the community can only be a secondary one that derives from the ability and excellence that is lived habitually in the usages of everyday life. The distribution of such high estimation should therefore be made according to the worth of a person, and this worth is measured by ability and excellence, i.e. if it is to be just, the distribution of honours and public esteem, must be proportional to each individual's respective ability and excellence inherent in themselves. It must be proportional to the individual merit that entitles to one's share or μέρος. Moreover, since being means ultimately presencing,[110] in order to be estimated, an individual's powers and abilities must *presence* and *show themselves* in the open temporal clearing in which all sociation takes place in order to be, even if, and especially their estimation in society at large is contested or their excellence is not appreciated at all, but rather ignored.

Indeed, since honour and esteem for an individual depend upon those honouring and esteeming, and thus upon the regard in which they hold the one esteemed, and regard is nothing other than a kind of opinion and view depending upon how the esteemed person appears to and is appreciated by those esteeming, the honour and esteem accorded to an individual is an extremely fickle and unstable thing infected also with distortion and illusion. Whereas the ability and excellence of an individual shows itself and is manifest in the life practices of that individual, and the worth of a person is measured in the first place by their own ability as they show themselves off as themselves to themselves in self-esteem, whether this self-showing is appropriately reflected in the views held by others about this individual must be viewed with scepticism. The truth of an individual in their own ability and excellence, and how that individual assesses his or her abilities in self-estimation, on the one hand, and who they are held to be in the view of others, on the other, invariably diverge. In fact, for Aristotle, such ability and excellence is only properly *recognized* and *estimated* by others in the highest kind of friendship by a friend who likewise possesses ability and excellence; cf. *Eth. Nic.* 1156b7). Such friendship is rare and even barely possible for those who are ahead of their time, i.e who do not fit the average understanding of a time.

The fundamental problem with any notion of a just distribution of the social good of esteem is that, barring a system for at least nominally distributing esteem according to a rigid social hierarchy, esteem itself arises ineluctably from sociating interplay itself as the mutual estimation of each other's abilities. That is to say, the good of esteem is essentially a *commutative* phenomenon of social interchange that evades any attempt to *distribute* it according to any criterion external to the interplay of mutual estimation itself. The concept of distributive justice, when applied to the phenomenon of the distribution of the basic social

---

110 Cf. my *A Question of Time* 2015.

good of esteem, can thus be seen to be an incoherent concept, even more so than the already untenable concept of redistributive social justice (cf. preceding section). If esteem and honour were to be distributed according to inherent ability, the game of social estimation would have to result in abilities being reflected in public esteem in proportion to intrinsic merit, that is, according to the ability and excellence that entitles to the individual's share. But how could this be at all possible? The myriad interplays of social living do not admit of any uniformity of estimation, to say nothing of estimation in proportion to intrinsic merit justifying a given reward, for what could be the measure of intrinsic merit? Since merit is a δύναμις, i.e. a potential, it must express, show, put itself to work in a movement that others can also see and assess, even when their estimation is often a misestimation.

There is also no conceivable instance, nor a system of social mores, that could enforce any posited 'just distribution' of public esteem and honour, since the esteeming and honouring lie in the realm of opinion, i.e. in how others hold somewho to be. Instead, only the merits of specific individuals can be publicly debated and whether their specific merits have been adequately rewarded and appreciated by the public for a time, by posterity, etc. There is certainly a notion of justice or injustice in this in the sense of just deserts, say, when an individual's excellence is publicly noticed and appreciated post mortem or only in a later age. According public honour to an individual's abilities and achievements remains always essentially controversial, and it is no injustice that the controversy may never cease. Not to mention fame and celebrity, whose allotment is even more capricious, relying as they do on the whimsy of mass public opinion.

On a more prosaic level closer to home, individuals can be happy and glad that their abilities are appreciated, acknowledged and esteemed in their own life-worlds, for this is how their standing as *who* they *are* is affirmed and assured in their everyday social world. But it hardly can be claimed that it is a socially actionable injustice when one's abilities are not recognized and appreciated by one's social milieu. In the first place, where is the judge who could decide? Moreover, since has been shown in Chapter 6.1 that the estimating of material goods is by and large equivalent to, or can be reduced to, the esteeming of abilities in the interchanges of daily life, this allows us to see also that even the just distribution of the material goods of living is an incoherent concept insofar as such factual, resultant *distribution* only comes about through the *commutative* interplay of having goods estimated *as* valuable through valuating interchanges.

The interplay of the exchange of goods would have to be itself abolished or tightly regimented in some way to impose some other distribution of material goods. But such an abolition would amount also to a violent distortion of the interplay of mutual estimation and appraisal of people's abilities that makes up the fabric of social life. Abilities to perform and produce could not be estimated in the mundane form of monetary reward in a free interchange, but rather their rewards would have to be allotted by some superior instance of social power, or perhaps by a rigid traditional hierarchical schema of social evaluation that assessed individual merit in some inevitably rigid fashion (cf. feudal and caste societies). The acknowledgement and rewarding of individual merit would become also the outcome of a political power play, for instance, over places in a rigid social hierarchy as it was, say, in feudal China.

Furthermore, the good (i.e. ability and excellence) that is embodied and lived by a particular individual may be completely misrecognized and remain unappreciated and unaffirmed by others, especially if that good is not one current, common, familiar and therefore easily recognized in practical everyday life. The others must at least understand in some way the excellence and ability of an individual who in order to assess and appreciate them, but this is often not the case. For people can only honour, estimate, appreciate and esteem something they understand in some way. Those abilities which cannot be easily understood by average understanding are likely to be misunderstood, with the consequence that the person embodying that good, far from being honoured and esteemed, is held to be a misfit, eccentric, strange and alien. This is the lot of those extraordinarily creative ones who are ahead of their time and bring something into the shared world whose existence was previously unheard of. The first hearing is usually a totally misunderstanding mishearing and thus recognition is denied, or granted on the basis of a gross misunderstanding, to a creative individual who brings forth and shapes something that breaks the mould of average understanding. Arthur Schopenhauer remarks in this respect, "Some merits lie completely outside the sphere of understanding of the great majority, others they understand and acclaim when such merits first occur, but afterwards they have soon forgotten them." (Manche Verdienste liegen ganz außerhalb der Sphäre seines Verständnisses, andere versteht und bejubelt er [der große Haufe], bei ihrem Eintritt, hat sie aber nachher bald vergessen.[111]) And, he notes, the fame of actions

> ...in der Regel sogleich eintritt mit einer starken Explosion..., während der Ruhm der Werke langsam und allmählich eintritt, erst leise, dann immer lauter, und oft erst nach hun-

---

111 A. Schopenhauer *Aphorismen zur Lebensweisheit* Chapter IV 'Von dem, was einer vorstellt' ed. Rudolf Marx, Alfred Kröner Verlag, Stuttgart 1956 p. 69.

dert Jahren seine ganze Stärke erreicht. [...] Bei ihnen liegt dagegen die Schwierigkeit im Urteil, und sie ist um so größer, in je höherer Gattung sie sind: oft fehlt es an kompetenten, oft an unbefangenen und redlichen Richtern. [...] Dieser Hergang [der Herausbildung des leichten, ephemeren, falschen Ruhms oder aber des tiefen, dauernden Nachruhms ME] beruht eigentlich darauf, daß, je mehr einer der Nachwelt, d.i. eigentlich der Menschheit überhaupt und im ganzen, angehört, desto fremder er seinem Zeitalter ist.

Schopenhauer 1956 pp. 113, 114, 115

...usually arrives with a strong explosion..., whereas the fame of works arrives slowly and gradually, at first quietly, then louder and louder, and often reaches its full strength only after a hundred years. [...] With them, the difficulty lies in judgement, and this difficulty is all the greater, the higher the genus in which they are situated; often there is a lack of competent judges, often a lack of unbiased and honest judges. [...] This sequence of events [in which lasting, ephemeral or false fame respectively is established ME] is really based on the fact that the more someone belongs to posterity, i.e. properly speaking to humanity in general and as a whole, the more alien is this person to their own age.

Certain rare, extraordinary individuals are, first of all, recipients of a message[112] for which they are sensitive that emanates from the mood of their time (or, more precisely: Zeitgeist, time-mind). The message itself may have been long coming from historical time, challenging a singular individual with his or her own idiosyncratic mixture of abilities to take on the task the message itself calls for, and thus developing his or her potentials to the full to be equal to actually being able to take in the message and energetically cast a singular work in casting his or her own self. The work cast contributes to casting the future, far beyond the individual's own time and the Zeitgeist of his or her time, in which the work's significance is often scarcely understood, grossly misunderstood, overlooked or ignored altogether.

I agree with Aristotle that honour and esteem accorded by others are "too superficial" (ἐπιπολαιότερον 1095b24) to be taken as constituting the end in which a good life is attained. Indeed, Aristotle provides as one possible definition of happiness (εὐδαιμονία *Rhetoric* I v. 1360b para. 3) in life together in a polity "independence of life or a life most agreeable with security [i.e. that cannot be brought to a fall]" (αὐτάρκεια ζωῆς, ἢ ὁ βίος ὁ μετ' ἀσφαλείας ἥδιστος 1360b para. 3). The Greek word for 'security' here is ἀσφαλεία, which comes from the verb σφάλλειν meaning 'to bring to a fall, to topple, to fell' which is also related to the Latin 'falsum', falsity. That which cannot be brought to a fall stands firmly and has a secure stand. An individual who has gained a firm stand

---

112 On messaging, cf. Capurro, R & Holgate, J. (eds.) *Messages and Messengers. Angeletics as an Approach to the Phenomenology of Communication* Fink, Munich 2011.

in existence stands in his or her own self-cast self and is insofar independent, does not waver and therefore cannot easily be brought to a fall. Such a life is happy and secure for it is not dependent on fickle affirmation by others.

Another meaning for the Greek word for independence, αὐτάρκεια, is 'self-sufficiency' or 'self-reliance'. According to Aristotle, a man who is sufficient unto himself is strong enough (ἀρκεῖν) in his self (αὐτός) and happy. But what is the sense of self-sufficiency in this context? It does not mean merely that one has sufficient material goods of life to survive independently of others, but concerns the self-standing that one has attained in one's self as somewho, that is sufficient unto itself and reliant on itself, nor in the sense that it is entirely independent of mirroring by others as who he or she is, but at least in the sense this who is able to fend off offence and attacks by others and draw on his or her own self-esteem to stand as self, despite others' misestimating his/her self. Without having the mode of being of whoness in view, this phenomenon of a self-sufficient self-standing must remain invisible as a fundamental ontological-existential phenomenon. Since whoness is the social phenomenon par excellence arising from the movement of sociation in mutual estimating, my stand in my self as somewho can never be entirely cast out of my self. Already who I have become is an outcome of my mirroring interplay with others in the world.

Can it, then, be said that an individual is self-sufficient in the sense that it does not depend on the honour and esteem accorded by others, but stands in itself, without need of mirroring estimation by others? For, it must be asked, how does an individual at all come to an independent stand as somewho? My gaining of my self is not possible without the mirroring through others who reflect who I am or *could* be. If I am in my own life-movement, in the first place, my existential possibilities and potentialities, how can I come to see them and grasp and develop them without some kind of mirroring through others? Is not such mirroring of some kind indispensable to become who I could potentially be? These questions concern self-becoming rather than the estimation given to already attained accomplishments and a firm stand in these accomplishments as somewho. (No thing can have accomplishments, only somewho.) Aristotle rightly points to attained accomplishments (ἀρεταί) in oneself as primary in determining a successful life in community, whereas the estimation of these accomplishments by others is secondary. On the other hand, accomplishments and abilities that remain wholly unreflected by estimation in the social environment leave the individual in isolation and perhaps desolate.

The greater the accomplishment and the harder it is to understand in general understanding, the greater must be the fortitude (one rendering of Gk. ἀνδρεία, 'manliness') of the individual to attain a self-stand and self-esteem *regardless* of the *regard* accorded or refused by others. For the most part, we depend to a greater or lesser extent on the mirroring reflection by others to *be* who we are, i.e. to confidently maintain our stands in our respective individual selves. This mirroring as necessary component of experiencing ourselves as who we are implies that we can never be wholly independent and autistically construct our self-stands as somewho from within ourselves. To achieve our potential in actual accomplishments and thus to become who we are, we need the *encouragement* of estimation by others. Encouragement gives the heart courage to reach out (ὀρέγεσθαι), to strive for what is not yet attained. Your encouragement gives me courage, enheartens me to become who I could be in casting my self into my ownmost possibility and achieving my potential in accomplishments.

Our ineluctable exposure as sociating beings to mirroring estimation of our who-stands means, however, that each of us is open to *flattery*. As shown in Chapter 3.3, flattery is the phenomenon of others falsely mirroring, for their own self-interested advantage, an aggrandized view of who one is in one's abilities, qualities and accomplishments. Since each of us strives to *be* somewho and to stand as tall as possible *as* somewho, each of us is prone to succumbing to the flatterer's flattery. From sheer vanity, i.e. the vacuousness of worth that is covered over by self-over-estimation, we like to look in a magnifying mirror to see who we are. Each of us therefore has to discriminate whether the estimation given by others is genuine, i.e. not just whether it is genuinely meant, but whether it genuinely and soberly reflects our self-stands as somewho as measured by what we are capable of and what we have actually accomplished. The question is always whether the esteem accorded to us truly reflects our abilities and accomplishments, thus bolstering our self-esteem. Thus on the one hand, we cannot know who we are in our selves without the mirror of self-recognition held in the hands of others, but on the other, we must also take care to preserve a sober, independent and self-critical self-assessment of who we are.

Even when others genuinely and truly mirror who I am, the very abilities and accomplishments that justify me in my high self-esteem can raise me beyond my self. I then tend to over-estimate the existential possibilities that are open to me on the basis of my accomplishments and thus cast myself into projects that are beyond my potential that are then abandoned. Or I pretend to my self that I have great potentials that I then never wager to test by actually developing them; in my self-delusion I remain in constant *procrastination*. All projects of self-casting involve a risk, a certain boldness and daring and self-confidence to become who I can be, so there is no sure way of knowing whether my future castings overstretch my inherent potential without tenaciously trying.

Moreover, in casting my self as a future possibility to be realized, I do not know where it will lead, for all self-casting is finite and bound by an horizon, namely, that of the open future into which I gaze in self-casting my self. The risk of failure in realizing my self in casting into the future must be somehow accepted. The courage to become my self is also the courage to risk failure as one of my future possibilities in the openness of 3D-time.

Nevertheless, there is a self-casting that amounts to *self-inflation* and *hubris* (ὕβρις), the central and constant theme of Greek tragedy. If I cast my self all too grandly into the future as a possibility of who I could become, the failure can destroy me utterly. The struggle to become my self is thus a dangerous game of self-casting out of the possibilities that I see or imagine arriving from the future. Since, as long as I exist, I continue to cast my self into the open temporal dimension of future, I am always becoming my self and there is the continual danger of over-reaching my genuine potential of self-becoming. Or avoiding perpetually the challenge of becoming my self through cowardly procrastination.

An independent self-stand means that life together in community requires that you do not necessarily share the views of what others hold you to be, but rather, on the contrary, you set a limit (πέρας) from within a firm stand enabling you to neglect or at least view at a distance the personal, individual regard and esteem in which you are held by others. Sharing the truth of presencing in the 3D-temporal clearing, insofar as it concerns the whoness of the individual self, thus assumes the form of fending off and critically assessing the particular regard in which you are held to be by others, thus maintaining the independence of your own self-assured truth of your self and also preventing yourself from being felled by the false, clueless or wavering and fickle views of others.

For the most part, and assuming that you do not simply conform to the views and visages that public opinion puts on offer as socially acceptable modes of self-casting, your own self, which is lived as your very own, singular existence within the openness of 3D-time, exercising your own abilities, has only obliquely to do with the regard, honour and esteem or otherwise in which you are held by others, i.e. with how you appear to and show off to others. Your very own truth in critical self-estimation and self-esteem, and the falsity or stupidity of others' opinions about who you are as somewho are separate and contraposed. You have to be strong and independent enough in your own whostand to set the limits of the disclosive truth of yourself against the false, reputation-felling or even reputation-boosting, flattering opinions of others, even though being somewho means precisely being exposed to the shared temporal clearing in which the mutually estimative interplay is played out through which you are held to be somewho or other by others. Even the honours accorded by others provide no firm basis for your own existence, that has to be led on the basis of your own insight into yourself, which is the same thing as your insight into your own world and your able or less than able practices and accomplishments within this world. Those who conform to the Zeitgeist, i.e. the time-mind, of their time, of course, have an easier time in being according self-affirmation and high estimation by their contemporaries.

There is something highly paradoxical, contradiction-ridden, about how individuals share a world ranked and graded according to who's who. Not only is it the case that the views which people hold about states of affairs in the world are highly divergent and conflicting, so that the shared understanding of world is for the most part the sharing of misunderstanding and diverging views, and a squabble and strife over truth, but also the views which 'people' hold regarding a particular individual are at best partial and in any case at variance with and alien to the lived existence of that individual. The others are the aliens who alienate oneself from one's self if one fails to draw the demarcation line and maintain a steadfast stand in one's own independent truth of one's own world-opening and one's own abilities and accomplishments. To be my self I have to cast my very own self-world which cannot be made to depend upon the honour and esteem and regard or otherwise in which I am held to *be* somewho by others. And yet, to be human also means to share the temporal opening of world in an ongoing interplay of estimation with others and to be somewho in that shared world, so that the estimation accorded to me as somewho affects my own stand within myself. As already remarked, my stand within my self cannot be hermetically sealed off from others in a shared world. "No man is an *Island*, entire of it self." (John Donne *Devotions*)

Aristotle does not treat this aspect of independence (αὐτάρκεια) but restricts his discussion to the security of ownership and the enjoyment of one's own goods, of what one has acquired and owns (κτῆσις *Rhet.* I v. 1351a para. 7). This is not only because the open clearing of 3D-time within which ἀλήθεια can play its game of revealing and concealing is taken for granted by Aristotle's thinking, but because the phenomenon of whoness situated within the temporal clearing enabling whos to show themselves as who they are in an interplay of first- and second-person and also third-person estimating opinion is not investigated explicitly. It is nevertheless whoness as an onto-hermeneutic dimension sui generis which complements that of whatness. Whereas whatness is the hermeneutic dimension corresponding to what became known in Greek and all subsequent grammar as the third person, whoness is the ontological dimension that corresponds, in the first place, to the mirroring interplay between first and second person. Grammatical categories are therefore not innocuous but themselves contain an implicit hermeneutic-ontological content that calls for explicit unfolding.

There is, however, another, more general concept of honour and esteem according to which the regard in which one is held by others does not concern the particularity of an individual existence, but rather only one's general standing as a fit member of society ("taugliches Mitglied der Gesellschaft" Schopenhauer 1956 p. 70). To be regarded as a reputable person (which has already been investigated in Chapter 3 under the rubrics of reputation and person) means only that the individual adheres to the general mores of intercourse in civil society such as fulfilling one's contractual obligations reliably and punctually, and not engaging in legally dubious practices to gain one's own advantage at the expense of others. Schopenhauer writes with regard to this kind of honour that it "is not the opinion about particular properties attributable to this subject alone, but only about those properties usually to be presupposed which also this subject should not lack." (Denn die Ehre ist nicht die Meinung von besondern, diesem Subjekt allein zukommenden Eigenschaften, sondern nur von den, der Regel nach, vorauszusetzenden, als welche auch ihm nicht abgehen sollen. 1956 p. 73) Schopenhauer contrasts this civil honour or respectability with fame and points out that honour "only implies that this subject is not an exception, whereas fame implies that the subject does represent an exception. Fame, therefore, first has to be acquired, whereas honour only needs not to be lost. Accordingly, the lack of fame is obscurity, something negative; the lack of honour is disgrace, something positive." (Sie [die Ehre] besagt daher nur, daß dies Subjekt keine Ausnahme mache; während der Ruhm besagt, daß es eine mache. Ruhm muß daher erst erworben werden: die Ehre hingegen braucht bloß nicht verlorenzugehn. Dementsprechend ist Ermangelung des Ruhms Obskurität, ein Negatives; Ermangelung der Ehre ist Schande, ein Positives. 1956 p. 73)

The reference to obscurity indicates that fame is the phenomenon of somewho appearing or rather, showing off, *as* somewho in the shared open 3D-temporal clearing of society in a prominent, exposed position where they are held in high regard by public opinion, this high opinion being attributable to the individual's perceived special abilities, merits and achievements. From the point of view of civic honour, a citizen can be content to live in obscurity in the sense that the honourability of an individual only becomes salient and visible in the temporal open when this individual's honour and reputation are put into question and are perhaps tarnished, so that the individual is forced to defend them. An individual's honourability in the sense of their standing as a respectable citizen is, as Schopenhauer says, "presupposed" and it only has to be defended when attacked by slander, i.e. when something is wrong and their standing *as* somewho in the community risks being brought to a fall by the dissemination of a questionable reputation. "The only counter-measure is a refutation of the slander with appropriate publicity and an unmasking of the slanderer." (das einzige Gegenmittel ist Widerlegung derselben [der Verleumdung], mit ihr angemessener Öffentlichkeit und Entlarvung des Verleumders. 1956 p. 73)

The heading of the chapter in Schopenhauer's book from which the above quotations are taken reads 'About what one represents' (Von dem, was einer vorstellt) and is concerned with "our existence in the opinion of others" (unser Dasein in der Meinung anderer, 1956 p. 57), so to speak, in the dimension of third-person otherness. The chapter title indicates that we present a view of ourselves to others in society and in turn, the others hold their own views about the view we present and represent, but it also indicates that Schopenhauer did not see the relational, not substantive phenomenon of whoness as such and the associated task of an ontology of whoness. Who we *are* in society is always a matter of presenting a view, representing ourselves hermeneutically *as* somewho (and not as a "what", as Schopenhauer's chapter heading suggests), showing ourselves off and, conversely, being held to be who we are in the mirror view of others both directly in first-and-second person encounters and in third-person opining. Being together in society is thus a phenomenon of truth also in the sense of mutually disclosing and showing-off *who* we are.

Disclosure here has to be understood in the broad sense which encompasses also its negation and deficient modes, including such phenomena as obscurity, misrepresentation of a person's reputation in public opinion, slander, misrecognition of an individual's special abilities and merits, and the like. Disclosure within the open clearing of 3D-time has to be distinguished from what Schopenhauer means by "representation" (*Vorstellung*) which for him is always representation within consciousness. For Schopenhauer, "the place in which all this ["What one is" and "What one has", the titles of the two preceding chapters; ME] has its sphere of influence in one's own consciousness. On the other hand, the place for "what" we are for others is inside alien consciousness; it is the representation under which we appear in it along with the concepts which are applied to this representation." (Denn der Ort, in welchem alles dieses [was einer ist und was einer hat] seine Wirkungssphäre hat, ist das eigene Bewußtsein. Hingegen ist der Ort dessen, was wir für andere sind, das fremde Bewußtsein: es ist die Vorstellung, unter welcher wir darin erscheinen, nebst den Begriffen, die auf diese angewandt werden. p. 58)

Society is thus conceived by Schopenhauer as the interrelations or communication between consciousnesses in whose interiors representations are formed, i.e. a realm of *intersubjectivity*, as noted already in the Foreword, a problematic notion still virulent today assumed as self-evident. The dimension within which these separate, isolated consciousnesses could have anything at all to do with each other, i.e. the 'inter-' of intersubjectivity, remains an unasked question in Schopenhauer's thinking, just as it is in all (explicitly or implicitly) metaphysical thinking, including pragmatism. In fact, it is unclear how such consciousnesses could have anything at all to do with each other or what the representations have to do with the persons in the world who are only 'represented', 're-presented' inside consciousness.

6.7 A just distribution of honour and fame in society? – The (non-)fame of creative recasters of an historical world

To return to the question of the just distribution of honour in society taking account of Schopenhauer's insights into the phenomena of honour and fame, it can now be seen that honour in the sense of the respectability of a member of society is distributed in modern times equally to each worthy person in general, unless that person, through unjust actions infringing the generally recognized mores and norms of intercourse in civil society, has partially or wholly forfeited his or her reputation. As such, the status of being an honourable or 'decent' person is general, and even abstract, and has nothing to do with the individual's particular abilities and merits or otherwise. The modern individual has an abstract worth (or dignity, as Kant would put it) corresponding to the abstractly sociating interplay of a market-mediated society. On the other hand, honour in the form of fame is only accorded to an individual insofar as the exceptional merits of that individual are seen, in some way understood, and estimated highly by society at large. Fame, or how somewho is talked about by others and so held to be, depends crucially on the famous who's self-presentation being easily understood by large numbers who today are reached by the mass media for whom the criterion of easy comprehensibility is paramount. Their condition of survival is never to pose or allow any fundamental questions that would challenge 'people's' average everyday understanding of how the world 'is', including of course, any questions even faintly touching upon the socio-ontological cast of world in our age.

But whether the exceptional merits of an exceptional, singular individual are understood by the broad majority or even a significant minority can be safely ruled out. Rather, in the case of exceptional individuals who create exceptional works, the broad majority estimates the greatness of these works not on the basis of its own understanding and insight, but rather mediatedly in placing its faith in the judgements of a relevant authority in these matters. And whether an authority can see, appreciate and esteem and acclaim exceptional merit depends, as Schopenhauer says, on whether "envy pressed their lips closed" (der Neid die Lippen zudrückte, 1956 p. 115). Or also on the ability, inclination and mood of the times themselves to understand what a singular individual has cast in his or her creative work, which goes far beyond envy into the realm of insight and wisdom. Envy, the "feeling of mortification and ill-will occasioned by the contemplation of superior advantages possessed by another" (OED), is the phenomenon of protecting one's own standing as somewho by refusing to estimate and by depreciating and even denigrating the superior stand of another. One's own who-stand must be shored up as superior at all costs, even and especially at the cost of denying another's superior merit in order to lower their standing, for being somewho means constantly comparing one's own stand in a vertical dimension with that of others.

By contrast, in the case of exceptional acts of merit which are easily understood, such as sporting excellence, fame can be accorded easily and indisputably. Whether an exceptional, singular individual who creates a work becomes famous, especially within their lifetime, is a matter of contingency and is invariably based on misunderstanding or an abridged or superficial understanding. For, an act of creation in a work is an accomplishment that opens up new insights and, in a sense, in bringing something to light and giving it shape in a work, helps hermeneutically recast the historical world in a hitherto unheard-of way that is always also a hitherto unknown way of thinking, because an historical world is opened up and cast by how it is *thought to be* (where thinking is not just a 'subjective' human activity). Such a recasting, by casting out into the future of historical time, needs time to even begin to be fathomed and understood as it arrives from the future, that is, presupposing that this alternative cast is not entirely ignored or suppressed. Such works live on in posterity because they are unfathomable and malleable and offer possible starting-points for later creative individuals engaged with their exceptional abilities in the task of recasting the historical future.

Just as has been shown in sections 6.1 and 6.6 above that it is incoherent to apply a concept of distributive justice to the commutative interplay in which esteem is accorded, it is also doubtful whether it is at all sensible to talk about a just distribution of fame in society. It is more likely the case that, if at all, only posterity can learn to estimate the name of an exceptionally creative individual, and that only under favourable circumstances, if the work is not lost or forgotten and comes, in time, to be appreciated. Fame is thus an extremely fickle, relative phenomenon of truth. For instance, it could be said that the undoubtably great Plato (and even this status is disputed) is esteemed for all the wrong reasons, i.e. on the basis of a merely superficial understanding. "Fame is based, properly speaking, on what one is in comparison with the others" (Der Ruhm beruht eigentlich auf dem, was einer im Vergleich mit den übrigen ist. 1956 p. 121)

> Auch wäre es eine elende Existenz, deren Wert oder Unwert darauf beruhte, wie sie in den Augen anderer erschiene [...] Vielmehr lebt und existiert ja jegliches Wesen seiner selbst wegen, daher auch zunächst in sich und für sich. — Was einer ist, in welcher Art und Weise es auch sei, das ist er zuvörderst und hauptsächlich für sich selbst: und wenn es hier nicht viel wert ist, so ist es überhaupt nicht viel. Hingegen ist das Abbild seines Wesens in den Köpfen anderer ein Sekundäres, Abgeleitetes und dem Zufall Unterworfenes, welches nur sehr mittelbar sich auf das erstere zurückbezieht. Zudem sind die Köpfe der Menge ein zu elender Schauplatz, als daß auf ihm das wahre Glück seinen Ort haben könnte. (1956 p. 121f)

> And it would be a miserable existence whose worth or lack of worth were based on how it appeared in the eyes of others... Rather, each being lives and exists for its own sake and therefore at first in and for itself. What somebody is, in whatever way, he is this primarily and mainly for himself, and if it is not worth much here, then it is not much at all. On the other hand, the image of its being in the heads of others is something secondary and derivative and subject to chance which is only related back to the former in a very mediated way. Moreover, the heads of the mass of people are much too miserable an arena for true happiness to have its place there.

The "heads" of others is, in truth, the open, shared clearing of 3D-time's enabling of truth in which each individual is somewho and in which each individual is held to be who they are in the opinion, view, regard and estimation of others.

Who I am, I am "primarily and mainly" for myself, and this self-stand demands a fortitude from my self. My existence in civil society depends on the estimation by others, primarily only in the general sense that I am regarded as a respectable person. My personhood, however, is only my general mask necessary for social intercourse and does not touch the singularity of who I am. It makes no sense to lay claim to a just social distribution of honour and esteem for the individual as this singular individual. The distribution of fame, too (which is the exaggeration of public honour and esteem), depends too much upon average understanding to be a true measure of individual worth and merit. And personhood is a sign of respect accorded generally by society to all its members who have not acted dishonourably and indecently. Aristotle's conception of the just distribution of honour according to the worth of an individual depends on a system of social ranking and hierarchy no longer applicable in the modern age in which each individual person has an abstract worth as a human, a kind of birthright. And even Aristotle sees that ability, excellence, accomplishment as a measure of worth is what it is as the lived practice of an individual living for itself, and not in how it is recognized, estimated and held to be by others.

A closer examination of modern civil society (which is still with us at the start of the third millennium) shows that each member of society is generally worthy of respect unless forfeited, on the one hand, and that the distribution of fame for exceptional individual merit, on the other, is entirely contingent and unreliable, and more illusion than truth in a time whose questions call for a radical alternative hermeneutic recasting. As Schopenhauer says, citing Osorius, "fame flees from those who seek it and follows those who neglect it, for the former accommodate themselves to the taste of their contemporaries and the latter defy it". (... daß der Ruhm vor denen flieht, die ihn suchen, und denen folgt, die ihn vernachlässigen: denn jene bequemen sich dem Geschmack ihrer Zeitgenossen an, diese trotzen ihm. 1956 p. 120) "For not that someone is regarded as a great man by the so frequently beguiled crowd, lacking in judgement, makes him enviable, but that he *is* one; nor that posterity learns something of him, but that thoughts are engendered in him which deserve to be preserved and pondered on for centuries to come is great happiness." ('About what one represents' Denn nicht daß einer von der urteilslosen, sooft betörten Menge für einen großen Mann gehalten werde, sondern daß er es sei, macht ihn beneidenswert; auch nicht, daß die Nachwelt von ihm erfahre, sondern daß in ihm sich Gedanken erzeugen, welche verdienen, Jahrhunderte hindurch aufbewahrt und nachgedacht zu werden, ist ein hohes Glück. 1956 p. 124)

The great thinker thinks thoughts which "deserve" to be pondered for centuries, and the thinker himself is the judge of this deservingness that may well be a misjudgement. The name of the thinker who first thought the thoughts may well be lost in oblivion. And precisely because they deserve to be pondered, great thoughts are neglected by all but the rare few, for what makes a thought great is that it is not run-of-the-mill and is therefore unpopular in a most literal sense. In challenging an hermeneutic cast of world, a great thought that recasts is a threat to the status quo and is suppressed by all means available. The great, recasting thought first has to be broken down into small change to enjoy popular dissemination and wide circulation, but even beforehand has to be engaged with by present-day thinkers. Such popular conversion inevitably amounts to putting a soft focus on the thought that facilitates its assimilation into the currency of 'people's' prevalent hegemonic average understanding. An established elite of thinkers is not at all inclined to countenance any hermeneutic recasting — quite the contrary.

Moreover, each of the great, recasting thinkers fails in working out the thought they are called on to think, for the thought and its folds and implications are too rich and inexhaustible to be exhausted by a finite existence. There is therefore always controversy and polemic surrounding the thinking of great thoughts. It is not that a philosophical thought is complex or complicated which makes it difficult, but that it is simple and apparently 'nothing', even trivial, and puts the dearest and most self-evident thought-prejudices of an age into question. The simplicity of the thought cuts through what has previously been established as self-evident to open up a new vista on the world as a whole. If you think (and therefore also feel) differently, the world itself is different and has a different mood. A new thought in its simplicity is potentially world-shaping and world-casting in casting out far ahead into the future. This disarming simplicity means that the significance of the thought is lost on most, including even the erudite and the educated. Especially among both natural and social scientists today, there is a strong proclivity in our age to mock philosophical thoughts as mere speculation which stands opposed to a down-to-earth understanding or well-founded scientific theories verified and established according to scientific method which are at least experimentally or empirically testable and thus putatively 'objective', i.e. generally verifiable and not restricted to a rare few who take it upon themselves to learn philosophical thinking.

Not only philosophical thinking and practical life are antithetical, but also philosophical thinking and modern scientific thinking. Strangely enough, despite the obstacles to gaining access to a simple great thought, philosophers' names are among those with the greatest historical longevity. They enjoy a quiet, often subterranean fame based upon multiple refractions of their thought into popular understanding, or are even taken seriously by a rare few, being taken up throughout the ages because their thinking addresses phenomena simply and raises inexhaustible questions. And because a simple great thought is inexhaustible, there will always be the rare new thinker at spasmodic, incalculable intervals in the openness of the historical time-clearing who engages with an ancient thought.

6.8 The gainful game among competitive players

The situation regarding the commutative justice of transactions can be made ever more complex by enriching the kind of transactions from a direct exchange of individual productive powers/abilities, of the products resulting from the exercise of abilities and the mediation of such transactions by money, to consider higher-order transactions involving higher-order (or derivative) goods. [113] Goods are then understood generally as all that contributes to living well within the customary practices of everyday life as shaped by the interplay of individual freedom of movement in its plurality. In extending to higher-order interchanges, the underlying conception of commutative justice as fairness remains unchanged, but the intricacies of transactions and the ontic possibilities for unfairness multiply exponentially.

The crucial socio-ontologically conceptual step has already been taken in Chapter 5, however: the *exchange-value* of labouring abilities or their products is exercised and comes about as a *power* to acquire in the reciprocal movement of interchange, by agreement, a good which another has. Exchange-value must therefore be understood as a power (for its exercise can bring about a change, namely, an interchange), but as a power sui generis, because its exercise is only possible by intermeshing, by agreement, with another who likewise has an exchange-value in the form of a potential ability or a finished product. Exchange-value is an elementary socio-ontological concept of *social power* in accord with freedom, whereas *physical violence against others* could be regarded as the most elementary concept of social power pure and simple (cf. Chapter 10.1).

What proceeds on a daily basis on the markets is hence properly called a *power interplay* of exchange-values based on *mutual estimation* of those powers. Once money comes to mediate exchange, it acquires as a mere thing the power to exchange for anything on the market and is therefore the crystallized, *reified* embodiment of universal exchange-value, a social power par excellence. This goes hand in hand with the real illusion that exchange-value itself is the inherent property of a thing and hence has a power (of universal exchange) residing in itself as such, an illusion which Karl Marx termed 'fetishism'. The social power of money is real enough, but it rests on a play of mutual estimation of human powers and abilities and thus on an interplay of human freedom. The essential socio-ontological structure of whoness remains hidden and unnoticed behind the real reified power and can be deciphered only by socio-ontological, 'speculative' thinking.

In a money economy, the daily lives of individuals necessarily assume the trait of *earning a money income*. Money must be had to mediate the exchanges that are part of shaping and leading a life. Hence *income-earning interplay*, too,

---

113 This and the following sections in this Chapter derive from my 'Anglophone Justice Theory, the Gainful Game and the Political Power Play' at URL www.arte-fact-org 2009.

must be regarded as an essential aspect of sociation emanating from free persons exercising their freedom of movement to shape their own lives. With the advent of money, a second possibility also arises: value reified in money can be employed to hire *labour power* which is set to work to provide services or produce finished goods for the market which are sold on the capitalist hirer's account, and not the labourer's. The labourer expending his or her labouring powers under the terms of a wage agreement with the capitalist enterprise receives for his or her troubles *wages* as income in estimation of his or her labouring powers, which are a further value-form. This is the emergence of *capital* as a socio-ontological category requiring the prior three value-forms of commodities and money and wage-labour along with their intermeshing in a kind of gainful social *movement* encompassing buying, production and selling.

The interplay of everyday life proceeding from the exercise of individual freedoms has become more complex and could be called specifically capitalist economic activity. Money has now assumed the *value-form of capital*, a further reified social power, which is also a characteristic movement from money advanced to an augmented money-sum returning, and income from transactions now has three value-forms: sales revenue, wages (including salaries, which are wages by another name) and profit. Gainful activity is conceptualized more complexly in terms of value-forms and the sociating movements enabled by them. As capitalist income-earning there is a power play not just on the markets on which abilities and products are traded, but also between the enterprising capitalists and those hiring out the exercise of their abilities, who can be termed the *employees* of the capitalist *employer* to avoid misleading exclusively 'blue collar' connotations of the word 'labourer' or 'worker'.

The refinement of the value-forms proceeds further, for (functioning) capital itself can split into productive and circulation capital concentrating respectively on the spheres of production and circulation, and also into functioning and finance capital with the latter lending money-capital to the former in return for *interest*, which is a further reified value-form. Furthermore, finance capital can *invest* capital in functioning capitalist enterprises in return for a cut in the net profits, which is paid out as *dividends*, i.e. a division of *profit of enterprise*. Through the mediation of finance capital, even income-earning employees can and do become lenders and investors in capitalist enterprises, thus deriving also interest and dividend income. All this is enabled socio-ontologically by the complex, interlocked structure of value-forms and the gainful movements of income-earning interplay they enable.

Finally, since the movement of value as capital requires also a *place* to take place, there is the value-form of *ground-rent* that arises from lease transactions between capitalists and landholders who can demand a rent for leasing access and use to pieces of the Earth's surface (of all kinds, including arable land, stretches of water, urban blocks of land) they monopolize through private ownership. All these many different kinds of transactions are, in the strict sense, social power plays among individual and collective players striving to earn income, now of all *four* kinds. Collectives arise naturally through individuals' agreeing to form a company of some kind or other and hence are also an expression of the exercise of the freedoms associated with earning income. Functioning capitals in production or circulation are a kind of company that can be called *enterprises*. Such companies based on a common interest may be organized more or less hierarchically with those higher in the hierarchy enjoying a certain *social power of command* over a workforce that is recognized on the basis of contractual agreement. Individuals and groups thereof *compete* on the many different kinds of markets distinguishable according to the value-forms within which they move. The entirety of this socio-ontological value-structure and its movement of interchange can be called the capitalist *gainful game* emanating ultimately from the power interplays among free individual players striving to earn income(s) of one kind or another that serves to support their lives according to their self-determined life-plans.

One could say that the gainful game among free individual players exercising their freedoms as persons estimating each other's powers results inevitably in this complex socio-ontological structure of interdependent value-forms. The superimposition of other, older social hierarchies, however, may hinder this unfolding of the gainful gain in pure form. The striving of free individuals for a life shaped by free will unfolds the various ramified reified value-forms and the economic movements within them, but starts with the lively striving of individual players, as sources of power residing in their own abilities, to have them estimated and validated. Capitalist society appears as an ongoing, daily competitive struggle among *revenue-source* (or *income-source*)[114] owners striving as competitive players to gain their respective kinds of revenue/income, namely: wages (including salaries), ground-rent, interest, and profit of enterprise, which latter is the residual remaining for the functioning capitalist enterprise, which may, in turn, be paid out to shareholders as dividends if it is a collectively owned joint-stock company. This completes the quadruple of basic value-forms that fit together to form the capitalist gainful game in which all income-earning individuals are involved.

---

114 For more detail on the revenue-source value-forms cf. Eldred, M. 1984/2015 §§ 7ff.

There is, of course, no end to deriving further higher-order value-forms, since money as reified value and contractual agreement as the form of interplay offer many opportunities for imaginatively inventing new tradable market values, odd hybrids and stratospherically derivative financial products such as discounted bills of exchange and accounts receivable, stock, bond and real estate investment funds, futures contracts, interest swaps, investment certificates, collateralized debt obligations, synthetic collateralized debt obligations, etc. etc. All the basic value-forms and the further, higher-order derivative value-forms of the gainful game are overlaid over the elementary value-form of the mutual exchange of individual powers and abilities, which is the as-yet (dialectically speaking in the thinking-through) non-reified interchange of mutual estimation in which sociating, social value first comes about socio-ontologically.

The development of the various value-forms is simultaneously the development of various kinds of *social power* that come into play in the competitive struggle. For instance, land has the social power to draw a ground-rent income for its owner by being leased to a capitalist enterprise. Because the complex interplay of powers takes place via the exercise of many free wills, it hovers over a *groundlessness* and is inherently *incalculable, risky* and subject to sudden game-changes. There are no guarantees in the striving for income, and no surely precalculable outcomes, but only potentially gainful power plays that may either win or lose. The competitive gainful game is one played on continually shifting sands, and firm contracts offer only temporary respite from market uncertainties. "Through their own free actions within the form of contract they [the subjects of competition = players in the gainful game] inaugurate their subjection to a process under no conscious social control."[115] This process result-

---

[115] Eldred 1984/2015 §23. A full, step-by-step development of the value-forms can be found in the Appendix to this work: 'A Value-Form Analytic Reconstruction of *Capital*' by Michael Eldred, Marnie Hanlon, Lucia Kleiber & Mike Roth. That the capitalist economic process is a game (an estimative value-interplay with competitive players) in a strict socio-ontological sense, as revealed by value-form analysis, has consequences for economics that can hardly be overestimated: "Form-analysis shows that there can be *no* economic theory in the sense in which this is attempted by economics. Economics (marxist and otherwise) is a futile attempt at a premonetary theory of capitalist economy. [...] Form-analysis restricts itself with good reason to the analysis of the contradictory form of bourgeois society. It does not need to engage in (endless) empirical research; the world to be conceptualised lies to hand in the form of everyday consciousness. Empirical details are merely embellishments, 'roccoco ornaments' to connect the general with a specific context. Those sociologists and economists who pursue their research of capitalist economies operate on the conceptual level of an avid newspaper reader. The complicated mathematical economic theories in vogue today are an obscene hoax which

ing from interplay can appropriately be called a game. The appropriate socio-ontological name for capitalism is therefore the *gainful game* (cf. also Chapter 9.6).

Thus insight is gained into the intimate intertwinedness between the play of individual freedoms and the riskiness of such freedom for individuals, groups thereof, and even the economy as a whole which is a power game beyond any instance's control. The socio-ontological structure and movement of the gainful game within this structure is not a 'model' constructed from reality (that could be empirically tested by empirical research), nor is it an imagined stateless state of nature, nor is it an hypothetical choice situation set up to choose 'principles of justice' by agreement, but rather it is an abstract thought-structure with full validity attained by thinking through certain well-known, incontrovertible elements abstracted from everyday life as we know it, moving dialectically from one appropriately conceptualized element to another to build up a connected socio-ontological structure *providing insight not to be had any other way*.

Despite appearances to the contrary, any way at all of approaching issues of justice in society has to be abstract in the sense that it focuses on certain elements while bracketing others off, but this is disguised by spinning an 'accessible', illustrative narrative or by presenting plausible explanations that leave the vital questions glossed over and unanswered. When a philosopher writes 'accessibly', it is a sure sign that the deeper philosophical question has been begged for the sake of not overstraining the reader's understanding. The reader therefore learns nothing. Even the socio-ontological structure of the gainful game as sketched above has gained a certain concreteness because it is the concretion of many determinations, starting with consideration of the simple exchange of individual abilities. The *ontic* complexity of the gainful game, the possible moves by the players within the game are sheer endless, for the socio-

---

appropriate social wealth for the ostensible solution of problems which are in principle insoluble" (Eldred 1984/2015 § 66Aa). Economists, economic historians, sociologists et al. who pursue economic research make a career in and are honoured, estimated and even celebrated by learned institutions precisely because their endeavours conform to the *will to effective power* suffusing the modern age. That the will to effective power is the underlying motivation remains more or less entirely hidden to the actors on stage in this age, who may even regard themselves as contributing disinterestedly to 'objective' social research and human well-being. To *be* a science, i.e. to be *estimated* and *validated as* a science in today's world, social science in all its variants must orient itself toward the mathematico-empirical blue-print for modern science already laid down explicitly in Descartes' *Regulae*. All else remains *invisible* to today's thinking, whose raison d'être is to deny the (socio-)ontological difference and keep it closed, which amounts to a closure and degeneration of the Western-cum-global mind.

ontological structure is not a rigid framework, nor does it aim at multifactorial ontic-causal explanation, but permits and enables infinitely varied moves motivated by gainful strivings and strategies.

The gainful game as both socio-ontological structure and movement is the appropriate initial situation for considering *commutative* justice among free individual players in power interplay with one another as abstract persons, for it covers the gamut of the possible kinds of social power plays in which issues connected with commutative justice arise. Moreover, the intermediate conclusion can already be drawn that it is commutative justice, and not distributive justice, that first arises as an issue from the social life generated by a plurality of freely interchanging players sharing a world. This represents a major objection against Anglophone justice theory, as will seen in more detail in following sections.

6.9 Recent debates on justice in Anglophone moral philosophy and the disappearance of commutative justice

> Regulae autem Iustitiae fundamentales, seu Utilitatis publicae sunt duae: (1) ut ne cuiqvam auferatur res (*sine vitio*) possesso [...] et (2) ut cuiqve tribuatur qvantum ipso opus est ad publicam utilitatem juvandam. [...] Illa regula juris stricti fundamentum est, haec aeqvitatis. [...] illa est justitiae commutativae, haec distributivae.
>
> Leibniz 'Brief an Conring' 2003 p. 328f

> Now, there are two fundamental rules for Justice or public Utility: (1) that no one will have taken away from him (*without fault*) a thing he possesses [...] and (2) that everyone is to be attributed the amount needed to promote public utility. [...] The former rule is the strict foundation of right, the latter of equity [...] The former is commutative justice, the latter distributive.

In the endeavour to connect the dots from Aristotelean justice to debates on justice in Anglophone moral philosophy in the second half of the twentieth century, it is striking that they focus on issues of distributive justice to such an extent that even the term 'commutative justice' rarely occurs. For instance, there is an entry on distributive justice, but astoundingly no entry on commutative justice in the *Stanford Encyclopedia of Philosophy*. Both these kinds of justice are named originally by Aristotle who, in the fifth book of the *Nicomachean Ethics*, deals with distributive justice as an issue concerning the fair and deserving apportionment of the goods of living to individuals on the basis of criteria of their individual worth, as discussed in detail in preceding sections. Such goods comprise not only material goods, including money, but also, and significantly, the good of honour and esteem (τιμή) which is a social good associated with an individual who's estimation by others as a worthy, honourable individual.

As far as I can see, the good of esteem and its distribution seldom (Michael Walzer is an exception) plays a role in modern philosophical debates over distributive justice, which instead concentrate on material goods and, perhaps, the 'distribution' of political rights such as freedom of speech and the right to stand for political office. Even libertarian positions in this debate tend to be subsumed under the heading of distributive justice[116] by foolishly considering individual liberty as just one more good to be distributed and weighed against other, competing goods, rather than as the fundamental starting-point for any consideration whatsoever of justice in the modern world. If the question concerning freedom is intimately linked with the question concerning justice, individual liberty and the way of social living in which it is at all possible cannot be simply up for grabs in weighing and trading them against other desirable goods of living handed out by distribution, but, at the very least, must be viewed as colliding and conflicting with proposed candidates for ultimate social goods.

The disappearance of commutative justice in recent Anglophone discussions of justice in political and moral philosophy as well as in social theory in favour of various schemes for purely distributive justice is no accident. There are those who deny altogether that there is even an issue concerning commutative justice, i.e. the justness relating to the transactions and interplay in civil society. It is important to deny that there is such a thing as commutative justice in sociating interplay in order to strip it of any status as having, of itself, just and fair outcomes that have to be 'lived with'. Rather, the outcomes, i.e. consequences, have to be measured against criteria of distributive or social justice, and therefore, for adherents of Rawlsian, utilitarian or egalitarian principles of justice, it is entirely just, even self-evidently so, to revise outcomes of the gainful game by means of the superior power of the state to meet distributive criteria of some kind. Instead of the fair interplay of *potentials*, of social powers at play, it is only the *actual, final, factual* outcomes of the power interplay that can be assessed 'objectively' as just or unjust. Hence there are countless empirical sociological studies on so-called 'social justice', simply because they are easier to carry out on factually available data.

---

116 Cf. the entry on 'Distributive Justice' in the *Stanford Encyclopedia of Philosophy* by Julian Lamont and Christi Favor at URL plato.stanford.edu/entries/justice-distributive/ Accessed December 2009.

One critic of the commutative/distributive justice distinction claims that "commutative justice, when not directly relying upon a broader distributive background [...], is merely a matter of fulfilling promises, or performing contractual obligations, and as such, is not a matter of justice at all".[117] Sadurski adduces two examples to prove his point:

> The payment of a salary by an employer may be considered both as the exchange of money for labour (commutative justice) and as the payment of a salary to an employee based on her rank (performance, qualifications, etc.) within a given structure (e.g., an enterprise), in a way that is proportional with the way salary is differentiated within that structure (distributive justice). And because the goods 'exchanged' (labour, money) are ultimately incommensurable, the only way we can assert our view as to the 'equality' in this exchange is against a background which is par excellence distributive: by comparing this particular employer with those who earn more and those who earn less, and checking if the salary paid is proportional to whatever we consider to be a morally proper basis for a salary differentiation.

and

> The case of a (putative) duty to fulfil an unjust promise (for instance, to murder someone), or to keep an unjust contract, [...] yes, we have a general duty to fulfil our promises and contractual obligations, but not necessarily when the consequences of such actions would prove unjust. And if this is the case, then it seems to me natural to say that principles of justice may, at times, collide with the general duty to keep promises. And if the latter can collide with the former, then the latter cannot be part of the former.

Is the situation of contract "merely a matter of fulfilling promises"? No. Contract is a form of intercourse between parties who first of all respect each other's free personhood, each other's life, liberty and property, and this applies also to the contract's content, which must not of itself violate free personhood. An agreement with a contract killer is therefore not a just contract at all from the outset, and not because of the agreement's unjust outcome (a dead person). With regard to the example of setting an employee's salary, the equality and fairness pertaining to it is whether the market negotiation between the two parties has an outcome, as assessed by both parties and also agreed, that is comparable to the going rate for the same type of work elsewhere. It is not a matter of applying one-sidedly the employer's criterion or convenient method for setting salaries by using a pay scale based on seniority and internal performance measures, but

---

117 Wojciech Sadurski 'Commutative, distributive and procedural justice – what does it mean, what does it matter?' *Social Science Research Network Electronic Library* URL ssrn.com/abstract=1471022 Accessed Dec. 2009.

of a bilateral, reciprocal agreement. The employee may not care less about how she has been ranked by the employer and find a better paid position elsewhere, or argue with the employer that the pay-scale criteria simply do not apply in her case or have been entirely misapplied.

Moreover, there are two intertwined aspects to the employer's applying a ranking to an employee to determine salary: firstly, the envisaged amount of pay, which is a matter of bargaining and commutative justice over what is a fair salary, and secondly, the *esteem* with which the employer estimates the employee according to her assessed performance, etc., which is a matter of distributive justice insofar as, to be fair, the employee must be ranked according to genuine merit and ability, quite apart from how that ranked position is remunerated. Thus, for example, the employer may express his/its (apparent) esteem for the employee by elevating the position's title, but without giving a pay-rise, which shows that the aspects of esteem and salary are separate. Therefore, there is no good reason to abandon a concept of commutative justice. On the contrary, it is important to learn to see socio-ontologically precisely why there are two major kinds of justice.

John Rawls' *Theory of Justice* from 1971 and Robert Nozick's libertarian reply, *Anarchy, State, and Utopia,* from 1974 stake out the territory for much of the Anglophone debate among professional, academic, political and moral philosophers since then. Rawls' book itself is a response to, a further development of, and a compromise between two positions on distributive justice dominant since the nineteenth century: egalitarianism and utilitarianism. What is to be distributed are primarily the material goods produced as an output by society as a whole, along with positions in hierarchies and political offices in the state. Hence there is a link to political economy, itself originally a branch of moral philosophy, and economics. By contrast, Nozick is concerned first and foremost with individual freedom, which is a power, potency or potential, and never a realized, finished, actual outcome.

6.9.1 Walzer's plurality of distribution systems

The third prominent figure to help stake out the area of Anglophone moral philosophical debate on justice is Michael Walzer, who gave a seminar together with Robert Nozick at Harvard in 1971 on 'Capitalism and Socialism' from which Walzer's 1983 book, *Spheres of Justice: A Defense of Pluralism and Equality,* finally issued. The first sentence of the first chapter of this work names its subject as "distributive justice". There is no mention of commutative justice in the entire book. This very first paragraph calls "human society" (ahistorically, anthropologically) a "distribution community", referring then immediately to the "distribution and exchange of things that brings us purposefully together". So why isn't human society, first and foremost, an exchange society? The glaring imprecision in Walzer's statement is not accidental, but essential for his entire study, for it relies on treating the "exchange of things" as distribution, thus allowing the issue of commutative justice, which is concerned above all with the fair exchange of things, to disappear from sight. The sleight of hand is hardly noticeable, for who would want to deny that the many *exchange* transactions of goods *results* in a *distribution* of material goods? Isn't it pedantry to insist on the distinction between exchange and distribution, (and ultimately between two distinct modes of presencing: δύναμις and ἐντελέχεια)? What hangs on this distinction, anyway? And, due to absence of any socio-ontological thinking, nobody seems to have noticed anything missing so far. All the worse for Anglophone moral thinking on justice!

Walzer's first chapter goes on to discuss a "theory of goods" in which material, economic goods play the dominant role. The market is treated as "one of the most important mechanisms for the distribution of social goods". Again exchange is treated *as* a mechanism and *as* distribution. By contrast, as has been shown in Chapter 5, exchange is to be grasped hermeneutically *as* an interplay of *potentials*, of *powers* among players striving for gain in which the outcome is uncertain, whereas, viewed from the total *output* of the social exchange process, the play of exchange, as movement itself a kind or 'sight' of ἐνέργεια, *results* in an *actual* distribution of material goods. The exchange process is where the exchange-*value* of goods *becomes actual* as a *power* to acquire another good, which is a gain for both parties to the transaction, but even actualized exchange-value must be distinguished from total social distribution. As *means of exchange*, and *not* as a 'means of distribution', money must be conceptualized as a reified value-form mediating the ongoing exchange metabolism of the economy. The connection between commodities as value-form and money as value-form is made through a *dialectic* (cf. e.g. Plato's *Sophist*) between ontological concepts that grasp the being of commodities and the being of money. In Walzer's scheme of things, however, money is made invisible as a means of exchange; it is subsumed beneath the determination of means of distribution. Instead of *being* a value-form as a reified social power, money as a tool, a "mechanism" for social distribution is muddled up with many other distribution systems of social values such as social status and social honour systems in all kinds of societies all over the world and at all historical times.

Hence, although Walzer quotes Marx on money copiously throughout his book, he nowhere grasps the socio-ontological *concept* of money in its significance. The issue of the free interplay on the markets mediated by money that is linked to the very possibility, historically, of the free individual, thus necessitating consideration of the commutative justice of this interplay (and not merely of its just distributive result), is glossed over and goes entirely unnoticed. An entire problem for the possibility of justice is made to disappear as a non-issue, and Walzer contents himself with gathering materials and examples from many different sources to underscore, in sociological fashion, his thesis of a plurality of spheres of justice. No attempt whatever is made to undertake a connected conceptual analysis of these different spheres that would bring their *mode of being as such* to light. A plurality of spheres of justice constituted by a disjointed jumble of different kinds of distributive justice jockeying alongside each other is supposed to justify Walzer's appeal for pluralism, while at the same time ignoring the deeper-lying conflicts between individual freedom as a social interplay of powers, and criteria for an attained, actual distribution of social goods of all kinds. Social and political power struggles can be talked about endlessly, drawing on historical and sociological material, but in this way the entirely familiar phenomena of power and power struggles can never come to their adequate socio-ontological concepts. Hence, for example, in Walzer's hands, Hegel's ontological phenomenology of a "struggle for recognition" becomes a bland "sociology of titles" (Chap. 11).

6.9.2 Conceptions of distributive justice and the welfare state

The elaborator of thinking on distributive justice after Plato, Aristotle, himself postulates four different criteria for the distribution of the goods of living, including, among others, material goods, namely: free birth, wealth, nobility of birth and merit/ability/excellence (ἐλευθερία, πλοῦτος, εὐγενεία, ἀρετή *Eth. Nic.* V 1131a27ff; cf. ii) above). Of these four, only two have weight in the modern era as justified criteria, namely, free birth (every human is born free since the century of the French Revolution and human rights) and merit and ability (an individual deserves a portion of wealth proportionate to his or her abilities), whereas wealth as a criterion for distributing goods is valid today mainly only among investors owning parts of companies, and nobility of birth has lost any traction as a criterion for allotting wealth and still has application perhaps only in distributing the good of respect and honour in certain traditional social customs.

Egalitarian doctrine proceeds on the basic premise of free birth as the criterion for the distribution of total social material goods: because each individual
human being is simply born free, it has putatively a right to an equal share in
the social product, and the political constitution of a just society must be such
that equal apportionment of produced material goods is guaranteed and realized. *Utilitarianism* is concerned with maximizing the utility or happiness of a
society which comes down 'materialistically' to maximizing the total income of
society's members: that distribution of total social material output is just for
which its maximization is attained. Rawls proposes a middle course, captured
by his "difference principle" which postulates that deviations from equal distribution of total material output are just insofar as the material standard of living
of the "least advantaged" is raised. In all three of these positions on justice,
society is regarded as a kind of machine for producing material well-being. For
such a conception, individual freedom becomes relativized to considerations of
productive efficiency, and it is precisely in such terms that individual freedom
has come to justify itself: 'we' as a whole are better off materially by virtue of the
productive efficiencies of incentivized individual freedom.

Moreover, since the orientation is toward maximizing and sharing out total
material output, the *secure precalculability* of such output gains in weight. The
total productive machine called society, to be just, ostensibly should securely
produce well-being for all, and the riskiness of freedom in its social interplay
becomes a negative to be avoided. Rather a bird in the hand than two in the
bush. The egalitarian, Rawlsian and utilitarian conceptions of distributive social
justice meet the requirements of social policy-makers advising the government
on issues such as redistributive taxation policy, and thus debates among moral
philosophers over the criteria for just distribution of total social material output
become 'politically relevant' and 'practically useful'. Apart from the issue of
supposedly inviolable individual human freedom, even the justness of distribution becomes subjected to criteria of measurability and practicability. An ontological determination of human being itself, that is, that the mode of being of
the human being is freedom, is not present in the debates weighing up the pros
and cons of different just 'distribution models'.

In contrast to a precalculable distribution of material well-being, the gainful
game as an interplay of estimating powers has an uncertain outcome for each of
the players and even for the totality of players. The powers at play start with
individual powers and abilities that have to be validated on the market in a
mirror game of estimation. The products of labour, too, have to validate their
power as exchange-value on the market. Then, as has been shown in section 6.8
above, there are the derived social powers associated with each of the reified

value-forms: the power of capital, of organized wage-labour, of finance capital, of landowners, each in a plurality. The fully-blown gainful game is generated by the exercise of the freedoms of private property under the motivation of earning an income of some kind. Individual freedom of the person is therefore a power, potency and potential, and not the finished presence, or actuality, of an achieved output of some kind or other (such as GDP or total well-being). For this reason, the libertarian position on justice is antithetical to all those positions on distributive justice that demand 'just' shares of the total social material product according to some criterion or other. If some version of distributive, so-called social justice holds sway, the freedom of the gainful game motivated by individual striving must be clipped and (partially) suppressed to fit an ostensibly just distribution of total social output, and the income outcomes of the gainful game must be redistributed, which is the socio-ontological origin of the *social welfare state*. It is therefore a major issue for theories of distributive justice to meet the challenges posed by an ontological hallmark of human being, viz. its freedom of self-movement.

One strand in this issue arises especially for traditional and Rawlsian egalitarianism when arguments are made along the lines that there are players in the gainful game, or on its sidelines, who, 'through no fault of their own', are at a disadvantage, e.g. if they are chronically ill or disabled, or simply have below-average abilities to offer to the market. Such natural disadvantages, perhaps reinforced by the social environment of someone's upbringing, are said to place such players at an unfair disadvantage that demands a compensatory redistribution of the output of total social production. But does the essential freedom of human being in itself demand such a compensation for unequal opportunities in the gainful game due to the natural distribution of individual abilities or the differences in social environment into which each individual is cast? In response to this question it must be pointed out that individual human freedom comprises not only the freedom to cast one's own life of one's own free will, grasping the opportunities that arise (or failing to do so), but also *having been cast* into a situation over which the individual has no control and for which no instance in particular can be blamed or praised. An individual cannot choose its parents, its natural innate abilities, its place of birth in a certain country at a certain historical period, the customs and traditions into which it is born, the Zeitgeist of a time, the way of thinking of an epoch. It is simply thrown, and this thrownness of having-been-cast is part of its freedom, namely, the negative side. Only from the present can an individual cast into the future and shape its own self in coming to terms with, exerting its own powers and making the best of, how it has *always already* been cast.

There is therefore no justification for a redistributive justice to even out the inequalities in the distribution of individual abilities and disabilities, but there is a case to be made for the injustice of social rules of interplay that unfairly rig the individual's starting-position in the gainful game, such as *social discrimination* where the abstract dignity of free personhood is denied. This is an important issue to which we shall return in section 6.12 below, taking care not to confuse issues of fake distributive (social) justice with genuine social (in-)justice in the proper sense relating to discrimination.

6.10 Critical appraisal of Nozickian libertarianism

6.10.1 The legitimate founding of a state

Nozick's 1974 book has set in train debates on various issues that continue to the present day. One such issue is the legitimate founding of a state with which Nozick deals in arguments against anarchism (that denies the legitimacy of a state altogether) within the framework of a notion of a Lockean social contract. The starting-point is therefore a 'state of nature' in which the plurality of individuals has natural rights of free personhood and property ownership, summed up by the Lockean formula of "Life, Liberty and Estate". Nozick conceives the state basically as an instance having an effective monopoly of coercive power over the inhabitants of a certain territory. Its role is to protect the lives and property, including the contractual intercourse, of its subjects and hence to exercise force against those who commit acts of violence, theft, fraud and breach of contract against its citizens.[118] In his argument against anarchist principles, Nozick is at pains to show that a state can be legitimate even without the consent of all its citizens. He therefore starts with the notion of individuals hiring private protection agencies to enforce their rights which is then widened to a dominant protection agency becoming gradually a state with "an effective monopoly on the use of force in its territory" (Vallentyne 2006.). The driving force for this gradual widening of a private agency's coercive power is that more and more individuals give their consent to subjecting themselves to this instance for the sake of their own protection. In a state of nature, by contrast, the

---

118 Cf. Peter Vallentyne 'Robert Nozick, *Anarchy, State and Utopia*' in *The Twentieth Century: Quine and After* (Vol. 5 of *Central Works of Philosophy*) edited by John Shand, Acumen Publishing 2006 pp. 86–103. URL klinechair.missouri.edu/on-line%20papers/Nozick.doc Accessed Dec. 2009.

individuals are said to have a right to protect their own lives and property, including by force, so the emergence of the state is a matter of a transfer of natural rights to a superior social instance which then monopolizes the effective use of force against offenders' bodies and their possessions.

The fallacy in this state-of-nature and social-contract way of arguing lies in the very imagining of an historico-chronological emergence, as if rights inhered in individuals who could only transfer them by consent. The dilemma can be seen already by considering that individual rights, and their enjoyment and exercise, are always already social; they only make sense for a plurality of individuals sociating with each other on the basis of their own free will. Free sociation takes place in the first place via an agreement called contract, according to which the contracting partners give their word to perform such-and-such for each other. Any contractual agreement is exposed to the *possibility of dispute* over what has been agreed. Even someone accused of blatant theft or robbery may claim legitimate acquisition of the thing allegedly stolen. Who is to decide? This is the crucial question, for even if a victim of theft takes back from the thief what has been stolen off him, who is to say that the victim is himself not a thief? Or if someone defends themself against assault, who is to say that he himself was not the assailant when each accuses the other and it is a case of word against word? Or if fraud has allegedly been perpetrated, who is to decide whether this is truly the case if the fraudster denies any wrong-doing?

Any interchange between individuals that has infringed the fairness demanded of transactions must be adjudicated by a *superior third party* above the fray of the two parties' self-interests, to which both parties must submit for judgement. Hence the demand that the judge be *impartial*. The interchange itself has generated something beyond the individual wills of the two parties to the agreement (or non-agreement), a 'we' with a will to a fair and just transaction that cannot be located solely in either of the parties, nor in the sum of the two individual wills, nor even in witnesses to the transaction, since one or other of the two parties may contest their evidence. Individual freedom and its exercise in an intertwining of free wills in an elementary 'we' necessitates both the will to fairness of the transaction and the will to have the fairness of the transaction adjudicated by a third party in the case of dispute. The case of dispute can never be ruled out in the mutually binding and intertwining exercise of free wills. In willing a transaction with each other, the two free-willed parties will willy-nilly a 'we' and the adjudication by a judge of any dispute that may arise, and have therefore implicitly already submitted to a judge as a legitimate instance.

This is already the kernel of an incipient government, no matter whether the individuals explicitly consent, in contractarian manner, to subjection to a superior instance or not. The very concept of individual freedom demands, via several mediations, subjection to impartial, superior, adjudicating instances which collectively may be called government or the state, unified under the initial determination that the judiciary is dedicated to righting (alleged) wrongs that inevitably occur wherever the freedom of interchanges among individuals is lived out. The state as protector of life, liberty and property is legitimate by virtue of its conformity to the *concept* of human freedom, i.e. the essential human condition of freedom in its power interplay, which is, at its core, *individual* freedom, regardless of whether it is explicitly consented to by individual citizens. If the term were not so hackneyed by common-sense, one could say the *nature* of human beings is to be free.

Those who argue over justice and legitimacy in the framework of a social contract theory have overlooked that a critique of the notion of a social contract is bequeathed to us by Hegel's *Philosophy of Right*, a work that refuted basic postures in recent Anglophone debates 150 years in advance. To argue from a speculative concept of freedom, of course, is anathema to Anglophone mentality, which is quick to level the charge of idealism. But freedom, if it is anything at all, is first and foremost an *idea*, that is, a *'look'* or *'sight'* of the being of human being itself, an ontological *sight* that can come into view as an *insight* for the thinking philosophical mind.

The above line of thought focuses on the conceptual (and not merely practical, ontic) necessity of a judicial instance that raises individual free will to a higher level beyond itself, and not on the necessity of a protective agency for protecting the lives and property of individuals, and therefore it deviates from Nozick's imagined historical line of reasoning about protective agencies which, as Murray Rothbard points out[119], is faulty anyway. Such protection can well be provided already by private security forces without these attaining the status of a rightful, superior instance. Indeed, the actions of private security forces are just as much subject to judicial scrutiny as those of private individuals, and conflicts may arise when a private security guard uses force against any person when fulfilling his protective duties, which conflicts in turn require adjudication by the acknowledged legitimate judicial instance to judge whether rights of person or property have been infringed. Similarly, a police force exercising

---

119 Murray N. Rothbard 'Robert Nozick and the Immaculate Conception of the State' in *Journal of Libertarian Studies* Vol. 1 No.1 1977 pp. 45–57. URL www.mises.org/journals/jls/1_1/1_1_6.pdf Accessed December 2009.

physical force over a populace in the name of protection of life and property is not the kernel of the state, for this function can be exercised also privately. Rather, a police force is, in the first place, the agent of the judicial instance which is charged with forcibly bringing parties to a conflict over an interchange before a judge when one or both of the parties refuses to appear. The physical force or threat thereof is just and rightful because the resolution of conflicts over interchanges among free persons itself is justly referred to a judicial instance. It is therefore an erroneous 'materialist' view to define the state in terms of holding a monopoly over physical violence, for the use of physical force or the threat thereof has to be *legitimated* cogently in the name of freedom.

6.10.2 The original appropriation of (landed) property

Nozick's theory of justice is a libertarian theory modelled on the Lockean fundamental rights of the individual to "Life, Liberty and Estate" and hence is weighted toward the freedom of private property. In line with social contract theory, an imagined, fictitious history is fashioned to account for how private property comes about in the so-called state of nature. Nozick's version of basic rights therefore includes "rights of *initial acquisition*: the right to acquire full property rights in unowned things..." (Vallentyne 2006). For any historical theory of justice it is a problem to account for the original appropriation of property. Once property has been appropriated it is easy enough to account for its just transfer through contractual agreement between private property owners. "Locke's version of [the right to initial acquisition] requires that one 'mix one's labor' with the thing and that one leave 'enough and as good' for others" (Vallentyne 2006), where the provision 'enough and as good' is termed by Nozick the "Lockean proviso". Since Locke there has been much debate over appropriation of property by 'mixing one's labour' with things, although, if one has any sense of history, the issue here is the original appropriation of *landed* property not by individuals as such, but by groups of people such as tribes. Only subsequent to the appropriation of a territory by a group can one speak sensibly of the allocation, *perhaps*, of land to individuals as private property, again a fictitious history. Hence the issue for rightful original appropriation in the Lockean proviso concerns land ownership and the social power to derive income from landed property as ground-rent.

All original appropriation of land back in the mists of time is most frequently an act of force where a group occupies land (a hunting ground, a fishing ground, pastures, fields, etc.), thus pushing out some other group, i.e. if one does not imagine the geographical spreading of a species called homo sapiens over the Earth. Wars and skirmishes over land may then establish habitual rights of occupancy over time in which the original struggles for the land are forgotten. For the original appropriation of land historically, right is might in the situation of a 'state of nature' in the sense that there is no acknowledged superior instance to appeal to for adjudication in the case of conflict, which is therefore, if diplomacy between the parties fails, decided by force of arms, perhaps according to acknowledged rules of war. As is apparent today, compensation for forceful and unjust occupancy of land by invasion only has relevance when the struggles over the appropriation of land are relatively recent historically and the details of previous land occupancy and land-use still alive in the memory, i.e. when it is 'as if' it were a case of a civil dispute over land rights rather than of land appropriation by conquest. Any theory of justice, such as social contractarianism, is on shaky ground in arguing historically, or even theoretically, from a purportedly innocent original appropriation of land. But such simple-minded thinking has the charm of easy comprehensibility.

Furthermore, it is a matter of mere historical fantasizing to imagine an original appropriation of land *as* individual private property. Groups, tribes, peoples originally appropriate land by force which then become their territory, within which land may (or may not) then be allocated to individuals, such as when a king rewards a lord, or a lord rewards a true vassal by awarding a stretch of land to him which then becomes a family estate that is handed down over generations through a line of succession. To speak of an acquisition of landed property by 'mixing one's labour' with land is a quaint notion, since territories are appropriated originally by mixing the bloody labour of warriors with the soil. Private landed property and the trade therein by transfer of title and lease are relatively recent historically, and, only once private landed property is established can its rights be determined as a matter of commutative justice which only makes sense in a society in which interchange is customarily practised.

Once the original acquisition of private property is widened beyond the appropriation of land it is easy to account for it, because private property in things can be acquired by hiring out one's labouring abilities. Such reified private property is then an individual's 'estate' which may be further accumulated. Upon further accumulation by means of saving, it may even become entrepreneurial or finance capital or landed property. The entire system of private landed property depends on the establishment of the various fundamental value-forms required to constitute the gainful game. Today, the entire surface of the Earth, its land and even its seas, has pretty much been carved up as sovereign state territories within which the rights of private landed property and sovereign territorial ownership apply.

For a discussion of issues of justice in today's world it is best to restrict it to those societies in which the socio-ontological constellation of the gainful game holds sway. Admittedly, this socio-ontological constellation of historical being can only be seen by the philosophical mind; it is invisible to historians, journalists, politicians, empiricists, moralizing philosophers, etc. who are blinded by its obviousness. Nevertheless, to say that today there is such a thing as a globalized capitalist economy is to admit implicitly that underlying it all there is a definite value-form-determinate constellation of social being. A focus on a socio-ontological constellation is the philosophical alternative to other approaches to the question concerning justice, including social contractarianism in particular. As I have repeatedly said, all these alternative approaches do not see the ontological difference at all.

6.10.3 An attack on libertarian freedom conceived as individual caprice

Hugh LaFollette's paper, 'Why Libertarianism Is Mistaken',[120] offers an attack on libertarianism which is instructive for bringing the issues to light. His article launches with the assertion, "Central to libertarianism is the claim that individuals should be free from the interference of others. Personal liberty is the supreme moral good." (LaFollette 1979) Why "moral good"? It should be noted that moral philosophy is concerned with what *ought* to be the case, and not with the socio-ontology of what *is as such*, i.e. the whatness of whats and the whonness of whos. This is a general weakness of Anglophone moral-political philosophy: it is an *ought* hovering over an *is*, with only tenuous ties between the two and without the 'is' itself being interrogated. It is therefore constantly endangered by that favourite, self-delusive, futile pastime indulged in by well-meaning people: Utopianism. The question concerning justice is, properly speaking, not a moral question, but one concerning what social interplay among human beings conforms to the essence, nature or concept of human being itself. Unjust social interplay violates the *mode of being* of human beings as such and, as established and entrenched social interplay, can lead to a degradation and destruction of human being itself. Such degradation can proceed

---

120 In *Justice and Economic Distribution* John Arthur and William Shaw (eds.), Prentice Hall, Englewood Cliffs 1979, pp. 194–206. URL www.hughlafollette.com/papers/libertar.htm Accessed Dec. 2009.

subtly without being noticed by people themselves, who may even unwittingly will and want it. The issue for any theory of justice is the historical possibility of a society in conformity with freedom, a 'look' of social movement. It cannot be assumed that 'people' unconditionally want to be free, and a theory of justice cannot proceed by arguments of the kind, "Most people think that x ought to be the case", which degrades the task of thinking to an expression of mere opinion.

LaFollette provides an example of how libertarian liberty is purportedly restricted: "The slave-holders' freedom [e.g.] was justifiably restricted by the presence of other people; the fact that there were other persons limited their acceptable alternatives. But that is exactly what the libertarian denies. Freedom, he claims, cannot be justifiably restricted without consent. In short, the difficulty is this: the libertarian talks as if there can be no legitimate non-consensual limitations on freedom, yet his very theory involves just such limitations. Not only does this appear to be blatantly inconsistent, but even if he could avoid this inconsistency, there appears to be no principled way in which he can justify only his theory's non-consensual limitations on freedom." (LaFollette 1979) The very nature of freedom, from the outset, must take into account that there is a plurality of human beings living *with each other* on Earth and that the question concerning justice arises only when there is such a plurality, for justice concerns always sociation with others. To imagine that there is first a solitary, free individual able to enjoy boundless liberty, who is then restricted in its liberty by the presence of others, is a rather bovine misrecognition of the very nature of freedom.

"So imagine with Hobbes and some libertarians that individuals are seen as initially being in a state of perfect freedom. In such a state, Hobbes claims, 'nothing can be just. Right and wrong have there no place.'[121] To introduce right and wrong of any sort is to put moral limitations on individual freedom. To that extent, everyone's freedom is restricted." (LaFollette 1979) The question concerning justice simply does not arise in an imagined state of nature, for it is a state of 'might is right' and anything but a "state of perfect freedom". LaFollette confuses freedom with the *arbitrariness of individual will that is able to realize itself without resistance*. Therefore, contrary to the assertion that the introduction of right and wrong puts "moral limitations on individual freedom", it is only when right and wrong are "introduced" that freedom comes about, for freedom means just sociation of free individuals respecting each other as persons and entering into interchanges with one another on the basis of mutual

---

121 Thomas Hobbes *Leviathan* ed. Michael Oakeshott New York: Collier Books 1973 edition p. 101.

agreement and with a view to mutual benefit. Freedom conceived erroneously — and childishly — as the arbitrary exercise of individual will is *always* restricted by justice by virtue of sociation itself being a power interplay. An individual does not have to "consent" to respecting others as likewise persons and private property-owners; rather, it is a *demand* of freedom to acknowledge other individuals as likewise free. LaFollette's line of argument is that, since even the rights of personhood and of private property require a non-consensual restriction of individual liberty (conceived as the caprice of individual will to do what it wants), and the libertarian is in agreement with such a restriction of individual liberty as just, then *a fortiori* the libertarian also cannot have any proper objection against distributive justice, which is likewise simply just another restriction of individual liberty conceived as caprice.

LaFollette further claims, "Libertarians seem to desire a totally individualistic system in which one's interests never have to be weighed against anyone (or everyone) else's. But that is impossible." (LaFollette 1979) Libertarians, it is true, are concerned with defending individual freedom, which, however, is not a stand-alone property of an individual, but is *of itself* a specific historical 'look' of sociation, of reified social interplay among human beings sharing a world. This holds true even though there are certainly strains of libertarianism that also misconceive individual freedom as arbitrariness of individual will. The phrase, "totally individualistic", suggests that the individual claims the 'liberty' to do anything he or she wants, without taking consideration of others' presence in the world. An individual's interests are always "weighed against" everyone else's when the individual enters into social interplay, which he must, in order to lead his or her life. It is the sociation, i.e. the interplay with others, that, in the first place, has to be free by virtue of mutual agreement, and only on this basis of mutuality can each individual's interests be furthered or frustrated. The interplay with others already offers *resistance* to individual will, especially capricious will, since some kind of mutual agreement has to be reached. Achieving such an agreement fairly, however, is a realization of freedom, not its frustration.

"I have shown that neither property nor liberty (as defined by the libertarian) should be seen as the only social good; singling these out as the only social values is unreasonable. Instead, these should be seen as two values among many, all competing for recognition." (LaFollette 1979) If the 'absoluteness' of freedom (not just individualistic liberty conceived as arbitrariness of will) is relativized among a gamut of other desirable 'values' or 'goods' of living, such as a secure material standard of living, then it has to be questioned the extent to which these other goods can at all be reconciled with freedom in the sense of a free sociation through estimating interplay. Otherwise, freedom becomes just one ill-defined 'value' among others on the shelf of the supermarket of values among which 'people' choose what they'd like to have in a 'free' society. Above in section 6.8 we have seen, however, that value is a socio-ontological concept of social movement requiring careful development. LaFollette's conception of what constitutes freedom in a free society is a perversion of freedom, which in truth is demanding and risky, and invariably a power play. If freedom is an essential hallmark of human being as such, and such freedom is and must be realized historically, apart from any other determinations, *as* the free individual, i.e. the freely sociating individual, then any undermining of the interplay of free individuals as the predominant ontological 'look' of sociation in a free society must be considered with due philosophical seriousness, and not by asking for 'people's' opinions and preferences.

By equating the libertarian conception of liberty with the arbitrariness of individual will and its exercise, LaFollette misses the mark in his critique of libertarianism. This is not to say that there are not strains of libertarianism that proceed from the same confusion. Indeed, Nozickian libertarianism has to be saved from itself by pointing the way to a genuine socio-ontological understanding of the *mode of being* called human freedom. From libertarianism and its critique we turn now to the other side, namely, to left-liberal justifications of distributive social justice, also known under the specious name of '*solidarity*'.

6.11 A closer look at Rawls

6.11.1 The "original position"

John Rawls' highly influential *Theory of Justice* represents another contractarian approach to the question concerning justice. It is as if the predilections of the Anglophone mind tend toward considering justice and freedom as issues revolving about what people would likely agree to in a social contract, i.e a question of the collective will of subjects. That sociating movement called living-with-one-another is thus supposed to grounded in subjective, i.e. underlying, will, that hidden god of the onto-theological thinking that reigns in the modern age. The "original position" in Rawls' theory is the setting analogous to the conception of a state of nature in political philosophy from Hobbes and Locke onward. The original position with its famous "veil of ignorance" is a setting set up in which willed subjects are to choose and agree to principles of justice containing an assortment of rights, these principles being two or three in number. These principles, or starting-points, are merely posited like self-evident or 'reasonable' axioms from which to proceed.

The First Principle of Justice: "First: each person is to have an equal right to the most extensive scheme of equal basic liberties compatible with a similar scheme of liberties for others."[122]

The Second Principle of Justice: "Social and economic inequalities are to be arranged so that: a) they are to be of the greatest benefit to the least-advantaged members of society (the difference principle). b) offices and positions must be open to everyone under conditions of fair equality of opportunity." (Rawls 1971 TJ:303).

"The basic liberties of citizens are, roughly speaking, political liberty (i.e., to vote and run for office), freedom of speech and assembly, liberty of conscience, freedom of personal property; and freedom from arbitrary arrest. However, he says: 'liberties not on the list, for example, the right to own certain kinds of property (e.g. means of production) and freedom of contract as understood by the doctrine of laissez-faire are not basic; and so they are not protected by the priority of the first principle.' (TJ:54 rev. ed.)"[123] A basket of basic liberties of citizens therefore is on offer in the First Principle, and classical libertarian rights of property are not in this basket, for that would be a barrier to the redistribution of wealth and income. This postulated basket of citizens' rights begs the question regarding the justification for such rights, for it must be asked whether each is in accordance with freedom or not, e.g. whether democracy as a form of government accords with freedom or not and why. Instead, a fully fledged democratic society with the usual rights is assumed as desirable.

The Second Principle formulates a qualified version of egalitarianism that admits deviations from "social and economic" equality if a) a so-called maximin condition for those worst off is satisfied and b) if such inequality ensures equality of opportunity in competing for positions in social hierarchies and running for office in government. Thus a finished political constitution of society familiar in Western liberal democracies is set before those with a sense of justice choosing principles of justice from behind the veil of ignorance. Isn't the "basic structure of society" assumed in the original position (such as "the political constitution and framework for the legal system; the system of trials for adjudicating disputes", etc.) already too rich for consideration (whether agreement is reached or not) of justice and fairness? In other words, doesn't this "basic struc-

---

122 Rawls *A Theory of Justice* The Belknap Press of Harvard University Press p.53 revised edition; p.60 old 1971 first edition.
123 See URL en.wikipedia.org/wiki/A_Theory_of_Justice Accessed Dec. 2009

ture of society" itself have to be developed via a path of questioning thinking to decide whether it is just?

The "veil of ignorance" is a way of abstracting from the particular interests aligned with the social situation of the social actors, in order to construct a hypothetical situation in which rational social actors with a sense of justice could reasonably agree on fundamental principles of justice. The veil indicates of itself that the question of justice is one concerning *universal* issues of justice, freedom, well-being, the goods of living, etc., rather than the *particular* self-interests that individuals have and strive for. The veil, however, still allows the self-interested individuals sitting behind it to *calculate* likelihoods of their being dealt a bad hand in the allotment of social status, interests and abilities, and to decide accordingly, perhaps in favour of minimizing the risk of being placed at the bottom of the social pile. Abstraction is certainly basic to any philosophical thinking-through of phenomena and works by leaving aside certain determinations of the phenomena to concentrate on abstract moments. Such abstraction can also be called "bracketing-off" (Ausklammerung, Husserl). Such abstraction or bracketing-off is of quite a different nature than setting up an hypothetical situation, thought-experiment or 'model', which is open to the vagaries of what is to be imagined as being the case and the motivations, etc. 'if the situation were such-and-such...'. What is the appropriate level of abstraction for considering a fundamental concept of justice? Can this appropriate level of abstraction be achieved by hypothesizing a social situation behind a veil of ignorance? It is easy to see that Rawls' original position is biased toward distributive justice at the expense of the commutative justice of free and fair interplay among individuals. What justifies this bias? Is the tension between distributive and commutative justice to be resolved by despatching the latter into oblivion, that is, by 'forgetting' that there is a crucial issue here? (see section 6.11 below) Above all, the socio-ontological dimension that is to be brought to light by asking what kind of *sociating movement* underlies the just distribution or commutation of the goods and bads of life is entirely lacking.

In contrast to an approach that poses the socio-ontological question, What is justice as such?, one commentator on Rawls, Fred D'Agostino, even claims that the *Theory of Justice* is not conceptual, but pragmatic, and from all that is assumed by the two principles of justice, this indeed seems to be the case. "Rawls's analysis was, then, what I will call *pragmatic*, not conceptual. ... It is, I repeat, a fact about how principles might *function* that justifies the choice of these principles as principles of social coordination for our society. That they enable 'each person to secure his ends' (Rawls), subject to certain circumstances, conditions, and constraints, is their justification, not that they reflect some antecedent understanding of what justice is, metaphysically or conceptually."[124] The principles of justice are to "function" efficiently to secure ends, to bring them forth as finished products on an ongoing basis, a *productivist* understanding of justice. Hence the bias toward distributive justice at the expense of commutative justice: with the modern welfare state there is an instance of control with the requisite 'vertical' political power that is responsible for distributing 'justly' material goods, at least, and *producing* a result, whereas commutative justice concerns the fairness of the games of estimation (esteeming each other, estimating each others goods = exchange-value) played 'horizontally' among the players of civil society. The fairness of such interplay concerns the starting-points, the potentials for playing, not the outcomes 'produced'. According to D'Agostino, "Rawls was trying to determine, in effect, which principles of sociability are fit to play a certain role in the organization of our collective lives", whereby he leaves the question of who 'we' are unposed and unanswered. The original position, he claims, is set up with an eye to achieving "an *overlapping consensus* of the main substantive ethico-political doctrines current in a community". What is up for discussion and choice are conventional notions of justice current in a given society, such as certain citizens' rights, and above all two influential theories of justice: egalitarianism and utilitarianism. Is a conventional theory of justice the best that moral philosophy can do?

This suggests that the original position is not so very original, that is, it is far from asking the originary question concerning what justice is *per se*, which is the truly philosophical, i.e. socio-ontological, question bequeathed from ancient Greek philosophy. D'Agostino admits this for, according to him, with Rawls' theory, "we are trying to design a tool for use by certain kinds of agents to accomplish certain sorts of purposes in a certain kind of environment, and our problem is one of practical functional design, not of conceptual analysis or metaphysical speculation about The Good or The Right." A tool purportedly has to be designed procedurally to achieve ends. But what if justice is not about achieving ends? Perhaps the answer to the originary question, What is justice *as such?*, is an unpleasant one for those behind the veil of ignorance seeking "an *overlapping consensus*" on a basket of conventional notions of justice, in the sense that they could not simply choose principles to *secure* their ends and well-being, but rather would have to accept that they not only come to enjoy a social life governed by principles of justice, but also have to live up to *demands* and

---

124 Fred D'Agostino, superseded entry on 'Original Position' in the *Stanford Encyclopedia of Philosophy* at URL plato.stanford.edu/archives/fall2008/entries/original-position/ Accessed Dec. 2009.

duties of freedom and justice. The original position as a setting for a procedure for constructing principles of justice presupposes that 'people' can pick and choose and calculate what they would prefer to have as principles to *secure* their ends connected with living well in society. It is not fortuitous that the proposed principles of justice in the original position are dealt with as if they were *distributive* principles, even those to do with civil liberties, as if they could be doled out and instituted by mutual consensus on the best arrangement for society, rather than being *demands* on and *duties* for free human being *as such* that guarantee no good as an end to be secured.

When Rawls speaks of duty, he speaks of political duties vis-à-vis *political* institutions, such as "the duty to support just institutions" (TJ:93 revised ed.), although, he concedes, there is no "duty requiring all to take an active part in political affairs" (TJ:200). The duty for a member of society, as far as possible, to earn an income to support a livelihood is not mentioned, but only the right of the "least advantaged" to a minimum income governed by the maximin difference principle. According to one of Rawls' editors, Samuel Freeman:

> The difference principle (the first part of the second principle, through (a)), addresses differences or inequalities in the distribution of the primary goods of income and wealth, and powers and prerogatives of office and positions of responsibility. It basically requires that a society is to institute the economic system that would make the least advantaged class better off than they would be in any other feasible economic system, compatible with maintaining citizens' equal basic liberties and fair equality of opportunity. Rawls defines 'least advantaged' as the class of those persons with the least share of the primary goods of income and wealth, and powers and prerogatives of office. He assumes the least advantaged are engaged in productive activity of some kind. Rawls then regards distributive justice as the benefits that accrue to persons for doing their part in socially productive cooperation. The class of unskilled workers receiving minimum income satisfies his definition of 'least advantaged.' Disability payments for citizens who are handicapped and permanently unable to work are not then a matter of distributive justice, as Rawls construes it, but are instead covered by principles of assistance, which he leaves unspecified.[125]

This passage tells us that the difference principle covers the least well-paid workers, but not the disabled, who have to rely on charity. This omits major areas of the activities of the welfare state, and hence major issues of so-called distributive social justice such as unemployment benefits. What is the situation with the able unemployed and what is the incentive for the "least advantaged" to be "engaged in productive activity of some kind"? The unemployed are not

---

125 Samuel Freeman, entry on 'Original Position' in the *Stanford Encyclopedia of Philosophy* at URL plato.stanford.edu/entries/original-position/ Accessed Dec. 2009.

even mentioned in *Theory of Justice* (rev. ed.). Are they covered by the difference principle or by "principles of assistance" which amount to charity? If this were so, how could it be that "Rawls is committed to policies such as universal healthcare and disability cover"[126] if these were not in line with his principles of *justice*? Are there any *rights* to assistance that go beyond the duty to help those in dire emergency? What is to prevent the emergence of a large population of welfare clients who calculate that they are better off living from hand-outs than from low-paid work (the problem of free-loading)?

Are "principles of assistance" to be complemented by illiberal prods to earn one's own livelihood, i.e. to engage as a player in the gainful game? Or is it simply assumed that all citizens are upright people who want to stand on their own feet economically for the sake of their own self-respect and self-esteem? (The socio-ontological grounding of the phenomena of esteem and self-esteem in mutually estimative interplay among whos, of course, is entirely lacking.) Are the inevitable bureaucratization and even minute administration of citizens' lives, and the inevitable intrusion of state agencies into the private sphere in order to administer, monitor and prevent abuse of measures aimed at keeping economic inequalities within the bounds of the difference principle an issue for Rawls and those who find his theory attractive because it furthers what they deem to be social justice? Does Rawls address such important issues relating to the modern welfare state and the demands placed upon it in the name of distributive social justice?

6.11.2 Property-owning democracy

These issues apply not just to the welfare state, but equally to Rawls' preferred model of a "property-owning democracy" (cf. esp. *Justice as Fairness: A Restatement* 2001) which is still concerned with providing redistributive social-welfare benefits, but *in addition* radicalizes the welfare state by demanding a break-up of concentrations of economic power (ownership of means of production and sheer wealth) in favour of wide dispersal, mainly with the aim of ameliorating problems of plutocracy, i.e. domination of the economy by a few super-wealthy, the undue influence of moneyed wealth on due democratic political process, thus perverting the equality of political liberties. Welfare-state capitalism, Rawls says, "permits very large inequalities in the ownership of real property

---

126 Martin O'Neill 'Liberty, Equality, and Property-Owning Democracy' URL mora.rente.nhh.-no/projects/EqualityExchange/Portals/0/articles/ONeill-2008.pdf Accessed Dec. 2009.

(productive assets and natural resources) so that the control of the economy and much of political life rests in few hands" (JF:137), whereas a property-owning democracy would "work to disperse the ownership of wealth and capital, and thus to prevent a small part of society from controlling the economy and indirectly, political life as well" (JF:139).

It could be said that concentrations of capital and wealth, as concentrations of a specific kind of *social power*, namely, that of social power *reified in value-forms*, distort both the playing of the gainful game and the political power struggles around the state, thus making both *unfair* in giving certain economic and political players too much weight against all the others in the power interplays. With regard to the economic gainful game, this distortion can be booked under the heading of *commutative* justice insofar as the conditions of fair play in the competitive struggle as a whole are distorted by monopolies and oligopolies. But Rawls argues for a breaking-up of concentrations of capital and wealth on the basis of considerations of *distributive* justice, namely, that they distort the *produced* distribution of incomes and of the weightings of citizens' rights in the political process, thus affecting its outcomes. Strictly speaking, the "fair equality of opportunity" (TJ:303) Rawls invokes is an equality of potential to engage in competitive struggles for positions and offices as distinct from a fair distribution of actual outcomes of these struggles, but this distinction is ignored as if only functions, effects, consequences were at stake. It is not only ignored, but Rawls and his ilk are oblivious to the distinction. The notion of "equality of opportunity" remains entirely diffuse due to utter neglect of the question concerning the ontological distinction in the mode of presencing between a power or potential, on the one hand, and that of a finished, actual presence, on the other.

The problems of capital becoming concentrated in few hands are thus recognized by Rawls and a counter-measure proposed, whereas the problems of society's underdogs pursuing life-strategies relying chronically on welfare benefits handed out by a totally life-administrating state are not addressed. This is presumably due to the egalitarian biases in Rawls' theory that allow some sympathizers in the area of social policy to interpret the break-up of large capitals and agglomerations of wealth in conciliatory, harmonizing terms: "The argument for the justice of taxing large-scale wealth in order to secure the fair value of political liberties, institute meaningful equal opportunity, and improve the lot of the least well off in turn mirrors the larger Rawlsian argument for understanding society as a system of social cooperation aimed at realizing a common life characterized by fairness, as opposed to a game in which the aim is to ac-

cumulate as many assets as possible within the permissible rules."[127] Fair "social cooperation" is here contrasted with "a game" of asset accumulation within
"permissible rules" which is presumably unco-operative and beyond the pale of
fairness and justice altogether.

For Williamson and O'Neill, "without the political capacity to break up
large accumulations of wealth in practice, Rawlsian aspirations for realizing a
just society based on the two principles of justice will remain tantalizingly out
of reach" (Williamson/O'Neill 2009). This raises the questions whether social
living could ever be characterized throughout by co-operation to the exclusion
of competitive power struggles in both the economy and politics, and whether
the gainful game is per se unfair and unjust. The favouring of co-operation over
competitive power struggles is an attractive moral stance for those seeking harmony and effective outputs but, measured against the socio-ontology of human
being itself, is it not self-delusory and therefore specious?

In his article 'Property in Rawls's Political Thought',[128] Quentin P. Taylor el-
oquently presses Rawls on the issue of his neutral, non-committal stance vis-à-
vis the property regimes of capitalism and socialism. Taylor quotes Rawls, "the
choice between a private-property owning economy and socialism is left open;
from the standpoint of justice alone, various basic structures would appear to
satisfy its principles" (TJ:228 rev. ed.) even while assuming a "competitive
economy" (TJ:137). The late Rawls apparently overcomes this neutrality on such
an important issue by coming down in favour of what he calls "property-owning
democracy" in which, one would assume, there are secure property rights. Taylor, however, shows us through a judicious choice of quotations that this is not
the case. The "allocation branch" of Rawls' proposed state is mandated with
effecting "changes in the definition of property rights" (TJ:244). The "distribution branch" has the task of making "necessary adjustments in the rights of
property [to] preserve an approximate justice in distributive shares" (TJ:245).
Taylor concludes, "Even in Rawls's 'property-owning democracy,' then, private-
property rights (outside of 'personal property') clearly are not secure. [...] The
insecurity of property rights and the shadowy nature of property relations under
Rawls's scheme would more likely create a climate of uncertainty, distrust, and
complacency" (p. 397). It goes almost without saying that neither Rawls nor

---

127 Thad Williamson and Martin O'Neill 'Property-Owning Democracy and the Demands of
Justice' in *Living Reviews in Democracy* 2009. URL democracy.livingreviews.org/index.php/-
lrd/article/viewArticle/lrd-2009-5/15 Accessed Dec. 2009.
128 *The Independent Review* Vol. VIII No. 3 Winter 2004 pp. 387–400. URL www.independent.-
org/pdf/tir/tir_08_3_taylor.pdf Accessed Dec. 2009.

Taylor know anything at all about a deeper socio-ontological grounding of private property in reified value-forms.

The conception of a property-owning democracy goes beyond breaking up concentrations of capital and wealth that pervert fair, commutative competition to hinder plutocratic control of the economy and politics, to also 'readjust' property rights for the sake of secured distributive social justice. Taylor therefore suggests that 'property-owning democracy' is a misnomer and asks, "should it not be more accurately characterized as a species of socialism?" (p. 397)[129] Indeed, it is apparent already from the "original position" that in his heart of hearts Rawls is an egalitarian:

> Since it is not reasonable for him [the hypothetical person in the original position] to expect more than an equal share in the division of social primary goods [including income and wealth], and since it is not rational for him to agree to less, the sensible thing is to acknowledge as the first step a principle of justice requiring an equal distribution. Indeed, this principle is so obvious given the symmetry of the parties that it would occur to everyone immediately (TJ:130).

Justice as fairness for Rawls means equal citizens' rights (including so-called 'real opportunities') and equal shares in material wealth output by the economy. A deviation from egalitarianism is admitted by his two principles of justice only on grounds i) of the necessity of positions of economic and political power which, however, "must be open to everyone under conditions of fair equality of opportunity" (TJ:303) and ii) of efficiency that the materially worst-off in society actually gain from inequalities in income and wealth i.e. that a market economy produces a larger pie through efficiencies brought about by the concentration of capital for large-scale production and by the greater productivity of individuals with greater abilities who are driven by the incentive to earn more. Fairness for Rawls has nothing to do with the fairness of the power interplays of potencies in the gainful game or democratic politics, where power implies potency, potential, possibility rather than attained actuality. Taylor has put his finger on a fundamental antinomy in Rawls' theory of justice: the freedoms of a market economy based on the gainful strivings of private property-owners are continu-

---

129 David Schweickart would answer this question affirmatively, just as he answers his own question, "Should Rawls Be a Socialist?", in the affirmative; cf. D. Schweickart 'Property-Owning Democracy or Economic Democracy?' in Thad Williamson and Martin O'Neill *Property Owning Democracy: Rawls and Beyond* (Blackwell-Wiley) URL www.luc.edu/faculty/dschwei/-articles.htm Accessed Dec. 2009.

ally curtailed and sacrificed to demands of modified distributive egalitarianism. And yet Rawls sails under the flag of liberalism!

This antinomy can be seen clearly from the vantage point of the socio-ontological constellation called the gainful game. The value-forms are generated originally by the movements of individual freedom at play already in the form of sociation constituted by the exchange of abilities and their products. Once value gains a reified form of existence in money, nothing can stop its further unfolding to the freedom to hire labour power, which is simultaneously the socio-ontological birth of capital itself as a reified value-form. Nothing, that is, except the suppression of the individual freedom of gainful interchange by a superior political instance, and even then, this is an ontic suppression, not a socio-ontological one. The nub is that where desirous, striving individual freedom is in interplay, there is also money as the reified, value-form medium of this interplay, and this reified social power, in turn, as capital, is able itself to set labour power and means of production into movement on leased land.

Rawls' conception of a 'property-owning democracy' contains an incoherence that necessitates draconian powers for a strong state that is assigned the task of continually curtailing and readjusting the individual freedoms of private property against immense resistance. The diverse private-property interests besieging the state have to be suppressed in favour of modified egalitarian redistribution not only of the economy's output as expressed in income through heavy taxation, but also of a politically coerced redistribution of the very income-sources of accumulated capital and land themselves. Given that Rawls nevertheless still proposes a market economy, this implies that the gainful game as a socio-ontological constellation could only go underground, being decreed unfair and unjust, or fair and just only up to a point, in Rawlsian terms. The inevitable result would include, on a massive scale proportional to the political suppression necessary, black markets and political corruption through which money would continue to unfold its irresistible social power nevertheless.

6.12 Anomalies in the gainful game and the political power play

Strangely (or perversely), it is precisely the reified social power, money, that enables an individual to *be* a free individual. With this thingly social power in my hand I am able to freely shape my life in my private sphere with considerable degrees of freedom without asking approval from anybody or any authority.[130] The constitution of who I am, and who you are, and who we all are through the interplays of estimating and esteeming each other becomes an intimate mirror game behind the wall of privacy that money income affords. Within this private garden of individuality, there may even be a flourishing of singular creativity, freed from the social rituals of public recognition with their inevitably levelling tendencies. Thus, individual freedom goes hand in glove with the reification of sociation via an abstract-universal thing from which, as outlined above, the gainful game unfolds through the many and various value-forms. The *garden of privacy*, that is, the freedom to lead one's private life with those one wishes, is the jewel of modern, bourgeois, individual freedom. Private individuality is endangered, however, by encroachments of the state's administering distributive justice. In this section the (re)distributive, social justice aspect of the state's raison d'être will be kept in the background, with the focus being instead on anomalies in the gainful game itself and the state's role in resolving them.

The first duty of the state is the protection of personhood and private property, a duty that arises, as has been shown, of necessity from conflicts over the commutations in civil life. Personhood is the abstract-universal status of the individual human being under abstract right, and this status is the *first civil right* guaranteeing human dignity. The protection of personhood, i.e. of this first civil right, by the state is a matter of *commutative justice*, not of distributive justice. This point cannot be overemphasized, for it is fatal for all those approaches to the theory of justice that neglect and suppress commutative justice and its social ontology of estimative interplay. *Civil rights movements against social discrimination* are movements against the wrong committed against the abstract and dignified status of personhood, and civil rights are grossly miscon-

---

130 Karl Marx clearly saw the connection between reified exchange relations and individual freedom and equality: "Hence, if the economic form, exchange, posits the equality of subjects in all directions, then the content, the material, individual as well as factual, that drives to exchange is *freedom*. Equality and freedom are thus not only respected in exchange based on exchange-values, but exchange of exchange-values is also the productive, real basis of all *equality* and *freedom*. As pure ideas they are only idealized expressions of the same; as developed in juridical, political, social relations they are only this basis with another exponent." (Wenn also die ökonomische Form, der Austausch, nach allen Seiten hin die Gleichheit der Subjekte setzt, so der Inhalt, der Stoff, individueller sowohl wie sachlicher, der zum Austausch treibt, die *Freiheit*. Gleichheit und Freiheit sind also nicht nur respektiert im Austausch, der auf Tauschwerten beruht, sondern der Austausch von Tauschwerten ist die produktive, reale Basis aller *Gleichheit* und *Freiheit*. Als reine Ideen sind sie bloß idealisierte Ausdrücke desselben; als entwickelt in juristischen, politischen, sozialen Beziehungen sind sie nur diese Basis in einer andren Potenz. *Grundrisse der Kritik der Politischen Ökonomie* Dietz, Berlin 1974 S. 156.)

ceived when they are treated as matters of social, distributive justice, i.e. as a matter of how citizens' rights are 'distributed' by the state and constitutionally guaranteed by it. It may disappoint some that civil rights movements could be booked first and foremost under the heading of abstract right rather than basking in the radiance of articles of the constitution, but the rights of personhood lie deeper than the state; they are a matter of *natural right*, properly understood as rights in the name of individual human freedom per se (insofar as we can still say today that it is the nature of human being to be free). The momentous struggles over the centuries for civil rights and against social discrimination should not be mixed up with issues of so-called distributive social justice. The ambiguity residing in the much employed and revered term 'social justice' is toxic and addles thinking on issues of justice. By banishing commutative justice from consideration, Anglophone justice theory has shot itself badly in the foot.

It is not enough, however, for the state to protect personhood and private property, which are the forms, i.e. ideas, 'looks', in which the various value-forms, hidden as such from both the state and the players (because they do not think socio-ontologically), are preserved that enable the very movement of the gainful game itself. Apart from the issue of the fairness of the commutations, i.e. the interchanges, that are the metabolic synapses, or 'touchings-together', of the gainful game's movement, there is the major issue of the *fairness of the gainful game as a whole*, commonly and aptly referred to as the issue of the *level playing field*. This playing field is not to be level in only one plane, since it has many, many facets and so could be called a multifaceted polyhedron. The gainful game cannot be left to play by itself, for it can get out of kilter through its own movements under the impetus of the many players' playing strategies for gain. Freely working markets do not simply self-correct, or rather, their eventual self-correction can be a violent, disruptive collapse of the entire game. Laissez-faire capitalism can also push some players to the wall and make playing conditions altogether unfair. A major problem of the gainful game is that some players can become very big, so big, that the other players with whom they play have to accept grossly unfair conditions — the perennial problem of monopoly, oligopoly and cartels on markets of various kinds.

Such monopolies may be *labour unions* which, through strike action, can hold an industry, a sector, the public or the government to ransom. Therefore the government legislates on *industrial relations* to lay down the rules under which industrial disputes over wages, working conditions, etc. are to be fought out. To be fair and just, the government must be even-handed in legislating to channel the ongoing struggle between functioning capital and labour (or, on an extended plane, between the state itself and its so-called public servants).

The tendencies for the formation of monopolies, oligopolies and cartels, however, is far greater with capital because capital accumulates of itself, and capital accumulation is a major way in which an individual capital (a company, an enterprise) ensures its survival in the competitive struggle against other capitals. A company that does not grow steadily becomes endangered gradually in its very existence, and may be swallowed by another company. Capital accumulation also enables investments in productivity-enhancing technologies that also improve survival chances in the competition. But once a company has reached a certain size, it attains a market-dominating position that affects the fairness of competition in that sector, including not only competition with similar companies, and also bargaining leverage with suppliers and the power to set selling prices to consumers. In the name of justice as competitive fairness, the government is called upon to redress the competitive balance, perhaps by compelling the company to reduce its size through spin-offs, or perhaps by forcing a break-up of a huge monopoly. In particular, there is the issue of *state-enterprise monopolies* when the state itself becomes an entrepreneur providing, say, infrastructure (public transportation, roads and railways, telecommunications, etc., etc.). Such state monopolies may decree 'fair' prices as they think fit, or, if privatized, crush all competition through sheer size or entrenched and lingering competitive privileges.

One particular sector in which the sheer size of companies is a crucial issue for the fairness of the gainful game is that of finance capital. Finance capital (the private, commercial and investment banks plus finance companies of various kinds) has the function, above all, of providing the interest-bearing loan-capital (called 'leverage' in the U.S., or 'gearing' in Australia) that lubricates the transactions in a capitalist economy. Such loan-capital is therefore the life-blood for the movement of the gainful game, and when it dries up temporarily, the movement freezes. The gainful game often gets out of kilter in the phenomenal form of a so-called 'credit crunch' that plunges the economy into recession or crisis. Recession is when the gainful game on the whole is not achieving gain, and crisis is when the gainful game is severely hampered, perhaps by the need for entire industries to restructure, which amounts to repositioning in the gainful game.

Because the financial sector is so vital to the economy as a whole and also looks after people's savings, its strategies and playing conditions in the gainful game demand especial oversight by the state. The government must legislate banking legislation to ensure a proper level of *prudence* in banking activities. Prudence means appropriately assessing risk, limiting it, avoiding it, making provisions for it, etc. It may be viewed simply as tough luck when an individual enterprise pursues a poor, imprudent, risky strategy and goes bankrupt, but, because of its linch-pin role, there must be state agencies to oversee the financial industry in particular to keep it within acceptable bounds of risk, say, by restricting lending activities or banning certain highly complex and potentially explosive financial products such as synthetic default swaps. Needless to say, overseeing risk and providing regulation for risk management is, of its nature, a risky undertaking, for the gainful game itself and the ever-new strategies pursued in search of gain are full of surprises never envisaged by financial legislation, and also entirely overlooked by supervisory authorities. The necessary regulation of rules of play in the financial sector is inevitably always behind the curve.

A further major problem (seen by Rawls in proposing his property-owning democracy) is the influence that huge, accumulated capitals (also private moneyed wealth, which in turn is always invested in some way or other) has on government and the democratic election process in particular. Private interests lobby government, and large moneyed private interests have the social power to lobby most strongly of all. They may also buy ownership control of the *mass media of public opinion* that sway it this way and that without ever posing any questions that dig beneath the surface of life. This is the issue of *political plutocracy* which, through the power of money, can severely distort the workings of government and the state to ensure the fairness and also the prudence and stability of gainful game as a whole. Money as reified social power thus distorts political power. The government may legislate to limit the political influence of accumulated wealth and the interests of big capital, but even this legislative activity is itself exposed to lobbying and hence may have its teeth drawn. Therefore fair play in the gainful game and the proper function of the state in ensuring fairness of play may be put in jeopardy by the power of accumulated capital and wealth.

Furthermore, actions by the government in pursuit of policies of (re)distributive social justice may not only impair the fairness of the gainful game (say, by legislating immoderate job protection), but restrict its overall functioning and success (say, preventing restructuring by protecting social inertia). For those under the influence of conceptions of social distributive justice, the freedoms of the gainful game are dispensable and even morally dubious. The claims of property-ownership and income-earning are subordinated to policies of redistribution for the sake of total social well-being and in the name of state-defined social justice. The fault line between commutative and distributive conceptions of justice, i.e. between the rights of property and striving for income, on the one hand, and the secured rights of material well-being, on the other, is one of the major splits in people's ways of understanding the social world. This right-left split is played out as a perennial power struggle in democratic politics (cf. Chapter 13) that never attains a final state of equilibrium, i.e. of final closure.

7 Interlude and recapitulation with some intermediate conclusions: Everyday living of finite human beings – Security and insecurity

7.1 Securing the polity of civil society – An initial determination of government (Schmitt, Locke, Kant) – The rule of law

Government, and democratic government in particular, is about securing and enhancing the quotidian, customary way of life of a given community or society as a whole, on the one hand, by protecting it from detrimental effects, and on the other, by enhancing it through forward-looking policies that meet the ever-changing challenges gathering and shaping up from the horizon of the future. The practical issues of everyday life in which government policy and government decisions are involved are limitless, ranging from the local level to the national and international levels. Government provides the framework within which the life of a society is lived, i.e. government erects, guides and protects a state of living and is in this sense a state of affairs which stands as a solid framework, a ground on which social living can stand. As Carl Schmitt notes, the Staat is first of all the "state of affairs of a people" (Zustand eines Volkes[131]). The state maintains the state of affairs of a way of societal living and is in this sense a bulwark against the contingency which besets human living and human endeavour and, above all, human enterprise. Seen in this way, the state exists for the sake of a people and its way of life, and not, as totalitarian thinkers such as Carl Schmitt have proposed, the people for the sake of the state and its power, of which more later (cf. Chapter 13).

All human undertakings *as* social movements are exposed to contingency, especially and essentially all those economic undertakings in which more or less freely working markets mediate. The socio-ontological underpinnings for this statement have been provided already in Chapter 5. Human existence has to take care to counter contingency, above all that contingency which arises from social interplay with other, free human beings who can act one way or another. The state erects and upholds a state of affairs in which existence is relieved of some of the care of contingency by making life secure in many and various

---

131 Carl Schmitt *Der Begriff des Politischen* 1932 Duncker & Humblot, Berlin 6th ed. 4th printing 1963 p. 20.

https://doi.org/10.1515/9783110617504-007

ways, such as preventing and redressing crime, providing necessary infrastructure and social services, or alleviating poverty. Security means being without care, Latin: se cura.

John Locke puts security at the heart of his reasoning why "men" in a "State of Nature" consent to put "on the bonds of Civil Society" (p. 375) "by setting up a known Authority, to which every one of that Society may Appeal upon any Injury received, or Controversie that may arise, and which every one of the Society ought to obey" (p. 369) when he states that men "joyn and unite into a Community, for their comfortable, safe, and peaceable living one amongst another, in a secure Enjoyment of their Properties, and a greater Security against any that are not of it." (p. 375) In short, "Government has no other end but the preservation of Property" (p. 373), a man's property being "his Life, Liberty and Estate" (p. 367). The security of the individual's life, liberty and estate is the raison d'être for the state of civil, law-governed society. This is a first, fundamental determination of a concept of state from the viewpoint of liberal individualist understanding of a free society, and its validity is not merely an historical curiosity, but applies wherever individual liberty is taken as the starting-point for thinking about government and its legitimacy, a theme that will be taken up again in Chapter 10.

The securing of property in Locke's broad sense is the securing of the framework of civil society, i.e. the polity, within which individuals act on their own account, interplaying with others to take care of their everyday concerns, especially their economic concerns to earn a living. The state is the guarantor of this formal framework by protecting property rights and thus securing basic individual freedom of interplay against incursions by others. This is a restricted, provisional but fundamental understanding of security as the *rule of law*. The core of the rule of law is to remove the insecurity relating to individuals not keeping their contractual word (cf. Chapter 5.6) by the state's enforcing contracts under law. Exchange contracts, which are the medium in which, the mediation through which the life of civil society moves, thus become secure once they have been entered into by free property-owners to a degree more secure than the mutual trust on which contracts already are based.

In the more expanded state, the concept of security is extended to cover also guaranteeing the basic material welfare of individual citizens. The state then not only guarantees a legal framework for individual interaction but positively intervenes in the distribution of the total wealth created by commutative economic interplay as a whole. This intervention of the welfare state is only seen to be necessary because earning a livelihood, even when the forms of property, namely "life, liberty and estate", are guaranteed, remains insecure. This kind of insecurity lies deeper and cannot be remedied simply by the state's erecting a secure welfare-state of affairs. Why not? Because, as we have seen following Hegel (*RPh*. § 245; cf. Chapter 6.5), a welfare state contradicts the principle of civil society, which is individual self-reliance in the ongoing interplay of powers. The dilemma is that freedom of property and the rule of law cannot provide for every single individual's well-being because earning a livelihood through the exercise of individual freedom is subject to the uncertainties of income-earning social interplay, which inevitably includes sudden, marked changes in the general interplay of the economy.

The state securely providing welfare benefits for its people is as contrary to individual freedom as the beneficence of an autocrat. As the great representative of German Enlightenment, Kant, puts it:

> Denn mit Freiheit begabten Wesen gnügt nicht der Genuß der Lebensannehmlichkeit, die ihm auch von anderen (und hier von der Regierung) zu Teil werden kann; sondern auf das *Prinzip* kommt es an, nach welchem es sich solche verschafft. Wohlfahrt aber hat kein Prinzip, weder für den, der sie empfängt, noch der sie austeilt (der eine setzt die hierin, der andere darin); weil es dabei auf das *Materiale* des Willens ankommt, welches empirisch, und so der Allgemeinheit einer Regel unfähig ist. Ein mit Freiheit begabtes Wesen kann und soll also, / im Bewußtsein dieses seines Vorzuges vor dem vernunftlosen Tier, nach dem *formalen* Prinzip seiner Willkür keine andere Regierung für das Volk, wozu es gehört, verlangen, als eine solche, in welcher dieses mit gesetzgebend ist: d.i., das Recht der Menschen, welche gehorchen sollen, muß notwendig vor aller Rücksicht auf Wohlbefinden vorhergehen, und dieses ist ein Heiligtum, das über allen Preis (der Nützlichkeit) erhaben ist, und welches keine Regierung, so wohltätig sie auch immer sein mag, antasten darf.[132]

> For beings gifted with reason, the enjoyment of the agreeableness of life apportioned to them by others (here, by the government) does not suffice, and the crucial point is the *principle* according to which they procure such agreeableness. But welfare does not have any principle, neither for the one receiving it nor for the one apportioning it (one person will posit it to be such, the next will posit it otherwise); because it depends on the *material* will, which is empirical and is thus incapable of the universality of a rule. A being gifted with freedom, therefore, conscious of its distinction from the reasonless animal, and according to the *formal* principle of its arbitrariness, can and should demand no other government for the people to which it belongs than one in which the people contributes to making laws; that is, the right of people who are supposed to obey must necessarily precede all consideration of well-being, and this is something sacred that is above any price (of usefulness) and that no government, no matter how beneficent it may be, may touch.

---

132 Immanuel Kant *Der Streit der Fakultäten* Zweiter Abschnitt 1798 A 147f *Werke* Band VI ed. W. Weischedel 1964 S. 360, emphasis in the original.

The sense of this passage changes in today's context when read against the backdrop of the rampant, debt-ridden welfare state and the ubiquitous political demands of so-called (distributive) social justice. The protection of individual freedom and its associated self-responsibility under the rule of law is a "formal principle" of universal applicability, arising as it does from a casting of human being itself as free, whereas enjoying an agreeable life and being cared for by the government, is "empirical", and can be posited to include all kinds of material comforts for human living. The agreeableness of living is like an endless shopping list that cannot have the dignity of a universal human right and must not be played out against human freedom, which is always also necessarily individual and risky, no matter what other guises it may assume. The inviolability of human freedom (which is manifested in social interplay as investigated in Chapter 5 and only visible socio-ontologically) and its precedence over material well-being have long since been violated not only in historical political struggles, but also and above all in a kind a 'social' thinking that has mixed up material well-being with individual freedom and sacrificed the latter to the former. Not only that: individual freedom has been defamed as mere individualistic arbitrariness, on the one hand, and as merely the freedom of a particular, purportedly privileged social class to the exclusion of the less well-off, on the other.

Freedom demands also that the people have a say in the laws that rule them which gives precedence to a form of government that Kant, in a time before the massification that democracy brings, calls "republicanism", but which today would be called democratic government. These laws are in the first place "formal" in Kant's sense of the term: pure, transcendentally a priori (to experience) and therefore ontological, capable of a universal formulation without favour or prejudice to any particular individuals or social groups, and having precedence over empirical government measures providing concretely for material well-being which may also be posited in the form of (administrative) 'laws' which are simply acts of the government's political will. Formal laws in Kant's sense are universal rules of play for individuals exercising their freedom in interplay with one another. They are "sacred" in the sense that freedom is "infinite" in the Hegelian sense, and cannot be compared or traded off with material well-being and security, which is a 'finite' state of affairs that can be set up by a state. The 'arbitrariness' of individual freedom so strongly denounced by critics of 'bourgeois freedom' or 'market consumerism' is only one side of the coin of individual freedom, which is always insecure and groundless through being exposed to social interplay. The other side of the coin is that the individual learns to exercise its powers and freedom in casting and caring for its ownmost course of existence across the seas of social vicissitudes.

7.2 Exchange as the starting-point of social living (Plato, Hegel)

Civil society is based on a division of labour which necessitates the exchange of the products of labour in some form or other. Earning a livelihood depends on offering something on the market, whether it be goods or services, including one's own potential to labour. Recall what Plato says about the ontic genesis of the polis:

Γίνεται τοίνυν, ἦν δ' ἐγώ, πόλις, ὡς ἐγῷμαι, ἐπειδὴ τυγχάνει ἡμῶν ἕκαστος οὐκ αὐτάρκης, ἀλλὰ πολλῶν ἐνδεής· ἢ τίν' οἴει ἀρχὴν πόλιν οἰκίζειν; (*Rep.* 369b)

which is standardly translated something like:

A city arises therefore, I said, it seems to me, because it happens that each individual one of us is not self-sufficient, but lacks much; or do you think that a city is established from some other beginning?

This translation takes the passage as the argumentation about an historical, chronological beginning and genesis of a city, but there is a deeper meaning embedded in the text if "polis" and "beginning" are understood in a more essential, ontological way. Polis stands for humans living together in some sort of community, a way of Mitsein, of togetherness, constituting a shared everyday life-world. Beginning (ἀρχή) is also the principle, which is a point of origin governing what proceeds from that origin. The principle here is that each individual is not self-sufficient and autonomous but, like Eros, lacks much, which can only be overcome through some sort of sociating intercourse among humans. This lacking of much should be understood not only more *broadly* than humans needing means of subsistence such as food, clothing and shelter (such needs being derivative of certain particular usages that determine, for instance, what, specifically, *is* food, clothing and shelter in a given society), being extendible to everything that humans lack which they can set their heart's desire on as enabling some agreeable, customary practice or other of social life, but above all more *essentially* as that human being *as* social is intrinsically interchange in both the sense of mutual estimation as somewho and also the intertwining of desiring wills in exchanges of all kinds, including giving, exchanging, trading, buying and selling.

Hegel puts it thus, "If for their consciousness it is need in general, benevolence, benefit, etc. that lead them to contracts, intrinsically it is reason, namely, the idea of real (i.e. existing only in the will) determinate being of free personhood" (Wenn für ihr Bewußtsein das Bedürfnis überhaupt, das Wohlwollen, der

Nutzen usf. es ist, was sie zu Verträgen führt, so ist es an sich die Vernunft, nämlich die Idee des reellen (d.i. nur im Willen vorhandenen) Daseins der freien Persönlichkeit. *RPh.* § 71 *Übergang vom Eigentum zum Vertrage).* In Hegel's thinking, Reason, Vernunft is the (ontological, i.e. speculative) "conceptual knowledge" (begreifendes Erkennen, *RPh.* end of *Vorrede, Werke* Bd. 3 S. 27) of the Gestalten of being which, when realized in a "conscious identity" (bewußte Identität, *RPh*:27) of reason and reality, constitutes the "philosophical idea" (philosophische Idee, *RPh*:27). The concept of freedom essential to human being itself demands that it be realized also in contractual intercourse.

The most elementary 'look' of intercourse is the exchange of goods, which, beyond the more primitive form of barter, is generally mediated by money. Money as medium is therefore constitutive of human society and human intercourse on a fundamental, practical level by facilitating the rudimentary social nexus. A more fundamental, socio-ontological level presupposed by human beings labouring within a division of labour and exchanging with each other is that human beings share the openness of 3D-time in its identity with mind, and therefore are able to labour on the basis of an understanding, to share an understanding of world including what is involved in exchanging one good for another, and also have intercourse in language with one another in which their understanding of the world is articulated and expressly shared. Aristotle says this most famously in his *Politics* by fundamentally linking human social being (ζῷον πολιτικόν) with human beings' having language and understanding (ζῷον λόγον ἔχον). As beings with understanding, humans are at play, buying and selling on the market to gain through interchanges what they lack for living within their usages.

Goods are always already understood as being able to remedy some lack or other and therefore as being good for this or that. As such, goods are *valuable* and show themselves off as such to human understanding. This has already been discussed (cf. Chapter 4.1). This game with commodified valuables, this interplay of exchange-values, is essential to everyday life both in earning a livelihood and enjoying it by consuming what can be purchased. Everyday life is negotiated on the market, with money serving as the conventional mediator for exchanging valuables. Money has to be earned to lubricate the movement of living by spending it to support a given way of life. The polyarchic interplay on the markets — which is more basically the interplay among free, individual human powers (δυνάμεις) — is subject to all sorts of contingencies and vicissitudes which are played out in supply and demand and ultimately in the prices of commodities of all sorts.

No matter what is done by the state to hem the contingencies of value-play in the market-place, say, by controlling prices or, more generally, in guaranteeing certain levels of income for the population, any such policies do not and cannot suspend and abolish the interplay of value-estimation through market exchange. Where total control is attempted, as in state socialist regimes, the market asserts itself nevertheless behind the state's back as a black market, driven by the motive force of individual self-interests and the simple social possibility of exchange, regardless of what the state determines to be legal prices and acceptable social practices. This is because value itself is a socio-ontological category, i.e. a look of being that shows itself already in things themselves showing themselves to understanding as being-good-for... Such a look of being cannot be effaced even by harsh state coercion, but simply goes underground.

Any scheme for managing value-interplay, which are expressed quantitatively in prices, works only as long as the unforeseen does not happen. Why is this so? To cite Hayek, "Surely Samuel Butler (*Hudibras* II, i) was right when he wrote, 'For what is worth in any thing, But so much money as 'twill bring'"[133], for value-estimations have no ground, but only an empirical validity which, however, can evaporate if the circumstances of social interplay on the markets change considerably all of a sudden. The exchange-value of things is not reliable because, as has been shown in Chapter 5, exchange-value only comes about through a bi-archic and polyarchic interplay. Nevertheless, the exchange of goods is a 'natural' elementary form of sociation that actually enables practical, everyday life. It is natural in the sense that, just as it is natural for human beings (i.e. corresponds to the way the world opens up for human understanding) to know how to make or do certain useful things for living and to use and enjoy them, it is also natural for them to exchange these goods one for the other to acquire what they cannot make or do themselves.

7.3   The reliability of things (Heidegger)

Let us return to the statement that the *exchange*-value of things is not reliable. The qualification is necessary because, in the sense of *use*-value, the value of things is entirely reliable, so much so that reliability can be said to constitute the being of things. How so? The value of the practical things of everyday life is

---

133 Friedrich A. Hayek *Law, Legislation and Liberty* Vol. 2 The Mirage of Social Justice, Chicago U.P. 1976 p. 179. Hereafter cited in the form *LLL2*:179.

their usefulness for quotidian uses in customary usages. Things are useful for, i.e. good for, a specific purpose or purposes, and this constitutes their being, i.e. their mode of presencing. Their being is thus a valuableness in the sense of being-good-for some purpose or other in existence's movement. Being-good-for is how Heidegger famously determines the being of pragmatic things (Zeug) in *Being and Time* (1927). In his similarly famous study on *The Truth of the Work of Art* a few years later (1935/36), Heidegger roots this being of things in a deeper "essential being" which he calls "reliability" or "dependability" (Verläßlichkeit). Through the reliability of things in everyday life, a certain world as a customary way of life is dependably kept open. Heidegger explicates this reliability in discussing the peasant woman's boots said to be portrayed in a painting by Van Gogh:

> Das Zeugsein des Zeugs besteht zwar in seiner Dienlichkeit. Aber diese selbst ruht in der Fülle eines wesentlichen Seins des Zeuges. Wir nennen es die Verläßlichkeit. Kraft ihrer ist die Bäuerin durch dieses Zeug eingelassen in den schweigenden Zuruf der Erde, kraft der Verläßlichkeit des Zeuges ist sie ihrer Welt gewiß. Welt und Erde sind ihr und denen, die mit ihr in ihrer Weise sind, nur so da: im Zeug. [...] die Verläßlichkeit des Zeugs gibt erst der einfachen Welt ihre Geborgenheit und sichert der Erde die Freiheit ihres ständigen Andranges.
>
> (*Holzwege* S. 19)

> The thingness of [practical] things consists in their serviceability. But serviceability itself rests in the fullness of an essential being of things. We call it reliability. By virtue of it, the peasant woman is let into the silent call of the Earth; by virtue of the reliability of things, she is certain of her world. World and Earth are only there for her and for those who are with her in her way thus: in [useful, practical] things. [...] only the reliability of useful things gives security/shelteredness to the simple world and secures the Earth the freedom of its constant surge.

Here Heidegger refers explicitly to security, the security of living in a world and belonging to the earth as a way of life. The peasant's boots are good for working in the fields, and they are dependably good for this labour as one crucial practice in a way of life. The peasant woman understands the boots as part of her peasant way of life and she has the boots under her own control. In this simple, rustic world, the boots can hardly fail to be reliable.

But it could be said that the being of technological things, too, consists in their reliable functioning in a certain context, which is presumably more complex than the simple world of the countryside. Perhaps boots can be said to be more reliable than a piece of electronic equipment such as a personal computer, but the being of a computer lies nevertheless in its being reliably serviceable for certain functions embedded in the interconnections of a modern way of living with the cyberworld.[134] In the modern world too, reliability of function is essential to the being of technological things, and such reliability is guaranteed by both quality control procedures and a service network of service providers who are supposed to speedily fix any function failures.

The reliability of things, both simple and complex, resides in their dependable use within a way of life, thus keeping a world open. Their reliability pertains to usefulness and usages in everyday life. Such reliability secures a world. The peasant woman can be sure of her peasant world, even if she has to worry "about securing bread" (S. 18) because of the dangers of bad weather and is therefore glad when she "once again survives hardship" (S. 18). The simple world described here is a world of quasi-self-sufficient production. The reliability of the peasant's boots is paralleled for us in the modern world by the reliability of the electricity grid: when we flick the switch, the power is reliably on.

7.4   Exchange essentially unreliable

But what if the elementary sociating practice of exchange is introduced to the simple peasant world? This is a phenomenon entirely overlooked and suppressed by Heidegger for thoughtful consideration throughout his entire writings. Even the simple peasant way of life is based on a division of labour and requires that the peasants exchange their grain for other things they need for their way of life, such as boots. How well this way of life succeeds and is kept open with its characteristic usages and ways of experiencing and understanding depends not only on whether the harvest is good, but on the value of the harvest on the market. If prices are depressed, this endangers the security of the peasant world just a much as bad weather — or even extremely good weather producing a bumper harvest and therefore a market glut — does. The market value of the peasant's grain is not dependable because there is no thing that can reliably fulfil the function of 'sale'. Sale is not a technical act, but depends on two parties reaching agreement on an exchange. Moreover, this exchange in turn depends on general market conditions, in which guise 'the others' penetrate into the peasant world. This dependency means that sale is *essentially*, i.e. in its very mode of being, not dependable, since the parties are just as free to enter into an exchange relation as they are to refrain from one. A sale has to be clinched in a moment of reciprocal interplay, and the bargaining over price may

---

134 Cf. Capurro, R., Eldred M., & Nagel D. *Digital Whoness: Identity, Privacy and Freedom in the Cyberworld* ontos/De Gruyter, Frankfurt/Berlin 2013.

lead even to the peasant's way of life being threatened by insufficient grain prices being attained.

Whereas in the functioning of a useful thing by a single person for a purpose others are present mostly indirectly in securing that function, exchange relations of their essence involve direct interchange between humans. Even in a simple, largely self-sufficient peasant world, exchange interplay, and thus the exchange-value of things, plays an essential part in keeping that world open and liveable as a way of life. But the sale of a harvest on the market, which is a social interplay rather than a practical thing, is not essentially reliable like a pair of peasant's boots. On the contrary, sale is an essentially unreliable social movement of relational interplay, and this unreliability means that even the simple world of the peasant is exposed essentially to insecurity. The peasant woman can only be sure of her world in being aware of the unreliability of the selling prices for grain. Security is essentially wedded with insecurity in any world in which social relations of exchange are part of the social fabric. Or rather: there is insecurity in any way of social living because there is no guarantee that others, as free beings, can be depended upon in the ongoing social interplay of all kinds. In a market economy, this insecurity of sociating interplay is mediated significantly via the reified relations of the marketplace.

It is safe to say, however, that most human society is characterized more or less by commodity exchange, including simple peasant societies and those socialist societies in which the state imposes a total social production and distribution plan. Even state socialism has not been able to elude the uncertainty of exchange relations. Insofar as things are always essentially of themselves doubled as use-values and exchange-values, i.e. in being good for a certain use and in being good-for-exchange and therefore abstractly worth a certain amount of money, it must be said that their mode of being resides both in reliability and unreliability. The social being, i.e. the sociating interplay, is unreliable. That is, the being of practically useful things spans the entire gamut of the dimension of reliability from reliability in use to its negation in the unreliability of exchange-value. The unreliability of things is essentially related to the nature of human being as being-in-the-world *with others*. The other as a free origin is essentially unreliable. The ontological source of this unreliability is the essential, groundless character of market exchange interplay which in turn is rooted more deeply in the essential freedom of individuals in power plays with each other (cf. Chapter 5.6). Here we will deal only with the first aspect.

7.5   Free market exchange as both an unreliable and reliable form of sociation

A closer look at exchange interplay shows that it is not only unreliable as social interchange, but that, if not reliable and dependable, it at least forms the basis for mutual relations of reliance and dependency. For, the very unreliability of exchange interplay in the quantitative sense of prices to be had on the market and fluctuations in supply and demand is embedded, in turn, in an essential interdependence among social members in maintaining a way of life. In being based on a division of labour, a way of life is only supportable and sustainable as a network of dependable exchange relations constituting a viable economy. The fluctuations in prices in such an economy are only the creaking of the living movement of interdependency that dovetails in an organic, albeit ever-changing division of labour that constitutes some sort of overall economic household.

As Plato points out, no individual is autonomous in providing for him- or herself what he or she lacks. This makes the individual dependent on others without the relations of exchange being dependable in the sense of guaranteed or even predictable, calculable availability or prices. Nevertheless, motivated by self-interest, each player will strive to be dependable in its interchanges with others, thus building a basis of *trust* with those (customers, employer, etc.) on whom she or he depends. Whether Heidegger's peasant woman can make ends meet even in her relatively sheltered, simple peasant world depends not only on the capricious weather that affects how the crops grow in the field but, among other things, also on the prices for grain on the market.[135] For, the boots she wears to the field and myriad other things that serve her dependable peasant way of life have to be bought with the proceeds from selling at least part of the grain harvest. Without market interplay being quantitatively dependable, those living in society, that is, all human beings who are not "useless or better than a human being" (φαῦλος ἢ κρείττων ἢ ἄνθρωπος Aristotle *Pol.* 1253a5), are neces-

---

135 "Here people are talking a lot about the fact that now so much cattle has been bought by the Jews out of the villages and that the purchase of meat will be at an end in winter. Don't you think we ought to buy some in advance if possible? [...] — the peasants up here too are gradually getting impertinent and we are inundated with Jews and black marketeers." (Hier spricht man viel davon, daß jetzt so viel Vieh aus den Dörfern von den Juden fortgekauft wird u. daß es dann mit dem Fleischkauf im Winter zu Ende sei. Meinst Du nicht, daß wir, wenn möglich, etwas vorkaufen sollen. [...] — die Bauern werden hier oben allmählich auch unverschämt u. alles ist überschwemmt von Juden u. Schiebern. *'Mein liebes Seelchen!' Briefe Martin Heideggers an seine Frau Elfride 1915–1970* ed. Gertrud Heidegger, dva Munich 2005, letter to Elfride from Martin in Meßkirch dated 20 August 1920, p. 113)

sarily dependent and reliant on that very market interplay (on which even the weather has an effect) that, for the most part, is dependable enough for enabling and keeping open a way of life in habits and routines of living.

This dependency on undependable exchange interplay which is played out routinely within dependable forms of property transactions secured by the state's rule of law is itself a source of insecurity. In a society based on a generalized, free market economy, the nexus between buyers and sellers, suppliers and consumers becomes the linch-pin holding the social fabric together. This nexus is the nodal point of both relations of necessary interdependency and incalculable undependability. Each member of society alternately takes on the role of buyer or seller, hirer and lender, supplier or consumer in earning a livelihood and enjoying a level of material comfort, but this social interplay shifts and twists, creaking and groaning of its own accord, depending on the anonymous movements of the myriad markets.

An enterprise supplying a certain kind of product can never be sure that the market prices attained will be sufficient to allow the business to prosper, or even survive in the long run, but nevertheless has its rules of thumb derived from what usually happens. Consumers, too, have to flexibly adapt their material standard of living to their available income and the prevailing prices of the goods and services they wish to purchase. This unpredictability and unreliability of a market-based economy derive ontologically not from the (ontic) complexity of the conditions of reproducing a total economic process, but arise originally from the inherent, essential groundlessness of the simple exchange interplay itself in which one human being meets and has an interchange with another.

Because the reproduction of a total economy is built on the shifting sands of groundless exchange interplay in which exchange-value is reified in money as means of exchange, this reproduction, too, is always at risk and subject to continual disequilibria which are in a constant process of correction through a kind of negative cybernetic feedback loop that weeds out (negates) attempts at gain that fail to be valued, i.e. estimated and validated, sufficiently on the markets in hard cash. This cybernetic, exchange-value-based feedback loop is nothing other than the simple, disciplining principle of a market economy that could also be called its boundary condition of movement. Each economic agent or group of economic agents pursues its own interests in entering into exchange interplay, the motive for each individual exchange being self-interest. But the totality of this exchange interplay bracketing the production and consumption of an entire economy constitutes a universal connection in which the particular interests are entwined, disciplined through the simple principle of value-gainful striving, and thus raised to a higher, social-universal plane. The pursuit of self-interest has to contend with the uncertainty of market interplay and adapt continually to it, with each economic agent making some contribution or other to total social wealth.

If, alternatively, a modern mass society is set up in such a way that the state attempts to lay down a total social plan for production, exchange and consumption, this project is not only fraught with having to precalculate every detail of a highly complex economic process, but, more essentially, the execution of such a total social plan does not accommodate the particular self-interests that are the motive force in a market economy. Particularity can then find its degree of freedom of movement within a universal, perhaps even democratically state-imposed blueprint, only by subterfuge. In this case the unreliability of social interplay no longer resides quintessentially in the simple exchange relation between two parties and its generalization in legal, reified, money-mediated markets, but directly in illegal negotiations of whatever kind, including deals, favours, bribes, kick-backs, etc.

These considerations indicate that, given that society as a totality of inter-meshing everyday practices is constituted on the most fundamental, mundane level by the social interchanges necessitated by a multitude of wants and desires corresponding to a more or less refined division of labour, the essential kernel of the insecurity inherent in human co-existence has to be located originarily already in the simple social interchanges among individual human beings, i.e. in the simple interplay of human freedom between two individuals (analogous to how Marx discovers the secret of exchange-value already in the simple exchange relation between two commodities). Even though the forces of nature make human living uncertain, it is social interchanges among human beings that are most unfathomable.

7.6   Money-mediated exchange abstract and reified (Marx)

Through market exchange, the unfathomability of the encounter between free beings as origins (ἀρχαί) of power (δύναμις including the power to act and powers in the sense of abilities) is at least reduced to a giving and taking of things, and the potential complexities and opacity of the interchange between human psyche and human psyche are left aside (cf. Chapter 5.6). All that matters is that an amount of money is handed over as compensation for giving something valuable. The particular qualities (we leave aside here the wage-labour relation for which particular qualities in the form of abilities are essential) and the singularity of the individuals giving and taking play no role in such an exchange interplay. It does not matter of what race or creed or worldview the exchangers are, and it is irrelevant that it is precisely this singular individual exchanging with that singular individual. Exchange is an abstract relation between humans in which things, money and commodities, mediate. It is this abstractness that makes exchange interplay practically simple and workable for daily life and capable of spanning the globe. The bearer of money has in his or her hands the universal key to the world of all useful things. Each of the parties involved in an exchange has a particular interest in the exchange, either to gain money, or some useful good (including service), and exchange takes place on the basis of a *mutual* satisfaction of the interests of the parties involved. The abstract relation of exchange provides a framework for the pursuit of particular interests and their mutual satisfaction, encompassing and subsuming all individual singularity, and it is this abstractly universal, flexible quality that makes exchange into the suitable, strong nexus constituting a large society, even a rudimentary world society, practically on its most rudimentary level.

The abstract simplicity of exchange interplay, the so-called cash nexus, is often maligned as *alienation* and *reification* because personal relations between humans are replaced by impersonal relations between things. On the one hand, reification is indeed an apposite term for money-mediated exchange. It is another matter, however, whether reification is a category implying critical rejection of a type of social interplay or whether reification per se represents a perversion of the human social essence. The notion of alienation, on the other hand, from Latin *alius*, 'other', implies that the products of labour confront the individual member of society as an other, a strange other, thus preventing individual belonging to society as a world in which individuals can constitute an identity. The supposedly cold, impersonal, estranged, reified relations of commodity exchange are contrasted with warm, personal, familiar, dependable human relations, say, in a village community. However, in such critique it is invariably overlooked not only that human being, as social being, is necessarily being with the other, but also that the warmth of personal, familiar relations harbours also the possibility of the heat of enmity, mistrust, prejudice and other destructive human passions as well as the entanglements of personal dependency. Abstract exchange abstracts from such entanglements without, on the other hand, having to totalize to exclude sociation of other kinds, such as friendship and intimacy. Some critics of commodity relations as the alienated, reified glue of society even suggest that social life, liberated from the exchange of products as private property, could have room for love in the practice of production and exchange. Thus the young Marx writes:

Gesetzt, wir hätten als Menschen produziert: Jeder von uns hätte in seiner Produktion sich selbst und den andren *doppelt bejaht*. [...] In deinem Genuß oder deinem Gebrauch meines Produkts hätte ich *unmittelbar* den Genuß, [...] sowohl in deinem Denken wie in deiner Liebe mich bestätigt zu wissen.

Karl Marx, Excerpts from James Mills' *'Élémens d'économie politique'* in MEW Erg. Bd. 1 p. 462

Assuming that we had produced as human beings [instead of exchanging our products as private property ME], each of us would have *doubly affirmed* himself and the other in his production. [...] In your enjoyment or your use of my product I would have had the *direct* enjoyment [...] of knowing that I am affirmed in your thinking as well as your love.

Where there is room for love, there is also room for hate. Marx casts his conception of production "as human beings" against the foil of the production and exchange of private property in which things are the mediators of human relations. Under such social relations, "Our *reciprocal* value for each other is the *value* of our reciprocal objects. Thus, the human himself is reciprocally *worthless* for each other." (MEWErg1:462) Exchange relations abstract from the persons exchanging, making them mere bearers of property relations. The act of exchange is indifferent to the particularity of the exchangers and also to their singularity as these unique individuals. It is the value of the objects exchanged, their being-good-for a particular use, that shows itself and motivates the exchange, not the value or worthiness of the human exchangers, which is irrelevant here and abstracted from. Their value can be at best only the reflection of the value of the goods exchanged.

To want to imbue exchange interplay with an appreciation and estimation of the other as such in his or her concrete particularity or even unique singularity would mean introducing the whole gamut of intricate interplay of estimation possible between two free beings, which would multiply infinitely the unreliability of simple market exchange relations. If exchange were practised on the basis of love, which is a deep human relation involving an appreciation and acknowledgement of the other in their totality as this unique individual, there would be little exchange and the social fabric would tear and cut into small, uneven patches based on personal dependency (such as clans and tribes) and the narrow radius of personal inclinations, dislikes, proclivities, fancies, etc. which abstract interplay leaves to one side. Even requiring brotherly love as a prerequisite for exchange would put the social nexus of exchange on a shaky footing, for it would make the business of exchange dependent on morally overcoming human likes and dislikes, inclinations and disinclinations, which are manifold and capricious. The exchange of the products of labour on the basis of their respective use-values as transformed in the medium of exchange-value and motivated by the reciprocal self-interests of the parties exchanging, puts social intercourse on an abstract, minimal, workable footing.

It could be a blessing for human social living that exchange interplay is reified and abstract, guaranteeing a certain distance and indifference. It is irrelevant whether I like or dislike the vendor from whom I buy a newspaper or the taxi-driver who drives me to the airport, or whether national economies trade with one another on the basis of a warm bond of friendship between peoples. Whether a commodity exchange transaction takes place depends on the respective self-interests of the parties involved. If these self-interests complement each other and each can be satisfied with a transaction, a deal is done to mutual satisfaction; if not, it can't be helped, and no love is lost. The parties remain independent of and indifferent to each other, and the exchange, if it takes place at all, is an act performed by free, independent, self-interested individuals who function in the exchange relation only as the bearers of goods and money. Even if the seller attempts to persuade the prospective buyer to make a purchase, this persuasion is directed at the buyer's imputed self-interest and is not, say, an appeal to the buyer's generous heart. Since a transaction may depend on the whim of a moment on the part of either party, there is no reliability or calculability in exchange relations despite all the attempts to manipulate the prospective buyer's desires. Even for the staple necessities of life, for which demand is highly inelastic, the prices at which goods are sold can swing wildly, depending on overall supply. Economic agents therefore not only cannot find personal warmth and comfort in economic relations, but they also cannot rely on their constancy. But neither, as a rule, will they find enmity and personal rejection in economic interchanges. Rather, economic life is an interplay of uncertainty requiring flexibility, adaptability, perseverance and even a tough skin to weather the indifference. Is such toughness a perversion of human nature or just one of its facets? (Cf. Chapter 9.1ff.)

7.7 Risky enterprise and secure jobs

Because economic life is a game, and therefore uncertain, there are losers as well as winners, and therefore also an inherent tendency of players in the economy to build hedges against risk as far as they are able. Prudent caution is one of the principal precepts of economic life and this can only be so because it is *essentially* risky, i.e. exposed to contingency, even apart from the minimum of trust required to engage in exchange interplay at all. The agent in modern economic life most exposed to such contingency is the entrepreneur, i.e. literally, the one who undertakes an undertaking whose success or failure depends on how a product finally fares on the market, how much revenue is generated and how much is left as net profit. But all the economic roles in a capitalist economy depend on the entrepreneur's success, whether it be the employees who have hired their power to labour to the entrepreneur at fixed, agreed wage rates, the financier whose has lent money at fixed interest rates, or the landowner who has leased land for a fixed rental.

The new value that comes about through the entrepreneur's operations in the process of market validation has to be sufficient to cover the costs of wages, interest, rent and means of production and also leave a residue of profit of enterprise. Whether sufficient new value gains market recognition as the validation of the enterprise's operations remains necessarily and essentially open, uncertain. It is not in the interests of employees to recognize the risk to which the enterprise for which they work is exposed. Their interests are rather to strive for secure, guaranteed jobs with assured income, regardless of the company's fortunes, and to call on the state to pass legislation to protect their jobs. Such protection is then regarded as a 'victory' for the working class and for 'social justice'. Bargaining on the market over jobs is then tendentially displaced or at least supplemented by state regulation and legislation that lay down a framework for employment that is as secure as possible and often even denies the company's risks of surviving in the economy. The state once again assumes its essential role of erecting a state of affairs, to be maintained by force of law, which keeps dangers to its subjects at bay. The core dangers to be warded off by the state, however, are those threatening the "life, liberty and estates" of its citizens, and this prime function and raison d'être for the state — the rule of law — is fulfilled in its guaranteeing the lawful form of fair interplay in civil society.

But the risks of losing out in the interplay of self-interests in civil society even *within* the lawful rules of play, in which citizens pursue their individual self-interests, can also be transferred to the state which thereby becomes a *welfare state* with the role of cushioning the impact of the risks of economic activity, of providing a social safety net, of spreading risk in a social security scheme of so-called social solidarity (paradoxically based on a collective self-interest — or rather, mass egoism — to being cared for). Through the exercise of state political power, the free play of economic interplay is suspended or curtailed, not by being subjected to lawful rules of play (which rather *enable* the interplay), but by certain market exchanges, such as the dismissal of workers (which is the termination of an exchange contract), being declared illegal by state will. The value criterion — according to which an enterprise must make money rather than losing it, and enhances its chances of survival in the market-place by mak-

284 — Interlude: Everyday living, security and insecurity

ing a comfortable profit, sufficient also for investments to maintain competitiveness — is thus insofar made ineffective as the principle guiding and disciplining the enterprise's strategy. In its place steps the uncertainties of the political power struggles, because a law posited by the state's will and under the political pressure of employees seeking job security can also be repealed or replaced by another law. Moreover, the cost of providing job security through state fiat is that the economic market interplay can no longer discipline the enterprises to adapt to changing exchange-value relations, thus enabling other economies to gain a competitive advantage. The respite from competitive interplay attained through job-securing legislation is a Pyrrhic victory for the organized employees, turning into its opposite, because international competition lessens the potency of domestic enterprises, lowering economic growth and perhaps, after all, inexorably endangering jobs through the bankruptcy or simply poor economic performance of domestic enterprises. We shall return to this theme in Chapter 9.

In the meantime, it is important to note that the *ontological* origin of the tension between risk and security lies in the nature of (social) movement itself, i.e. between the ontological plane of δύναμις power, potential, potency, ability, on the one hand, and the plane of the ἐντελέχεια, actuality of the material goods people actually have, on the other. *Any* movement at all, proceeding as it does from potential, potency to actuality bears within itself the possibility of missing its end, its τέλος, but the movement of social interplay, in particular, is doubly, or exponentially, exposed to risk, proceeding as it does from at least two free starting-points (ἀρχαί). Put succinctly, since all human living is socially shared, life itself, at its socio-ontological core, is risky. Like all deep ontological truths, this sounds like a platitude, but no matter, for it is destined for certain, highly receptive ears only.

8 The short reach of Cartesian certainty and Leibniz' principle of reason into the social science of economics

8.1 Leibniz' principle of reason as a general "grand principle"

I return to the theme of the Cartesian cast of economics first treated in Chapter 4.3. The triumph of the modern age heralded in philosophically by Descartes in the seventeenth century derives from the success of the mathematized natural sciences. The names of Galileo, Newton, Descartes, Leibniz, along with those of many other mathematicians and natural scientists, resound to the present day. The mathematized natural sciences also formed the foundation for the industrial revolution that revolutionized not only the economy, but — with its technical innovations — the way of life as a whole. The metaphysical underpinnings of the modern age consist firstly in the Cartesian positing of the ego cogito as the fundamentum inconcussum, the unshakeable foundation upon which certain knowledge is to be founded, and secondly, in Leibniz' principle: nihil est sine ratio, nothing is without reason or, formulated affirmatively, every being has a reason. The full version of Leibniz' "grand principle" is "nothing happens without a sufficient reason" (rien ne se fait sans raison suffisante[136]). These two metaphysical postulates together were thought to constitute a secure building which was designed to house and has housed at least the natural sciences, physics, chemistry and molecular biology.

But what do the firm, grounding foundations and indubitability of knowledge they enunciate have to do with the security of living on an everyday basis, as addressed in the preceding chapter? Although the law-like nature of the universe was 'discovered' (i.e. cast) first of all for the movement of (initially: celestial) physical bodies which allowed a mathematical grasp of them in both a conceptual and technologically palpable sense, the metaphysical reach of mathematico-rational laws was by no means restricted to the realm of motion first studied by Galileo and Newton, but was extended in the shape of Leibniz' "grand principle" to a general principle governing all beings. Thus, the claims

---

136 G.W. Leibniz *Principes de la Nature et de la Grace, Fondés en Raison* Werke, Wissenschaftliche Buchgesellschaft, Darmstadt 1985 Bd. I, Para. 7 S. 426.

https://doi.org/10.1515/9783110617504-008

of reason extended to all areas of knowledge, to all sciences, even beyond the domain of nature to that of social phenomena.

To prevent an infinite regress of reasons, Leibniz derives from his "grand principle" a "last reason for things", a "substance" and "necessary being" which "bears the reason for its existence within itself" (portant la raison de son existence avec soy; Para. 8) which "is called God" (est appellée *Dieu*, Para. 8). God is the theological anchor in Leibniz's onto-theology complementing the ontology of his grand principle. "This simple, primitive substance" (Cette substance simple primitive, Para. 9) guarantees not only the existence but also an order of the universe which, moreover, can be seen by human beings through the power of reason. By "choosing the best possible plan" (choisi le meilleur Plan possible, Para. 10), God has set up the universe in such a way — "the most perfect possible" (le plus parfait qui soit possible, Para. 10) — that it is "possible to render a reason why things tend to run thus rather than otherwise" (possible de rendre raison, pourquoy les choses sont allées plustôt ainsi qu'autrement, Para. 10) Human reason is able to render (rendre raison, Para. 11) to each being the sufficient reason for its existence, no matter what it is, and all sciences are now subjected to the demand to find the sufficient reasons for the phenomena they investigate.

In the late eighteenth and nineteenth centuries, the budding social science of political economy, which grew out of moral philosophy, was subsumed under the Leibnizian principle and subjected to its imperative just as, say, the sciences of chemistry or psychology before it. Political economy was the 'test case' for the establishment of a social science. When Karl Marx arrives on the scene in the second half of the nineteenth century, he is able to draw on an entire body of writings in French and English in the area of political economy in order to subject it to critique. His endeavours explicitly take their orientation from the paradigm of the natural sciences, as evidenced not only by the chemical analogies that abound in *Das Kapital*. This thread will be taken up again in section 8.2 after the digression.

8.1.1 Digression: The principle of reason further considered

8.1.1.1 Leibniz

The principle of reason was first enunciated in the seventeenth century by Leibniz. It states: "Nihil est sine ratione", or more fully, "nihil existere nisi cujus reddi possit ratio existentiae sufficiens"[137]: "Nothing is without reason" or "Nothing exists whose sufficient reason for existence cannot be rendered". The sufficiency of the reason will be of special interest here. Expressed positively, the principle states that everything has a sufficient reason that can be rendered (from L. reddere 'to give back') why it is so rather than otherwise. "Everything" here refers to facts (fait[138]) expressed in true propositions or "enunciations" (Enonciation veritable, Para. 32).

The German word for reason is 'Grund', and the principle of reason in German reads 'Der Satz vom Grund', which, because of the ambiguity of 'Satz', can also mean 'the leap from the ground'. In English, too, one synonym of 'reason' is 'ground'. The principle therefore provides the ground upon which truths stand by assuring, i.e. by 'giving back', that every state of affairs indeed has a ground, indeed, grounds that are sufficient to support the state of affairs. 'To suffice' comes from Latin sub- 'under' and 'ficere 'to make', suggesting that the principle slips in a ground underneath all states of affairs that happen to support them in their being thus rather than otherwise. Leibniz distinguishes between two sorts of truths, truths of reason (Raisonnement, Para. 33) and truths of fact (Fait, Para. 33). The former truths can be analyzed by reason into simple, basic truths requiring no proof, so that all truths logically derived from them are "necessary" (necessaires, Para. 33).

The latter sort of truths, Leibniz claims, can also have a "sufficient reason" (raison suffisante, Para. 36), even though they are "contingent" (contingentes, Para. 36) and not necessary like the truths of reason. The reasons for the truth of contingent truths (that can possibly be otherwise) can be either "cause efficiente" or "cause finale" (Para. 36). Leibniz asserts that an infinite number of both final and efficient causes goes into his present activity of writing his manuscript. The distinction between these two kinds of causes is of the utmost importance for Leibniz, for he claims that without final causes it is not possible to sufficiently ground certain important states of affairs. His standard example that recurs throughout his writings, and thus has the status almost of a paradigm, is that of the Newtonian laws of motion which, he asserts, cannot be provided with sufficient reason solely through efficient causes. The Newtonian

---

137 Leibniz *Werke* Beilage: II. Communicata ex literis D. Schull(eri) no. 23, cited also by Heidegger in *Der Satz vom Grund* Neske, Pfullingen 1957 S. 64, abbreviated *SvG*. (with "potest" instead of "possit"), or, more colloquially, "rien ne se fait sans raison suffisante" i.e. "nothing happens without sufficient reason", *Principes de la Nature et de la Grace, Fondés en Raison* Werke Bd. I, Para. 7 S. 426.

138 G.W. Leibniz *Monadologie* Werke Bd. I, Para. 32 S. 452.

laws of motion, enunciated first of all with regard to the motion of celestial bodies, quickly come to dominate minds, for they show that the language of mathematics can be employed to understand elegantly and predictively the motion of physical bodies. This ushers in the striving, buoyed by tremendous confidence, that mathematics will be able to unlock the secrets of nature so that it can mastered by human reason (god-like will to power).

Leibniz regards it as indispensable to consider final causes with respect to the laws of motion because their elegance and simplicity cannot be otherwise explained, i.e. given a sufficient reason. Since the laws of motion are not truths of reason, they are not necessary, and therefore contingent. They therefore could have been otherwise. But Leibniz introduces besides the principle of necessity, the "principle of convenience" (principe de la convenance[139]) according to which the laws of motion are subject to a "choice of wisdom" (choix de la sagesse, Para. 10), namely a choice made by God. Being a matter of "choice", the laws of motion are chosen thus and not otherwise for a particular end or τέλος, namely, the end of a highest possible degree of perfection of the world. God as the supreme, omnipotent and perfect being has the power to choose the laws that govern the world to be as perfect as possible (*Monadologie* Para. 54).

The return to a sufficient reason on which all the states of affairs of the world, no matter how contingent they are, can be grounded leads Leibniz back to a "sufficient or ultimate reason" (raison suffisante ou derniere, Para. 37), an ultimate ground on which everything that exists can stand and be what and how it is. This ultimate ground is God, who has "the reason for his existence within himself" (la raison de son existence en luy même, Para. 45). God is thus self-grounding and as such the ultimate guarantor that the world has been set up in such a way that it is "convenient" in the sense that human reason can gain the most elegant possible insight into the grounds of even the most contingent states of affairs down to the last "detail" (detail, Para. 37). The principle of reason guarantees that the world has an order and a sense that can be seen by human reason and, even if it cannot yet be seen clearly by human reason, because the individual "monads" (Monades) are "limited and distinguished by the degree of distinct perception" (limitées et distinguées par les degrés des perceptions distinctes, Para. 60), it guarantees that there is a divine plan underlying the world whose set-up has been chosen by God according to the greatest possible "measure of perfection" (mesure de la perfection, Para. 54) and "the greatest possible order" (le plus grand ordre qui se puisse, Para. 58). Precise observation

---

139 G.W. Leibniz *Principes de la Nature et de la Grace, Fondés en Raison* Werke Bd. I, Para. 10 S. 430.

of the details of nature, such as the bodies of living organisms (cf. Para. 64), shows that each of the organs "in their smallest parts" (dans leur moindres parties, Para. 64) has been fashioned and produced for a particular end and purpose by "divine art" (l'art Divin, Para. 64) since "the universe is regulated by a perfect order" (l'univers étant réglé dans un ordre parfait, Para. 63).

8.1.1.2 Hegel

So far we have seen that the sufficiency of the sufficient reason for each being, according to Leibniz, cannot be provided solely by efficient causes according to the mechanical schema of cause and effect, but requires recourse to final causes, i.e. to ends and purposes. This is taken up also by Hegel, who deals with Grund (reason/ground) and the Leibnizian principle of reason (Satz vom Grund) in his *Logik* under the Doctrine of Essence. The addition to § 121 on Grund in the *Enzyklopädie* makes explicit reference to Leibniz' demand that one go beyond efficient causes to final causes. "According to this difference, light, warmth, moisture, for instance, would have to be regarded as *causae efficientes*, but not as *causa finalis* of the growth of plants which *causa finalis*, however, is precisely nothing other than the concept of plant itself." (Nach diesem Unterschied würden z. B. Licht, Wärme, Feuchtigkeit zwar als *causae efficientes*, nicht aber als *causa finalis* des Wachstums der Pflanzen zu betrachten sein, welche *causa finalis* dann eben nichts anderes ist als der Begriff der Pflanze selbst. *EnzI* § 121 Add.)

Hegel juxtaposes the concept to ground/reason, the concept being a final cause. But not all final causes have the status of the concept, and Hegel distinguishes "the *finite*, the *extraneous* expediency" (die *endliche*, die *äußere* Zweckmäßigkeit, *Enz.* § 204 Note) from the "*inner* expediency" (*innere* Zweckmäßigkeit, § 204) brought into play by Aristotle and revived by Kant which corresponds to a concept of life. There may be "*extraneous* expediency" in a thief stealing to satisfy his hunger or a soldier running away to save his life, and these ends of the satisfaction of hunger or saving one's life are certainly grounds for the thief's or soldier's action, and even sufficient grounds. "If a soldier runs away from battle to save his life, he acts in breach of his duty, but it cannot be maintained that the reason/ground that determined him to act in this way was not sufficient because otherwise he would have stayed at his post." (Wenn ein Soldat aus der Schlacht entläuft, um sein Leben zu erhalten, so handelt er zwar pflichtwidrig, allein es ist nicht zu behaupten, daß der Grund, der ihn so zu handeln bestimmt hat, nicht zureichend wäre, da er sonst auf seinem Posten geblieben sein würde. *EnzI* § 121 Add.)

It is therefore not enough to point to sufficient grounds for an action resid-ing in an extraneous purpose or end; rather, this end itself must be justified against a concept of justice and the good. The principle of reason is therefore unable to deal with the indispensable distinctions between inner and external expediency, good and bad actions, just and unjust actions which require a fur-ther dialectical unfolding of thinking to the plane of the speculative concept and the idea.

Hegel therefore emphasizes in the section on "Teleologie" (*EnzI* § § 204ff) that "the difference between the purpose as *final cause* and the merely *efficient cause* [...] is of the highest importance" (ist der Unterschied des Zweckes als *Endursache* von der bloß *wirkenden Ursache* [...] von höchster Wichtigkeit, § 204 Note) and he characterizes the latter as "belonging to not yet uncovered, blind necessity" (gehört der noch nicht enthüllten, der blinden Notwendigkeit an, § 204 Note), whereas the former "only effects itself and is in the *end* what it was at the *beginning* in its origin" (bewirkt nur sich selbst und ist am *Ende*, was er im *Anfange*, in der Ursprünglichkeit war, § 204 Note). The end is already *seen* from the beginning and is brought forth. "The ground/reason still has no determinate *content* in and for itself, still is not *purpose*, and therefore it is neither *active* nor *productive*; but rather, an existence only *proceeds* out of the ground/reason." (Der Grund hat noch keinen an und für sich bestimmten *Inhalt*, noch ist er *Zweck*, daher ist er nicht *tätig* noch *hervorbringend*; sondern eine Existenz *geht* aus dem Grunde nur *hervor*, Enz. § 122 Note) Purposive action sees its end 'ideal-ly' in a 'look' from the beginning from within itself and, guided by this sight of the ideal, negates objectivity to bring forth, to produce the fore-seen end-result.

This line of thinking echoes Plato's and Aristotle's determination of the es-sence of τέχνη ποιητική as a starting-point in know-how that knowingly fore-sees the end-product to be produced and governs the actions that lead to bring-ing forth this end-product. A τέχνη ποιητική is a δύναμις μετὰ λόγου, where the λόγος has the task of fore-seeing the end, of bringing it knowingly into view and gathering into a know-how the actions required to achieve the desired final result. For Hegel, however, the end in view is not merely the finite, 'technical' ends seen by understanding, but infinite ends that conform to the speculative, i.e. ontological, concept. Whereas for Leibniz, God is the ultimate reason or ground upon which all that happens in the universe rests, for Hegel, it is the speculative concept that fulfils this role insofar as the concept in correspond-ence with objectivity is the Idea in its truth (*Enz.* § 213), and the Idea is the Abso-lute, God.

The many individual steps in dialectical thinking leading from abstract be-ing in its immediacy to the Idea are to provide speculative insight into how it is that the world is in conformity with the thinking of God in the Idea. Hegel therefore agrees with Leibniz that God is the ultimate reason for the world, however, not as a blind ground, but rather as a concept in accord with divine wisdom that can be humanly attained in absolute knowing. The "infinite purpose", according to Hegel, is realized in the world. "The execution of the infinite purpose is thus only to lift the illusion as if it were not yet executed. The good, the absolute good, is accomplished eternally in the world... The Idea in its process makes this illusion for itself, posits an other opposite itself, and its action consists in lifting this illusion." (Die Vollführung des unendlichen Zwecks ist so nur, die Täuschung aufzuheben, als ob er noch nicht vollführt sei. Das Gute, das absolut Gute, vollbringt sich ewig in der Welt... Die Idee in ihrem Prozeß macht sich selbst jene Täuschung, setzt ein Anderes sich gegenüber, und ihr Tun besteht darin, diese Täuschung aufzuheben. *Enz.* § 212 Add.).

The world is thus shown through the dialectical movement of speculative thinking to have a purpose, an infinite, divine purpose in the sense that the concept corresponds to objectivity, despite the illusory appearance that it is otherwise. The end-result is the same as Leibniz', but it is reached via many more mediations in thinking. Hegel, indeed, is the thinker of mediation, of Vermittlung, so that nothing is simply accepted in its immediacy.

8.1.1.3   Nietzsche

This philosophical confidence in the existence of an ultimate, divine reason for the world dwindles during the course of the nineteenth century until Nietzsche finally proclaims in 1888 that "*nihilism* as a *psychological state* will have to set in" (Der *Nihilism* als *psychologischer Zustand* wird eintreten müssen[140]) when it is realized that there is no sense, no direction in the happenings of the world, "that something is supposed to be *attained* through the process itself, and now one grasps that with becoming *nothing* is achieved, *nothing* attained... Thus the disappointment over a purported *purpose* of *becoming* as a cause of nihilism" (daß ein Etwas durch den Prozeß selbst *erreicht* werden soll: — und nun begreift man, daß mit dem Werden *nichts* erzielt, *nichts* erreicht wird... Also die Enttäuschung über einen angeblichen *Zweck* des *Werdens* als Ursache des Nihilismus, *KSA13*:47). With this pronouncement, an ultimate, unifying purpose for the world is seen to be null and void, so that a final cause for the world, an end

---

140 Friedrich Nietzsche *Nachgelassene Fragmente* November 1887 - March 1888 11 [97–99] *Kritische Studienausgabe* Bd. 13 S. 47 = KSA13:47.

toward which it progresses, no matter what this end-purpose might be, whether divine or profane, dissolves into nothing.

For Nietzsche, this first state of nihilism is accompanied by a second and third state. The second state comes about when it is realized that there is no unified "*organization* in all happenings" (*Organisirung* in allem Geschehn, *KSA13*:47) so that human beings could believe and be settled "in a deep feeling of connectedness with and dependency on a whole infinitely superior to humankind, a mode of divinity" (in tiefem Zusammenhangs- und Abhängigkeits-Gefühl von einem ihm unendlich überlegenen Ganzen, ein modus der Gottheit, *KSA13*:47). And finally, the third state of nihilism sets in when it is realized that there is no "*true* world" (*wahre* Welt, *KSA13*:48) behind a world of illusion so that a state of "*disbelief in a metaphysical* world" (*Unglauben an eine metaphysische* Welt, *KSA13*:48) sets in and one "concedes the reality of becoming als the *sole* reality" (giebt man die Realität des Werdens als *einzige* Realität zu, *KSA13*:48), without "any kind of secret paths to hinterworlds and false divinities" (jede Art Schleichwege zu Hinterwelten und falschen Göttlichkeiten, *KSA13*:48). In such a state of nihilism, there is no longer any possibility of lifting the illusion of which Hegel speaks to reveal an "infinite purpose" of the world, the "absolute good" that is "accomplished eternally in the world". For Nietzsche nihilism means, "the aim is missing; the answer to the question asking Why? is missing" (es fehlt das Ziel; es fehlt die Antwort auf das 'Warum?', Autumn 1887, *KSA12*:350). He thus denies the principle of reason with respect to the ultimate reason and ground on which the world is supposed to rest. But more than that — he questions the very category of purpose:

> ...warum könnte nicht ein Zweck eine Begleiterscheinung sein, in der Reihe von Veränderungen wirkender Kräfte, welche die zweckmäßige Handlung hervorrufen - ein in das Bewußtsein vorausgeworfenes blasses Zeichenbild, das uns zur Orientirung dient dessen, was geschieht, als ein Symptom selbst vom Geschehen, nicht als dessen Ursache? - Aber damit haben wir den Willen selbst kritisirt: ist es nicht eine Illusion, das, was im Bewußtsein als Willens-Akt auftaucht, als Ursache zu nehmen? [...] Es verändert sich, keine Veränderung ohne Grund - setzt immer schon ein Etwas voraus, das hinter der Veränderung steht und bleibt. Ursache und Wirkung: psychologisch nachgerechnet ist es der Glaube, der sich im Verbum ausdrückt, Activum und Passivum, Thun und Leiden. (*KSA12*:248, 249)

> ... why couldn't a purpose be an epiphenomenon in the series of changes of efficient forces which call forth the purposeful action - a faint, symbolic image projected ahead into consciousness that serves us for orientation about what is happening, as itself a symptom of the happenings, not as their cause? - But with this we have criticized the will itself: is it not an illusion, to regard what crops up in consciousness as an act of will as a cause? [...] Something changes; no change without a reason - already presupposes a something that

stands and remains behind the change. Cause and effect: recalculated psychologically, it is the belief that is expressed in the verb, active and passive, acting and suffering. (*KSA12*:248, 249)

In these passages Nietzsche denies the categories of purpose and causa finalis altogether, preferring instead the sole schema of blind cause and effect, thus doing away with what Leibniz regards as indispensable for gaining insight into how the world is set up. We will return to this Nietzschean questioning of the category of purpose further on, asking whether it would be more appropriate to restrict instead the applicability of the schema of cause and effect in favour of an interplay of rival and complementary purposes.

8.1.1.4 Heidegger

For the moment we turn to Heidegger's discussion of the principle of reason in lectures delivered at the University of Freiburg in Winter Semester 1955/56 at a time that could be characterized as an advanced stage of nihilism. In any case, Heidegger will not even mention final causes when interpreting Leibniz' principle of reason. Instead he evades the entire issue of teleology in his exposition of what is meant precisely by "sufficient reason". Instead of shifting from efficient cause to final cause to expound the meaning of "sufficiency", as Leibniz does, Heidegger claims that the sufficiency of the reason resides in its "perfection". "In the background of the determination of sufficiency (of suffectio) there stands a guiding idea of Leibniz' thinking, that of perfectio" (Im Hintergrund der Bestimmung des Zureichens, der Suffizienz (der suffectio), steht eine Leitvorstellung des leibnizischen Denkens, diejenige der perfectio, SvG:64).

Heidegger interprets the "existere" of the being in the formulation of the principle of reason cited at the outset as a "Ständigkeit", i.e. as a "standingness" of the object, which is "thoroughly secured, perfect" (durch und durch sichergestellt, perfekt, SvG:64) by a complete rendering (giving-back) of the grounds for its standing in existence. This "Voll-ständigkeit" (SvG:64), i.e. "fullstandingness" or "completeness" of the object's grounds that secures its existence is, according to Heidegger, a completeness of efficient causes, as he immediately makes plain: "The ground (ratio) as cause (causa) is related to the effect (efficere)" (Der Grund (ratio) ist als Ursache (causa) auf den Effekt (efficere) bezogen, SvG:64).

But this means for Heidegger that the principle of reason is unleashed historically as a principle of total calculability of all beings. "Its [ratio's] pretension to power unleashes the universal and total accounting for everything to make it calculable" (Deren [der Ratio] Machtanspruch entfesselt die universale und totale Verrechnung von allem zum Berechenbaren, SvG:138). The "perfection" of grounds is now a "completeness of accountability" (Vollständigkeit der Rechenschaft, SvG:196), and "only this guarantees that every representational thought can count on and calculate with the object everywhere at any time" (verbürgt erst, daß jedes Vorstellen jederzeit und überall auf den Gegenstand und mit ihm rechnen kann, SvG:196). The principle of reason now means, "any being is regarded as existing if and only if it has been secured for representational thought as a calculable object" (Jegliches gilt dann und nur dann als seiend, wenn es für das Vorstellen als ein berechenbarer Gegenstand sichergestellt ist, SvG:196).

Heidegger thus brings the Leibnizian principle of reason to resonate with the ostinato of his theme of modern technology that is "rasende Technik" in the twofold sense of 'mad' and 'racing'. "The perfection of technology is only the echo of the pretension to perfectio, i.e. the completeness of grounding" (Die Perfektion der Technik ist nur das Echo des Anspruches auf die perfectio, d.h. die Vollständigkeit der Begründung, SvG:198). And this perfection is no longer a perfection of God as the perfect, supreme being who guarantees that the universe has been set up in the most "convenient" way possible with the purpose of harmonizing with God's infinite goodness, but the perfection of total calculability, another 'god'. "The perfection is based on the thorough calculability of the objects. The calculability of the objects presupposes the unrestricted validity of the principium rationis" (Die Perfektion beruht auf der durchgängigen Berechenbarkeit der Gegenstände. Die Berechenbarkeit der Gegenstände setzt die unbeschränkte Geltung des principium rationis voraus, SvG:198). And this is "the essence of the modern technical age" (das Wesen des modernen technischen Zeitalters, SvG:198).

But Heidegger seeks a way out of this "destiny of being/sending from being" (Seinsgeschick, SvG:187) of the modern age and he does so by means of a leap that depends on listening to the principle of reason in a different, "second key" (zweite Tonart, SvG:177 and passim) which hears it as saying, "Being and ground/reason: the Same" (Sein und Grund: das Selbe, SvG:178 and passim). Being is the ground upon which beings as such are cast by being, the ground upon which beings shape up and stand and *are* or *presence as* the beings that they are. The original word for ratio is the Greek λόγος, whereas the Greek word for being, εἶναι, means "presence" (anwesen, SvG:177). "Clarified in the Greek sense, 'being' means: shining into and over to unconcealment and, thus shining, enduring and whiling" (Im griechischen Sinne verdeutlicht, heißt 'Sein': ins Unverborgene herein- und herbei-scheinen und, also scheinend, währen und weilen, SvG:177). The task of λόγος in this eventuation of the shining of beings as such into presence is to glean them into a saying. Why? "Because λέγειν means: to gather, to glean, to lay next to one another. Such laying, however, as gathering, gleaning, saving, preserving and keeping, is a letting-lie-before that brings to shining in appearance that which lies before us" (Weil λέγειν heißt: sammeln, zueinander-legen. Solches Legen aber ist, als sammelndes, aufhebendes, bewahrendes und verwahrendes, ein Vorliegenlassen, das zum Vorschein bringt: das Vorliegende, SvG:179).

By allowing beings as such to lie in front of us in presence, the ground is laid for allowing other things to lay beside and be thus grounded. "Λόγος names the ground. Λόγος is presence and ground at one and the same time" (Λόγος nennt den Grund. Λόγος ist Anwesen und Grund zumal, SvG:179). But in this gathering into presence that allows beings as such to appear and shine as that which lies before us, being itself remains hidden in withdrawal. Being (= originary 3D-time) itself remains in hiding as it sends the shapes of beings as such within historical sendings that Heidegger calls the "destiny of being" or "sending from being" (Seinsgeschick, SvG:187). "Rather, being, in hiding its essencing, allows something else to appear, namely, the ground in the shape of the ἀρχαί, αἰτίαι, the rationes, causae, the principles, causes and rational grounds" (Vielmehr läßt das Sein, indem es sein Wesen verbirgt, anderes zum Vorschein kommen, nämlich den Grund in der Gestalt der ἀρχαί, αἰτίαι, der rationes, der causae, der Prinzipien, Ursachen und der Vernunftgründe, SvG:183). The ἀρχαί, αἰτίαι, as thought by the Greeks are the grounds upon which beings can be grounded and thus known.

Aristotle says that knowledge is that which can be derived from ἀρχαί, i.e. first principles. An ἀρχή is a 'wherefrom', a 'whence', an origin from which something else can be led forth, derived in such a way that the origin governs the presence of that which is derived from it. Similarly, an αἴτιος, a cause in the Greek sense, is that ground which can be 'blamed' for something else. One being is caused by another insofar as its existence is due to another. By attributing and showing an origin of beings in their presence, by 'blaming' their presence on other beings, the λόγος or reason accounts for their presence as the beings which they are and show themselves to be. This accounting-for, according to Heidegger, finally unfolds in the course of history to thoroughly calculative reason that calculates and precalculates the presence of beings in their totality on the grounds of a chain of efficient causes. There is no longer any purpose or end or τέλος in this calculating grounding of beings, but only what Heidegger calls a "will to will" (Wille zum Willen) that brings forth beings into presence merely for the sake of bringing-forth (a perverse version of τὸ ἀγαθόν).

Whilst grounding all beings in their coming forth into and whiling in presence, however, being itself remains ungrounded. "Being as being remains without ground, without reason" (Sein bleibt als Sein grund-los, SvG:185). Being itself is therefore groundlessness, the "Abgrund" (SvG:185), the abyss. On hearing the principle of reason in its "other key" (andere Tonart, SvG:178 and passim), beings in their presence can no longer be accounted for on the ground of an ultimate ground called God who bears the ground for His existence within Himself. The ultimate ground is now being, which is itself groundless. Because the sendings of being are themselves groundless, they are, according to Heidegger, a "game" (Spiel, SvG:186). The leap from the ground of the principle of reason is therefore a leap into the groundlessness of a game "into which we mortals are brought by dwelling near to death" (in das wir Sterbliche gebracht sind, [...] indem wir in der Nähe des Todes wohnen, SvG:186).

The measure of this groundless game in which we mortals are brought into play, according to Heidegger, is death. "Death is the still unthought measure for the immeasurable, i.e. the supreme game" (Der Tod ist die noch ungedachte Maßgabe des Unermeßlichen, d.h. des höchsten Spiels, SvG:187). No longer is there a supreme being as a ground for reason, but a supreme game of life and death of mortals dwelling on the Earth. The as yet unthought thought of death as the measure for the groundless game of being, i.e. presencing and absencing, is the concluding thought in Heidegger's lectures on the principle of reason. Such a game can no longer be conceived in terms of efficient causes or final causes, which always recur to a being as ground, and not to being itself in its groundless play.

But is this the final, ultimate move in the movement from the ground of the principle of reason into groundlessness? Is only a "jump into being" (Satz in das Sein, SvG:98, 98, 103) possible from the firm ground of the ground of reason upon which beings must account calculatively for their presence? Could it be that beings themselves are at play *with one another* in such a way that this play eludes the grasp of the reach of grounds in the sense of efficient and final causes? Isn't a game understood already in a normal, everyday sense already beyond the reach of a calculability in terms of causes on which the moves in the game could be 'blamed' in a way that could be followed deductively, causally, calculatively by reason? Is there another way to jump into the groundless game? Such a jump would require in the first place letting go of the striving of calculative reason to secure every being completely in its standing presence.

8.1.1.5 Anaximander and the fairness of interplay

While leaping into the groundlessness of being, it is worthwhile considering whether there is already an other groundlessness that lies closer to hand and which has always already undermined the pretensions of reason to know the phenomena and have things in its grasp. No leap is required to reach this groundlessness, but rather a side-step, as we shall now see. Furthermore, we will discover that the leap into the groundlessness of being goes hand in hand with the groundlessness reached by the side-step. The two kinds of cause on which everything has traditionally been blamed are efficient cause and final cause, with the latter kind of cause receding more and more into the background as the historical hegemony of the mathematized sciences has been established, consolidated and unquestioningly accepted as the sole site of truth, namely scientific, causal explanation. Causa materialis (the weak and insipid reminder of the Earth) and causa formalis (the weak reminder of being's 'looks') had already faded from the scene with the advent of the modern age, being taken for granted without a thought. Whereas Hegel holds onto a supreme ground for the world that can be thought by dialectical-speculative thinking as the Absolute, Nietzsche, in recurring to the sole schema of cause and effect, puts the entire schema of final cause into question, and Heidegger leaps from the ground of the principle of reason altogether to think the groundlessness of the game of being, i.e. of presencing and absencing, itself.

The two kinds of cause, however, have traditionally worked in tandem, with the purpose of the final cause making use of the concatenations of cause and effect by what Hegel calls the "cunning of reason" (List der Vernunft, *Enz.* § 209). The will sets itself a purpose which it strives to achieve through its actions that are guided by a know-how that has insight into the interconnections of cause and effect and thus can manipulate the materials or objects in such a way that *in the end* the desired product can be brought forth. This productive way of thinking is transferred also to practices in fore-knowingly bringing about practical results. The human being in this way of thinking is an ἀρχή, i.e. a 'whence' or origin whence the movement of other beings is knowingly controlled. Hegel formulates this purposive mastery as a "power" (Macht, *Enz.* § 208 Note) of the "subjective purpose" (subjektiver Zweck, § 207) over the object through which "the object is posited as *inherently* null" (das Objekt als *an sich* nichtig gesetzt ist, § 208 Note). Nullity resonates already with the nihil of nihilism.

But what happens when there is not just one human being or 'the' human being as the master of beings and practitioner of 'instrumental reason', and instead a multiplicity of human beings, each of whom is thought as its own origin of movement, of action? One purpose then meets up with another purpose or other purposes in interchanges of all kinds. Failing the subjugation or submission of one source of action to another, there can only be either a conflict or a congruence, a clash or complementarity between different purposes. A congruence of purposes is brought about by agreement, but there is no saying in advance whether such an agreement will be reached. Where there is a conflict of purposes, there is no fore-saying which purpose will win out or even if one purpose will win out or if a compromise will be reached according to which the parties 'promise together' (Fr. com- 'together' and promittere 'to promise', 'to send forth'), thus sending forth into the future what they have agreed upon. Each individual as free is its own groundless ground confronted with other independent, free, groundless grounds. As long as each of these individual grounds or groundless origins recognizes the other in a process of mutual estimation as independent, none is a controlling ground. Instead, the individuals, whether there be two or many, are involved in a groundless interplay of powers of movement in which many purposes are hazarded.

Only if the process of mirroring each other in mutual estimation leads to one estimating the other as superior does submission take place and the one individual becomes the tool of the other. In this case, the schemata of efficient causes and final causes are once again applicable insofar as the superior individual is established as an origin with the *power* to control the other's movements. But such *social power interplay* depends essentially on the submission of one to the other within the movement of estimation, and this movement always remains in play. It is never concluded once and for all. The interplay among the individuals remains a continual power play based on a dialectic of mutual estimation and submission (whether voluntarily by free will or involuntarily under duress, in which case the submission is a *subjugation*).

As long as the process of estimation is a mutual mirroring of each other as formally equal origins without the submission of one to the other, the outcome of interactions between the individuals can be only the outcome of a game, an *interplay*, which is unpredictable because the two or many points of origin in interplay offer no secure ground 'wherefrom' such a prediction could be foreknowingly made (a circumstance that must be denied by modern scientific psychology). The interplay itself is groundless and its outcome is always uncertain, insecure. Both or all individual origins maintain their power, albeit that the power may consist only in the power of persuasion. The only ground for interplay can be agreement based on *trust*. Trust becomes an always retractable ground upon which interplay becomes reliably possible, and only on this ground does the result of the interplay become securely predictable, but always within the terms of the agreement and under the proviso that the basis of trust is not destroyed.

Trust, which is engendered and supported by making and keeping promises mutually 'sent forth' (L. pro-mittere), is one of the basic elements enabling interplay to go on without the intervention of a superior social power or physical violence which degrades the other to a mere object. Such an interplay on the basis of mutually esteeming each other at least as formally equal players depends on the players adhering to fair rules of play for the interplay. Such fair rules of interplay do not guarantee any particular outcome but only that, whatever the outcome, all players will estimate the outcome as just and equitable, even if some players lose. The entire interplay depends upon the players esteeming each other as players without taking unfair advantage of each other. Although each player may have a different aim, it is possible that, through the interplay of estimation and the power plays among equal individuals, a mutually satisfying outcome can come about, but such an outcome is beyond the reach of the principle of reason, which can never render the sufficient reason for one outcome rather than another.

This leads us to the question of the fairness and rightness, or justice, of interplay, which cannot be mastered by any principle of reason since it presupposes a superior governing origin whence the other is treated as an object, even though this other may be itself an origin potentially governing its own movements. The question concerning the fairness of interplay goes hand in hand with the question of the *legitimacy* of social power. These intimately related questions do not arise only with the modern age in which the individual, 'bourgeois' subject comes into its own, and nor do they concern only the foundations of metaphysics with Plato and Aristotle; rather, they go back even to the origins of philosophy.

The oldest philosophical fragment handed down from the Greeks is that of Anaximander. It reads: ἐξ ὧν δὲ ἡ γένεσίς ἐστι τοῖς οὖσι καὶ τὴν φθορὰν εἰς ταῦτα γίνεσθαι <κατὰ τὸ χρεών· διδόναι γὰρ αὐτὰ δίκην καὶ τίσιν ἀλλήλοις τῆς ἀδικίας> κατὰ τὴν τοῦ χρόνου τάξιν, where only the part in pointed brackets is today regarded by philologists as genuinely Anaximander's words.[141] I will first prepare a translation before providing a first one below and a second in the next section.

This fragment has traditionally been read as the wisdom of a 'Pre-Socratic natural philosopher', a φυσιολόγος, as Aristotle and Theophrastos, and then the entire tradition, have characterized him. Heidegger, however, is at great pains

---

141 Cf. Heidegger's 1946 essay 'Der Spruch des Anaximander' *Holzwege* Klostermann, Frankfurt/M. 1950, 6th corrected printing 1980 and also Martin Heidegger *Der Spruch des Anaximander*, the script of a lecture course that was not delivered and presumed written in summer/autumn 1942, (ed.) Ingeborg Schüßler *Gesamtausgabe* Band 78 Klostermann, Frankfurt/M. 2010 *GA78*.

to show that Anaximander's fragment concerns *all* beings, τὰ ὄντα, including natural things, made things, gods and human beings, circumstances, moods, social practices and usages, etc.

The saying is obviously about right or justice (δίκη) and wrong or injustice (ἀδικία) (assuming for the moment that these standard translations are adequate) and the key to understanding it is to interpret the phrase, δίδοναι [...] τίσιν ἀλλήλοις. Δίδοναι means 'to give' and ἀλλήλοις means 'one another'. So the saying concerns at its heart a giving to one another. But what do they give to each other? Τίσις is what they give to each other. Τίσις can mean simply 'penance', 'penalty' or 'payment', a negative meaning relating to compensating a wrong, as if they had done wrong to each other, but it is related more fundamentally and positively to τιμάω 'to esteem, value, worth, honour, revere' and τιμή 'esteem, value, estimation, honour', a word and phenomenon that plays an important role throughout Plato's and Aristotle's political and ethical writings as one of the major goods of living striven for and prized by human beings living together, sociating in society. Both goods and people can have τιμή (value, worth) and therefore be esteemed, estimated, valued by others. Goods, for example, are 'estimated' in being worth something in exchange for each other. This is their exchange-value as expressed in another good. Goods 'esteem' and 'estimate' each other in the market-place in competitively showing off their value (what they are good for) to each other and expressing their value in each other. In this sense, they 'give' worth to each other.

The competition arises of itself from the many beings in interplay, each of which vies to display its value in comparison to other beings' value, matching themselves against each other in rivalry. Goods and people esteem and estimate each other in assessing and acknowledging each other's value; a thing does this by showing and offering itself in its valuableness for a human usage which humans appreciate. Human beings estimate and esteem each other's worth in all their encounters *as* who they are, i.e. *as* they present themselves. The intercourse between individuals is based essentially on mutual esteem, even though, in the modern age, this estimation may be only the formal estimation of each other as a person who is regarded and respected as such, masking a deeper-seated indifference. For the most part, each individual is estimated in vieing to have the abilities he or she has on offer and display recognized and adequately estimated.

Anaximander's fragment therefore says something about the esteem which people and things give to each other through assessing and acknowledging each other's value. Esteeming each other amounts to conceding each other the opening in presence to show off the value inhering in each thing or person in a competitive interplay. Only in granting each other this opening to present themselves as valuable and estimable, only by holding each other rightly in estimation is right satisfied and wrong overcome. The Greek word for right, δίκη, means a state of affairs, i.e. a conjuncture, in which everything is in joint. Κατὰ τὸ χρεών, with which the first half of the saying ends, has usually been rendered as "according to necessity", but, as Heidegger points out, χρεών is related to ἡ χείρ, 'the hand' which in this context would be the hand of the destiny or dole of being that hands (or doles) out presence for the presentation of beings' value to each other, thus overcoming the out-of-jointness that arises from wrong self-presentations and from not paying due heed to each other's worth. Such habitual practice of mutual esteeming among all beings is the core of ethics, i.e. of right as second nature, as custom. A first, rough rendering of Anaximander's fragment that formulates the thoughtful experience it embodies would be accordingly:

> Whence all beings come to presence, however, thither they also depart <according to the handing-out into presence, for they do right by giving each other due esteem, thus bringing everything into joint> according to the arrangement of time.

"According to the arrangement of time" in the above translation renders κατὰ τὴν τοῦ χρόνου τάξιν. Its appropriateness will be discussed in the next section.

In thus hearing the echo from Anaximander with Heidegger's help, we begin to understand, provisionally, that right is done in the interplay among *all* beings insofar as they estimate each other's worth in contesting with each other in self-presentation, each striving to attain its end: an acknowledged, worthy stand in presence according to the arrangement of time. The perversion, hindering or prevention of this free interplay for the sake of wrongly gaining a stand in the opening for presencing and absencing beyond or higher than one's due is the highest wrong of an unfair, ugly conjuncture that is out of joint.

For the sake of gaining a stand in presence, for instance, the intervention and support of a higher power in the interplay may be welcomed, but at the cost of spoiling the chances of other players' self-presentations in the arrangement of time, thus putting the game out of joint and making it ugly. The principle of reason is the ground upon which the power of knowledge, and hence control, is one-sidedly exercised over other beings from a governing origin, thus positing them as "null" (nichtig, *Enz.* § 208 Note), i.e. as of no value and importance, for the sake of a purpose that has been posited one-sidedly, whereas the side-step into the groundlessness of interplay opens the possibility of each being's showing itself in its valuableness, vieing fairly in mutual estimation with all other beings for appropriate presencing. Only thus can everything come into joint, and the interplay show a fair face.

8.1.1.6 Deepening the interpretation of Anaximander

But, it will be objected, this interpretation and translation of Anaximander's saying comes only from overlaying it with Plato's and Aristotle's metaphysical ethics, and even with later, modern, liberal conceptions of right as fairness. Perhaps, however, fairness has something to do with the Greek experience of τὸ καλόν, the fair, just as the English word 'fairness' itself is derived from its signification as 'beauty'. Heidegger's interpretation in 'Der Spruch des Anaximander' from 1946 and his earlier 1942 lecture script under the same title (see the preceding footnote) attempts to unearth a more originary saying of the saying and hence a more adequate translation into German. Here an attempt will be made to distil a quintessence from Heidegger's interpretations, briefly sketching a twist to them that offers an alternative accentuation in which the interplay itself comes more to the fore. The crucial key that Heidegger employs to open the enigmatic archaic saying is a temporal meaning of being as Anwesen (presence, presencing). What vista does this key open up?

The saying speaks of τὰ ὄντα, of beings in the very broadest, all-inclusive sense, of how their coming comes to them as present in the arrangement of time and of how their going away takes them out of the present of presence to absence, which is itself only another 'look' of presence. They come from among beings that are absent and they also return there. The first part of the saying reads in translation: "From those, however, becoming (γένεσίς) comes to beings, also comes their passing-away (φθορὰν, perishing) back into them." Beings in their being are 'die Anwesenden' or 'das Anwesende', 'that which is present', which unfortunately must be rendered in English in this clumsy way (cf. however below).

Heidegger discusses at length in *GA78*:48ff why it is justified to render in German the Greek plural τὰ ὄντα in German as the singular 'das Seiende' rather than 'die Seienden'. In German, beings in the unity of their being are 'das Seiende'. By rendering the Greek plural as singular in German, there is nevertheless the acute danger of obscuring that the very being of beings depends upon their plurality, as will be worked out in the interpretation offered below. In English, by contrast, the appropriate rendering of τὰ ὄντα is 'beings qua beings', maintaining the plural. 'Beings' can mean both entities in their plurality and beings in their being, an ambiguity serving to obscure the ontological difference between being and beings. Because beings come and go from absence to presence and vice versa, they are what is present or absent in the clearing of presence, for which I now propose the unusual translation as 'occurrents' in order to avoid having to render 'die Anwesenden' as 'those which are present', and also because beings themselves are 'the presents' given (and used) by being, i.e. by presencing and absencing itself. An obsolete signification of 'presents' is 'things present, circumstances' (OED) which is herewith revived. 'Occurrents', however, cover both 'presents' and 'absents', i.e. all that which occurs in either presencing or absencing. 'Presents' present themselves in presencing, whereas 'absents' absent themselves in absencing. The temporal interpretation of being itself as presencing and absencing and beings as 'occurrents' finds support already in Anaximander's saying itself, which speaks of the coming and going of beings "according to the arrangement of time", even if this addendum is not originally from Anaximander.

Heidegger interprets τὸ χρεών as "the oldest name in which thinking brings the being of beings to language" (der älteste Name, worin das Denken das Sein des Seienden zur Sprache bringt. HW:334), thus implicitly naming the ontological difference between being and beings as the difference between τὸ χρεών and τὰ ὄντα. This ontological difference is now said temporally as the difference between Anwesen und Anwesendem, presencing and presents, i.e. that which is present. If τὸ χρεών is thought from 'hand', it is the handing-out that hands out presencing (or withdraws into absencing), using beings as the occurrents that occur in coming to present themselves in the present and also withdrawing into absence, all within the open clearing for presencing and absencing which encompasses also the two modes of absence, earlier and later necessary for both temporal movements: presencing and absencing. Handing-out itself is thus first of all the three-dimensional time-clearing itself for presencing and absencing. Beings themselves are the occurrents handed out and thus used by time that present and absent themselves within the clearing of three-dimensional time. As occurrent, beings are *used* by time itself to present themselves as presents and to withdraw as absents. Insofar, τὸ χρεών is a handing-out and withdrawing that uses, i.e. a usage (χρῆσις). Heidegger therefore hazards a rendering of τὸ χρεών as "der Brauch" (usage, custom HW:338, *GA*78:134) instead of "Notwendigkeit" (necessity). This is in line with the insight that needs arise from usages, not conversely: being needs beings, i.e. time needs occurrents, because it uses them, not conversely.

The present (Gegenwart as one dimension of Anwesenheit, presence) itself is the conjuncture, i.e. the joining-together, in the time-clearing between the two modes of absence whence occurrents come and whither they go in the sense of becoming and passing away. The presents come into and while for a time in the present before going back into absence, and in this sense they are temporally finite, even the 'immortal' gods. Presents *are* only within this three-dimensional time-clearing, and each has its while in the present. Their presence as presents in the conjuncture of the present joining past and future is only in joint for as long as they present themselves for the allotted time of presence, according to usage, without striving to exceed finite limits into τὸ ἄπειρον, i.e. limitlessness, of which Anaximander is also said by Simplikios to have spoken (cf. HW:339 and *GA78* §§25–27). Such excessive striving for presence marks, above all, human being and can be seen in the phenomenon of hubris. This reading, of course, presupposes a *linear* conception of time as a kind of movement from absence to presence and back to absence (cf. below).

In the conjuncture of the present, beings enjoy their worth in being estimated, esteemed, heeded by the other presents that are also presenting themselves rivalrously for a time in the present. In this way they give δίκη which, according to the dictionary, would be rendered as 'custom, usage or right as dependent on custom, law'. Heidegger therefore translates δίδοναι δίκην as 'sie geben Recht', i.e. 'they give right', and makes a connection between right and "rectus, 'straight', 'upright' (rectus, 'gerade', 'aufrecht', *GA78*:161) as well as "Richtung" (direction) and "Weisen" ('to direct', including in the sense of a 'to give a directive'). Hence I hazard to say, bringing in an alternative accentuation to Heidegger's, beings 'give right' to themselves and their handing-out by presence by taking a 'right', upright stand, each showing itself off in the present *as* it is, thus disclosing its powers forthrightly. Heidegger then interprets δίκη from its related verb, namely, δείκνυμι in the sense of 'weisen' (*GA78*:161), i.e. 'to show, point, direct', so that δίκη itself would be a 'showing, pointing, directive', and 'giving right' would be 'giving a directive into an upright stand', thus being used 'rightly' by the 'timely' handing-out which is being/presence itself. Being uses beings in giving them the directive to while uprightly as presents with one another in the present for a time. This translation of δίκη is prior to and hence free from any legal meaning, referring instead to how beings themselves stand and show themselves in presence, namely, rightly, uprightly, forthrightly. Correspondingly, ἀδικία as the negation of right is wrong in the sense of a self-presentation that is deceptive, i.e. not upright, lacking in rectitude, as a consequence of not following the directive of the handing-out of presence. Accordingly, an interpretive English rendering of the saying now reads:

> Out from among the absents in absence whence a coming-to-stand in the present is granted to presents, back to the same does their going-away withdraw them into absence, <thus [occurrents are] used by the handing-out that hands out into presencing and withdraws into absencing, for they do right by following the directive into their upright stands, giv-

ing one another due worth in estimation, thus bringing the present conjuncture of presents into joint> according to the three-dimensional time-clearing's arrangement.

Beings (τὰ ὄντα) are the presents and absents, or occurrents, handed out and
used by being (presencing) into the time-clearing's conjuncture of the present,
whiling there for a time, giving each other their due worth, coming from absence and withdrawing again into absence. Heidegger barely speaks of absents
(die Abwesenden) and absence (Abwesen, Abwesenheit) in connection with the
interpretation of ἐξ ὧν and εἰς ταῦτα, and does not speak at all of the three dimensions of the time-clearing in the context with his interpretation of Anaximander. Instead he relates both these plural expressions (GA78 §§11f) to the
singular τὸ χρεών which he interprets as "presencing itself" (die Anwesung
selbst, GA78:125) whence beings have their emergence into presence and whither they are withdrawn. As far as I can see, Heidegger speaks of absence only at
GA78:116, where he interprets φθορά as "escape/going-away in ab-sencing"
(Entgehen im Ab-wesen, *not* Entgehen ins Ab-wesen) and as that "wherein that
which escapes/goes away out of presencing into absence comes to stand"
(worin das aus der Anwesung heraus Entgehende in die Abwesenheit zu stehen
kommt). Only in this latter formulation can a being standing in absence be construed, but Heidegger does not take this further, except much later and en passant when he mentions that "γένεσις and φθορά name the emergence (coming-
to-stand) from absence into presence and the escaping (going-away) from presence into absence" (γένεσις und φθορά nennen das Entstehen aus dem
Abwesen in das Anwesen und das Entgehen aus dem Anwesen in das Abwesen.
GA78:158). The two ecstatic temporal dimensions of absencing are not named,
and his remark in passing has no effect on the translation of the fragment. In
particular, χρόνος (time) is not interpreted as the three-dimensional time-
clearing, not even later on in § 21, where Heidegger interprets the final phrase of
the saying, κατὰ τὴν τοῦ χρόνου τάξιν. There χρόνος is translated as "Erweilnis"
(GA78:200), a neologism that can be rendered as 'enwhiling'. The "order of
enwhiling" is then the "allotment of and directive into whiling" (der als Erweilnis fügenden Zu- und Einweisung, GA78:201).

But χρόνος suggests, and is invariably interpreted as, a linear time of succession tracing movement/change, thus resulting in presencing for a while
along a time-line, whereas the presencing and absencing of occurrents need not
at all be conceived according to any linearity, but according to an 'arrangement'
(τάξις) that need not be successive, linear. In what sense is time an arrangement? Or in what sense is the time-clearing itself arranged? The question here is
whether the genitive in τὴν τοῦ χρόνου τάξιν is to be understood as genitivus
subjectivus or genitivus objectivus. Is it the time-clearing that arranges pres-

encing and absencing or is it presencing and absencing that arranges time? Or is it both, i.e. a dialectical interplay between the time-clearing itself (the Da) and the presencing and absencing of occurrents in the time-clearing?

The mind, which is nothing other than human being's (Dasein's) openness for time's presencing and absencing of occurrents, is not tied to linear succession, but can leap back and forth in recalling both presents and also absents in their twofold 'looks' of past and future. If this is so, then whiling itself need not be continuous and linear, but discontinuous and abruptly scattered. The mind can direct itself intentionally (from L. intendere 'to direct toward, to stretch forth') toward what is past or futural, allowing such absents to presence in absence, without adhering to any continuity, for it can leap effortlessly between the three temporal dimensions according to its very own motivation. In this sense, it would be the mind that 'arranges' the time-clearing in arranging its own intentional movements of presencing and absencing. Conversely, it is time's enabling the presencing and absencing of occurrents that draws the mind's attention to such occurrents, thus 'arranging' the mind in its involvement in the play of presencing and absencing. Hence, both genitivus subjectivus and genitivus objectivus are applicable. The interplay of estimation between and among occurrents plays out not only in the present, but also in the two dimensions of absence, viz. past and future. Historical events, for instance, are interpreted as an interplay among absents to assess them justly. Or what may occur, presencing from futural absence, is estimated by the mind in considering an interplay of as-yet absents, for instance, in deliberating on a future plan of action, weighing up alternatives that 'estimate' each other. Such absent occurrences thus 'rightly' call the mind's attention to themselves "according to time's arrangement" in the sense of a genitivus subjectivus.

'Right' (δίκη), i.e. the directive into an upright stand in the present conjuncture, is that state of affairs in which the occurrence of occurrents in the time-clearing is mutually an upright, forthright self-presentation to each other and thus in joint, i.e. fair. Such fairness is τὸ καλόν. From a linear conception of chronological time, each present can be interpreted as having its own allotted finite time in the present where it can shine like gold for a while, being estimated in its worth in an interplay with one another which the mind takes in and understands. But if time is the non-linear, three-dimensional openness for presencing and absencing, such occurring of occurrents is haphazard with its own 'timely' arrangement of such presencing and absencing in an interplay ultimately of a plurality of powers that only potentially come to presence as a movement, change or interchange, depending on how the play plays out with other powers.

The occurrents handed out and used by time include both human beings and things, whos and whats. Things include, in particular, useful, practical things and also nature regarded practically, whose worth in presencing and absencing comes about in an interplay of mutual estimation of worth of inherent potentials and powers as presented. In the case of practical things and useful pieces of nature such as areas of land and stretches of water, these potentials are their use-value in the usages of human living, and when they presence and for whom is itself a matter of power interplay among occurrents. In the broader sense, however, the sky can be said to 'esteem' the Earth, for instance, in an interplay in which rain falls upon the Earth. In the case of mortals, i.e. human beings, the coming into and going out of the present in the merely *chronological*, linear time of succession, is the initial coming of birth (γένεσις) and the final passing-away in dying (φθορά), since human beings are those beings who are ex-posed to, stand-out toward death, death itself being a present withheld for a life-time in absence toward which each mortal is ecstatically stretched as his or her final existential possibility of which all are 'capable'.

But also *within* the allotted time of a mortal lifetime there are those special conjunctures in the present when a human being shines and is esteemed most radiantly in the present, as when an athlete wins a contest, and such moments amount to a repeated coming and going from the radiant light of high estimation and accolades in the temporal clearing that may be more or less haphazard, depending upon how the interplay with other athletes plays out in a power play of sporting abilities.

Like useful things, human beings vie for their appropriate stand in the present, coming to shine and estimating each other's worth in an interplay enabled by presencing itself, through which those who present their excellence tower above the rest for a moment or durably or haphazardly. But even those excellent ones have their own time to while — or merely pop up briefly like a 'flash in the pan' — in the present, enjoying the reflections of estimation by others. Or their past excellence may be recalled from absence for reappraisal. Their share of worth in such a reappraisal is allotted according to shared mind's (re)assessment of the rivalrous interplay that determines each human being's worth, often fortuitously, including that of a 'has-been' athlete. The interplay of mutual estimation always has an onlooker, which is the mind itself which we all share as human beings, partaking of the movement of absencing and presencing of occurrents in their interplay with each other.

The worth of an athlete is exemplified by Pindar's Fifth Isthmean Ode that Heidegger interprets in extenso in *GA*78:65–101 § 8. This ode relates to the contests at the Isthmean games where young men, in displays of their athletic and other abilities, show themselves off in phallic stands in the temporal clearing where they have come together in the present and which Pindar now evaluates and estimates in his ode. The competitors vie to hear the "fair word of fame" (εἴ τις εὖ πάσχων λόγον ἐσλὸν ἀκούῃ. Isthm. V line 15) that acknowledges their worth, and Pindar is one whose saying of their feats establishes their fame. Although tied to a particular present moment of victory, now past, such fame then may resound throughout a lifetime and perhaps even beyond, enhancing the winner's stance, his reputation, within a community, i.e. fame is a present that persists in the present, as if the athlete were quasi-immortal and did not have to go away into absence.

His achievements — and thus in a certain sense, he himself — are recalled recurrently to the present when the mind turns its attention to such feats. Or he may be forgotten, thus disappearing into hiddenness within the temporal dimension of absence. Line 15 is followed immediately by a warning against the hubris of striving to become Zeus, thus standing too high in the time-clearing, for "you have everything if the allotted share of the fair reaches you; mortal things befit mortals" (εἴ σε τούτων μοῖρ" ἐφίκοιτο καλῶν. θνατὰ θνατοῖσι πρέπει. Isthm. V lines 16–18). There is rivalry among beings, especially human beings, in striving to have their worth estimated and validated in the clearing of the present when they present themselves and put their powers on display, but even beforehand, there is a rivalry among *ambitious* mortals striving for glory and casting their selves toward this future possibility of victory or success. And for those who have enjoyed a moment of radiant success in the present through high estimation by others for their achievement, there is also the retrospective striving to maintain the sight of their achievement in memory. A moment of radiance in the present may extend into a whiling of enduring high estimation by others, or, depending on the complex interplay of powers, it may not. The injointness of δίκη as a fairness or unfairness/ugliness of presencing and absencing in "time's arrangement" is itself an interplay of the shared mind's estimation of the power play of mortals over the worth or otherwise of individual whos. I say " shared mind" because mind and the time-clearing are the same in the sense of belonging together as two sides of the same coin. We mortal human beings ineluctably share the time-clearing with each other for as long as we 'stand out' (ex-sist) into it, and therefore we also share mind in this sense.

A phenomenological interpretation of the extant fragment of Anaximander's archaic saying allows deeper insight into the *temporal* meaning of being as presencing and absencing in its relation to (human) beings in their estimating interplay than that provided, say, by the fifth book of the *Nicomachean Ethics*, not to mention modern discussions of commodity exchange-value in political economy and its critique from Adam Smith on in which all trace of being *implicitly* understood by Greek thinking as standing in presence has been lost to oblivion. Commodity value (τιμή) and the striving for τιμή (esteem) among men already abundantly thematized in Plato and Aristotle are shown to be more deeply interplays of presencing and absencing played in the 3D-time-clearing. In particular, they are games among mortals vieing for estimation of their finite, mortal powers by others. Through such insight, rivalry among individual mortals is not done away with, but *seen* no longer merely in the light of individual personal ambition or striving to gain wealth. Rather, in one mode of play of presencing and absencing, such mortals are first of all granted presence as the presents of presencing, and strive and vie with each other to stand phallically in the shining light of the present for a while or a moment or enduringly. The temptation of hubris, however, misleads them to strive to present themselves not uprightly or more highly than their abilities warrant, or to extend their time in shining presence by all means of power available, thus putting the fair interplay of mutual estimation out of joint.

By contrast, Heidegger suggests in the following passage that a recasting of being and human being from the insight into its temporal nature as presencing amounts to an overcoming of so-called individualism altogether, which he locates solely in the modern age. "Insofar as they are human beings out of the essence of their presencing in the gleaming of the pure clearing, they have already, through themselves as presents, met each other in the sending of destiny." (Insofern sie Menschen sind aus dem Wesen ihres Anwesens im Erglänzen des reinen Lichten, haben sie [sich] einander, durch sich als Anwesende, schon im Geschick getroffen. *GA*78:93) *Insofar* as he conceives such individualism as "some sort of non-destinal meeting-together of the already individualized multitude of people in some sort of agreement [that] effects community" (Nicht irgendein geschickloses Zusammentreffen der bereits vereinzelten Vielen der Menschen in irgend eine Übereinstimmung bewirkt Gemeinschaft, *GA*78:93), his rejection of the individualism of an imagined social contract is justified. Human beings have *always already* met each other in their destiny in sharing the 3D-temporal clearing with each other. But, within this clearing that is 3D-time, they are also *always already* sociated with one another and have therefore *always already* "met each other in the sending of destiny" in this sense, too, in having to share a world with each other and therefore sociate. Heidegger's conception of individualism has itself overlooked that the modern individual itself is already enabled by, and goes hand in hand with, and *is*, a kind of sociation mediated by a reified medium, namely, value, an insight to be had from the mature

Marx and from Hegel. This kind of sociation is itself a destinal sending from the temporal clearing 'arranging' its own kind of *reified* interplay among beings.

Heidegger does not conceive value as a reified medium of sociation (in the various value-guises of money, commodity, capital, wages, interest, etc.; cf. Chapter 6.8) in the gainful game of estimation among things and mortals. Rather, he asserts that value as "the goldness of gold has dissolved into an effectiveness within the circulation of payment transactions" (Das Goldsein des Goldes hat sich aufgelöst in eine Wirksamkeit innerhalb des Umlaufs des Zahlungsverkehrs, *GA*78:70) in an "effectiveness in causing effects" (Wirksamkeit im Verursachen von Wirkungen, *GA*78:70). Heidegger thus has a technical-causal conception of value and money, and displays a patent lack of elementary understanding of the *interplay* of a market economy. Moreover, (exchange-)value in its various masks is the reification of what the Greeks experienced as τιμή. Heidegger ignores that value in the modern age is, and has already been disclosed by Marx to be, a reified medium for estimating the value of things and people in an "exchange process" (Austauschprozeß) that, more properly, is to be seen as a gainful game of mutual estimation ungraspable by any schema of cause and effect. Would the gainful game be overcome when human beings knew themselves as presents of the giving of presence into the finite, temporal clearing? Or would it be only gotten over in a stepping back from an unconditional striving for gain and estimation that puts the game out of joint?

Human being itself is used by time as the destination for the presencing of beings as such. Their shining in the present would have no recipient, their being no radiance, were it not for recipient human being existing as Da-sein in the Da of the time-clearing which is 'the same as' the mind. Hence human beings, as those exposed mindfully to the clearing of 3D-time in which the interplay of mutual estimation takes place, are never 'out of play'. They are the presents needed as *witnesses* to the spectacle of beings' interplay of presencing and absencing in all its, perhaps haphazard, temporal moves. Anaximander's saying points to the interplay of estimation among *all* beings in their plurality and even in *all* three temporal dimensions. Only by virtue of this interplay do beings come to shine and hence *be* in having their shine in presencing and absencing in twofold absence, e.g. in commemoration or aspiration, reflected in due heed and esteem. They would have no worthy stand in presence or absence *as* disclosed without such interplay and without such interplay being witnessed in the shared mind. Insofar, their very being as occurrents depends not only on the granting-withholding handing-out by the time-clearing itself, but also on the interplay of estimation among beings of all kinds to which human beings as such are witness. The plural forms employed in Anaximander's saying are therefore indispensable and should be given due regard explicitly, and not conflated carelessly with the singular, as is natural in German. The in-jointness of justice can then be seen as *fair* interplay among a plurality of occurrents in time's three-dimensional openness for their presencing and absencing.

8.2 "The economic law of motion of modern society" (Marx)

We now return to considering how the principle of reason unfolded its effects also in the budding social science of political economy and Marx's critique thereof. Marx writes already in the preface to the first edition of *Das Kapital* Volume I from 1867 that "it is the ultimate purpose of this work to uncover the economic law of motion of modern society" (es ist der letzte Endzweck dieses Werks, das ökonomische Bewegungsgesetz der modernen Gesellschaft, MEW23:15). Marx understands this economic law of motion in the first place as a law of historical development of societies in which the capitalist mode of production gains a foothold and comes to dominate the entire economic movement of life of those societies. Thus he writes in this vein that modern society "can neither skip over natural phases of development nor decree them to disappear" (kann sie naturgemäße Entwicklungsphasen weder überspringen noch wegdekretieren, MEW23:16). And Marx has indeed generally been read in the Marxist tradition as inaugurating a theory of law-like historical development of capitalist society, usually up to its historically inevitable self-overcoming in socialism and communism.

But there is another reading of the sense of "economic law of motion of modern society" which is more pertinent to an economic science of society, and this reading concerns the concept of value that constitutes the cornerstone of Marx's entire Critique of Political Economy in *Kapital*, its first, fundamental concept and, as law, its scientific first principle. The law of labour value is not a law of historical development, but a *quantitatively* conceived law that is said to underlie, directly or indirectly, the exchange relations among commodities in a capitalist economy, in a way precisely analogous to how the movement of a physical body obeys Newton's mathematically formulated second law of motion $f = ma$. This quantitative law of value is supposed to be the fundamental governing principle through which the movement of capital itself, on its various levels of abstraction right down to the concrete levels of the intertwining of individual capitals in reproducing a capitalist economy, is progressively to be theoretically grasped by means of conceptual mediation. This way of proceeding is entirely analogous to mathematized physics insofar as the Newtonian laws of motion, with successive elaboration of the mathematically formulated theory of mechanics, are able to account for increasingly complex movements of natural bodies in particular circumstances, thus resulting in theories of hydrostatics, hydrodynamics, aerodynamics, and so on. When Marx introduces this quantitative law of value, it is no coincidence that he refers specifically to one of the laws discovered by Newton, namely, the law of gravity:

> Es bedarf vollständig entwickelter Warenproduktion, bevor aus der Erfahrung selbst die wissenschaftliche Einsicht herauswächst, daß die unabhängig voneinander betriebenen, aber als naturwüchsige Glieder der gesellschaftlichen Teilung der Arbeit allseitig voneinander abhängigen Privatarbeiten fortwährend auf ihr gesellschaftlich proportionelles Maß reduziert werden, weil sich in den zufälligen und stets schwankenden Austauschverhältnissen ihrer Produkte die zu deren Produktion gesellschaftlich notwendige Arbeitszeit als regelndes Naturgesetz gewaltsam durchsetzt, wie etwa das Gesetz der Schwere, wenn einem das Haus über dem Kopf zusammenpurzelt. Die Bestimmung der Wertgröße durch die Arbeitszeit ist daher ein unter den erscheinenden Bewegungen der relativen Warenwerte verstecktes Geheimnis. (MEW23:89)

> It requires completely developed commodity production before the scientific insight grows out of experience itself that the private labours which are performed independently of each other, but which depend all-round on each other as naturally emerging members of the social division of labour, are continually reduced to their socially proportional measure because, in the contingent and constantly fluctuating exchange relations of their products, the labour-time socially necessary for their production violently asserts itself as a regulating law of nature, like the law of gravity, for instance, when a house tumbles down over your head. The determination of the magnitude of value by labour-time is therefore a secret hidden beneath the phenomenal movements of the relative values of commodities.

Marx's law here relies first of all on the Hegelian distinction between essence and appearance operative already in the treatment of understanding in the *Phänomenologie des Geistes* which is itself tacitly modelled on a conception of Newtonian laws of motion behind the appearances. Hegel's Doctrine of Essence in his *Logik* develops the ontology of essence and appearance that Marx draws on. The determination of the apparent magnitude of value by its putative essence, labour-time, is a reformulation of Ricardo's law of value (although also supplemented by a thorough philosophical and thus 'qualitative' or 'metaphysical' or 'ontological' analysis of the value-form, i.e. the ontological 'look' of value), which is subjected to the same metaphysico-mathematical demand laid down in Descartes' *Regulae* (cf. Chapter 4.3). A *reason* is rendered for the exchange relations of commodities, and these relations are themselves conceived from their *quantitative* aspect amenable to mathematical treatment, for which a

sufficient, quantitative reason is sought and found to reside in labour-time under a definite qualification of being "socially necessary".

It cannot be said, however, that the law of value has been empirically underpinned in the way that this can be and has been asserted for Newton's second law of motion, which initially drew its empirical evidence from the regular
motions of celestial bodies. Furthermore, the debate among economists which
Marx's theory of labour value inaugurated has led to its being largely rejected,
for neither empirically nor through reasoning (cf. Chapter 6.3) and the elaboration there of Böhm-Bawerk's critique) is it possible to shore up such a quantitative law for magnitudes of labour-time regulating the exchange relations between commodities, even very indirectly through steps of conceptual mediation
(as attempted in solutions of the so-called transformation problem[142]). If established, such a quantitative law would have indeed provided the foundation for a
'theory of motion' of capitalist economy and allowed reliable, predictive mathematical calculation of its movements.[143] As has been shown in Chapter 5, the
reason for the lack of a science of economics analogous to the natural sciences
is ontological, residing in the socio-ontological structure of social interchange
itself.

8.3   Adam Smith's notion of labour-value

Looking back at the inaugural hours of political economy in 1776, in Adam
Smith's seminal discussion of exchange and exchange-value, it is apparent that
he was not intent on formulating a quantitative law of motion akin to Newton's
laws of motion, for labour itself, which for Adam Smith is essentially the expenditure of effort required to acquire a thing and as such the "real measure" of
value, is not simply measured in time. He writes:

> The real price of every thing, what every thing really costs to the man who wants to ac-
> quire it, is the toil and trouble of acquiring it. What every thing is really worth to the man
> who has acquired it, and who wants to dispose of it or exchange it for something else, is
> the toil and trouble which it can save to himself, and which it can impose upon other peo-
> ple. What is bought with money or with goods is purchased by labour, as much as what
> we acquire by the toil of our own body. That money or those goods indeed save us this toil.

---

142 An example of a mathematical approach to the transformation problem is to be found in
Chapter V of Shinzaburo Koshimura *Theory of Capital Reproduction and Accumulation* Jesse G.
Schwartz (ed.), Toshihiro Ataka (transl.) DPG Publishing, Ontario 1975.
143 On the untenability of the law of value cf. Eldred 1984/2015 and Eldred 2000/2015. Cf. also
the work of Christopher J. Arthur, and G. Reuten and M. Williams.

> They contain the value of a certain quantity of labour which we exchange for what is sup-
> posed at the time to contain the value of an equal quantity. Labour was the first price, the
> original purchase-money that was paid for all things. It was not by gold or by silver, but
> by labour, that all the wealth of the world was originally purchased; and its value, to
> those who possess it, and who want to exchange it for some new productions, is precisely
> equal to the quantity of labour which it can enable them to purchase or command.[144]

This is how Smith introduces the concept of labour-value. It is based on a common-sense notion of what things are worth. They are worth the bother and toil
of acquiring them, he says, and they are presumably acquired because they are
practically useful — and in this sense valuable — for one employment or another. Labour has to be 'invested' as the 'purchase price' of every thing, but this
already implicitly presupposes that what is produced is valuable for use within
the context of everyday social practices, or, put negatively, labour that does not
produce use-values is in any case worthless, non-value-producing, no matter
how much labour is expended. This common-sense notion of labour-value, i.e.
of what things are worth, is based on a qualitative insight into social exchange
and is aimed not so much at erecting an empirically applicable, quantitative
theory of exchange relations, i.e. a labour theory of value.

The qualitative insight consists in seeing that the exchange-value of a thing
consists in "the quantity of labour which it can enable them to purchase or
command". This amounts to saying that in exchange it is not so much the finished goods in themselves as reified entities, but ultimately the *services* of
providing those goods that are honoured and paid for in exchange, i.e. the exchange relation of purchasing a commodity is at base a relation of *estimation*
and *social validation* of the labour or service required to provide that commodity. What is directly purchased is mostly the finished product, but more or less
indirectly it is the provision of a labour-service, i.e. the exercise of labouring
abilities of whatever kind, that is paid for, and that is why money is valuable,
because it can "command" others' labour, i.e. their service-provision. The kernel of truth disclosed in a distorted way by the so-called labour theory of value
is therefore that 'labour value' is a social relation of estimating and esteeming
the labour expended in providing services to others. The services provided are
the exercise of abilities, powers that reside in individuals. The abilities that an
individual is able to exercise and hire out as a service to the market, and above
all the productivity of those abilities depend of course crucially on the
knowledge and skilled know-how this individual embodies, and this knowledge
and know-how is a *shared* social good, albeit that it has to be *individually* ap-

---

144 Adam Smith *The Wealth of Nations* Bk. I Ch. V p. 33f.

propriated. This will be investigated further in Chapter 9.2ff, where the care-structure of exchange is examined.

Adam Smith qualifies the insight into labour-value as follows:

> But though labour be the real measure of the exchangeable value of all commodities, it is not that by which their value is commonly estimated. It is often difficult to ascertain the proportion between two different quantities of labour. The time spent in two different sorts of work will not always alone determine this proportion. The different degrees of hardship endured, and of ingenuity exercised, must likewise be taken into account. There may be more labour in an hour's hard work than in two hours easy business; or in an hour's application to a trade which it cost ten years labour to learn, than in a month's industry at an ordinary and obvious employment. But it is not easy to find any accurate measure either of hardship or ingenuity. In exchanging indeed the different productions of different sorts of labour for one another, some allowance is commonly made for both. It is adjusted, however, not by any accurate measure, but by the higgling and bargaining of the market, according to that sort of rough equality which, though not exact, is sufficient for carrying on the business of common life.[145]

The terms hardship and ingenuity refer to the dimensions of the intensity and productivity of labour, respectively. A more intense labour is a compression of time, and a more highly skilled labour produces a qualitatively better product than unskilled labour could do or more in a given time. These factors, along with others, come into play in determining the price on the market in the groundless interplay of supply and demand which finds its expression in what Smith calls "higgling and bargaining", i.e. the interplay of reciprocal estimation. The upshot of these qualitative considerations is that it is untenable to posit a quantitative law of labour value regulating exchange, and Adam Smith is quick to concede that what he calls "real price" measured by labour expenditure diverges from "nominal price". His intention is to establish a qualitative insight into "exchangeable value" and not to erect a quantitative theory which would satisfy the rules for acquiring certain knowledge as laid down in Descartes' *Regulae*. Labour value for Smith is thus a measure of "rough equality which, though not exact, is sufficient for carrying on the business of common life". This is in line with the Aristotelean insight that the exactness of knowledge demanded has to adapt itself to the phenomena being investigated (cf. Chapter 12.3 below; *Eth. Nic.* I iii 1094b11–25).

A further indication that Adam Smith is not concerned with establishing a quantitative law of exchange-value regulated by labour-time is that when he comes to consider market price, i.e. the prices actually attained for products on

---

145 Adam Smith *The Wealth of Nations* Bk. I Ch. V p. 34f.

the market, he treats not their deviations from their "real price" as expressed in labour expenditure, but from their "natural price" based upon customary or "natural rates of wages, profit, and rent, at the time and place in which they commonly prevail" (*The Wealth of Nations* Bk. I Ch. VII p. 62). This has often been regarded as a theoretical inconsistency which later theoreticians have attempted to reconcile. Thus the so-called 'transformation problem' of values arose in which labour-value 'prices' are transformed into prices expressing the average prevailing rate of profit (cf. Chapter 6.3). From the perspective of Smith's intentions, these efforts at establishing quantitative relations are a red herring, a red herring drawn across the trail by the quantitative Cartesian casting of scientific methodology which grasps beings exclusively by their magnitudes.

It should also be pointed out briefly in conclusion that what something is worth to me in the expenditure of my labour on it must gain social estimation if this labour is to count as socially value-creating labour or, what amounts to the same thing, there must be a market for the products of a given particular kind of labour for it to be sensible to talk of labour 'creating' exchange-value. What is worth the bother and trouble of producing for myself may be considered a total waste of time and effort by others, and therefore not enter the dimension of marketable exchange-value, which is a *sociating* dimension, at all. Thus, for example, an artist's work to which the artist has devoted his or her life may be regarded as worthless by others, i.e. by the market-place. Or the lifetime's work of a philosopher has no market value because others cannot see any value in this labour, and that because they cannot, or cannot be bothered to, understand it, or because this kind of labour seems to be useless for anything.

8.4 Economics as a quantitative empirical science (Aristotle, Hayek)

Even with the rejection of the labour theory of value as a quantitative theory of exchange relations as outlined in the above passage from Marx's *Kapital*, economic science has not ceased to be subjected to the principle of quantifiable — and preferably: mathematizable — reason; indeed, it has become a highly mathematized science, but the magnitudes with which economics deals, apart from physical magnitudes which do not cause problems of principle, are essentially monetary magnitudes. There is, however, no fundamental law for determining monetary magnitudes since they depend on the vagaries and essential groundlessness of markets, including the "higgling and bargaining" to which Adam Smith refers. That is, they come about through the groundless interplay of mutual estimation. The theory of marginal utility and marginal costs, too, as a theory of prices is only a way of conceiving marginal demand and marginal supply (in an emulation of the differential calculus) without, however, being able to render a ground for either demand or supply, both of which are ways of estimating goods. Economics therefore has to rely on empirical, quantitative, monetary data with which it can mathematically 'model' economic motion and draw provisional conclusions using statistical and other probabilistic means that allow regularity to be distilled from data. But distilling regularity from data, even through highly complex stochastic mathematical models running on powerful computers, precisely does *not* satisfy the requirements of science (ἐπιστήμη) as conceived since Aristotle, which demands governing first principles, not merely empirical regularities.

Modern economics lacks a theory of the essence of money, i.e. a theory of what money essentially *is* (as a fundamental, elementary, reified, mediating medium of practical sociation and interchange). It cannot deny the phenomenon of money itself, but the theories of money it develops lack a socio-ontological foundation, despite all their subtle and complicated elaboration and treatment of different kinds of money, its circulation and volumes, the role of the central bank, etc. Modern economics is much like an empirical science in the Aristotelean sense of providing knowledge of how the phenomena will behave "for the most part" (ἐπὶ τὸ πολύ) but not in principle, i.e. as governed by an underlying point of origin. This is because, as has been shown in Chapter 5, the elementary economic phenomenon of exchange (μεταβολή) does not fit the cast of "productionist metaphysics" (Michael E. Zimmerman[146]) that has dominated Western thinking from the beginning in which μεταβολή only in the sense of change, but not in the sense of exchange and interchange, is ruled by a principle, an ἀρχή.

Mathematical statistical methods are able to extract regularities from empirical data which provide some sort of guide to the course of a given capitalist economy when worked up into models for calculating various scenarios (including investment strategies that may work well "for the most part" but also suffer the fate of suddenly going horribly wrong), along with experientially based rules of thumb, which are hardly knowledge at all. Computers are able to perform highly complicated and otherwise laborious calculations on economic data to model economies in simulation programs, but again, all these calculations are built on the shifting socio-ontological sands of estimating interply. Thus

---

146 Michael E. Zimmerman *Heidegger's Confrontation with Modernity: Technology, Politics, Art* Indiana University Press, Bloomington 1990 pp. xii-xxii.

economics is bolstered by quantitative mathematical methods which serve to create the delusion, including self-delusion, that it is a serious science. However, it cannot guarantee law-like necessity but deliver only empirical patterns with restricted and revocable predictive, precalculative power based on a more or less sophisticated extrapolation. These empirical, mathematical-statistical methods are what Hegel would call *begrifflos*, i.e. they are not based on the insight of reason into necessary, governing principles, nor do they have any speculative insight whatsoever into the socio-ontology of the phenomena they process. Leibniz' principle of reason therefore comes to grief on the rocks of uncertain and unpredictable and fathomless economic, i.e. *social*, relations which defy forecasting, i.e. reliable precalculation.

Where it does not proceed by empirical methods, economics builds theoretical models on the basis of assumptions that are supposed to at least approximate empirical economic reality. Above all, assumptions are made about price data and it is assumed that the economist-theoretician has a god-like knowledge of the "facts". Friedrich Hayek puts it thus:

> Economic theory can elucidate the operation of this discovery procedure [in economic competition ME] by constructing models in which it is assumed that the theoretician possesses all the knowledge which guides all the several individuals whose interaction his model represents. We are interested in such a model only because it tells how a system of this sort will work. But we have to apply it to actual situations in which we do not possess that knowledge of the particulars. What the economist alone can do is to derive from mental models in which he assumes that, as it were, he can look into the cards of all the individual players, certain conclusions about the general character of the result, conclusions which he may be able to test on artificially constructed models, but which are interesting only in the instances where he cannot test them because he does not possess that knowledge which he would need. (Hayek *LLL*3:69f.)

This is indeed what economic theory does: it denies the phenomena, namely the phenomenon of exchange, and misinterprets this phenomenon within the paradigm of productionist metaphysics. Hayek rightly conceives of economic competition as a game among human actors. Exchange on the markets, which Hayek terms "katallaxy", is indeed an interplay. What Hayek consistently does not see, however, is that even if the economist theorist were able to "look into the cards of all the individual players", this would not enable the game to be predicted because i) the economic players in truth do not have this omniscience, ii) even if they did, the game would still have many variants and iii) the interchanges among the players would remain fathomless even with 'perfect knowledge' of the conditions of competition, because each player is a free origin of its own social movements, including its economic exchange decisions one way or the other, so that there is also no way for the economist to look into his 'cards', which themselves are potentialities, not actualities. It also does not help one wit to proceed in an empiricist fashion and to try to compare a theoretical model with empirical data in order to test the model (say, on the basis of so-called Big Data), because the very way in which the phenomenon of exchange is conceived socio-ontologically in the first place does violence to it. This phenomenological violence can be seen without having to compare the concept with empirical data. The violence consists in giving a groundless phenomenon — namely, the estimating interchange among human beings — a ground, a principle, thus denying the fathomless interplay evident in the phenomenon itself, indeed even and crucially in the simplest case of an exchange between two players. We can see this groundlessness in the phenomenon of exchange if we are prepared to look at the simple phenomenon and rethink, breaking the thoughtless habits of entrenched, centuries-old thinking (cf. Chapter 5 *Ontology of exchange*).

Both Descartes and Leibniz had theological recourse to a supreme being called God as the final guarantor of certain truth and as the ground-giving principle of reason, respectively. God is for their metaphysics the posited producing entity bridging the gulf between subject and object, between human knowing consciousness and world. For Descartes, God in his perfect goodness could not allow the conscious ego to be systematically deceived in its perceptions of the world. For Leibniz, God as the ultimate ratio of all beings also guarantees that, in view of the supposed 'windowlessness' of the monad and thus also the soul, the representations within the consciousness of the windowless ego were co-ordinated precisely with the movement of physical beings in the external world. This co-ordination he named "pre-established harmony" (harmonie préétablie). As the omniscient, omnipotent supreme being and ultimate ground, the postulated God secured the reach of truth as certainty and the reach of the principle of reason to the totality of beings. This ultimate ground has since fallen away through having been called into question by thinking. Today's science cannot accept an ultimate explanatory ground residing in God. Moreover, the insights we have gained in the course of our discourse on social and economic phenomena show that subjective reason is by no means able to rely on the discovery of a certain, rational order in the phenomena. Social interplay is a realm and kind of movement in which no pre-established harmony reigns or could reign, and in which movement and change cannot be traced back and attributed to a unified starting-point, a governing ἀρχή. Leibniz's concept of pre-established harmony is a way of warding off cognisance of the everlasting, unpredictable *power plays* inherent in the social world.

8.5   The disclosive truth of markets

If it is not possible to emulate Newton and formulate quantitative laws of market exchange which would allow a mathematical grasp of economic phenomena, and this *not* because of the complexity of markets and other economic phenomena, but because of the simple, essential groundlessness at the heart of the social interplay of exchange, then the truth of markets has to be approached not through a Cartesian or Leibnizian ontological precasting of how beings are to show up in the world. In fact, the phenomenon of the market itself has to be seen as a phenomenon of truth in the sense of disclosure. The social science of economics does not see this phenomenon, but skips over it, taking it for granted.

The question is: What is a market? This is the classical philosophical form of question known from Greek antiquity. The answer usually runs that a market is a place where goods of all sorts are exchanged. A market is an exchange. In order to exchange, goods must be offered for exchange. For the sake of simplicity, it may be assumed that the goods are offered for exchange against money, i.e. they are offered for sale at a price, although this presupposes that what money and price are is known. At first they are known only in the sense that we are entirely familiar with them and understand them; the (preontological) phenomena have not yet been brought to their (ontological) concept. This said, a market is a place where goods of whatever kind and in the widest possible sense come together and are offered for sale by suppliers of all kinds and may be sold to bidders of whatever kind. The possibility of sale is prior to any sale or exchange actually taking place, and the possibility of sale itself depends on the goods being offered for sale, and more deeply, on their being seen and understood *as* saleable and, more fundamentally, *as* valuable-in-use (every being is always understood *as* something — this is the hermeneutic AS). This offering of goods for sale is itself a showing of the goods, a showing-off of the goods in which they with their useful attributes are put on display. Any market depends on displaying the goods offered on the market for potential buyers. The market is thus a place of possibility, of potential exchange, a situation δυνάμει that offers opportunities to buyers and sellers. As a place of possibility, the market is open and oriented toward the future in which those opportunities will be realized or not.

What is shown in the showing of goods when they are put on display on the market? What becomes apparent about them to prospective, potential purchasers? The goods offered and displayed must be *worth* something to someone. As

David Ricardo puts it, the goods must be "objects of desire".[147] Desire is directed at the objects because they are good for something or other, whether it be the immediate "necessaries and conveniencies of life" (Adam Smith) or in a more derivative, higher order way, such as stock in a publicly listed company which offers the promise of further monetary income yield or price gains. What market goods (including all sorts of services) are good for is either some immediate use in being consumed, like a tube of toothpaste, or in the production of further goods, such as a machine or land, or in the appreciation of its beauty, or in further trading for monetary gain, or even (most abstractly) as an entitlement to future income (such as interest). The showing of goods on the market is a showing of them in their being good for fulfilling the desire of potential buyers. The desiring buyers reach out (ὀρέγεσθαι, ὄρεξις, appetite) for the goods as being good for a future possibility of their living well or living better (I buy a drink to quench my thirst). This being-good-for is a kind of usefulness in the broadest sense, such uses being embedded in the usages customarily practised and cultivated by a given historical way of life. This presupposes, in turn, that potential buyers in that culture understand goods in term of their usefulness and thus appreciate their value in use, i.e. the potential purchasers are human beings with an understanding of what things are good for. In this case, the understanding is *essentially* an appreciation, an estimation of value, and use-value constitutes the very being of the goods.

A market is therefore a clearing, a site of presencing where the goods show themselves, disclose themselves in their truth. Truth is the disclosure of beings in their being for human beings, i.e. those beings who understand this disclosure. They understand this disclosure, moreover, with regard to the goods' potential for realizing a future possibility of their own existence, and are hence insofar self-interested. This possibility can only be realized through the mediation of exchange. Goods in the widest sense display themselves in the showcase of the market for prospective buyers who understand and appreciate, i.e. estimate, what these goods are good for. Standard examples of goods are things like corn or textiles, but goods in the present context is meant to comprise more broadly everything that can be offered on a market of whatever kind. The focus at this point is not so much on the circumstance that all this manifestation of value is reduced and channelled into a quantitative manifestation, i.e. that things showing themselves on a market have a price and are estimated quantitatively in money value. We have already treated the abstractly quantitative

---

147 David Ricardo *Principles of Political Economy and Taxation* 1821, Prometheus Books, New York 1996 p. 18.

nature of value in market economies in a previous chapter (Chapter 6.3). Where money reigns as the universal embodiment for the manifestation of value, what goods are good for gains a derived expression in a one-dimensional quantitative measure. Things offered on the market are always already understood as something valuable, i.e. they are appreciated and estimated, and this estimation takes its quantitative measure in monetary price. The goods of life are thus quantitatively estimable. Here, however, the focus is on the showing itself.

A particular manifestation of disclosive truth is associated with those goods which are themselves income-generating and not destined merely for consumption. Whereas means of personal consumption or productive consumption realize their potential for use in a kind of directly useful consumption and/or enjoyment, loan capital and stocks in a capitalist enterprise are not directly consumable goods. Loan capital has a lending-price, called interest, because it enables the borrowing capitalist to generate profits by employing the capital, by 'clothing' or investing it in a particular garb of concrete, productive employment. A part of the projected profit to be generated is paid to the lender of money-capital. The lender must have faith that the loaned principal will be repaid along with interest on the due date; he is a believing creditor who gives credence to the borrowing debtor and therefore also bears a risk. The interest price paid depends on the supply of loan capital (itself affected by central bank policy on interest rates and money supply as well as many other factors), the expected profit, the security for the loan and the risk of the enterprise in which the borrowed capital will be employed. The loan-capital market is an exchange where these various factors in interplay which refer uncertainly to the future are envisaged, i.e. the market foresees and forecasts the use of loan capital and puts a quantitative price on it in the shape of the going market interest rate for the specific market sector concerned. This foreseeing estimation carried out through the medium of the loan-capital market includes an estimation of risk, i.e. it includes an estimation of what *cannot* be foreseen, and this estimation of risk is included quantitatively in the ongoing market determination of interest rates. This is usually referred to as the market 'discounting' a certain risk premium which is reflected in the going market rate for a given loan-security; the higher the risk perceived by the financial market, the lower the price for the bond. The loan-capital market thus puts a price on what it does *not* and *cannot* see, based on rules of prudence derived from past experience of similar situations, but also on *sentiment*, i.e. the *mood* regarding future prospects.

Moreover, the risk premium to be paid by the borrowing company depends in part also on what asset security it can offer if the business goes very wrong and capital is lost. The higher the break-up value of a company as measured by its net asset value, the less risk premium it has to pay by way of a higher interest rate when taking up loan capital on the financial markets. The financial markets assess and evaluate the securities offered to cover a loan, thus bringing the uncertainty of measuring the risk of loss back to the estimable value of assets already in possession of the company and assignable to creditors as loan security. The risk-averse investor wants to avoid the uncertainty of the future by estimating what the company in question already has (ἔχειν) in asset substance (οὐσία). Standing presence within grasp is to be preferred to a projected presence that has yet to arrive, even though the assets securing the loan can only be realized as monetary value through exchanges that are themselves subject to uncertain market interplay. This uncertainty, in turn, is compensated for by demanding loan security in assets that is generously in excess of the amount loaned. The risk associated with loan capital can only be adequately conceptualized soundly on the basis of a socio-ontological insight into the groundless nature of interplay itself. This goes hand in hand with an ontological insight into truth itself as a disclosure in the time-clearing of that which withdraws, an insight radically unfamiliar to today's Cartesian cast of thinking, i.e. the ubiquitous modern mind-set.

8.6   Stock market estimations of the future

The forward-looking, fore-seeing and fore-casting nature of the market, which only fore-sees by working out *possible* future scenarios of interplay against the background of the present mood or sentiment, is even more striking in the case of stock markets which trade in the ownership titles for publicly owned enterprises. A publicly listed company always has a current market capitalization which is simply the total market value of the shares in the company as quoted on the stock exchange. This valuation depends on what the company owns, i.e. its assets, as well as its prospects, i.e. its chances of generating net profit and thus growing in value as an undertaking for generating further profits, thus capable of paying a larger dividend yield to shareholders. So-called joint-stock companies (which are today more often called publicly listed, publicly quoted or simply public companies) are commonly divided into value stocks and growth stocks depending upon whether the company is seen to be valuable mainly because of its already accumulated assets and established markets, or mainly because of its future prospects for generating ever larger profits on growing sales revenues from growing markets, and therefore growing stock-market capitalization in the future. If a company is valued mainly on the basis of its already accumulated assets, it is the value of the assets which is implicitly priced on the stock market through the company's capitalization. These assets could potentially be sold if the company were wound up or taken over. Value stocks are therefore valued conservatively with a view to even the worst-case scenario of a possible demise of the company.

By contrast, growth stocks are valued as a kind of capitalization of expected future earnings, which are expected to grow at a rapid rate due to growing markets and hence growing sales revenues. The greater the growth in earnings expected (e.g. through new markets being opened up or increased market share or a new market altogether), the greater the price of the stock on the stock exchange. Future earnings growth is treated notionally as interest on invested capital. If this expected earnings growth rate is high compared with current market interest rates, the company's capitalized market value will be all the higher. If these prospective earnings growth expectations wane, however, the capitalized market valuation of the company will fall dramatically with a leveraged effect equal to the 'lever' of the lower expected profit growth rate. In the case of growth stocks in particular, the stock market is a place where a company's future earnings growth is put on display as a potential, a possibility of successful, competitive economic interplay. Since it is future earnings growth which the stock exchange is estimating, based on an assessment of the company's potential, this assessment is subject most of all to uncertainty, and therefore the share price of growth stocks is more volatile than that of value stocks. In the case of value stocks with steady earnings from established market shares and constant dividend payments, by contrast, the market valuation is weighted to what the company is already worth in terms of accumulated assets and its established earnings' performance to date, but even for value stocks, the share price valuation of the company assigned by the stock market depends partially also on expected future earnings because they are the source of dividend payments.

The stock exchange is thus a market-place on which *estimated insight into the future* is valued and traded, either in the stocks of companies, or in derivative instruments, such as call options, that estimate only future earnings without taking a stake in the company's assets. The stock market is a place for speculation in the sense of seeing and not-seeing, i.e. guessing, into the future and assessing future profit-generating prospects in a continual competitive market interplay that can alter sharply and suddenly if profit-generating prospects or merely 'sentiment', i.e. mood, change. Since future earnings *cannot* be foreseen with technological certainty, the market puts a negative value on this inability to see with a risk premium, i.e. the *non*-foreseeability is appreciated and estimated in money terms as a *risk discount* on the stock. For this reason, stock

markets are among the most volatile of all markets. This is due also to the leveraged nature of stock market capitalization valuation that rests on a notional
market interest rate. If the current earnings prospects for a company rise or fall,
the share price rises or falls with a multiplier effect. Similarly, even if general
interest rate levels rise or fall, this fluctuation is transmitted to share prices with
a leveraged effect not only because the cost of loan capital (a deduction from
company earnings) rises or falls with interest rates, but also because the stock
market competes with the bond market for available investment funds. The
higher market interest rates are, the less attractive the more uncertain dividend
yields of stocks become.

The stock market is an exchange where stock companies are put on display
and the risk of capitalist enterprise is estimated monetarily in a concentrated
way. The valuations generated willy-nilly from day to day and second to second
on the stock market express to a greater or lesser extent the expected earnings
of the individual companies listed there. Since the net profit generated by a
company in a given future period is subject essentially to uncertainty (because
all market valuations are essentially fathomless), the assessment of future prospects of a given company, its earnings' potential (δύναμις) is always open to
guesswork as to the ongoing outcome of the gainful interplay. The valuation of
a given company always involves projecting past earnings performance into the
future whilst taking into account foreseeable economic and political factors
which could impair or enhance future earnings performance, but also the general economic mood. This kind of analysis of companies provides some sort of
guide to the justifiable present valuation of a given publicly listed company, but
the assessment remains largely a matter of mooded opinion, or δόξα. Δόξα is
formed on the basis of how things δοκεῖν, i.e. how things seem. On the stock
exchange, companies display themselves in what they are worth, and what they
are worth is by no means merely dependent on the current market valuation of
the assets they own (less company debt, etc.), but on future prospects for generating net earnings. Future net company earnings depend on future interplay on
many different markets, future state interference with the economy (especially
taxation policy) and other (geo)political factors that make for uncertainty (since
the political realm, too, is an ontologically fathomless social power play, as we
shall investigate further in Chapters 10 and 12).

8.7 Market irrationality, sentiment and psychology as phenomena of mood

It is often said that stock markets are 'irrational' and that they are driven 'eighty per cent' by psychology. Psychology and irrationality are two misnomers for a genuine phenomenon. Markets would be rational if they could be brought down to a ratio, i.e. if they could be calculated and precalculated from a starting-point, a principle. But all sorts of markets, and especially stock markets, always have a prospective element of valuation that is mood-dependent. A price is put on what the market as a whole expects in future, which it fore-sees without being able to see. That markets are places for seeing and not-seeing, and thus surmising into the future makes them irrational in the strict philosophical sense of the term. Whereas Leibniz's "grand principle" announces that nihil est sine ratio, i.e. nothing is without a reason or ground, the stock market in particular is a phenomenon which gives this principle the lie: social interplay is sine ratio. The future play of social interplay, and in particular, economic interplay, can only be foreseen by way of expectation and prudent estimation based on likely scenarios. Whereas the essence of technology consists in a know-how of how to bring forth (this knowing forming the governing starting-point or ἀρχή for bringing forth), and is thus insofar a way of reliably foreseeing the future, markets are a *social* exchange interplay among human beings not amenable to technological reduction. They are ontologically groundless, an interplay of polyarchic origins of human, sociating movement. An essential part of human being is to fore-cast the future in the double sense of fore-seeing the future and also of casting oneself forward into the future with one's projects that grasp possibilities of existing (Seinkönnen). This forecast, or casting forward, in the realm of social interplay and exchange is always, i.e. essentially, subject to uncertainty, despite all the ontologically misguided efforts of science in modern times to provide grounds for prediction. Because the social world is essentially interplay, the social science of economics is reduced to modelling regularities of observed economic phenomena and extrapolating them in more or less sophisticated ways into the future to produce different scenarios depending on different assumptions.

Whereas Newton's laws of motion gave modern science the wherewithal for predicting the motion of physical bodies, starting with the 'eternal' motions of celestial bodies, there are no equivalent laws in the realm of economics because of the essentially abysmal nature of the phenomena of exchange and exchange-value which, in turn, derives ultimately not only from the essentially abysmal nature of human being itself which is essentially *free*, i.e. open to the future into which it freely casts itself in choosing and grasping its possibilities, but also from the free *interplay* among free human beings which amounts to a quadratic potentiation of freedom. Stock markets are therefore essentially irrational in the sense that, as places for foreseeing and risking the future, they are exposed to the groundless uncertainty of the future as it unfolds in human exchange and interchange of all kinds for, although I can be sure of how I aim to cast myself into the future, in any interchange I cannot be sure of how the other or the others will comport themselves — and markets are sites where many gather in interchange.

The stocks listed on the stock markets parade themselves in their potency for generating profit which can be expected of them, since the dividends a given stock can pay depend crucially on what earnings the company itself generates. The assessment of this potency ultimately precipitates quantitatively in the stock price which investors are prepared to pay to participate in this profit-generating undertaking (which is not simply a predictable, controllable machine). This quantitative assessment is oriented toward future earnings prospects, including risk-probability calculations. Even what *cannot* be foreseen, which presences as absent from the future, but there withdraws into hiding, is converted into a quantified estimate reflected in the present facticity of the stock price. What the company has already generated by way of profit is secondary and interesting only insofar as past earnings can provide some guide to future earnings by way of extrapolation. There is therefore something intrinsically indefinable and uncertain, unfathomable and thus irrational (sine ratio) in the market valuation of stocks.

This indefinability means that there is always a certain mood and sentiment prevalent on the stock market which tells of the way the market is currently assessing and appreciating and estimating the prospects of individual companies, particular sectors or an economy as a whole. This assessment is necessarily nebulous and is experienceable only in an holistic mood, which is called 'investor sentiment'. This is the reason why capitalist stock markets, apart from being essentially irrational, i.e. without ground, are also driven by psychology, for the psyche is simply another name for human being in its openness to being, i.e. its openness to the quivering time-clearing, including especially its dimension of the future. We human beings resonate with this quivering.[148]

On the stock market, the many human players involved are exposed to the expected future of earnings, which is necessarily an opinion open to error and therefore diffuse and nebulous, supported only by indications and extrapola-

---

148 Cf. Eldred, M. *Thinking of Music* CreateSpace, North Charleston 2015.

tions of past experience and 'reasonable' expectations. This diffuse and obscured future hangs in the air as an holistic market mood. The quantitative valuations of stocks which factually come about on the stock market in the present, by expressing expectations for earnings and earnings growth, manifest most of all an indefinable mood with regard to future market prospects. The *indefinability* is the way in which this human openness toward the future is made manifest first and foremost in a mood, in an attunement to the whole of future prospects, i.e. in so-called market psychology and sentiment, which nevertheless is precipitated of necessity in a fluctuating, *definite* quantitative day-to-day market valuation. The human *psyche* itself may be regarded as our openness to the time-clearing that is not only understanding, but also mooded. Price volatility is an expression of an essentially indefinite and indefinable mood, a *resonance* with the temporal dimension of the future. Quantitative fluctuations in price arise from future earnings and future earnings growth eluding the market's attempt to tie them down quantitatively with any certainty. Price volatility and market sentiment are essential moments of human being's openness to market valuation which in turn is embedded in human beings' openness to the temporal dimension of the future in their interplay with one another.

The truth of the stock market, first of all with respect to growth stocks, is the disclosiveness of a momentary market mood manifesting the potential of stock companies — individually, sector-wise or as a whole — to generate profits. In particular, the outlook for an economy as a whole is affected by the political situation, from the local to the global level. Stock market behaviour and the ups and down of stock market valuations are driven by the mood of expectation with regard to future profit generation. This makes it clear why stock markets are irrational, i.e. groundless, and driven by so-called investor psychology and sentiment. Because the future always remains essentially uncertain, especially with regard to human economic affairs (which are based on myriad social interchanges among human beings), stock markets function as mood barometers, i.e. as indicators of how the future is opening and shaping up and what the future is offering by way of prospects of gain. It is often said that stock markets hate uncertainty, and become skittish when uncertainty looms.

But it must be seen that the truth of stock markets lies *essentially* and *invariably* in an uncertain and indefinable disclosure and estimate of future earnings prospects, i.e. stock markets live from uncertainty; that is the kind of disclosive truth they continually generate as a matter of opinion in estimating what of its nature is withheld from presencing and is indefinite, uncertain. Because they constantly peer into the future, stock markets are constantly climbing a 'wall of worry' about everything adverse that *could* happen in social interplay to thwart profit-making. By contrast, when a mood of complacency descends on the market, this is a bad sign because it indicates that the market players have become too certain about their fore-seeing guesses. Such a complacent mood can therefore turn suddenly into panic if something unforeseen crops up suddenly on the futural horizon of the time-clearing which may or may not arrive in the present.

These reflections on the disclosive truth of stock markets show from another perspective why an economic science conceived within the Cartesian axiomatic-mathematical casting of modern science is essentially ill-conceived and does violence to the phenomena. The phenomenon of (exchange-) value is the fundamental economic phenomenon for capitalist market economies. But this foundation is itself groundless, as has been shown. The attempt to get the stock markets within the grasp of a quantitatively predictive grip in analogy to the physical sciences is based on an essential misrecognition of the socio-ontological structure of the fundamental phenomena involved, namely, μεταβολή in the sense of *exchange* and *interchange* among human beings, and not merely in the sense of *change* in some *thing* else governed by a principle. The approach to economic phenomena prescribed by the modern, essentially Cartesian, understanding of science is a misguided way of access because it does not fundamentally consider the being, i.e. the ontology, of the phenomena which it attempts to get within its grasp. Such foundational questions, however, must be posed, for they have an impact on the adequacy of the science, including on what is to be understood at all by knowledge, and also on how we as human beings are to come to terms not only with economic phenomena, but with the temporal dimension of the future itself.

9 Sociation via reified interplay, the invisible and the visible hand

9.1 Social democracy, reified sociating interplay and caring-for in a capitalist economy – Caring for one's own world and indifference to others (Heidegger's *Being and Time*)

As we have already seen briefly in Chapter 7.6, ever since the early Marx, capitalism has been damned as an economic set-up in which humans, in particular, the working class, are ruled by things: money and capital. Economic imperatives compel people to adapt to undesirable options. Politics, it is lamented, is not in charge, but itself is subject to and subjugated to the compulsions emanating from a reified capitalist economy. A cornerstone of social-democratic politics is that the capitalist 'market economy' *should* be managed by a collective will for the sake of the citizens' welfare, that enterprises *should* be socially 'responsible', etc., and not the other way round.

To see what is at issue here, I turn first briefly to look at the idea of social democracy via a work of social theory rather than social ontology.[149] If, as one commentator on Berman's book, Henry Farrell,[150] claims, "she decisively demonstrates the importance of ideas to politics", this could perhaps be turned into an argument for a socio-ontological approach to the question of social democracy, for it is ideas as the looks of beings qua beings that have been at the vital focus of philosophy ever since Plato. It is the looks of beings as being that shape our shared mind and thus guide any of our actions. To practise social ontology, however, would be to renounce the explanatory ambitions of social theory to provide an account of the "causal power of ideas" (Farrell, 2006) in underpinning the emergence of social democracy, stepping back from explanation in favour of thinking through the ideas themselves under the aegis of the lead question, Who are we human beings? This would allow an approach to the question of human freedom itself. Philosophy as social ontology is prior to social theory because it aims to clarify the prejudicial preconceptions that the latter has always already tacitly activated to even start a coherent discourse that expounds causal explanations for ontic-historical happenings such as the rise of social democracy. Considering all that apparently needs to be explained in

---

149 Berman, S. *The Primacy of Politics: Social Democracy and the Making of Europe's Twentieth Century* Cambridge U.P. 2006.
150 URL www.henryfarrell.net/berman.pdf, accessed Nov. 2006.

https://doi.org/10.1515/9783110617504-009

the world, what social ontology has to offer seems to be too little, and indeed, what philosophical thinking has to offer is the precious little that is nonetheless indispensable. This precious little is invariably swamped by the putative wealth (or rather: poverty?[151]) of empirical facts that call for being 'analyzed' and worked up into cogent explanations for social developments such as social democracy.

The purported recipe for success of post-WWII social democracy of "using markets for their clear economic benefits, while protecting citizens from their worst depredations" (Farrell summarizing Berman, 2006) certainly has plausibility, but it leaves out of account the issue of human freedom in its singular individuality that can never be swapped for economic prosperity. How can singular individuality be saved, if at all, despite the necessity of sociation? Following on from Berman's account, Farrell points out that "If social democracy and fascism are cousins-german, then there's a very plausible risk that social democracy, if it goes too far in this direction, can lapse into a sort of fascism-lite", by which he understands a kind of xenophobic nationalism that he would like to see avoided by a "a social democracy that at the very least leavens its communitarianism with a broader, more international set of solidarities" (Farrell, 2006). But this consideration, too, leaves out of account an inherent tendency of social democracy toward social totalitarianism that extinguishes the individual per se as singularly free. I will return to this crucial issue in Chapter 11. Is it not this tendency that makes "social democracy and fascism [...] cousins-german"?

In the same collection of short commentaries on Berman's book, Mark Blyth asks, "If social democracy was a species of fascism (or vice versa), do we need a re-born fascism now to (re)energize the 'dead-men walking' parties of social democracy in the present?". The same worry could also instigate a radical rethinking of liberalism — rather than merely a polemic against so-called neoliberalism — that would descend into the socio-ontological depths of the question of freedom, thus becoming unrecognizable to those versed in the habits of thought of social theory, and of liberal social theory in particular, by questioning the apparently self-evident, but tacitly socio-ontological, preconceptions on which it rests: the question of free sociation itself. In Berman's own response to her critical commentators in the same collection, she claims that "the heart of classical liberalism, both ideologically and as a matter of historical practice, was an emphasis on the rights and interests of individuals[...]", and this, indeed, is the nub of the issue, viz. that social democracy willingly surrenders

---

151 Cf. the first section of Hegel's *Phänomenologie des Geistes* (*PhdG*) on "sinnliche Gewißheit" (sensuous certainty).

individual freedom, replacing it with an illusory surrogate of freedom, namely, freedom understood as democracy. It also does not pose the question concerning the individual as a 'look' of human being itself and how the individual is itself a form, i.e. a look, of sociation.

With regard to Berman's own "notion that social democracy has an inherently communitarian nature", she claims that "if you want an order based on social solidarity and the priority of social goods over individual interests, some basic sense of fellow feeling is required to get that order into place and keep it politically sustainable". (Berman 2006) Is it matter in the first place of what we want, what we will? Apart from the issue as to whether "fellow feeling" in truth turns out to be the totalitarian creep of bureaucratically administered state care, this makes individual freedom in its essential and therefore indispensable singularity dispensable for the sake of setting up a controllable order, for which purpose, refractory, idiosyncratic singularity has to be tamed and averaged out into a "sense of fellow feeling". Hence, freedom in its singularity (which is not to be calumnied as mere individual egoism or consumerist capriciousness) is sacrificed on the altar of solidarity (which turns out to be in political struggle a mask for mass egoism), instead of bearing the rending, contradictory tension in human being itself between its free singularity and its sharing of the world with others, for which latter a feeling for others' predicaments is not out of place. Is individual singularity reconcilable with social living in a kind of sociation that allows room for singularity to move while at the same time also allowing individuals to care for each other on a quotidian basis? This question will continue to occupy us in the following.

At the opposite end of the political spectrum to social democracy, the proponents of liberal free enterprise point to the problem-solving cybernetics of unfettered markets which are said to be superior to bureaucratically implemented, conscious political policy worked out through the complex institutional mechanisms of democratic government with all its inertia and distortions through political power plays (cf. Chapter 10 on the ontology of social and political power). The implication is that the markets unknowingly 'know' better than the politicians what is good for society. Through a kind of corrective or negative cybernetic feedback loop that governs social interplay, sifting out failures, they purportedly can deliver better results, viz. prosperity, more efficiently and with less friction and resistance than deliberate government policies with their unavoidable concomitant of bureaucratic regulation and lobby-driven protectionism. The much maligned laissez-faire or 'neo-liberal' approach to economic life relies on the corrective cybernetics of market interplay, whereas a state charged with positively delivering good living to its population through its complex of intentionally organized apparatuses is operating teleologically toward some end that it has posited, through a political power play resulting in a compromise, as the general good of society as a whole (or merely a compromise reached among the mass egoisms of various interests?). This topos of conflict between left and right in capitalist democratic politics is very familiar (cf. Chapter 13).

Allowing markets to bring about what they bring about is rejected by the left as social Darwinism, a charge that is not without irony.[152] The topos is also reflected in works of sociology, economics and political philosophy going back at least to the eighteenth century, when the term 'laissez-faire' was coined as the maxim of French free-trade economists.[153] Despite the familiarity of the topos and its persistent controversial rehearsal throughout the decades and centuries, it can still be asked whether it can be taken deeper into the socio-ontological grounds of possibility of such a conflict between opposed conceptions of the socio-economic set-up. What is to be said socio-ontologically about reification and of the invisible hand, two sides of the same coin, the one implying something deleterious about so-called market mechanisms, and the other implying something benign and beneficial about market interplay for living well in society?

---

152 "The first [misunderstanding ME] is the erroneous belief that it [evolution ME] is a conception which the social sciences have borrowed from biology. It was in fact the other way round[...] It was in the discussion of such social formations as language and morals, law and money, that in the eighteenth century the twin conceptions of evolution and the spontaneous formation of an order were at last clearly formulated, and provided the intellectual tools which Darwin and his contemporaries were able to apply to biological evolution." (Hayek *LLL*1:22f) And Hayek cites in a footnote, "The doctrine of evolution is nothing else than the historical method applied to the facts of nature, the historical method is nothing else than the doctrine of evolution applied to human societies and institutions. When Charles Darwin created the philosophy of natural history (for no less title is due to the idea which transformed the knowledge of organic nature from a multitude of particulars into a continuous whole) he was working in the same spirit and towards the same end as the great publicists who, heeding his field as little as he heeded theirs, had laid in the patient study of historical fact the basis of a solid and rational philosophy of politics and law. Savigny, whom we do not yet know or honour enough, or our own Burke, whom we know and honour, but cannot honour enough, were Darwinians before Darwin. In some measure the same may be said of the Great Frenchman Montesquieu, whose unequal but illuminating genius was lost in a generation of formalists." Sir Frederick Pollock *Oxford Lectures and Other Discourses* London 1890 p. 41 cited in Hayek *LLL*1:153. The moot point here is whether it is "historical fact" that serves as the (empirical, positivist) basis of a theory of social, market-mediated selection.
153 Cf. 'laissez-faire' OED.

The paradigm for and core of reified sociation is money-mediated commodity exchange. As a thingly mediator and medium of commodity exchange, money is itself a thing, i.e. a reified sociating medium that brings people together in com-merce, i.e. that sociates through bringing goods together. But the commodity goods offered on the market, too, are things that refer in their being qua commodities to others, namely, to potential buyers, and are therefore also reified sociations as potentialites. Commodity services, too, however, (and the 'service' of wage-labour power in the present context could also be considered as a commodity service) are reified by being subject to the reified, mediating medium of money.

One option for investigating the social ontology of reified social interplay is to take the social ontology implicit or only sketched in Heidegger's *Being and Time* (*Sein und Zeit*), unfolding it into an explicit social ontology of commodity exchange. This is what will be attempted first here in rough outline. Later on, we will investigate briefly the capitalist wage-labour relation in particular.

Sein und Zeit offers a fundamental ontology of human being, which is conceived as Dasein. The foundation here is not a universal anthropology of humankind, but Western thinking on the beingness of beings, starting with the Greeks. The being of humans, or simply, human being, is existence.[154] With the determination of human being itself as existence, Sein und Zeit introduces already a deviation from the Western tradition of ontology, for which existence is that of things, i.e. that they exist, i.e. are, in their whatness, rather than in their whoness (Wersein in *Sein und Zeit*). The phenomenological interpretation of Dasein's existence results in the ontological-existential analyses of Sein und Zeit whose culmination at the end of Part I, Division 1 is the three-dimensional ontological structure of care (Sorge), whose details will not be further elaborated here. (I note here only that the three-dimensional existential-ontological structure of care maps isomorphically onto the three-dimensional ontological structure of temporality itself in Part II.) Human beings' everyday existence is a taking-care-of..., a Besorgen. This taking-care-of the 'business' of everyday life involves human beings with practically useful things that are used within the possibilities for existing that Dasein has chosen in leading its life, i.e. its existence. The being of these practically useful things (Zeug, equipment, stuff, πράγματα) resides in their being-good-for a definite application or range of ap-

---

154 As explicated in a further unfolding of Heidegger's thinking in preceding chapters, the Da of Dasein can be conceived as the openness of human being to the 3D-time-clearing to which human being is exposed and in which it ex-sists first of all. Cf. for details my *A Question of Time* 2015.

plications within the context of Dasein's shaping its existence, i.e. these practically useful things offer themselves to Dasein as enabling a possibility of its existence, thus enhancing it. Only in understanding (albeit pre-ontologically and self-evidently) the being of useful things, i.e. their specific being-good-for..., their use-value, can Dasein exploit the possibility offered by them in enabling a concrete option of existence. Everyday existence is an involvement with taking-care-of everyday affairs employing useful things for doing so, such as shoes for walking and telephones for talking.

But everyday existence involves not just taking-care-of affairs by using practically useful things. It involves also involvement with others, human beings who are also Dasein. *Sein und Zeit* terms the being of the others who are also human beings Mitdasein. The others are also (mit) there in the Da in which the world itself is located, i.e. takes place. Since Dasein shares the world in its temporal openness with others, all Dasein is Mitsein with others, or Mitdasein. The ontological-existential structure of sharing the world with others is worked out in *Sein und Zeit* as caring-for... (Fürsorge) which is the 'social' complement to taking-care-of... (Besorgen) in using things. Caring-for... has to be read here in an ontologically neutral and broad way, without restricting it to the 'positive' connotations of nurturing, looking after, etc. *Sein und Zeit* introduces the concept of caring-for as follows:

> Das Seiende, zu dem sich das Dasein als Mitsein verhält, hat aber nicht die Seinsart des zuhandenen Zeugs, es ist selbst Dasein. Dieses Seiende wird nicht besorgt, sondern steht in der Fürsorge. [...] Die 'Fürsorge' als faktische soziale Einrichtung zum Beispiel gründet in der Seinsverfassung des Daseins als Mitsein. Ihre faktische Dringlichkeit ist darin motiviert, daß das Dasein sich zunächst und zumeist in den defizienten Modi der Fürsorge hält. Das Für-, Wider-, Ohne-einandersein, das Aneinandervorbeigehen, das Einander-nichts-angehen sind mögliche Weisen der Fürsorge. Und gerade die zuletzt genannten Modi der Defizienz und Indifferenz charakterisieren das alltägliche und durchschnittliche Miteinandersein.

Martin Heidegger
Sein und Zeit 1927/1984 § 26 S. 121

> The being toward which Dasein comports itself as Mitsein, however, does not have the mode of being of useful things at hand (zuhandenes Zeug), but is itself Dasein. This being is not taken care of (besorgt), but rather is cared-for (steht in der Fuersorge). [...] 'Caring-for' (Fuersorge as social welfare) as a factual social institution, for instance, is grounded in the ontological constitution of Dasein as Mitsein. Its factual urgency is motivated by the circumstance that, at first and for the most part, Dasein keeps to the deficient modes of caring-for. Being for, against, without one another, passing each other by, having nothing to do with each other, are possible modes of caring-for. And precisely the last-named modes of deficiency and indifference characterize everyday, average being-with-one-another.

Is this last statement that deficiency and indifference predominate in everyday life as modes of caring-for merely an empirical observation? Is it ideological, i.e. deceptive? Or do such deficient and privative modes of caring-for have the upper hand only in a certain kind of society, such as, or, above all, capitalist society? Marxists never tire of employing the argument that bourgeois thinkers 'eternalize' and proclaim as 'natural' social relations that are merely historically specific to the capitalist mode of production. What, then, speaks in favour of giving the above assertion of the everyday predominance of deficient and privative modes of caring-for socio-ontological weight? Does this weight arise only with the historical rise of the possibility of mass sociation that, in turn, requires its own historically specific medium? It should be underscored here once more, that socio-ontology does not aim at the 'eternal truths' of a philosophia perennis, but at insight into the socio-ontological casts of an historical age within Western history.

Human being (Dasein) exists in leading its own life, an ontological-existential characteristic designated in *Sein und Zeit* by the term Jemeinigkeit, i.e. individual my-ownness. Its own, individual existence is an issue for it about which it cares, and has to care for as long as it leads and shapes an existence in the Da. The world opens for Dasein in the twofold of understanding and mood first of all individually, from an individual perspective rooted ultimately in Dasein's individual bodiliness, even though this individuality is embedded in an historically universal, shared opening of world. The individual perspective should therefore not be understood as merely 'subjective' in today's thoughtless sense of the word. This does not mean at all that Dasein is essentially egoistic, selfish, etc., but that its truth of the world, although necessarily also shared, universal, is at the same time, individual, and has to be mediated with others through interchange of all kinds including, crucially, exchanges of views in dialogue.

Furthermore, it means that Dasein builds and cares about its own world to which certain others belong whom it positively cares about and therefore cares for. Each human being has an individual world around it, i.e. an Umwelt, to which certain other individuals belong — "not only we ourselves, but all the objects of our kindest affections, our children, our parents, our relations, our friends, our benefactors, all those whom we naturally love and revere the most"[155] —, and the perspective and focus that a given human individual has on

---

[155] Adam Smith *The Theory of Moral Sentiments* (1759) Prometheus Books, New York 2000 Part VI, Section II Chapter II, 2nd paragraph p. 334.

the world is given by the individuality of its individual, practically shared world with its changing situations.

Certain features of the world show up as having an effect on its individual world, whereas others remain in the background. To lead its life, individual Dasein has to take care of matters which concern it and care for those who are close to it. Each individual human being is an individual opening of a perspectival view on the world that defines also the proximity of those few who are close to it. Because of this essential focus of the world-opening of each individual, most others do not belong to individual Dasein's world; rather, they are in the background, and therefore the caring for others is, for the most part, a matter of indifference, a "passing each other by". We have to bear looking at the disclosive truth of the existential-ontological statement that, at first and for the most part, I couldn't care less for you. This 'at first' indifferent mode of caring-for, however, can quickly change within a situation to a positive mode when, for instance, you notice an anonymous passer-by on the street who has inadvertently dropped something and kindly call his attention to it. Such practised kindness, of course, is not so-called social solidarity.

A collectivity of caring for others in a more abstract manner, i.e. caring for those who do not belong to one's own everyday world, has to be constituted through a mediation (such as a social institution which is a Gestalt of shared human being or, in Hegelian terms, 'objective spirited mind'; cf. Chapter 11) that gives even those at one remove from one's own circle a weight in caring-for. This accounts for the predominant privative mode of indifference in caring-for in everyday existence, which amounts to a kind of ontological-existential bias, a 'default setting' of socio-ontological self-centredness of each individual's world that should not be confused with selfishness. At first and for the most part, the others hardly even appear on the horizon of one's own world and are not understood as being part of one's care for one's own circle. They remain for the most part inconspicuous, taken for granted (Unauffälligkeit und Selbstverständlichkeit *Sein und Zeit* § 26 S. 121), and do not elicit any positive mode of caring-for. In its everyday 'default setting', Dasein is more or less inconsiderate. Even when others who 'need' caring-for do present themselves in one's own world, outside of a personally experienced, concrete situation, these others are levelled to an anonymity, thus making even any altruistic response itself anonymous, general, abstract, as exemplified by making cash donations to an established charity.

The principal positively deficient mode of caring-for is being-against-one-another (Wider- oder Gegeneinandersein). This implies that there is a clash between individual human beings in caring about their daily affairs for they are moving existentially in opposed directions. Everyday life is essentially concerned with acquiring the goods for living, no matter whether these goods be material (ranging from the so-called basics of food, clothing, housing to the endless array of goods, including services, that contribute to agreeable living) or more intangible (such as honour, reputation, prestige, seniority, social status, political power, etc.). We have discussed these goods of living copiously in preceding chapters. This acquisition of goods has to be negotiated with others in a kind of interchange understood in the broadest sense, and such interchange is inevitably marked by competition, not only because the supply of such goods may be limited (in fact there may even be a surfeit), but because one's own standing as somewho is only defined in comparison to others' who-status. Here, at first, material, economic goods will be considered.

Whatever kind of society, the finite wealth of what is good for living (produced by the exercise of that society's sum total of human abilities in combination with the other natural, produced and financial factors of production), has to be distributed in some fashion, either via some distributing power or as a factual result of interplay, among its members. Such distribution, even if carried out according to some principle of equality of the members of society by a powerful superior instance, gives rise to difference in the material interests of the members of society, either individually or collected together into communities of interest. The distribution of the goods for living, no matter how egalitarian it may be, is essentially contentious, if only because, even if there were solid agreement that the distribution of wealth in society should be egalitarian (in some sense or other of 'equal'), the understanding of what, concretely, is egalitarian and how this egalitarianism should be particularized would still remain an eternally contentious issue for a shared way of living in a given society.

Apart from the essential differing of individual perspectives in understanding the world, there is therefore also the essential differing and conflicting and rivalry among self-interests (which may also be collective self-interests) in sharing the material goods of society. This makes caring-for in everyday life also a rivalry, a conflict of interests, a being-against-one-another, i.e. a deficient or negative mode of caring-for. The self-interested particularity of human being as outlined here does not depend on assuming a market-mediated society. The point to note is that the self-interested situation of Dasein's existence implies necessarily conflicts of interest with other Dasein, i.e. with Mitdasein, even in an egalitarian society based upon an ideal or ethos of material equality.

If other, more intangible societal goods beyond material, economic goods and their distribution in society are included, then it can be seen all the more clearly that vieing for the goods of life brings individuals and interest groups into competition and conflict with one another. (We have already discussed in extenso the (im)possibility 'just distribution' of that social called esteem in Chapter 6.7). Because human being understands what is good for living, and because it is individualized, the striving to gain what is good for living must be, at first and for the most part, an everyday being-against-one-another, i.e. a competition, which may or may not be resolved by some kind of social mediation, negotiation and 'elevation' (Aufhebung) into a compromise. Caring for one's own, individual world inevitably (i.e. as essential to the socio-ontological structure of human existence sharing a world) implies also conflict, or at least rivalry, with others caring for their own respective worlds, a conflict or rivalry that can assume and has assumed countless phenomenal forms throughout Western history — and presumably all over the Earth. The vieing against one another, under the impetus of personal ambition, for position in the social hierarchy assumes phenomenal forms in all kinds of social practices and rituals, but all such vieing emerges socio-ontologically from the whoness of human being, i.e. from the existential challenge to bring oneself to a self-stand and to be estimated as having such-and-such a social standing as somewho within the social clearing.

The more basic, latent, quotidian mode of sharing the world with others is the privative mode of indifference in which others do not figure in one's caring for one's own world, not even as rivals. They remain inconspicuous and invisible, even though they are implicitly, subliminally understood as also being there in the world — in the background. There is a socio-ontological predisposition toward the self-centredness of world, whereby this self-centredness is to be understood neither merely as naturally determined in the sense of a biological given (since human being always has a self-reflective distance from its bodiliness and is not merely instinctually driven), nor as a kind of egoism or inconsiderateness, but rather as a focus of Dasein's caring about its own world that, of itself, leaves the others in an indeterminate, background inconspicuousness. Dasein is absorbed with its world as its own casting of self in which only certain others figure as 'mattering', i.e. as having weight in the valency of caring for one's own world, and most others figure as not 'mattering'.

Dasein's selfhood consists in its choosing and grasping (including failing to do so) its very own possibility for existing in casting its self in a definite direction, into a particular, individually chosen project. This means that you are not concerned and involved with most others, and that, if at all, they mostly figure in your own world under some collectivity that draws your attention. The inconspicuousness of the others in your world is a neutral 'basic setting' for caring for others, and does not yet amount to an inconsiderateness in failing to behave adequately toward an other who has entered your world (usually understood as 'common decency and politeness'), or ruthlessness, which consists in positively riding roughshod over others who presence in your world, which is a deficient, negative mode of caring-for.

But it would be wrong to envisage social relations merely as 'dog-eat-dog' competition and rivalry among opposing self-interests because, although individuals are necessarily against each other in some respects and by and large indifferent to each other, social living, as has been shown in Chapter 5 within the historical specificity of a market-mediated society, is, in its socio-ontological structure, also an estimating interchange with others from which, in particular, my own self-standing is derived or confirmed in estimating interplay. Sociation through interchange means that none of my projects for living well with those who are close to me can be realized or even attempted without social interchange with others based not merely on rivalry, but on mutual benefit and mutual sympathy. In particular, economic exchange relations of all kinds are based on mutual benefit to both parties. They are a win-win situation of some kind or other. Exchange transactions are entered into because there is a mutual advantage to be had on both sides, and individual interests can only be furthered by sublation (Aufhebung: elevating) through some kind of interchange, including mutually advantageous co-operation with others. The sociation of self-centred individual human being intertwines self-interests in such a way that they are elevated of themselves to mutuality, a kind of 'we' (cf. Chapter 11) which could be regarded as a kind of Aristotelean mean between selfish egoism and selfless altruism.

9.2 Self-interest and mutual caring-for in exchange interplay

What, more particularly, is the situation with caring-for in a market economy in which the material goods (including services) for living are produced for a market? We will consider a specifically capitalist market economy based on wage-labour later. On any market there are buyers and sellers. What kind of caring for one another are they engaged in? Clearly, the participants in a given market are not indifferent to each other, although they figure in each other's worlds only abstractly as one of many buyers or sellers who are understood merely as such buyers or sellers of a certain kind of good, leaving aside all else that makes up each individual's concrete particularity. Moreover, when a particular buyer and a particular seller perform a sales transaction for a certain good, each is taking care of daily affairs, the one by acquiring something useful for living, the other by earning money as part of the business of everyday life. For the buyer, the seller figures not in his or her full, concrete particularity but only insofar as the buyer is focused on acquiring the good in question. Conversely, for the seller, the buyer does not figure in the seller's world in his or her concrete particularity, but only abstractly as a bearer of money, as a potential customer. Buyer and seller care for each other (and are therefore not indifferent to each other) in the first place only as the bearers of a particular good and the abstract, universal equivalent, money, respectively, with the aim of acquiring what the other has.

In order to actually make the sale, however, the seller must care at least for the buyer's motivation to buy the product (either a good or a service), which is to realize a possibility for the buyer's living well, since the good for sale offers itself in its being as being-good-for..., i.e. as a use-value. The seller (even when aiming at a mass market) endeavours to make the good, valuable qualities of the product plain to potential buyers and thus assumes a definite positive mode of caring-for vis-à-vis the latter, bringing into focus of his (the seller's) attention at least a segment of the potential buyer's concrete particularity. This endeavour is a kind of rhetoric that attempts to win the buyer over to a positive decision in favour of purchasing the product on offer by presenting all the persuasive 'selling arguments' to the potential buyer that speak in the product's favour. Insofar, the potential buyer is no longer in the seller's sights merely abstractly, as the bearer of a certain quantitative purchasing power, and the (potential) market interchange has already entangled buyer and seller in a more concrete engagement with one another.

If the product is presented to the potential buyer as that which it is not, then the caring-for exercised by the seller is deficient (fraud, misrepresentation). Since what a product is good-for, i.e. its being, can be presented in the medium of the λόγος in many different ways, whether the seller presents the product as that which it genuinely is in truth — as a use-value — may become a contentious issue. Since the seller's interest is to acquire the buyer's money, there is always a potential divergence and discrepancy between this interest (a caring for oneself) and caring for the potential buyer in presenting the product's qualities as enabling a possibility for the potential buyer's existence and therefore as being valuable for this potential buyer (customer satisfaction). The potential buyer, on the other hand, is interested only in the product and what it enables within the context of taking care of his or her own daily existence. The product must show itself as being good for the sake of the buyer's existence. It must reveal itself to the potential buyer as being valuable in this regard, and the seller's motivating rhetoric in favour of a purchase is supposed to match how the use-value in question shows itself of itself. Otherwise, the good is misrepresented to the prospective customer.

The seller figures in the potential buyer's world only as the bearer of the product, and thus the potential buyer's comportment toward the seller is only a neutral, indifferent mode of caring-for. The potential buyer is indifferent to the seller's caring about his or her own existence by earning a living, whereas the seller cares for the buyer's existence only insofar as this is a mediating step to gaining the buyer's money. The seller therefore cares whether the customer is satisfied or not, albeit mediatedly as a way of maintaining the buyer's custom and keeping the door open for further sales in future. And the buyer, in being directly interested in the good offered for sale for his or her own use, indirectly contributes to the seller's well-being. Self-interest is thus mediated via the reified exchange interplay with caring for the other in a positive, albeit restricted sense.

Buyer and seller each enable the other to take care of him or herself in acquiring what is good for living: either a particular, useful product, or money-income as the universal means for acquiring goods. Each mediates the other's well-being in striving, in the first place, directly or im-mediately only for his or her own well-being, namely, taking care of his or her own being-in-the-world. In this way, each individual is raised willy-nilly out of its merely self-interested particularity to a universality that is more than merely the sum of two particularities.[156] In the quid pro quo of exchange, each enables a possibility of the other's taking care of his or her own existence. Paradoxically, in each pursuing

---

156 "Needs and means become as real, determinate being a *being* for *others* through whose needs and labour satisfaction is mutually dependent. The abstraction which becomes a quality of needs and means [in a highly refined division of labour ME] becomes also a determination of the mutual relations of the individuals with one another; [...] By virtue of the fact that I have to orient myself toward others, a form of universality enters. I acquire from others the means of satisfaction and accordingly have to accept their opinion. At the same time, however, I am compelled to produce/bring forth means for the satisfaction of others. The one thus plays into the other and is interconnected with it. Everything particular becomes insofar something social; [...]" (Die Bedürfnisse und die Mittel werden als reelles Dasein ein *Sein* für *andere*, durch deren Bedürfnisse und Arbeit die Befriedigung gegenseitig bedingt ist. Die Abstraktion, die eine Qualität der Bedürfnisse und der Mittel wird (s. vorherg. §), wird auch eine Bestimmung der gegenseitigen Beziehung der Individuen aufeinander; [...] Dadurch, daß ich mich nach dem anderen richten muß, kommt hier die Form der Allgemeinheit herein. Ich erwerbe von anderen die Mittel der Befriedigung und muß demnach ihre Meinung annehmen. Zugleich aber bin ich genötigt, Mittel für die Befriedigung anderer hervorzubringen. Das eine also spielt in das andere und hängt damit zusammen. Alles Partikulare wird insofern ein Gesellschaftliches; Hegel *RPh.* § 192, 192 Add.). The universality of market-mediated economic activity is given by one particularity playing into the other, i.e. through an estimating interplay of particularities that brings forth willy-nilly, behind the backs of the players, a form, a 'look' of universality.

their self-interest lies unintentionally — and, so to speak, behind their backs — the opposite of a mutual caring for each other, no matter how limited; neither has to have the immediate intention of acting altruistically in a positively caring way for the other, but through the mediation, each becomes the agent of the other's self-caring.[157] Strictly speaking, each is indifferent to the other, but through reciprocal, intermeshing self-interests exercised in exchange, each unintentionally becomes mediator of the other's well-being by contributing to the other's taking care of daily life. In the unintentionality lies the invisibility of the "invisible hand". Thus, from one perspective, an indifferent mode of caring-for on both sides of the exchange relation enables nonetheless, through interchange, each side to take care of itself and is beneficial for both sides. In partic-

---

157 Cf. Hegel: "In this dependency and reciprocity of labour and the satisfaction of needs, *subjective self-seeking* turns into a *contribution to the satisfaction of the needs of all* — into the mediation of particularity with universality as a dialectical movement so that through everyone acquiring, producing and enjoying for themselves, they precisely thereby produce and acquire for the enjoyment of all the others." (In dieser Abhängigkeit und Gegenseitigkeit der Arbeit und der Befriedigung der Bedürfnisse schlägt die *subjektive Selbstsucht* in den *Beitrag zur Befriedigung der Bedürfnisse aller anderen* um, — in die Vermittlung des Besonderen durch das Allgemeine als dialektische Bewegung, so daß, indem jeder für sich erwirbt, produziert und genießt, er eben damit für den Genuß der Übrigen produziert und erwirbt. *RPh*. § 199). For Hegel, this dialectical mediation of particularity with universality means that civil society, along with the family, forms the "second basis" for the State as concrete, actual universality: "This is so important because the private persons, although self-seeking, have the necessity of turning outward toward others. Here is thus the root through which self-seeking links up with the universal, with the state, whose care and concern it must be that this connection be a solid and firm one." (Diese ist um dessentwillen so wichtig, weil die Privatpersonen, obgleich selbstsüchtig, die Notwendigkeit haben, nach anderen sich herauszuwenden. Hier ist also die Wurzel, durch die die Selbstsucht sich an das Allgemeine, an den Staat knüpft, dessen Sorge es sein muß, daß dieser Zusammenhang ein gediegener und fester sei. *RPh*. § 201 Add.) In Hegel's thinking, the State as the concrete, actual, universal instance becomes a law unto itself and can therefore relativize the rights of civil society (essentially the rights of personhood and property), subjugating them to its own self-posited aims for the universal good. This is against the liberal-democratic conception of the state, according to which the state itself, i.e. government, must be itself relativized in being subjected to democratic elections, thus being linked back to civil society (including the family unit as the cell of civil society) as the ultimate source of political power. It is not merely fortuitous that in German 'Staat' is synonymous with 'country', i.e. with the whole, whereas in the liberal tradition, 'government' is only one function in the polity. The liberal conception maintains the dialectical tension between civil society and government, and more generally between particularity and universality, so that it never comes to a final resolution in which the State gains the upper hand and subjects civil society to its own purposes. In a democratic polity, the universal itself remains fractured and therefore in continual movement from one relative point of equilibrium to another. See Chapter 12 for more on this.

ular, out of self-interest, the seller has, mediatedly, an interest in caring for what the customer wants, i.e. in cultivating customer care. This may be contrasted, for instance, with the situation of a bureaucrat exercising power within a hierarchy of political power, which has to be distinguished socio-ontologically from the powers at play in market interplay (cf. Chapter 10).

The mediation of furthering one's own self-interest only by catering to the other's self-interest, so that a mutually satisfying transaction comes about on the basis of intermeshing self-interests, even though there may be struggle and haggling over the terms of the transaction, gives the lie to the well-worn, not to say, hackneyed moral dichotomy between egoism and altruism so firmly anchored in Western thinking like second nature, mainly through the Christian tradition, according to which a 'good person' can only be an altruistic person, whereas all 'self-seeking' is more or less bad and sinful and subject at least verbally to opprobrium as 'greed'. However, a look at the phenomena of daily practice immediately shows how inadequate this moralistic dichotomy is. For the most part, at least in average everyday life, we get along well with each other in exercising our abilities for each other's benefit on the basis of mutual self-interest, which is neither purely egoistic, nor purely altruistic, but a mutually beneficial and satisfying relationship, despite the opposed interests that are necessarily part of the interplay for, if the two parties did not opposed (but complementary) interests, no transaction at all would come about. Even apart from market exchange in which money serves as the yardstick of equivalence, sociating customs, too, invariably have the structure of give and take even when at first they seem to be based one-sidedly on generosity. Consider, for example, customs of hospitality, according to which the guest unavoidably becomes 'indebted' to his or her host and later issues a return invitation.

The interchange based on mutual self-interest in which each provides the other with a useful good is situated in the middle between the extremes of altruistic self-sacrifice and ruthless, egoistic self-interest, and such an intermeshing of self-interests that cater to each other, albeit that they sometimes also clash, is the fabric of market-mediated, economic life. Social interchange based on mutual self-interest is certainly mundane and mediocre rather than heroic or otherwise positively praiseworthy, and thus accords with life as it goes on for the most part. Market interchange is a practice that of itself lifts mere self-interest beyond itself to a kind of mutuality and thus represents a form of sociation in which particularity is unspectacularly mediated with universality, or self-interest with the common good. Such mediation has to be clearly distinguished from the suppression of particularity in favour of universality, whether it be by morally castigating egoism in favour of altruism or by moralistically rejecting 'bourgeois' individualism in favour of 'socialist' solidarity. If particular self-interest belongs essentially to human being, then its condemnation by moral opprobrium is an impotent, merely moralistic act that not only inevitably ends up in a dichotomy of its own making, viz. hypocrisy, but, more significantly, refuses to look more closely at the contradictory, torn nature of human being itself, just as it *is*.[158]

Advertising is a good example showing how self-interests have to intermesh in everyday life. The rhetoric of advertising is directed at making the product desirable for potential customers in fulfilling an attractive possibility of existing, and this is not altogether disingenuous. Advertising aims at presenting the product as providing a valuable service to the potential buyer. In attempting to arouse the potential customer's desire to acquire, advertising is a mixture of genuine disclosure of the product's use-value, and disingenuous pandering to customers' supposed desires, i.e. a kind of flattery consisting in associating an uplifting mood with the product. To characterize advertising as mere manipulation of the consumer amounts to denying the consumer's freedom, i.e. the possibility that each free individual is able to *assess for itself* whether a use-value on offer is genuinely useful, rather than being taken in. The denial of freedom corresponds to the standpoint according to which human beings are thought as manipulable objects, i.e. in the third person. Such a denial of freedom is indeed, for the most part, a *self*-denial of freedom according to which the individual understands and explains itself in terms of the circumstances it finds itself in which 'force' it to (re-)act in a certain way.

---

158 Nietzsche offers trenchant criticism of Christianity and socialist doctrines which, he asserts, are based upon a morality of the "weak and those who have come off badly in life" (Schwachen und Schlechtweggekommenen, *Nachgelassene Fragmente* Spring 1888 14 [5] KSA13:220), that is, of those who are not up to the sometimes tough interplay and would much rather seek security. For Nietzsche there is a boundless egoism underneath the Christian and secularized Christian, i.e. socialist, teachings of altruism (otherwise known as solidarity): "[...] hidden beneath the universal praise of 'altruism' lies the instinct that if everybody cares for each other, the individual will be best preserved [...] it is the *egoism of the weak* which has created the praise, the exclusive praise of altruism" ([...] unter dem allgemeinen Lobe des 'Altruismus' verbirgt sich der Instinkt, daß wenn alle für einander sorgen, der Einzelne am besten bewahrt bleibt [...] es ist der *Egoismus der Schwachen*, der das Lob, das ausschließliche Lob des Altruismus geschaffen hat, 14 [5] KSA13:219). The ideology of solidarity is thus, according to Nietzsche, merely a cover for the weak which blocks the strengthening and enhancement of abilities through the incentives offered to self-interest. The morality of the underdog always looks sympathetically toward the weak rather than the strong, and disparages the latter as selfish rather than praising their excellence and achievements. Nonetheless, Nietzsche, paradoxically, like so many intellectuals, retains a dim view of business and commerce.

Because the exchange between buyer and seller involves money, the transaction always essentially has also a quantitative dimension, viz. *price*. The good offered for sale is always good-for a certain application or range of applications in living; that is, the good's mode of being resides in its applicability and aptitude, and that is what makes it valuable. This is its use-value, its value in the primary sense. But its value in the secondary, derived or second-order sense, (as already discussed in Chapter 4.1; cf. Aristotle *Pol.* Book I iii 1257a7) consists in its being exchangeable for money, the universal means of exchange that enables its owner to acquire any of the myriad goods offered for sale on the countless markets. The exchange-value of a good is thus necessarily quantitative and measured in the monetary dimension; its exchange-value is simply an amount of money, a price.

What a good is worth in money terms is determined by the market interplay. The ongoing transactions on the market always provide a range of prices for the good in question which sets the going rate or *market value*. The market price of a good is set as a (changeable) brute fact as the ongoing outcome of an anonymous process and it can be found out by all those engaged in the market, both buyers and sellers. The price set by the market, as a quantified, reified social relation, is indifferent to the well-being or otherwise of the market's participants. Assuming that a 'caring' (welfare) state does not intervene in the market, the price is not set by some caring agent so that certain sellers in the market will earn enough to support their families; nor is it set sufficiently low by force so that certain buyers will be able to afford it. Rather, the going price is a given fact that may fluctuate from day to day and even hour to hour, independently of either buyers' or sellers' endeavours to take care of themselves. The going market price, expressed in money, is a reification of mutually indifferent caring-for and caring about one's self.

Nevertheless, precisely in this indifference, it enables participants in the market to go about their daily business, i.e. to take care of their daily lives in mutually beneficial exchanges. The facticity of going market prices forces all participants in the market, buyers and sellers, to adapt and adjust their daily practices. Structural market anomalies such as monopoly or cartels, however, will give certain participants (in this case, the monopolist or cartel member) the power to set market prices to their own advantage, thus positively harming the others. Although buyer and seller have opposed interests with respect to the price to be paid for a given good, they can nevertheless reach agreement with an eye to the going market price, thus mutually furthering each other in taking care of their own individual worlds.

The buyer purchases the product because it offers something good for, i.e. valuable to, the buyer's own existence. The product itself is produced by a kind of labour or labours, more or less complicated. The price paid for the product is therefore always also an abstract, quantitative validation and estimation of the labour provided by all those contributing to producing the product, and the exchange relation is a kind of relation of estimation and validation of the labour represented by the product as being valuable for a concrete use in the purchaser's existence. The exchange relation abstractly mediated by money, may therefore be regarded as an abstract relation of social estimation of the labour involved in providing the product, thus serving the customer. Providing a product is hence equivalent to providing a service to the consumer. The price the consumer pays is ultimately an abstract form of estimation of the labour of providing, of performing some kind of service. Thus, although the exchange relation is abstract and reified (through the abstractly social thing, money), it is nevertheless a relation of social estimation of the provision of a more or less valuable service to the consumer mediated by a mutually beneficial furthering of self-interests in exchange. As touched upon in Chapter 8.3, the so-called labour theory of value is a disguised and distorted way of seeing in the exchange relation an interplay of abstract mutual estimation in providing services to each other, i.e. of exercising labouring abilities or individual powers in favour of each other. These services may be immediately beneficial to consumers leading and enjoying their lives, or they may be mediatedly beneficial by providing the means of production for providing those services.

9.3   Reified sociating interplay and purportedly 'inhuman' alienation of human being

The lament about the 'uncaring', reified sociating interplay on the market goes back at least as far as Karl Marx's thoughts on alienation in the 1840s. It is important to note that, strictly speaking, the lament is independent of the critique of capitalist exploitation of the worker and therefore also has to be assessed independently of the latter critique. With regard to exchange relations of one good for another (and not for money, as has been assumed above) Marx writes:

Ich habe für mich produziert und nicht für dich, wie du für dich produziert hast und nicht für mich. Das Resultat meiner Produktion hat an und für sich ebensowenig Beziehung auf dich, wie das Resultat deiner Produktion eine unmittelbare Beziehung auf mich hat. D.h. unsere Produktion ist keine Produktion des Menschen für den Menschen als Menschen, d.h. keine *gesellschaftliche* Produktion.

Karl Marx, Auszüge aus James Mills *Élémens d'économie politique*, transl. by J.T. Parisot, Paris 1823, in MEW Erg. Bd. 1 S. 459

I have produced for myself and not for you, just as you have produced for yourself and not for me. The result of my production has in itself just as little relation to you as the result of your production has an immediate relation to me, i.e. our production is not production of humans for humans as humans, i.e. it is not *social* production.

In producing a good for the market, each of us is taking care only of his or her own world and the interests that arise within it. We are indifferent to each other. There is no directly intended caring for the other in our productive activity and therefore, according to Marx, "it is not *social* production". Nevertheless, the exchange of the products is indeed a social relation that sociates us via the market, but in an indifferent mode of caring-for that, behind our backs and willy-nilly, is mutually beneficial and therefore in this sense mutually caring. Hence — pace Marx — our production *is* also "*social* production".

Die einzig verständliche Sprache, die wir zueinander reden, sind unsre Gegenstände in ihrer Beziehung aufeinander. Eine menschliche Sprache verständen wir nicht, und sie bliebe effektlos. [...] So sehr sind wir wechselseitig dem menschlichen Wesen entfremdet, daß die unmittelbare Sprache dieses Wesens uns als eine *Verletzung der menschlichen Würde*, dagegen die entfremdete Sprache der sachlichen Werte als die gerechtfertigte, selbstvertrauende und sichselbstanerkennende menschliche Würde erscheint. (*MEWErg1*:461)

The only understandable language that we speak to each other are our objects in their relationship to each other. We would not understand a human language, and it would remain without effect. [...] We are mutually alienated from human being, so much so that the direct/unmediated language of this being appears to us as a *violation of human dignity*, whereas the alienated language of reified values appears as justified, self-assured human dignity recognizing itself. (*MEWErg1*:461)

The exchange relation between us is not primarily that of talking to each other in the medium of the λόγος, thus exchanging views and perhaps directly catering to and caring positively for each other, but rather, the social interplay between us is mediated by things and is thus a reified social interplay. Each of us is interested only in acquiring the other's product which offers itself in its being as being valuable, i.e. useful, for some application, thus enhancing a way of life. Hence our mutual understanding of each other's products is primarily at play as motivation for the exchange in the first place. We may even, and mostly do, talk with each other about the possibilities in use offered by the other's product, thus entering into an interchange on how each other's product could enter into each other's taking care of everyday existence. Nonetheless, each of us has his or her own interest in the exchange and is not motivated by being able to help the other care for his or her own existence. The exchange, if it takes place, is predicated on a *mutual satisfaction* of what each of us sees as beneficial, and the exchange itself is a reciprocal interplay of *estimating* the other's product, and thus the labour embodied in the product, as being valuable for a possibility of living.

Marx claims that this mutual self-interest amounts to an alienation from genuine human being, from the human essence and thus as a "violation of human dignity", genuinely understood from its essence in human being. The appeal of one of us to make the exchange because one of us urgently needs the product in question would be "without effect" and would amount to a loss of "human dignity" because commodity exchanges take place only on the basis of reciprocal, complementary self-interests. But Marx suggests that this state of affairs is beneath human dignity once human being itself is understood in its genuine, non-alienated, 'authenticity'. The call here is for a positive mode of caring-for that would make our social relation of exchange genuinely dignified by acknowledging neediness.

> Unser *wechselseitiger* Wert ist für uns der *Wert* unsrer wechselseitigen Gegenstände. Also ist der Mensch selbst uns wechselseitig *wertlos*. (*MEWErg1*:462)

> Our *mutual* value is for us the *value* of our mutual objects. The human being himself is thus for us mutually *worthless*.

Within the context of exchange, each of us is focused on the use-value promised as a possibility of living well by using the other's product. This use-value makes each of our products valuable, estimable and therefore worthy of acquiring in exchanging some other value for it. Given this focus, we are indifferent to each other as worthy human beings *per se* who may possess many other excellences or human qualities. The exchange relation is not the place where we undertake a mutual and comprehensive appraisal of each other's merits as human beings. Nor is it the place where a recognition of the other as 'one of God's creatures', independently of any merits and merely by virtue of the fact of being a human being, takes place. Nor is it the place where the other's neediness is recognized and compensated (as if neediness itself were the hallmark of human being). Despite this lack of interest, this disinterest in the value or otherwise of each of us as human beings, in exchanging products we can be mutually beneficial to each other. Moreover, we mutually estimate the products as valuable, and thus also the labour embodied in the products, and hence also the exercise of the human abilities required to make the products.

> Gesetzt, wir hätten als Menschen produziert: Jeder von uns hätte in seiner Produktion sich selbst und den anderen *doppelt bejaht*. [...] 2. In deinem Genuß oder deinem Gebrauch meines Produkts hätte ich *unmittelbar* den Genuß, sowohl des Bewußtseins, in meiner Arbeit ein *menschliches* Bedürfnis befriedigt, als das *menschliche* Wesen vergegenständlicht und daher dem Bedürfnis eines andren *menschlichen* Wesens seinen entsprechenden Gegenstand verschafft zu haben, 3. für dich der *Mittler* zwischen dir und der Gattung gewesen zu sein, also von dir selbst als eine Ergänzung deines eignen Wesens und als ein notwendiger Teil deiner selbst gewußt und empfunden zu werden, also sowohl in deinem Denken wie in deiner Liebe mich bestätigt zu wissen, 4. in meiner individuellen Lebensäußerung unmittelbar deine Lebensäußerung geschaffen zu haben, also in meiner individuellen Tätigkeit unmittelbar mein wahres Wesen, mein *menschliches*, mein *Gemeinwesen* *bestätigt* und *verwirklicht* zu haben. (*MEWErg1*:462)

> Assuming that we had produced as humans: Each of us in his production would have *doubly affirmed* himself and the other. [...] 2. In your enjoyment or your use of my product I would have had *directly* the enjoyment as well as the consciousness of having in my work satisfied a *human* need, of having objectified the *human* essence and therefore of having created the object corresponding to the need of another *human* being, 3. to have been the *mediator* for you between you and the species, that is, to be known and felt by you yourself as a complement to your own being and as a necessary part of your self, that is, to know that I am affirmed in your thinking as well as your love, 4. in my individual expression of life of having directly created your expression of life, that is, in my individual activity of having directly *affirmed* and *realized* my true essence, my *human* essence, my *communal/political essence*. (*MEWErg1*:462)

According to Marx, what stands in the way of this genuine expression of the true "*human* essence" is "private property" (Privateigentum, *MEWErg1*:459), under the "basic presupposition" (Grundvoraussetzung) of which "the purpose of production is to *have*; [...] it has a self-interested purpose" (der Zweck der Produktion ist das *Haben*. [...] sie hat einen eigennützigen Zweck. *MEWErg1*:459). In having produced to satisfy the need of another human being and in knowing that the other affirms me in his "thinking" and "love", a positive mode of caring-for would be constitutive of economic life in general. Economic life would be a theatre of universal love driven by (mutual?) need-fulfilment. Self-interest as the motive for exchange would give way to knowing that I have "satisfied a *human* need". Our exchange would then be "the mediating movement in which it has been affirmed that my product is for you because it is an *objectification* of your own being, your need" (die vermittelnde

Bewegung, worin es bestätigt wurde, daß mein Produkt für dich ist, weil es eine *Vergegenständlichung* deines eignen Wesens, deines Bedürfnisses ist. *MEWErg1:459*).

As it is, however, abstract, reified exchange interplay is nevertheless in truth a form of social estimation of each other as providing something valuable to each other as a possibility of existence. The exchange relations of products are relations of mutual recognition and estimation in providing services to each other. This does not amount to relations of total concrete recognition of each other as human beings resembling a love relation, but it does constitute a social nexus and enable a social way of living in which self-interested actors nevertheless mutually benefit each other. Why should it be alienating? Indifferent self-interest is willy-nilly mediated with caring for another and thus raised up dialectically, whereas the above-quoted passage from Marx is undialectical in failing the think the mediation of opposites with one another. Just as any service can be regarded as a product, so too can any product be regarded as a service, i.e. the purchaser purchases the exercised abilities embodied in the product as a kind of service and thus abstractly esteems in the purchase the labour of service-provision. This falls short of love, nor is it a one-sided satisfaction of the other's neediness, but it is no injury to human dignity. Moreover, as has been shown in Chapter 4.5, neediness is not a fundamental category of human existence but derivative of the usages which people habitually practise.

The barrier to the realization of "true *human* being" in Marx's view are private property relations, which distort this "true *human* being". This barrier could be overcome through an act of political revolution in which private property were abolished, thus also revolutionizing historical human being itself into a way of sharing the world with others in which a positive, affirmative mode of caring for others purportedly would become 'natural' in everyday sociation with one another. Against this assertion we have a fundamental socio-ontological structure of human being as care and of shared human being as caring-for in which social relations such as private property have to be thought as being more fundamentally rooted. As we have seen above, the predominant modes of caring-for arising from everyday life are deficient and privative modes, *not* because of private property relations but, more deeply, because human being itself is individualized and cares in the first place about casting and shaping its own existence and its own world in a small, familiar circle, whether it be a nuclear family, an extended family, a clan, a neighbourhood, etc. It exercises its powers and abilities, in the first place, for its own sake, i.e. for the sake of its own world. Only those who are close to me are part of my world; others figure in my world "at first and for the most part" in a background mode of indifference.

This prevailing indifference, however, in no way precludes mutually beneficial interplay driven by self-interest from arising and thus an interplay of mutual estimation of each other as being valuable to and appreciated by each other (rather than being weak and needy, and therefore pitied).

The 'wanting to have more', the πλεονεξία, the Habsucht discussed in Chapter 4 is — pace Marx — not a consequence of private property, but rather conversely, private property, which deprives others of access to what I have got for myself and for those close to me, corresponds to a deeper proclivity to take care of one's own first and to exclude others from using and benefiting from those material goods acquired that contribute to living well. Is this merely a proclivity of the historical Western world? At least in Western traditions, it is not beneath human dignity to care for oneself and one's own first, but wholly in line with a deeper socio-ontological structure of human being as experienced and thought through in Western history.

The socialization of property therefore presupposes another, 'higher', historical fundamental — and more than merely self-deluding, Utopian — recasting of human being itself (a 'new' human being) in which some positive, more inclusive, non-indifferent mode of caring for others would become a 'natural', ubiquitous human condition, a condition of ethical "second nature" (*RPh.* § 151). Marx and other socialists have regarded such an elevation of human nature to a higher plane to be historically possible, whereas a more sober and insightful view of how human beings fend for themselves in the world — which can be clarified by ontological-existential concepts forged from everyday life — suggests that Marx's alienation is Utopian, i.e. that it has no place on this Earth and therefore amounts to positing a mere Ought that can only wreak havoc in history by suppressing the self-interested particularity of human being. Rather, social interplay of mutually beneficial self-interest arises of itself (and in this sense is φύσει, i.e. 'natural') from individuals and groups of individuals striving to take care of themselves in going about the business of everyday life. Caring for oneself thus becomes of itself, i.e. naturally and willy-nilly, a mutual, although restricted, caring for each other, and the abstract, reified interplay of the market is nonetheless a social interplay in which we estimate each other abstractly, and in part even concretely, through money as being mutually beneficial to each other — despite and precisely because this mutual estimation is mediated *through* our self-interests.

When the young Marx strikes the theme of love in social relations, he is of course taking up a motif of Christian discourse, the ἀγάπη, 'charity' or 'brotherly love' which makes a Christian a good person pleasing in God's sight. The virtues of liberality, generosity and beneficence, too, have been regarded since ancient Greek philosophy as most praiseworthy, whereas stinginess, miserliness and meanness have been among the most blameworthy traits of human nature that were to be overcome by becoming virtuous. With the advent of Hobbes, however, the bar was lowered. Since men were after glory, were self-interested, did not keep their word, did not trust each other, etc., the best that could be hoped for was that a Leviathan be set up to "keep them all in awe" (*Lev.* p. 62 cf. Chapter 10), so at least they did not kill each other. The social ontology developed in the present inquiry, however, has asked what the nature of human sociation is and uncovered that the bland term, 'social relation', has to be regarded more deeply as sociating, estimating interchange and interplay, whose ontology has been analyzed in Chapter 5.

The ubiquitous nexus of everyday life is a mutually beneficial and mutually self-interested interchange which is neither praiseworthy nor blameworthy. Everyday life is a give and take. This contrasts with the altruistic virtues of giving without taking, up to the extreme of sacrificing one's life for others (as a soldier may do to defend his country or for the sake of fulfilling one's own ideal 'look' of oneself). And it contrasts also with egoistically taking without giving as happens in phenomena such as stealing, fraud (taking whilst pretending to give), robbery (taking under the threat of physical violence) or the extreme case of murder (taking another's life), or in simply being egoistically ruthless in all one's dealings. All these phenomena, from one extreme to the other, may be regarded as social interchanges, from the most praiseworthy to the most blameworthy and punishable. The mean is constituted by the mundane exchange of estimated equivalents, the give and take of everyday life in which most people earn a livelihood in a society characterized by a division of labour which thus motivates exchanges on the basis of what we, through the exercise of our diverse abilities, can do for each other to enhance each other's lives by providing something useful that serves one or other of the usages that go to make up our habitual quotidian lives. This is the socio-ontological middle ground, which is neither imbued with Christian virtue, nor stained by the violence of a Hobbesian state of nature.

9.4 The wage-labour relation and caring-for – Co-operation and conflict – Hierarchy and reified discipline – Economic democracy and total economic control

We turn now to capitalism and the relationship between capital and wage-labour to consider it from the perspective of the socio-ontological structure of caring-for. Marx conceives wage-labour *as* alienated human activity in which, moreover, the labourer is sorely exploited. The alienation is said to stem from i) the labourers' not owning and therefore controlling their means of production, which are the private property of the capitalist and ii) the reification of social relations in money-value which, once it is set into motion as the movement of capital, subsumes wage-labour beneath it as a mere factor of production. The exploitation is said to originate in the appropriation by the capitalist of a portion of the product value as surplus value, the basis for this claim being the labour theory of value, according to which the product's magnitude of value is determined by its labour content. If the claim that capitalism is based in its essence on the exploitation of wage-labour through the extraction of surplus value is disposed of in refuting the labour theory of value (cf. Chapter 6.3), the alienation-reification critique of capitalism still has to be considered.

Seen from the opposite perspective, the alienation-reification critique of capitalism is Adam Smith's felicitous "invisible hand", since this latter means nothing other than that economic activity is undertaken via the market under the guiding facticity of reified sociating interplay that functions as a simple, ubiquitously applicable, disciplining, social filter, i.e. as a kind of ingenious cybernetic feedback loop that sifts out failed attempts, and validates, esteems and rewards the best attempts.[159] When the production of use-values, i.e. of what is good for living, is undertaken privately but for the market, the product's use-value becomes exchange-value and, quantitatively, price, a reified expression of what the product is worth in sociation. But reified social interplay does not stop there.

Once the valuableness of goods attains a reification in money, this thing itself becomes the embodiment of value and, as universal equivalent, is itself able to acquire all else that human being values, i.e. everything that is good for living including, for instance, even honour, social prestige, public office, political influence, etc. etc. In particular, and essentially, reified value can be employed gainfully, i.e. money can be employed self-reflexively, i.e. invested, to make more money $M-C-M + \Delta M$, thus setting itself into a peculiar kind of movement, a *social, sociating* movement which, through its movement, sociates. This gainful, self-reflexive, self-augmentative movement of money-value is capital in its primary and fundamental determination as expressed in the above simple formula for the movement of value as capital. As mercantile capital, money-

---

159 "Just as Adam Smith was the last of the moralists and the first of the economists, so Darwin was the last of the economists and the first of the biologists." Simon N. Patten *The Development of English Thought* New York 1899 p. xxiii cited in Hayek *LLL*1:153.

value is put into motion to bring goods together on the market, i.e. com-merce, but as productive capital, money-value is set into movement, bringing together or sociating the factors of production (labour power, raw materials, means of production and land) into a production process.

Essential to setting up a capitalist production process is the wage-labour relation between the capitalist and the labourers (where the labourers in this general context can be anyone who works for money, i.e. employees, including managers, and not just 'blue-collar' workers. The capitalist here is nothing other than the personification of money-capital, i.e. of a reified social relation, and is therefore not necessarily a natural person but perhaps merely a legal entity, a non-natural person. This legal entity can even be a co-operative in which the owner-workers as capitalist owners employ *themselves* as wage labourers. Such owner-workers therefore wear two character-masks. Money-capital has the power to purchase an essential ingredient of the production process, labour power, which is embodied in the labourers. For this to happen, the capitalist and the workers do a deal, an exchange: wages for labour power expended for a certain time. Of course the capitalist also has to purchase raw materials, means of production and lease land, but that is left to one side here. We are concerned here only with considering the capitalist wage-labour relation from the perspective of caring-for.

The wage-labour deal is an exchange between two parties. The capitalist hires the labourer as the bearer of labour power with the aim of making money. The employees hire out their labour power with the aim of earning wages to support their way of living. The employees are making a living, and the capitalist is making money, and indeed, only remains a capitalist for as long as he is making money, i.e. augmenting money-value rather than diminishing it. The capitalist (who, on a more concrete level, could be, say, shareholders living off dividends, or employees themselves as part-owners of a co-operative for which they work) will live off the money made, but also reinvest the money made to make even more money, thus enhancing the enterprise's chances of survival in the competitive economic interplay. Both sides of the wage-labour hire transaction are therefore interested in making money, at least in part, for a livelihood. They are not directly interested in each other's welfare or in supporting a comfortable way of living for the other. They are both self-interested. Moreover, each side has opposed interests with regard to the amounts of wages paid since, for the capitalist, the wages are a cost and therefore a deduction from potential profit, whereas for the employees, the higher the wages or salaries, the better. Thus, to start with, the capitalist wage-labour relation could be characterized as a mode of indifferent or — with respect to their opposed interests with regard to wage levels — even deficient, negative or antagonistic caring-for mediated by the reified sociation via money-capital — but only to start with.

Why? Because, although each side is (self-)interested in earning money and these interests are quantitatively opposed, the wage-labour relation brings the two sides together in some sort of ongoing production process in which labour power is expended in a labour process (which may be also a service-provision process). This ongoingness amounts to a way of everyday working life in whose continuation both sides have an interest. The capitalist must be interested in the quality of the product produced; the employees must be interested in the quality of the working conditions. These interests may be aligned (in which case there is an easy mutuality of interest) or they may conflict (in which case there is a caring-for as Gegeneinander, as opposition). Maintaining product quality or enhancing productivity may entail paying higher salaries and wages, and providing good working conditions and auxiliary benefits, or it may entail co-operative, minimally hierarchical organization of the labour process in teams, or it may entail paring costs by sacking employees, or strict labour discipline in 'sweatshops' enforcing a high intensity of labour at low wages.

The essence of capitalism, the gainful game (cf. Chapter 6.8), which for the present purposes may be defined from the capitalist side as the striving for monetary gain through advancing money-capital, does *not*, however (pace Marx's immiseration theory), necessarily dictate poor wages and poor working conditions as in inevitable outcome of the interplay of opposed interests. The (abstract, simple) essence of capital is infinitely more versatile, more Protean than that. Above all, where employees embody special skills, these skills are worth something to the capitalist which is acknowledged in the level of wages and salaries and in enhanced working conditions, side benefits or even bonuses. Moreover, the organization of wage-labour into labour unions (and, assuming a democratic public sphere, the formation of public opinion) is an alternative way for employees to improve the outcome of their struggle with capitalist employers over wage levels and working conditions when the capitalist's money-making strategy is to ruthlessly minimize costs. The bargaining advantage of the employing capitalist in negotiations over wages and conditions is then weakened by workers presenting a united front in negotiations (or bringing public opinion behind them on the issue of what is regarded socially as fair conditions of employment). The employees' bargaining position can also be improved (or worsened) simply by the conditions of capitalist competition, such as a shortage (or surfeit) of labour power.

The ongoing capitalist production and circulation process therefore involves both positive and negative modes of caring-for, i.e. there can be both mutual co-operation and sharp conflict between capitalist and workforce in concretely shaping the production or circulation process and how it is remunerated. Thus, reified social relations (money, capital) by no means entail merely indifference or conflict among the participants in the economy but may elicit also positive modes of mutually caring-for in the way the two sides comport themselves toward each other. The wage-labour relation with capital is thus *socio-ontologically ambiguous*, containing both the possibility of mutual co-operation and benefit and even satisfaction, on the one hand, and that of bitter conflict, on the other. Those with highly prized skills on the employment market, for instance, will more easily enjoy an employment relationship describable as a mutual caring-for in the positive sense. Others, who are less skilled and in abundance on the job market, will experience employment as dreary or a hard slog.

Furthermore, the continuity of the production and circulation process[160] and the mutual dependence of capitalist and workforce on each other mean that a way of working life arises around the capitalist enterprise. Each side, in taking care of its self-interest in earning money, indirectly cares for the other side's taking care of everyday working life on a continuous basis. As long as the capitalist enterprise remains profitable by conforming to the simple value-form conditions of the movement of value as capital, the production or circulation process can continue, and both capitalist and workforce can earn their livelihood and mutually benefit from each other. The enterprise's profitability constitutes the 'boundary conditions', the reified value-parameters for whether the enterprise's production process can continue in its present shape or at all. Maintaining or enhancing profitability, enforced by competition among the capitalist enterprises, dictates continual changes to the enterprise's production and circulation process, which may include retrenchments of the workforce, intensification of the labour process, a worsening of working conditions or wage cuts.

The continual struggle over jobs, wage levels and working conditions with the capitalist employer is waged within the boundary conditions of the enterprise's overall profitability, i.e. if the employees' side pushes too far to assert its self-interests, it may bankrupt the enterprise altogether, thus terminating a possibility of working life altogether. The pursuit of self-interest by both capitalist and employees is thus mediated with the other side's interests, so that there

---

160 Production and circulation of capital are the two complementary parts of the circular movement of capital, for the produced product also has to be brought to market and sold for advanced capital to complete its augmentative circuit, and this latter role may be undertaken by a separate commercial, rather than productive, capital.

is both co-operation and conflict, i.e. both positive and negative modes of caring-for. Moreover, the reified, money-mediated social interplay enforces mutations in the enterprise to secure or enhance its chances of survival, i.e. the enterprise is a mode of movement of social life that is not decided by political institutions and the eternal interplay of negotiating political powers, but by the anonymous workings of market cybernetics that is able to dislodge the entrenched inertia of an habitualized way of working life for the sake of enhancing the value of the enterprise's product that is achieved on the market. The term 'market mechanism' or, more properly, 'market metabolism' is justified only as a term for reified social interplay, i.e. for sociation accomplished through things, above all, through money. The movement of prices on the various markets, which is itself a reified sociating movement, has a cybernetic feedback effect on the production processes and the way of working life in the enterprise.

The criticism of capitalist-waged employee labourer interplay — that the waged employees do not control their own working conditions but are subject to the capitalist's command — can be answered as follows: First of all, any modern production (or circulation, which will here be left to one side) process in the broadest sense (including service provision) that has even a moderate scale must have some sort of hierarchy that structures the productive organism. A thorough-going 'direct' democracy in the production process is unworkable. Secondly, large or medium-sized production processes can be organized with more or less steep hierarchies, and productivity may well be enhanced by instituting team-work organized in shallow hierarchies and by encouraging individual employee responsibility. Such measures will give employees more control over their own work processes, but within an overall working structure that aims at efficient, productive production as measured ultimately by success in quantitative value terms. Thirdly, capitalist enterprise allows also the variant of a co-operative in which the employees own their own company but, even in this event, there must be some sort of hierarchy and chain of command to organize the production process, and the co-operative, too, is subject to the discipline of the boundary conditions of self-augmenting value. Fourthly, the lack of control over working conditions is not merely a matter of a capitalist boss dictating how the employees are to work, but is due above all to the capitalist enterprise being exposed to market conditions and especially to the competition with other capitalist enterprises. The value-reified conditions of markets and competition enforces discipline in the company's production process itself, and the capitalist entrepreneur or the managers are only the mediators or 'messengers' who pass on the necessary adaptations down the chain of command in the hierarchy. Even a co-operative is exposed to capitalist competition.

Fifthly, *any* kind of sociation of a single production process in an overall economic system, whether it be mediated by reified market relations or whether it be controlled politically through political power play as in state-owned enterprises, takes away autonomous control of the production process and how it can be organized. Even a totalized system of economic democracy in which normal employees would have a say in how the overall economy is organized and what and how it is to produce would not do away with relations of domination and subordination, i.e. with the social power play. The politicization of the production process on a total social scale would mean that the struggles that are carried out via the medium of reified value on competitive markets under capitalism would assume the form of ongoing political power struggles within the enterprises and the political institutions themselves. This would amount to an intensification of political power struggles, since the cybernetic functioning of reified market interplay would no longer provide some externally imposed, reified and therefore neutral discipline and dispensation from continual, internal struggle. No matter how the sociating interplay of production may be historically modified and reconstellated, social power play remains a predominant, ineradicable phenomenon in countless and ever-changing forms of manifestation. We shall return to a consideration of the ontology of social power in Chapter 10.

9.5 The invisible hand and the ontological possibility of a caring capitalism – Unlimited economic growth through caring for each other

Undoubtedly the most famous turn of phrase from Adam Smith's pen is that of the "invisible hand" which works mysteriously in markets purportedly for the general good of society. The phrase occurs in a chapter of *The Wealth of Nations* headed "Of restraints upon the importation from foreign countries of such goods as can be produced at home" (Book IV Chapter II) in which Smith discusses the detrimental effects of trade protectionism by means of import prohibitions and customs duties, etc. which allow a domestic industry to thrive behind artificial trade barriers erected and maintained by the state in its exercise of political power. Political power therefore in this case trumps the power interplay among the various economic resources, each with its own potential when sociated via the medium of reified value.

The basic idea is that protectionism distorts the allocation of wealth-creating resources of a nation in favour of protected industries from how they otherwise would be allocated if the profit-making self-interest of entrepreneurs alone were to direct their allocation. A protected domestic industry can afford to be less efficient in its use of economic resources than foreign competitors. The removal of protectionist barriers would lead to a reallocation of resources toward what that nation's domestic economy does better, i.e. more productively and efficiently, which it could then trade to gain the goods produced in foreign parts more efficiently, and therefore more cheaply, than the domestic economy is able to produce, thus bringing about a win-win situation. Smith writes:

> But it is only for the sake of profit that any man employs a capital in the support of industry; and he will always, therefore, endeavour to employ it in the support of that industry of which the produce is likely to be of the greatest value, or to exchange for the greatest quantity either of money or of other goods. [...] He generally, indeed, neither intends to promote the public interest, nor knows how much he is promoting it. By preferring the support of domestic to that of foreign industry, he intends only his own security, and by directing that industry in such a manner as its produce may be of the greatest value, he intends only his own gain, and he is in this, as in many other cases, led by an *invisible hand* to promote an end which was no part of his intention. Nor is it always the worse for the society that it was no part of it. By pursuing his own interest he frequently promotes that of the society more effectually than when he really intends to promote it. I have never known much good done by those who affected to trade for the public good. It is an affectation, indeed, not very common among merchants, and very few words need be employed in dissuading them from it.[161]

The good of society is here taken to be attained with the maximization of the "annual revenue" which is "always precisely equal to the exchangeable value of the whole annual produce of its industry, or rather is precisely the same thing with that exchangeable value" (p. 484). Today this would be termed the Gross Domestic Product (GDP). The good of society is thus seen to have a quantitative measure residing in the total monetary value of the annual produce of a nation's industries and it is only with regard to this quantitatively maximized general good as a sum of commodity values, and against the foil of the 'visible hand' of government interference, that the phrase "invisible hand" is to be understood. In later liberal economic theory, however, the invisible hand has misleadingly come to mean something much more encompassing, viz. the general good of society as such and not a value-determinate magnitude that comes about only through the intricate estimating interplay on the world's markets, both domestic and international.

---

161 Adam Smith *The Wealth of Nations* 1776 Bk. IV Ch. II pp. 484, 485, emphasis added.

The agents of production "of the whole annual produce" are the society's entrepreneurial class who as 'undertakers' take it upon themselves to bring together the factors of production and organize them in diverse production processes, thus 'energizing' their potentials. Each entrepreneur has the individual aim of making a maximum amount of profit, which is the residue left from the sale of the product after all the costs of production consisting of rent, wages, means of production costs and interest have been paid. In other words, the entrepreneur strives to maximize the individual bottom line in both an absolute and relative sense. Ultimately, the measure of his success is the rate of return on capital (ROC), another simple quantitative measure expressing the efficiency with which a single capital bears its offspring, namely, net profit. The measure of entrepreneurial success and of social wealth, as the simple aggregation of individual capitals' value-products, is thus a measure of sociating movement in the dimension of monetary value. It is the annual rate of value augmentation that serves as measure for both individual and overall social economic success.

The maximization of annual total social value augmentation is in effect the solution to a kind of differential equation to calculate a maximum. Each component of the total social capital must add its maximum possible increment to the annual total value creation for the overall maximum total to be achieved. The notion of the invisible hand says that, compared with the alternative of government intervention that interferes with the striving of *entrepreneurial* self-interest for gain, it is better for each component part of the social capital to seek maximum gain in the competitive economic interplay. Put another way, the exercise of political power, say, through the imposition of import tariffs or the subsidization of certain domestic industries, can indeed alter, i.e. distort, the value relations that come about through estimating market interplay from where they would otherwise be, and such a shift is only ever paid for caeteris paribus with a *diminution* (in mathematical terms: a negative first differential) compared to allowing the market interplay to have full sway in determining value-outcomes. The argument of the invisible hand does not depend on assuming some such thing as 'perfect' or 'free' competition, but is only a comparison with regard to value enhancement between the interventionist exercise of political power on the one hand, and the power play of market interplay *among entrepreneurs*, on the other.

How is the Smithian notion of the invisible hand to be modified when not just the entrepreneurial players, but all the players striving for income in the gainful game (cf. Chapter 6.3) are taken into account? Or does it need no modification? The entrepreneurs are the functioning capitalists who undertake to set up and operate a production or circulation process within the reproductive circulation of total social capital. They bring together labourers (employees), means of production, finance capital and land for the enterprise's operations. The value generated by the enterprise and realized on the markets by selling the product, whatever it might be, is divided among the four basic types of income: wages, interest, ground-rent and the residual income: profit of enterprise, along with the costs of the means of production themselves, which have to be replaced either straight away (circulating capital) or after some time (fixed capital). This division of the realized product value can be viewed from the viewpoint of a single enterprise, an industry or a nation's aggregate social capital. How this division turns out depends upon the power interplay among the various classes with their different kinds of revenue.

The share of total sales revenue left as profit of enterprise limits that enterprise's ability/power to *invest* to enhance productivity which, in turn, affects its competitiveness with other enterprises. Or aggregate social revenue in the form of profit of enterprise in a given industry affects how much enterprises in that industry can invest in enhancing the industry's productivity which, in turn, affects their overall competitiveness globally in that industry. Since the other income-earners in an enterprise or an industry, i.e. the employees, the lenders of loan capital and land-owners (assuming these character masks are worn by different players), depend on the enterprise's or industry's successful valorization to generate total sales revenue, their own self-interests lie in not pushing the enterprise to the wall in demanding excessive wages, interest and ground-rent, since this would amount to killing the golden goose. Although all the income-earning stakeholders in an enterprise or industry have opposed interests in the power play over how total sales revenue is carved up, they also are interdependent. Ultimately it is the enterprise's or the industry's survival in the competitive struggle that serves as the invisible hand that cybernetically regulates the power interplay over dividing up gross sales revenue. The Smithian invisible hand is therefore, via the mediation of competitive struggle among enterprises, still a guiding hand for the power play among the four basic kinds of income-earners. Under pain of the enterprise's or the entire industry's 'death', whether they want to or not, they must reach a compromise with which each of the players can 'live'. No intervention from a superior instance is needed for this cybernetic feedback to work and, indeed, such meddling can only makes things worse. I shall return to this topic in section 9.7 below.

This is a restricted, economic view of the Smithian invisible hand, but it can be seen to be, more deeply, an attribute of anonymous steering, i.e. cybernetics, of an economic way of living that is mediated by reified sociating value, viz. money and capital, that cannot be attributed to any underlying subject. The market interplay power-interplay, although essentially groundless, nevertheless tends through the individualized strivings toward an optimum value power-interplay outcome by continually disciplining and correcting each partial play in the overall interplay according to its relative success or failure as measured, relatively simply, by reified value magnitudes. Smith's argumentation of the invisible hand aims at a quantitative justification of market-mediated economic activity driven by the pursuit of self-interests as against the possibility of a conscious 'visible hand' of state dirigisme in the hands of those vested with political power, to wit, politicians and bureaucrats. But for a capitalist market economy driven in its movement by the pursuit of self-interest on the part of myriad individuals, all the various income-earning players can also be thought through in connection with the existential structure of care (Sorge) that has already been introduced above in section 9.1.

We have already seen that through the estimating interplay which is essentially constitutive of capitalist economic life, self-interested, income-earning individuals come into contact and do a deal that is and must be mutually beneficial to both sides and hence accepted as more or less fair. The mutual benefit consists in making a living or acquiring goods and services that contribute to living well. Thus, despite the necessarily opposed interests of the parties in the exchange interplay, there is at the same time a mutuality of interest in that each furthers the other's interest. David Hume puts it thus, "I learn to do a service to another, without bearing him any real kindness."[162] Even more than that, there must be also a level of *trust* between the parties to the exchange relation for it to be practically viable as an everyday practice. Each must accept the other's word that they will fulfil their end of the bargain. Each must be reliable in the performance of contract if any kind of stable relationship is to come about. Especially the wage-labour relationship reveals a level of mutual trust and reliability that amounts to caring for each other in a positive mode of the existential of care. This can be seen above all from the negative phenomenon of when the wage-labour relationship breaks down and the employee is dismissed, for there is always, in some sense, a breach of trust involved on one side or the other.

Seen more generally in the context of generalized exchange interplay in a capitalist market economy or "katallaxy",[163] the intertwining of self-interest and

---

162 David Hume *Treatise, Works* II p. 289 cited in Hayek *LLL2*:185.
163 Friedrich A. Hayek proposes the term 'catallaxy' as an alternative to 'economy' (which latter, in the literal sense, is a managed, organized household) to capture the notion of a social fabric or social network that comes about through the intertwinings of people exchanging services among one another. "Since the name 'catallactics' has long ago been suggested for the

mutual interest that is part of the socio-ontological structure of estimating interplay itself (a win-win game) to weave a social fabric justifies the (sober rather than ebullient) use of the term Fürsorge or caring-for to describe capitalist economic market interchange. All the players in a capitalist economy are dependent on the economic interplay to acquire goods (both material and immaterial) that they require and desire to live well. All these goods can be regarded ultimately as services provided by others, either directly or indirectly, and are paid for. The 'others' in the economy thus, in the neutral sense of a socio-ontological existential, play a positive role in caring for the economic actor, and capitalist economic life can be thought of as *that intermeshed, complex web of intertwined, money-mediated, mutually beneficial economic activities and estimating interplay, a movement without an underlying subject disciplined and guided by value magnitudes, that provides for the livelihood of individuals through these individuals' caring for each other in the sense of providing services to each other.* "They are led by an invisible hand [...] and [...] without intending it, without knowing it, advance the interest of the society..."[164]

Caring-for, of course, must always be taken to mean caring-for in all possible shades and variants within the entire spectrum of the existential of care, ranging from the attempt to simply exploit and take advantage of the other, through callous indifference to genuinely wanting to serve the other's requirements in good faith. Nevertheless, in a fundamental sense, even the pursuit of self-interest in a capitalist economy is not incompatible with positive, satisfying modes of caring for others. In fact, caring for contractual partners whether they

---

science which deals with the market order (Richard Whately *Introductory Lectures on Political Economy* London 1855 p. 4) and has more recently been revived (especially by L. von Mises *Human Action* Yale 1949 passim.), it would seem appropriate to adopt a corresponding term for the market order itself. The term 'catallactics' was derived from the Greek verb καταλλάττειν (or καταλλάσσειν) which meant, significantly, not only 'to exchange' but also 'to admit into the community' and 'to change from enemy into friend'. From it the adjective 'catallactic' has been derived to serve in the place of 'economic' to describe the kind of phenomena with which the science of catallactics deals. The ancient Greeks knew neither this term nor had a corresponding noun [This seems wrong, since Democritus used καταλλαγή for 'exchange' ME cf. Liddell and Scott]; if they had formed one it would probably have been καταλλαξία. From this we can form an English term *catallaxy* which we shall use to describe the order brought about by the mutual adjustment of many individual economies in a market. A catallaxy is thus the special kind of spontaneous order produced by the market through people acting within the rules of the law of property, tort and contract." *Law, Legislation and Liberty* Vol. 2 The Mirage of Social Justice, Chicago U.P. 1976 pp. 108f.
164 Adam Smith *The Theory of Moral Sentiments* (1759) Prometheus Books, New York 2000 Part IV, Chapter I, near end of penultimate paragraph pp. 264f, cited in Hayek *LLL2*:186.

be customers and clients or employees and suppliers, and taking their interests into account can be a successful formula for the long-term satisfaction and furthering of one's own self-interests. Conversely, ruthlessly asserting one's own self-interest vis-à-vis all the other players engaged with in the economic game can be, and often is, a formula for one's own long-term demise in the value interplay. This, of course, leaves aside the question of the justice or fairness of the rules of play for the economic interplay as investigated in Chapter 6. It also leaves aside the question concerning how fair, general rules of play for the interplay are laid down more or less cleverly and wisely by the state in the form of enforceable laws and regulations. Such laying down of rules of interplay through fiat of political power must be distinguished from state interference in the economic game itself, thus unfairly benefiting certain particular players to the detriment of certain others and distorting the value outcomes of the interplay.

From the perspective of the ontological concepts of existence, care and caring-for, it also comes to light that economic activity need not be regarded simply as productive activity or the rampant exploitation of the earth's non-renewable resources for the sake of providing material consumer goods. Capitalist economic growth is often (mis)understood and harshly criticized as essentially productive activity that rapaciously exploits the earth's finite resources and places a burden on the environment. Of course, material goods and the use of the earth's resources are an essential part of any economic activity because material goods make up an essential part of the goods required to live at all well in any way of social living. But the exploitation of resources and their consumption by no means exhaust the repertoire of possibilities under the constellation of capitalist, market-mediated social interplay, and, precisely because of the abstract nature of estimating interplay mediated by reified value, compatibility with environmental friendliness is not essentially excluded for a prospering configuration of global economic interplay.

If capitalist market economy is conceived (thus showing itself in its presencing) *as* a kind of mutual social caring-for in interchanges of all kinds, then it can be seen that the countless ongoing exchange plays among the economic players are ways of *serving each other in exercising individual abilities*, i.e. individual, developed powers that can be more or less 'productive' or 'performative', depending upon the knowledge, know-how and skill each individual has appropriated through practice and hence embodies. This serving, of course, must be taken in a socio-ontological-existential sense of including also the negative mode of doing a disservice to the other and merely exploiting the other 'carelessly' and callously to one's own advantage. But it means that capitalist economic growth can conceivably (i.e. in a thinking guided by the ontological sight of beings) consist in expanding and intensifying economic interplay in which the economic players serve each other by selling service commodities — from which all sides benefit.

This implies that there are *no necessary, essential limits to economic growth* because there is no end to the possibilities for how human individuals even via the mediation of reified value can care for and serve each other whilst mutually satisfying their self-interests. The kinds of service commodities possible through realizing individual potentials are limited only by human ingenuity and inventiveness, for human being itself in relation to the world is always a casting of possibilities of living well. Such possibilities of living well can include also finding ways of getting around the finiteness of the earth's non-renewable resources, including above all technological advances — and that even under the self-interested incentive of gain. Thus, not only are new commodity gadgets, both small and large, continually and endlessly being invented, but also new services, new ways of serving each other. Seen from this perspective, which can only come from thoroughly rethinking the socio-ontology of value, there can be no 'limits to growth' and no danger that jobs or the need for labour could 'dry up' in a 'jobless economy'. John Stuart Mill expresses an analogous thought already in 1857:

> It is scarcely necessary to remark that a stationary condition of capital and population implies no stationary state of human improvement. There would be as much scope as ever for all kinds of mental culture, and moral and social progress; as much room for improving the Art of Living and much more likelihood of its being improved.[165]

An even earlier, not unrelated source is Virgil, who writes in *Georgics* 1.123 of "curis acuens mortalia corda", "sharpening the vital tension of mortals' wits by care".[166] Such a sharpening of wits through care is always also an enhancing of individual abilities. Care as the existential constitution of human being pricks (acus) us to tighten the vital tension of the gut-strings (chordae) of our wits in tuning our abilities, and these abilities are invariably exercised not only for oneself, but also in caring for each other in the estimating interplay of daily life.

165 J.S. Mill *Principles of Political Economy* 1857 in *Collected Works* eds. V.W. Bladen and J.M. Robson, University of Toronto Press 1965 p. 756, cited in *The Limits to Growth* D.H. Meadows, D.L. Meadows, J. Randers, W.W. Behrens III, Earth Island, London 1972 p. 175.
166 Cited by David Hume in 'Of Commerce' Essay I in *Essays Moral, Political, and Literary* Part II 1752, reprinted Liberty Fund, Indianapolis 1985 p. 267.

One could object that this understanding of endless economic growth amounts to a view of human living as endless economic materialism and consumerism, but that would be to regard the possibilities of caring for each other in a capitalist economy cynically only from the hard-nosed viewpoint of making money and to regard the other merely 'instrumentally' as a potential source of income for oneself. Why should the conception of economic life as the interchange of services for each other be labelled across the board as materialism and consumerism? Are goods merely 'matter' that is 'consumed' — to the neglect of the 'conservation' of the 'spirit'? The implicit invocation of a transcendent spirit is more than questionable today, but that does not dispense with the lively human spirited mind with its endless possibilities of enrichment rather than degeneration. Nothing prevents the hard-nosed, self-interested, 'capitalist' perspective from being *seen through* and thus complemented and intertwined with the possibility of catering to each other's desires and enhancing each other's lives by providing immaterial goods and services that contribute to living well, or that economic interchanges can be mutually satisfying and even mutually enriching. The Janus-faced possibilities of the simple socio-ontological structure of capitalist sociating interplay remain historically in Protean flux. Serving each other, even under the impetus of earning incomes of all kinds (cf. Chapter 6.8), need not be regarded as merely mercenary, but as a rewarding possibility of combining the necessity of earning a livelihood with the satisfaction of positively caring for others. 'Rewarding' thus gains a double meaning. Notwithstanding ineradicable predilections for underdog sob stories, not only can economic interplay be mutually beneficial whilst being based on self-interest, but it can also provide a framework for genuinely rewarding, satisfying possibilities of caring for others, despite the less satisfying and often downright disheartening exigencies of coping with the market competition in which such caring-for is necessarily estimated. Indeed, as a existential possibility held open by the socio-ontological existential structure of caring-for, the possibility of serving each other in economic life *must* have its place in one mode or the other.

As has been shown, positive, negative and indifferent modes of caring-for necessarily intermingle in economic interplay, if only because human being is shared being-in-the-world also in the sense of mutual economic interdependence. Seen as an historical socio-ontological existential possibility of humans living together, there is nothing to prevent thinking from casting something resembling caring capitalism as a possibility of shaping the future. In truth, even thinking this possibility in a socio-ontologically well-founded way is the recasting itself. Since caring-for as a socio-ontological existential always encompasses the full gamut of positive, negative and neutral modes, the casting of an historical possibility of a caring, katallactic capitalism by no means amounts to proposing the fanciful Utopia of an harmonious, idyllic way of economic life, but rather to opening up the vista, and thus the option, of a more affirmative stance toward the historical possibilities still lying dormant in the schema of reified estimating interchanges under capitalism. It may be that the pressures of competition go hand in hand with a tendency to better serve one's customers, not merely by offering the lowest prices, but by catering to customers' desires and even awakening and engendering desires by offering new possibilities of living that do not necessarily have to be booked under the heading of mere shoddy 'consumerism'. Such competition to invent new ways of caring-for (which, since human being is essentially openness to possibility, are endless in a good sense) could even turn out to be a virtuous circle that offsets the more grinding aspects of tough economic competition, which is also an integral part of market-mediated interplay. Much depends upon the socio-ontological clear-sightedness of mind, but also on power struggles to make manifest and assert alternatives to an all-too-grasping capitalism.

9.6 The set-up and the endless cycle of self-augmentation of reified value (Marx, Heidegger) – The historical possibility of the side-step into endless mutual caring-for

There remains yet another critique of capitalist market economy and the invisible hand to be considered that consists in claiming not so much that capitalist social relations are uncaring and alienating, but that the process of capitalist economy as a whole is a way of living, now globalized, that has gotten out of hand and is in its essence a senseless process that, besides ruthlessly exploiting natural resources, demeans human being itself and alienates it from the historical alternative of an authentic mode of human being.[167] Elements of such a critique can be unearthed in Marx's critique of capitalism as a process without a conscious social subject,[168] but they can also be found, with an entirely different

---

[167] This section is a thoroughly revised and altered update of Chapter 7 of my *Kapital und Technik: Marx und Heidegger* Röll, Dettelbach 2000. English version: 'Capital and Technology: Marx and Heidegger' in: *Left Curve* No. 24 May, 2000 Oakland, California USA. Revised and republished in 2015.
[168] Cf. Marx's investigation of the total, social circulation process of capital in *Das Kapital* Band II and the 'Value-form Analytic Reconstruction of *Capital*' (Michael Eldred, Marnie

focus, in Heidegger's questioning of modern technology against the foil of the alternative of humankind dwelling poetically on the Earth. We shall start with Marx.

9.6.1 The gainful game

According to the late Marx, who radicalizes the concept of alienation laid out in his early works, the essence of capital, its whatness, is the endless, limitless valorization of value, the endless deployment of reified value for self-augmentation through never-ending cycles of money-capital being advanced and returning bloated with a surplus. This is a sociating movement which sets itself up and asserts itself "behind the backs" of people, as Marx often puts it (hinter dem Rücken, e.g. Gr.:136, 156, MEW23:59). Valorization is the translation of German 'Verwertung', which can mean simply 'use', 'utilization', 'drawing the value or benefit from something', but in the context of Marx's thinking it signifies above all the 'use' of reified value to make more reified value through the circular movement of the advance and return of capital. Valorization is the movement characterizing what capital is, whereby the movement here cannot be thought in terms of human action, but as a destiny, an historical sending as a cast of being that prevails over everything, enticing with its possibilities. To think valorization as attributed to historical destiny goes against the grain of Marxian thinking, of course, for which something destinal would have to be treated as an ahistorical fetishism which could be dissolved as a figure of "bourgeois false consciousness" by deciphering value and valorization as os-tensibly a "social product just like language" (MEW23:88) that is attributable ultimately to human subjectivity.

Hanlon, Lucia Kleiber & Mike Roth) in *Critique of Competitive Freedom and the Bourgeois-Democratic State* 1984/2010 § 65. The total social circulation process of capital must be regarded as a social movement that is mediated by, i.e. which takes place within, the socio-ontological structure of the fully developed value-forms developed step by step in the value-form analysis. The primary value-forms in order of conceptual development are use-value/exchange-value, commodity, money, capital, surplus value, wages, profit of enterprise, interest, ground-rent, and the quadruple of these last four as revenue- or income-sources (cf. Chapter 6.8). This complex socio-ontological structure can be termed a "constellation" or "cast" of being in the Heideggerian sense. In my *Capital and Technology* 2015, I have termed this constellation "das Gewinnst", "das Gewinn-Spiel" or the "gainful game" in which human beings are caught up as players competing for income.

Nevertheless, just as we shall see, when discussing Heidegger's thinking on the set-up, that the essence of technology is nothing technical, the essence of capital is nothing economic; the valorization of value cannot be thought ultimately as an economic phenomenon but solely as an historical casting of human being and the beingness of beings within the 3D-temporal clearing for being itself. Marx's critique of political economy is not a theory of capitalist economy with the appropriate specialized concepts; rather, as critique, it is a questioning and a presentation of the socio-ontological essence of capital which — now expressed in Heidegger's language — is not merely a human machination. The analysis of the value-form, that has plagued and puzzled readers of the first chapter of *Das Kapital* ever since its first publication, is a socio-ontology of value, as the very word 'form' indicates, a term that goes back to Plato and Aristotle as the Latin translation of ἰδέα and μορφή, terms coined to formulate the beingness of beings, their 'looks' *as* beings.

If the valorization of value expresses the essence of capital, i.e. its whatness, then capital is gathered into the various modes of valorization. In this gathering, everything that *is* reveals itself to be valorizable, i.e. as capable of being drawn into a circuit of valorization, i.e. of self-augmentation of reified value. Value is neither money nor capital but the essence of valorizing, which lets all beings appear as valorizable. With the reification of value in the sociating thing, money, and the self-movement of this value-thing through transformations into commodities and production process in circuits of self-augmentation, the connection of reified value-movement with being valuable for human beings is lost, alienated. The movement is out of human hands and instead humans themselves are enticed and motivated to move by an eery power of endless augmentation of value. Whereas previously (Chapter 5.1) we have seen that the phenomenon of value is to be uncovered first of all in things and people being valuable for living, i.e. in enhancing a way of life, and exchange-value is to be understood as a derivative form of value that arises in the social practice of exchange, Marx traces an inversion of value in which it becomes a self-moving subject of its own augmentation and as such a reified social power (cf. Chapter 10.1). This is the Marxian concept of fetishism, which assumes various phenomenal 'looks', including commodity fetishism, money fetishism, capital fetishism, interest fetishism (cf. Chapter 6.8). The common essential trait of these fetishisms is that value has assumed a reified look remote from any human appreciation of value as value for living that initiates a movement within a topsy-turvy world of self-augmenting self-movement of reified value. "It is only the determinate social relation of humans themselves which here assumes for them the phantasmagoric form of a relation among things." (Es ist nur das bestimmte gesellschaftliche Verhältnis der Menschen selbst, welches hier für sie die phantasmagorische Form eines Verhältnisses von Dingen annimmt. MEW23:86)

Value expresses itself quantitatively as well as qualitatively in the potential or realized exchange against money, but, despite the real appearance of reification, it cannot be identified with the thing 'money', for this is already an inversion. Exchange-value comes about, in the first place, in the sociating movement of estimating interplay of commodity goods. Nevertheless, once this value reification and fetishism are established (preontologically in understanding, ontologically in philosophical thought and historically in the world), the essence of capital expresses itself above all in money and money-capital's augmenting self-movement. The capitalist world gathers itself in money; in the thing 'money', the world 'worlds' capitalistically, as soon as the movement of valorization, i.e. the augmenting deployment of all beings *as* values, achieves an absoluteness. The absoluteness consists in reified value no longer having any relation to how things and people's abilities are valuable for human living. In the capitalist world, all beings have a direct or indirect relation to money; the totality of beings passes like Alice through the value-mirror, money, into an inverted world of capital valorization. The critique of capitalist economy amounts to deciphering this inversion.

If reified value is the way the totality of beings opens up and shows itself in its being, and also is kept in perpetual movement as a metabolism of value-forms, the question arises as to what the gathered gathering of valorization should be called. With this naming, the essence of modern capitalist society would also be named. Instead of tracing back value to social labour in an abstractly universal form (as Marx does, thus suggesting that a socialized human subject could re-invert the reification of value into a conscious sociation of labour according to a total social plan that would do away with reified social relations), labour itself now also has to be thought in tracing it back into its groundless ground in the never-ending movement of valorization, since labouring humans, too, are merely used by this essencing that holds sway historically as a way in which the world shapes up and manifests itself in our age. We call the gathering of valorization that attains domination in the capitalist world in an essential sense the *gathering of the gainable* or, simply, the *gainful game* (*Gewinnst, Gewinn-Spiel*). The gainful game as the gathering of the gainable is here neither profit nor winnings nor a purely economic magnitude, nor the successful result of a human struggle or human labour, but the *open gathering of all the risky opportunities for gain through reified, estimating interplay*, which holds sway groundlessly as the essence of capitalism's truth. The gainful game offers itself to view *as* a world of apparent opportunity for human being whilst appropriating human being to itself. Within this gathering as a constellation of being, human beings are enticed to cast their selves into the endless, uncertain pursuit of gain as its unwitting agents.

According to Grimm: "Winnings (*Gewinn*) are associated with winning (attaining something through struggle, labour)." With this definition, only a human action would be addressed. The definition also takes account of the contingency — the fortune, chance, hap, luck — at play in the pursuit of winnings. The manifold of winning as the essence of capital's sociating movement signifies more originarily and more uncannily the gathering of all modes of possible gain in which humans, too, are drawn into and are (or can be) used by the circular self-movement of valorizing value. Only from a human perspective does the gathering of the gainable appear as a goal that is achieved by struggle and labour, viz. earning a livelihood. The gathering of the gainable as a constellation of being's disclosive truth in historical time, however, makes everything that *is* (exists) present itself *as* valorizable material. In this way, it entices and ensnares humans in grasping striving. Everything *is* only to the extent that gain can be had from it. Everything that does not allow itself to be drawn into the circuit of valorization, through which advanced capital can be augmented, *is* not (is worthless). Everything *is* only insofar as a capital sum can generate from it winnings as offspring. The gathering of the gainable challenges all beings — both whats and whose — to allow themselves to be drawn into the circuit of valorization and thus to contribute to the growth of capital. The gathering of the gainable thus sets all beings into motion by sucking everything a priori into the risk-taking calculus of valorization, of winning and losing.

The essence of capital (that calls for an historical, hermeneutic recasting) is thus not anything merely capitalist but rather the reified historical consummation of what Plato and Aristotle call πλεονεξία (cf. Chapter 4.1, 4.4, Chapter 6.1), the striving for more. It is neither the principal sum of money that is augmented, nor merely the ethos of a subject that is greedily or otherwise after monetary gain. It is neither money nor the lust for money, neither something objective nor subjective, but a calculating, 'gainful' mode of revealing the totality of beings in whose 3D-temporal clearing everything appears valuable as having the potential for winnings, so that humans are enticed by the gainful game as players and compelled to think in a thoroughly calculative, albeit risk-taking, manner that sets up everything in images and representations of potential for gain. *The gainful game is a constellation of being, an historical hermeneutic cast of being, that holds sway as a way in which the totality of beings discloses itself.* Since it is an historical sending, a cast of the beingness of beings, the essence of capital, cannot be tied down to any 'thing', even though everything that can be valorized ultimately has a relation to money, i.e. a price. Nor is capital the self-interested 'invention' of a social class, the 'bourgeoisie'. Marx speaks of value as a social relation, which suggests that it is constituted by sociated humans themselves, of course, without them knowing what they are doing, i.e. unconsciously. ("They don't know it, but they do it." Sie wissen es nicht, aber sie tun es. MEW23:88) The concept of the gainful game, by contrast, does not aim at anything made by human subjects and *a fortiori* not at anything merely social, but at an historical way of disclosure of beings as beings in their totality that has always already targeted possibilities for gain and which calls forth the corresponding human re-actions and social structures, i.e. the corresponding modes of being-together in estimating interplay. The sociating of human beings accomplished by the historical socio-ontological constellation of the gainful game does not posit merely capitalist, gainful social relations among (pre-existing) human beings, but constitutes human beings themselves *as* competitive players, i.e. human beings' very being is constituted by the gainful game.

In Marx, the value relation remains in the economic and social realm; it is the money-mediated social relation of commodities to each other which covers up and distorts the relations of working people to each other. Capital as a social relation mediated by things provides the economy with its ontological form and form of self-movement and also constitutes the basis upon which a superstructure is erected. The other social instances — the state, the legal forms, morality, culture, ideologies, philosophy, etc. — are supposed to be thought proceeding from this basis and in a correspondence to it. According to the (never completed) program of Historical Materialism announced by Marx, a social whole is to be thought in this way: the bourgeois social totality, that is, a structured totality of beings. Here in the present study, by contrast, an attempt is being made to take capital and the valorization of value back to something more originary, namely back to a constellation of disclosive truth in an historical age (our own) in which all beings appear *as* what and *as* who they are.

In the constellation of being called the gainful game, everything is disclosed in the light of being potentially good for bringing in winnings. All beings must have a potential use for gain, however indirect, otherwise they are worthless and do not 'register' in this historical cast of being. All beings appear refracted through the prism of reified value. Use for humans is not the criterion, but use for a circuit of valorization, i.e. ultimately, for the gainful game which turns endlessly within itself, throwing off winnings and gain for all the income-source owners. Even untouched nature can be and is valorized in the gainful game, not only through the exploitation of natural resources, but also, say, as a recreational value for valorizable humans, who in turn are employed by the circuit of valorization as labourers and clerks and managers. A valorization of untouched nature is even conceivable via the value-category of ground-rent whereby the Earth's capacity to absorb pollutants such as carbon dioxide is marketed and thus valorized.[169] That is, even the Earth in an untouched state, without being drawn into an exploitative capitalist production process of whatever kind, presents itself *as* valorizable for the gainful game.

Valorization is here no longer, as in its Marxian guise, only the augmentation of money-capital in a circuit, but is conceived more broadly as exploiting to achieve success, and as *winning and gaining in general,* and more especially as the earning of the four basic kinds of income by the competitive players (cf. Chapter 6.8). Such gaining and winning always has a more or less tenuous monetary aspect, i.e. it can be expressed directly or indirectly in costs, savings, profits, surpluses, asset-values, goodwill, brand-value, celebrity-value, prestige-value, political influence and suchlike. Insofar, all beings can be quantified and incorporated into calculations on the basis of which the success or failure can be measured in a universal measure of value: money. The estimating interplay among whos in esteeming each other (cf. Chapter 5.6) is thereby reified in being 'monetized' in some fashion. The gathering of opportunities for gain entices and ensnares humans in a competitive struggle for gain in the broadest sense, where they struggle with each other, and in this way, the gainful game valorizes and deploys human beings themselves. The value for valorization cannot be restricted directly to monetary value but indirectly covers everything that can be won from beings as gain and success. Even though certain kinds of success cannot be turned directly into cash, a connection with money-value is nevertheless maintained insofar as success appears valuable. Success can show itself simply in the form of a gain in social status and prestige, i.e. as gaining a successful stand in whoness, which can then, in turn, be deployed in the pursuit of monetary gain. The striving for gain in this case assumes the phenomenal form of vanity as a thirsting to have one's who-status estimated highly by others, and this thirsting, in turn, sprouts also a striving to have more of those "conveniencies of life" (Adam Smith) which one 'deserves'.

As sketched above, the value-form, i.e. the socio-ontological 'look' of value, analyzed by Marx can be traced back to a more originary valorization in an historical hermeneutic constellation in which the totality of beings opens up and beings show themselves a priori from the perspective of potential contribution

---

169 Cf. M. Eldred 'Questioning the Earth's Value — Including a proposal for a capitalist carbon sink industry' 2005/2006.

to gain. The reason for the non-originariness of the Marxian analyses of the value-form is that they mainly tease out the contradiction between private and social, i.e. particular and universal subjectivity with the aim of relating every-thing back to the historical possibility of a consciously sociated universal sub-ject that would underly the total economic process. Insofar, Marx's thinking is situated within the subjectivist metaphysics of modernity in the particular form of Feuerbachian anthropology in which all beings in their being are traced back to humankind and in particular to 'productions' and 'projections' of the labour-ing human as the underlying subject. The fetish character of the value-form includes that the products of human labour have assumed an autonomy vis-à-vis human subjectivity and therefore evade its control. Subjectivity as the meta-physical environment in which Marxian thinking abides is, however, not origi-nary, but is in turn grounded in a clearing of historical truth that decides *as* what the totality of beings reveals itself, without lying simply at the disposition of human actions as a 'production'. Rather, a recasting requires our receptivity for an hermeneutic message. Marx wants to bring renegade objectivity, which is thought under the rubric of fetishism, back into a non-reifiedly, authentically sociated subjectivity, in which collectivized human beings are consciously me-diated social subjects, but this by no means implies that the totality of beings would cease to reveal itself as a gathering of opportunities for gain or even that there would be a twist in such revelation.

If, therefore, to see more clearly, we must take leave of the modern meta-physics of human subjectivity in the form of labouring human being as what is, or ought to be, underlying, this leave-taking does not have implications solely for the value concept, which now can no longer be traced back *ultimately* to human labour as abstract value-substance. Accordingly, the value concept must now be thought without a pro-ductive relation to human labour as that which ultimately underlies, as the valuableness of beings themselves which, con-ceived in a more Hegelian way, is neither purely subjective nor purely objective, but rather subjective-objective.

The valorization of value cannot be traced back to a production, i.e. to a bringing-forth, by human labour in which surplus value is siphoned off, but as a bringing-about (Zeitigung) in a mutually estimating interplay of competitive struggle, i.e. a power play in which abilities of all kinds, including entrepre-neurial abilities, vie for tangible, monetary, value estimation and validation. The totality of beings opens itself to us human beings as valuable, estimable — and therefore worth desiring, as desirable — in the broadest of spectrums that includes also what is worth-less, value-less, but also whos as well as whats. The whos are not subjects and the whats are not objects. Valuableness comprises not only things' being useful (being-good-for...) in the broadest sense of being appreciated, estimated and valued, but also the value of being seen as somewho and reflected in a good light by others, being appreciated by others, in the first place, in having one's abilities estimated, validated and rewarded through reflection in the "value-mirror" (Wertspiegel, MEW23:72). Money is the highest embodiment or crystallization of this value-being as the reified, tangible mediator in the dimension of valuableness that provides also the universal reified measure for all that is valuable. Money itself as the representative of wealth in general is the universal key to what is valuable by means of exchange and so itself becomes desirable as the focused aim of the striving for gain. The open gathering of opportunities for gain entices human beings into a striving for gain that, from another perspective, is nothing other than the reified movement of money as capital which sets all beings into motion for the sake of gain, thus becoming a circular end in itself and insofar senseless.

9.6.2 The set-up

In order to assess the uncanny nature of the gainful movement set in train by fetishized sociation through reified value and put it into relation with the socio-ontology of exchange, interchange and interplayas well as the notion of the invisible hand, all of which have been developed in earlier chapters, it is helpful to draw on Heidegger's thinking on the set-up (Gestell) as the essence of modern technology. We read in a lecture given by Heidegger in Bremen in 1949:

> Das Bestellen stellt. Es fordert heraus. Das Bestellen geht jedoch, wenn wir es in seinem Wesen bedenken und nicht nach möglichen Wirkungen, keineswegs auf Beute und Gewinn, sondern immer auf Bestellbares. 'Immer', das sagt hier: im vorhinein, weil wesenhaft, das Bestellen wird nur deshalb von einem Herstellbaren zum folgenden fortgezogen, weil das Bestellen zum voraus alles Anwesende in die vollständige Bestellbarkeit hingerissen und dorthin gestellt hat, mag das Anwesende im Einzelfall schon besonders gestellt sein oder nicht. Diese alles überholende Gewalt des Bestellens zieht die gesonderten Akte des Bestellens nur noch hinter sich her. Die Gewalt des Bestellens läßt vermuten, daß, was hier 'Bestellen' genannt wird, kein bloßes *menschliches* Tun ist, wenngleich der Mensch zum Vollzug des Bestellens gehört.
>
> ('Das Ge-Stell' *GA79*:29f, emphasis in the original)

Setting-up sets up by order[170]. It challenges. If we consider it in its essence and not according to possible effects, however, ordered setting-up does not aim at booty and gain/winnings (Gewinn), but always at what can be ordered to set up. 'Always' means here: a priori, because essentially, ordered setting-up is only dragged forth from one being that can be pro-duced to the next because ordered setting-up has from the outset always already torn everything present into a total availability for being set up by order and sets it up in this total availability — no matter whether in an individual case the present being may be specifically set up or not. This violent force of ordered setting-up that surpasses everything only draws the specific acts of ordered setting-up in its wake. The violent force of ordered setting-up suggests that what is called 'ordered setting-up' here is no mere *human* act, even though humans belong to the execution of ordered setting-up. ('Das Ge-Stell' *GA*79:29f, emphasis in the original)

Despite all this "violent force of ordered setting-up" that "surpasses everything", the chain of ordered setting-up, according to Heidegger,

> läuft auf nichts hinaus; denn das Bestellen stellt nichts her, was außerhalb des Stellens ein Anwesen für sich haben könnte und dürfte. Das Be-stellte ist immer schon und immer nur daraufhin gestellt, ein Anderes als seine Folge in den Erfolg zu stellen. Die Kette des Bestellens läuft auf nichts hinaus; sie geht vielmehr nur in ihren Kreisgang hinein. Nur in ihm hat das Bestellbare seinen Bestand.
>
> ('Das Ge-Stell' *GA*79:28f)

comes to nothing, for ordered setting-up does not set up anything in presence that could have or could be allowed to have a presence for itself outside setting-up. What is ordered into the set-up is always already and always only set up in order to set up in success an other as its successor. The chain of ordered setting-up does not come to anything; rather, it only goes back into its circling. Only in this circling does what can be ordered into the set-up have its stand.

Heidegger thinks here ordered setting-up as the essence of nihilism, that comes to nothing, circling only in its "aim-lessness" (Ziel-losigkeit[171]) and senselessly drawing all beings into its incessant circular movement. Human beings themselves cannot be the subject of this constellation of being called the set-up because they, too, are drawn into "absolute servitude" (unbedingte Dienstschaft, XXV *V&A*:87), degraded to the status of mere "employee" (Angestellte) inserted into the set-up and employed as its "most important raw material" (XXVI

---

170 'Setting up by order' or 'ordered setting up' renders 'Bestellen' and aims at capturing the polysemy of ordering as commanding, putting into order and placing an order (for some commodity). Beings are ordered into position, they are put into the order of the set-up and they are ordered just like items in a mail order catalogue.

171 Martin Heidegger 'Überwindung der Metaphysik' XXI in *Vorträge und Aufsätze* Neske, Pfullingen 1985 S. 85, *V&A*:85.

V&A:91). The quintessential formula for Heidegger's questioning of the modern world is the "will to will", a formula forged from his long critical engagement with Nietzsche and the latter's formula of the "will to power". The ghostly absolute 'subject' of the ceaseless circling of the set-up is named as "the will to will", a will that wills only "the absolute and complete securing of itself" (Wille zum Willen [...] die unbedingte und vollständige Sicherung seiner selbst, *V&A*:84). The will to will is thus but a ghostly presence and an enticing siren in whose presence all beings are drawn into a circular movement of setting-up for the senseless sake of setting-up. The origin of this setting-up, according to Heidegger, is the productive know-how that has its beginnings in Greek τέχνη (ποιητική) and which provides the paradigm for all Western metaphysical thinking, including its theological thinking. The ancient Greeks already thought being as having-been-produced (Hergestelltsein), as having been brought forth into standing presence, and Heidegger sees modern technology, enabled by the exact sciences that arose in the seventeenth century, in its absolute domination as the historical culmination of this metaphysical destiny.

Because of his single-minded focus on production, Herstellung, which conforms with the asserted one-dimensional constellation of being he calls the Ge-Stell, Heidegger has to assert, as quoted above, "ordered setting-up in no way aims at booty and winnings, but always at what can be ordered to set up" ('Das Ge-Stell' *GA*79:29). But how is this assertion to be squared with Marx's insight into the essence of capital as the "restless movement of winning, gaining" (die rastlose Bewegung des Gewinnens, MEW23:168)? Heidegger remains totally blind to the phenomenon that all that is *produced* by the Gestell also has to *estimated* and *validated* in an interplay *as value* in order to *be*. This may seem at first sight to be an overly strong assertion.

Marx's thinking, in contrast to Heidegger's, focuses not only on the capitalist production process, but also on the exchange process, the interplay, through which the phenomenon of value first becomes visible in its *form*, its 'look', i.e. first comes about *as such. The concept of value is the foundation of Marx's socio-ontology of capitalism.* This concept of value remains ambiguous in Marx because, on the one hand, only through exchange does the form, the 'look' of value itself come about (and this *form* or look of value must be regarded as the *beingness of the exchangeable*), but on the other, value is said to have a measurable quantitative *substance* residing in the "productive expenditure of human brain, muscle, nerve, hand, etc." (produktive Verausgabung von menschlichem Hirn, Muskel, Nerv, Hand usw., MEW23:58) whose agglomeration *produces* value (and not just brings it about in the estimating interplay of exchange). Value in Marx's thinking is thus thought ambiguously both as coming about through the mirror interplay of exchange and also, true to the age-old paradigm of productionist metaphysics, as being produced by labour expended. We have criticized this latter conception of labour-value, which forms the basis of the famous labour theory of value, in Chapter 6.3. We have also seen (Chapter 8.2) that this conception enables Marx to construct a Cartesian, 'law-like' type of theory of capitalist economy because, if labour is the substance of value, capital-value can be continually augmented through the extraction and reification of this substance by having labourers labour under the command of capital. Value is accordingly pro-duced, brought forth through the production process, and the exchange of produced commodities on the market is then only the realization of already produced, substantial value, including a component part of surplus value, in money.

Against Heidegger's single-minded focus on production and the totalized, "pre-calculable" (vorausberechenbar, 'Die Frage nach der Technik' in *Vorträge und Aufsätze* S. 25) bringing-forth and setting-up of all beings in the Gestell, and also against Marx's postulation of labour as a value-substance with a standing presence that can be calculably produced in a production process through extracting this substance from living labour power, it has been shown that value is not produced, but comes about (sich zeitigt) as the ongoing *outcome* of an estimating interplay on the markets in which what is offered is subjected to a competitive valuation in the mirror of money. The *form* of value, i.e. its look, is nothing other than this social process of estimation and validation. Value *is* only in being seen *as such* by human being which is itself involved in the mirror play of exchange. The markets as a whole are an ongoing interplay of estimation and validation, and thus coming-about as valuable of all the abilities of those involved in the competitive struggle to have their abilities and efforts recognized and rewarded in a social metabolism of estimation mediated by the sociating thing, money. Value can only be thought in its being as a *social* concept which means, it can only be thought *relatively*, i.e. as a relation of estimating interplay.

Moreover, because value is a relational, ongoing outcome of a value mirror play, it can also *circulate* as capital. Produced products and abilities and services offered directly or indirectly to society can only become and *be* values through the mirror of estimation in other goods and abilities similarly offered. Because Marx, at least in his dialectical value-form analysis, locates value in the exchange process, his determination of the essence of capital as a restless movement of self-augmentation of value is closer to the phenomena as they show themselves in the market-mediated striving for gain. The goal of competitive striving, money-income, is conceived by Marx as reified value, and the incessant striving for money-income holds the capitalist economy in its characteristic restless, augmentative movement which Marx ultimately thinks through in concrete, complex, conceptual detail in the (relatively neglected) Volume II of *Capital* on the Circulation Process of Capital. Heidegger's conception, by contrast, can only postulate a ghostly, god-like and therefore quasi-theological "will to will" that asserts itself in an endless bringing-forth and setting-up without being able to conceptualize how this postulated "will" as essence appears, i.e. is mediated with the phenomena of everyday life in which the mobilization of beings is apparent. The very *being* of what is pro-duced by the Gestell is *value*, and such value only comes about as an outcome, and not as a product, through the sociating interplay in which these beings are *estimated* and come to *belong as such* to sociated human being. This, too, is a possible rendering of Parmenides' famous Fragment 3: τὸ γὰρ αὐτό νοεῖν ἐστίν τε καὶ εἶναι "Being and human being belong together." Why? Because the estimating interplay of valuation presences in the 3D-temporal clearing *as* such to the human mind.

Marx's analysis of capitalism is also able to show precisely how the striving to increase productivity through the application of all sorts of technology — the power of bringing-forth — meshes with the essence of capitalism which he formulates as the valorization of value. The connecting link is what he conceptualizes as "relative surplus value production" in Part 4 of the first volume of *Das Kapital*. Even when the value-substance of labour-content is purged from the value concept as untenable, the striving to augment value considered in its money-form, i.e. in its 'money-beingness', can nonetheless still be enhanced by producing more productively because, other things being equal, greater productivity in comparison to lower productivity is invariably 'honoured', estimated and valued by the market in the ongoing competition with a greater monetary reward. All that is important here is the comparative or marginal or differential perspective: greater productivity, whether it be more quantity or better quality, gives an edge over competitors. In other language, the concept of relative surplus value production says that the employment of technology is a means of enhancing the chances of gain within that constellation of being called the gainful game.

Technology is and can be employed as such a means because money-capital has the social power of developing or acquiring such technology by employing people in research processes. The power of bringing-forth is thus endlessly furthered because it intermeshes with the endless pursuit of monetary gain which, in turn, must intermesh with products being estimated and validated in the market mirror play *in their being as valuable*. Since Heidegger's conception of the set-up entirely lacks socio-ontologically founded concepts of value and money, the phenomenon of the link, through the mediation of a socio-ontological concept, between the striving for gain and the striving to continually enhance productivity must remain in his thinking invisible and unfounded.

Both Heidegger and Marx, of course, diagnose the state of the world as being out of kilter. Heidegger focuses on "the mad race of technology" (das Rasende der Technik, FndT VA:39), whereas Marx damns not only class exploitation (which depends on the untenable labour theory of value), but also the uncontrollable, subjectless process of valorization of value (to be remedied — purportedly — historically through socialism and the construct of a totally socialized subject). For Heidegger, a major consequence of the unleashed technological way of thinking is the "devastation of the earth" (Verwüstung der Erde, 'Überwindung der Metaphysik' XXVIII *Vorträge und Aufsätze* S. 95).

> Aber die Erde bleibt im unscheinbaren Gesetz des Möglichen geborgen, das sie ist. Der Wille hat dem Möglichen das Unmögliche als Ziel aufgezwungen. Die Machenschaft, die diesen Zwang einrichtet und in der Herrschaft hält, entspringt dem Wesen der Technik, das Wort hier identisch gesetzt mit dem Begriff der sich vollendenden Metaphysik.
> ('Überwindung der Metaphysik' XXVIII *Vorträge und Aufsätze* S. 95)

> But the earth remains sheltered in the inconspicuous law of the possible which the Earth is. The will has forced on the possible the impossible as aim. The machination that sets up this compulsion and holds it in domination arises from the essence of technology, the word here being set identical to the concept of metaphysics in its self-consumption.

Heidegger's diagnosis depends entirely on how he thinks Western metaphysics onto-theologically. The primary thesis, first formulated in 1922, remains to the end "being means having-been-produced"[172]. In the late text, 'The Question Concerning Technology', we even read, "Even φύσις, the emergence from within itself, is a bringing-forth, is ποίησις" (Auch die φύσις, das von-sich-her Aufgehen, ist ein Her-vor-bringen, ist ποίησις. FndT VA:15) When Heidegger looks for that which could save the earth from devastation and the human essence from total absorption in calculative thinking and disclosure from being exhausted in "ordering setting-up" (Bestellen, FndT VA:38), he points therefore to something "related" because "any saving [power] must be of a higher, but at the same time related essence to that which is endangered" (alles Rettende höheren, aber zugleich verwandten Wesens sein muß wie das Gefährdete, FndT VA:38). This related something that could save is therefore, Heidegger proposes, itself a kind of ποίησις, namely "art" (Kunst, FndT VA:39). All of a sudden,

---

172 "Sein besagt Hergestelltsein" M. Heidegger, 'Phänomenologische Interpretationen zu Aristoteles (Anzeige der hermeneutischen Situation)' in *Dilthey-Jahrbuch* Volume 6 1989 MS:26.

Heidegger switches from his talk of τέχνη pure and simple, without qualification, to τέχνη ποίητική whose *poietische* character as art now becomes pertinent. But otherwise, he totally ignores τέχνη κτητική., the 'art' of acquiring, which involves exchange. With his concept of Gelassenheit or 'letting-be', Heidegger also sees the possibility of an alternative in dealing with the "mad race of technology" by stepping back from its imperious challenges. In both cases, however, he misses the possibility of the side-step into estimating interplay.

Gelassenheit could serve as a mild injunction to the siren calls of the manifold gathering of opportunities for gain that constitutes the constellation of being under capitalism and lead to a re-evaluation of what is valuable for dwelling on earth. Refusing to heed and follow without limit the enticements of the possibility of gain in favour of living well within appropriate mortal limits is an echo of Aristotle's distinction between economics and chrematistics, as discussed in Chapter 4.1. It is an exercise of human freedom to set a limit to the pursuit of gain and, ultimately, only the free individual can say 'Enough!' and draw that line beyond which it refuses to participate in the hard, competitive power play of striving for gain. Such a freedom, of course, is not possible for an individual living on the edge of destitution. But even this stepping-back from the gainful game leaves out of consideration that the gainful game itself can be seen through and seen *as* a mutual caring-for. Namely, we have already pointed to another possibility lying at the heart of metaphysics from its beginning, a possibility which Heidegger did not see. The fixation on ποίησις and production comes from the way δύναμις (power, potential) is thought ontologically by Aristotle as being the "governing starting-point for a change in something else" (ἀρχὴ μεταβολῆς ἐν ἄλλῳ *Met*. Theta 1, 1046a9f). In this formula for a key ontological structure, however, there is an ambiguity residing in the term μεταβολή, which can mean both 'change' and 'exchange' or 'interchange'. This ambiguity opened the way for us to think through in Chapter 5 a socio-ontology of exchange distinct from traditional productivist metaphysics. Μεταβολή is the *fulcrum* where the lever of rethinking can be placed to pivot productivist ontology into an other ontology of interchange that is, with a shift of perspective from what to who, at the same time an ontology of whoness: the other as a starting-point of its own freedom of movement. This alternative understanding of μεταβολή must be regarded as "related" in Heidegger's sense, and within this alternative understanding, exchange and interchange must be thought as a groundless, estimating mirror interplay of powers, in contrast to production, which is the exercise of a grounded power of knowing on a passive 'material' to bring forth a change in something else, namely, the 'material', which may even be a human being. Furthermore, as shall be investigated in Chapter 10, *social* power in general cannot be thought as a production but — as long as it is not the exercise of brute physical violence — only through a relational process of mirroring estimation and validation in which a superior power is recognized *as* superior (if only as potentially physical violent) by a free human being and thus submitted to.

What is saving in this pivoting side-step from productionist metaphysics, as indicated in Chapter 9.5, is the possibility of thinking the competitive interplay of a capitalist market economy also in its ambiguous, Janus-faced possibility as an interchange of caring-for based on mutual self-interest and even on mutual satisfaction. An intensification of caring for each other in the mutual exercise of abilities of all kinds that are estimated and appreciated *as* valuable in the ongoing metabolism of social interchange could represent an alternative to the "devastation of the earth" that concerns not only Heidegger. The Janus-faced possibility lying dormant in the ambiguity of human interchange must be seen as a complement to the possibility Heidegger sees in the set-up:

> Zwischen den epochalen Gestalten des Seins und der Verwandlung des Seins ins Ereignis steht das Ge-stell. Dieses ist gleichsam eine Zwischenstation, bietet einen doppelten Anblick, ist — so könnte man sagen — ein Januskopf. [173]

> Between the epochal Gestalten of being and the transformation of being into propriation stands the set-up. This is, so to speak, an intermediate station, offering a double sight, is — one could say — a Janus-head.

If the set-up (Ge-stell) as the gathering of all possibilities of bringing-forth and the gainful game (Gewinn-Spiel) as the gathering of opportunities for gain in gainful interplay are complementary constellations of a twofold way in which the world opens up for human being, which is invariably also a striving for what contributes to living well or better, including mutual esteem, estimation and validation, then the alternative to the restless pursuit of gain that resides in seeing social interchange as opportunities for caring-for, albeit under the impetus of mutual self-interest, must also be brought clearly to light as an historical possibility. Such a possibility of rethinking, of hermeneutic recasting, itself cannot be had without power struggle among those who genuinely dedicate themselves to thinking.

---

[173] M. Heidegger, Transcript of a seminar on 'Zeit und Sein' in *Zur Sache des Denkens* Niemeyer, Tübingen 1969 S. 56f.

9.7 State intervention in the economic interplay of civil society

The modern state, equipped as it is with a full panoply of powers financed by prodigious taxation, can intervene in the economy in all sorts of ways to divert the economic resources of a nation into endeavours whose aims are political. A political aim is an aim set by the polity whose constitution — assumed here to be democratic, on which more in Chapter 13 — provides for the state, led by the government, to legislate and devise policy in all areas of social life and action, including the economy, ostensibly for the sake of the well-being of society as a whole. This conscious, knowing, political positing of a conception of social well-being may well, and mostly does, cut across the grain of where an invisible hand would lead. A political aim which goes against economic rationale is, for example, to maintain a domestic coal-mining industry for the sake of having an independent national energy supply, even though the domestic coal-mining industry is less efficient, i.e. more expensive, than other energy resources available from abroad. National interest in self-sufficiency is then said to have priority over economic efficiency.

Another example of a political aim which goes against economic rationale, at least in the short term, is to subsidize renewable energy technologies or specifically tax coal-generated energy for the sake of diminishing the dangers of global warming. The subsidy in this case is intended to kick-start a new industry until it becomes technologically cost-efficient and stand on its own feet in the competitive, gainful, economic, interplay. The examples of state intervention in the economy are myriad and for myriad political reasons, some of which are based on a more or less genuine conception of national well-being and others which are based merely on the compromise outcome of a power struggle among the vested self-interests of segments of the population, and yet again others deriving from the power struggles among nation states (such as championing the national economy, or for military strategic reasons). In intervening in the economy, the state posits by will and its political power a shaping of economic activity that diverges from what it would be if left to the laissez-faire gainful striving of economic self-interests alone. Such intervention is made in the name of the good of society and especially in the name of that ubiquitous slogan, (redistributive) social justice (cf. Chapter 6.5).

State *intervention* in the economy must be distinguished from state *regulation* of markets for the general well-being, e.g. to ensure that those offering services (such as health services) on the market are actually qualified to provide them, or to ensure that companies present accurate accounts of their financial situation when floating publicly on the stock exchange, or to prevent price collusion among the member companies of oligopolies, etc. etc. State regulation has to do with the state setting up and overseeing the (formal, legal) rules of play under which the pursuit of economic self-interest can be played out in power interplay. It is an aspect of the rule of law in the name of (commutative, including reciprocal) justice in its guise as *fair rules of play* for the strivings of economic self-interests in a competitive game. We speak of state regulation providing for a 'level playing field' for all those competing on various markets for *possible* successful outcomes. Regulation does not posit or guarantee certain outcomes, but only sets the formal boundary conditions that are supposed to be fair and just and also protect members of society from abuse at the hands of some players. Good state regulation does not merely *hinder* the free movements of individuals competing in the interplay that is civil society, but rather *enables* it as *fair* interplay. Such regulation, if it is to facilitate rather than impede fair gainful interplay, should be 'light-touch' rather than bureaucratically heavy-handed.

As discussed in section 9.5 above, Adam Smith's notion of the invisible hand can be extended beyond entrepreneurial action to include also the other income-earning players or character masks in the gainful game, namely, the land-owner, the wage-earner and the financier (cf. also Chapter 6.8). These players, too, strive to maximize their incomes relative to what they give in return on the relevant markets and this leads to a certain distribution of economic resources under the managerial command of the entrepreneurial class. As has been shown, the market metabolism, whose inner spring is the individual striving to further self-interest in a mutually beneficial way, induces an efficient allocation of resources which will maximize overall wealth-creation measured in the dimension of monetary value (and also provide for a sharing of the annual value generation among the various classes of players within certain disciplining limits; cf. section 9.5). Adam Smith argues that state planning could not achieve the same degree of efficient resource allocation as the working of markets:

> What is the species of domestic industry which his [the entrepreneur's] capital can employ, and of which the produce is likely to be of the greatest value, every individual, it is evident, can, in his local situation, judge much better than any statesman or lawgiver can do for him. The statesman, who should attempt to direct private people in what manner they ought to employ their capitals, would not only load himself with a most unnecessary attention, but assume an authority which could safely be trusted, not only to no single person, but to no council or senate whatever, and which would nowhere be so dangerous in the hands of a man who had folly and presumption enough to fancy himself fit to exercise it. (p. 485)

Here Smith claims not only that knowing (or guessing), willed state-allocation of economic resources through various sorts of policies is inefficient, but furthermore that it is dangerous. The danger lies both in the presumption that a conscious plan could foreknowingly lay down the best allocation of resources and also in political economic decisions being made that further only the ends of politicians or other powerful and influential persons or interest groups who have the ear of government (lobbying), or satisfy clamouring desires of a part of the electorate for the sake of re-election. It is a question of "an authority which could safely be trusted", a recurring motif in all liberal thinking on the state. Against the concentration of power in the hands of political agents who enjoy the backing of the state's overwhelmingly superior power, Adam Smith, and all liberal thinking, urge a 'healthy' mistrust of political power of whatever kind and, in its stead, the kind of sociation provided by money-mediated markets which allow great individual degrees of freedom with better economic results. The sociating, estimating, gainful interplay of the economy is thus modified by the interplay of political powers in the state (cf. Chapter 12.1).

The value-creation of a society, which is measured in money, is itself the outcome of economic competition on the market-place and thus of an interplay of social powers that decides ultimately what economic effort is worth. It is not necessary for the aim of total social value-creation to be in view in advance; on the contrary, it is hidden and cannot be shown as the result of consciously planned social action, not because an economic process is too complex (ontically), but because (socio-ontologically) value-creation itself is 'simply' not the outcome of any kind of pro-duction (a μεταβολή in one sense of the word), but of myriad social interchanges (μεταβολαί in the other sense of the word) that are in principle (i.e. from the starting-point of a knowing ἀρχή) unpredictable, unforeseeable. The productionist kind of thinking that advocates concerted, willed, totally controlled social action may be appropriate for a military machine, but it suffocates the free metabolism of civil society.

Market interplay as a whole knows what is best for the whole without knowing, i.e. without the whole as such ever becoming transparently visible for a foreknowing insight. The knowledge of the optimization of economic resource allocation is available only retrospectively and indirectly by means of a kind of mathematical differential reasoning such as was inaugurated by Newton and Leibniz. The invisible hand provides an optimum solution to a practical differential function of individual strivings to do well in earning income without this optimum being foreseeable in advance. This mathematical differential reasoning is only possible because there is a reified entity called total social wealth at all which is quantifiable as the ongoing outcome of monetary market interchanges. The quantifiability of social wealth is only possible because there is such a thing as value measured in monetary terms, a 'natural product' of social interplay. The quantitative-qualitative dimension of reified value first enables and sociates definable, measurable economy, and only in the mirroring estimation of money is the result of individual strivings measured. This circumstance, in turn, seduces political economy to emulate mathematized physics' astounding success by likewise mathematizing to become the social science of economics. As discussed in Chapter 7, these efforts are socio-ontologically misguided.

Total social wealth and total social wealth creation are magnitudes possible only in the dimension of monetary value, and insofar Adam Smith's quantitative reasoning in favour of the invisible hand rests upon socio-ontological preconceptions, namely, that society itself is sociated via interplay among individual players who, of course, must also be free to play in the gainful power interplay. The dimension of reified value is what sociates modern society in the first place by sociating a priori the dissociated, private activities of individuals striving for monetary gain. By a priori here I mean that the aim of monetary gain through estimating interplay is already a sociating aim, albeit an abstractly sociating, quantified aim that is pre-ontologically already in view. The social formation is formed first of all through the value-form[174] 'looks' of market interchange, i.e. through the cash nexus. The value-forms as such, however, remain invisible socio-ontologically. Moreover, total social wealth and total social

---

174 Hans-Georg Backhaus has perseveringly pointed out the importance of the value-form and the concept of value for grasping the "sensuous-supersensuous" (Marx) essence of capitalist society. In a recent paper he comments on the question of social phenomena with reference to the economic sociologist, Carl Menger, "But in contrast to the economistic restrictedness of his discipline, he [Menger] recognized yet another, important problem. Like the young Marx, he saw that the 'social phenomena' religion, state, the 'manifestations of the markets, competition, money' are not the 'result of an agreed convention'. Similarly to Liebrucks and also Marx, he includes language in the series of social formations and conceives as a remarkable, 'perhaps the most remarkable problem of the social sciences' the question set in italics and bold-faced type: 'How can significant institutions serving the general well-being arise without a **common will** directed at their establishment?" Hans-Georg Backhaus 'Über den Doppelsinn der Begriffe politische Ökonomie und Kritik bei Marx und in der Frankfurter Schule' in *Wolfgang Harich zum Gedächtnis* Band II Stefan Dornuf and Reinhard Mitsch (eds.) Müller & Nerding, Munich 2000 p. 186f, my translation. This raises the question of the commonality of this purported common will, i.e. the question of *sociation* of will. Cf. also the valuable collection of Backhaus' papers in his *Dialektik der Wertform: Untersuchungen zur marxschen Ökonomiekritik* 1997, which includes his series of four papers 'Materialien zur Rekonstruktion der Marxschen Werttheorie' which, not yet published, in turn, were taken up in "reconstruction" efforts in Eldred 1984/2015.

wealth creation are each simple sums of individual, dissociated wealth and value-creation that have come about through the strivings of market interplay. The individual, dissociated striving to maximize income returns through reified sociation in a given period such as a year leads in the sum to a maximization of total social value creation by maximizing the individual marginal contributions. Any thwarting of this individual striving for whatever (qualitative, political) reason leads to a marginal diminution of the magnitude total annual social value creation.

But Adam Smith's reasoning of the invisible hand does not depend necessarily on the players in the economic interplay striving to *maximize* monetary gain through the exercise of their various powers. The *differential* nature of the reasoning in favour of the invisible hand says only that it is always advantageous to allow the economic players *themselves* to decide how best and to what extent and intensity they exercise their powers in striving for gain *compared to* the state *interfering* with them and *directing* them to act economically in a certain way, especially directing them negatively by placing obstacles in their way such as controlling prices or wages, or hindering investment. Not only does the state, through its apparatuses, not have any better insight into the state of play of the economic interplay (for it is in principle impossible to plan the outcome of interplay), but blunting the motivating incentive of individual gain through onerous interference can only spoil the value-performance of the interplay. One must therefore not be misled by an exclusively quantitative focus on the economic metabolism of civil society (even though money itself, as a unique kind of social quantitative measure, enables such a viewpoint), but must consider also the qualitative comparison between leaving the economic players to make their own gain-promising decisions and having the state dictate the terms of play themselves rather than restricting itself to ensuring the boundary conditions for fair play.

Liberal thinkers argue in favour of the blind 'wisdom' of market metabolism for distributing social economic resources, whereas opponents argue that markets lead to distortions averse to overall social well-being, and above all detrimental to (redistributive) social justice. Liberal thinkers, however, easily concede that monopolies, cartels, oligopolies, in particular, are themselves distortions of market mediation which require the oversight of state regulation. Proponents of reliance on markets as the medium of economic sociation, today called neo-liberals, are criticized for reducing 'everything' to monetary terms, for, it is said, how can overall social well-being be measured quantitatively by such a soulless thing as money? This raises the issue of money as a 'look' of reified value, and the striving to acquire it, as a medium of reified sociation versus politics (its institutions, deliberation, discourse, power struggles, etc.) as a medium of λόγος-facilitated sociation. Both media are media of social power (cf. Chapter 10.1): reified value through the estimating interplay of individual powers on the markets in countless interchanges, and politics through the power plays in the institutions of state that can work only by being invested with a superior power capable of overwhelming any individual or interest group in civil society. Both are sociating media and as powers they also have an interplay with each other that is visible already, say, in money's powerful influence in politics, a more than familiary phenomenon whose socio-ontology, however, still awaits explication.

9.8 Uncertainty of income-earning – The 'law' of social inertia and the tendency toward conservation of a way of life – Openness to the future vs. risk-aversion – The ensconcing of particular interests behind protectionist barriers

In the context of existential care, earning a living is one of the cares whose taking-care-of is subject to the vagaries of contractual exchange interplay on the market. Selling a self-produced good or service piecemeal on the market depends on fluctuating market conditions that vary from day to day. Even though the good (including service goods) may be reliably producible, its sale and thus how it is valued on the market are insecure, unpredictable variables. For some ways of earning a living which are exposed to the bounty or niggardliness of nature (e.g. fishing, agriculture), even the production of goods may be a cause for concern. Human being, whose existence includes essentially taking care of matters to lead a life, has an inherent tendency to secure its conditions of living, i.e. to lessen the cares of life and thus be se cura (L. lit. 'without care'). For those earning their living by hiring out their labour power, there is specifically the tendency to seek a secure job. The original meaning of job as a one-off task has become the term for a position of employment on a lasting basis that is conceived quasi as a thing that an employer 'gives' to an employee, thus inverting the employee's giving his or her labouring powers to the employer. Continuity of employment provides security in the sense of removing the care of having to confront the market interplay every day from scratch. An individual entering an employment contract is just as much concerned with being paid as well as possible for services rendering as with securing a long term contract with guarantees against being laid off. A secure job is a kind of shelter against the cares whipped up by the continually changing seas of the market-place, which is the site for the power interplay of all the economic players.

This is not mere (ontic) description, but illustrates rather an existential-ontological tendency of human existence to achieve a relative state of security, i.e. to relieve itself as much as possible of its cares. If human existence is in essence care (Sorge), this tendency implies a weighting toward removing negative cares that arise from the unreliability (cf. Chapter 7) of social power interplays of all kinds, thus being freed to care, in the positive sense, for those matters and those others that are closer to home and heart. Since specifically market exchange relations of all sorts, with their inherent, irremediable uncertainty, lie paradigmatically at the core sociating practices constituting society, there is necessarily a tendency for human existence to secure itself against this uncertainty in particular. Secure employment enables individual employees to plan, i.e. to cast their existences in the future and forecast what means will be available for their self-chosen casting. It also provides a space for an inherent tendency of human practices to become habituated, thus gaining an inertia of their own. Human existence, which consists on a quotidian plane of a multiplicity of practices, has an essential inherent tendency to inertia by virtue of the everyday practices and their overall structure and intermeshing becoming, or already having become habituated as usages. Individuals both understand and practise their existences in a frame that tends to relatively fixed habituation. An essential aspect of existential security, of being without care, is not having to care, bother or worry about changing one's understanding, practices and habits in order to get by in life. Existential security consists in part of having a constant and steady 'formula' for leading one's life and, in particular, for earning one's livelihood. This 'formula', which is a kind of habituated understanding and structure of practices, allows each individual to 'calculate' and reckon with its existence. Human existence likes a life which is secure, without cares, whilst plodding along straight ahead and persevering in a rut unless acted upon by and thus having to suffer the forces of momentous external circumstances. Newton's first axiom or law of motion (Axiomata, sive leges motus) for physical bodies can also be interpreted existentially in the social context: "Corpus omne perseverare in statu suo quiescendi vel movendi uniformiter in directum, nisi quatenus a viribus impressis cogitur statum illum mutare." (Every body perseveres in its state of rest or in moving uniformly straight ahead as long as it is not compelled to change by forces impressing upon it.) One could even say that the 'law of inertia of social life' is the true origin in social living itself of the physical law of inertia.

This could be called a *conservative* or *inertial* tendency of human existence to prudently conserve and secure its livelihood, to remain stalwartly within the usages of a given, reliable way of life, to resist change and stick to the path that one already knows. Prudence (φρόνησις) here consists in the insight into the insecure nature of practical human interplay, including especially that mediated via markets, along with precautionary action to counteract this insecurity. The conservative tendency of human existence makes it risk-averse. It tends to turn away from the risks inherent in shifting valuation by the market and to prudently build a hedge against the risks of economic life. Such hedges can take many different forms, such as savings accounts, insurance policies of diverse types, superannuation, investments, or dependency on a spouse, etc. The former kinds of hedges all employ reified value in its function as a store of value, and thus of social power, to counter insecurity.

Everything saleable on the market has a quantitative value put on it consisting in the amount of money, i.e. the price, to be had for it. This holds in particular for an individual's labour power which it hires out to earn a living. Everything that *is* (exists) in a social world shows itself also from the aspect of having a market value. Since what can be traded in today's world is virtually unlimited, everything that is, including even the most intangible of entities, has potential monetary value. Being worth something in monetary terms on some market or other is an essential aspect of social being, i.e. being-in-the-world-with-others, Mitwelt. The all-pervasiveness of tradability and monetary value in the social world has assumed global proportions today, but that things show themselves off in the social world *as* being worth something is a phenomenon familiar from ancient times whose socio-ontology has intensively occupied us in previous chapters. Reified value as medium of sociation is today ubiquitous. This means that the household management of human existence, its economy, is embedded in a totalized market economy and is thus dependent on the shifting sands of how the myriad markets put values on things.

Critics of laissez-faire or let-it-happen capitalism are not satisfied with Adam Smith's reasoning for the maximization of value-generation. Instead of value-maximization they want to posit other, qualitative objectives for total social economic activity, such as social security (an unconditional hedge against the insecurities of reified-value interplay guaranteed by the state) and preservation of the so-called 'quality of life', which override the 'one-dimensional' striving for monetary gain. They point, for instance, to the social dislocation caused when the economy is forced to structurally readjust under the impact of massive market forces. In this section we shall consider only the supposed imperatives of state interference in the economy for the sake of securing a people's way of life.[175] Value-generation itself, because it only comes about through the inter-play of countless individual forces on myriad markets, is a fickle thing that changes direction unpredictably, leading perhaps even to the obsolescence of entire industries. This reallocation of resources through market metabolism may indeed be efficient for maximizing monetary value-creation, they say, but it costs the price of social disruption and upheaval. People have to change their way of life. The settledness of a way of life with its customs and ingrained, but cherished habits (say, of a coal-mining community) is then put at the disposi-tion of anonymous market forces that seem arbitrary and brutal in their effects.

Much of the critique of the invisible hand comes from the quarter of the in-ertia of social life, i.e. from its tendency to persist without change in the course of its customs, habits, routines and ruts unless disturbed by intervening forces. As already noted, this is the social equivalent of Newton's first law of motion. The preservation of a given way of life in a specific locality or province, interpo-lated 'linearly' and 'endlessly' into the future, is posited as an end in itself, as an ideal of living well and comfortably, against the quantitative end of the striv-ing for monetary gain, thus furthering total social value-generation for the sake of raising material standards of living, and against the claimed 'injustice' of rough, disruptive market capitalism. A qualitative end is set against a quantita-tively measurable end (such as growth in gross domestic product). The satisfac-tion of living within the customs, usages and routines of a way of life is weighed up against the opportunity of 'ruthlessly' increasing the wealth-generation of a nation by obeying market forces, flexibly taking advantage of market opportuni-ties, or responding to competitive challenges from other national economies by maintaining and improving a competitive edge, both of which require change. A tendency to conservatism in an established, self-contained, social environment and set of customs counterweighs the incessant dynamism of capitalist markets not only with their opportunities for enhancing wealth whilst demanding a willingness to adapt one's way of living, but also with their compulsion to con-tinually adapt to continually changing competitive conditions of economic

---

175 Other state interference, say, for the sake of environmental protection, raises the question concerning how wisely and cleverly the state can steer the economic interplay in a certain, environmentally friendly direction, thus harnessing and staying aligned with the forces of individual incentive for monetary gain, including through the development of new technolo-gies, on the one hand, as opposed to the state simply prohibiting or inhibiting certain econom-ic practices deemed to be environmentally harmful, on the other. Φρόνησις in its guise as practically wise policy of the state or multi-state treaties is one way in which the Earth as per-haps the most precious 'boundary condition' for living well can be spared from exploitative ravages.

survival. The settledness and satisfaction of routine everyday living that poses no challenges to good living is counterposed to the demands of flexibility and adaptability on pain of going under in capitalist competition which today is a *global* interplay of powers.

The competitive state of play is continually changing, and this change is not simply for the sake of maximizing economic wealth generation under shifting circumstances, but rather, the market competition is a cybernetic feedback loop that responds sensitively to shifts in demand (value estimation) and available resources, i.e. supply as estimated in reified value. The markets aggregate countless individual economic movements on the part of all those engaged in economic interplay on both the demand and supply sides. They do this of themselves, without any conscious, intentional control by a superior social power. Such aggregation is the resultant, or rather multiple, multifaceted outcomes of power plays, of economic movements initiated by countless individuals pursuing their own particular interests, whether it be as income-earners or as consumers, thus engaging in interchanges with each other. The changes in these aggregate outcomes manifest themselves as economic changes that in turn force the adaptation of economic players. The ever-changing interplay between demand and supply, when it takes the form of opening new markets, translates phenomenally into new goods appearing on the markets, and these new goods must be understood ultimately as new ways in which the economic players exercise their abilities for each other's benefit, which leads to an enhancement of the quality of life, even though, in some cases such 'enhancement' is dubious or double-edged.

The question arises as to whether these enforced changes are benign or malign for social living. No matter how this question is answered, it can be seen that markets as the socio-ontologically simplest and most rudimentary form of social interchange bring individuals from diverse places, and even worldwide, willy-nilly into social interplay with one another. This social interplay of countless social forces emanates from individuals as sources of power and will, i.e. as individual, dynamic ἀρχαί, whose ongoing, dynamic outcome is an aggregate response to polyarchic social movement.

The inertial tendency of a way of living is therefore invariably manifested as a resistance to the web of market relations that enmesh and entangle a local or regional community in dynamic, global, social interchanges mediated by sociating value-things (commodities, money, money-capital, finance capital) that bring change. The conservative inertia of a local or provincial or even national way of living is thus an aversion to the dangers and risks of having to change that all social interchanges with others, no matter whether on a small or large scale, bring. It is not merely 'big multinationals' 'hungry for profit' that force change worldwide on people and their ways of life, but rather, these large capitalist corporations are only the entrepreneurial nodal points, themselves embedded in the web of economic social interchanges in which humanity is today enmeshed worldwide. One may lament that this is so, but one must also learn to see that it is the *socio-ontological* fluidity of social interplay with others itself (laid out in Chapter 5) that underlies the continual economic changes with which all are challenged to cope. All the defensiveness against changes induced by social interplay with the 'outside' is ultimately a kind of provincialism. And the obverse side is that all change also harbours the *challenging possibility* of the world opening up for understanding and practice in a more life-enhancing way. The question of social conservatism and inertia thus turns upon how open a community or society is to the open horizon of the future on which more or less historically momentous possibilities for human living appear.

Since the necessity and/or enjoyment of earning a living is embedded in a market economy, it is necessarily buffeted by the winds and storms occasionally whipped up by groundless, unfathomable and therefore unpredictable changes and upheavals in the markets. The market economy opens up, i.e. reveals itself, as a possibility of casting one's self both in the sense of offering the opportunity of gain, but also in the sense of exposing oneself to the risk of loss. Those enterprising spirits who set out on the seas of unfathomable, uncertain markets must be prepared to accept risk for the opportunity to also make a good profit. Enterprise as a basic existential possibility could be understood in this sense of a casting into the uncertainty of human interplay in the widest sense. Such an existential possibility demands flexibility and agility, that is, the willingness to adapt one's practices and the alertness to see the necessity of modifying or even completely changing one's 'formula' for personal gain in response to ever-changing katallactic seas.

The conservatism of a way of living makes itself felt also once the state has intervened in the economy for political reasons, that may even be well-justified in terms of overall social well-being, to protect certain markets by means of subsidies, import duties, restrictions and prohibitions, quotas, state monopolies, or the like. The market barriers erected by the state for whatever political reason (e.g. maintaining the nation's self-sufficiency in the production of some commodity or industry deemed to be in the national interest or for national security) afford a protective wall behind which some of the nation's wealth-producing resources are diverted by particular interests that there seek and enjoy an economic advantage and security. Economic resources are diverted from where they otherwise would be allocated without the protection of trade barriers. Once these barriers exist, a whole industry and an associated way of life can prosper artificially and become comfortably ensconced within a protected, 'greenhouse' economic and social environment.

The state's economic policy then becomes hostage to those (usually democratic voters; cf. Chapter 13) whose living depends crucially on the trade barriers, and any subsequent attempt on the part of the state, when circumstances and political priorities have in some way altered, to do away with or modify the trade barriers will be met with stiff resistance born of conservative self-interest. In any even vaguely democratic system of government, vested interests will lobby the state (i.e. the government of the day) to prevent any change whatsoever, and they will bemoan the threatened loss of a way of life. What may have once been a policy introduced genuinely in the national interest (at the cost of a less than optimally efficient allocation of the nation's economic resources measured in monetary terms) thus becomes a factor in protecting merely the self-interest of a particular social group under changed circumstances, which depends on the trade-protected industry, and a fetter for which society at large has to pay. The general well-being of society is then infected by particular self-interests, and the state, especially through its democratically elected politicians, becomes the agent for upholding these vested interests. The immovability of a way of living then translates into the political immovability in the state's trade-protection policy. This immovability is the (socio-ontological) viscosity of the medium of political power itself (and democratic political power in particular; cf. Chapter 13) that in turn is rooted in the tendency to inertia in ways of living. In contrast with the (socio-ontological) fluidity of the reified sociating medium of value that enables continual adjustments according to countless 'molecular' market movements which, as has been shown above, are only a particular, rudimentary manifestation of the essential socio-ontological fluidity of social interchanges as a whole, especially when they are the interchanges among free individuals in power interplays with each other.

It is this kind of protectionist anomaly which Adam Smith has in view when he uses the felicitous phrase "invisible hand" in referring to the beneficial effects of the profit incentive acting in free markets as opposed to trade protectionism initiated and upheld by the nation state. Today, however, the notion of the invisible hand is taken to mean, much more broadly, the open slather of market forces without any state intervention whatsoever. The terms 'liberalism' and 'neo-liberalism' are often used these days as derogatory appellations purportedly signalling 'profit before people', as if it were not people themselves who strove for monetary gain.

Adam Smith's use of the notion of the invisible hand, however, does not exclude the necessity that the state ensure that markets work in an orderly and above all, fair fashion. Nor does it simply reject a political 'visible hand' as anathema. As already noted, state regulation to prevent, say, the formation of monopolies, cartels or some other manipulation of the market, is absolutely necessary to ensure that the invisible hand has room to move. Other markets may get into an unsustainable, speculative fever driven by gainful prospects whose eventual collapse severely disrupts the entire economy due to the interdependence of all sectors mediated by finance capital whose gainful activities require stricter regulation. Furthermore, rules of play to protect, say, the populace's health are indispensable, and these may include restrictions on weekly working hours, child labour, etc. The notion of the invisible hand represents rather a caveat regarding the dangers of interfering with the largely beneficial market medium of sociation driven by the inner spring of the striving for monetary gain and replacing it with some sort of visible hand in the shape of conscious state policy that rests upon the interplay like a lead weight and iron hand. For it has to be asked: i) Is the visible hand of conscious policy posited by the state really in the best interests of society as a whole or is it instead, precisely because it is visible, open to political manipulation and horse-trading and to political-social inertia under the effects of social lobbies and even corruption by powerful individuals and corporations? ii) Can a consciously posited state economic policy match the efficiency in allocation of economic resources achieved by market cybernetics under the individual incentive of monetary gain in guiding privately dissociated economic activities which are associated only via the market-place? and iii) Is the diversion from the presumed outcome of the workings of the invisible hand for the sake of important universal, overarching political goals, which are thus given precedence, justifiable, purdent and necessary? There are therefore constant tensions between justifiable state interference and judicious state guidance of the economic interplay.

State policy on market intervention to direct the allocation of the economic resources of society is invariably justified in terms of the general good and, more often than not, in the name of social justice. For instance, the national defence is indisputably part of the general good, and the defence budget could in this context be regarded as an economic intervention for the general good, even though the concrete details of the defence budget and defence policy will always remain a contentious political issue, also favouring a particular sector, viz, the defence sector. The visible hand of state economic policy is supposed to rise above the merely particular interests of social groups that are self-interested in policy taking a certain direction. Such justification of state or government economic policy takes place and is fought out in the arena of political debate and dispute in which all sorts of viewpoints and arguments are brought forward, especially by associations representing sectoral interests (for, any state policy whatsoever, even that of the highest national interest, affects also particular interests one way or another). Whether these viewpoints and arguments are genuinely for the general well-being of society or are merely camouflage for vested self-interests is often unclear and is inevitably a contentious political issue.

Even assuming that the debates and conflicts over state economic intervention policy are fought out in the spirit of a genuine interest in social well-being as a whole, the political disputes and conflicts inevitably remain infected by particular economic interests. Every issue in social-political life has elements of both particular and universal interests. Universal interests concern das Allgemeine, τὸ καθόλου (literally, 'the on-the-whole, the toward-the-whole') that is above particular interests. Given the inevitable infection of the universal interest by particular interests, in particular, by the tendency of social groups to want to persevere in an established way of life, it can be beneficial for the social whole if the viscous sociating medium of political power is complemented and balanced by the more fluid, change-friendly invisible hand of the reified power of markets that not only *compels* individuals to change the way they live, but also *enables* them to do so, often for the better.

The infection of the universal interest of a society by particular interests is achieved above all through the specious notion of universal social justice in whose name a 'just' distribution of the goods of living is demanded (cf. Chapter 6.5). Vested interests become embedded in the social welfare state whose policy represents a concrete conception of internal social well-being. The outcomes of the competitive game of earning income through market interchanges are 'corrected' in the name of such social justice. The particularized strivings of all players in the gainful game to have more (πλεονεξία) that have room for play in the game of economic competitive katallaxy are now thwarted and diverted to the competitive *political* struggle over shaping state social policy so that the concretely realized conception of social justice, which putatively aims at caring for the populace, is in truth shaped by various particular social groupings of differing strengths, each striving to have more, or fighting at least not to have anything less than what it has already achieved. Mass egoism goes under the sheepskin of social solidarity.

9.9 The manifestation of the visible hand in the shape of bureaucracy

Once a policy of state economic intervention has been resolved on, it still has to be implemented by means of knowingly social, and therefore politically visible organs and institutional organs distinct from the un knowingly sociating, value-mediated market interchanges which sociate dissociated economic activities solely through the market-place. The imposition of import duties, for instance, represents a relatively simple economic intervention, because only a protective trade barrier is erected behind which a domestic industry can seek shelter. The only executive organ required is a customs bureaucracy to collect the duty on the relevant imported goods entering the country. If a more qualitative objective is posited for the state's policy of economic intervention, such as furthering certain kinds of energy sources deemed to be socially desirable, say, for the sake of protecting the environment, or supporting agricultural use and cultivation of the countryside or providing services deemed to be a universal right of all citizens independently of their financial means, then an entire, elaborate bureaucratic apparatus has to be conceived and set up to execute and administer the policy. What the economy achieves through the interplay of self-interests has to be implemented instead through executive organs of state carrying out, and above all enforcing, a political will.

Such an execution of will through bureaucratic organs can only be had at the price of multiple frictions, because in the place of market-mediated, individual strivings for economic gain driven by nothing other than each individual's estimation of its best earning opportunities must step a bureaucratically regulated process that ensures that the state's will is indeed being properly executed. The conduct of the economic players must be explicitly regulated by numerous regulations that have to be overseen and enforced. Individual economic players have to make applications on forms to the bureaucracy which then have to be processed through more or less lengthy and elaborate procedures. The bureaucracy's clients have to provide detailed relevant information about themselves which then has to be checked and evaluated. Their privacy as private citizens thus has to be breached to this extent, and the state encroaches on the private sphere. All this regulation must be performed in some way through the medium of the λόγος in its guise as 'paper-work' and 'red tape'. Such paper and tape represent sources of friction to social movement that may even strangulate it, and, finally, the entire bureaucratic process of execution and regulation represents a social cost because it requires resources of all kinds. State economic intervention that sets goals, purportedly for the general good, that differ from the direction in which the economy would head under its own estimating power interplay therefore needs to be carefully considered and weighed against its costs in resources and bureaucratic friction.

Whether and to what extent the 'visible hand' policy is cleverly conceived, and effectively and efficiently implemented in a given bureaucratic apparatus and whether and to what extent the bureaucratic procedures can be abused by clients who now engage in power play with the state are important questions. Even granted, against all likelihood, that the visible hand of government economic policy is adequately implemented by an efficiently conceived and functioning bureaucratic apparatus, this visible hand remains a social cost demanding political justification and furthermore, any subsequent change in government economic intervention policy is then exposed to multiple *sources of inertia* deriving from the state bureaucracy itself with its own vested interests, political institutions with their power struggles, the formation of public opinion, and especially the inertia of a given way of life in certain sections of society that has adapted to and ensconced itself comfortably behind a given state policy of economic intervention. Such multiple sources of inertia and 'perseverance of motion' (cf. Newton's first law of motion adduced in the preceding section) have to be contrasted with the oft-noted flexibility of markets which, under the guidance of the invisible hand of the income-earning motive, can (some would say: ruthlessly) compel changes in economic activity in short periods of time. Such market compulsion, as has been mentioned, is standardly criticized as causing social dislocation. (cf. section 9.8 above). Bureaucratic complacency and the leaden inertia with which state bureaucracy, in its viscous creep and impenetrable lianas of red tape, can and do weigh upon the dynamic interplay of civil society. These features speak to that side of human existing that tends to hang on to old ways simply because they are well-known, familiar and therefore present no challenges.

9.10 State intervention as a visible helping hand for the invisible hand – An asserted unconditional right to be cared for – Caring-for that "leaps in" vs. caring-for that "leaps ahead" (Heidegger)

A third possible variant for state intervention in the economy is situated 'midway' between the state intervention already adumbrated and unfettered market interplay. It consists in providing assistance in the transitions enforced, sometimes suddenly and drastically, by the markets mediating the economy's movement. Such economic policy could be called a visible helping hand for the invisible hand. Since the markets change unpredictably through the groundless interplay of sociating interchanges and sometimes with surprising rapidity, in some cases state economic intervention could be justified on a temporary, transitional basis to ease the pain of social adjustment whilst at the same time encouraging economic change rather than merely reinforcing 'second-nature' resistance to it. Such a transitionary visible hand is a political force to overcome social inertia and works in alignment with, rather than against, the direction in which the workings of the market economy are pushing at a given time. The dynamism of capitalist economies is then not simply negated, but conceded, and the social dislocation of people having to change their livelihoods is ameliorated. The sociating medium of political power thus seeks an alignment with economic life that is mediated by reified value and driven by self-interests partly in mutual co-operation and partly in competition with each other. A vision of the social good has to be cast that is compatible with the sometimes unpleasant rigours of capitalist market dynamism. Social inertia and movement in the customary movements of social life themselves have to be mediated with each other by a state policy of social transition.

The classic example of the visible hand of state intervention in the economy as a transitional corrective for the workings of the capitalist economy is that protective trade barriers are set up to give an infant domestic industry time to adapt to the rigours of competitive conditions on the world market. Another policy option is to pay subsidies to the domestic industry for a transitional period. Such economic policies are of course well-known, but the question here is how their deeper "speculative" (Hegel), socio-ontological meaning can be brought to light. The character of state economic intervention as transitional indicates a mediation between two extremes. On the one hand, there is the liberal conception of social living that is based on a conception of individual freedom of interplay and its associated economic self-reliance. The individual members of society have the freedom to find a niche in the capitalist markets and earn a living and are, at the same time, also responsible for looking after themselves and their own life-worlds. This is the much touted freedom of private property wedded with self-reliance. Such an individual strives for economic gain within the forms of freedom enabled by private property, i.e. more deeply by reified value as sociating medium, and may either prosper or fail. The world opens in this socio-ontological casting of individual freedom as a gathering of opportunities for gain through social interplay (cf. Chapter 6.8). The state has only the role of guaranteeing and preserving the proper, just forms of (especially contractual) social intercourse and interplay through law. The 'downside' to this liberal conception of social life is that the dynamic and ever-changing workings of the capitalist economy itself themselves produce 'failures', i.e. those who do not manage to gain a viable foothold in the economy.

This leads, on the other hand, to an opposed conception of social life according to which the individual member of society has a more or less unconditional right to be cared for by society as a whole insofar as the disruptions in social life brought about by the dynamics of capitalist market interplay also inevitably generate those who cannot earn a living. Self-reliance and independence are thus substituted by unconditional conceptions of social security and social solidarity as a counterweight and correction to the "indifference" of reified social relations (cf. section 9.1 above). The transitionary conception of state economic intervention as a helping visible hand to smooth out the dislocations of social life caused by the continually shifting sands of capitalist economic metabolism mediates between the liberal and solidaric conceptions of social life and is their Aufhebung or sublation.

The socio-ontological condition of possibility of a free individual at all is the sociation via the medium of reified value which appears on the surface as the market-mediated sociation of owners of private property (including labour power free to be hired out by labourers who enjoy the liberty of their own person). There is a social individual only where there is also a private sphere, i.e. a sphere of life into which the individual can withdraw and to which the rest of society and especially the state is deprived access. Such an 'access-depriving', private individual whose private sphere is protected from interference is only possible because the pecuniarily reified social interchanges of markets provide a form of sociation apart from regulating social life through explicit exercise of social power in the guises of political struggle and deliberation, positive state legislation, enforced religious-ethical prescription, etc. etc. Sociation is performed primarily through reciprocating, estimating interplay free individuals governing their own life-movements rather than through submission of free, individual self-movement to a superior authority and power. Sociation through the medium of reified value goeshand in hand with the abstract rights of personhood which guarantee the individual's freedom to be indifferent to others' individual 'truths' (Chapter 10.6) on how one 'should' live, whilst at the same time making it more difficult for the individual to become its self, lacking as it does the orientation provided by traditionally prescribed ethical usages when shaping its own individual existence.

In the context of an individualized society, which is enabled in the first place the sociating medium of reified value, the opposite conception of *social solidarity* arises as a palliative for the essential indifference, isolation, competition and ups and downs of fortune in market-mediated competitive life. Not only the risks of fluid, social interplay in a reified medium are to be shared through social insurance schemes, but the cold anonymity and isolation of reified social interaction are to be ameliorated by a social disposition akin to, and historically derived from Christian ἀγάπη (brotherly love and charity). To be an individual self shaping one's own life-world in the midst of an uncaring society is regarded as a fate too harsh, and even 'inhumane', so that solace and shelter are yearned for and sought illusorily in a notion of social care and solidarity that is to become institutionalized in the state's bureaucracy, especially in its social-work apparatuses to care for the weak.

Accordingly, a genuine conception of the good of living well is said only to be realized when the individual member of society has a claim to be supported if it loses its footing in the money-mediated competition, which mostly means that it becomes unemployed. The state is then called on to 'leap in' to help those individuals who have fallen by the wayside in the economic competition. The individual is said to have a rightful, just claim to being cared for temporarily by society, regardless of its ability (δύναμις) to earn its own livelihood. One speaks of social security as a safety net for those who have fallen through the web of market-mediated interchanges in the effort to earn a living. A society of individuals striving to get by without the safety net of social security is said to be a society set up as a ruthless Darwinian struggle for the survival of the fittest and therefore unworthy of basic human dignity. As has been shown in Chapter 6.4, however, to provide a social safety net for those temporarily unable to help themselves need not stand in contradiction to individual freedom; the social safety net becomes problematic when it becomes a permanent way of life for welfare-benefit recipients. Furthermore, the polemicism of a so-called 'ruthless Darwinian struggle for the survival of the fittest' calumniates freedom overlooks the dilemma of the inherent tension between individual freedom and subjugation to social power, i.e. being cared for by society — today: a social welfare state — is itself a *social power play* to which the state's welfare clients must submit (cf. Chapter 10.1 and 10.2). Once more as a reminder: preceding chapters have shown through a socio-ontology of freedom that it resides first of all in individual powers and abilities as origins of self-determined movement in shaping one's own life and thus casting one's self. Such individual powers and abilities are energized, i.e. put to work, in mutually estimating power interplay with others through which the individual gains his or her own self-esteem.

There is a further, related dilemma hiding in the conception of an individual being unconditionally cared for by society because the creation of social wealth (a universal aim) is only spurred on by the incentive of individual striving for gain (a particular aim), which in turn depends upon the self-reliance of individuals exercising their powers who will to shape their own lives in a social sphere of privacy that is protected against outside interference. Even if employment is regarded as being beholden to an irksome relations of dependency, these relations i) are at least based on mutually estimating interchange, ii) are not absolutely without alternative among the possibilities opened by market interchanges, iii) are themselves malleable through (collective) power plays, and iv) enable through monetary reward the free shaping of a private life-world. If the spur to earn a living through exercising one's own abilities is blunted, self-reliance recedes and the individual becomes dependent on being looked after and thus dominated by another power, which in itself attacks self-esteem, i.e. the estimation of one' own powers and abilities. The individual's existence is then no longer accepted as its very own, free existence which it itself has to lead and shape together with those dear to it, but rather, the individual passes on responsibility for its self to another, in this case, the state in its function of providing social security. Social security support as an existence without care (se-cura) is an enticing but dangerous, potentially ruinous situation for human being since human freedom is only grasped in its possibility through individuals accepting the challenge of casting their own, individual shared life-worlds. Social security as *transitional assistance* to help an individual again find its feet arises from the insight that an individual's self-reliance should not be undermined or even extinguished by receiving social welfare benefits but, on the contrary, it should only be helped to get back on its own self-reliant feet by finding a niche in which to earn its own livelihood.

Such a conception of social security as transitional, temporary assistance can be taken back to two different basic positive existential possibilities of caring for others (Fürsorge) which, according to Heidegger in *Being and Time*, stake out the extremes of the spectrum of caring for others.

> Die Fürsorge hat hinsichtlich ihrer positiven Modi zwei extreme Möglichkeiten. Sie kann dem Anderen die 'Sorge' gleichsam abnehmen und im Besorgen sich an seine Stelle setzen, für ihn *einspringen*. Diese Fürsorge übernimmt das, was zu besorgen ist, für den Anderen. Dieser wird dabei aus seiner Stelle geworfen, er tritt zurück, um nachträglich das Besorgte als fertig Verfügbares zu übernehmen, bzw. sich ganz davon zu entlasten. In solcher Fürsorge kann der Andere zum Abhängigen und Beherrschten werden... Ihr gegenüber besteht die Möglichkeit einer Fürsorge, die für den Anderen nicht so sehr einspringt, als daß sie ihm in seinem existenziellen Seinkönnen *vorausspringt*, nicht um ihm die 'Sorge' abzunehmen, sondern erst eigentlich als solche zurückzugeben. Diese Fürsorge [...] verhilft dem Anderen dazu, *in* seiner Sorge sich durchsichtig und *für* sie *frei* zu werden.
>
> Martin Heidegger
> *Sein und Zeit* 1927/1984 § 26 S. 122

> Caring-for has two extreme possibilities with regard to its positive modes. It can, so to speak, lighten the other of his 'cares' and put itself in the other's position in taking care of things, *leap in* for the other. This caring-for takes over what is to be taken care of for the other. The other is thrown out of his position; he steps back in order to subsequently take over what has been taken care of as something completed and available, or to completely disburden himself from what has to be taken care of. In such caring-for, the other can become dependent and dominated... Opposed to this, there is the possibility of a caring-for that does not so much leap in for the other, but rather *leaps ahead* of him in his existential ability-to-be, not to lighten him of his 'cares' but to properly give them back to him for the first time. This caring-for [...] helps the other to become transparent to himself *in* his care and to become *free for* it.

This is said in *Being and Time* with regard to the fundamental existential possibilities of human being (Dasein) in its relations with other human beings (Mitdasein). Care is the ontological structure of human being as it exists in the world of everyday life, taking care of its affairs. This caring involves both taking care of things and caring for others, both dimensions being conceived in the broadest possible sense as encompassing also the negative, privative and deficient modes of caring for one's own existence in sharing a world with others. For instance, caring-for is "at first and for the most part" in daily life in the mode of indifference to the other, i.e. of *not* caring less about the other. Note that caring-for that leaps ahead gives back to the individual its own care for its self and thus its *freedom*. Our purpose here, however, is not existential analysis of human being, but existential-ontological investigation of social being on the level of society and state in a Western modern society based on a capitalist economy. In such a society one is faced with the dilemma that the dynamics of the capitalist economy itself generates through its uncertainty failures. For the sake of simplicity, let us assume that these failures are the unemployed who, for whatever reason, cannot find gainful employment in the economy.

As members of social welfare society (which is first and foremost a way of *conceiving* sociated existence as such-and-such, i.e. an hermeneutic 'mind-set', and not a real, 'thingly' set-up of state apparatuses actually doling out benefits), the unemployed not only have the aim of earning a living but also even an ostensible guaranteed right to have enough to live on, i.e. a so-called 'living-wage'. The *conception* of well-being in such a society includes that not only a part of society should win in the competitive struggle for income, but that some acceptable standard of material well-being of the entire population must be a component part of 'living well' for society as a whole. Such an all-encompassing, all-inclusive conception of social well-being is the basis in understanding for the social security benefits provided by the welfare state. Here we are considering only unemployment benefits for those potential members of the workforce who are out of work. These unemployment benefits are a way of caring-for the other which the welfare state takes upon itself through a redistribution of created wealth. This caring-for can be either a caring-for that leaps in for the other or a caring-for that leaps ahead of the other. On this distinction hangs the circumstance whether the one helped is made dependent and is dominated and thus becomes unfree, or whether the social welfare recipients are helped to become free for their own individual existence in taking care of it on their own responsibility through the exertion of their own powers.

9.11 The paternalistic 'all-caring' state – Taxation and its tendentially asphyxiating hold on civil society

Caring about and caring for one's own, self-cast existence, as we have already considered earlier, does not mean that the individual human being is cast as a selfish egoist. Caring about (Sorge) one's own existence means caring about one's own life-world both in taking care of (Besorgen) things and in caring for (Fürsorge) those with whom one lives.[176] Moreover, caring about one's own existence necessarily requires intermeshing with others on mutually agreeable terms, whether it be for economic benefit or estimating interchange in some other sense. The underlying understanding of human being is that each individual human being as a freely deciding point of origin governing its own self-movement is free in taking care of and shaping its own existence within its given possibilities, and that, by giving up this care and responsibility to another, whether it be another human being or a state institution, the individual thereby becomes unfree, dependent and dominated, perhaps only to some degree and gradually, in a scarcely noticeable encroachment on the individual's self-standing and hence self-esteem. Being-cared-for, especially when it becomes (regarded as) a human right, as in modern welfare states, is a way in which individuals will their own unfreedom and domination by the state, their own subjection to the state, which thereby becomes a paternalistic state that 'knows better'. Such a putataive human right is bereft of anchoring in sociating existence.

---

176 Cf. Chapter 9.1 where Adam Smith has already been cited; "not only we ourselves, but all the objects of our kindest affections, our children, our parents, our relations, our friends, our benefactors, all those whom we naturally love and revere the most" (Adam Smith *The Theory of Moral Sentiments* 1759/2000.).

To the extent that a social welfare recipient becomes unfree and dependent, the welfare state that administrates this dependence becomes more powerful. Even and especially those citizens who are *not* welfare benefit recipients become dependent on and dominated by the welfare state through their *expectations* of being secured. The institutions of the welfare state themselves, as apparatuses ostensibly for the good of the whole of society, become consolidated and entrenched in their existence with their own inertia and momentum, and they achieve this by being underpinned by a 'socially minded' way of pre-ontological thinking. Their social welfare clients serve as their raison d'être, and they unfold their power over the lives of these clients, who lose not only their independence but even the desire to be independent and self-reliant. Instead a symbiosis is nurtured and unfolds between social welfare institution and client in which, on the one side, the client learns to manoeuvre within its dependent power relationship and to gain from it and, on the other side, the welfare state apparatuses consolidate their 'indispensability'. The welfare client by no means gives up his or her striving for gain, the appetite to get more thus rendering even life within the social welfare apparatuses a derivative kind of gainful game.

In the course of time, the social welfare state thus has the tendency to perpetuate its own existence and to thoroughly undermine and destroy the self-reliance and independence of sections of the population. This is the look assumed by the existential of caring-for that leaps in, now transposed to the context of the modern social welfare state. The welfare-benefit recipient (and, through its expectations and orientation in thinking, also the population at large) loses its independence, its stand within itself, and its self-standing, or lack thereof, is mirrored not only in its self-image, i.e. its ἰδέα of itself, but also in its social interchanges with others, all of which are kinds of estimation. The social welfare state, in unfolding its power over its clientele, undermines the self-esteem of those whose welfare it 'manages'. It provides social security and renders the individual social welfare recipient se-cura, 'without care'. But since human being itself — as the free origin of its own life-movements — is structured ontologically as caring for one's self in the 3D-time-clearing for as long as it is exposed to it, to be disburdened of one's cares, especially the care of having to earn a livelihood, by another agent is to be robbed of one's *own* existence and standing in it. The social welfare state that guarantees social security as a citizen's 'right' is therefore rightly called a *paternalistic* or a 'nanny' state that regulates and interferes with its citizens' lives in reducing them to the status of dependent children, and that without the citizens even noticing their loss of independence. On the contrary, the citizens clamour to be cared for even better and better as an unconditional right.

This state paternalism is reflected in the conception of law itself. The very conceptions of Sozialpolitik (social policy) and Sozialgesetz (social welfare law) are products of 19th century German legal positivism, that is antithetical to a conception of inviolable individual liberty and self-reliance (Selbstverantwortung):

> Für eine individualistische Rechtsordnung ist das öffentliche Recht, ist der Staat nur der schmale schützende Rahmen, der sich um das Privatrecht und das Privateigentum dreht, für eine soziale Rechtsordnung ist umgekehrt das Privatrecht nur ein vorläufig ausgesparter und sich immer verkleinernder Spielraum für die Privatinitiative innerhalb des all umfassenden öffentlichen Rechts.[177]

> For an individualistic legal order, public law, the state is only the small protective framework that revolves around private law and private property. Conversely, for a social legal order, private law is only a provisionally spared and continually diminishing room for play for private initiative within an all-comprehensive public law.

By contrast, state unemployment benefits to the unemployed conceived as strictly transitional assistance toward finding one's foothold again in the economic interplay can be booked under the heading of a caring-for that leaps ahead and gives back to the individual its responsibility in caring for its own existence and leading its own life. The transitional, temporary nature of this assistance must be apparent in clearing the way for the unemployed individual to see for itself a viable way of getting back on its own feet, especially by developing its own potentials, also *for the benefit of the greater society*. The unemployed individual must be motivated to re-establish its independence, to bolster its self-standing and thus self-esteem, and not develop the comfortable expectation of being cared for by the welfare state. This way of understanding its world makes the individual defensive of its welfare-state-derived benefits, and the moves of other, independent players in the economic competition seem all the more threatening, so that it calls for even more protection (say, against 'foreigners') from its all-protecting state whose subject it is.

When society is conceived first and foremost *as* a whole that must provide securely for its members, including all the social welfare benefits that are regarded as making up a socially acceptable way of secure living such as (social) housing, health care and old-age pensions, economic activity to earn of living in market rivalry is regarded as some kind of necessary 'asocial' evil to acquire the means for financing 'genuinely social' living away from the workplace. The

---

177 Gustav Radbruch 'Vom individualistischen Recht zum sozialen Recht' (1930) reprinted in *Der Mensch im Recht* Göttingen 1957 p. 40, cited in Hayek *LLL*1:179f.

expectation of being cared for by the welfare state becomes an anchor-point of orientation for living, a purported 'achievement of social progress', thus affirming a dependency on the social welfare state, which, in turn, not only assumes a paternalistic stance toward its clients, but also has to finance its tasks of providing social welfare through *taxation* (including social security contributions of all kinds). The more that is expected from the state, the more it becomes a matter of course that the state has the 'right' to tax and otherwise siphon off and hijack more and more wealth from civil society for the sake of financing its welfare and other activities for the 'universal good', otherwise known today as so-called social solidarity.

The gainful outcomes of competitive economic interplay are thus subject to greater or lesser revision by how the state intervenes in the economic game through imposing taxation policy (above all in the name of social, 'redistributive' justice; cf. Chapter 6.5). Paying one's taxes becomes a social duty for the sake of contributing to universal social welfare. With the growth of dependency on social welfare benefits of all kinds, and under the constant pressure of all wanting to have more, the greater the burden of taxation and the intricacy of taxation legislation and regulation, along with the inevitably ever-increasing incursions into the private sphere, become. The tendency of the state to augment its power, that goes hand in hand with the tendency of society's members to increase their dependency and demands upon the welfare state, assumes the particular form of a tendency of the state tightening its stranglehold on the economic interplay of civil society through the tax burden and the intricacy of a taxation system designed to catch every possible tax dollar.

Every dollar earned in economic activity is subjected to state inspection and control, because the state has a 'taxation stake' in each and every dollar earned, and so has to constantly increase its surveillance of economic activity to prevent personal income from 'disappearing' tax-free. Every new technological possibility of financial surveillance of its citizens inevitably, sooner or later, becomes a means of state control over civil society formulated in positive law. The tendency of political power toward totalitarianism (that must be countered by counter-powers — hence the liberal conception of a 'division of powers' and democratic scrutiny of all taxation; cf. Chapter 12) assumes under the particular constellation of sociation mediated by reified value in the interplay of private property owners, the form of an evermore asphyxiating stranglehold of taxation legislation, regulation and bureaucracy that successively hollows out the private property rights of citizens, thus undermining their individual freedom and their ability to care for themselves through their own efforts. It turns out that what is my property is, strictly speaking, not my own, but the state's. In its thirst for taxes and social security levies, under the impetus of the populace's unquench-able thirst to have ever more, the modern welfare state bloats into a kind of Frankenstein that demands its ever greater taxation tribute. The state itself thus becomes a kind of player in the gainful game, enjoying an unfair monopoly advantage of being able to legislate its interventions in civil society, purportedly justified by its role as agent for the social good. With its voracious appetite for taxation revenues, the state is perhaps the most avaricious player. The populace at large, in turn, acquiesces so long its expectations of being cared for are more or less fulfilled. Otherwise, a so-called crisis of the welfare state develops.

The diametrically opposite understanding of state welfare benefits is that they are not justified, because the individual must remain unconditionally re-sponsible for itself, no matter what its social predicament is. Any state welfare is then regarded as unjustified and as undermining the individual's self-reliance in fending for itself within the context of its own life-world, which includes its family and other loved and close ones. The individual is conceived as uncondi-tionally responsible for its own success or failure, thus overlooking that the individual itself is socio-ontologically itself an historical form of sociation. Situ-ated between these opposed ways of understanding state welfare benefits there is a whole range of possible amalgams with the mean being that the state must only assist in emergency situations and on a temporary, transitional basis, and that, for the sake of its own freedom, the individual must remain responsible for regaining its own independent stand in social life, which is also of benefit to the larger society, which profits from individuals exerting their own powers.

Insofar as the visible helping hand of state assistance is conceived as a temporary corrective to the workings of the invisible hand through the markets, an understanding of caring-for that leaps ahead has the upper hand, giving back to those individuals suffering distress their independence (Ger.: Selbstän-digkeit = lit. self-standingness). Such a pre-ontological conception corresponds knowingly or unknowingly to the deeper-lying socio-ontological conception of freedom. Caring-for that leaps ahead can consist of training, retraining and re-educating the social welfare client, thus developing his or her own potentials, with the aim of improving his or her prospects of finding an appropriate job in which his or her *own* abilities are estimated and valued (monetarily). Education is indeed the paradigm for such leaping-ahead because all learning is necessari-ly self-learning (and not 'knowledge-transfer' from one to another), an activa-tion of one's own powers. The teacher only has the role of arousing and encour-aging and guiding the pupil's or student's self-learning in which they have to work through and appropriate what is to be learned for *themselves* by *exerting* themselves. A welfare state can assist its clients by retraining them in such a

way that they are able to again find a niche in the interplay of capitalist economy. It may also prime a start in economic life by providing grants to start an
enterprise or a career. Such a state policy can and must be complemented by
state economic policy that aims to structurally shape and further the kinds of
industry with which the nation's economy will do well in the competitive economic power play both domestically and internationally. Such shaping does not
have to amount to overbearing state intervention in the economy, but can be
more a 'helping hand' that propels the economy in a propitious direction.

In contrast to state welfare, the estimating interplay on the markets, including especially the hire relationship for labour power are based on mutual gain.
The contractual parties meet each other with their respective interests and negotiate some sort of contract acceptable to both. There is a mutually beneficial
interchange. In the case of an employment contract, the inclusion of company
welfare benefits for employees does not indicate a caring-for on the part of the
employing company, but is rather a matter of negotiation in which the prospective employee is estimated and esteemed in relation to his or her potential contribution to the enterprise's own striving for profit. Paradoxically, both sides are
caring for themselves in caring for the other; the estimating power play is mutually beneficial.

When employees are laid off for economic reasons, this is done from a position of neutrality or indifference within the spectrum of caring-for on the understanding that an employment contract can only be maintained on the basis of
mutual gain for both parties in the gainful game. The ethos of a capitalist market economy, its habitual mode of life and stance toward living, is that each
economic player has the possibility, liberty and responsibility of looking after
him- or herself, and insofar, the social relations of capitalism correspond to a
deeper understanding of human being itself as individually mine, i.e. jemeinig,
associated with a prevalent mode of caring-for that must be described as calculating *indifference*, i.e. as a deficient mode of caring-for but also, remarkably
also as mutually estimating and beneficial. Within this basic indifference, interchanges of mutual benefit and usefulness nevertheless continually take place,
and such reciprocal usefulness is not an injury to human dignity for they are
also an interplay of genuine mutual estimation. Being useful to each other in
the gainful game may be precisely the bond that holds social life together in a
satisfying, peaceful way, despite the ongoing competitive struggles and the
conflicts that arise. The movement of social life, because it is a movement of
interplay, is maintained by the tension of contradictions, of conflicting opposites, of opposed but nevertheless co-operating powers.

10 Social power and government

10.1 Ontology of social power

Has an ontology of social power ever been adequately worked out in political philosophy and modern social science? The answer is: No. As noted in the Foreword, modern social science is per se blind to the ontological difference, and, for reasons investigated in previous chapters (cf. especially Chapter 5)), political philosophy has never succeeded in developing a socio-ontology of power interplay. Political and social power are such ubiquitous, thoroughly familiar phenomena that it seems possible to skip the question concerning what they *are*, to *presuppose* a preconception of the spectrum of phenomena (which are, indeed, *very well* understood) and to talk endlessly *about* them in a pseudo-philosophical, mostly narrative, or perhaps logically syllogistic fashion (e.g. so-called consequentialism). This is the usual situation with simple, fundamental phenomena: they seem to be so well-known and familiar and self-evident that it would be superfluous to try to give anything more than a definition of the concept. Familiarity with a phenomenon in all its nuances generally makes us blind to questioning its mode of being, thus posing a genuinely ontological question. There seems to be no point at which thinking could gain a purchase on it so that it would open up its depths and mystery, its questionableness. Thus we remain blinded by obviousness and dismiss the suggestion that there could even be a depth to what seems self-evident, obvious and even trivial.

"We": that is all except a handful of singular individuals who suffer themselves to be drawn into that deeper kind of ontological interrogation of the phenomena bequeathed to us by the Greeks as encapsulated in the inconspicuous word 'as'. And yet, there is a way to make the phenomenon of power reveal its ontological secrets by returning to the metaphysical tradition, for it has by no means been entirely neglected. Aristotle offers a source which, to the present day, has not been tapped with respect to the question of the ontology of specifically social and political power, the socio-ontological question par excellence that has been pursued and unfolded in preceding chapters. The philosopher whose name in recent years has most been associated with the phenomenality of political and social power is Michel Foucault, and yet he and his many disciples never raise the question concerning the *ontological structure* of political and social power as modes of *social, sociating* movement. They are wilfully blind and oblivious to it, and therefore perforce implicitly, unwittingly and unavoidably adopt the ontology of *productive* power. In the absence of an ex-

https://doi.org/10.1515/9783110617504-010

plicit ontology of social power, the phenomena of social power can only show themselves in a distorted fashion through pre-ontological misconceptions.

It has to be said that the phenomenon and concept of power lie at the heart of Aristotle's ontology under the names ἀρχή and δύναμις in connection with the problem of grasping the phenomenon of movement/change *as* a mode of being — a major issue for Greek philosophy from Parmenides on. Chapter 5 on the Ontology of Exchange[178] has explored δύναμις with regard to the phenomena of commodity exchange and social interchange, which already represents a side-step out of traditional metaphysical ontology. Why? Because the ontology of power offered by the tradition, starting with Aristotle, is exclusively that of *productive* power (δύναμις ποιητική, a collocation occurring in Aristotle at *Met.* Delta 1021a15 and generally mistranslated as 'active potential', is the complementary concept to δύναμις παθητική (1021a15), the passive power to suffer the energy of a productive power). This ontology of productive power has only, by sleight of hand, been thoughtlessly transferred to phenomena of social power (δύναμις κοινωνική a collocation that, as far as I know, does not occur in Greek philosophy).[179]

Here I will focus on the phenomenon and concept of ἀρχή which is dealt with first of all in the famous book of definitions, Book Delta of the *Metaphysics*, as the very first chapter. Like all elementary, simple concepts, ἀρχή, too, is "said in several ways", and all but one of Aristotle's definitions of ἀρχή start with saying that ἀρχή is ὅθεν, i.e. "from where" or "whence" something has its beginning. Aristotle says explicitly that "of all the various meanings of ἀρχή what is common is to be the first whence something either is or becomes or is known" (πασῶν μὲν οὖν κοινὸν τῶν ἀρχῶν τὸ πρῶτον εἶναι ὅθεν ἢ ἔστιν ἢ γίγνεται ἢ γιγνώσκεται· 1013a17). An ἀρχή is therefore a "whence".

The concept of ἀρχή is essential to Aristotle's treatment of one of his most important and characteristic ontological categories, that of δύναμις, for the latter is defined in Book Theta of the *Metaphysics* to be a kind of ἀρχή having dominion over change in something else. According to the seminal Book Theta, and thus unquestioningly and implicitly for the entire philosophical tradition, power is always power to effect a change in something else. It makes not one

---

178 The terms 'metaphysics' and 'ontology' are distinguished by virtue of the former's character as onto-theology, i.e. as both ontology and theology. The latter is the investigation of a supreme being that may be a god, but can also be a highest first principle such as will to power; cf. the Foreword.

179 Stimulation for the additions to the first two paragraphs of this chapter came from an e-mail exchange with Stuart Elden on 24 June 2011.

iota of difference when synonyms for social and political power such as 'control', 'governance', 'force', 'violence', 'coercion', 'discipline', etc. are employed, as if these words captured the essence or essential ontological differences. Such proliferation of synonyms only muddies and covers up the ontological issue in more or less sophisticated, sophistic ways. The guiding, paradigmatic phenomenon for Aristotle's consideration of δύναμις (power) is that of productive τέχνη, i.e. the know-how to effect a change in something else in bringing something forth, in pro-ducing. And this understanding of τέχνη is also explicitly linked by Aristotle with political power in his run through various meanings of ἀρχή in Book Delta when he writes:

ἡ δὲ οὗ κατὰ προαίρεσιν κινεῖται τὰ κινούμενα καὶ μεταβάλλει τὰ μεταβάλλοντα, ὥσπερ αἵ τε κατὰ πόλεις ἀρχαὶ καὶ αἱ δυναστεῖαι καὶ αἱ βασιλεῖαι καὶ τυραννίδες ἀρχαὶ λέγονται καὶ αἱ τέχναι, καὶ τούτων αἱ ἀρχιτεκτονικαὶ μάλιστα. (*Met.* Delta 1 1013a10)

Another meaning of ἀρχή is that of a deliberate purpose according to which something which is moved moves or something which is changed changes, such as political magistracies (ἀρχαί), and régimes (δυναστεῖαι) and kingdoms and tyrannies are said to be ἀρχαί, and also the know-hows (τέχναι) and of these most of all the architectonic know-hows.

This linking means that power in the sense of political rule and dominion is said to have the same ontological structure as that of the power (δύναμις) of productive technical know-how (τέχνη ποιητική) in the sense that both, as modes of being, are the starting-point governing, or a whence having dominion over, a change in something else (ἀρχὴ μεταβολῆς ἐν ἄλλῳ *Met.* Theta 1, 1046a9f). But the "something else" is different in each case. In the case of technical know-how, the power is a power to bring about a change in manipulable things considered in the 'third person'. The example of medical knowledge makes this particularly clear, since medical know-how is able to bring about a change in a human considered as a body, i.e. *as* a 'thing', rather than *as* a free-willed being. Once again, the inconspicuous Greek word ἧ (as, qua) plays a crucial role (cf. Foreword).

Political power, on the other hand, concerns the rule over human beings and is insofar a *social interplay* between and among human beings. Political power is an estimating social interplay in the sense of being, still in line with Aristotle's productive definition of δύναμις, a point of emanation (a principal, head, leader) for bringing about a change in other human beings according to a deliberate plan or purpose. As Joseph Nye puts it, unknowingly echoing Plato's

Gorgias, power is "the ability to obtain the outcomes one wants".[180] Such a change can be understood as obedience to a command, an order, which may or may not be formulated as a law or, in a 'softer' version, compliance with one's wishes, or in an even softer version, making an impression on others (e.g. a man's expensive hand-made shoes, a woman's flashing red lips[181]). For example, a magistrate holding an office entrusted with the administration of justice can, i.e. has the power to, order an offender who has infringed the law to be fined, imprisoned or otherwise punished. The magistracy is thus a source of emanation of political power over others, and the holder of this office holds and exercises specifically political power, here in the garb of judicial power. This ontologically unclarified preconception of political power is echoed even more than two millennia later in the modern social science of sociology, when Max Weber e.g. defines the phenomenon of ruling others, of rule or *Herrschaft*, "Rule, i.e. the chance of finding obedience for a certain command."[182] This definition at least implicitly admits the uncertainty of political power, but by no means approaches an adequate socio-ontological conception.

Those subjected to political rule, namely, are humans regarded as humans, and not humans regarded as bodies (as in the case of medical know-how), and thus the relation of political power is one of power over beings in the 'second person', as an other human being, and not merely power over things (or humans regarded as bodily things, as 'patients' in the 'third person' who 'suffer' passively (πάσχειν) to have changes made to them). The relation of political power is that of the subjection of one human will to another, dominant human will in contrast to, say, a relation of agreement (a concurring of wills) on a course of action as in the case of the exchange of commodities or an interchange of views on how best to proceed regarding some practical issue (such as organizing a work process within a company).

To get a better overview of what the phenomenon of Greek δύναμις encompasses, it is instructive to look first at the range of lexicographic meanings, not in order to do 'dictionary phenomenology', but to allow related phenomena to pass review before the mind's eye. The basic meaning is 'force', 'Kraft' or 'power'. This force may be the physical force of brute physical strength (e.g. to bend

---

180 Cited in *Fortune* magazine, Vol. 156, No. 11, 10 December. 2007 p. 38.

181 "... and the love of power, which sleeps in the bosom of the best of little women, woke up all of a sudden and took possession of her" L.M. Alcott *Little Women* Folio Society, London 1966 p. 242.

182 "Herrschaft, d.h. die Chance, Gehorsam für einen bestimmten Befehl zu finden." 'Die drei reinen Typen der legitimen Herrschaft' in Max Weber *Soziologie Universalgeschichtliche Analysen Politik* Kröner Verlag, Stuttgart 1973 p. 151)

steel or knock someone out using one's fists), or the force of armed forces such as an army or navy (e.g. to defeat an enemy in combat, which depends ultimately on the power to physically kill by destroying the body as a thing using suitable weapons). In armed combat, two (or more) opposed military forces estimate each other *as* enemies, estimating, in particular, the enemy's potential military force. Military force can be employed to 'beat an enemy into submission' but, significantly, the act of submission is performed *by the enemy* in estimating that the other side is a superior military power. Hostilities may cease also by the two sides achieving a political resolution, again on the basis of mutually estimating each others strengths, including military strength.

Δύναμις is also the power of an ability, a competence or skill based on know-how, such as knowing how to play the guitar or make a bookshelf, both kinds of productive power. In particular, it is also rhetorical skill, the power of persuasion to win trust and bring others around to a particular view by force of *what* the speaker says, *how* winningly he says it and and the charisma of *who* is speaking. In the social realm, δύναμις is 'influence', 'personal importance and prestige that carries weight', i.e. the power to *impress* others, and also specifically the 'political power' of public office, but all these are no longer simply productive powers, but power interplay. Δύναμις is also 'the meaning of a word', 'valuable assets' or 'the monetary value of something', i.e. the power of one thing (assets, money) to bring something else into one's possession. One signification of the related verb, δύνασθαι, is 'to be worth', as in 'five shoes are worth one table', i.e. five shoes have the power to exchange for, i.e. to acquire, to bring into one's possession, one table. *Exchange-value* is therefore a *social power*, an observation whose importance cannot be overemphasized. The standard Latin translation of δύνασθαι is 'valere'[183] which means 'to be strong, powerful, influential; also, to have value, including monetary value, to be worth'.

The phenomena of social and political power are therefore situated in the realm of mutual estimation and esteeming among human beings and their goods, and therefore they cannot be approached without a clearsightedness for the dimension of *whoness*, of estimating who-interplay. Of course, the ontological question concerning social and political power arises only with a *plurality* of human beings sharing a world and concerns *power-playful relations*, not substance. A determination of human being, say, as animal rationale (which *includes* animal irrationale) therefore leaves the problematic of social and political power grossly underdetermined.

---

183 Cf. Georges *Ausführliches Lateinisch-Deutsches Handwörterbuch* Bd. II 'valeo'.

The power of money can be understood from the ontology of exchange as laid out in Chapter 5. As underscored already many times, it is not a power like productive power, which is the power to "bring forth a *change* in some*thing else*", but the power to purchase in *exchange* any*thing* or any*one*, i.e. anywhat or anywho, offered for sale or hire, which depends firstly upon what is offered itself being estimated as a value (and thus as having a power of exchange, such as labour-power that is valuable in producing things or performing services, or commodity goods that are valuable for some use or other), and secondly upon the possessor of that offering being *willing* to offer and to actually exchange, so that *two* powers (in the sense of being valuable) must reciprocally intermesh concurringly in an interchange, which is therefore always also an estimating interplay, a power play, and *never the one-sided exercise of a power or force having dominion from a single origin to cause an effect, i.e. never simply productive power*. The game that is the interplay of exchange can never be adequately grasped ontologically in terms of the schema of cause and effect derived from productionist ontology, but only through its ontological structure sui generis.

The terms "game" and "power play" do not imply here an ontologically lightweight, merely playful, frivolous phenomenon; rather, here they are accorded the grave ontological weight due to them as fundamental 'speculative' concepts of human sociation in society. One immediate corollary of this insight into the ontological structure of social power as mutually estimating interplay is that *social* freedom itself can never be conceived as the freedom of individuals to do what they like, for *all* social freedom in its exercise or ἐνέργεια is an intermeshing with others, and therefore the individual comes up against the other as a likewise free individual exercising its own powers, whatever they may be. In this sense, freedom is always essentially negotiated in a power play. Even the freedom to withdraw into one's private sphere and exercise one's caprice within this sphere is the ongoing outcome of a social power play in which it is decided politically where, precisely, the limits of the private sphere are to be drawn. Individual freedom, considered as social freedom, can only ever be the freedom of the individual to play in a power play with others according to rules of justice that are more or less fair, more or less beautiful. The notion of an individualist society of individuals being free to arbitrarily exercise their individual will denies the ontological insight that human social living is essentially, ineluctably a power interplay whose outcome, moreover, is ongoing, shifting, always becoming.

But let us continue our review of the various phenomena of social power.

The possessor or owner of money and assets furthermore has power and influence *mediated* through the power of money to acquire all sorts of material and more intangible goods simply because money is a *reified social power* that literally, as *res* or thing, can be handed over to another. These are interchanges played out in the sociating medium of reified value. In this way, money becomes the social power of *capital*, which can command not only labour power, but means of production and land, and also a lending price called interest. The reified power of money and capital extends to social status, prestige and influence, including political influence, enjoyed above all by the wealthy, thus demonstrating how one kind of social power can encroach on and commingle with another.

There is also political power proper within the state by virtue of holding some public office, whether it be that of a magistrate, a king, a member of parliament, a minister in the government, a government bureaucrat, a police officer, a military officer, a customs official, etc. within a constituted polity. Such power is not exercised merely through brute physical force, which is the exception, even though political power is backed up by the *possibility* (δύναμις) of exercising brute physical force against people through, say, a police force, but in general, the application of physical force against bodies is not necessary because the subject subjugated to political power *estimates* the political power as a *superior* power and submits to it, i.e. in this estimation there is an act of *legitimation* of and *submission* to the superior political power. Only through this act of submissive estimation is the superior political power able to issue commands that will be obeyed without the need to use physical force.[184]

---

184 And even more than that, it can be questioned whether the obedience to commands can ever be compelled by physical force (e.g. arrest or punishment by the state apparatuses). Hegel writes on this from one aspect, "[...] that there is no such thing as compulsion and there has never been a person who has been compelled. [...] Thus, if somewhere the existence of compulsion is to be demonstrated, there precisely the opposite can be shown with regard to the selfsame phenomenon, namely, that it is not compulsion, but rather an expression of freedom; for through the fact that this phenomenon is taken up into the form of imagination and thus becomes determined by interiority, by ideality, the subject is at liberty/in freedom vis-à-vis this phenomenon. [...] The possibility of sublating/cancelling the determination which is imagined and is supposed to serve as compulsion is absolute;" ([...] daß es gar keinen Zwang gebe und nie ein Mensch gezwungen worden sei. [...] Wo also irgendwo die Existenz von Zwang aufgewiesen werden soll, da kann von einer und ebenderselben Erscheinung gerade das Gegenteil gezeigt werden, nämlich daß sie nicht ein Zwang, sondern vielmehr eine Äußerung der Freiheit sei; denn dadurch, daß sie in die Form der Vorstellung aufgenommen und hiermit durch das Innere, Ideelle bestimmt wird, ist das Subjekt in der Freiheit gegen dieselbe. [...] Die Möglichkeit, die Bestimmtheit, welche vorgestellt wird und als Zwang dienen soll, aufzuheben, ist absolut; 'Über die wissenschaftlichen Behandlungsarten des Naturrechts, seine Stelle in der

By the same token, any holder of political office only ever has the back-up of the option of physical force insofar as the public forces such as the police and the army in turn *estimate* and *esteem* the political leaders and their political apparatus and officers *as* a legitimate, superior, political power and *submit* to them in obedience. Political power is therefore *essentially, inherently* based originarily on estimation in which subjects estimate another, usually an office-holder in the structured hierarchy of the polity, whether it be based on a written constitution or not, as *superior*.[185] Just as *trust* (a concept that only makes sense in considering the power interplay between *free* human beings) is essential to the interchanges of civil society, and is itself a mutually estimating interplay, estimation of a political instance *as* superior is essential to the life of a polity and constitutes the core of its *legitimacy*.[186] A political instance such as a court,

---

praktischen Philosophie und sein Verhältnis zu den positiven Rechtswissenschaften' (1802/03) *Werke* Bd. 2 S. 513).

185 David Hume puts it thus: "...we shall find, that, as FORCE is always on the side of the governed, the governors have nothing to support them but opinion. It is therefore, on opinion only that government is founded; and this maxim extends to the most despotic and most military governments, as well as to the most free and most popular." D. Hume 'Of the First Principles of Government' Essay IV, Part I *Essays: Moral, Political, and Literary* Eugene F. Miller (ed.), Liberty Fund, Indianapolis 1987 p. 32. "Opinion" in Hume's usage means 'a holding to be legitimate'.

186 In his 2003 paper 'Social Ontology and Political Power', John R. Searle approaches the problem of the ontology of social power from within subjectivist metaphysics. "The important point to emphasize is that the essence of political power is deontic power. [...] It is a matter of rights, duties, obligations, authorizations, permissions and the like. Such powers have a special ontology." (All further quotes in double inverted commas are from Searle's paper.) This "special ontology" is said to reside in "status functions", as distinct from 'objective' "physical functions" such as 'Rain makes you wet'. Status functions, "imposed" by the "collective intentionality" of human beings "can be represented in the form, 'X counts as Y in C'". The "brute fact" of a physical phenomenon such as expressed in the statement "It is raining" or 'George is sitting at his desk' is superimposed with a status that allows, for example, the statement "George W. Bush is president" to fit the model 'X counts as Y in C': Bush counts as President in the context of the institutions of democratic elections. "Counts as" here is synonymous with 'is valid as' or 'is recognized as'. The status accorded to Bush through this putative projection of collective intentionality confers on him deontic powers such as the power to command the armed forces, which are obliged (deontically) to obey, or the power to veto legislation which Congress is obliged to acknowledge. Furthermore, Searle asserts, "Where political status functions are concerned it is [sic] almost invariably linguistic.", an example being the linguistic thought, "He is president". Hence, according to Searle, political power is constituted "almost invariably" by certain linguistic conventions that confer "rights, duties, obligations, authorizations, permissions and the like". Likewise, Searle regards the social power, money, as a thing (paper) accorded a "status function" by convention according to the formula, 'This paper

estimates a citizen as answerable before the court, and conversely estimates the court itself as legitimate and submits to its summons. Political power sanctioned by the constitution is always estimated and submitted to, a people's constitutional polity with its multiple interplays of estimation, legitimation and submission, being its *historical second nature* by virtue of its living-together.

Why is this interplay of legitimating estimation and submission *essential* for political power? Regarded as a social interplay among human beings, each of whom is a free starting-point (source of power, ἀρχή) of self-movement (i.e. an individual endowed with free, spontaneous will), whether this movement be in understanding or in practices, specifically political power can only be under-

---

counts as means of payment (money) in the context of market exchange'. This counting-as-money is presumably accompanied by the linguistic thought, 'This is money'. Searle's problematic of social and political power is thus isomorphic with Neo-Kantianism's (e.g. Heinrich Rickert) account of values, according to which 'values' are overlaid over 'objective reality'. In Searle's terminology, such 'values' are status functions projected onto "observer-independent", objective, physical things and physical people by "collective intentionality" and are therefore "observer-dependent". The key distinction between "observer-independent" objectivity and "observer-dependent" subjectivity, however, is untenable. Why? Searle's root concern is with the question "How can there be *political* reality in a world consisting of physical particles?". Hence the dichotomy between physical objectivity and social reality, which latter, it is claimed, is "observer-dependent" in the sense that it depends on a projection of "collective intentionality" onto physical things of the kind 'X counts as Y in C'. But *all* beings in the world, including bare, physical beings, are 'counted as' in the sense that they are understood as, say, "physical particles". Such understanding-as... is only possible in the modern scientific age within the Cartesian cast of being (which Searle obviously believes is the unquestionable, rock-bottom, scientific truth), and "physical particles" *are* such only for the scientific subject of the modern age, i.e. 'physical reality' is not "observer-independent" and "objective", but is conceived and cast *as* such by an historical way of human thinking. Even the innocuous, brute, factual statement adduced by Searle that "it is raining" depends upon the apophantic *as* according to which the observed phenomenon of precipitation is understood *as* rain. There can be no "observer-independent" objectivity because objectivity is such only *for* a human subject within an historical world that is cast within its own epochal understanding of the world. Moreover, human beings are always already in the world engaged in practices with each other, i.e. in interplay, taking care of their lives, and are never merely subjective consciousnesses separated from objective reality. In the context of these practices of interplay, and not merely linguistically through representations in consciousness, individual or collective, they estimate, value and evaluate things and people based first of all upon what they are good for and worth in the context of such daily, individual and shared, practices. The stepwise path in thinking via value (τιμή) as it emerges from the practices of everyday life through to specifically political power has been adopted in the present inquiry to bring the power play among human beings in all its facets socio-ontologically to light. For Searle, mired as he is in subjectivist metaphysics, for which 'collective intentionality' serves as theological anchor, such a social ontology can make no sense.

stood as the submission of one free source of power to another in estimating the other source of power *as* superior. The superiority consists in the superiority of the willed purposes posited by that superior ἀρχή, i.e. what the superior holder of political power posits as a purpose can — has the power to — assert itself vis-à-vis the inferior, subjugated subject, who estimates the superior ἀρχή and its purpose *as* legitimately superior and therefore obeys. The hierarchy of political power thus necessarily depends on acts of submissive estimation. Without this submissive act of estimation, power in the guise of superior physical, coercive force would have to be applied ubiquitously in which the superior political power proves at least its physical superiority through the exercise of brute physical force carried out by its agents who, in turn however, must recognize their superior *as* superior (perhaps for the sake of some advantage this superior provides, such as comparatively lucrative pay for the security forces). Such a state is a police state lacking in legitimacy, for the state may be feared by dint of its superior brute force, but it is not estimated highly. Even the exercise of superior physical force cannot force the act of submission and estimation by the inferior subject (as evidenced by the phenomenon of *political dissidence* ubiquitously practised in the name of freedom). At most it can only physically restrain, confiscate, threaten physical violence, incarcerate, etc.[187]

The act of estimation is a kind of interchange (cf. Chapter 5.6) in which the superior individual sees itself mirrored in the other's comportment in an act of submission *as* superior, and the inferior individual sees itself mirrored in the comportment of the superior individual *as* an inferior individual who will submit to and obey commands, and is, perhaps, under the superior's protection. The power game is apparent in the reciprocal mirroring, that is, in the reflective

---

187 Hegel puts this point as follows: "As a living being, a human being can well be *overpowered*, i.e. his physical and otherwise exterior side brought under the power of others, but the free will in and for itself cannot be *forced* (§ 5) except insofar as *he himself does not withdraw from the exteriority* on which is held fast or from the imagination of such exteriority (§ 7). Only he can be forced into something who *wills* to allow himself to be *forced*." (Als Lebendiges kann der Mensch wohl *bezwungen*, d.h. seine physische und sonst äußerliche Seite unter die Gewalt anderer gebracht, aber der freie Wille kann an und für sich nicht *gezwungen* werden (§ 5), als nur sofern *er sich selbst aus der Äußerlichkeit*, an der er festgehalten wird, oder aus deren Vorstellung *nicht zurückzieht* (§ 7). Es kann nur der zu etwas gezwungen werden, der sich *zwingen* lassen *will*. *Rechtsphilosophie* Werke Bd. 7 Suhrkamp, Frankfurt/M. 1970 § 91). The body and external property can be ontically, physically overcome, but freedom is nothing ontic. The free will externalizes itself in exterior things and is embedded in a physical body, but it can withdraw into its proper domain, that of the psyche in its belonging to the 3D-temporal clearing, beyond the reach of any physical force. Hegel misplaces such freedom in a subjective interior.

interplay of mutual estimation in which rituals of submission are paramount. Therefore there can be no political power without this reciprocal mirroring as superior who and inferior who, even though the act of legitimating estimation may be feigned, i.e. a false semblance effected by the presentation of false masks of self-comportment, and it may be grudging. If the estimation of the superior instance *as* superior is freely given, it is *legitimized.*

The one holding political power is literally the governor who governs the subject by imposing its will on the governed subject (a will usually, but not always, formulated within the framework of the rule of law, at least in modern democracies, but possibly also the capricious will of a despot). The holder of political office is a governing origin for bringing about a change in another, namely, the politically governed subject, through an imposition of will. The political subject, in recognizing, grudgingly or otherwise, the one holding political power *as* superior, obeys the command of the 'governor'. Imposition and obedience are therefore always already an *interplay*, and never one-sided. The relation between governor and governed, once constituted more or less permanently, is one-sided, unidirectional in the sense that the governor is the starting-point who governs the other through an imposition of will by command, whether it be a direct, specific command, or the indirect command by promulgated laws that prescribe rules of conduct, often negatively in the form of prohibitions, or indirect commands in the form of regulations issued by authorities under the control of the governor or government (which is itself an hierarchically organized, collective governor with a president, prime minister, premier or similar at its head). The change (μεταβολή) is brought about one-sidedly in the other by the one governing. But this one-sidedness of having the power to issue commands that will be obeyed, i.e. the one-sidedness of being able to bring forth a change in another, inferior individual, is itself embedded in a deeper-lying two-sided or reciprocal act of estimatioin in which the respective superior and inferior statuses of the two individuals are acknowledged and thus established in the first place. Because the necessary estimation which forms the basis of the political power play is invariably overlooked, political power can seem to be simply a 'technical' relation of one-sided governing of changes (viz. performed, obedient behaviour) in the political subject. But the political subject is itself irrevocably an ἀρχή, a free, spontaneous will, who must *renounce* its individual will and power to determine its own movements, and sight must not be lost of this if socio-ontological insight is to be gained.

The governor's imposition of will through commanding the governed subject in some way (e.g. a magistrate sentencing an offender to some punishment or other or, more mediatedly, a parliament promulgating a law) has to be distinguished from a technical relationship such as a doctor treating a patient, because τέχνη ποιητική — which, like political power, is indeed an ἀρχή, i.e. an origin having dominion over change in something else, namely the patient's body — is based on knowing how to bring about an envisaged change without one (superior) will being imposed on another (inferior) will. A carpenter, for instance, knows how to transform wood into a table, but the wood that is thus transformed has no will of its own. The phenomenon of a physician treating a patient is situated between purely technical manipulation of things and the exercise of political power because the patient is a human being endowed with free will who acknowledges the physician as superior only with respect to the medical know-how that will hopefully bring about a cure. The patient *concurs* to being treated by the physician for the sake of a purpose which the patient has set for him or herself, namely, to be cured. Without the patient's permission, the physician can do nothing. Insofar, the physician treating the patient is the patient's agent, acting at the patient's behest as a service-provider, and the patient's will and purpose remain the point of origin and thus ultimately superior, even though the physician has superior knowledge with regard to how to cure sick people. There is no imposition of a superior will when the physician manipulates the patient's body or prescribes how the patient should behave to get well.

The relationship between physician and patient is that of an *interchange* between free sources of power in the sense that there is an agreement between the two for the physician to render a service, and not a relationship of one-sided social power between a superior source of power and a submissive one, despite the physician's superior know-how (which may be factually intimidating for the patient — but this is another facet of who-interplay). The patient obeys the physician not by dint of the physician's superior political power (in holding some political office or other), but by dint of the physician's superior knowledge which the sick patient *ultimately wills* and *wants* to have applied to him or herself. The patient can even refuse treatment by the physician. This shows that the patient remains the starting-point for what happens in the treatment, including even the termination of treatment. The patient remains in control, a point of origin, and does not submit to the doctor as a superior, governing source of power. The patient's obedience to the 'doctor's orders' is still relative to the patient's having ultimate control over being treated by the doctor (assuming that the patient is, say, not mentally ill and has lost the ability to be responsible for him or herself, or is unduly intimidated by the doctor's superior social status, etc.).

10.1.1 Recapitulation: Various kinds of social power

As noted above, there are different kinds, or 'looks', of δύναμις, and even differ-ent kinds of social δύναμις, of social power. A social power is, on the one hand, an estimating interplay *among* powers inhering in different human beings on a basis of formal equality or, more decidedly, a power of human beings *over* hu-man beings, i.e. one or several human beings as a free ἀρχή are the starting-point for governing the actions of other human beings who submit, willingly or unwillingly (grudgingly, resentfully, …), to this principal ἀρχή. The act of sub-mission to specifically political power (literally, the prince), as has been shown, is an act of estimating the superior ἀρχή *as* superior in which the subjects *sup-press themselves* as the free point of emanation of their own self-movements. For the sake of clarity, these different kinds, or phenomenal looks, of social power should be laid out to view in summary fashion. There is:

i) Brute physical, bodily strength that is superior to another's physical, bod-ily strength and can therefore be employed to subdue the weaker one. The supe-riority can also be a superiority of cunning in subduing the opponent. This is a power in the sense that the superior physical force is a starting-point (ἀρχή) for bringing about a change (μεταβολή) in another, namely, another human being, by either killing him or forcing his submission, i.e. by breaking the opponent's will, which amounts to subduing the other as a free ἀρχή, a free starting-point governing its own self-movement in the sense of its own actions. Since the one to be subdued resists this 'change', this μεταβολή, there is here a physical *struggle*, ultimately of life and death, between two ἀρχαί in which it is decided who is stronger. One can therefore not speak simply of a one-sided exercise of physical power from a single source, but must have the interchange of physical struggle, a physical power play, in view.

ii) Brute physical, bodily strength can be assisted by banding together and by technical means, i.e. weapons, which makes it brute physical, armed power. As Rousseau points out, "La force est une puissance physique; le pistolet que le brigand tient est aussi une puissance".[188] To be an effective power that can ac-tually (ἐντελέχεια) bring about change in the opponent or enemy, i.e. actually defeat the enemy, this military power must be superior to the enemy's. The military forces are matched in a struggle with each other, and one power achieves victory over the other. Victory is only finally achieved when the enemy admits defeat and *estimates* the victor *as* victor. Within an established polity,

---

188 *Contrat social* I, 3 cited in Carl Schmitt *Politische Theologie* 1922 S. 20.

the superior armed brute physical force is the police or national guard that exercises physical violence against law-breakers.

iii) The power of money in acquiring goods both tangible and intangible is a reified social power insofar as it can be employed to purchase the services of others. In employing workers to clean the windows, there is power exercised in that my purpose, namely, to have clean windows, is carried out by the window cleaners who submit freely, in exchange for money-wages, to my will. Even the purchase of material goods can be regarded as the purchase of services insofar as indirectly it is command over the labour of others. Money can also buy a person more or less entirely to become totally subservient and do one's bidding. Furthermore, all capitalist enterprise depends on the power of money to purchase labour power, i.e. to hire employees. The entrepreneur or chief executive then exercises social power over others in the enterprise's organizational hierarchy who submit to the superior entrepreneurial or managerial will in exchange for wages or salary. The exchange is an interchange as a kind of estimation of the enterpreneur's power to exercise command over labour power in exchange for money and other benefits. The legitimacy of this power is expressed by saying that the enterprise has acquired, by exchange for money, the *right* to command others' labour power, and those who have sold their labour power in this way will not object to the employer's right of command, because they have agreed to it, and have a reciprocal right to be paid. The workforce's obedience to directives from above in the hierarchy is the change (μεταβολή) effected by the entrepreneur's or chief executive's order, albeit that the boss, a superior ἀρχή, can only exercise this power mediatedly by virtue of the power of money to purchase others' labour power in the first place. Finally, there is the power of money as capital addressed by Karl Marx in his socio-ontological determination of the essence of capital as the endless movement of the self-augmentation of reified value in which this self-augmentation has become a fetishized end in itself, divorced and alienated from any human purpose (cf. Chapter 9.6).

iv) Political power is a special case of social power. It is the power to manage the affairs of a community or a society and in particular, to make and promulgate laws and decrees according to which the members of that community or society must conduct themselves. The citizens of a polity submit to a political power, which is institutionalized and constitutionalized in some way or other, by acknowledging it, emphatically or tacitly, as legitimate. The organized institutions of political power include a head of state with ministers forming a government, a law-making body, an executive body in the form of a bureaucracy of some kind. (The details of these constitutional institutions, whether democratic or not, are not of concern for the moment.) These institutions must ultimately be backed by brute physical force in the shape of military forces and a police force in order to quell resistance by those individuals who will not submit willingly to the exercise of political power, i.e. its ἐνέργεια, its being-at-work or 'energy'. The legitimacy of a political power is the act of estimation and acknowledgement of and submission to that superior power by its subjects who, with greater or lesser insight, affirmatively or grudgingly, regard the political power as being for the good of social living or at least a necessary 'evil' to enable social cohesion and peaceful order.

v) The special social power, *rhetorical power*, the paradigm of so-called "soft power" (Joseph Nye), which has been investigated in Chapter 5.3 in the context of commodity exchange and social interchange, will be considered further below. It is the power of persuasion through speech to win others' trust and bring them around to a point of view. It is not a power of suppressing the other as a free ἀρχή, but a power for winning others over of their own free will so that there is agreement, i.e. a congruity and unification of free ἀρχαί, on a given issue, course of action, business deal, sale transaction, etc.

These different 'looks' of social power, i.e. powers of human beings over other human beings bringing about specific changes, although ontologicially distinct, merge ontically into and intermesh with one another. There are countless sorts of mixtures and transitions between these kinds of social power one into the other. For instance, the power of money can be exercised (illegitimately) to purchase brute physical force (e.g. thugs, contract killing) or political influence (e.g. bribery of holders of public office, illegally funding political parties). Or conversely, an officer of the state can use his politically invested power to coerce citizens to pay illegitimate 'fees'. A public servant is employed by a state department for money, but the loyalty demanded by the state from its employees goes beyond mere provision of service, i.e. there is an element of political power exercised over the public servant to loyally and dutifully serve the public and the state. Rhetoric as power of persuasion is employed in all social contexts (political deliberation and debates, economic exchange and other deals, combat pep talks, advertising, etc.) to win others over, to gain their trust and even build their confidence. Political power is (legitimately) exercised economically to purchase goods and services on the markets and, especially, to raise *taxes* to gain money to finance the government's budget. Political power also has legitimate disposal of armed physical force in the guises of the military forces and the police force. Or it can be exercised illegitimately by holders of public office to gain favours from enterprises (e.g. free flights, free hotel accommodation and countless other perks) in illegitimate exchange interplays.

Here we are not interested in these endless ontic mixtures and variants of social power in all their empirical richness, but in the invariably overlooked, simple ontological outlines of social power, and political social power in particular. It is the ontological structure of social power that is more difficult to see as a problem, not the 'sociological' investigation of how social powers intertwine ontically in ever new and hitherto unforeseen combinations in different times and places. The endless ontic variations of intertwinings form the stuff of thick narratives in sociology that may even have misplaced philosophical pretensions.

All social power, based socio-ontologically on an interplay of mutual estimation, is power to bring about changes in others (in what they do, in what they refrain from doing, etc.). Just as for technical power, which is power to produce changes in things, or in people *as* mere things, there is no inherent limit to the striving to augment its productive power, so too is there no inherent limit to social power. Its dynamic is to augment itself, so that one could speak of a dynamic of social δύναμις, an inherent acceleration of social power that lies in the nature of social power itself for the sake of higher estimation that ends in hubris. (In Chapter 9.6 special attention is paid to the tendency of the social power of money, i.e. value, to continually augment itself as capital to become a more powerful player in the competitive economic interplay.) The limit to social power ultimately can only come from the resistance of those who are subject to it, who do not go along with its essential tendency to encroach ever more. Because social power is always a power interplay, it is held in check only by the counterpowers at play in the interplay itself.

In the particular case of political power, which ultimately is based on legitimacy, the limit to its inherent self-augmentation resides in the resistance of those over whom it is exercised to the office-holders of political power within a constitutional framework that provides for members of society to resist the ever-encroaching exercise of political power. (The topic of the constititution of a polity is taken up in Chapter 12.) This resistance invariably amounts to putting the legitimacy of the exercise of political power *into question*. This question is always the question concerning by what *legitimate right* a particular political power is exercised, and the question of right is always intimately connected to the question of freedom which, ultimately, is *essentially* individual freedom since individuals are the ultimate origins of free, spontaneous movements of all kinds, including acts of willing submission.

10.1.2 Aristotle on social and political power

When Aristotle comes to consider the constitution of practically shared human living in his *Politics*, he starts by saying that "every sociation comes about for the sake of some good" (πᾶσαν κοινωνίαν ἀγαθοῦ τινος ἕνεκεν συνεστηκυῖαν *Pol.* I i 1252a2), just as he says at the beginning of the *Nicomachean Ethics* that "every action and deliberate purpose seems to aim at some good" (πᾶσα ... πρᾶξίς τε καὶ προαίρεσις, ἀγαθοῦ τινὸς ἐφίεσθαι δοκεῖ· *Eth. Nic.* I i 1094a1). Sociation in practice, i.e. in action, is the germ and fabric of society. The supreme sociation comprising all others (ἡ κυριωτάτη καὶ πάσας περιέχουσα) is the political association (κοινωνία πολιτική *Pol.* 1252a8). The polis and its polity as the supreme and most comprehensive form of human sociation are thus the subject of investigation. The very next sentence then introduces various kinds of rule and rulers: "the rule of the statesman and royal ruler, of the head of a household and the despot" (πολιτικὸν καὶ βασιλικὸν καὶ οἰκονομικὸν καὶ δεσποτικὸν *Pol.* 1252a8) and points out that these are all different kinds of association and differ not only in size but "in kind" (εἴδει 1252a10), i.e. in the 'look' of their specific being. The investigation of the polis will therefore be an investigation of the sociation between ruler and ruled, of those who govern and those who are governed (ἄρχον δὲ καὶ ἀρχόμενον 1252a21, 17). Human political sociation thus always involves social interplays of power, where power, to start with, can be understood ontologically by keeping Aristotle's key ontological concept of δύναμις, i.e. power, together with its complementary sister concepts, ἐνέργεια and ἐντελέχεια, in mind and, as laid out in the preceding section, *developing it further for the realm of sociation as a power interplay*.

The first good postulated by Aristotle in his *Politics* as a ground for sociation is that of progeneration, begetting (γένεσις 1252a28) and the sociation is that between a man and a woman. The second good postulated as a ground for sociating is that of safety, security (σωτηρίαν 1252a31) and this gives rise to a sociation between "ruler and ruled according to nature" (ἄρχον δὲ καὶ ἀρχόμενον φύσει 1252a31). The "naturalness" of this sociation and power interplay lies in the nature of human understanding: "the one with the ability to foresee through understanding is by nature the ruler" (τὸ μὲν γὰρ δυνάμενον τῇ διανοίᾳ προορᾶν ἄρχον φύσει 1252a32). The nature of human being, its essence, is to have understanding, and the power of understanding varies from individual to individual. The kind of understanding addressed here is that of being able to foresee, this foresight being with regard to safety. This says first of all that human living is exposed to danger from what is detrimental to it. Such dangers are possibilities of what can happen and are thus situated in the prospective, i.e.

forward-looking, futural dimension of human existence. Human existence always has to look forward and anticipate and cast its own future, and such casting of one's own existence has to take into account what could be, in the future, detrimental to living, its risks. The one who is able to foresee and assess possible dangers by virtue of his (or her) understanding is in a superior position with regard to shaping his existence. It is this superiority with regard to fore-seeing danger, according to Aristotle, which justifies one ruling the other.

Transposed to today's context, such a superiority of foresight with respect to providing safety and protection in living could well be regarded as a *leadership* quality by virtue of which those with less foresight and insight are willing to obey and follow. There can be no doubt that leadership qualities play a decisive role in today's politics (including demagoguery, i.e. (mis)leading the people) and that therefore Aristotle's text can be read not merely as an historical document from times far off, but as applicable also today. The submission to a leader for the sake of safety would then be an act of estimation that first establishes the positions of superior ruler and subordinate ruled with respect to relations of social power, i.e. of the ruler being able (having the power) to command, to rule the ruled. Submission to another's rule is the price for safety and protection, and the individual is willing to renounce its individual freedom for the sake of living securely, without care (se-cura) under a government whose principal task is to ward off the dangers that may and do 'arrive' from the future. Already here, with Aristotle's primal postulation of a social power relation of ruler and ruled, we see a trade-off between individual freedom and security. Trade protectionism, for instance, is today a ubiquitous phenomenal form of this protectionism in which a state's subjects seek shelter from the rigours of competitive market rivalry, with all its uncertainty and insecurity, in the state's power to impose customs duties, import quotas, and the like. The subjects thus increase their dependency on the state and its power in exchange for protection of their livelihoods.

The willing submission to a ruler for the sake of safety presumably is also to be seen in relation to being able to defend oneself against others exercising brute physical force of arms (today these arms have high technical sophistication and deadliness which is, in turn, a kind of brute 'productive' power). Brute physical force is an effective social force, i.e. an effective force over others, only if it is a *superior* brute physical force that is able to (has the power to) overwhelm the resistance of those (an opposing brute physical force) this force is being exercised (ἐνεργέιᾳ) against. There is therefore sense and necessity in banding together for the sake of the good of safety against attack from others, and this banding together requires some kind of leader-follower structure, i.e. a hierarchy, in order to be able to act in concert against an enemy, which also is organized in some kind of hierarchical structure to be able to act as a unified, collective armed force. A leader arises who rules by virtue of being *estimated by others as* able to better assess and counter the external dangers than others. This is a germ, i.e. a ground for existence, of political power relations between a ruler and ruled for the sake of safety and security. In this case the ruler would be a general, and estimation of this leader *as* a commander for the sake of safety is a way for the subjects to achieve free and peaceable living under the protection of an able, far-seeing general.[189] With this example it can be seen already that free individuals would be willing to recognize and submit to a superior power, thus forfeiting in some measure their freedom, precisely for the sake of safely enjoying their individual liberty in other respects.

The above is an alternative reading to the usual interpretation of Aristotle's passage, according to which it is simply a justification of master-slave relations, and Aristotle seems to be saying that some are "naturally" masters and others are "naturally" slaves. However, reading this Aristotelean passage in our modern context would suggest rather a relationship of political leadership based upon the ('natural', individual) superiority of the leader's understanding and foresight with regard to the practical casting of shared everyday life. If only this superiority of foresight can be inkled and estimated by those with a more limited horizon, a basis of trust for being led, along with a readiness to willingly follow and obey, is established. In that case, the leader has authority. Insofar as Aristotle says that all sociations exist for the sake of some good, he is committed to showing that settled social power plays, i.e. relations between ruler and ruled, are for the good of both the ruler and the ruled, and are not merely a matter of one being factually and arbitrarily subjugated by the other through superior brute force, for such brute subjugation could not be regarded as being for the good of the one subjugated. Even where political power relations of ruler and ruled are established initially through an act of brute violence (δύναμις in the sense of brute, physical, military force), there is still an act of estimation involved insofar as the subjugated subjects surrender and acknowledge the superior power of the ruler and his armed forces and submit (for the sake of their, the subjugated subjects', own lives and safety). Within this act of estima-

---

189 David Hume puts the point (ontogenetically) thus: "It is probable, that the first ascendant of one man over multitudes begun during a state of war; where the superiority of courage and of genius discovers itself most visibly, where unanimity and con-/cert are most requisite, and where the pernicious effects of disorder are most sensibly felt." D. Hume 'Of the Origin of Government' Essay V, Part I 1752 p. 39f.

tion of a superior *physical* force as superior and of submission to it, the ruler can then rule peaceably and *political* power and authority are established. If those defeated by military force do not submit and estimate the superior power as superior, this refusal of estimation amounts to a denial of a state of peace, and political power cannot be said to be properly established.

To recapitulate: The good of safety and security (which ensures an *absence* of what is *detrimental* to living, i.e. a kind of double negation) means that human beings sociate also for the sake of saving a way of life (especially against an enemy composed of many hostile ἀρχαί or, in a milder form, a foreign 'enemy' that 'conquers' domestic markets by dint of superior economic power) and moreover that, for the sake of this good, established social relations of political power are necessary and acceptable and thus consented to, i.e. are regarded as *legitimate* (cf. below, section 10.3). Those with superior understanding and foresight with respect to practical human affairs are 'born leaders' who are *estimated* as such and willingly followed and obeyed by others with less understanding and foresight. The leader-follower or superior-subordinate relation is also a social power play, although not necessarily a *political* social power play (e.g. leadership in a commercial enterprise). The leader has power (δύναμις) in the sense that the orders he gives to achieve a purpose he has set in accordance with his foreseeing understanding of what is good for a community or society (or even an organization or enterprise within the realm of social power) are the point of origin for governing the actions of others, just as analogously the foresight of technical know-how is the point of origin for governing changes in things in order to bring forth a fore-seen product.

The carrying-out of the ruler's commands is the ἐνέργεια of his δύναμις, his power, and the state brought about through carrying out the ruler's commands, in line with the purpose envisaged by the ruler, is the ἐντελέχεια, the perfected presence, the actuality of the ruler's political δύναμις. A relationship of leadership in politics is also usually acknowledged on the basis of age and experience, which provides more insight into practical, political affairs and thus also a reason not only why those who are older have an authoritative leadership role vis-à-vis the young in political matters, but also why those younger and less experienced estimate the one who is older and wiser and more experienced *as* superior and submit voluntarily to his or her leadership (cf. Aristotle's remark that "hence the young are not suited to be auditors in politics; for they are inexperienced in the practices of life" διὸ τῆς πολιτικῆς οὐκ ἔστιν οἰκεῖος ἀκροατὴς ὁ νέος· ἄπειρος γὰρ τῶν κατὰ τὸν βίον πράξεων, *Eth. Nic.* I iii. 1095a2).

10.2 Two related social powers: Rhetoric and the political power of government – Legitimacy, punishment, terror

The essential difference between a social relation of power and a technical relation of power over things (or humans qua things), as we have seen, is that power over other human beings as free ἀρχαί always involves, of its essence, their willing or unwilling submission, i.e. an ontologically prior interchange of estimation with the ruler in which the ruler is acknowledged *as* a superior power to be obeyed. The priority here is not a temporal one but a priority in the order of thinking-through that reveals the ontological structure of the world. Willing submission may be either a renunciation of responsibility for shaping one's own existence, thus disburdening oneself of the care for one's own existence, or it may be in exchange for something else, such as money or protection, or it may be the estimation that the ruler or leader has a superior understanding for shaping a shared existence on the basis of the association. In the latter case, one could speak of a legitimate sociation through political power, accepted and affirmed by those being led and ruled. Unwilling submission may be coerced through the use of violent force or the threat thereof. Such submission under duress is the hallmark of *illegitimate* political power.

As has been shown, sociation through *political* power has to be distinguished not only from the technical power to transform things (the know-how of τέχνη ποιητική), but also from sociation through mutually estimating interchange in which humans freely give and take goods in the broadest sense, including the exchange of commodity goods, services, honour and prestige, esteem, gifts, views, opinions, pleasantries, kindnesses, insults, glances, etc. (as investigated in Chapter 5.6). Such a free give-and-take is not based on power in which one is ruled by the other, but on the equality of the exchangers in a *power play*,[190] even when a wealthy individual 'buys' others to do his or her bidding

---

190 Nietzsche comes close to seeing this ontological power play in his critique of the cause-effect relation, although in other places he happily makes use of the cause-effect schema — an aspect of the muddledness of Nietzsche's thinking. The muddledness in this case has to do with his failure to distinguish conceptually between the ontologies of physical power and social power. He writes, for instance: "Two consecutive states, the one cause, the other effect : is false. The first state has nothing to effect, the second has nothing effected. : it is a matter of a struggle between two elements unequal in power: a rearrangement of forces is achieved according to the measure of power in each. The second state is something fundamentally difference from the first (not its effect): what is essential is that the factors in struggle emerge with other power-quanta." (Zwei aufeinander folgende Zustände: der eine Ursache, der andere Wirkung : ist falsch. der erste Zustand hat nichts zu bewirken den zweiten hat nichts bewirkt. :

(thus exercising a kind of venal power over others, i.e. a social power mediated by the power of money). But sociation through political power must proceed from an act of estimation in which the ruled submit, i.e. renounce their status as being free, unrestricted ἀρχαί, free points of emanation of their own self-movement for the sake of some good (which may be simply the absence of a bad).

As announced in the previous section, there is a further art investigated by Aristotle at the founding moment of Western metaphysics which does not fit the paradigm of know-how as a starting-point for governing change in things considered merely as physically manipulable. This art is the art of *rhetoric* which is the know-how of persuasion, i.e. the art of knowing how to bring an audience around to a given point of view aligned with what the orator is aiming at. The change which the art of rhetoric aims at is engendering and winning trust and confidence on the way to bringing about a change of viewpoint on the part of the audience (those who hear), a change in how they hold the world or a particular aspect or situation in the world to be, often with a view to their action, and this change is to be brought about by (verbal, rhetorical) means of persuasion, i.e. of persuasive speech, and the movement itself is persuasion, and what is changed is how the world is held to be on the part of an audience in a certain aspect and a certain situation. Such a change ostensibly governed by the orator (e.g. a salesperson's pitch ending with the customer's decision to buy, thus 'clinching the deal', or a politician's speech that attains the end of convincing

---

es handelt sich um einen Kampf zweier an Macht ungleichen Elemente: es wird ein Neuarrangement der Kräfte erreicht, je nach dem Maß von Macht eines jeden. der zweite Zustand ist etwas Grundverschiedenes vom ersten (nicht dessen Wirkung): das Wesentliche ist, daß die im Kampf befindlichen Faktoren mit anderen Machtquanten herauskommen. *Nachgelassene Fragmente* Frühjahr 1888 14 [95] KSA13:273) Different powers are in struggle with each other, and there is an outcome of this struggle that depends on the interplay of the various "power-quanta". In particular, this means that there can be no calculus of power analogous to the calculus of forces in classical mechanics in which force vectors can be simply added and their resultant force calculated mathematically. But Nietzsche does not unequivocally formulate this, and employs the ambiguous term, "power quanta". Where powers are in play with and against each other, one cannot speak of cause and effect (which would be in principle precalculable), but only of the outcome of a power play in which there is indeed calculation, but calculation on all sides which amounts to various power strategies, even in the most 'innocent' case of negotiating over a sales/purchase transaction. What is most striking in Nietzsche is that, although the "will to power" plays such a dominant role in his thinking, there is no onto-logical-conceptual clarification of what power as such is, i.e. there is no ontology of power in a well-founded sense in Nietzsche's thinking, and this has to do with his contempt for conceptual thinking — to his own detriment, it must be added.

the listeners to vote for him/her) is not a merely real change in a thing, i.e. in a being regarded simply as a thing in the third person, but a change in a being or beings addressed in the *second person* who, as outlined in previous chapters, has that openness to 3D-time that can be called a *psyche and mind*.

Such addressing presupposes that the ones addressed are themselves open to the world in its disclosive truth (such disclosure happening through undistorted presencing and absencing in the 3D-temporal clearing) and that they hold the world to *be* in a certain way, which is their opinion (Dafürhalten, δόξα), and that the way they hold the world to be is articulable in language and therefore also open to the flux of communication and argument in speech, in language which they can hear and understand. Such second person beings are human beings, i.e. beings themselves exposed to the open time-clearing who understand the world in a certain way and are *receptive* to it. The change which the art of rhetoric aims at has to be regarded as a change in how the world reveals itself to an audience and not merely as a real (or 'thingly') change in things.

The words spoken by the orator — *what* is said in the rhetorical arguments aimed at entering the hearts and minds, i.e. ψυχή καὶ νοῦς, of the listeners, and *how* they are spoken (their moodful intonation, the way the speech is 'delivered' to its auditors) — are supposed to woo the audience over to another viewpoint favourable to the orator's intentions and interests. The audience can also be persuaded especially by the status of *who* is speaking, i.e. by the orator's authority, status, reputation and charisma, *as* who he shows himself to be in how he presents himself in the comportment-masks (cf. Chapter 5.6) of his speech as well as the aura of his charisma and reputation.[191] Charisma is the aura emanating from somewho's physical presence, whereas reputation is how a person is held to be by what is said generally about who this person is in his or her physical-sensuous absencing, which consists of a general opinion about the person's goodness, where goodness is not understood in the moral sense, but in the sense of whether this person is good for anything (e.g. competent, an expert in a field relevant to what is spoken about, reliable, trustworthy, etc.), or good for nothing.

The who-status of who is speaking is a powerful 'argument' in itself, and who-status in itself, independently of any overtly rhetorical situation in which words are spoken, must be considered as an aspect of social power in the basic

---

191 "In the λέγω it is at first manifest who somebody is, an upright man or an hypocrite." (Im λέγω zeigt sich zuerst, wer einer ist, ein rechtschaffener Mann oder ein Heuchler. Peter Trawny *Sokrates oder Die Geburt der Politischen Philosophie* 2007 S. 18)

and very simple sense that an individual will show itself off as somewho or other in order to *make an impression* on others. Making an impression on others, albeit diffusely, is a kind of change (μεταβολή) brought about in others (in their perceptions) and therefore fits, at least from one side, the ontological structure of δύναμις, of power, as laid out by Aristotle in the *Metaphysics*. Making an impression can be simply the beauty a woman puts on display to affect her public, or the clothes a man or woman wears in order to create a certain impression of wealth, stylishness, social stratum, up-to-dateness, hipness, conservative solidity, or whatever. Fame and renown have the social power aspect that the mere physical-sensuous presence of a famous person, a celebrity, statesman or who-have-you, is sufficient to make waves in an audience. The who-status of fame is in itself a social power in the power play of estimation.

It must not be overlooked, however, that the social power exercised by showing oneself off in one's who-status in a certain way to make an impression is always a two-way, reciprocating situation in which an audience has to estimate and acknowledge and be receptive for the display and showing-off of who-status. The change wrought in making an impression on others is therefore in truth always and essentially an estimating *inter*change that depends on the audience's active receptiveness. Even the simple physical presence of beauty, for instance, can fail to make an impression if the audience cannot properly read that beauty, so that beauty as a social power can only be exercised within a definite socially established, customary understanding of what constitutes beauty in any given time and with an audience that can 'see' and estimate such culturally cultivated beauty. Making an impression on others by the way one shows oneself off as who one is, is inchoate compared to the explicit exercise of social power in being able to command others. It is a more subtle, implicit sort of social power that may attempt and expect to get others to behave in a certain way, but may just as easily exhaust itself in simply quietly enjoying the feeling of power in the mirrored estimation of one's impress-ive presence by others.

In listening to rhetorical arguments which aim at entering the heart, mind and soul in order to engender trust and bring the listener or listeners around to another viewpoint in swinging their mood, by gaining their confidence, it is the audience's soul as a whole that is aimed at, i.e. its openness to the 3D-time-clearing in which the world shows itself either *as* it is or *as* it is *not* within a given hermeneutic cast of an age, and is grasped thus by understanding. The limitations of the social power of rhetoric thus lie within the nature of the human soul, which is the unique mode of being of human being itself. The limitations of the power of rhetoric therefore lie ultimately in human being itself as ex-sistent exposure to the open clearing of 3D-time, which cannot be manipulated like a builder may manipulate a beam or a doctor a dislocated shoulder. By virtue of this exposure to the temporal clearing, human beings are free ἀρχαί of their own self-movement. The limitations are therefore ontological in nature, not merely ontic or physically 'real'.

There is no precalculable certainty with which a listener or an audience can be swayed in its mood and brought around to a given point of view through the employment of words for, how auditors see and understand the world lies at the core of the freedom of human being itself. The manipulability of an audience has its limits in the audience's very otherness as free, which is an ontological otherness that essentially remains untouched by ontic manipulation and effect (such as the collision between physical bodies), despite all attempts to influence its mood. The words employed by a skilled speaker are not like the hammer employed by a builder in effecting real changes to nail and timber as things. Rather, they speak to the other revealingly or concealingly or distortingly and call a state of affairs to presence within the other's world and from within a certain mood and ontological preconceptions. To win over an audience, to bring someone around by talking, to gain the trust of another person, depends on the other *giving* the speaker its trust and confidence, and this can be freely refused.

Thus we can see that the rhetorical situation is not and can never be one-sided, but is always a mutually estimating *exchange*, an *interchange*, an *interplay* of powers (cf. Chapter 5.6), even when only one person is doing the talking. The act of persuasion depends essentially also on a reciprocation in the listener or listeners giving the speaker their trust and confidence. This reciprocation, as has been shown, is a kind of *estimation* and *mirroring*, which underlies *all* interchange between human beings in their ineluctable casting as somewho or other.[192]

Does the phenomenon of political power, as Aristotle suggests (cf. above *Met.* Delta 1 1013a10), have the ontological structure of a *pro-ductive* δύναμις in that the one wielding power, the ruler or governor or government, is the starting-point governing a change in the other, i.e. the ruled or governed, in the sense that the ruled obey the ruler's commands under pain of punishment? We have already seen that this is not the case because obedience presupposes submission, which is a kind of estimation accorded by the governed. The terms ruler/ruled or government/governed are employed here for convenience only, on a general level of consideration of the phenomenon of *political* social power *pertaining to how a polity is structured according to power plays*, and could be

---

192 Cf. my study 'Assessing How Heidegger Thinks Power Through the History of Being' 2004.

substituted by sovereign/subject, governor/governed, magistrate/accused, commander/commanded, but not the social power of master/servant, superior/subordinate or employer/employee, etc. *mediated by reified value*. Sociation through political power involves a government and the governed, commands and obedience to commands. Political power is the power to get somebody else to do something or refrain from doing something in line with a ruler's will. This obedient action in response to a ruler's command constitutes the change (μεταβολή) that is brought about in the other being, the one ruled, analogously (but by no means identical) to the case of the art of rhetoric, in which the change brought about is a change of viewpoint on the part of the audience. In both cases, it is words, speech which apparently effect the change, the words of command, on the one hand, and the persuasive words of rhetorical argument, on the other. The change wrought in each case is active obedience itself or a change of viewpoint and in both cases depends upon a receptiveness — of 'hearingness' in the former case and listening in the latter.

Words do not and cannot 'effect' a change in a free human being. They are not 'effective', 'actuating'; they are *heard*. Obedience to a command is literally a 'hearingness', deriving from Latin 'ob-' 'toward' and 'audire' 'to hear' or 'obœdire'(L. 'to give ear, hearken, obey'), which presupposes that the commanded subject hearkens and gives ear, just an audience gives ear to and allows itself to be swayed by an orator. Hence there is an essential ontological link between political social power and the social power of rhetoric which is also manifest in the ubiquitous *rhetoric of political power*. This giving of ear is already an estimation of the ruler or governor or commander *as* such. The willingness to obey is the governed subject's free decision and amounts to a submission on the part of the governed subject itself of its own will in favour of the ruler's will.

And what if the governed subject does not give ear to the ruler's command, e.g. what if it does not obey the laws promulgated by the government? Such disobedience can go so far as that of a *political dissident* who questions the government's very legitimacy and not merely one of its actions. Then it must be punished, perhaps even for sedition. *Punishment* can take the form of physical harm to the subject or those close to it, the restriction of the subject's freedom of physical movement by imprisonment, the total or partial loss of the subject's property (e.g. a parking fine or confiscation of assets). Even punishment cannot force obedience, for the act of giving ear is a free one by a free ἀρχή. Under pain of punishment, however, this free ἀρχή may acquiesce grudgingly to comply. Apart from any consideration of due process of law, which is here put to one side, a subject that does not obey its government's commands in the form of law, etc. must be punished, and this punishment must be carried out by the government's agents (bailiffs, police force, prison officers, etc.) entrusted with the task of punishing offenders. The agents of punishment, in turn, must obey the commands to carry out a punishment, and this presupposes that these agents *estimate* appropriately the hierarchical power structures in which they are embedded and perform their duty.

This estimation can be given, on the one hand, because the government's agents estimate the government *as* legitimate and understand themselves *as* loyal government officers, or on the other hand, they may estimate the chain of command from the government down for fear of punishment themselves if they do not properly carry out orders. There is thus a kind of regressive alternating chain of legitimacy and punishment that must underlie any form of politically sociating power in a community or society. In this chain, the alternating links have a different ontological status because legitimacy is an act of human freedom and punishment is ultimately an act of physical force and coercion directed at things and human bodies. Both work in tandem. Physical force and violence can confiscate, restrain, kill and maim, banish, incarcerate, intimidate, but it cannot force anyone to esteem a government *as* legitimate. Any individual as free principal is (ontologically, i.e. by virtue of exposure to the clearing of 3D-time) beyond the reach of the power of physical force emanating from another principal, in this case, the hierarchical organization of a state's repressive apparatus.

Furthermore, a government that relies primarily on a system of punishment carried out by its agents to enforce its will whilst not being estimated *as* legitimate by large parts of the citizenry must be a system of *terror* with a nested organizational system of agents of physical force who themselves fear punishment by other sections of the repressive apparatus if they do not efficiently carry out orders. (For instance, the secret police oversees the police.) The tyrant who rules through an organized system of terror (consisting of arbitrary punishment and also arbitrary rewards) must himself even fear being killed because the legitimacy of a government can only be given by a people that is not in constant fear of being subject to arbitrary, violent, physical force exercised by the tyrant's agents. Friedrich A. Hayek points out the crucial importance of legitimizing opinion among the people even for a tyrannical system of government:

> As dictators themselves have known best at all times, even the most powerful dictatorship crumbles if the support of opinion is withdrawn. This is the reason why dictators are so

concerned to manipulate opinion through that control of information which is in their power.[193]

A system of sociating political power plays constituting the government of a society can only be regarded as free insofar as the citizens of that society freely, willingly estimate, through their own judgement, the government *as* legitimate. Kant puts it thus:

> Vielmehr ist meine äußere (rechtliche) *Freiheit* so zu erklären: sie ist die Befugnis, keinen äußeren Gesetzen zu gehorchen, als zu denen ich meine Beistimmung habe geben können.
>
> Kant *Zum ewigen Frieden* 1983 S. 204

> Rather, my outward (rightful) *freedom* is to be declared as follows: it is the authority not to obey any outer laws other than those to which I have been able to give my assent.

This implies that the citizens then freely submit to the government's superior power and obey its laws and other decrees, edicts and regulations that shape how the citizens are to conduct themselves in social intercourse with each other and with the state itself. The exercise of political power is then not based largely on the threat of punishment, and even offenders who infringe the law accept their punishment as legitimate (presuming due process of law, which is an essential part of demonstrating the law's legitimacy and consists largely in acknowledging the accused as free and equal before the law). The 'hardened criminals' in society, who do not esteem any political power as legitimate and have to be restrained by physical force, remain a small minority, and the free citizens legitimize the regime only because they reconcile the existence of a superior, governing instance in some way or other with their own individual freedom exercised in manifold power plays in civil society.

A government also gains legitimacy through rhetorical means in the broadest sense insofar as it wins the 'hearts and minds' of its citizens, who signal that they have been won over by estimating the government as legitimate in their own minds. Political power therefore intermeshes with both rhetorical power (e.g. attempts on the part of the government to win the people over to a certain

---

193 Friedrich A. Hayek *Law, Legislation and Liberty* Vol. 1 Rules and Order, Chicago U.P. 1973 p. 92. Hayek is presumably echoing a thought of David Hume's: "No man would have any reason to *fear* the fury of a tyrant, if he had no authority over any but from fear; since, as a single man, his bodily force can reach but a small way, and all the farther power he possesses must be founded either on our own opinion, or on the presumed opinioin of others." 'Of the First Principles of Government' Essay IV Part I 1752 p. 34.

policy) and physical social force (the state's so-called repressive apparatuses, as last resort, in particular, to maintain the polity as the play of political powers that it is). Only the last form of social power is pro-ductive power *at all* in the sense investigated in the metaphysical tradition as a point of emanation governing changes in something else (the offender's body, property,...), and even this point of emanation, a physically repressive force (such as a police force) is, in turn, organized internally as a hierarchy of command and obedience that is a political power play based on estimation of superiors by subordinate officers who are and understand themselves as dutiful servants of the state.

Furthermore, the offender as a human being can *resist* the attempt to restrain and subdue him physically, and may not simply *submit* to the state's agents of repression. Such an act of submission, in turn, is, as we have already seen, a free act of estimation beyond the reach of any physical force (even physical torture). Thus *all* forms of social power are structured ontologically as an estimating interchange between free principals. This is because *all* sociating power plays between human beings without exception involve some form of mutual estimation, no matter how deficient. In the case of specifically political power, the governed subjects estimate the superior powers as such, give ear and obey. Within the recognition of a government as legitimate, the government can indeed give commands (above all in the form of laws) that will be obeyed.

10.3 Legitimacy of government further considered – Acceptance and affirmation of government

In the case of legitimate government, as opposed to a tyranny based on a system of state terror, the subjects accept and assent or at least acquiesce to being governed by their government which has legitimate authority to do so in their eyes and for the sake of some good which could be formulated generally as enabling and protecting the citizens' customary way of life. Where a ruler rules or a government governs not solely by virtue of the threat of punishment (which is always ultimately physical force and violence), it rules by virtue of the acknowledged legitimacy of its rule, i.e. because its subjects are *willing* to obey its commands, i.e. its laws, displaying even *reverence* for, say, a country's monarch or its constitution. Insofar as a subject is willing to obey, paradoxically, the use of physical force and coercion is unnecessary. One could even say that the ultimate basis of government is not, as a Leninist would say, 'organized state violence': even if the society in question is ruled tightly and repressively by a tyrannical system of terror, physical force is not an ultimate means but can only be exercised by the government's agents because the government is estimated in some way as legitimate by the population at large which, say, may consent to being governed by a 'strong hand' for the sake of security and law & order or certain welfare benefits such as cheap housing. Legitimacy given by free consent thus becomes, and must become, the ultimate ground of government, not the threat of physical force and violence, since all social power, including political social power, is a mutual estimating.

Legitimacy here is understood not as a synonym for legality in the sense of "conformable to law or rule; sanctioned or authorized by law" (OED), if law is taken to mean law promulgated by a legislature as written law, for this would be a formal conception of legitimacy as conformity merely to *positive right*, i.e. to right posited by the state in the form, the 'look' of law. Rather, legitimacy in the present context means conformity to law in the sense of natural right, which is ontologically prior to merely state-posited right. Natural right is 'natural' in the sense of being a state of affairs, a polity that is in-joint and conformable with 'human nature', i.e. with an historically cast essence of human being that is lived and practised ethically-habitually in the framework of certain shared usages or, in other words, with Greek νόμος. Legitimacy depends essentially on the insight of understanding into such conformity with νόμος, i.e. on the insight that how society is set up as a polity is in conformity with what is good and necessary for human beings living together in society in an historically rooted, customary way of living that at the same time engenders and preserves human freedom.

Legitimacy of government or of the government's laws thus depends in turn on the people's accepting it as in accordance with what is right, with law in the deeper sense of an in-jointness (δίκη) of social living within established and proven usages (νόμος). In Hegelian terms, legitimacy is an "Erfahrung des Bewußtseins", an experience that reflective consciousness goes through, and not merely a question of the procedure according to which laws are posited and promulgated. Legitimacy in the sense understood here is intimately associated with the liberal tradition of thinking for which government's raison d'être is the good of its citizens and in conformity with their individual freedom, rather than the authority of tradition or the like.

The present inquiry has taken the notion of 'natural right' deeper by bringing to light the hermeneutic socio-ontology of sociated freedom *as a mutually estimating power interplay* among whos. It is in this sense that human being is 'naturally' free. The sociating power interplay among all the social players in society or the state is 'naturally rightful' if it accords to freedom which, in turn, consists in the *fairness* of the sociating power plays.

This 'naturalness' of right implies, in particular, that even the legislator within an acknowledged form of government has to be estimated *as* legitimate. It does not suffice for the legislator to baldly posit the laws for those laws to be legitimate. Friedrich A. Hayek puts it pre-ontologically thus:

> The authority of a legislator always rests ... on something which must be clearly distinguished from an act of will on a particular matter in hand, and can therefore also be limited by the source from which it derives its authority. This source is a prevailing opinion that the legislator is authorized only to prescribe what is right, where this opinion refers not to the particular content of the rule but to the general attributes which any rule of just conduct [in civil society ME] must possess. ... In this sense all power rests on, and is limited by, opinion...[194]

This conception of legitimate legislation is an injunction against the unlimited power claimed by a positivist conception of law, including an absolutist conception of democracy. There is an established, customary and thus ethical (in the sense of the connection between ethos (ἦθος) and habit (ἔθος)) way of life in civil society that must be respected by the legislator's laws if those laws are to be estimated by the subjects as legitimate.

Full legitimacy of government (not just a particular government, but a polity as a whole and in general as a system of political power), as opposed to grudging acceptance or mere acquiesence to being governed, amounts to its estimation and acceptance and even affirmation by those governed in the sense that the government's subjects view the world in such a way that holds the government's rule to be good for a given way of social living and therefore necessary and acceptable and welcome. Such legitimacy may consist in a high estimation and acceptance of ancestral authority as a good way of social living, namely, according to tradition (cf. the comments on Leo Strauss' thoughts on ancestral authority in Chapter 6.1). Legitimacy of rule in the modern era, however, is *given* to the government by the subjects only in affirming that this rule is ultimately good for their *own* way of life, including their individual liberty, their freedom of movement in shaping their lives, and not merely as an act of reverence for traditional authority. There is no force or threatened use of force which could enforce legitimacy, since legitimacy is beyond the reach of any physical power, just as a person's political convictions are beyond the reach of torture. In another context, Thomas Hobbes puts it thus: "It is true, that if he be my Soveraign, he may oblige me to obedience, so, as not by act or word to declare I

---

194 Friedrich A. Hayek *Law, Legislation and Liberty* Vol. 1 Rules and Order, Chicago U.P. 1973 p. 92.

beleeve him not; but not to think any otherwise then my reason perswades me."[195]

How "my reason perswades me" to hold the world to be is an ontological, or at least pre-ontological, condition of how the world shows itself to be in its truth and untruth. Insofar, the situation of legitimate rule by a sovereign or government is similar to the rhetorical situation in which the audience is persuaded, brought around, coaxed, won and wooed over by a speaker to see the world or a situation in a certain way, i.e. to freely adopt a certain view of the world as its own. Legitimacy of rule in the modern age can only be granted by a subject who freely affirms being ruled by a superior sovereign or government for the sake of some good, which must include also its *own* good social living. Otherwise, a government governs (or vainly attempts to govern) only by coercion and ultimately — if the citizens thoroughly refuse recognition of the government as legitimate — by terror, i.e. by virtue of being able to (threaten to) do physical violence to the subject, to exercise physical force against the subject's body and property. As Hegel notes in his scholia to the *Rechtsphilosophie*: "Absolute subjectivity cannot be forced" (Absolute Subjektivität kann nicht gezwungen werden, *RPh.* [zu § 139]).

The question of the legitimacy of government is at the heart of the liberal question concerning government which was first posed by Thomas Hobbes and taken up again by John Locke in seventeenth century England. Although Hobbes is usually assigned to the school of "absolutist" political thinkers, both Hobbes and Locke must be regarded as the fathers of liberalism in the thinking of political philosophy, at least in the sense that the government now has to legitimize itself, i.e. to justify itself, to the reasoning of the individual subject for the sake of whom government exists. Government must now justify itself to "Laws of Reason" rather than simply being accepted as divinely ordained in a monarch's rule. In the incipient modern age emerging from medieval times, the individual subject (understood both in the political sense as the subject of a sovereign and also in the ontological sense of the reasoning, conscious subject as the underlying locus of representations of beings as such in consciousness) becomes the touchstone for all questions of truth, including the question of how society is to be set up or whether a polity's existence is justified at all. This contrasts with the medieval age in which all questions regarding truth or the legitimacy of the social order were referred back ultimately (via the ostensible media-

---

195 Thomas Hobbes *Leviathan* eds. Richard E. Flathman and David Johnston, Norton, New York/London, Ch. XXXII p. 196. Page references to *Leviathan* are consistently to the Head edition of 1651.

tion of God's representative on Earth, the Church) to the supreme subject, God, as the creator of the universe and the instance responsible for the highest good of humankind (salvation of the sinful soul).

The question of the legitimacy of government for the individual subject is a renaissance of the Greek question concerning the polis insofar as Greek thinking, too, understood the polity of the polis solely in terms of its existing for the sake of some human good, namely, good living, i.e. εὖ ζῆν. But the *individual* subject and the conception of a state of nature as a pre-social situation composed of individuals is a modern conception necessitated by having to free all questioning from the oppressive authority of the Christian church which theologically usurped questioning in favour of the dogmas of faith "to the Honor and Dignity of God Almighty".[196] The historical condition of possibility of questioning authority and tradition is the emergence of the human being *as* an individual which, in turn, as thoroughly investigated in preceding chapters, goes hand in hand with the sociation of human beings abstractly via reified value, whose ascent sets human beings abstractly free *as* individuals.

The Hobbesian conception of the state of nature is the (inept, because in large part ontic-genetically conceived as a chronologically prior period of history) attempt to start again with a clean slate in order to legitimize the mode of sociation, including government, to individual consciousness itself in the light of its 'natural', individual reason. That is why the state of nature and a law of nature in both Hobbes and Locke are synonymous with the state of reason and a law of reason. Reason is rendered by the individual subject asking why, and it is human nature itself to reason. As Leibniz formulates around the same time, nothing exists without sufficient reason, i.e. for the sake of some good, a τέλος (cf. Chapter 8.1ff). This "grand principle" of reason is equivalent to the relentlessness of the individual subject of consciousness in asking the question, "Why?", which does not shrink back even from questioning the legitimacy of government equipped with political power in a fundamental sense by demanding its raison d'être.

The posing of the question as to why a state must exist at all, or its constitution, has traditionally taken the form of a rationalist justification consisting in logical deduction from self-evident premises or axioms. The rationalist mode of thinking was first formulated explicitly by Descartes. In the present context, this subjectivist rationalism has the curious side-effect of imagining (vorstellen) an

---

196 Edward Hyde *A Brief View and Survey of the Dangerous and Pernicious Errors to Church and State in Mr. Hobbes's Book, Entitled Leviathan*, London 1676, reprinted in part in Leviathan, 1651/1997 p. 286.

isolated, pre-social, individual subject in a state of nature = state of reason try-ing to reason about society, sociation with others, the necessity of government, etc. as if social being itself could be a logical deduction preformed by con-sciousness. This is akin to Descartes' solitary subject reasoning about the candle wax in his chamber. This solitary subject is in truth the result of a metaphysical positing of the ego cogito, cogito ergo sum, i.e. positing 'I am' as the self-certain foundation for knowing and assessing the world. As should now be apparent from the minute investigations in previous chapters, the socio-ontological route taken in the present inquiry is very different.

To return to the specific question at hand, we now see that the power which a government exercises over its subjects has two essentially different sources. The one, primary source is the affirmation by the subjects on the basis of insight and conviction that they be ruled by a superior, sovereign subject, i.e. a gov-ernment, and the other, secondary source is the fear of punishment which is based always ultimately on (the potential use of) physical force exercised against bodies and property. The subjects only assent to being governed be-cause, on balance, they regard it to be for their own good and preferable to an-other kind of polity or no polity at all and in this way they reconcile the possible use of superior force against them with the restriction of their own individual liberty. Insofar, the subjects regard their being ruled by the government as nec-essary, justified and legitimate, in that the government's rule is affirmed as being good for a given social way of living. It is accepted that social life would be impossible without a superior, powerful subject "able to over-awe them all" (*Lev.* p. 61), which is what Hobbes means by the Leviathan.

The granting of legitimacy to the government is a renunciation on the part of the subjects in the sense that subjects subject themselves willingly, i.e. freely, to a superior will, namely, that of the government (which, in the present con-text, may be monarchical, democratic, oligarchic, aristocratic or whatever). They are in agreement with and assent to being governed by the government, in its Hobbesian formulation, *for the sake of living peaceably with one another* and insofar *give* the government power over themselves, which makes the use of force superfluous. Otherwise, they resist the government's power and attempt to delegitimize this power, which latter is at core a rhetorical enterprise, since all questions of legitimacy stand or fall ultimately with regard to the question of what is the best government or best form of government for those living under it or whether government is necessary at all. Such questions are dealt with in words, reasoning, argument. Force and violence against bodies and property, by contrast, can never touch the question of legitimacy because legitimacy is situated in the realm of how the (social) world is held to be, i.e. ultimately within the openness of being's truth revealing itself in the 3D-temporal clearing, whereas physical force and violence can only restrain, injure, damage and destroy physical bodies or reified property.

To reason for the necessity of government for the sake of peaceable living is still that kind of pro and con arguing back and forth with oneself that never enters the realm of genuinely socio-ontological thinking which has to grapple with modes of sociation not in terms of advantages and disadvantages, but guided by insight into human being itself as free. Freedom itself becomes the criterion for judging the sociation practised by a given way of social living. Social ontology must therefore ask what human freedom consists in at all and how freedom in sociation is possible.[197]

10.4 The "restlesse desire of Power after power" and the necessity of the Leviathan – Straussian "vanity" and the inevitable ongoing mutual estimating of who-status and individual powers – The modern individual subject as the foundation and starting-point for deriving the Leviathan

In average everyday life, people live according to the government's laws out of a mixture of acknowledging their legitimacy and wanting to avoid (the chance of) punishment for their violation. Affirmation of or acquiescence to being governed is paired with the fear, ultimately, of having violence done to one's body or estate by the government's forces. Hobbes' political thinking is concerned

---

197 When Hobbes says that government is necessary for the sake of or "peaceable, sociable, and comfortable living" (*Lev.* p. 80) or Hayek says that "all power rests on, and is limited by, opinion", they are arguing on the basis of an understanding of what is good for living. Hume's and Hayek's emphasis on the importance of "opinion" still does not penetrate to the level of the philosophical distinction between positive and natural law as developed in Hegel's speculative philosophy, for which opinion is not the criterion for legitimacy, nor simply peaceable living, but the *concept of freedom* itself as thought through by speculative reason. Only that government and that government's laws which are in conformity with the ontological concept of freedom, and thus with natural right, are legitimate and ultimately historically viable for, according to Hegel's *Rechtsphilosophie*, speculative reason can gain insight into human social being and see that this being is nothing other than freedom, so that any reality that does not conform with this ontology of freedom must crumble of itself. In particular, this implies that the basis for legitimacy cannot be opinion, but rather that opinion itself must become aligned with the concept of freedom as it becomes concretized in an historical people, and that this latter concept (which is never anything merely 'thought up' by human beings) is the deeper ground of history.

with the question of why men should reasonably assent or acquiesce to being ruled by a "common Power to keep them all in awe" (*Lev.* p. 62), i.e. that such a superior power should exist at all for the sake of men living well together in society, or "peaceable, sociable, and comfortable living" (*Lev.* p. 80). The alternative to setting up an artificial social subject, a Leviathan "that *Mortall God*, to which wee owe ... our peace and defence" (*Lev.* p. 87), according to Hobbes, is inevitably a "condition which is called Warre, and such a warre, as is of every man, against every man" in which "the life of man, [is] solitary, poore, nasty, brutish, and short". (*Lev.* p. 62) These ideas and formulations of Hobbes' are well-known; indeed, in part they are famous standard quotations, and from the start Hobbes' views were strongly attacked, in particular, his dismal view of human nature and his dishonouring of the divine creator. But we have to ask whether there is a possibility of reading them more deeply in a way that undercuts the controversies surrounding Hobbes both in his own time and in present-day scholarly debates. I will attempt a socio-ontologically rooted reading in the following.

Hobbes poses the decision of individual subjects in the situation of confronting each other as individual centres of power (like Leibnizian monads, themselves a modern transposition of Aristotelean ἀρχαί as governing sources of free self-movement) as to whether they can agree to renounce the use of violence against each other in favour of being governed and "kept in awe" by a superior power whose primary function is to maintain a peaceable way of living among its subjects. The proposed reason for the existence of the state is pacification of a warlike state of (human) nature. Who are the subjects confronted with this decision? Why are they so warlike? Hobbes casts human beings as such, i.e. ontologically, as desirous subjects of power.

> Nor can a man any more live, whose Desires are at an end, than he, whose Senses and Imagination are at a stand. Felicity is a continuall progresse of the desire, from one object to another; the attaining of the former, being still but the way to the later. ... And therefore the voluntary actions, and inclinations of all men, tend, not onely to the procuring, but also to the assuring of a contented life; ... So that in the first place, I put for a generall inclination of all mankind, a perpetuall and restlesse desire of Power after power, that ceaseth onely in Death. (*Lev.* p. 47)

The "Power after power" referred to here implies a continual, endless accretion and augmentation of power, an "Übermächtigung" (Heidegger *Die Geschichte des Seyns* 1938/40 GA69:62) and a will to power, a Nietzschean Willen zur Macht, for the sake of the "Felicity" of "assuring ... a contented life" or, as Aristotle would say, εὐδαιμονίας ἕνεκα (for the sake of happiness, cf. *Nic. Eth.* 1176b30). But the difference from Aristotle's τέλος of εὐδαιμονία is that "Felicity is a continuall progresse of the desire", i.e. it is ἀτελής, without end, like πλεονεξία, i.e. the desire to have more, that has played a leading role in preceding chapters, starting with Chapter 4.1. And what is power for Hobbes?

> The POWER of a Man, (to take it Universally,) is his present means, to obtain some future apparent Good. ... *Naturall Power*, is the eminence of the Faculties of Body, or Mind: as extraordinary Strength, Forme [i.e. appearance ME], Prudence, Arts, Eloquence, Liberality, Nobility. *Instrumentall* are those Powers, which acquired by these, or by fortune, are means and Instruments to acquire more: as Riches, Reputation, Friends, and the secret working of God, which men call Good Luck. (*Lev.* p. 41)

In contrast to Aristotle, who envisages a τέλος or end-state in the strivings of men living together in society, Hobbes posits an endless, restless desire for more which, moreover, has an essential link with comparing oneself to others:

> ... as men attain to more riches, honours, or other power; so their appetite groweth more and more; and when they are come to the utmost degree of one kind of power, they pursue some other, as long as in any kind they think themselves behind any other.[198]

Leo Strauss comments:

> Das Selbstbewußtsein konstituiert sich aber nur durch die Vergleichung des Individuums mit anderen Individuen: nicht überhaupt nach immer weiteren Zielen strebt der Mensch, sondern nach immer weiteren Zielen als sie je *ein anderer* erreicht hat. Gibt es also Angenehmes, das der Rede wert ist, nur in der Vergleichung mit andereren, nur im Sichmessen mit anderen, nur *gegen* die anderen... (*HpW.* p. 131)

> Self-consciousness is constituted, however, only through comparison of the individual with other individuals: human beings do not just strive for one goal after another without qualification, but for one goal after another more than *any other* has attained. If there is anything pleasant worth mentioning, then only in comparing it with others, only in measuring oneself against others, only *against* others... (*HpW.* p. 131)

> ... das Streben nach Ehre und Ehrenstellungen, nach Vorrang vor den anderen Menschen und nach Anerkennung dieses Vorrangs durch die anderen Menschen, den Ehrgeiz, den Stolz, die Ruhmsucht... (*HpW.* p. 21)

> ... the striving for honour and positions of honour, for precedence over other people and for recognition of this precedence by other people, ambition, pride, thirst for fame... (*HpW.* p. 21)

---

198 *Elements of Law* E I, VII 7 cited in Leo Strauss *Hobbes' politische Wissenschaft* Luchterhand, Neuwied 1965 on the basis of the German manuscript from 1934/35 p. 131.

The individuals each stand in a status as somewho, and this who-status is what it is only in the comparison with the stands of other individuals who likewise are cast into the socio-ontological mould of whoness. It is therefore not just self-interest and egoism that drive human beings to strive for more "power", i.e. the goods of living, but their mutual, differential measuring of each other's who-status in each other's mirrors, which reflect how high or how low one stands in the hierarchy of possible who-stands. Leo Strauss calls this the essential "vanity" ("Eitelkeit" *HpW*. p. 20, p. 144) or "boundless self-love" ("schrankenlose Selbstliebe" *HpW*. p. 148) that drives human beings and, together with the fear of violent death, necessitates a superior instance, viz. the state, to pacify the war over precedence in who-standing, and it is indeed the essential endangeredness of each individual's stand as who in the comparison and rivalry with others' who-stands that characterizes the socio-ontological predicament of humankind. What Hobbes calls a "comparison" and Strauss a "recognition of precedence" have been shown to be aspects of the sociating of human beings via mutually estimating power interplay.

This ontologico-existential whoness of human being must not be conceived merely as a human failing or as a dismal aspect of human nature but in all explicitness as an historical socio-ontological destiny that entered into (at least) the Western way of conceiving the world's social constitution and questioning reflection upon it with Greek philosophy (and presumably universally into human *experience* and *narrative* since time immemorial). Although, as Leo Strauss is at pains to emphasize, Hobbes saw the phenomenon of human pride and gave it a central role in his political thinking (for instance, by choosing the name Leviathan from the book of Job because "the state resembles the Leviathan, since it too and precisely it is the 'King of all the children of pride'" *HpW*. p. 22), this nevertheless does not amount to a socio-ontology of whoness but rather outlines a universal anthropology. To return to the exposition in *Leviathan*:

Such desirous subjects of power seeking their own apparent good inevitably come into conflict with each other. "Competition of Riches, Honour, Command, or other power, enclineth to Contention, Enmity, and War." (*Lev.* p. 47f) This can only be so because the claims to goods are mutually exclusive — or at least comparable as more and less, higher and lower — so that the powers to obtain such goods are opposed to each other; they are *rival* claims. Desirous subjects of power are in a permanent state of differentially measuring, estimating their respective powers against each other. In the first place, the goods of life are all those material things comprising a man's estate which contribute to living well. In the second place, the goods of life are the command over servants (today we would say service-providers) who perform services that enhance living. In the third place, there is the derived, intangible good of honour which, for Hobbes, resides in the estimating acknowledgement of a man's powers:

> The *Value*, or WORTH of a man, is as of all other things, his Price; that is to say, so much as would be given for the use of his Power: and therefore is not absolute; but a thing dependant on the need and judgement of another. ... The manifestation of the Value we set on one another, is that which is commonly called Honouring, and Dishonouring. To Value a man at a high rate, is to *Honour* him; at a low rate, is to *Dishonour* him. (*Lev.* p. 42)

The constant measuring, estimating and esteeming of each other's powers (especially abilities) as the means to acquiring other goods is itself, for Hobbes, a good, namely, the derived or second-order good of honour. Such a good presupposes already that the subjects live together in a world, that they regard themselves in having self-esteem and that they have social intercourse with each other in mutually estimating and esteeming each other, including, of course, also the negations and deficient modes of self-esteem and esteem. Such subjects continually eyeing and sizing each other up and exercising their individual powers with and against each other in the acquisition and enjoyment of the goods for living is what Hobbes calls a "condition of warre one against another" (*Lev.* p. 63), i.e. a *social* state of vieing, which arises from

> three principall causes of quarrell. First Competition; Secondly, Diffidence; Thirdly, Glory. The first, maketh men invade for Gain; the second, for Safety; and the third, for Reputation. The first use Violence to make themselves Master of other mens persons, wives, children, and cattell; the second, to defend them; the third, for trifles, as a word, a smile, a different opinion, and any other signe of undervalue, either direct in their Persons, or by reflexion in their Kindred, their Friends, their Nation, their Profession, or their Name. (*Lev.* p. 62)

Such a "condition of warre one against another" as name-bearing whos is not empirically, i.e. experientially, alien to us, even and especially today in the twenty-first century. There are, for instance, stateless regions of the world where a state of continual or intermittent war reigns with shifting alliances between warlords involved in various rackets or with feuds of honour between clans. But the 'war' of competing for reputation is entirely familiar to us and closer to home in our everyday lives. And, as Hobbes points out,

> yet in all times, Kings, and Persons of Soveraigne authority, because of their Independency, are in continuall jealousies, and in the state and posture of Gladiators; having their weapons pointing, and their eyes fixed on one another; (*Lev.* p. 63)

This is the state of affairs among the individual nation states of the world which have no "common Power to keep them all in awe" (*Lev.* p. 62). Hobbes, too, is undoubtedly referring also to an empirical, historical state of affairs in the seventeenth century present in men's minds. His proposal that men agree to set up a sovereign power to rule them all (whether it be a single sovereign or an assembly, i.e. a monarchy or "an Assembly of All that will come together, ... a DEMOCRACY or Popular Common-wealth" *Lev.* p. 94) could thus also be regarded as a practical political proposal in a specific historical context. Such an interpretation is too easy and unphilosophical, however, since the "condition of warre one against another" has to be understood not merely as some empirical, particular, historical overall state of affairs present or past, but *socio-ontologically* as a "condition" of human nature itself. Such an socio-ontological condition of humankind, or human being itself, is open to view for reflection or speculation even within our highly *civilized* conditions of everyday life, namely, as a "condition of warre one against another" which is only kept in check and repressed, or merely mediated, by a superior power.

It should also be noted here that only a superficial reading of Hobbes could assert that he argues exclusively for an absolutist monarchy as opposed to a democracy, a line often adopted even today in readings of Hobbes. For Hobbes, the "common Power to keep them all in awe" can indeed be a democratic government, whether it be a democracy of an assembly of all, or a representative democracy. The core, essential argument for the existence of the Leviathan, in the first and fundamental place (prior to any arguments in favour specifically of absolute monarchy), is indifferent to whether the political form of this monstrous monster demanding utter subjection to itself is monarchical, democratic or otherwise. What Hobbes argues is that this sovereign power, whether it be monarchical or democratic, must have *absolute* (rather than relative) power to make laws and that no individual subject can opt out — a situation not entirely inconsistent with the understanding of legitimate democratic sovereignty today as absolute, despite (or even because of) the refinement of the idea of legitimate democratic sovereignty through the addition of ideas of a division of powers within the state, revisions to the constitution through referendum, etc.

Absolutist democracy is not a contradiction in terms and indeed, it is the form that our modern democracies, especially in the name of social justice (cf. Chapter 6.5, Chapter 9.10f), have increasingly assumed (in negating and restricting the interplay of individual liberty). But neither the absolute nature of Hobbes' Leviathan — which therefore with some justification could be called a Frankenstein, and even more so as the dispenser of so-called social justice — nor his preference for absolute monarchy is the fundamental point. Hobbes' innovation in political philosophy is that he poses the decision as to whether individual subjects of power could assent, through the use of reason and for their *own* sakes, to set up a superior sovereign power *at all*, thus asserting the modern subjectivity of human subjects as fundamentum absolutum in the context of the question concerning social political power. The fundamental modern question of the legitimacy of government is how the polyarchic rivalry among many human beings — their unceasing mutually estimating power plays — each conceived of as an individual centre of power (ἀρχὴ δυνάμεως) comes, through the use of reason, to willingly relinquish its individual powers in favour of a unifying, pacifying, superior power. Leo Strauss makes an equivalent point on the underlying subjectivity of individual human subjects for the state when he writes in *Natural Right and History*:

> If we may call liberalism that political doctrine which regards as the fundamental political fact the rights, as distinguished from the duties, of man and which identifies the function of the state with the protection or the safeguarding of those rights, we must say that the founder of liberalism was Hobbes.[199]

Attributing fundamental, primordial rights to individuals (namely, their individual freedoms in who they are and what they have in their social interplay with one another) amounts to making individualized human subjectivity the basis, the ὑποκείμενον, on which all social power must be legitimized through an act of reason (not a factual act) that constitutes a state. This individualism of human subjectivity — the hallmark of the modern era — has been noted by a trenchant critic of Hobbes when he writes that Hobbes' politics

> is itself based ... on assumptions representing an extreme form of individualism: an individualism more uncompromising than that of Locke himself.[200]

The individualism here repudiated is not merely the individualism of self-interest and arbitrary liberty, but must be seen to lie deeper in the socio-ontology of a world in which individual humans have (been enabled by value as pervasive reified sociating medium to) become freely playing subjects, thus fundamentally transforming the problematic of political power and the state:

---

199 Leo Strauss *Natural Right and History* 1953 p. 181f.
200 C.E. Vaughan *Studies in the History of Political Philosophy Before and After Rousseau* Manchester 1925 I p. 23 cited in Leo Strauss *HpW*. 1965 p. 151.

> While modern thought starts from the *rights of the individual,* and conceives the State as existing to secure the conditions of his development, Greek thought starts from the right of the State.[201]

It is a moot point whether the Greek πόλις can be regarded as a "State". That said, the individualized subjectivity of modern man means that the very existence of the sovereign state has to be instituted by an act (in thought that grants legitimacy) of collective individual will (based, according to Hobbes, on the primal fear of violent death at the hands of other individuals — but this is secondary and presupposes the fundament of individualized, free human subjectivity):

> A *Common-wealth* is said to be *Instituted,* when a *Multitude* of men do Agree, and *Covenant, every one, with every one,* that to whatsoever *Man,* or *Assembly of Men,* shall be given by the major part, the *Right* to *Present* the Person of them all, (that is to say, to be their *Representative*;) every one, as well that *Voted for it,* as he that *Voted against it,* shall *Authorise* all the Actions and Judgements, of that Man, or Assembly of men, in the same manner, as if they were his own, to the end, to live peaceably amongst themselves, and be protected against other men. (*Lev.* p. 88)

This passage, no doubt, can be read as a description of an historical practical political situation in which men institute a commonwealth, and there are indeed historical examples which need no mention here, the most notable being perhaps the founding of the North American colonies. Such a reading is from within a problematic of the history of ideas which investigates the ideas that thinkers have and how they have influenced the course of history by being taken up by socio-historical movements. 'Ideas' are then conceived of as final-causal, 'influencing' elements in a chain of historical, ontic events.

But we need to dig deeper to unearth a socio-ontological reading of the constitution of social power. The situation in which "a *Multitude* of men do Agree, and *Covenant*" that a "*Man,* or *Assembly of Men,* shall be given by the major part, the *Right* to *Present* the Person of them all, (that is to say, to be their *Representative*;)" presupposes that there is a basis for agreement at all, which must consist in some kind of apriori shared understanding of the world motivating such agreement that Hobbes has already adumbrated as a "condition of warre one against another" (*Lev.* p. 63). I have also already noted that these "Men" are all whos in rivalrous power play with each other. Against this background, the socio-ontological question is that of the legitimacy of a superior political power

---

201 Ernest Barker *Greek Political Theory: Plato and His Predecessors* 1964 p. 27 cited in Leo Strauss *HpW.* p. 149f.

which necessarily involves a *relinquishing and giving of power*, not factually in an empirically given historical situation, but in an act of legitimation – even here and now –, i.e. through assent to a superior power which could and must be given even in an already constituted society and state. This relinquishing and giving of power to a superior governing subject, an ἄρχων, is said to be for the sake of a definite τέλος or end of government, namely, to enable men to "live peaceably amongst themselves".

Hobbes thus makes the question of the legitimacy of a superior social power into a question of war and peace and, ultimately, life and death. As an individual, the security of one's own life and estate, he says, demands a superior social, political power to prevent violence being done to oneself by others. Such a superior political power can only be constituted by men banding together to form an "Artificiall Man" (*Lev.* p. 1) (although, in the first instance, we may object, this does not have to be a "Common-wealth, or State"), for no individual is strong enough to defend himself alone. Such banding together must be a unification of will of some kind, i.e. there must be some kind of agreement to act together in some way and insofar a subordination of individual will to a collective will formed by agreement on how to act against dangerous, hostile individuals and groups of individuals.

10.5 Legitimacy of the Leviathan – An arbiter in the "Competition of Riches, Honour, Command, or other power" – The predicament that "nothing is more easily broken than a mans word"

In any kind of agreement to act together, men must come to a common view regarding a situation and a course of action. The particular situation which Hobbes sets up is that of a multitude of individuals striving to satisfy their desires through the exercise of their powers through which they inevitably come into competition and contention with one another. These powers include the powers to do violence by killing or robbing each other. Such powers provoke the counter-powers of defending oneself against physical attack and robbery. Such a situation is said to be antithetical to men living well, for then, "the life of man, [is] solitary, poore, nasty, brutish, and short". (*Lev.* p. 62) The situation of a clash of interests among men leading to serious dispute and contention, Hobbes says, must have a solution other than the use of force, i.e. acts of physical violence, against each other, which would amount to a permanent state of war. The state of war is a direct consequence of the state of nature, which means, more precisely, the socio-ontological state of human nature as desirous individual centres of power and, more specifically, as desirous individual centres of power pitted against each other in a comparison of their respective who-stands. This makes individualized humankind both mutually dangerous and mutually endangered.

The strife among men means in the first place that there must be a superior arbiter and judge to decide cases of dispute over the goods for living well, which are primarily material goods and the intangible good of honour, which latter the Greeks call τιμή and Hobbes calls "Glory" and "Reputation" (*Lev.* p. 62). This amounts to a modification of the Greek concept of justice according to which "the distribution of esteem, wealth and other divisible goods" (*Eth. Nic.* 1130b32) must be "fair" (ἴσος 1129a35). This Greek concept of distributive justice differs from Hobbes' concept of justice, viz. "That men performe their Covenants made" (*Lev.* p. 71), which is restricted to voluntary dealings among men. In the Aristotelean tradition, this latter kind of justice has been called commutative or corrective justice (cf. Chapter 6) relating to commutatio or social interchange. The reason for this restriction is that Hobbes conceives society itself as being constituted by the covenants among a multitude of individual subjects who acquire and *trade* the goods of life, thus leading society itself back to the posited ultimate subjects, namely, individual human subjects who freely enter into interchanges with each other for the sake of enjoying the exercise of each other's powers.

But already the phenomena of "Glory" and "Reputation" show that these goods are not merely traded by covenant and contract, but that they are in part constituted in their very being through social intercourse and the mutual mirroring of social estimation. To *be* who he is, an individual is reliant on the confirming mirroring by others of his who-status. Esteeming, respecting, honouring, offending, insulting, etc. each other are only possible in the mutual mirroring of social interchange and are socially 'distributed' through this interplay according to worth of each individual as constituted in this interplay itself, "which is commonly called Honouring, and Dishonouring" (*Lev.* p. 42). (Because of this constitution through commutatio itself, it is misleading to speak here of distribution.) Is dishonouring an act of injustice? It is certainly an injury and a cause for offence and conflict among men, and it concerns a misdistribution of a social good, but it does not involve breaking a covenant, but, say, stealing, too, does not involve breaking a covenant, but is an injury that falls under the heading of corrective or commutative justice, so it would seem that Hobbe's definition of justice is too narrow, encompassing only "Covenants made" and not the implicit covenant not to harm each other in social intercourse by injuring each other's goods, whether tangible or intangible. That is, just interchanges demand first of all the mutual respect for each other as persons, as whos.

As laid out in Chapter 6.7, there also do not seem to be any ready criteria available for a fair and just distribution of honour by some superior instance. Honour, rather, is a good that results first and foremost from the estimating power interplay among whos. In contrast to the criteria for individual worth specified by Aristotle, namely, free birth, wealth, nobility of birth and ability/excellence (*Eth. Nic.* 1131a28), in the modern era of individual human subjects sociated through the commutations of everyday life, the socially guaranteed acknowledgement of individual worth has to be restricted to a guarantee of abstract estimation as a free and equal person within the domain of commutative, and not distributive justice. Hobbes himself implies that there are no readily available criteria available for assessing the individual worth of a man by claiming that it is only the result of a kind of market transaction, "his Price; that is to say, so much as would be given for the use of his Power: and therefore is not absolute; but a thing dependant on the need and judgement of another". (*Lev.* p. 42) Price, however, is an abstract quantitative (ποσόν) phenomenon of estimation or mirroring of worth that itself comes about only in relation to others (πρὸς ἕτερον) and not automatically on the basis of any 'substantial' (οὐσία), intrinsic worth such as an individual's inherent abilities. So there can well be a rivalry and contest over the estimation of men's value, but this contest must take place within certain rules of fair interplay that safeguard against doing positive harm to each other in *who* he *is* and *what* he *has*.

The rivalry and strife among men means in the second place that justice, which guarantees men their just deserts as the outcome of an interplay, must not only be arbitrated by a superior instance but must also be enforced, if needs be, by a superior power against individuals and groups of individuals who act unjustly. Such a superior power must be capable of exercising physical force and must be great enough to overwhelm resisting individuals and groups of individuals within the given community. This is the germ of Hobbes' Leviathan, and its legitimacy is acknowledged by all those with insight into the understanding of justice as the fair interchange of both tangible and intangible goods among formally free and equal individual centres of power. The judicial, arbitrating function of the superior instance is primary here, and its superior force is secondary, that is, derivative of its judicial function ── something that is not made clear in Hobbes. No other or greater sovereign power can be derived from the Hobbesian situation of "Competition of Riches, Honour, Command, or other power" (*Lev.* p. 47). To be a legitimate arbitrating and enforcing power, this superior power must be above the fray of particular interests, for only if this be the case can it decide what is fair in a case of contention over the goods of living. The very concept of fairness demands impartiality of justice, which is a kind of absoluteness in the sense that true justice, i.e. justice that corresponds to its concept, cannot be relative to any particular interest within society. The superior power must therefore be above society, independent and stronger than any interest group.

From here it can be seen that Hobbes does not just set up an ontic situation which calls for decision, but rather, read on a deeper plane, he sets up a fundamental socio-ontological dilemma confronting individual human beings as a *plurality* of individual centres of power sharing a world. It is not enough for human beings to agree to be fair in pursuing their desires or that they concur with adhering to the moral precept, "Do not that to another, which thou wouldest not have done to thy selfe" (*Lev.* p. 79), for this is not sufficient to prevent strife and ardent contention over the goods of living from arising. Not even an agreement to comply with what Hobbes calls the third law of nature, viz., "That men performe their Covenants made" (*Lev.* p. 71) is sufficient to prevent strife for, as Hobbes points out, "nothing is more easily broken than a mans word" (*Lev.* p. 65). Apart from a man thoughtlessly giving his word and then, subsequently, dishonestly wheedling his way out of it, the breaking of a man's word can be interpreted in two ways; in the first place, that men are inclined to break their word for the sake of their own self-interests, or alternatively and more innocently, that the individual situations of men desiring to pursue their interests and enjoy the goods of life (both useful goods and esteem as somewho) inevitably give rise to differences in viewpoint, even when the men involved are genuinely trying to behave fairly and above mere blinkered self-interest.

Hobbes is generally attributed with having a 'pessimistic' view of human nature according to which his statement, "The force of Words ... [is] too weak to hold men to the performance of their Covenants..." (*Lev.* p. 70) could be interpreted merely as a more or less cynical observation on human moral weakness. Such a 'pessimistic' interpretation is supported also by many other passages such as Hobbes' "three principall causes of quarrell. First Competition; Secondly, Diffidence; Thirdly, Glory." (*Lev.* p. 62) for, even in agreeing to curb their vieing for material goods and glory in line with the moral precept of "Do not that to another, which thou wouldest not have done to thy selfe" (*Lev.* p. 79), there is still a further cause for strife arising, namely, diffidence. That is, human beings simply do not trust each other because they have learned that, under the mantle of trust, the other is inclined nonetheless to deceivingly pursue his self-interest. Trust is easily betrayed in interchanges among men.

But, taking leave of Hobbes' dismal view of human nature which is not at all implausible, granted even that human beings genuinely agree and strive to trust each other (an 'optimistic' view of human nature as upright and honest), it cannot be avoided that contention and strife arise among human beings. Why not? Because human being itself is ontologically exposure to the truth of being and this exposure is always essentially *individual*, i.e. each individual human being is exposed individually to his or her own truth or perspective, despite every willingness and good will to understand another human being's point of view and to act fairly (or even altruistically, i.e. one-sidedly to the other's benefit). Even a genuine willingness to relativize one's own self-interest in favour of an impartial fairness and to well-meaningly trust other human beings and their good intentions and to stick to contracts which one has entered into cannot prevent a difference and clash of viewpoints from arising.

Such a clash of viewpoints, when it is associated with desires in a practical situation having effects on individuals' ways of living, i.e. when it affects practical self-interests, inevitably leads to strife and fervid contention over useful goods and honour (esteem). Such strife and contention or, more mildly, 'misunderstandings', can perhaps be resolved through argument and controversy between or among the parties involved, but, when the fragile ground of trust given in mutual estimation breaks and diffidence gains the upper hand and a kind of blindness of self-interest sets in, the only way out is for a third, impartial, superior power to intervene to conciliate, arbitrate and adjudicate. Such a superior power is superior in a threefold sense: i) estimated as standing above the fray of the conflict of self-interests and thus empowered to adjudicate as a universal instance, ii) estimated as this superior, governing source of power and iii) backed by superior means of physical force (cf. the first two sections of this chapter). This, in germ, is Hobbes' Leviathan, which ─ conceived now as a superior power over human beings living together in a society to adjudicate conflicts of interest ─ is socio-ontologically essential given the individual exposure of human being to splintered, perspectival truth (cf. the next section below). Inevitable differences in viewpoint inevitably lead also to practical conflicts in action, quite apart from any distortion of individual viewpoints through egoistic, single-minded self-interest.

The 'best will in the world' of human beings to keep their word and trust each other cannot avoid contention and strife, especially over the goods of life both tangible and intangible, not simply because of the moral weakness of humankind or the ineradicability of human egoism and selfishness, or even because of self-interest which distorts one's perspective, but, at its ontological root, because of the individuality of disclosive truth in individual situations in the world, even independently of self-interest, egoism, pride, etc. which blind individuals. By contrast, Hobbes relies on a pessimistic ontic, empirical assessment of humankind:

> The force of Words, being ... too weak to hold men to the performance of their Covenants; there are in mans nature, but two imaginable helps to strengthen it. And those are either a Feare of the consequence of breaking their word; or a Glory, or Pride in appearing not to need to break it. This later is a Generosity too rarely found to be presumed on, especially in the pursuers of Wealth, Command, or sensual Pleasure; which are the greatest part of Mankind. The Passion to be reckoned upon, is Fear; ... (*Lev.* p. 70)

The weakness of the force of words, according to Hobbes, resides in the self-interest of the "pursuers of Wealth, Command, or sensual Pleasure", etc. which can often make "men" reluctant to perform their "Covenants". But the non-performance can also lie, even *independently* of self-interest, in a dispute over the interpretation of the word given in the contract, whether this dispute is motivated by self-interest or not, i.e. self-interest may make men blind by allowing only a self-interested interpretation of a word given in a contract, or there may be a more genuine 'disinterested' dispute over the terms of the word given and agreed in a contract. The agreement made in any "Covenant" may be simple and straightforward, leaving little room for diverging interpretations or, more often, it may leave much room for interpretation and therefore dispute, or it may offer another interpretation at a later point in time when the situation has changed. The words employed in making any "Covenant" ultimately fail to tie an agreement down unambiguously in every instance; they scatter and disperse into the scattering of truth passing through several or many individuals' understanding. Agreements made in words always remain essentially tenuous, ultimately because truth necessarily always manifests itself individually in individual perspectives. Social being of human beings is a *sharing of a splintered truth of being eventuating in the open 3D-temporal clearing* within the practices of individual lives. Such splintering is apparent, for instance, in the law of contract which develops its own elaborate, even contorted language in the vain attempt to tie down and precisely define the "Covenants" that men are obliged to "performe".

Hobbes' by no means implausible dismal view of human nature is echoed through the tradition both before and after. In Kant's thinking, for instance, it is taken up again as the ground for a repressive state power when he refers to "the maliciousness of human nature that makes coercion necessary" (das Bösartige der menschlichen Natur ... welches den Zwang notwendig macht[202]) and "the malice of human nature that is [...] very much veiled in the state of civil law due to the coercion of government" (die Bösartigkeit der menschlichen Natur, die sich [...] im bürgerlich-gesetzlichen Zustande durch den Zwang der Regierung sich sehr verschleiert, *WVI*:210). The propensity for malice among human beings can hardly be overestimated, but this should not allow the more fundamental, and even more tragic human predicament of being cast individually into the shared openness of being's truth to become invisible. The splintering of the both pre-ontological and ontological truth of being goes hand in hand with human being as individually free because to be a free individual means to be a groundless point of emanation of both one's actions and also one's understanding of the world.

10.6 The individualization of the truth of being (Protagoras, Heidegger) – The ultimate socio-ontological source of strife – The finite process of resolving differences among individual perspectival views

Sogar im Denken, wo alles doch logisch und sachlich zusammenhängt, [...] anerkennt man die überlegene Überzeugung eines anderen gewöhnlich bloß dann vorbehaltlos, wenn man sich ihm auch auf irgendeine andere Weise unterwirft, sei es als einem Vorbild und Führer, sei es als einem Freund oder einem Lehrer. Ohne ein solches Gefühl, das nicht zur Sache gehört, macht man sich fremde Meinung aber stets nur mit dem stillschweigenden Einspruch zu eigen, daß sie bei einem selbst noch besser aufgehoben sei als bei ihrem Urheber;

Robert Musil
Der Mann ohne Eigenschaften II Tl. 3 Kap. 48

Even in thinking, where everything is connected logically and matter-of-factly, [...] one acknowledges unreservedly the superior conviction of someone else usually only when one subjects oneself to him also in some other way, whether it be as a model and leader, whether it be as a friend or teacher. Without such a feeling that does not belong to the matter at hand, one only adopts an alien opinion with the tacit caveat that it is better preserved with oneself than with its author;

Individual perspectives on truth cannot be reduced to what today is called 'subjective' truth as opposed to 'objective', general truth that is regarded as the only

---

202 I. Kant *Zum ewigen Frieden* BA 20 *Werke* Band VI ed. W. Weischedel 1964 S. 244. Abreviated *WVI*:244.

genuine truth (which, above all has to be 'established' via 'scientific method'). The individualization[203] of truth as the disclosure of the world in individual situations does not amount to an inferior kind of truth vis-à-vis a superior, firmly established, 'hard', 'objective' truth said to be 'independent' of subjectivity. Rather, there is truth only *within* and *arising from* the identity or belonging-together of being and human being endowed with understanding, i.e. of 'objectivity' and 'subjectivity', so that truth is neither an objective nor a subjective phenomenon, but a fundamental phenomenon of human-being-in-the-world arising only from the belonging-together of Zeit and Geist, i.e. the 3D-temporal clearing and mind. Moreover, it has to be seen that the truth of being *universally* lays claim on human being *individually*, and that the individual human being coming to the truth of the world in its unconcealment is, paradoxically, at the same time the very individuation[204] of that individual. Protagoras is famously attributed with having had the first insight into the individuality of truth:

πάντων χρημάτων μέτρον ἐστὶν ἄνθρωπος, τῶν μὲν ὄντων ὡς ἔστι, τῶν δὲ μὴ ὄντων ὡς οὐκ ἔστιν.

(according to Sextus Empiricus; cf. Plato
Theaitaetos 151c)

Of all 'things' (which humans beings use in the usages of practical daily life – i.e. χρήματα [practically useful things including money ME], χρῆσθαι) the (individual) human is the measure of beings present that they present themselves in the way they do and also of beings denied presence, that they do not present themselves.

(interpretive translation adapted from
Heidegger *Nietzsche II* S. 135)

---

203 OED: individualize, v. [f. individual + -ize.] 1. trans. To render individual or give an individual character to; to characterize by distinctive marks or qualities; to mark out or distinguish from other persons or things.
204 OED: individuation [ad. med.L. individuation-em, n. of action f. individua-re: see individuate v.] 1. a. The action or process of individuating or rendering individual; that of distinguishing as an individual. spec. in Scholastic Philosophy. The process leading to individual existence, as distinct from that of the species. Principle of individuation (= med.L. principium individuationis): the principle through which the individual is constituted or comes into being. In Scholastic Philosophy this was variously held to be Form (by most Realists); Matter (by the Nominalists); and Matter as limited in the individual (by Albertus Magnus and Thomas Aquinas).

Socrates paraphrases this in *Theaitaetos* thus:

οὐκοῦν οὕτω πως λέγει, ὡς οἷα μὲν ἕκαστα ἐμοὶ φαίνεται τοιαῦτα μὲν ἔστιν ἐμοί, οἷα δὲ σοί, τοιαῦτα αὖ σοί· ἄνθρωπος δὲ σύ τε κἀγώ; (*Theaitetos* 152a).

Does he (Protagoras) not understand this roughly in the following way: as what an individual thing shows itself to me, such a look does it have for me; as what it shows itself to you, on the other hand, thus is it, in turn, for you; for you are a human being and so am I?

(translation adapted from Heidegger
Nietzsche II S. 136)

Heidegger comments:

Die Art, wie Protagoras das Verhältnis des Menschen zum Seienden bestimmt, ist nur eine betonte Einschränkung der Unverborgenheit des Seienden auf den jeweiligen Umkreis der Welterfahrung. Diese Einschränkung *setzt voraus*, daß die Unverborgenheit des Seienden waltet, noch mehr, daß diese Unverborgenheit bereits als solche einmal erfahren und als Grundcharakter des Seienden selbst ins Wissen gehoben wurde.

(*Nietzsche II* S. 139 emphasis in the original)

The way in which Protagoras defines the relation of human beings to beings is only an emphatic restriction of the unconcealedness of beings to the individual horizon of experience of the world. This restriction *presupposes* that the unconcealedness of beings holds sway, and even more, that this unconcealedness was already experienced as such and elevated into knowledge as the fundamental character of beings themselves.

The clearing of the truth of being holds sway, i.e. prevails over human being and thus over all human beings, but in relation to individual human beings in their individual situations in the world and individual experience of the world, it holds sway in an individually "restricted" way so that the way beings present themselves to me in their looks is the way they are *in their disclosure (truth)* for me, whereas the way beings present themselves to you in their looks is the way they are *in their disclosure (truth)* for you. Despite human longing, there is no 'objective' truth that hovers over all individuals in general and on the whole (καθόλου), no 'catholic' truth (whether it be religious or scientific), but there is an open 3D-temporal clearing for unconcealment and concealment within which all beings can present themselves and also not present themselves or present themselves only distortedly or partially *as* what or who they are or *as* what or who they are *not*. Moreover, this very *as* is historical, temporal, i.e. cast and defined by an historical time.

Protagoras says that each of us as individual selves is the measure of the truth of beings in the sense that i) each of us (as νοῦς, mind, understanding) is an *individual* site for the disclosure of beings, where this disclosure is taken in the broadest sense of including also its negative and privative modes, and ii) the truth of beings in their being, which belongs to human being as such, must pass through human beings individually, thus individuating them *as* selves. Beings present themselves to each of us individually in our understanding, and if they do not present themselves, i.e. if they are not disclosively present or disclosively absent at my or your individual site — not even in the mode of ab-sence as memory or as phantasy of the future or as the imagining of a possibility — then we are unaware of them, i.e. they 'are' not. Or if they present themselves to my or your understanding in a partial or distorted way, i.e. as what they are not, then their disclosure is an untruth of which you or I are not aware (but about which we may become aware).

I hold the world to *be* in a certain way according to how it presents itself and discloses itself to me in my daily practical situation, and you hold the world to *be* in a certain way according to how it presents itself and discloses itself to you in your daily practical situation. Such presentation must be conceived not only as a presencing in the present (whether sensuously or not), but also an absencing from one of the other two temporal dimensions of past (or better: been-ness) and future, for beings (all that occurs in the temporal clearing) can disclose themselves also as what-has-been (say, in historical memory) or what-may-come (say, in expectation). That is, absencing is also a kind of presencing that may be disclosive or obscure or veiled in hiding.[205] This three-dimensional temporal possibility of disclosure must be kept in mind even when, in the following, I speak only of the temporal dimension of the present.

The disclosure of beings to you or to me does not remain static, however; it moves, for life itself is a movement with shifting perspectives. I go through the experience that beings present themselves to me, i.e. become present for me in how I understand them (pre-ontologically), in differing ways, showing different faces and facets, so that I also go through the experience, in a dialogue with myself,[206] that how things present themselves to me may be misleading because I am not yet aware of other facets (my view is too simple), or the view I have is too superficial (it has no insight into the deeper essence of how things are, which would be an ontological understanding), or it turns out to be not only partial but downright deceptive and false (not only as a matter of fact, but as a

---

205 Cf. my A Question of Time 2015.
206 Cf. Plato *Theaitetos* 189e: "A dialogue which the soul as self goes through with itself about beings it may look at/contemplate." (Λόγον ὃν αὐτὴ πρὸς αὑτὴν ἡ ψυχὴ διεξέρχεται περὶ ὧν ἂν σκοπῇ.).

conception of the nature of the world). This means in particular that my 'truth' of the world in particular and in general shifts and, although it differs from your truth of the world, there is still the possibility that with regard to a particular issue we can come to reconcile our individual truths with one another so that we end up seeing 'eye to eye', i.e. the issue becomes present for both of us showing the same face. This movement is only possible within the temporal clearing for being's truth that we, as human beings inhabiting the clearing, ineluctably share. This possible reconciliation of our differing disclosive truths may take place simply over time through the experience of living, but its more direct mode of possibility is that we talk and argue with one another, but always within an overall, binding hermeneutic cast of the beingness of beings in a given age of which pre-ontological understanding is entirely unaware but which nevertheless forms the ground upon which we can come to any sort of agreement in our views.

In this dialogue, the way the world or a situation or an issue presents itself to me and to you alters. Each of us starts to understand things differently through trying to see each other's point of view. The disclosure of world becomes fluid through other aspects of beings' self-presentations coming to light and distorted views of things being corrected or discarded. Thus it can be seen that the inevitable individuality of truth by no means amounts to an irrevocable, rigid 'subjective relativity' of truth. Both my truth and your truth rely on the strifeful holding sway of the clearing for being's truth in which there is a dynamic of disclosure, distortion and hiddenness in all three temporal dimensions. Because each of us is a finite being, this dynamic of disclosure and hiddenness does not necessarily lead to a convergence of our viewpoints, but may end merely in the consolidation of divergent, intransigent, opposed, albeit modified viewpoints.

This individuality of the truth of beings to individuals, its *splintering* within the 3D-temporal clearing for the truth of being, is the *ultimate ontological* source of strife among men, and not only the (never to be under-estimated) clash of differing and opposed egoistic practical self-interests and self-seeking (Selbstsucht, Habsucht), narcissistic fixation on one's own stand as somewho, or that men do not keep their word (moral failing). Human beings may have differing worldviews on the whole (e.g. different religious or political convictions), but this by no means prevents them from having practical dealings with one another in an agreeable way, and this is because the horizon of a shared practical situation such as a business transaction is restricted and abstracted enough to allow it to show itself to both parties in the same way. As noted in the preceding section, the individualization of truth in practical everyday affairs demands that there be a superior subject (a judge, not necessarily a ruler who issues commands) to arbitrate the conflict that necessarily arises — despite the 'best will in the world' and despite men even being inclined to trust each other, i.e. "the litigants may differ in good faith".[207] But Hobbes and all philosophers of the modern age[208] before Heidegger are far removed from any insight into the

---

207 Hayek *LLL*1:100. Hegel, too, points to the inevitability of collisions between rights in the domain of property rights and contract, calling it "unintentional wrong" (unbefangenes Unrecht, *RPh*. § 84ff). Both parties will and recognize the rights of property in their generality or universality, "so that the thing should belong to the one who has the right to it" (so daß die Sache dem gehören soll, der das Recht dazu hat *RPh*. § 85). But since the contract is a particular expression of will and there are various rightful grounds for the ownership of a given thing, these various grounds can and do come into collision with one another, so that "the subsumption of the thing under property" (die Subsumtion der Sache unter das Eigentum, *RPh*. § 85) is in dispute. "In the parties, the recognition of right is conjoined with opposing particular interests and views" (In den Parteien ist die Anerkennung des Rechts mit dem entgegengesetzten besonderen Interesse und ebensolcher Ansicht verbunden. *RPh*. § 85), thus engendering a collision between universality and particularity.

208 Even Hegel's discussion of Protagoras in his *Lectures on the History of Philosophy* interprets the human being as the "measure of all things" in a distinction between "everyone according to his specific particularity, the contingent human being can be the measure, or self-aware reason within the human being, the human being according to his reason-imbued nature and his universal substantiality is the absolute measure. Taken in the former way, all self-seeking, all selfishness, the subject with its interests the centre (and even if the human being has the aspect of reason, even reason is something subjective, and also he, the human being is something subjective)" (jeder nach seiner besonderen Partikularität, der zufällige Mensch, das Maß sein kann, oder [...]. die selbstbewußte Vernunft im Menschen, der Mensch nach seiner vernünftigen Natur und seiner allgemeinen Substantialität das absolute Maß sei. Auf jene Weise genommen ist alle Selbstsucht, aller Eigennutz, das Subjekt mit seinen Interessen der Mittelpunkt (und wenn auch der Mensch die Seite der Vernunft hat, so ist doch auch die Vernunft ein Subjektives, ist auch er, ist auch der Mensch); *VGPI Werke W18*:430). On the side of human "universal substantiality", the subjective human being is the absolute measure insofar as he gives "the absolute the form of thinking subjectivity" (das Absolute die Form der denkenden Subjektivität, *W18*:430) The tension Hegel formulates here is that between the self-seeking, everyday human being and the reason-imbued, thinking human being who "gives himself a universal content" (sich einen allgemeinen Inhalt gibt, *W18*:430), but this pulls the contradiction too far apart. On the one hand, the essential and therefore ineluctable individuality of truth for an individual human being must by no means be self-seeking and selfish. The different perspectives on truth lie in the finiteness of human individuality, not especially in self-seeking human individuality. On the other hand, the identity of thinking human being and beings as such is nothing other than the absolute that overcomes the human being as a merely subjective, relative measure, but this overcoming is possible, for Hegel, only in the absolute knowing of philosophy (contemplative, theoretical life) in which beings as such are brought to their ontological concepts. Before this explicit ontological knowing there is the shared pretemporal clearing for the truth of being as the play of unconcealment and concealment, of ἀλήθεια and λήθη, that encompasses both the theoretical and practical realms.

Hobbes claims that only fear can hold most men to their word. Fear is ultimately the fear of having physical violence done to one's person or one's estate in the broadest sense, including confiscation by force. One can lose one's liberty or property through the exercise of a superior physical force capable of violence, if necessary. But men's failing to keep their word by wilfully breaking it is only one of the contentious situations that can arise with regard to "Covenants" or contracts. And contention can also arise — outside contract in the narrow sense — over the exercise of an individual's rights of liberty or property, and that even without the contending subject having malicious designs on that individual's liberty or property. So fear of punishment cannot be a universal means of preventing strife from arising among men. Contentious issues can and do arise even when men honestly intend to keep their word and respect the other's liberty and property. When a dispute over an issue is theoretical, i.e. situated in the realm of contemplation and a speculative mirroring of the world, men may 'agree to differ', but, more often than not, even philosophical disputes are inexorable struggles over who-status aiming at who-annihilation. Disputes over the truth of an issue also often have practical implications, i.e. they impinge on how men act in the realm of daily action in dealing with their property, exercising their liberty in practice and enjoying the goods of living, both tangible and intangible. The intangible goods over which a theoretical dispute can arise include above all the good of *reputation*, the status and standing in whoness an individual enjoys, which in turn can have considerable effects on the individual's material wealth by affecting what job and/or public office that individual holds as an acknowledged expert of whatever kind.

Disputes over an issue with practical consequences arise not just from individuals' having different perspectives, but also from their having differing practical situations, i.e. differing interests with regard to action in pursuit of the goods of living. Self-interest is the way an individual self is situated 'amidst beings', i.e. inter-esse. The individual's practical situation affects, focuses, circumscribes and even partly defines how it sees the world, i.e. its individual perspective on the truth of the world. In the multiplicity of individual practical

---

ontological understanding of an historical world in which human beings implicitly share an understanding of the universal in their practical lives in the sense of an historical, epochal casting of the being of beings, including above all the casting of human being itself as free or unfree and its associated ethical life.

situations in their respective truths lies also the germ for strife over practical issues arising from differing and therefore also often opposed self-interests.

The individuality of truth (the world discloses itself individually and in diverse, particular and even idiosyncratic perspectives) and the associated individuality of practical situations (as experience of the world) are ontologically prior to the individuality of desire in desiring, willed subjects as free centres of power and thus also ontologically prior to the "three principall causes of quarrell" proposed by Hobbes, "First Competition; Secondly, Diffidence; Thirdly, Glory" (*Lev.* p. 62). The truth of being in the open 3D-temporal clearing is ontologically prior to will and desire (which are always practical), i.e. we always already understand the world and in some way or other prior to any action. The necessity for the mediation of conflicts of interest thus derives originarily not from desiring human nature and a natural propensity for men to do violence to one another in a "State of Nature", but from human being itself being cast individually as free into the truth of being. A 'pessimistic' casting of human nature (e.g. as malicious or as inclined to break covenants) is ultimately too superficial a ground for the necessity of government over society. The superior arbitrating instance required to mediate conflicts between individuals is an instance to find out the truth of the matter of contention in a practical situation in accordance with the truth that is brought to light through mediation (which necessarily includes the presentation of evidence to prove the 'true facts' of the matter).

The individuality of truth, its diversity for individuals in a multiplicity of perspectives, is an ontological condition of finite human being and has nothing to do with a supposed fictitious or non-fictitious "state of nature" temporally prior to the constitution of society and government in which only egoistic, self-interested, asocial individuals exist. Such imaginings of a state of nature represent a crudity in thinking that is unable to distinguish between the ontological (with its requirement of abstract thinking that proceeds step by step) and the ontic (apparently nitty-gritty, empirical reality of 'real' genesis), and also covers up the tragic depth of the human dilemma. It is impossible that there could be anything resembling a chronologically prior asocial state of nature, because human beings, even in the rudest of circumstances, are ineluctably social, i.e. they relate to each other (πρὸς ἕτερον), they estimate each other in some way or other, even when the mode of estimation is asocial, i.e. deficient, e.g. hostile. An *a*-social mode of mutual estimation is still a-*social*, i.e. one possibility of sociating through social relations. Both Hobbes and his critics can be blamed for setting up the blithely naive, ontic misconception of a state of nature which leaves traces throughout political philosophy, especially in the empirically-minded Anglo-Saxon and French traditions for which the ontological difference is 'nothing at all'.

The ontological individuality of truth, along with the derived particularity and singularity of perspectives in practical situations of individuals which necessarily gives rise to diverse self-interests, has, in the first place, nothing to do with egoism. Rather, each individual human being has a world and a worldview on a world which is always already shared, i.e. there is no state of human being, either ontically or ontologically, prior to a shared world in its open truth (of disclosure *and* concealment) in the 3D-temporal clearing. The self-interests which arise naturally in a shared practical world (a world of everyday practical interchanges concerned with striving for and acquiring the goods of living, both tangible and intangible, through give and take) always also involve others, namely, the others who belong to one's own world with whom one shares one's practical, quotidian life. Self-interest must therefore not be confused with egoism according to which an individual greedily and ruthlessly seeks to satisfy its desires regardless of the others in its life-world. Neither is this world of individuals with their individual perspectives and particular practical self-interests an asocial world.

The world of human beings is always already ineluctably sociated through interplays of mutual estimation as whos. Exposure to the openness of being is always already also exposure to others — who are *understood* and *estimated* (no matter how minimally or deficiently) *as* other whos — and all practical life necessarily involves others, even when one lives ontically in splendid isolation. No individual has a world in which others are not present, even if this presence is not the bodily presence of direct, practical dealings with one another but encompasses also both temporal modes of absence. Even a withdrawal from the society of others into an isolated, reclusive way of living in total solitude cannot escape the originary ontological sharedness of world nor the presence of others in their absence in one's world, nor even the practical importance of what others can provide for daily living. The abstract construction of a so-called state of nature thus has to be conceived as the situation of diverse individuals each with its own perspectival truth and associated practical self-interest. The question of society and government has to be conceived as the question of how these individual perspectival truths and associated practical self-interests can be mediated with each other in such a way that a shared practical way of social living in freedom is possible. The enablement of practical social living through interchange, of course, is a much more modest problem than the pretension that a community must share holistically the same worldview, so that much room is left for divergent individual liberty. Such modesty in casting a social world is crucial for the issue of freedom.

As all philosophers at the latest since Plato know, truth first has the form of opinion, δόξα, Meinung, opinion. Hegel says that my Meinung is meins (mine), i.e. opinion is my individual way of holding the world to be in how it discloses itself to me in my individual perspective on the world. Shared opinion is only a shared way of holding the world to be, i.e. shared conviction, and can be just as wayward and unsteady as a single opinion. The way toward a shared truth, if at all attainable, requires the mediation of a dialectic, a dialogue which discursively passes through the various (opinionated) views of the world in order finally to converge on a view on which all can agree on the basis of an insight that can cope with counterviews by showing up their inadequacies with judiciously chosen words. A dialectic in this sense has to pass through all the negations of a perspective on an issue in order to arrive finally at an unencumbered view of the issue and establish the perspective in question in its well-grounded truth — well-grounded through the medium of the dialogical λόγος that has the role of disclosing (apophantically) the world in how it shows itself. An unobstructed view of an issue in the clearing of 3D-time, whether theoretical or practical, on which all participants agree, however, is extremely rare, if only for want of motivation to engage diligently in a (possibly strenuous) dialogue. The various views of an issue always remain in a difference, borne apart (διαφέρειν) from one another and therefore remain debatable, or even implacably opposed. Philosophers, too, are inclined to evade the rigours of having it out with an opposed position, especially if that position does not enjoy acknowledged 'mainstream' status and therefore does not seem to be 'worth' the trouble. What establishes itself as truth in an historical age depends crucially on the interplays of mutual estimation as somewho or other, with the views of some being estimated highly and others estimated as unworty of attention at all. Since an historical age is dominated by a prevailing hermeneutic cast of the beingness of beings, i.e. the whatness of whats and the whoness of whos, only those who conform to this cast can achieve a high status as somewho in the temporal clearing of an age. Those who offer a counter-casting or recasting are at a disadvantage in achieving notice as somewho in the power interplays of estimation.

Because finite human beings lead finite, mortal lives, in the realm of collective practical action, the dialogical process mediating diverse views on an issue at hand with one another necessarily becomes the finite process of *deliberation* in which finally a decision has to be made on a course of action to be taken. The participants in the process of deliberation reach some sort of consensus or take a vote that enables a practical resolution; the final truth of the issue itself remains undecided and is clarified only to an extent that reveals a feasible course of action. The diversity of views on a practical issue is inevitably associated also with practical consequences which favour or prejudice the self-interests of the various participants in their differing individual situations. The resolution of an issue can then no longer be a matter of disinterestedly uncovering the truth of the matter but in reaching a compromise with which each of the participants 'can live', each with their own interests, i.e. their individual ways of being amidst beings (inter-esse) in their respective situations, being partially fulfilled. Since practical situations in which deliberation takes place invariably depend also on what is likely to happen, and this view into the future more often than not is only incompletely revealing, or entirely misleading, even the individual truth of a practical situation can never be complete. The assessment and judgement of a practical situation are not of the totally disclosed truth of the situation (which cannot be had for finite human beings), but are guided by experience and prudence, experience of what has already happened in similar situations in the past, and prudence regarding the risks of possible adverse happenings in the future. By contrast, insofar as a theoretical debate in the modern sciences over an issue involves only speculating without practical consequences, the differences in viewpoint remain in suspense. Only mathematics, which deals with pure, simple entities such as number and figure that are abstracted from the world, is able for the most part to finally settle its issues with a proof.

To summarize: the bedrock of difference among 'men' is not the conflict of opposed interests of desiring, asocial egoists in an uninhibited state of nature but, more innocently and more tragically, the individualization of truth in human individuals with diverse perspectives in a world which is always already shared with others, both in how it is understood contemplatively and in everyday practical situations. The problem, on the fundamental level, is not the moral problem of how to get 'men' to restrain their egoistic desires and 'do unto others as thou wouldst have done unto thyself', but how to mediate the myriad individual perspectives on the world in such a way that a social world is practically liveable and also free. It is in this context of the necessity of mediating differing, conflicting, practical, self-interested points of view with one another to enable viable, free living that a superior, arbitrating social, political instance, which is stronger than individuals and acknowledged by them as superior, itself becomes necessary.

Self-interest arises only with an individual self's existing in the world in its individual situation, i.e in its own individual truth, which, as we have seen, is not merely 'subjective', i.e. 'inside' consciousness, but possesses its own validity. The individual situation shapes the practices that are practised which the individual regards as favourable and desirable and good for its existence. The clash of practical self-interests is therefore inevitable and has to be mediated or aufgehoben in the Hegelian sense, i.e. the conflict of practical self-interests has to be waived, saved and raised to a higher, more unified plane of some kind of 'we'. The clash of practical self-interests is waived insofar as the parties' conflict is settled by the intervention, mediation and judgement of the superior, adjudicating instance and the parties forbear to claim or demand; it is saved insofar as, according to the judgement, not all the self-interests of the parties are fully satisfied; and it is raised insofar as what is right is laid down in the higher judicial instance's judgement that overrules each party's conflictual viewpoint.

10.7 Ontological powerlessness of the metaphysical, productive conception of power – The ultimate impotence of both political power and rhetoric – Ineluctably sharing an hermeneutic cast of the truth of beings in an historical age – Embeddedness of individual truth in a shared, historically cast truth – The Geist-Zeit and the enpropriation of human being to the clearing of 3D-time – Powerlessly free, mutually estimating power interplay, pluralism and benign indifference – Fairness as the ethereal ethos of a free society

Is the powerlessness of rhetoric as a technique for bringing the other around through talking, a powerlessness arising in the face of the ontological otherness of the other with whom there must be interchange and some sort of process of mutual estimation — as sketched above in section 10.2 and in more depth elsewhere[209] —, itself related in essence to the powerlessness of being itself as the temporal openness for presencing and absencing? That is to say, is it not the case that the other human being as an other individual site for the openness to being is beyond the reach of any technically conceived productive power and machination? Does the merging of the openness of being in its temporality as shared individually by each and every human being require an essentially different approach to the question of specifically *social* and *political* power? Does

---

209 Cf. my 'Assessing How Heidegger Thinks Power Through the History of Being' Section 3 'Rhetoric as a test case for power over the other', URL www.arte-fact.org/untpltcl/pwrrhtrc.html

the question concerning the possibility of constituting a We at all (cf. Chapter 11) have to be posed anew from a perspective that has clearly taken leave of the traditional, one-sided, mono-archic metaphysical, productive conception of power? Within such a conception of power, a social power such as rhetoric is regarded as a technique that (mis)understands its powerlessness over the other as merely an impotence that could be overcome through improvements in technique, and not as an ontological powerlessness that resides ultimately in one origin of free movement encountering another origin of free movement, both of whom are free only because of their exposure of mind and psyche to the 3D-time-clearing.

As Heidegger points out, powerlessness has to be distinguished from impotence. Powerlessness is situated outside the dimension of power altogether, whereas impotence is a lack, a deficiency of power. "Power-lessness is not impotence that, lacking power and having to do without it, still remains related precisely to power." (Das Macht-lose ist nicht das Ohn-mächtige, das immer noch und gerade auf Macht — sie entbehrend und sie missend — bezogen bleibt. *Besinnung GA*66:188) Even when an other human being is coerced through (the threat of) the use of physical force to obey a command, such subjugation under duress does not impinge upon the other's freedom, which, as has been shown, remains in essence untouched by such subjugation. Such subjugation through the use of physical force or its threatened use is based on force directed physically, i.e. ontically, against the other's body or property or the bodies of persons close and dear to the other. The other's body or the other's property can be physically restrained or maimed or confiscated or injured and damaged, or even destroyed by a superior force, but the other as another human being is situated ontologically in a temporal clearing altogether outside the realm of exercise of such violent power which is thus altogether powerless, and not merely impotent, in this respect. Why is this? Because the other as another human being is an individual site within the clearing for being with its own perspective on the disclosure of beings in the temporal clearing.

How the other holds the world to be in the openness of the clearing for being's truth is essentially individual and therefore untouchable by means of violent force. Holding the world to be within the open clearing for being's disclosure and concealment is constitutive of human freedom, which is always essentially and ultimately individual freedom, even when practical consensus has been attained through some kind of deliberation, or certain truths, as we shall see below, are necessarily shared, 'common property' in any given epoch. The truth of being is situated outside the reach and scope of any possible one-sided exercise of political or other social power, which is directed at another being, but not another being in its being. Strictly speaking, there can be no such thing as a one-sided exercise of political or other social power for, as has been shown in detail, all social power is a mutually estimating power interplay, and such estimating remains always a matter of individual opinion, i.e. an individual way of holding the other to be and estimating who she or he is.

That is why the means of rhetorical power are primarily words, and these means come up against and are faced with the essential limit of the other's very being in its freedom, i.e. of the other human being's essential individuated situatedness within the openness of being in its truth and its corresponding practical self-movement within this openness emanating from it as a point of origin. All the means and techniques of rhetorical persuasion, no matter whether they reside in the arguments presented to enter and sway the heart and soul of the audience, or in the reputation and charisma of who is speaking and how the speaker projects his character and who-standing to the audience, or in the way in which the arguments are delivered through the tone, inflection and drama of the voice, have to win the confidence and trust of the audience and somehow mesh with its worldview to have their effect. Such winning of confidence and trust is thus always essentially a free reciprocation that depends on the willingness of the audience to go along with the speaker in an implicit exchange of views on how the issue at hand is to be seen. An audience cannot be simply rhetorically manipulated (passively), but must allow itself to be so, especially by (freely) allowing itself to be swayed hither and thither by cleverly manipulated moods (e.g. fashion in advertising, or fear in political campaigns).

As has been presupposed throughout this inquiry, from Heidegger we can learn that being and the truth of being needs human being as the open site for truth, as the Da. In thinking on further from Heidegger we have brought to light that the Da, in turn, is identical with the clearing of 3D-time for presencing and absencing of 'occurrents' whether they be whats or whos. Being and human being belong to each other in the open temporal clearing. That is Ereignis or propriation, and such belonging is at the same time the groundless exposure of humans to freedom of thought, whereas freedom of action depends on outcomes of mutually estimating power interplays. Only through being and human being belonging to each other does world open and beings as a whole and as such, both *as* what they are and *as* who they are, come to show their multifaceted faces to human being in some hermeneutic casting or other. But the clearing for the truth of being is occupied existentially by human being individually; each human being ineluctably partakes individually of the open clearing of the truth of beings in their beingness so that the constitution of a We has to be approached as an explicit philosophical problem of how the truth of being, in its singularity, particularity and universality, comes to be shared. A We is not merely a bunch of individual humans taken collectively.

At the same time, each individual participation of human being in the truth of being is also essentially shared; in being human beings, we essentially and necessarily share the openness of being in its temporality with other human beings. No individual is able to 'make up' its own world entirely in how it discloses itself. Moreover, each individual world only ever opens also through others' opening to the world. Each individual experience of world is mediated essentially also through the experience of others, i.e. world opens for each of us also through the mediation of other human beings in their own openness to being from whom we learn in countless ways, be it through communication or simply by adopting others' views or practically imitating. Thus, traditions, which are always also ways of understanding the world, are handed down. This means that each individual truth, each individual point of view is mediated by practically sharing a life-world with others through education.

But even more deeply than that, i.e. ontologically: Each individual truth is also a shared truth with others within a shared historical world that has a given, universal cast, i.e. an hermeneutic cast of mind in a given age. No matter what differences in individual, singular views exist, these differing individual views and how each individual holds the world to be (Dafürhalten) are all situated and are mediated with one another within a shared, universal-historical world in the 3D-time-clearing with its fundamentally shared understanding of that world in the basic ontological outlines and building blocks for its truth that define in advance or apriori what the truth of beings as such can be in that historical time. The historical opening of world in how it shapes up in a given, universal hermeneutic cast is ontologically prior to the individual or any collectivity of human beings, and is an 'always already', ineluctably universal given whose givenness is only co-shaped and co-moulded by those rare, exceptional ones who find themselves called to the abyssal task of co-casting an historical world. The 'always already' only becomes malleable and revisable in a creative re-casting that must first dare to question. At first and for the most part, the truth of an historical world is simply given and shared — unquestioningly — thus forming the basis within which innumerable differences arise in all sorts of configurations of mutually estimating power interplays.

The universality of an hermeneutic ontological casting of an age may well be shared with another one. In our own age this is the case, for instance, with the overlapping of a modern scientific cast of world with a Christian one with all the incoherence and inconsistency this often brings with it.

Nevertheless, a shared historical truth of the world in all its particularity (specific areas of what is understandable and knowable in the world) has to be appropriated individually. There is thus an essential embeddedness of individual (*singular*) truth in a shared (*universal*, historical) truth of being which provides the basic casting for all *particular* truths. The clearing for being's truth, although ineluctably individually, mortally and therefore also finitely ek-sisted, is essentially also ineluctably shared with the other in the other's exposure to the same temporal clearing in which a given, historical, universal cast has taken shape. An individual opening of world in all its singular idiosyncrasy and particularity is willy-nilly a shared opening of world mediated not only by the countless others, near and far, intimately close and anonymously average, present and past, together with whom we are cast into and share an historical world, but also by the mind of the time, i.e. the Geist-Zeit, as a universal casting of historical world that confronts humankind, unquestioned and seemingly unquestionable, like an uncanny destiny which, however, is experienced simply as self-evidence and obviousness. How an individual understands and holds the world to be is always a configuration, perhaps singular, unique and quirky one, of ontological building blocks provided by an historical epoch. Radical singularity only comes about when an individual questions the very self-evidence of a given hermeneutic cast of world, thus breaking with all possible configurations.

Sharing an understanding of world with other human beings takes place primarily through language (leaving aside the powerful possibility of imitating through which, especially when young and not yet our selves, we appropriate others' understanding and way of being in the world in a kind of one-sided mirror-game with 'identification figures'). The other's world is evoked, called to presence primarily through language. But even more than that: Insofar as the stillness of the being's truth in the temporal clearing of an age makes its way to human language, an historical world opens up and takes shape in language's casting definition, which can be shared among humans through this language, albeit always accompanied by a mood of the time that makes its way to music.[210] The casting of an historical world is a shared epochal human project in which individuals participate not only through listening to each other in dialogue, but also by listening and being open to the hitherto unheard-of, silent sendings from the temporal clearing with messages about how the beingness of beings can be recast through fundamental ontological concepts that *as* ontological

---

210 Cf. M. Heidegger 'Der Weg zur Sprache' in *Unterwegs zur Sprache* Neske, Pfullingen 1959 and my *Thinking of Music* 2015.

remain hidden to those living in a given age. Nevertheless, we can listen to each other both preontologically and ontologicaly because human being itself is first and foremost openness and exposure and a belonging to the temporal openness for the truth of being in its stillness from which an historical world emerges and assumes shape and within which it *can* even change how it shapes up epochally in historical time.

The enpropriation of human being to where it belongs, namely, in the clearing of 3D-time, from which beings as such emerge in their ontologically defined outlines, is powerless. It is 'only' a possibility that cannot be denied or refused, since we are powerless to refuse, knowingly or unknowingly, our enpropriation to being or how an historical world shows up and shapes up for our understanding. It is the possibility of all human possibilities to gain such insight. The eyes of understanding cannot banish an insight once they have caught a glimpse of it. There is no power which can either coerce or prevent such knowing belonging, just as there is no power which can either coerce or prevent the oblivion to such belonging to the truth of being. Ultimately, each individual must decide for him- or herself.

One specific powerless possibility for a shared historical truth that breaks the mould and initiates a hermeneutic recasting is to come to conceive social and political power differently from how it has hitherto been conceived, mostly implicitly, throughout the history of metaphysics. As has been shown in previous chapters (Chapter 5.3, 5.4, 5.6, Chapter 9.2, Chapter 10.1, 10.2), the phenomena of human beings sharing the world in mutually estimating interchange with each other point to the limits of mono-archically conceived productionist, metaphysical power, for metaphysically conceived, productive power is always thought as a starting-point residing in one being governing a change, a μεταβολή in another being. Monotheism, in particular, thinks within this mono-archic paradigm by positing the ἀρχή as a supreme being, but also all onto-theological thinking that posits some kind (look) of first principle, such as a will to live, as an anchor.

In questioning powerlessly, we have asked: Does not the reciprocity of the free, mutually estimating exchange and interchange (μεταβολή in its other sense) between and among human beings, even today, still await its appropriate conceptualization, no longer subsumed (implicitly) under key metaphysical concepts from δύναμις and ἐνέργεια through to Nietzschean will to power in which power is always thought mono-archically? By virtue of the ontological peculiarity of human beings as ineluctably free beings cast individually and singularly out into an historically shared, universal, temporally open truth of being in its beingness, all interchange among them is a who-power-play that, paradoxically, is situated essentially outside the reach of any metaphysically conceived power and therefore within a realm of powerlessness. In particular, there is no metaphysically conceived power capable of achieving a lasting unity of truth (e.g. a theocracy) or even practical agreement among a plurality of individual emanations of freedom; any unity is a unity on recall, until the next outbreak of dissent and conflict. The yearning for the one (τὸ ἕν) must give way to acceptance of the many (τὰ πολλά) whereby such acceptance of difference, paradoxically, is a kind of unity.

A free society sociated via mutually estimating power play is necessarily *pluralist*, for there can be no unified truth for a way of living in it, but only a plurality of different ways of living mediated with one another by sociating interchanges in the medium of abstract, reified value that leave each other in peace, and indeed, in a guaranteed, but benevolent *indifference* to each other. The preservation of freedom demands conceding the *powerlessness* of government to bring about certain envisaged outcomes of the power interplay at the heart of social living.

The mutually estimating power plays among individuals and associations therefore contains many contradictory possibilities, including the following: rivalry and teamwork, competition and co-operation, appreciation and depreciation of abilities, vanity and self-esteem, flattery and esteem, winning and losing, greed and moderation, mutual benefit and one-sided advantage, uplifting exhilaration and downcasting disappointment. The power interplay cannot be governed, controlled to produce certain desirable outcomes rather than others, nor can it be quelled to prevent the savage struggle over who-status among the players (over standing presence in the mirroring shine of public or private estimation) that rages everywhere and everyday, mostly covertly.

Political power is not cybernetic, but can only arbitrate conflicts and right wrong through a judiciary and seek to maintain fair boundary conditions of the game as a whole. Fairness cannot be calculably set up. When the power play among individuals and their associations is fair, it is beautiful like a fleeting, mild summer's day, but, more often than not, it is unfair and ugly. The government is only one instance mandated to fight for fairness by laying down rules of play. Fairness, however, is not so much a matter of implementable government policy; rather fair play is a shared *ethos* in which the players are immersed that imbues the power interplay with a certain attunement. An ethos is an aether which the players breathe habitually like a fairer, higher atmosphere; it is not a higher power.

11 The socio-ontological constitution of 'we ourselves'

11.1 Dialectical movement from the sensuous givenness of world to the identity of ego and world – The dialectic of recognition – "*Ego* that is *we* and *we* that is *ego*" (Hegel's *Phenomenology*)

The individualization of truth in myriad individual perspectives (Chapter 10.6) poses a problem for how individual humans are to share the world in social living. The historical emergence and institution of a polity can be regarded as a response to this splintering of truth by institutionalizing how individual truths are to be 'aufgehoben' or raised to a higher, pre-eminent plane of shared, social, lived truth. A study of Hegel's *Phänomenologie des Geistes* is one way of approaching this question of how individual selfhood in its individual truth is to be socially integrated or mediated (vermittelt), i.e. how individual self-consciousnesses can come together and share the "truth of the certainty of one's self" (*PhdG*. B Selbstbewußtsein IV Die Wahrheit der Gewißheit seiner selbst).

Doubtless the phenomenology of self-consciousness and especially the "process of recognition" (Prozeß des Anerkennens *Enz*III § 425 Add., § 430) constitute a crucial, pivotal point in the phenomenology of spirited mind (Geist),[211] not only in Hegel's famous 1807 publication, but also in the section on the phenomenology of mind in the 1830 edition of the *Encyclopaedia* §§ 413–438. Even on a merely formal level, this can be seen by perusing the table of contents of the *Phänomenologie des Geistes* and the *Enzyklopädie der philosophischen Wissenschaften*. In the latter, the phenomenology of mind is broken down into three sections, "a. Consciousness as such", "b. Self-consciousness" and "c. Reason", and section b. in turn is broken down into "α. Desire", "β. The recognizing self-consciousness" and "γ. Universal self-consciousness". Finally, proceeding back up the scale of the table of contents, the phenomenology of

---

211 "Geist" in Hegel's speculative-philosophical sense is difficult to render adequately in English, since Geist can mean either 'mind' or 'spirit' or something that is a bit of both, hence 'spirited mind'. 'Mind' in philosophical English is inevitably connoted with philosophy of mind which, in an Anglo-Saxon manner, usually implies something 'cognitive', which misses the point entirely, for Geist is, among other things, the translation of Greek νοῦς which is much more than merely cogitating consciousness. Hence νοῦς in Anaxagoras or Plato connotes something like a 'world-mind'. The 'spirit' of an age, for instance, is its Geist, its spirited mind.

https://doi.org/10.1515/9783110617504-011

mind in the *Encyclopaedia* is itself the second section of three making up "Subjective mind".

The formal structure is similar in the *Phänomenologie des Geistes*: "B. Self-consciousness" is sandwiched between "A. Consciousness" and "C. Reason", and the middle section of "B. Self-consciousness" is the famous "dialectic of master and servant" or the "process of recognition". But why should the process of recognition between self-consciousnesses constitute such a pivotal point in the movement of consciousness through to reason and absolute knowledge? The 1807 *Phänomenologie des Geistes* was first titled "Science of the Experience of Consciousness" (Wissenschaft der Erfahrung des Bewußtseins, cf. editors' note to Hegel's *Werke* Band 3). The German word 'Erfahrung' should be rendered by something like 'an experience gone through' because 'er-fahren' is literally 'to travel through'. The phenomenology is what consciousness or knowing awareness goes through step by step in knowing the world from its first, abstract beginnings through to absolute knowledge. It is consciousness itself as self-consciousness that carries on a dialectic with consciousness in which it step-by-step uncovers the inadequacy of how it conceives the world, moving on progressively to higher 'truths' of its conceptions, while we as readers, who already have the τέλος of absolute knowing in view, look on this dialectical movement. The possibility of this dialectical dialogue between consciousness and self-consciousness is given already by the structure of consciousness itself as con-science, i.e a co-knowing of its self being conscious of the world represented in itself; its perception of the world is always also an *apperception* of its self perceiving. Every ego cogito is an ego cogito me cogitare.[212] And we are the onlookers of this dialogue between consciousness and self-consciousness in the course of consciousness' going through its experiences.

---

212 Descartes says in § 9 of the first part of the *Principia philosophiae* from 1646, "Cogitationes nomine, intelligo illa omnia, quae nobis consciis in nobis fiunt, quatenus eorum in nobis conscientia ist" (I understand by the name cogitation/thinking all those things that happen in us which we know along with ourselves insofar as there is a co-knowing of them in us. Descartes *Principia philosophiae* Oeuvres de Descartes. Publ. Par Charles Adam et Paul Tannery, Paris 1897–1910, Vol. VIII, p. 7. Heidegger comments on this passage, "Consciousness is not merely perceptio, grasping re-presentation, but apperceptio, a presenting to *us* co-grasping *us* also. [...] consciousness of things is *essentially* and *properly speaking self*-consciousness, although mostly a consciousness of self which the self mostly does not represent explicitly and therefore in a certain way forgets." (Das Bewußtsein ist nicht bloße perceptio, fassendes Vor-stellen, sondern apperceptio, ein *uns* mitfassendes Auf-*uns*-zu-stellen. [...] das Bewußtsein von den Dingen ist *wesentlich* und *eigentlich Selbst*bewußtsein, obzwar meist ein solches, das das Selbst nicht eigens vorstellt und so in gewisser Weise vergißt. *Hegel GA*68:76)

The dialectical movement of thought in the *Phenomenology* is the movement of knowing awareness loosening, dissolving itself from (ab-solvere) any dependence on the givenness of the world in its objectivity so that ultimately, after it has travelled through all the stages of merely relative knowing and finally unfolded itself in absolute knowledge, knowing awareness knows itself to be knowingly one with the world in the "unentzweiteste Identität", the "most un-dirempted identity"[213]. Absolute knowing is not relative, i.e. it is not dependent upon any outer givenness of what is to be known and is thus infinite, unbounded, independent, unconditional, in short, absolute. The movement of thinking takes place in the medium of the λόγος and is a movement through the various forms in which knowing consciousness gets to know, i.e. becomes knowingly aware, of the world. The movement is therefore dialectical in the original sense of the word in Plato as διαλέγεσθαι, i.e. as a talking-through in the course of which the contradictions in what is said are overcome step by step. This going-through as a talking-through is at the same time 'absolvent', a 'loosening-from' in the sense of consciousness knowingly penetrating the world and becoming one with it, integrating it, so that ultimately it knows that in the objective world it experiences only itself, namely, as reason in the unity of the Idea.

Knowing awareness or consciousness starts at the beginning of the *Phenomenology* with the immediate *sensuous* givenness of the world which it takes in as "sensuous certainty" (sinnliche Gewißheit). What it takes in are the colours, sounds, odours of the world in their singularity, but in insisting that it is knowingly experiencing the world in its sensuous singularity, this sensuous certainty is driven beyond itself and has to admit that, even though it intends the unique singularity of 'this' in its sensuous givenness, 'this' is itself a universal category, and it is forced to *say* something universal, namely, that it knows a *thing* (Ding) with its many *properties* (Eigenschaften), and is thus compelled to move beyond itself. This new knowledge is taken from the thing in its sensuous givenness as *perception* (Wahrnehmung). Wahrnehmung means etymologically a 'taking-true', i.e. taking something in its truth. But in taking things in their truth through the senses, consciousness is merely exposed to and dependent on how things are given to it in a bewildering variety of endless properties. Confronted with this multiplicity, it cannot even keep the thing together as a unity, but is forced to move from one property to the next, one thing to the next, taking in each in its truth in perceiving it sensuously, and forced to connect these sensuous truths with a mere 'and'.

---

213 G.W.F. Hegel W2:46, cited in Heidegger *Vier Seminare* Klostermann, Frankfurt/M. 1977 S. 55, 57.

The knowing awareness represented by sensuous perception is thus, in turn, driven beyond itself to embrace the supersensuous world of simple laws in order to be able to explain, in a simple, unified way, the sensuous world of things in their endless variety and movement. It resorts to a "calm realm of laws" (ruhiges Reich von Gesetzen, *PhdG*:120) from which it can account for the continually shifting sensuous phenomenality and thus becomes understanding (Verstand). The laws form the basis for knowing the world as a "play of forces" (Spiel der Kräfte, *PhdG*:116). But such a split between a supersensuous "calm realm of laws" (such as the Newtonian laws of motion) and the movement of sensuous appearances means that movement is not understood as movement in itself, which requires that the many laws have to be unified in a single law, and that this law has to differentiate *itself* as a law of movement into its various moments residing in the *interior* of the moving object itself. In knowing the law, knowing consciousness thus finds *itself* in the interior of the object and their difference is aufgehoben, i.e. waived and simultaneously raised to a higher plane, namely, to that of self-consciousness. The object becomes something living, with its own principle of movement, i.e. its own soul (ψυχή), and thus identical with living consciousness, which now knows *itself* in the object. Just as the differences in the object become moments in the self-unfolding of the law and are thus, in truth, not differences at all, so too does consciousness differentiate itself from itself as ego but, since the ego is identical with itself in always already co-knowing itself (I = I), this difference is also no difference at all (cf. *Enz.* § 423 Add.). In being compelled to regard this self-movement of something living, understanding is on its way to becoming reason.

> Am Bewußtsein dieser *dialektischen*, dieser *lebendigen* Einheit des Unterschiedenen entzündet sich daher das *Selbstbewußtsein*, das Bewußtsein von dem sich selber gegenständlichen, als in sich selbst unterschiedenen einfachen *Ideellen*, das Wissen von der *Wahrheit des Natürlichen*, vom Ich. (*EnzIII* § 423 Add.)

> *Self-consciousness*, consciousness of the simple *ideal* that is objective to itself, that is, differentiated within itself, the knowledge of the *truth of what is natural*, of the *ego*, is therefore ignited in the consciousness of this *dialectical*, this *living* unity of what is differentiated.

Knowing awareness thus comes to know itself as a self; consciousness becomes self-consciousness, a knowing awareness of itself in its selfhood, and in knowing myself I know the world.

> In dem Ausdruck Ich = Ich ist das Prinzip der absoluten *Vernunft* und *Freiheit* ausgesprochen. Die Vernunft und die Freiheit besteht [...] kurz darin, daß ich in einem und demselben Bewußtsein *Ich* und die *Welt* habe, in der Welt mich selber wiederfinde und umge-

kehrt in meinem Bewußtsein das habe, was *ist*, was *Objektivität* hat. Diese das Prinzip des Geistes ausmachende Einheit des Ich und des Objektes ist jedoch nur erst auf *abstrakte* Weise im *unmittelbaren* Selbstbewußtsein vorhanden und wird nur von *uns*, den Betrachtenden, noch nicht vom Selbstbewußtsein selber erkannt. (*EnzIII* § 424 Add.)

In the expression I = I, the principle of absolute *reason* and *freedom* is expressed. Reason and freedom consist [...] concisely in the fact that in one and the same consciousness, I have *ego* and the *world*, that I find myself again in the world and conversely that I have in my consciousness that which *is*, that which has *objectivity*. This unity of ego and object constituting the principle of spirit, however, is present at first only in an *abstract* way in *immediate* self-consciousness and is only recognized by *us*, the onlookers, and not yet by self-consciousness itself.

At first, self-consciousness, i.e. the knowing awareness of self, is achieved only abstractly, and the unity of this knowing awareness of self with the objectivity of the world is apparent only to *us* who, from the start, have already assumed the standpoint of absolute knowledge and are the onlookers looking on how consciousness itself goes through the experience of working its way, in its own thinking, toward this standpoint of absolute, totally free unity of itself with the world. Self-consciousness is thus at first immediate, unmediated and insofar still captive to the standpoint of consciousness confronted with a given world in its objectivity which it strives to overcome in its instinctual drive (Trieb) of desire (Begierde). The unity of myself and world is at first immediate or "*an sich* or according to its concept" (*Enz.* § 425, an sich oder ihrem Begriffe nach, *Enz.* § 431 Add.), i.e. potential or δυνάμει, and not yet *für sich* or actually present, 'energized', ἐνεργείᾳ, maintaining itself in presence as a substance.[214] Dialectical, speculative thinking, the movement of theorizing (looking) that goes through the experience of the world, still has to move from what is only potentially identical with it and still only given to the senses as a "given objectivity" (gegebene Objektivität, *Enz.* § 425) to gain what is actually present for its knowledge in which it knows itself in its truth as identical with *being*, with "that which *is*". The first steps in this movement of self-consciousness toward its identity with the world in spirited mind are a three-step of the stages of "desire", the "process of recognition" and "universal self-consciousness", which make up the three sections on self-consciousness in the *Encyclopaedia*.

Desire is still the situation of "unmediated, [...] individual self-consciousness" (das unmittelbare [...] einzelne Selbstbewußtsein, *Enz.* § 425 Add.) in its relation to "an external object" (ein äußerliches Objekt, § 425 Add.).

---

214 Cf. *Vorlesungen über die Geschichte der Philosophie I, Werke* Vol. 18, S. 39, the concept of development, Entwicklung.

Through individual, desiring self-consciousness "egoistically, selfishly" (selbstsüchtig, *Enz.* § 428) consuming and annihilating the object, its unity with the object in the satisfaction of desire is only short-lived, transient, passing (Vorübergehendes, *Enz.* § 428 Add.) and it is drawn into an endless process of desire and held fast "in the boring alternation of desire and its satisfaction that continues endlessly" (in dem ins Unendliche sich fortsetzenden langweiligen Wechsel der Begierde und der Befriedigung derselben, *Enz.* § 429 Add.). It can only escape the tedious endlessness of desire by raising itself beyond the standpoint of immediate desire, in which its subjectivity confronts an external object, to a confrontation with an other that is likewise a self, i.e. another free ego.

> Indem ein Selbstbewußtsein der Gegenstand ist, ist er ebensowohl Ich wie Gegenstand. — Hiermit ist schon der Begriff *des Geistes* für uns vorhanden. Was für das Bewußtsein weiter wird, ist die Erfahrung, was der Geist ist, diese absolute Substanz, welche in der vollkommenen Freiheit und Selbständigkeit ihres Gegensatzes, nämlich verschiedener für sich seiender Selbstbewußtseine, die Einheit derselben ist; *Ich, das Wir, und Wir, das Ich* ist. (*PhdG*:145)

> Through self-consciousness being the object, the object is both ego and object. — With this, the concept *of spirited mind* is already present for us. What happens further for consciousness is to go through the experience of what spirited mind is, this absolute substance which, in the complete freedom and independence of its opposition, namely different self-consciousnesses existing for themselves, is the unity of these self-consciousnesses; *ego* that is *we* and *we* that is *ego*.

Not only does self-consciousness have to attain its unity with the world considered as a world of objects, but also its unity with other self-consciousnesses in a sharing of spirited mind (an ontological cast of world). The individual, self-conscious ego is thus destined to become unified with others into a We by going through the experience of dialectical thinking. I, we and the world will thus become one in the absolute independence and freedom of spirited mind that becomes objective in ethical life, its mores and institutions. The unity with the objective world in a We is to be an identity in the sense of a knowing belonging-together or Zusammengehörigkeit. But first of all, self-consciousness has to raise itself beyond its "singular individuality" (Einzelheit, *Enz.* § 430) through the "process of recognition" (Prozeß des Anerkennens, *Enz.* § 430).

 "At first there is a self-consciousness *unmediatedly* for a self-consciousness as an other for an *other*" (Es ist ein Selbstbewußtsein für ein Selbstbewußtsein zunächst *unmittelbar* als ein Anderes für ein *Anderes, Enz.* § 430). I "look at myself as ego in the other but also see in the other an immediately existing other object, absolutely independent [and standing over ME] against me as an ego" (Ich schaue in ihm als Ich mich selbst an, aber auch darin ein unmittelbar daseiendes, als Ich absolut gegen mich selbständiges anderes Objekt, *Enz.* § 430). The other is a mirror for myself as ego, but a mirror that is also completely independent of me, which gives me "the drive to *show* myself as a free self and to be *present* as such a free self for the other" ("den Trieb, sich als freies Selbst zu *zeigen* and für den Anderen als solches *da* zu sein, *Enz.* § 430). I cannot *be* a self without showing my self as such to others, without presenting my self to the other and being present for the other as a self, as somewho. What drives the "process of recognition" is

> ...der ungeheure Widerspruch, daß — da Ich das ganz *Allgemeine*, absolute *Durchgängige*, durch *keine Grenze Unterbrochene*, das *allen* Menschen *gemeinsame* Wesen ist — die beiden sich hier aufeinander beziehenden Selbste *eine* Identität, sozusagen *ein* Licht ausmachen und dennoch zugleich *zweie* sind, die, in vollkommener *Starrheit* und *Sprödigkeit* gegeneinander, jedes als ein *in sich Reflektiertes*, von dem Anderen absolut *Unterschiedenes* und *Undurchbrechbares* bestehen. (*EnzIII* § 430 Add.)

> ...the monstrous contradiction that, since the ego is the wholly *universal*, absolutely *uniform* essence *common* to *all* human beings that is *not interrupted by any borders*, the two selves here relating to each other constitute a *single* identity, a *single* light, so to speak, and nevertheless at the same time are two which, in complete *rigidity* and *aloofness* toward and against each other, each exists *reflected into itself*, absolutely *different* from and *impenetrable* by the other.

Each of the two individual self-consciousnesses as selves is "absolutely aloof", "impenetrable" and "rigid" in their independence from each other, but at the same time, in their essence, both are immersed in and share the same "light" of ἀλήθεια (disclosive truth) and therefore belong together in the same "identity" of essence. I see in the other myself and at the same time the absolute other. From this "monstrous contradiction" ensues a "struggle" (Kampf, *Enz.* § 431) that aims at overcoming the other self in its otherness. This struggle aims at the other's independence at first by attempting to overcome the other self in its immediate presence and independent "bodiliness" (Leiblichkeit, *Enz.* § 431), with the ego risking its own life, for it can appear at first glance that the other's independent individuality resides in its separate, sensuous, ontic bodiliness as a natural thing. But this first appearance is only an illusion because risking one's own life in struggle with the other does not aim at physically destroying the other, but only in showing and demonstrating that one is not merely a natural being tied to its physical bodiliness, but rather a free being, and this freedom is mutually demonstrated and recognized through a struggle over life and death in which the natural, ontic, living bodiliness of both selves is put at risk.

A life-and-death struggle is a struggle at the *extremes* which reveals how the selves can come to recognize each other *as free selves* and thus as ontological

beings. Freedom cannot be located in ontic, natural bodiliness but only ontologically in human being itself in its free selfhood. "This freedom of the *one* in the
other unites humans in an inward way, in contrast to which *need* and *distress*
bring them together only outwardly" (Diese Freiheit des *einen* im *anderen* ver-
einigt die Menschen auf innerliche Weise, wogegen das *Bedürfnis* und die *Not*
dieselben nur äußerlich zusammenbringt, *Enz.* § 431 Add.). Instead of an interaction of forces according to some inner law, as on the level of understanding,
here, on the level of knowing selves in interplay with each other in a process of
recognition as free human beings, we observe an extreme game of life and death
in which both selves demonstrate their freedom to each other in each other as
mirror. Only free human beings who *are* selves can play this game of putting
themselves physically at risk for the sake of showing off and demonstrating
their freedom.

Hegel is quick to avoid the misunderstanding that he is propagating the ad-
visability of his students engaging in life-and-death duels to prove their status
as free beings, pointing out that the struggle of life and death is applicable only
in the "*state of nature* where human beings are only *individuals*" (*Natur-
zustande*, wo die Menschen nur als *Einzelne* sind, *Enz.* § 432 Add.) and not in
"civil society and the state" (der bürgerlichen Gesellschaft und dem Staate, *Enz.*
§ 432 Add.) because in society they are always-already recognized as free persons, i.e. in civil society the spirited-mindful We of the abstract-universal person has already been constituted and realized. In a social, sociated state, the
singular, individual self is already mediated with its universal status as a free
person, and is no longer only immediately free and independent in its own individual, singular self-consciousness. The social objectivity in which it is embedded is then a law-governed realm of social intercourse that is an objectivation of
freedom in concrete institutions. Freedom is no longer only an sich, potential,
but also für sich or actually present and 'energized' (ἐνεργείᾳ) for itself in the
state's laws that guarantee the freedom of the individual as person. Not only
formally as person (especially before the law), but also substantially, the individual member of civil society and state, i.e. the citizen, is recognized in being
accorded "honour through the office that it holds, through the business it operates and through its other working activity. Its honour thus has a substantial,
universal, objective content no longer dependent on empty subjectivity" (Ehre
durch das Amt, das er bekleidet, durch das von ihm betriebene Gewerbe und
durch seine sonstige arbeitende Tätigkeit. Seine Ehre hat dadurch einen substantiellen, allgemeinen, objektiven, nicht mehr von der leeren Subjektivität
abhängigen Inhalt, *Enz.* § 432 Add.).

The life-and-death struggle is obviated in a state of society because the "process of recognition" already has attained the objectified form of honour that derives from the individual self's standing as somewho in the ensemble of objective, ethical, social relations in which it is embedded. Individual selfhood of free self-consciousness has to be mirrored and affirmed in the honour which derives from an individual self's social standing. The corollary to this is that the individual self is 'socially dead' if it is not acknowledged by being honoured in some way as a somewho with social standing and an assured place in the overall ensemble of ethical social life. The mirror of social honour and esteem is necessary for the individual to *be* a self; its self must be reflected in the world as a shared, social world. If this recognition is only formal, i.e. acknowledgement of the individual citizen's status as person, this socially guaranteed status remains abstracted from the individual's concrete life and place within the social whole, and the individual is confronted with an indifferent, blank, abstract mirror in the other.[215]

---

215 This notion of being 'socially dead' if recognition is refused presupposes a concept of whoness according to which the human being *is* a human being only insofar as he or she is somewho as constituted by the estimating mirror play of social interchange and recognition. As ηασ βεεν σηοων in earlier chapters, especially Chapter 5, it is above all each individual's *abilities* that gain recognition or fail to gain such esteeming recognition in social interplay. This mirroring is the social phenomenon of individual *value*. Although the individual must actually have ability for it to be recognized (that is, if the individual does not merely generate an illusion of ability that deceives others), social being as such depends on ability being recognized, esteemed. The individual whose abilities fail to be mirrored must have the strength of independence, through the ongoing dialogue of the self with itself, to maintain a sober self-estimation which is nothing less than a valiant attempt at mirroring oneself, despite the refusal of recognition by others. Otherwise, such an individual is downcast and dead, i.e. *mortified*. Such a phenomenon of refused recognition of abilities is what is aimed at when referring to the possibility of 'social death', which, in turn, opens up the possibility of thinking death differently from the usual metaphysical conception, according to which death is the event that physically ends an individual life when the soul (the concept of life or the being of life) and body part company. Thus, for example, Hegel conceives of life as a correspondence between soul and body, and death as a non-correspondence between soul and body: "Truth in philosophy means that the concept corresponds to reality. A body, for instance, is the reality, the soul the concept. Soul and body, however, should be adequate to each other; a dead human being is therefore still an existence, but no longer a genuine existence, a conceptless existence; wherefore the dead body decays." (Wahrheit in der Philosophie heißt das, daß der Begriff der Realität entspreche. Ein Leib ist z.B. die Realität, die Seele der Begriff. Seele und Leib sollen sich aber angemessen sein; ein toter Mensch ist daher noch eine Existenz, aber keine wahrhafte mehr, ein begriffloses Dasein: deswegen verfault der tote Körper. *RPh*. § 21 Add.). Death is accordingly, in this metaphysical way of thinking, an extreme that marks the end of life when body and soul part company, so that death is necessarily thought physically. But the phenomenon of

But on the prior level of the struggle over life and death between two self-consciousnesses, any kind of social recognition in "the ethically holding-relation" (dem sittlichen Verhältnis, *Enz.* § 432 Add.) of honour has not yet been gone through by knowing self-awareness. Instead, the life-and-death struggle has at first the outcome of the relationship between master and servant (*Enz.* § 433) in which the servant, for the sake of saving his life, subjugates himself to the master. Instead of insisting on his independent, free individuality, the servant now serves the master.

This could be regarded as the first lasting (i.e. habitual and thus ethical) *social* relation that arises in the phenomenology of spirited mind, a "*communality* of needs and the care for their satisfaction" (*Gemeinsamkeit* des Bedürfnisses und der Sorge für dessen Befriedigung, *Enz.* § 434). The self-consciousnesses are thus on their way from a confrontation of self-seeking, singular individualities to the constitution of a universal connection in which it is no longer a matter of the immediate satisfaction of desire (to prove the independence of self-consciousness from objectivity) but rather of mediated "caring- and providing-for" (Vorsorge, *Enz.* § 434) in social relations of labour in which "the two extremes of independence and dependency close together" (die beiden Extreme der Selbständigkeit und Unselbständigkeit sich zusammenschließen, *Enz.* § 434) in a "conclusion" (Schluß, cf. the third and final part of Hegel's *Logik*). Whereas the master can look upon the prevailing of his own individual, selfish being-for-itself in the servant and his service to the master (hat in dem Knecht und dessen Dienst die Anschauung des Geltens seines einzelnen Fürsichseins, *Enz.* § 435), the servant is raised above the standpoint of the merely immediate,

---

'social death' opens up another perspective on death which now shows itself in life itself as a constant accompaniment of life present in certain moods that could be called downcast moods, in which the individual does not have a firm stand in the world as somewho and feels weak rather than strong and robust. Such death-like states occur not merely fortuitously when the individual is lying down, especially in a sleepy state. Lying down, human being is vulnerable, and sleep has long been compared to death as a state in which the individual has temporarily withdrawn from the exertions of having to maintain a stand as somewho in (social) life. Being down in the sense of a physical position or a depressed mood signifies the constant, felt, hovering presence of death in life. Death is always with us more or less. It makes its withheld presence felt as a possibility that mingles with life, and not merely as an extreme that will arrive sometime in the future, at the end of life. Such attention to the phenomenon of death in life as an intertwining tango of Eros and Thanatos is not a memento mori in any religious sense but an aspect of our human status as constant intimates of death, of human beings who can die because we are selves who have always already assumed a more or less knowing stance toward our constant, silent companion, death.

selfish singularity of the satisfaction of desire to a more mediated, shared, communal, universal standpoint.

Moreover, there is a further twist in this dialectic of a power interplay between master and servant, viz. that through the work which the servant performs at his master's behest, he develops also his own potentials into powers put to work that ultimately can be turned against the master. Hegel does not see this twist which could be regarded as the historical possibility of changing the rules of power interplay to those of a power play between and among formal equals which would accord better with Hegel's dialectical move to "real universality as mutuality" among self-consciousnesses as we shall now consider.

11.2 Universal self-consciousness and irrepressible, questioning, singular individuality – The ever-broken mediation between singularity and universality concretely realized in ethical life

The upshot and culmination of the dialectical process of recognition among independent, self-knowing selves is the attainment of "universal self-consciousness" (das allgemeine Selbstbewußtsein, *Enz*III § 436) which knows its free self as affirmed in the other self-consciousness and as a "real universality as mutuality" (reelle Allgemeinheit als Gegenseitigkeit, *Enz.* § 436) which forms the "substance" (Substanz, *Enz.* § 436 Note) that is objectified in ethical social relations, i.e. in "every essential spirituality, of family, fatherland, state as well as all virtues, of love, friendship, bravery, of honour and fame" (jeder wesentlichen Geistigkeit, der Familie, des Vaterlandes, des Staats, sowie aller Tugenden, der Liebe, Freundschaft, Tapferkeit, der Ehre, des Ruhms, *Enz.* § 436 Note).

> Wir haben daher hier die gewaltige Diremtion des Geistes in verschiedene Selbste, die an und für sich und füreinander vollkommen frei, selbständig, absolut spröde, widerstandleistend — und doch zugleich miteinander identisch, somit nicht selbständig, nicht undurchdringlich, sondern gleichsam zusammengeflossen sind. Dies Verhältnis ist durchaus *spekulativer* Art; [...] Das Spekulative oder Vernünftige und Wahre besteht in der Einheit des Begriffs oder des Subjektiven und der Objektivität. Diese Einheit ist auf dem fraglichen Standpunkt offenbar vorhanden. Sie bildet die Substanz der Sittlichkeit, ... (*Enz.* § 436 Add.)

> We have here therefore the mighty diremption (sundering) of spirited mind into distinct selves who are completely free, independent, absolutely aloof, resistant in-and-for-themselves and for each other — and nevertheless at the same time identical with one an-

other and thus not independent, not impenetrable, but, as it were, confluenced, flowed-together. This relation is of a thoroughly *speculative* kind; [...] What is speculative or reasonable and true consists in the unity of the concept or the subjective element with objectivity. This unity obviously exists at the standpoint in question [namely, the final subsection of self-consciousness at the transition to reason, ME]. It forms the substance of ethical life,...

The dialectic of recognition among self-consciousnesses is the way in which, the path on which, according to Hegel, consciousness finally attains the standpoint of Geist, of spirited mind, where it knows itself to be identical with, i.e. as belonging to, the world, namely, a shared social, ethical world in its substantive objectivity. Reason is nothing other than the speculative, i.e. ontological, insight into the beingness of being, and such reason attains truth for Hegel as an adequation of the ontological concept to objective reality. Such is the consolation and reconciliation offered by speculative thinking to human being as a self-aware self that it find its place in the world by merging with other self-consciousnesses and becoming integrated into society's habitual-ethical practices, customs and institutions, thus becoming *substantial*. Only speculative thinking, i.e. thinking that reflects on and has insight into *being*, can see the unity of many different, independent self-consciousnesses in a shared ethical world that has gained substance, οὐσία, standing presence.

The merging with other self-consciousnesses is the experience that self-consciousness goes through in its dialectic with itself; for *us*, however, looking on from an absolute standpoint, there is no merging but rather the opposite: a sundering diremption of the always already unified spirited mind (Geist) into "distinct selves who are completely free, independent". Hegel's speculative-dialectical thinking is therefore the very opposite of subjectivist metaphysics, including in today's Anglo-Saxon analytic philosophy, for which consciousness is located somehow individualized 'inside'. For analytic philosophy as the hand-maiden of today's neuroscience, this 'inside' location is the brain.

Is Hegel's resolution of the question of the identity of self-consciousness with the world satisfactory? To *be* a self, singular, individual self-consciousness requires the recognition-mirror of the world to confirm its place in the world, which can only be a social world (cf. Chapter 3.3.1). The "certainty of one's self" is achieved only through the self's being reflected in the other and the others who acknowledge it affirmatively *as* self. Hegel himself points out in passing the problematic nature of the recognition and acknowledgement of self-consciousness in the other. The problem resides in the "*substance* of every essential spirituality" (*Substanz* jeder wesentlichen Geistigkeit, *Enz.* § 436 Note) and its discrepancy from its "universal reflected appearance" (allgemeines Widererscheinen, *Enz.* § 436 Note) or "universal shining-back" from social objectivity for, "this *appearance/shining* of what is substantial can also be separated from what is substantial and be held onto for itself in honour void of substance, vain fame, etc." (dies *Erscheinen* des Substantiellen kann auch vom Substantiellen getrennt und für sich in gehaltleerer Ehre, eitlem Ruhm usf. festgehalten werden, *Enz.* § 436 Note). The reflected standing that a self-consciousness enjoys in the recognition shone back by others and in ethical objectivity as esteem and honour can be mere appearance, a tinselly, tawdry fake, an illusion and a delusion of prestige (from L. præstigium a delusion, illusion, usually in pl. præstigiæ, illusions, juggler's tricks).

The individual's genuine "substance", its substantial, intrinsic (hence singular) powers in the sense of abilities, excellences, can blatantly diverge from the individual's socially mirrored standing by virtue of its merely derived, extraneous powers (wealth, social position and connections, official position in a hierarchy, etc.). But if this "substance" consists in an individual's powers and abilities, these are precisely *potentials* that refer of themselves to their exercise, i.e. their being put to work in active movement to bring forth some sort of work. In the context of a society, this work must be estimated in some way or other, and this movement of estimation is itself a power play between self and society, and therefore relational rather than intrinsic, substantial. Coming to stand as somewho in society is therefore fraught with the contradication that, on the one hand, the 'shining-back' from the others may be tawdry celebrity, fame, etc. but, on the other hand, some kind of affirmatively estimating reflection is necessary to *be* somewho at all.

The "form of awareness" (Form des Bewußtseins, *Enz.* § 436 Note) of this "substance", Hegel says, is "universal self-consciousness" itself, "i.e. that free self-consciousness for which the other self-consciousness standing over against it [...] is an *equally independent* self-consciousness" (d.h. dasjenige freie Selbstbewußtsein, für welches das ihm gegenständliche andere Selbstbewußtsein [...] ein *gleichfalls selbständiges* ist, *Enz.* § 436 Add.) thus constituting a unity "of subjectivity and objectivity" (des Subjektiven und der Objektivität, *Enz.* § 436 Add.) that is "the substance of ethical life" (die Substanz der Sittlichkeit, *Enz.* § 436 Add.). Only in recognizing each other in a mirror interplay as free, independent self-consciousnesses is any form of social being such as "family, love between the sexes (here this unity has the form of particularity), patriotism, this willing of the universal aims and interests of the state, the love of God..." (Familie, der geschlechtlichen Liebe (da hat jene Einheit die Form der Besonderheit), Vaterlandsliebe, dieses Wollens der allgemeinen Zwecke und Interessen des Staats, der Liebe zu Gott..., *Enz.* § 436 Add.) at all possible.

The substance, according to Hegel, is thus the universal that overcomes and elevates singular individuality and the self-interest of particularity to enable an ethical We composed of free self-consciousnesses in a customary way of life. But the substance can also be corrupted in fake forms of "affirmative knowing of one's self in the other self" (das affirmative Wissen seiner selbst im anderen Selbst, *Enz.* § 436) such as "in honour void of substance, vain fame" (in gehalt-leerer Ehre, eitlem Ruhm, *Enz.* § 436 Note). Honour and fame as forms, 'looks' in which self-consciousness mirrors, and thus consolidates, itself in other selves accordingly can only be genuine if the honoured or famous, celebrated individual concerned genuinely embodies the universal and stands above its own singularity and selfish particularity, i.e. if singularity is genuinely mediated with the universal (assuming that such a mediation is at all possible). The individual who insists on its peculiar, *singular* idiosyncrasy only conceitedly delectates itself in the mirror of the honour accorded to it by others, whereas the selfish individual only exploits the honour of public office to covertly further its own *particular* interests. Such a universal standpoint for self-consciousness is possible through self-aware human being — which is always already reasonable an sich, i.e. potentially in itself — raising itself above itself to become "reason" (Vernunft, *Enz.* § 437) conceived as a thinking correspondence to the beingness of beings as Idea, and through this, reason's constituting a true or genuine communality. Reason itself as an ontological casting of the beingness of beings is then objectified in ethical life, especially in the institutions of state, in such a way that the universal standpoint attains a solidity that no longer has to rely on the fickleness of individual self-consciousness with its proneness to self-interest or capricious idiosyncrasy.

Nevertheless, can reason itself, especially in its objectified forms of ethical life, be *unreasonably*, i.e. against the thoughtful hermeneutic recasting of the beingness of beings, repressive of individual singularity that does not conform to, is not identical with reason's solidified universality (cf. Heidegger's Mansein, i.e. the mediocre averageness of 'people', in *Being and Time*) and itself questions the validity of an all-too-consolidated historical mode of ethical life in given, unquestioned mores of an age? That is, can singularity and universality dirempt, i.e. fall apart, and switch roles and valencies in such a way that singular individuality — "the principle of individuality and personhood" (das Prinzip der Individualität und Persönlichkeit, *LII* W6:297) — that is non-identical with, i.e. does not belong to, *realized* reason, stands higher than universality as precipitated in an ostensibly 'reasonable', 'substantial', ethical social objectivity that has attained all-too-standing presence? Can reason itself become overbearing, repressing individual singularity's struggle to cast a facet of an other historical vista of how being could shape up as a world? Does Hegel's attempted dialectical mediation of singular individuality with the universality of reason gloss over the irremediable contradictoriness and fracturedness of such a mediation?

> Im Staate sind der Geist des Volkes, die Sitte, das Gesetz das Herrschende. Da wird der Mensch als *vernünftiges* Wesen, als *frei*, als Person anerkannt und behandelt; und der Einzelne seinerseits macht sich dieser Anerkennung dadurch würdig, daß er, mit Überwindung der Natürlichkeit seines Selbstbewußtseins, einem *Allgemeinen*, dem *an und für sich seienden Willen*, dem *Gesetze* gehorcht, also gegen andere sich auf eine *allgemeingültige* Weise benimmt, sie als das anerkennt, wofür er selber gelten will, — als frei, als Person. (*Enz.* § 432 Add.)

> In the state, the spirited mind of the people, ethical custom, law rule. Here, a human being is recognized and treated as a *reasonable* being, as *free*, as a person; and the singular individual for its part makes itself worthy of this recognition by overcoming the naturalness of its self-consciousness and obeying something *universal*, the *will that exists both in and for itself*, the *law*, and thus conducts itself toward others in a *universally valid* way and recognizes them as that which it itself wants to be regarded — as free, as a person.

Can a universal We constituted in conformity with reason (thinking insight into being), despite all recognition of and respect for the individual as a person, be stifling and repressive? Is the universal form of human being represented by personhood merely *abstractly* universal and therefore also potentially repressive of concretely individual singularity? Or is it rather the *concretization* of personhood in ethical life and state rule by law that is tendentially repressive, whereas precisely the *abstractness* of personhood, guaranteeing as it does *mutual indifference*, leaves room for play of the freedom of an individual singularity with an other perspective on being? Does the triad of universality, particularity and singularity remain always unreconciled, broken, beset by inner turmoil, a Zerrissenheit, not only through the distorting incursions of particular self-interests, but also through singular individuality that freely questions realized reason's self-sufficient concrete solidity, the final closedness and complacency of its mores, the oppressiveness of a purported 'closing-together' of singularity and universality in which the individual has to choose its self from among the masks of identity offered by the world? Does freedom itself depend upon singularity and universality remaining precisely *not* closed together in a consolidated, reasonable con-clusion? Does human being itself in its whoness, despite all pacification and reconciliation of its contradictions among singularity, particularity and universality through reason that has shaped a social world as objective, ethical spirit, remain nevertheless ultimately torn and turbulent, a turbulence that is embodied above all in singular individualities that break out of all conformity and identity, and engage in questioning, *keeping the very question of human being historically open toward the future* so that the present time can always be either a point of historical continuity or of historical rupture?

Such an openness would imply that the three moments of the Hegelian concept do not form an absolute closure, i.e. that, perennially exposed to the finiteness of human being-in-the-world, they invariably never quite fit together, rubbing against each other in a friction of discontent, alienation and strife. If, according to Hegel, "the singular, individual being is the same thing as what is real and actual, only that the former has gone forth from the concept, thus as universal" (das Einzelne ist dasselbe, was das Wirkliche ist, nur daß jenes aus dem Begriffe hervorgegangen, somit als Allgemeines, *EnzI* § 163 Note), we now have to contemplate — pace Hegel — the possibility that "the singular, individual" *human* being 'goes forth' from the concept, the universal, in such a way that breaks with historically realized and accepted forms of We that, as finitely human, have always already been corrupted by becoming solidified into a conventional, unfree conformism.

If the question of human being in its belonging to being (for Hegel: the Idea, but for us the open 3D-temporal clearing) always remains open, doesn't this mean that the shapes of objective, spirited mind, namely, the institutions of ethical life, themselves remain always unsettled in a double sense, questionable and revocable? The always unsettled and unsettling questions to be posed can only be posed by singular individuals who do not and cannot accept that reason has consummated itself and come to rest in offering singularity its identity as self only in the reflection of a people's given ethical mores and institutions, especially the political institutions of state. In a globalized world in incessant, intermingling movement is the ethical life of a unified people still at all appropriate for thinking through historically cast human being? *Within* Hegel's system it is possible, at least according to Hegel's intentions, for singular self-consciousness, by going through the experience of dialectical-speculative, phenomenological thinking, to ultimately attain undirempted, substantial, standing presence in the identity with a final, consolidated, social whole that is this singular self-consciousness's speculative mirror of (a people's) identity.

But does there not always remain an unmediated contradiction between singularity and universality and, in the case of the singularity and universality of human being, an unsettledness and uneasiness, especially about ways of political and social thinking, i.e. widespread preontological preconceptions, that have become all too complacently objectified in accepted institutions of political life and conformity to established mores? Doesn't precisely the *abstract* freedom of personhood allow the singular individual the recognized and guaranteed freedom of movement, albeit in a niche, to question concrete ethical practices and thus shift them even from *within* the guaranteed abstract ethical institutions of personhood, above all freedom of speech, that enable traditional understanding and practices that have been handed down to be prevented from being passed on all too unquestioningly and ungainsaid into the future? Can it not always be questioned by singular individuals whether the mores of a people and the laws of its state are truly in conformity with freedom, which could be open to ever new historical castings? The very question of freedom hence remains always open and unsettled.

For as long as there remains a kind of questioning thinking beyond or outside or beside reason consummated in a purportedly final, settled, absolute knowledge and ethical life, a kind of thinking in the lacuna outside reason's ambit *hitherto* more or less in conformity with an historically given cast of the beingness of being, the recognition accorded to individual self-consciousness as citizen by the "honour through the office that it holds, through the business it operates and through its other working activity" (Ehre durch das Amt, das er bekleidet, durch das von ihm betriebene Gewerbe und durch seine sonstige arbeitende Tätigkeit, *Enz.* § 432 Add.) itself becomes vain and empty and cannot satisfy vital, singular, thinking, questioning individuality. An uncanny hiatus, be it at first ever so slight and inconspicuous, opens up, or rather, singularity and universality were never truly closed together in a final historical conclusion.

Even in being acknowledged abstractly in its individual human rights and enjoying the freedom of movement of particularity (which are the great historical achievements of the West that have disseminated worldwide), singular individuality therefore remains always eerily unhoused, 'unbelonging' and isolated (vereinzelt, singularized, individualized) in the midst of historically realized, ethically cemented reason, for it is left ill at ease with the claim of infinite, absolute reason to have attained final historical consummation in the social institutions of substantive, consolidated, objective spirit that purportedly constitute self-consciousness's highest identity, its ostensibly unsurpassable, sublime belongingness to the world. In such an ever-broken mediation between singularity and universality concretely realized in ethical life, the open clearing of historical time sprouts single eruptions of free singularity.

If this is so then, in particular, universal human rights cannot be declared as the ideal toward which history is or ought to be moving as its final destination, its τελός. The present phenomenology of whoness as a genuine social ontology can remedy this delusion by introducing ontology of sociating through mutually estimating power interplay.

11.3 The question of who: Selfhood, my self, you-and-I (Heidegger's 1934 lectures and *Being and Time*)

If, within German Idealism, Hegel thinks the Absolute as infinite and philosophy as the possibility of absolute knowing, a century later Heidegger takes human being back to the finitude of Dasein whose truth is also finite, limited by
the horizon of the historical 3D-time-clearing (Zeitlichkeit) within which the
beingness of beings is hermeneutically cast and, furthermore, by the individual
and particular situation within this temporal clearing. Whereas Hegel proceeds
from the subject, from self-consciousness, seeking reconciliation and consummate identity in the Idea as subject-object, Heidegger is presumably the first
thinker in the Western tradition to pose explicitly the question of who, the Werfrage as an *ontological* question. He does this in *Sein und Zeit* as a prelude to
undertaking an ontological analysis of human being itself, which he calls
Dasein.[216] In contrast to metaphysical ontology, which has always asked the
question of *what* a being is *as* such, investigating τὸ ὄν ᾗ ὄν, Heidegger pursues
the question of *who* the human being is and analyzes this mode of being as the
3D-temporal structure of existence that enables selfhood. Existence is thus rede-
fined and comes to designate, as an ontological concept, the specific way human being stands out (ek-sists) in the three temporal ecstatic dimensions of
future, 'past' (Gewesenheit, beenness, yesterness) and present. This has crucial
implications for how the socio-ontological constitution of 'we ourselves' is to be
conceived as part of the problematic of the question concerning whoness. The
We can no longer be thought through a process of recognition between self-
cousciousnesses, as we shall see below. Another task is to assess how far
Heidegger gets in delving into the question of whoness.

Heidegger takes up the question, "Who is the human?" at some length in
his lectures in Summer Semester 1934,[217] immediately after his resignation from
the rectorate at Freiburg University:

> Die echte und angemessene Vorfrage ist nicht die *Was*frage, sondern die *Wer*frage. Wir
> fragen nicht '*Was* ist der Mensch?', sondern '*Wer* ist der Mensch?'. [...] Auf diese Frage
> antwortet der Angefragte 'ich' oder, wenn es mehrere sind, 'wir'. Oder es wird mit einem

---

216 "A being is either a who (existence) or a what (present-at-hand in the broadest sense)"
(Seiendes ist ein Wer (Existenz) oder ein Was (Vorhandenheit im weitesten Sinne).
M. Heidegger *Sein und Zeit* Niemeyer, Tübingen 1927 S. 45.
217 Published as Martin Heidegger *Gesamtausgabe* Band 38 under the title *Logik als die Frage
nach dem Wesen der Sprache* ed. Günter Seubold, Klostermann, Frankfurt/M. 1998.

Eigennamen geantwortet. Die Vorfrage lautet daher immer: 'Wer bist du?' — 'Wer seid ihr?'— 'Wer sind wir?'. (*GA*38:34)

The genuine and appropriate preliminary question is not the *what*-question, but the *who*-question. We do not ask, '*What* is the human?', but, '*Who* is the human?'. [...] The one asked answers this question with 'I' or, if there are several of them, 'we'. Or it is answered with a proper name. The preliminary question is therefore always: 'Who are you?' — 'Who are you all?' — 'Who are we?'.

If confronted with the question 'Who am I?', I answer in colloquial English, 'It's me' or 'I'm Michael Eldred', or, more philosophically, 'I am I myself', an unsatisfying, tautological answer of the sort I = I suitable perhaps for a god. The natural, colloquial answer, 'I'm Michael Eldred', reveals that I am a singular individual and bear a proper name to denote that singularity. The proper name goes no further than a denotation of this individual singularity *as* a difference addressing somewho *as* somewho, since there can be no identity without difference. Michael Eldred, Socrates, Louis Firestream are simply proper names for singular individuals, even though, to pass the time, one could still ask about the etymology of such proper names, or the family lineage, or what they signify in themselves. I myself bear a singular proper name that is supposed to point to nothing and no one other than me.

That different singular individuals coincidently bear the same proper name is a cause of confusion, for proper names are intended to hold singularities apart. Despite any traditions of naming within families, such a singular proper name is not merely a particularization of a universal, but aims at naming me in my unique singluarity. My selfhood is thus marked by a *proper-namedness*, a general or universal ontological-existential category that encompasses denotation of a singular self.[218] I am not a singular *thing*, a τόδε τι, but a singular *self*, a

---

218 "Das männlich ichhafte Dasein, d.h. sofern es unter der Form des Ich existiert, ist sogleich mehr als 'Bewußtseinsmitte' und mehr als ein x-beliebiges Ich; es west immer als ein bestimmter Jemand. Diese Jemandheit wird erst durch ein bestimmtes Zeichen, ein bestimmtes *Wort*, einen Namen, einen Eigennamen ins Sein gerufen, d.h. das Sein ruft das männliche Dasein als eigengenanntes Ich (und allgemeiner als Selbst) an, es schickt ihm von Anfang an sein Wersein als Eigennamenswort. Der Eigenname als Zeichen der ersten Besitznahme der Lichtung und des ersten In-Besitz-genommen-werdens durch die Lichtung unterscheidet den männlich Seienden von allen Anderen und hebt ihn als *besonderen, einzelnen* heraus." M. Eldred *Phänomenologie der Männlichkeit: kaum ständig noch* Röll, Dettelbach 1999 S. 22. English translation: "Masculine, ego-structured Dasein, i.e. insofar as Dasein exists under the form of the ego, is immediately more than a 'centre of consciousness' and more than an arbitrary, anonymous ego; it exists always as a definite somebody. The somebodiness is only called into being by a definite sign, a definite *word*, a name, a proper name, i.e. being calls masculine Dasein as a

τόδε τις, and in order to capture this singularity in the medium of language, I must have and bear my own, singular, proper name. And the same goes for you whom I encounter in the world.[219] Thus, even to say that I am a 'singular self' is to employ a general term that is already at one remove from my unmistakable, unique singularity as Michael Eldred, my proper name as a senseless sound that differentiates (or is supposed to differentiate) me *as* singular.

Heidegger at least implicitly recognizes this problem of singularity when he follows up the question, "How is the we and you all and I and you to be determined?" (wie das Wir und Ihr und Ich und Du zu bestimmen sei, *GA*38:35) and first answers with, "they are said to be persons and associations of persons" (sie seien Personen und Personenverbände, *GA*38:35). "But what is to be understood by the term 'person'?" (Aber was sollen wir unter dem Titel 'Person' verstehen? *GA*38:35) Heidegger does not pursue the question further, but we will provide at least an indication. 'Person' is related to Greek πρόσωπον, 'face', 'visage', 'mask', 'outward appearance', 'beauty', 'a person'. To be a person, I show my face, I present a mask to the world as a persona on stage; I show myself off in the world in an outward appearance. This self-presentation as a showing-off (Sichzeigen) of my face is the mirror reflection, the mirror *image* of the ἰδέα or εἶδος that metaphysics thinks as the look or face or sight which whats show of themselves in presenting themselves *as* whats in their whatness.

When Heidegger writes, "that the what-question hits back at us" (...daß die Wasfrage auf uns zurückschlägt, *GA*38:45), this can be interpreted as meaning that the metaphysical question concerning the whatness or the essence of beings hits back at us in the question of whoness, for now it is we ourselves who bear masks, show off a face, present a look *to* the world and are mirrored *by* the world to *be* ourselves. I am myself only in showing myself *as* someone, *as* somewho, just as a thing *is* a thing only in showing itself *as* something in its look of the εἶδος and in having this εἶδος *understood as such* by human being. But more than that: I can only show myself off *as* who I am in the mirror of the

---

proper-named ego (and more generally as self), it sends it from the outset its whoness as a proper-name-word. The proper name as a sign of the first taking-possession by the clearing and the first being-taken-into-possession by the clearing distinguishes the masculine being from all others and sets him apart as a *particular, singular* human being."

219 "Du unaussprechlich Einziger bist der Wer, [...] und erst, wenn nichts mehr von Dir ausgesagt wird, was Du bist und Du nur genannt bist, wirst Du als einzigartiges Wesen anerkannt." (You inexpressible unique one are the who, [...] and only when nothing more is said of you and you are only named do you become recognized as a unique being.) Karl Löwith *Das Individuum in der Rolle des Mitmenschen* (1928) reprinted in *Sämtliche Schriften* Bd. 1 ed. K. Stichweh, Metzler, Stuttgart 1981 S. 196.

others who estimate and either affirm or deny my self-standing. The others must see and understand *who* I am for me to *be* anywho. Such self-disclosure occurs in the 3D-temporal clearing.

Traditional ontology is now reflected back onto me myself and us ourselves when we take up and take on the question of who we are in our whoness. As has been shown already in Chapters 2 and 3 — and this is the all-important, pivotal point — the self-showing-off of who, i.e. the Sichzeigen of the phenomenon of whoness, must not be confused and coalesced with the self-showing of what, i.e. the Sichzeigen of the phenomenon of whatness. Whereas modern metaphysics, starting with Descartes, turned back and reflected back onto the ego cogito as ego cogito me cogitare, thereby positing as the fundamentum inconcussum and ultimate, substantial subject of self-certain truth, thus becoming self-consciousness, i.e. a co-knowing of self, as the starting-point for all certain knowing of the world, today we have to gain the insight that this self-reflection that essentially characterizes modern metaphysics *missed* its proper target because, in allowing the metaphysical what-question to "hit back" at us, Descartes and his successors, through to Hegel and beyond, all failed to translate the what-question in its hitting back into the appropriate who-question, thus missing the phenomenality of encounter and intimacy.

The question of the whoness of human being was therefore given a what answer: the *anonymous* ego, res cogitans, the cogitating thing, the conscious subject, self-consciousness, and the dimension of whoness in its ultimate singularity, of first-and-second person-being that comes about only in an ongoing, mirroring interplay among proper-named singularities, remained sealed off. All these what-answers to the question of the whoness of human being remain within the bounds of the Western metaphysics of substance, of that-which-underlies, of ὑποκείμενον, of standing presence, whereas genuine access to the phenomenon of whoness shows that human being is a site of temporal groundless, mutually estimating interplay that only strives to come to stand in a singular, proper-named showing-off of *who* it is in a mirror interplay of powers.

Both Hegel and Heidegger fail to properly enter the dimension of whoness in their thinking. The deficiency with Hegel lies in the circumstance that self-consciousness is thought in the third person, even though, to his credit, he underscores that "self-consciousness [...] is only as recognized self-consciousness" (Das Selbstbewußtsein [...] ist nur als ein Anerkanntes, *PhdG.* S. 145). The dialectic of recognition remains 'impersonal', however. Nevertheless, Hegel has the great merit that he shows that "the concept of this its [self-consciousness's] unity in its doubling [...] is a multilateral and polysemic intermeshing" (Der Begriff dieser seiner Einheit in seiner Verdopplung [...] ist eine vielseitige und vieldeutige Verschränkung, *PhdG*:145), without however draw-ing the conclusion that self-consciousness therefore cannot be a subject, a sub-stance, a self-standing presence at all.

The situation with Heidegger is more complex because, on the one hand, he clearly sees and emphasizes that all Dasein is Mitsein (e.g. "this being qua Dasein is always already with others"; dieses Seiende qua Dasein ist immer schon mit Anderen, *GA26*:245), i.e. that all human being is shared, sociating human being with one another, so that it makes no sense to talk of a self with-out others. But on the other hand, in his engagement with dialogical philosophy he asserts repeatedly that "selfhood, however, is never related to you, but ra-ther — because it enables all this — is neutral vis-à-vis I-ness and you-ness..." (Nie aber ist die Selbstheit auf Du bezogen, sondern — weil all das ermög-lichend — gegen das Ichsein und Dusein [...] neutral. [220]). The neutrality of hu-man being in a self-standing selfhood is thus given *ontological* priority over being you-and-me, i.e. the self is assertedly thinkable prior to its engagement and "intermeshing" with the other,[221] rather than you and me coming about as selves only in the mirroring interplay of our "multilateral and polysemic inter-meshing" (Hegel).[222] The very selfhood of Dasein, according to Heidegger, con-

---

220 M. Heidegger 'Vom Wesen des Grundes' (1929) in *Wegmarken* [2]1978 S. 156. Cf. also the discussion of these issues in Chapter 7 of my *Phänomenologie der Männlichkeit: kaum ständig noch* Röll, Dettelbach, 1999, and also in my 1997/2010 essay *Worldsharing and Encounter: Heidegger's Ontology and Lévinas' Ethics* at URL www.arte-fact.org/wrldshrg.html

221 Cf. however M. Heidegger *Die Grundprobleme der Phänomenologie* Gesamtausgabe Band 24 ed. Friedrich-Wilhelm von Herrmann, Klostermann, Frankfurt/M. 1975, where Heidegger explicitly thinks the constitution of self as a "shining back" (Widerschein) from the world. Thus he writes e.g., ". "The self radiating back from things [...]" (Das von den Dingen her widerscheinende Selbst [...], *GA24*:229). One could say that this is a truly speculative insight into the nature of selfhood on Heidegger's part: Dasein can only see its self in the mirror (spec-ulum) of the world. This insight blatantly contradicts what he claims about the self-contained self-standing of the self. Cf. on "shining back" also the digression Chapter 3.3.1, 'Dialectic of self and other – Wrestling with Plato, Hegel, Heidegger'.

222 Nevertheless, at least in his correspondence with his wife, Elfride (in 1918) — but, as far as I know, never in his philosophical writings 'proper' — Heidegger admits that selfhood and you-and-I are intimately intertwined. "Das 'Du' Deiner liebenden Seele traf mich. Das Erlebnis des Getroffenseins war der Anfang des Aufbruches meines eigensten Selbst. Das unmittelbare, brückenlose 'Dir' Gehören gab mich mir selbst in Besitz. [...] Da wurde das Grunderlebnis des 'Du' zur daseindurchflutenden Totalität. [...] Die Grunderfahrung lebendiger Liebe u. wahrhaf-ten Vertrauens brachte mein Sein zur Entfaltung u. Steigerung." (The 'you' of your loving soul hit me. The experience of *being* hit was the beginning of breaking out into my ownmost self. The immediate, bridgeless belonging to 'you' gave me my self into my possession. [...] The fundamental experience of 'you' became a totality flooding my existence. [...] The basic experi-

sists in its Seinkönnen, i.e. in its ability to cast itself into its future in choosing and moulding possibilities of its existence, an ability first enabled by Dasein's moodedly understanding and thus belonging (anonymously) to being.

But this possibility of self-casting, of realizing one's abilities, of bringing them to presence and into play in the world as acquired abilities that belong to one's self and therefore make up the core of one's identity, is in truth only given through the estimatively mirroring power interplays with others, especially intimately between me and you, in which each of us comes to stand, through estimation both affirmative and detractive, *as* our own, singular, proper-named selves. In ourselves, without this enabling interplay of mutual estimation, each of us is nothing, a blank, non-existent in the sense of not standing out into the shared world. This means that selfhood on its very deepest socio-ontological level is a reciprocal interplay of each of us casting each other affirmatively or disparagingly into our very own individual possibilities. This must be kept in mind when following further Heidegger's treatment of the question of who in 1934.

> Wer bist du? Wer bist du selbst? Wer bin ich selbst? Wer sind wir selbst? Die Werfrage zielt in den Bereich von solchem Seienden, das jeweils ein Selbst ist. Wir können jetzt die Antwort auf die Vorfrage so fassen: Der Mensch ist ein *Selbst*. Wenn wir jetzt nur wüßten, was ein Selbst ist. Hier fehlt uns völlig der Begriff. (*GA*38:35)

---

ence of vital love and genuine trust brought my being to unfold and rise. *'Mein liebes Seelchen!' Briefe Martin Heideggers an seine Frau Elfride 1915–1970* ed. Gertrud Heidegger, dva Munich 2005 p. 315) Here Heidegger touches upon the mutual co-casting of selfhood through the coming about of you-and-me in a love relationship. Elfride notes drily on the back of this letter, "Aus einem Brief v. Martin 1918 Modell für all seine Liebesbriefe an die vielen 'Geliebten'" (From a letter from Martin in 1918 model for all his love letters to his many 'lovers', Heidegger 2005 p. 316). Having pushed aside the Buberian problematic of you-and-I in the 1920s, Heidegger interestingly returns to it upon reading an essay by Buber in 1952. "Und es bleibt eine Frage, ob wir Sterbliche durch unser sterbliches Zu-einander Du-sagen unser ewiges Du (B. meint: Gott) ansprechen, oder ob wir nicht erst durch den Anspruch des Gottes in die Entsprechung zueinander gebracht werden. Die Frage bleibt, ob dieses 'entweder-oder' überhaupt zureicht oder ob nicht das Eine u. das Andere noch ursprünglicher vorbereitet werden muß [...]" (And it remains a question whether we mortals address our eternal You (B. means God) through our mortal saying You to one another, or whether we are only brought into correspondence with one another through being addressed by the God. The question remains whether 'either-or' is at all sufficient, or whether the One and the Other have to be prepared even more originarily [...], 12 Aug. 1952 p. 279). This deeper origin, for Heidegger's thinking at least, is presumably that of beyng or Ereignis.

> Who are you? Who are you yourself? Who am I myself? Who are we ourselves? The who-question aims at the domain of such beings that are in each singular case a self. We can now formulate the answer to the preliminary question in the following way: The human is a *self*. If we now only knew what a self is. Here we are completely lacking a concept.

Heidegger sees clearly that the question asking in the first person, '*Who* am I myself?' or '*Who* are we ourselves?', has a tendency to drift off into a question asked in the third person, '*What* is the self?'. The question concerning who seems to naturally transform itself into a question concerning what. We seem to naturally push the question away from us into the third person. Hence it could be said that the phenomenon of whoness loves to hide even more than the phenomenon of whatness, thus presenting even more a challenge to ontological thinking by hiding behind whatness. The direction in which the who-question asks is therefore constantly in danger of being brought off course into a question concerning what, the classical question of metaphysics, τί ἐστιν; or 'What is...?'. This tendency to drift off course is inherent in language itself — at least in language *hitherto*, whose grammatical structure is thoroughly metaphysical —, for the use of words itself transports each singular thing or singular individual into a universal or general realm.

This was seen clearly by Hegel at the beginning of the *Phänomenologie des Geistes* in the section on "sensuous certainty" (sinnliche Gewißheit), for sensuous certainty wants to hold onto its singular sensuous experience of this singular, sensuous thing here, e.g. this singular keyboard here at this very moment, and thus simply *points* at this singular, sensuous thing. Even by naming it as 'this thing' or 'this', a universality is said that is not intended, for 'this' can be everything that *is*, i.e. a universal. 'This' always misses its singular mark. Similarly with me, Michael Eldred. As soon as I say, 'I, Michael Eldred, am a self', I have already been deflected from my singularity and have used a general, universal term, namely, 'self'. It is therefore not easy to approach the question of who, the question of 'Who am I?' or 'Who are we?'. I would have to say tautologically, "I, Michael Eldred, am as self I myself." The reflexive pronoun, 'myself', refers back to me, not as *a* self, but as I *my*self; thus even I myself requires a mediation that breaks with brute tautology.

Nevertheless, apart from the self-reflexive proposition in which I as self bend back upon myself, each of us is a 'self', so that the singularity of my being myself and you being yourself and we being ourselves cannot escape, in some sense, subsumption under the universal of selfhood. How is our respective singularity to be preserved when you and I encounter each other? This subsumption may be not at all pernicious so long as we are aware of and think through carefully the translation of unique singularity into a universal category of selfhood through language itself and are not seduced by this translation into a comfortable, unquestioning subsumption under massive, substantivized concepts. There is even a peculiar doubling of singularity when I come to consider certain singular things that belong to myself. This singular fountain pen, for instance, is my very own. As something singular it could not even be named a 'fountain pen' (a universal denotation), but could only be pointed to; it is doubly singular, however, for it is not only a singular thing as 'this', but it is my very own and entertains a singular *relationship* (πρός τι) to my singular self, my Jemeinigkeit, expressed by saying, for instance, it has 'sentimental value' or that it is 'priceless'.

It is no coincidence, but inherent to the nature of (our Western) language, considering the work of the first grammarians in Alexandria, that the grammatical term 'substantive', meaning 'noun', is essentially related to Greek οὐσία, i.e. substance, standing presence, and that the concepts of our thinking are solid substantives in standing presence *designed from the outset to grasp the whatness of whats*. With regard to the phenomenality of whoness and the singularity of my self and our selves, a good measure of circumspection must prevail regarding the validity of substantive concepts that lay a claim on defining the phenomena of being 'who' by confining them in an ὁρισμός, a conceptual horizon of standing presence. The exertion and toil of the concept — Hegel's Anstrengung des Begriffs — must gain a new, more delicate, evanescent meaning in the realm of the question regarding who I am and who you are and who you-and-I are. Indeed, we must be prepared to use entirely unusual language to gently bring these light-shunning phenomena out into the open.

> Wir verstehen, was *Wir selbst, Du selbst, Ich selbst* heißt. Aber die Wesensbestimmung verlangt immer den Begriff. (*GA*38:35)

> We understand what *we ourselves, you yourself, I myself* means. But the determination of essence always demands a concept.

Are we looking for an "essence" of who? When posing the question of who, is it still possible, in the train of the philosophical tradition, to demand the concept? Does the concept always transform the who into a what? And singularity into universality? The two questions must be distinguished from one another, for it may be possible, after all, to situate singularity within a universal concept, namely selfhood, without thereby sliding unthinkingly and unawares from who (first and second person in mutually estimating interplay) into what (third person). It should be noted that Heidegger asks — and we, too, ask — the question regarding who not in the third person, 'Who is he?', 'Who is she?', 'Who are they?' because the third person already has the proclivity to drift into a what. People in the third person can be thought just like any*thing* else (which is why today's social science also talks invariably in the third person, because such talk is 'scientific', 'objective'). People are already easily assimilable to being thought of and treated as things, as 'facts'. The phenomenal immediacy of selfhood is preserved only by asking in the first or second person. As yet we do not quite fathom why this is so.

In posing the question of selfhood in 1934 and also earlier on, especially in *Sein und Zeit*, Heidegger focuses on gaining one's self by casting oneself into one's ownmost possibility of existing — without any mention of you. This is the *authenticity* of the self. At first and for the most part, he says, we are not our selves, but lost in the inauthenticity of understanding our possibilities of existing only from the tasks of taking care of things in which we are immersed and absorbed in everyday life and from the opinions of 'people' (das Man). Thus we are ourselves, i.e. understand our selves, only from everyday busyness, and this busyness is conceived as an involvement first and foremost with *things* that have to be taken care of in an average, conventional way under the watchful eye of people's opinions.

Even though Heidegger has provided an ontological-existential place for others in the world under the headings of Mitsein and Mitdasein, and points out that taking care of things always involves also having to do with others, the phenomenality of what this Mitsein entails with regard to understanding one's self is spelt out only as adopting the average, conventional opinion of "man selbst" (what 'people' 'think') in understanding oneself. It is to be noted and underscored here, that the entire discussion of the self, selfhood and das Man in *Sein und Zeit* takes place in the *third* person within a landscape of heavily substantified concepts.[223] This is not without consequences for the very thinking of Mitsein. In the 1934 lectures, the situation is similar, although now Heidegger situates his inquiry under the question, "Who are we ourselves?", i.e. genuinely in the first person (plural), noting that

> ...wir zunächst und zumeist nicht bei uns selbst sind, uns in Selbstverlorenheit und Selbstvergessenheit herumtreiben. (*GA*38:49)

> ...at first and for the most part, we are not with our selves but rather gallivant about in self-lostness and self-oblivion.

---

223 Cf. my attempt to break out of all-too-solid substantivity in considering how you-and-I come about fleetingly in a gap "scarcely in-between" in Chapter 6 of my *Phänomenologie der Männlichkeit* 1999.

The meaning of this lostness of and oblivion to the self is seen to lie in not grasping a genuine possibility of one's own existing through an authentic decision regarding how to cast one's very own, singular existence and resolutely pursue this possibility once adopted:

Wir sind *eigentlich* wir nur in der Entscheidung, und zwar, jeder vereinzelt. (*GA*38:58)

We are *authentically, properly* we only in the decision, and indeed, each of us individually.

A We comes about authentically solely in a decision? If only it were so easy! Where is the Auseinandersetzung, the having-it-out with one another, the conflict and debate through which we come to a common, shared decision in which the *power interplay of mutually estimating who each of us is mediates*? Where is the controversial interchange of views and arguments contro-verting, i.e. turning against, each other through which we win each other over, persuade each other and gain each other's trust and become confident in each other with regard to a proposed course of action, and so come about (zeitigen) in the first place as a unified, resolved We that mediates, as much as humanly possible, the gulf between us as singular individuals? Or does Heidegger, along authoritarian lines, envisage only that each of us individually decides to follow a leader or to commit oneself without altercation to a cause or a (predefined, uncontroversial) shared futural historical possibility of existing? How could such a unisonous commitment to a leader come about if not by miracle? Or seduction by clever demagoguery?

Furthermore, this account of self-lostness disregards an important, indeed crucial, aspect of the phenomenality of how we come adrift from our possible, very own self that is hidden in the word "Eigenname", "proper name", that Heidegger introduces but does not explore and develop further. We have already seen above that being who, i.e. being I myself, necessarily involves bearing a proper name that denotes me in my singularity. My proper name is my very own, strictly senseless, name, something almost intimate, belonging only to me myself.

But this name exists nevertheless in language and can thus also be appropriated by everyone else. In the social intercourse I have with others, my proper name is employed by you and them in appellating me, i.e. in calling, invoking me. And I, too, call or appellate you in addressing you with your proper name. We call each other by our very own proper names, and that is the proper domain for our proper names: calling, or appellating each other's selves in our intercourse with each other, an intercourse that sociates us, perhaps intimately. This proper domain for our proper names, however, is not walled off, and so my proper name and your proper name can be appropriated by others as well in referring to us in the *third person*. Our proper names thus come into circulation among the others, 'them', as mere signs marking individuals used to 'identify' them among others. This possibility of (our Western) language is inherent in the universal nature of language itself, in which designating substantives play a primary, leading role. In employing my proper name not to address, to call me, but rather to designate me, I have myself become a sign that can be circulated in the language spoken by others. *Who I am* is then decided upon in part by *what* is said about me by others, which reflects or shines back on my self. They, too, play a part in moulding and casting who I am, and who I can be, in my existential possibilities in the world.

As has been shown in Chapter 2, what is said about me by others is my *reputation*, my Ruf or 'calling' or 'vocation'. In and through my reputation in the eyes of others, I myself have been appropriated by language in the language of others, who may be completely anonymous, and I thus succumb to the eery power of the third person which also contributes to delineating who I am and can be in the exercise of my potential, above all, my abilities. For my reputation is ineluctably also an estimation of my abilities. The calling into my reputation provides me with a stand in the world of others, by virtue of which I can also enjoy a certain supportive Ansehen (standing, repute, face, sight) — or also lose face. How I stand, my standing, depends on how the showing-off of my face is reflected in the estimation of others, even and especially when this estimation does *not* take place in a face-to-face encounter. Through reputation I am *alienated* from my own self through others in the third person defining who I am.

This delineation of who I am in my reputation is a co-determinant of my self in the sense that it co-determines *as* who I can cast my self in the social world. In this sense and to this extent, with language, especially in the mouths of others, I have always already lost my self to the others (although at the same time it is also only *within* language that I can even cast, define, gain and be my own self). But it is not just in reputation and in the use of my proper name by others that I lose my self; it is in the very casting of possibilities of existing by a third person language that I come to cast my self by mirroring these third-person possibilities (each of which is a *universal*) into my self. I adopt or reject them and cast my self accordingly. I come under the sway of anonymous, circulating public opinion not only with regard to my own reputation that is circulated in this medium but also with regard to the possibilities of existing that I can see against the horizon for my self in how existential possibilities are cast as desirable or undesirable by public opinion or certain others. And whether I can realize a possibility of existing I have adopted as my own through exercising my potential, my abilities, depends also crucially on whether *others* estimate and mirror those abilities affirmatively, thus either opening up or closing off possible self-castings for developing my abilities and putting them to work.

To be my self, I must first of all cast my self into my ownmost possibility of existing, but how am I to decide which of these possibilities is my very own? How am I to decide whether I have been alienated from my self from the start by being swayed by the spectrum of existential possibilities that 'society' and the 'spirit and mood of the times' offers me? How am I even to attain my self-chosen self-casting if not through power interplays with others? Since it is impossible for me to cast myself in a void that is not already precast by public opinion and the thinking of the times in the language of the third person, and since I am always dependent on my social standing as defined by my reputation, how it is possible that I could *not* be selbstverloren, lost to myself?

Since I am always already exposed to the eery medium and power of third person language circulating about who I am, my abilities, etc., being my self must always be a *becoming* my very own self through winning my self *back* from its having been always already articulated, defined, precast by others, by anonymous common sense, by what others 'think' about me, how 'they' assess my potential, by what the conceptions of the times already pre-conceive, etc. This is the uncanny power of das Man, but now put explicitly and emphatically into relation to the phenomena of proper-namedness and reputation. Becoming my self is thus, in a certain sense, a rite of passage from the medium of the third person, in which I have always already been predefined and precast in my existential possibilities by the others, through a process of extracting myself from conventional, average normality, to the first person in which I myself choose and cast my singular self as my very own possibility of existing in the world, even though this very own possibility as a standing-out in the world is ineluctably and always an exposure of my singularity to universality, a more or less broken mediation of my singular individuality with the world.

In this passage from the third person of predefined and pregiven possibilities of existing (from the temporal ec-stasis of beenness, yesterness, Gewesenheit) to my very own, 'first person', in which a possibility of existing, insofar as this is humanly possible, becomes my very own, the second person plays an essential role, since the delineation of my possibilities of existing and thus becoming my self is mediated by an estimating mirroring in *you*, who, too, is always singular, and who confirms, supports and *enables* me in my choice of my very own possibility of existing as genuine, i.e. as genuinely belonging to my self. (Confirmation and support here must be understood in the broadest sense, encompassing also the deficient and detractive modes of refusing affirmation, disapproval, indifference, disparagement, putting-down, undermining, depreciation.) My self is therefore never a pure creation ex nihilo out of some purely autistic 'interiority' but mediated especially by a singular other, namely, you, who, in the intimacy of you-and-me, can say to me who I *could* be in and through the power interplays of the world.

In this sense, the alienness of an other, a singular other — you — as mirror, is a condition of possibility of my very self, but only in this alienness having become assimilated to me in a belonging together in the trusting intimacy of you-and-me, no matter how momentary it may be. Because you-and-me is fleeting, evanescent, anyone can be you for the momentary cast of a glance, or perhaps a little longer. (In German: Du sein kann jeder für einen entwerfenden Augenblick.) Since my singular interplay with you, a singular other, is essentially also an estimating mirroring of who I am, it is reciprocal; within our relationship of you-and-me I, too, play a role in casting who you can be; I, too, am your enabler, your co-caster. We mirror each other in shining back our self-castings of who I am and who you are. Thus I myself am mediated through you yourself, and you yourself are mediated through me myself in estimating interplay.

Pace Heidegger's conception in *Sein und Zeit*, Je*mein*igkeit is not a 'standalone' concept but coupled and interwoven with the Je*dein*igkeit (sic!) of you in your interplay with me, through which I can filter out the precast possibilities of existing preformulated in public opinion and everyday understanding's prefabricated roles that do not authentically belong to me, i.e. that do not form part of my very own, unique *identity* as self and are thus not part of the *manifold of faces* I present to the world in showing off who I am. Because Heidegger (seduced by the overly substantivized German language) too quickly substantivizes and thus substantifies his concepts and because he only mentions in passing (*GA*38:34), but does not pursue, the phenomenon of proper-namedness, his account of Mansein and Selbstverlorenheit remains deficient as a 'third person' conceptual hermeneutic that does not adapt itself adequately to the ontological-existential folds of first-and-second person as I have attempted to explicate concisely above. Heidegger also overlooks that the very ontological constitution of selfhood passes, in particular, through the mutually estimating, intimate interplay between you-and-me, and therefore asserts inappropriately, as we have noted above, "Selfhood, however, is never related to you, but rather — because it enables all this — neutral with regard to I-being and you-being".

A further deficiency in Heidegger's thinking on self and selfhood concerns his assertion that "The self is neither assigned primarily to the I, nor to the you, you all or we." (Das Selbst ist weder vorwiegend dem Ich zugeordnet noch dem Du, Ihr, Wir. *GA*38:50) This is stated in the first place with regard to the primacy of the ego-subject in modern metaphysics which, according to Heidegger, has to be overcome. But a phenomenological case can be made nevertheless for giving a certain priority to the I — albeit an I who is always already in estimative power interplay with others — when considering the self, for human existence is first and foremost individuated. My existence is my very own. I cannot escape my self, but have to cast it myself in the interplay. Ich bin jemeinig, i.e. I am individually my own self, even when I am lost as self to the anonymous others and conventional existential possibilities, and thus exist in a deficient, conformist mode of Jemeinigkeit.

All understanding of being, all attunement to being must pass through me individually, even when and even though I necessarily always already share this understanding and attunement with others because we are inescapably together-in-the-world. My individuality is also rooted in my very own body that can be nobody else's body, and my body is gendered.[224] From my body (which in this context must be distinguished from a physical corpus) embedded in its momentary surrounding, temporally quivering situation with which it resonates, my moods emerge as if from an abyss. There is an interplay, too, between my individual body and my individualized psyche into which the psyche as openness for the 3D-temporal clearing per se is scattered. My existence is necessarily bodily, and my mooded body, too, is necessarily, in the first place, individual. I, myself, feel my own joy and pain, and joy and pain have also a somatic texture, even when I share my joy or pain with others in shared attunement with a situation in the world quivering with the resonance of the time-clearing. This primacy of my individual and individualized I when considering the self is also brought to expression in the above quote:

Wir sind *eigentlich* wir nur in der Entscheidung, und zwar, jeder vereinzelt. (*GA*38:58)

We are *authentically*, *properly* we only in the decision, and indeed, each of us individually.

---

224 "Dasein per se shelters within itself the inner possibility for factual scattering into bodiliness and thus into genderedness. [...] Dasein as factual is inter alia always splintered into a body and, along with this, inter alia always split into two in a definite genderedness." (Das Dasein überhaupt birgt die innere Möglichkeit für die faktische Zerstreuung in die Leiblichkeit und damit in die Geschlechtlichkeit. [...] Das Dasein ist als faktisches je unter anderem in einen Leib zersplittert und ineins damit unter anderem je in eine bestimmte Geschlechtlichkeit zwiespältig. M. Heidegger *GA*26:173) Here Heidegger hints at the possibility of an ontology of gender as modes of being, but conceived as modes of bodiliness, which I have critically pursued in my *Phänomenlogie der Männlichkeit* 1999.

Why should "and indeed, each of us individually" be added if it were not for the peculiar priority and primacy of I myself as a singular conjunction in the 3D-temporal clearing, both in itself and in the constitution of we ourselves? We must consider more closely how 'we ourselves' are constituted. In doing so, we will be able to see even more clearly why 'I myself' has a certain ontological priority. Despite this priority of 'I myself', but not as something 'substantially' given, the phenomenon of the mutually estimating power interplay with an other and others in the ontological constitution of selfhood must not be neglected.

11.4 How do we ourselves come about? – Belonging together in a situation

> Die Persönlichkeit ist verändert, man kann fast sagen, unter der Haut gegen eine weniger eigentümliche umgetauscht: an die Stelle des Ich ist der erste, deutlich als unbehaglich und eine Verminderung empfundene, aber doch unwiderstehliche Ansatz eines Wir getreten.
>
> Robert Musil
> *Der Mann ohne Eigenschaften* II Tl. 3 Kap. 8

> The personality has changed; one can almost say, subcutaneously swapped for a less singular personality: in place of I, the first germ of a We has stepped, clearly felt as uncomfortable and as a diminishment, but nevertheless irresistible.

How is a We constituted? How do we ourselves come about? Heidegger says in the specific situation of his holding lectures before his students as the auditors of these lectures:

> Wir, die wir in einem bestimmten Auftrage stehen, uns in einer besonderen Lage befinden. [...] Die Zusammengehörigkeit zur Vorlesung ist das Wesentliche, sie gründet sich auf das Mithören, auf die Einbezogenheit des einzelnen in die Hörerschaft. Dieses Ihr der Hörer gliedert sich in die Du, die als solche, aus solchem Verhältnis, angesprochen werden. (*GA*38:41)

> We, we who stand in a certain task/mission, who find ourselves in a particular situation. [...] The belonging-together in the lecture course is what is essential; it is grounded in the listening-in, the listening-along-with, in the inclusion of the individual into the audience. This 'you all' of the auditors is articulated into the you's who as such, out of such a relation, are addressed.

We are constituted *as* we in a "particular situation", in "belonging-together" in a particular situation in which we "stand" in a "certain task/mission". "What is essential" for our constitution as we ourselves is this "belonging-together", into which each individual one of us is integrated as part of a whole we. We gain our *identity* as we our*selves* in this situated belonging-together. The audience, although articulated grammatically as a substantive, a noun, *is* only in the belonging-together in the particular situation. The audience *is* only in the "relation" (Verhältnis, πρός τι) of lecturer and students through the giving of the lecture and the listening by the auditor-students. It has no substance, no enduring, standing presence of its own. The 'you all' of the students vis-à-vis me as the lecturer *is* only in the belonging-together of you all, the individual students, in the situation. The we is thus situational presencing, not substantive οὐσία.

We arise only ephemerally in the conjunction of a situation that brings us together into an identity *as* we ourselves. The individuals, each of us, situated together in a "certain task" focused on a definite issue, are thus the ontic *and* ontological presupposition for constituting we ourselves. This shows that each of us as individual self has a certain ontological primacy in constituting 'we ourselves' as a certain kind of situational relationship. Whereas we ourselves *are*, i.e. presence, only in a situation in which we have taken on a certain task, I *am* myself in countless different situations with and without others. There is a certain continuity and permanence of I myself that endures through all the different situations in which I find myself — and find my self — as belonging together in one situational we or another. My finding myself in a certain situation is my Befindlichkeit, my particular situational *mood*. Sitting in the lecture theatre, I can be still in the mood of a situation now absent (a quarrel, perhaps) which, however, continues to presence as this absent, mooded situation, thus distracting me from my present situation. We ourselves, constituted as belonging together in the lectures' audience, are borne by a mood of belonging together as we ourselves in our particular present shared situation and task. Our situation as we is passing, transient, whereas each of us is I myself in various situations, either on our own or in sharing particular we-constituting situations such as a football game in a stadium or on television, or a debate in an auditorium or in the letters to the editor of a newspaper. :

It should be noticed that with Heidegger ("Dieses Ihr", "die Du") there is a tendency to shift into the third person and substantivize in formulating philosophical concepts, in staking out, marking out and defining the phenomenon in the horizon, the ὁρισμός, of its concept. This tendency would seem to be inherent in the attempts hitherto to move back philosophically into the ontological grounds of the phenomena. Today we must be aware of this tendency of language and thinking, and counter it in our own thoughtful language in order to capture evocatively the fleeting presencing and absencing of the first-and-second person.

In the pages cited above from Heidegger's lectures in Summer Semester 1934, he also goes through some of the possible deficiencies in the constitution of we ourselves that may consist of, say, those students who do not genuinely listen to the lectures and do not actively participate in learning (which in itself is already an indication of the fragmentedness of the we; those unfocused students are temporally absent in other situations that have been or might be), or the "certain number of countable exercise books" (bestimmte Anzahl zählbarer Hefte, *GA*38:42) that are administered by the university administration through which the we of the student audience is degraded into "certain numbers under the rubric of the professor's lecture course" (bestimmte Nummern in der Rubrik der Vorlesung des Professors, *GA*38:43). Through this ontological degradation, the we of the lecture course becomes, vis-à-vis the university administration, not just a collective you of more or less anonymous 'you students', but a *third person*, even reified, merely quantitative collection of student enrolment numbers. The transformation into a third person collectivity is an ontological tendency of we ourselves through which we slip into substantial being as a substantivized entity, say, as 'student enrolment numbers'. As student enrolment numbers, others now have a substantive linguistic 'handle' on us and we become manipulable in the third person under a label, and, in a further abstraction, even calculable as quantified entities devoid of quality, perhaps for the purposes of the university administration's planning, or in social research.

To take another example of a privative form of 'we ourselves': Even the crowd that gathers after a car accident (bei einem Autounfall ansammelt, *GA*38:42) forms, according to Heidegger, a kind of diffuse, transient we-self who presences with the situation of the accident. Nevertheless, all the myriad possible deficient and privative forms of we ourselves are only possible within the all-encompassing ontological dimension of the first person plural, where the plurality here, as Heidegger points out, is not a mere number greater than one, but some kind of belonging-together in a definite situation, including even a diffuse or banal one.

The situation does not have to be a present one, presently presencing, but can just as well be one in which we have been, such as the heady times of an earlier decade that can still be recalled out of its absence to presencing in its very absence, along with the specific moodful 'flavour' of that time as evoked, for instance, by the music of that time. Or 'we ourselves' can be constituted in considering a future challenge, say, of coming to terms with oncoming technological change presencing from a still absent future. We ourselves can thus be constituted throughout the 3D-temporal clearing, even in a now absent 'past' or a still absent future in which each of us has not or will not individually participate, such as the commemoration of long 'past', but still presencing as now absent, momentous historical events.

11.5 Constitution of an historical people – Heidegger's authoritarian, anti-liberal casting of "we the people" – The historical decision to open up to the future – "We are the coming about of time itself"

... so erfuhr man auch, daß der Grad der wahren Originalität nicht im eitlen Besonderssein beschlossen liege, sondern durch das Sichöffnen entstehe, in steigende Grade des Teilnehmens und der Hingabe hinein, vielleicht bis zu dem höchsten Grad einer Gemeinschaft der ganz von der Welt aufgenommenen, vollendet Ichlosen, den man auf diese Weise zu erreichen vermöchte! ... Ulrich war ärgerlich über dieses abergläubische Geschwätz.

Robert Musil *Der Mann ohne Eigenschaften* I
Tl. 2 Kap. 113

... thus one also found out that the degree of true originality does not reside in vainly being special, but arises through opening oneself up, in increasing degrees of participation and surrender, perhaps to the highest degree which one could attain in this way, of a community of the completely egoless, wholly absorbed by the world! ... Ulrich was annoyed by this superstitious drivel.

If we ourselves only come about through a situation in which we belong together and thus constitute an identity of difference, when it comes to the constitution of an historical people as a kind of 'we ourselves' in our own selfhood, the situation in which this founding of identity takes place must be an historical situation, an historical moment that carries weight, a 'casting-weight'. For this question we will continue to engage with Heidegger's lectures of Summer Semester 1934 (*GA*38), taking note of the special historical moment in which Heidegger poses the question, "Who are we ourselves?" (Wer sind wir selbst? *GA*38:109) and answers "We are the people." (Wir sind das Volk. *GA*38:109). This answer is to be a self-assertion of the German people in its authentic selfhood as an historical people for, according to Heidegger, a people, just like an individual human being or a group of human beings, can be estranged from its self and thus be unhistorical. Therefore he asks, "Are we historical?" (Sind wir geschichtlich? *GA*38:109), i.e. are we ourselves in the time-clearing of history? Heidegger makes the transition from 'we ourselves' arising out of a situation via institutions to the state and the people in a few bold brushstrokes:

> [...] wir sind eingelassen in das Erziehungsgeschehen einer Schule, die die Hochschule der Wissenserziehung sein soll. Wir unterstellen uns den Forderungen dieser Erziehung, machen uns bereit für Berufe... Wir legen unseren Willen voraus in diese Berufe, die als solche dienen, sei es der Erziehung, sei es der Erstarkung und Ertüchtigung, sei es der inneren Ordnung des Volkes usw. Indem wir eingefügt sind in diese Forderungen der Hochschule, wollen wir den Willen eines Staates, der selbst nichts anderes sein will als der Herrschaftswille und die Herrschaftsform eines Volkes über sich selbst. Wir als Dasein fügen uns in eigener Weise hinein in die Zugehörigkeit zum Volk, wir stehen im Sein des Volkes, wir sind das Volk selbst. (*GA*38:57)

> [...] we are inserted in the educational happenings of a school that is supposed to be a Higher School (university) of education to knowledge. We submit ourselves to the demands of this education, prepare ourselves for vocations... We put our will into these vocations from the outset which as such serve the education, the strengthening and physical fitness, the inner order, etc. of the people. By being inserted into these demands of the university/Higher School, we will the will of a state which itself does not will to be anything other than the will to rule/dominate and the form of rule/domination of a people over itself. We as Dasein insert ourselves in our own way into belonging to the people; we stand in the being of the people; we ourselves are the people.

This constitution of we ourselves as the state and people demands not just a belonging-together, i.e. an identity, but a unified identity into which "we" "insert" "ourselves", with a totalitarian form of rule or domination of "a people over itself" that is achieved via willing where now, for the first time, Heidegger explicitly introduces the *will* to his chosen example. (Heidegger does not consider the possibility of the state's rule over another people or the Schmittian distinction between the people and its enemy that elicits unity.) The transient situation in which we ourselves were first thought to come about, perhaps even *against our will*, by, for instance, 'finding ourselves' in the crowd of spectators at a car accident, is now reified, stabilized in institutions and a state of affairs that make up the complex totality of a nation state as a form of "domination" to which we will our belonging, i.e. to which we *will-ingly subjugate ourselves*. The will is the medium through which this constitution of national identity is said by Heidegger to take place. This will as unified will will brook no difference; on the contrary, it must be suppressed and repressed.

We as the people will the state in its stable, substantial institutions that rule over us as a people, and we will that we belong to this form of rule and domination of ourselves by "inserting" ourselves into it and "submitting" ourselves to it. Heidegger does not pose the question concerning state rule/domination/power (Herrschaft) as a mode of being (the question of δύναμις or *power* as a *social, sociating* phenomenon; cf. Chapter 10.1), but now selfhood as we ourselves consists in our *submitting* ourselves to the state's own hierarchically organized and institutionalized will to power and in serving the will of the whole. The mutually estimating power interplay among many selves is obliterated. Our belonging-together is now a *permanent, unified* submission to a superior, ruling, dominating will as the "state of affairs of a people" (Schmitt), and no longer a transient belonging-together that arises out of a passing situation, an ephemeral moment in which we find ourselves together, say, in a rock concert or a football game. Nor is it any longer a situation to which we can decide individually, through an act of will, to either belong to or to leave, as in the case of the student auditors of a lecture. We ourselves as the people under permanent, stable state rule have now passed over into the realm of "objective spirit" (Hegel), for which the individual *decision* and *will* to belong or not to belong no longer has any meaning; the people is a compulsory community. What the state wills is also not the ever-changing outcomes of mutually estimating power interplays among political players in compromises of various sorts.

Heidegger bases the constitution of 'we ourselves' as a people in the state on the observation that "human happenings [...] are *deliberately willed* and therefore *knowing*" (Das menschliche Geschehen [...] ist *willentlich* und deshalb *wissend*, GA38:86). Knowing and willing are said to be a presupposition for the constitution of ourselves as an historical people. Such knowing and willing are fully redolent of metaphysical ontology of pro-ductive, effective movement. The passage cited above is only the beginning of Heidegger's questioning of how this knowing willing of ourselves as a people takes place in the time-clearing of history. This historical time-clearing will be investigated in more detail by Heidegger (see below), but from the outset he is at pains to distance this willing that wills ourselves as a people through the state from any form of subjecticity: "This being is never a subject and not even a collection of several subjects who only found a community on the basis of agreements; rather, only this originary unifying entity bearing exposure, ecstatic transport, tradition and a mission can be what we call 'a people'." (Dieses Seiende ist nie Subjekt, auch nicht eine Ansammlung mehrerer Subjekte, die auf Grund von Abmachungen erst eine Gemeinschaft gründen, sondern das ursprünglich einige, Ausgesetztheit, Entrückung, Überlieferung und Auftrag tragende Seiende kann nur sein, was wir 'ein Volk' nennen. GA38:157) The disparaging distancing from any "contract theory" (Vertragstheorie, GA38:143) as a "concept of state" (Staatsbegriff, GA38:143) formed by a compact of many individual subjects is thereby signalled. The state cannot be a unification coming about as originating from many individuals' agreeing, but rather, the unification of Volk comes about by its being overcome by an historical destiny.

Subjects for Heidegger can only be worldless, Cartesian egos; he never engages with the thought that these subjects could be individuals always-already embedded in a world constituted by mutually estimating sociating interplay, including especially economic interplay, nor that the privacy of the private individual is *essentially* enabled by sociation being mediated by reified value, i.e. money, markets and capital, as we have investigated in earlier chapters. Heidegger (mis)identifies without further ado the ego-self of "liberalism, the age of the ego" (Zeit des Liberalismus, der Ich-Zeit, *GA*38:51) with the asocial, non-sociating, ego-subject of Cartesianism as the foundation of the mathematico-scientific casting of the modern world, and thus evades the task of engaging philosophically with the specifically *political* thinking of liberalism, which would require having to consider the sociating of humans through exchanges and power-playful interchanges of all kinds, which must be regarded as predominating modes of the *movement* of Mitsein-in-der-Welt.

Moreover, the ongoing mutually estimating interplay of exchange and interchange in civil society (which already is ontologically prior to any sort of mere 'compact' or 'agreement') could also be regarded as a mode in which 'we ourselves' are constituted in our identity as citizens engaging in the fair play of civil society, an identity that differs fundamentally from the constitution of 'we ourselves' through a power relation of subjugation to state domination, for it does not demand the suppression of difference. The ethos of fair play permeates a civil society based on free and fair interplay, whereas a people constituted by belonging to a state demands submission to the state's will, no matter how construed. Such a problematic is totally absent from Heidegger's thinking, but not so from Hegel's and Marx's. These latter two German thinkers *do* engage seriously with liberal political thinking.

Far from being inclined to think through a 'we ourselves' formed in a liberal society based on fair power interplay among individuals, Heidegger proceeds from the Tönnian distinction between community and society, Gemeinschaft und Gesellschaft, where the former is conceived of as rooted, say, in "the everyday life of communal Dasein of the sequence of its temporal happenings of birth, marriage, death and changes of season" (das Tägliche des gemeinschaftlichen Daseins in der Wechselfolge seiner zeitlichen Geschehnisse von Geburt, Heirat, Tod und Jahreszeitenwechsel, *GA*38:66), whereas the latter is composed of modern abstract individuals who presumably do not, or hardly belong together, including "the many in the back-yard houses of the big city for whom there is not even an inclement weather" (die vielen in den Hinterhäusern der

Großstadt, für die es nicht einmal eine Witterung gibt, *GA*38:66[225]). This implies that, in Heidegger's view, there is a more originary belonging-together as a people than in the state, namely, in the *established, customary way of life of a community*, as opposed to the ostensibly purely abstract sociation of "individuals conscious of themselves" (der Mensch als ein seiner selbst bewußter einzelner, *GA*38:143) in society who, apparently, do not belong together as 'we ourselves' and therefore have no identity.

In his 1934 lectures, Heidegger does not think through this 'we ourselves' in community as a possibility of selfhood that consists in a traditional, static, rooted way of life with its own ethos, usages and habits, but rather proceeds straight from a situational constitution of 'we ourselves' to the constitution of a people institutionally in the state that is willed by us in serving it and by subjugating ourselves to its rule and its will. Nor does he entertain that a community, too, must have ongoing contractual exchanges of some kind, and thus a kind of interplay, even — God forbid — business intercourse. Nor does he consider that a society composed of individuals engaged in mutually estimating interplay with one another on the basis of contractual interchanges, among other kinds of interchange, could have its *own traditions and ethos* (of liberal fair play) with their own dignity which constitute a customary way of life that has its own permanency and continuity despite the constant changes in the specific individuals, along with countless other changes composing that way of life at any one time in any one situation or locality.

We have to ask — contra Heidegger; cf. Chapter 11.7 below — why a customary *social* (as distinct from a communal) way of life cannot constitute our selves as 'we' or even a people and ground a belonging-together and a people's identity that in no way depends on the members of that 'we' remaining constant, as in the case of settled rural village life rooted in the ever-recurring cycles of nature that Heidegger seems to take as implicit paradigm. On the contrary, the way of life could be in constant flux with regard to its specific members, and may also itself be in flux through modifications and adaptations over time whilst retain-

---

225 This echoes an ostinato running throughout Heidegger's statements on 'modernity'. Twenty-five years earlier, Heidegger was already writing the same kind of lamentation on the decadence of the 'big city', "Allerseelenglocken läuten – läuten in den Trauermorgen. Die Menschen der Großstadt hören sie nicht. Sie hassen das Läuten, sie wollen die Lust, sie suchen die Sonne und wandeln in Nacht, in schwarzer, quälender Nacht." (Allerseelenstimmungen Heuberger Volksblatt, Jhrg. 11, Nr. 133, 5. November 1909) English: "All Souls' bells are ringing — ringing into the mourning morning. The people of the big city do not hear them. They hate the ringing; they want pleasure; they seek the sun and wander in night, in black, tormenting night."

ing its customary modes of social intercourse and a sense of belonging-together in civil society, despite the fact that this civil society *does not have to constitute itself as a unified will*, but rather consists in the spontaneous, unplanned power interplay of a multitude of individual wills, each pursuing its aims and interests in interchange with others. If these considerations are plausible, then indeed there can be a rootedness of 'we ourselves' as a people consisting in our embeddedness within the customary, traditional, *universal forms* and *ethos* of (fair, and therefore just) interplay of civil society, albeit that these socio-ontological modes of sociating enable an historically unprecedented dynamism of social living and can also assume countless, unforeseen, concrete, historical guises.

Let us return to time-clearing of history to consider more deeply how, according to Heidegger, it is involved in constituting a people. It must be kept in mind that Heidegger is speaking at a particular historical moment, 1934, with the National Socialists in power, giving lectures to his students whom he confronts with the questions, "Are you yourselves genuinely, authentically a part of the people?", "Are we an historical people?" This is a rhetorical situation structured according to first and second person, and the questions are not merely rhetorical but are intended to go to the heart of what it means to be I myself, we ourselves, you yourselves. Despite the historical moment of 1934 being an historical situation into which the German people, i.e. *we* have been cast without any act of will, just like the we formed by a crowd *as* crowd spontaneously and will-lessly gathering at the scene of a car accident, he claims that this question regarding being ourselves as part of history can only be settled through will, through a decision.

> Irgendeine Entschiedenheit macht unser Selbst jetzt aus. Das kleine und enge Wir des Augenblicks der Vorlesung hat uns mit einem Schlag in das Volk versetzt... (*GA*38:58)

> Some decisiveness or other now constitutes our self. The small and narrow we of the moment of the lectures has transposed us in one fell swoop into the people...

This decision and decisiveness concerns "whether we want to co-operate in acting or whether we want to act against" (ob wir mithandeln wollen oder zuwider, *GA*38:72). Act for or against in which direction? Is it a simple either/or decision that makes the incision between us, who willingly submit, and them, the unwilling ones who must be forced into submission against their will? The decision and decisiveness do not merely concern affirming the status quo, but, according to Heidegger, are only genuine, authentic decision and decisiveness if the Entschiedenheit is Entschlossenheit. Entschlossenheit is standardly rendered as 'resoluteness', but this is entirely misleading, for Heidegger thinks

Entschlossenheit as a "Sichöffnen" (GA38:75), as an "opening up of oneself". Entschlossenheit must therefore be thought as a resolute, decisive opening up of myself, of ourselves to possibilities which, of course, can only arrive from the future:

> Es gilt, in eine *Entschlossenheit zu kommen* oder die Möglichkeit dafür vorzubereiten. [...] In der Entschlossenheit ist der Mensch vielmehr in das *künftige Geschehen eingerückt*. Die Entschlossenheit ist selbst ein Geschehnis, das, jenem Geschehen *vorgreifend*, das Geschehen ständig mit bestimmt. (GA38:76, 77)

> What counts is *to come into a resolute openness* or to prepare the possibility for it. [...] In resolute openness, rather, people have *moved out into future happenings*. Resolute openness is itself a happening that, *anticipating* [lit. pre-grasping, ME] those happenings, continually co-determines those happenings.

Hence, after all, it is not possible to merely decide to be a people. What counts, according to Heidegger, is not simply a decision and a decisiveness, but an openness to possibilities that can only arrive from the future. It is not even possible to decide, through an act of will, to be resolutely open, for we have to *come* into such an openness and may even only be able to *prepare* the possibility of so coming into an openness for future happenings that can be fore-seen (perhaps?) in their historically imminent arrival. The possibility of moving into resolute openness does not lie within the power of our will, but remains at one remove from us. To put it in German: Die Möglichkeit des *Einrückens* in die Entschlossenheit ist der Macht unseres Willens *entrückt*. Das *Einrücken* ist dem *Entrücken* ausgeliefert. Even once we have come into a resolute openness (not through our own mere act of will), we only anticipate or 'pre-grasp' future happenings and are able to co-shape and co-cast them. The decisiveness that Heidegger appeals to is thus much mediated and concerns only a readiness to be open to future possibilities rather than insisting on and setting ourselves up comfortably in the status quo of what has been and continues to be thoughtlessly reproduced. And do not future possibilities demand an interplay of powers to adequately assess them as possibilites and not as certainties? With the above-quoted passages we can see, however, how the decisiveness that is necessary for even the possibility of becoming ourselves as a people turns upon an openness to happenings in the time-clearing. To become an historical people requires of us to be open to the happenings (Geschehen) of history (Geschichte). This makes our very selfhood as ourselves into a temporal determination:

> Wir dürfen uns selbst nicht mehr als in der Zeit Vorkommende verstehen, wir müssen uns erfahren als die, die von früher her wesend über sich selbst hinausgreifend aus der Zu-

> kunft sich bestimmen, d.h. aber: als die, die *selbst die Zeit sind*. Wir sind die Zeitigung der Zeit selbst. (*GA*38:120)

> We may no longer understand ourselves as beings occurring in time; we have to experience ourselves as those who, presencing from earlier and grasping out beyond themselves, determine themselves out of the future, and that means, as those who *are themselves time*. We are the coming about of time itself.

The radicality of this statement — which now goes far beyond the constitution of we ourselves in a situation — cannot be over-estimated, for it formulates the dissolution of the substantiality, the standing presence of us even as a people in time itself. But time in what sense? With this statement Heidegger shows himself as a radical, and by no means a conservative thinker. Our connection with temporality could not be more intimate, for, Heidegger claims, we are *ourselves* the coming about of time in its three-dimensional extension. We ourselves come about *as* the coming about of time itself. This is the temporal sense of Dasein, of human being itself, now pluralized as we. We can only become our selves in time and *as* time by answering, responding (Verantwortung, *GA*38:121) to the happening of history. History is no longer to be thought as significant occurrences *in* time, but as the happening *of* historical time itself.

> Geschichte überliefert sich in die Zukunft, gibt von dort her vor, wer und was sie sein kann. [...] Zukunft und Gewesenheit sind in sich einige Zeitmächte, die Macht der Zeit selbst, in der wir stehen. Wir sind nur zukünftig, indem wir die Gewesenheit als Überlieferung übernehmen. (*GA*38:124)

> History delivers itself over into the future and from there it lays down who and what it can be. [...] Future and beenness are in themselves unified temporal powers, the power of time itself, in which we stand. We are only futural by taking on beenness as tradition.

Tradition, Überlieferung is literally that which has been handed over, delivered over. We take on and accept the tradition out of the future in shaping the happenings that come toward us. This is our historical being as the coming about of historical time itself. According to Heidegger, our decisiveness in the historical moment is only the openness to the coming about of we ourselves as historical time itself. We can only become we ourselves in deciding to be *open-minded* in a radical sense of an open-mindedness toward the arrival of the future. The division between us and them, between those who "want to co-operate" and those who "want to act against" (*GA*38:72), would therefore be the opposition between open- and closed-mindedness toward futural historical possibilities. Only from this perspective can Heidegger say that there is a possibility that we are not ourselves, that we are not historical as a people. We close off the possibility of becoming ourselves by closing ourselves off to the still living tradition as it is delivered over alive to the future that comes toward us as a way of co-casting our selves into our future in a mode of living together. Such closing ourselves off is a kind of mental blindness. The so-called "power of time" is not something that stands at our disposition; rather we bring ourselves to a stand in taking on what the temporal power of beenness or yesterness delivers over to us as an open task and mission. We stand in responsibility to history as a responding and answering to historical time, not in any moral sense (cf. *GA*38:121), but in the ontological sense of the *possibility* of becoming and being who we are ourselves.

Our *ontological responsibility* is to respond to possibilities which we can only see, or rather, inkle *as* possibilities — and not as predictable certainties — inchoately shaping up by taking on and engaging with the tradition that has already shaped who we have been. In this sense, history, as the happening of time itself, is open, i.e. open to recasting, not by way of casting a fore-seeable, fore-knowable plan, but through an open engagement with who we have been that loosens up the tradition, thus enabling, perhaps, other possibilities of self-casting to gain historical shape through power interplays with each other into the temporal dimension of the future. The (decisive) question remains, however, concerning precisely *what* historical possibilities can be made out taking shape on the horizon of the future through engaging with what has been handed down, and the (divisive) strife and conflict over such possible arrivals. We can in any case see that, insofar as Heidegger's conception of the constituting of we ourselves as a people in and as historical time through openness toward the future is accepted on its word, it differs radically in its non-closure from Hegel's conception of the "world spirit" (Weltgeist, *RPh.* § 352) coming to itself in world history, consummating itself in the highest stage of its unfolding as the "Germanic Reich" (das germanische Reich, *RPh.* § 358).

The "time" that Heidegger conjures is not the traditional 1D-linear conception of time, but the 3D-temporality of the time-clearing for which there is the possibility of moving easily from what has been in one temporal dimension to what is possibly coming toward us from another temporal dimension, viz. the future. This originary 3D-temporal clearing is prior to movement, whereas the traditional 1D-linear conception of time is merely lifted off movement. Therefore it is entirely misleading of Heidegger to speak of we ourselves as the coming-about of time itself. Rather, we ourselves are engaged, through mutual estimating power plays, in casting how the world could shape up hermeneutically in future by retrieving former casts of our historical world and recasting them. The issue of blindness toward the future concerns above all the denial of the possibility of recasting and co-casting hermeneutically within the temporal clearing of history. An assessment of what has been requires an ontological thinking that can at all see the hermeneutic casting of the beingness of beings in an age, *thus keeping the ontological difference open*. Resistance comes most of all from those conservative quarters with their vested interests in the status quo that assert that 'we' have already reached the end of history, its final τελός and that only further 'progress' along the same line is to follow.

11.6 We the people and singular, rare individuals – The ethos of open-mindedness – Abstract personhood, interplay through a reified medium and the historical possibility of the free individual – The impossible mediation between universality and singularity – Singularity's shelter in the abstract rights of particularity – Heidegger's conjuring of a "fundamental attunement" among the people to support the work of a rare, singular individual

> Ταύτας τοίνυν τὰς τῶν μαθημάτων ἡδονὰς ἀμείκτους τε εἶναι λύπαις ῥητέον καὶ οὐδαμῶς τῶν πολλῶν ἀνθρώπων ἀλλὰ τῶν σφόδρα ὀλίγων.
>
> Plato *Philebos* 52b

> Then it must be said that these pleasures of learning are unmixed with pain and are not for the many but only for the very few.

In the preceding there has been talk of 'we ourselves' taking on the challenge of history in answering to the tradition. But is there really the possibility of an authentic we as a people constituted in this way through decision, resolute openness and answering to the call of history, and that through the mediation of the state, as Heidegger outlines in 1934? Heidegger himself makes a distinction during this very discussion between the community and certain special, rare, lonely individuals:

> Es gibt Dinge, die für eine Gemeinschaft wesentlich und entscheidend sind, und gerade diese Dinge erwachsen nicht in der Gemeinschaft, sondern in der beherrschten Kraft und Einsamkeit eines einzelnen. (*GA*38:15 cf. *GA*38:56)

> There are things that are essential and decisive for a community, and precisely these things do not arise in the community, but in the controlled, disciplined power and lonely solitude of an individual.

These rare and lonely individuals gifted (poisoned?) with a special creative power, who remain always singular and can never be absorbed by a we, are essential and crucial for something — precious little — to arise in the community that otherwise would be missing. These individuals must have some sort of forecasting fore-sight or fore-inkling into the historical time of hermeneutic casting, having received some sort of message. *They* (if it is at all admissible, rather than impossible, to refer to such singular individuals in the plural) are the singular ones, apparently eluding any we, who take on and engage critically with the tradition (of whatever kind) and are therefore in a position as an avant-garde to co-cast and recast how the future *could possibly* arrive in the present of a people. The people themselves, 'we ourselves' as a whole, can never see or know about the hidden transmission lines between the tradition that has been and its reshaping and recasting by exceptional, rare individuals as it arrives from the future. Keeping in mind Heidegger's starting-point in "willing" and "submitting", how could a people ever be authentically historical through a decision, decisiveness and resolute openness? Could it not ever only blindly submit? To what? Or is an hermeneutic recasting of an historical world so rare and so unheard of that another world shapes up historically more or less noticed and is never, in any case, seen to be an ontological recasting *as* such, but perhaps is noticed only in certain symptoms of a deeper change.

Aren't there "things that are essential and decisive for a community" on which the community cannot decide? After all, a community or a people lives only within preontological conceptions, never comprehending the hermeneutic As as such. Furthermore, isn't a people, immersed as it is in the well-worn ruts of normal, customary everyday life, always, at least tendentially, suspicious of those rare, creative individuals in its midst whom it cannot understand? Isn't there an essential friction and conflict between the conservative inertia of an established, ingrained, also cherished, traditional way of life of a people and its recasting through impulses emitted by possibilities arriving from the future that are defined, precast and moulded, at least in ontological outline, by the works of certain rare, fore-seeing or at least fore-inkling individuals, the people's (or, more cosmopolitanly, the world's) thinkers? Aren't these rare, fore-casting individuals, sacrificial midwives of coming historical truths they help shape, more often than not *singular outsiders* who do not succeed in life in any conventional sense because their contemporaries do not and cannot see and recognize them for who they are, caught as they are in the ambiguity of being regarded as either a far-seeing, gifted genius or as a blinded autist, a dangerous, poisonous radical or even an irrelevant crackpot or pitiable madman?

Doesn't the future come to be recast, if at all, in the crucible of the historical time-clearing precisely *against* the friction and positive resistance of an invariably 'conservative' people and all the institutions and 'accepted values' supporting this people? Isn't it above all the elite within a people, including the intellectual elite, that is invested most of all in the status quo? Doesn't the reshaping of the historical way of living of a people, the recasting of historical time take place *willy-nilly* and *behind the backs* of the people constituted as 'we ourselves' in the sense of belonging together in a settled, customary way of life? Aren't 'we ourselves' for the most part backward-looking rather than forward-looking? And is it not the case that Heidegger (and I) are talking here only in a *singular* conjuncture of Western history when former time meets an oncoming future in a present that calls for an hermeneutic recasting precisely because the ontological cast of world hitherto has become historically exhausted? Preceding chapters have shown in detail that the metaphysical ontology of movement *as* productive, effective, efficient has run its course and has been consummated.

If a disparity exists between a people and singular thinkers, then how could the *will* of a people, as Heidegger claims (*GA*38:57), play any crucial role in constituting it as an authentic, historical people? Aren't we the people introduced willy-nilly into an oncoming historical time only through being overwhelmed by changes that simply 'happen' to us, without us knowing whence such changes, such recastings of social living come? Could there not merely be at most a will, if at all, — or rather, an *ethos* — of *open-mindedness*, i.e. an ethos of a people being receptive for and supporting and perhaps even celebrating those unique, eccentric individuals in its midst, conveyors and heralds of strange, historically incipient truths, whom it does not (yet) understand? Would this not amount to an ethos of the preservation and protection of and receptiveness for the *singularity* of human being, an appreciation of why such singularity and even eccentricity of a biographical orbit must not be subsumed violently under the universality of a community, a society or a state by being compelled to conform to mores, but rather granted degrees of freedom of movement to follow its singular course?[226] Or is this asking for far too much, because an alternative cast can only

---

226 Nietzsche's liberal conception of the State, which excludes the State from having a purpose in world history, meshes with his estimation of genius, whilst aristocratically (Nietzsche stands against the incoming tide of Here Comes Everybody) depreciating the value of the multitude. "Der Staat ist aber immer nur das Mittel zur Erhaltung vieler Individuen: wie sollte er Zweck sein! Die Hoffnung ist, dass bei der Erhaltung so vieler Nieten auch einige mit geschützt werden, in denen die Menschheit kulminirt. Sonst hat es gar keinen Sinn, so viele elende Menschen zu erhalten. Die Geschichte der Staaten ist die Geschichte vom Egoismus der Massen und von dem blinden Begehren, existiren zu wollen: erst durch die Genien wird dieses Streben

come to light and find dissemination through bitter struggles? Could we as a people (no matter how homogeneously or heterogeneously such a people is conceived) nurture an habitual, customary sensibility, an ethos, for protecting human singularity against the violence of all-too-common sense? If openness toward the future is what is called for, would this not presuppose and demand that the people precisely *not* decide resolutely on a unified act of will that results in submission to the state, as Heidegger suggests, but rather cultivate a civil-social ethos of open-mindedness that enables singularities to flourish, thereby loosening the state's rule over society to the maximum possible extent?

If singularity requires mediation with the universal, whilst nonetheless never gaining perfect identity with it, but rather remaining forever rent with an unresolvable contradiction and opposition, this can only be achieved, if at all, through the mediation of particularity, which breaks down the claim of unified, identical universality into differing parts, insofar admitting difference, diversity, specificity under which singularity, too, in its eccentric uniqueness and therefore painfully broken, has at least some room to breathe and sometimes – in the coming about of an historically propitious, unusually *receptive* time – is perhaps even able to thrive. The freedom of particularity with which we are familiar in the West (and now worldwide, at least ideally) has the *form* (i.e. the ontological look) of the rights of the individual human being, i.e. the rights of civil freedom that came about and shaped up historically (especially in the seventeenth century with its singular thinkers, including Hobbes and Locke) as the modern age within historical time and were nurtured under the auspices of liberalism.

The core of individual liberty in the modern age consists in the freedom of exchange and interchange, and this metabolism of civil society is a power interplay among individuals endowed with abstract, universal rights that lend them the dignity of personhood. The very abstractness of the rights of personhood which abstract from the concrete living situations of members of society and guarantee their indifference toward each other, although so often deplored as an alienation from the social nature of human being, is the condition of possibility not only for the pursuit of particular self-interest in social interplay, but

---

einigermassen gerechtfertigt, insofern sie dabei existiren können." (Summer-Autumn 1873 29 [73] KSA7:661) "The state, however, is always only the means for preserving many individuals; how is it supposed to be an end! The hope is that with the preservation of so many no-hopers, a few are also protected in whom humanity culminates. Otherwise it makes no sense at all to preserve so many lousy people. The history of states is the history of the egoism of the masses and the blind desire to exist; only through the genii is this striving justified to some extent insofar as they, too, can exist."

also for the private sphere as the place of guaranteed withdrawal from society, and such a private sphere, guaranteed by natural right and law, is the sine qua non for singular individuality to find shelter from the conventional, conservative ethics of social reality and to assert and live also its *non*-identity with, its *not* belonging to the historically already realized, concrete ethical institutions of universality. Such singular individuality must not be maligned as mere caprice and arbitrariness, for it is also the ultimate source of freedom in its actual reality from which a more or less far-reaching recasting of world can emerge in a re-generation within the time-clearing of history.

As we have seen throughout this study, liberalism is intimately and in essence related with a market economy based on private property that admits, through the reification of its value-medium, the ongoing power interplay of particular self-interests in a *spontaneous* sociating power play not controlled and directed by an overarching, ruling state will. The liberal state's foremost task is to preserve the framework or *playform* of civil society, i.e. above all its forms of intercourse as forms of fair interplay, and not to intervene in civil society with aims (especially of paternalistically caring for the people) posited by will, but rather to allow the concreteness of civil society to come about as the ongoing outcome of a power plays among social players. The liberal state as the guarantor first and foremost of *abstract* personhood remains in essence *indifferent* to the concrete particularity and especially the individual singularity of members of society. This abstract indifference signals the state's distance from the private sphere, the hesitation of the state as the institution of concrete universality to differentiate or particularize itself into the particularity of different, particular, prescribed ways of living. The organic whole of a viable society comes about only as the ongoing, spontaneous metabolism of civil society with its interplay of particularity. Within this interplay, whose forms remain abstract and guaranteed through abstract personhood, individual singularity, for better or worse, finds its niche.

Abstract personhood is that socio-ontological state which historically enables the free individual for the first time, dis-sociating human beings from each other as sociated primarily through the mediation of an abstract, reified interplay. Contrary to modern, natural-right conceptions of the state that proceed from the premiss of pre-social, isolated, free individuals, it must be seen that the free individual is always already an individual engaged in the reified interplay and that without such a reified form of sociation there is no free individual at all. This reified form of sociation that engenders and preserves the private individual as free and dis-sociated nevertheless has its own strength and resilience.

Such a free individual did not exist in antiquity, although its germ was already present in ancient Greece.

The ancients, including Aristotle in his ethical and political writings, Hegel notes, were "unfamiliar with the abstract right of our modern states which isolates the individual, allows it to do as it likes (so that it is regarded essentially as a person) and nevertheless holds them all together as a more invisible spirited mind" (unbekannt mit dem abstrakten Recht unserer modernen Staaten, das den Einzelnen isoliert, ihn als solchen gewähren läßt (so daß er wesentlich als Person gilt) und doch als ein unsichtbarerer Geist alle zusammenhält, *VGPII* W19:36). Such a "holding together" recalls already Aristotle's formulation of how usage and money hold everything together (cf. Chapter 4.5 and passim), whereas the "more invisible spirited mind" is an echo of Hegel's reading of Adam Smith's "invisible hand", translated into the speculative language of "objective spirited mind", i.e. of socio-ontological forms.

Liberal theory itself has only ever concerned itself, in Hegelian terminology, with the mediation between universality and particularity, i.e. between the claims of society and the rights of individuals. Insofar, freedom in the liberal sense can be understood in a relatively bland way as the particular individual's (strictly speaking, an oxymoron) right to do what it wants as long as it does not infringe the exercise of other particular individuals' rights. Freedom then seems to be a matter of individual, arbitrary caprice and can be understood merely as the pursuit of average, normal happiness, including tawdry consumerism, which therefore can well be sacrificed for a purportedly higher, social good or, in pure liberal theory, at least guided cleverly by the state, as the instance of the universal, into alignment with the general good. But this casting of human being to consist of two moments is truncated, omitting as it does the third moment of singularity, the existential-ontological site of genuine individuality. Whereas particularity is the particularization of universality into parts, allowing particularity (as, say, a system of the totality of needs in their particularity) to be contained within universality through liberal forms of intercourse, there is no such easy mediation of the gulf between particularity and singularity. No matter how concrete the manifold determinations of particularity become, they can never capture singularity, which always eludes them. This is to say that human being itself is existentially rent in a primal split (Urteil; cf. Chapter 3.3.1.5) between the extremes of universality and singularity, with the mediating moment of particularity being unable to close the extremes together into an identity.

As singularly individual, human being itself is contradictory and torn in being simultaneously a part of the universal, i.e., in this context, a social being that shares the world with others. The moment of singularity reaches into the abyss, beyond any possible reconciliation with universality in an identity. It can only ever be repressed and kept at bay in a kind of normality of the individual, or at most granted a certain freedom of movement beneath abstract-universal social forms. The exceptionally able individual is recognized by others, if at all, only in particular terms assimilable to a general, universal understanding that does not and cannot reach into singularity, no matter how much average understanding may try. As essentially abyssal, singularity itself is unsayable. It only ever erupts with fragmentary forms of meaning in art and philosophy. Individual singularity can therefore only ever seek shelter in the particularity of individual freedoms abstractly guaranteed through the universal form of personhood, and this is a great merit of liberalism, although scarcely recognized as such. Precisely the 'cold' abstractness of reified social forms enables hyperborean singularity to breathe. As noted above, such hyperborean singularity is needed today for hermeneutic recasting.

As has been shown, however, Heidegger explicitly rejects liberalism, which he regards (very superficially for a philosopher) as the capricious individualism of abstract, uprooted, 'worldless' individuals that can result only in the 'decadence' of modern life. He yearns instead for the unity of an autochthonous, homogeneous people rooted in a substantive way of life, and constituted in an act of decisive, resolutely open willing that conforms seamlessly with the "will of a state". (GA38:57) Even when Heidegger imagines that the resolute openness of a people can only be "prepared" (GA38:76, cf. above) or could take fifty or so years to come to fruition (as he suggests in two talks he gave in 1933; cf. GA16 No. 155 and Chapter 12.2.1), this hope must be regarded as wishful and dogmatic thinking founded not merely on a political, but on a *philosophical, i.e. ontological* lack of understanding of the (impossible) mediated relationship among universality, particularity and singularity. The mediation between politico-social universality and singularity posited by Heidegger is that of authoritarian subsumption, leaving no room for an interplay among universality, particularity and singularity which, as has been shown (Chapter 3.3.1.3), Hegel at least attempts to think through dialectically. Let us further examine how Heidegger outlines the constitution of 'we ourselves' as an historical people.

Heidegger characterizes the constitution of the, presumably homogeneous, German people as 'we ourselves' *in* historical time and, purportedly, *as* historical time as an experience of going through (Erfahrung, GA38:126) our determination or even destiny (Bestimmung, GA38:127ff). We have to ask whether "we" "go through" (erfahren) our historical determination and destiny. The "fundamental attunement of a people" (Grundstimmung eines Volks, GA38:130) is said to support and enable "a great work" (ein großes Werk, GA38:130) of creative individuals living and working in the people's midst. Could such a "fundamental attunement" possibly be, as suggested above, that of open-mindedness?

> Die Gewesenheit als Überlieferung und die Zukunft (als auf uns zukommend) als Aufgabe halten das Dasein im Grunde und schon immer in einer Entschränkung. Ausgesetzt in die Stimmung und entrückt in die Arbeit, sind wir geschichtlich. Die Macht der Zeit zeitigt ursprünglich und nicht nachträglich die Entrückung des Daseins in die Zukunft und Gewesenheit. (*GA*38:155)

> Beenness as tradition and the future (as coming toward us) as task and mission hold Dasein fundamentally and a priori in a removal of barriers. Exposed to attunement and transported into work, we are historical. The power of time brings about originarily and not subsequently the ecstatic transport of Dasein into the future and into beenness.

The temporal structure of the historical time of a people *as* which, according to Heidegger, it is to come about (sich zeitigen), is the temporal structure of individual Dasein as developed in *Sein und Zeit* but now writ large, as the existence of an entire people, a whole nation that comes to its we-self. What is the mediation between individual Dasein which recollects its beenness and casts itself into its very own, individual future and the historical Dasein of a people? How is this gulf to be bridged, given that, at least as late as 1928, at a time when he engaged in debate with Max Scheler, Heidegger still regarded it as "a problem how Dasein as essentially free can exist in the freedom of factically bound togetherness"? (es ist ein Problem, wie das Dasein als wesenhaft freies in der Freiheit des faktisch gebundenen Miteinanderseins existieren kann[227]) And this problem is, ironically, the *fundamental question of that liberalism* which Heidegger so contemptuously rejects! Heidegger offers us little to go on in searching for mediation. For instance,

> [...] ist, aus der ursprünglichen Erfahrung des Menschseins aus der Zeitlichkeit und damit des geschichtlichen Seins verstanden, Vereinzelung auf echte Weise möglich und notwendig, nur dürfen wir den einzelnen nicht nach der Vorstellung des Subjektes denken. Die Vereinzelung in der Einsamkeit kann in einzigartiger Weise für das Ganze wirksam sein. Umgekehrt beweist betriebsames Dabeisein noch längst nicht die lebendige Volksverbundenheit; sie versteckt vielmehr Eigensucht. (*GA*38:157)

> [...] understood from the original experience of human being from temporality and thus of historical being, singularization in a genuine way is possible and necessary, but we must not think of the individual according to the idea of the subject. Singularization in the

---

227 Martin Heidegger *Metaphysische Anfangsgründe der Logik im Ausgang von Leibniz* Summer Semester 1928 ed. Klaus Held, Klostermann, Frankfurt/M. 1978, 2nd ed. 1990 *GA*26:175.

sense of solitude can be effective for the whole in a unique way. Conversely, busy involvement with what is going on does not prove a lively bond with the people; rather it hides self-seeking egoism.

This structurally unified coming-about in historical time which an historical people is supposed to *be* depends upon an overcoming or a suppression of the Unwesen or 'degenerate essence' of the people as a collection of self-seeking egoists. Such individual self-seeking has no place in Heidegger's casting of the temporality of an historical people; it is for him degenerate human being, i.e. an Unwesen, an outgrowth of the modern age of subjectivist metaphysics and its purportedly associated "liberalism" (*GA*38:51, 149, cf. *GA*38:143) of arbitrary and capricious individualism. Such individual self-seeking, it would seem according to Heidegger, needs to be morally, and then politically suppressed (instead of particularity, at least, being mediated dialectically and spontaneously with the universal, as in Hegel's thinking). According to Heidegger's peculiar version of "socialism" (Sozialismus; *GA*38:165), we become ourselves as an historical people in *deciding* to be unified and *knowing* ourselves unified in the shared work of a task and mission arriving from the future that has arisen from the tradition having delivered over its destinal mission to the future, and we are borne in this shared task by "grand fundamental attunements" (große Grundstimmungen, *GA*38:130). But are not attunements, no matter how grand, fickle and open to conflicting interpretations?

How can we as an historical people *know* of the necessity of " singularization in the sense of solitude" which "can be effective for the whole in a unique way"? Or is it a matter only of the people *inkling* — in an attunement of openmindedness that is nothing other than openness and receptivity for an ontological recasting of world in the 3D-temporal clearing of an age, our own — the importance for its own selfhood *as* a people of certain rare individuals? How is the individual who hears the calling to work in solitude to find a niche for this work within the bosom of the people and the established institutions of state? How is a singular, creative individual to find the freedom to pursue his or her calling, given the unified, totalized will of the people and state? Is it enough for the individual "to have the urge within him/herself which authorizes him/her to solitude" (der freilich in sich den Drang haben muß, der ihn zu der Einsamkeit berechtigt, *GA*38:56)? Does this amount to a kind of (arbitrary, nay, capricious) self-authorization on the part of the individual who feels an "urge"?

Whence does this urge, in turn, receive its authorization? Whence does it receive its guaranteed freedom of expression within the social whole? Indeed, how is a National Socialist "hierarchy according to vocation and work" (Rangordnung nach Berufung und Werk, *GA*38:165) to come about and be reconciled with the singular urge of an individual to work in solitude? Who is to have the power of determining this "hierarchy"? Is it to be decided on the basis of merit and competition among individuals exercising their individual powers and abilities? How is the structure, i.e. how are the banal, everyday social *power* plays of this envisaged National Socialist society to provide for the *individuation* of its singular individuals as a vital possibility and necessity? How is the "individual" invoked here by Heidegger to be distinguished from the (liberal, metaphysical) "subject" he so disparagingly rejects? It is hardly sufficient merely to proclaim with a vacuous rhetorical gesture that the appropriately attuned "individual" could be concretely embedded in the bosom of the people, whereas the "subject" of the liberal era remains an abstract, uprooted figure lacking an historical world.

Heidegger's casting of a kind of (National) Socialism as a way in which an historical people could bring itself about as 'we ourselves' pretty clearly excludes the rights of particularity, i.e. the highly proclaimed individual civil rights of the liberal age, including above all private property, which provide the room for movement, not only for self-interests to play themselves out in sometimes unseemly rivalry, but also for singular, individual independence to be maintained from both the concrete institutions of established political power and the social pressures of conventional ethical life. The caprice which individualized, private property rights enable under the mantle of the abstract, universal recognition of each individual as a person, may well be lamented by those 'intellectuals' who condemn the 'alienation' of reified 'social relations' and decry the descent of the individualized masses into tinselly, tawdry, tacky consumerism, but personhood, through its very abstractness and guaranteed indifference, also opens and protects a precious little space for certain singular, rare individuals to devote themselves to their ownmost calling and work of recasting — perhaps a people's — historical future behind its back, despite the cold indifference and/or heated resistance of the recognized, traditional institutions (especially of learning and of culture) in which a people's Geist hitherto has been supposed to be at home, ensconced in the comfortable exercise of their power and recognizing only those as estimable somebodies who adhere to the rules of power play of their established power game. It must not be forgotten that the transmission lines of historical truth are power lines.

This brings the phenomenon of whoness back into play, since those singular, creative individuals who have a special, irreplaceable role in co-casting the inkled possibilities (not the foreseeable certainties) in the historical time-clearing by casting a work of historical truth are whos and jemeiniges Dasein. Even when working in "lonely solitude" (*GA*38:15) in a laboratory of the future, these rare individuals can nevertheless only be who they are through the ongoing interplay of estimation through which an individual Dasein comes to stand as who he or she is, choosing and grasping his or her ownmost possibilities of existing from all the masks mirrored to it by others, especially those supportive others such as a teacher, mentor or a patron. The power play of the estimation interplay with others in coming to one's self and learning who one is to be must be, if not free and fair, then at least must provide a crevice to allow the necessary "lonely solitude" and individuation in which these rare, gifted individuals can devote themselves to their respective individual, ownmost tasks in exercising their creative abilities for the sake of something (that may turn out to be) "essential and decisive for a community". (*GA*38:15)

Since any genuinely creative task and mission (and in our present conjuncture this is a task of ontological rethinking) is historically fore-casting, it cannot be understood by the people. It must be a casting ahead of its present time to be genuinely what it is. The exceptional individual exists in an interstice between dimensions of the historical time-clearing. This means that the appropriate estimation of a special, creative individual *as* such in the present time may be *refused* altogether, as if this individual's whoness had evaporated and counted for nought. In a more favourable case, it is only through struggle and controversy that this singular individual may be able to overcome the crudest misunderstandings and present the outlines of what is gathering and shaping up from the future as an historical possibility of hermeneutic recasting, and perhaps even gain recognition by others that the work performed has value (if not market value).

11.7 The socio-ontological critique of liberalism – Contract as the abstractly universal shell-form for the metabolism of civil society – The possibility and ethos of a liberal We in free and fair interplay

Through this discussion it should have become apparent that Heidegger's conception of 'we ourselves' as an historical people and its relation to those singular individuals who, he claims, have an indispensable role in casting and shaping the time-clearing of a people's history, remains highly problematic and, not just *politically* (say, merely because it is 'anti-liberal'), but, more deeply, *socio-ontologically* ill thought out. The "problem" of reconciling "how Dasein as essentially free can exist in the freedom of factically bound togetherness" (*GA*26:175) is in the first place a philosophical, socio-ontological problem that goes to the heart of the question of human being itself, and not merely a prob-lem of how a society is to be set up politically with an appropriate constitution. Moreover, Heidegger's statement of a "problem", perhaps despite his inten-tions, can be regarded as a formulation of the *socio-ontological* problem of lib-eralism with which the tradition of liberalism itself has not confronted itself, instead taking individual freedom as an axiomatic given, as somehow self-evident, which is, philosophically, always a bad sign.

One could very well claim that liberalism has already long since had its hey-day and its day. After all, its fathers, Hobbes and Locke, lived already in the seventeenth century, and in the meantime, liberalism has been much maligned and unmasked, including as an 'ideology representing the class interests of the bourgeoisie', or as a 'capitalist free-market ideology' that serves to ride rough-shod over the poor and disadvantaged or to blithely neglect major issues such as today's environmental problems, or as 'Neo-liberalism' which aims at turning back the historical clock by undoing the 'achievements' of the modern social-welfare state. Furthermore, philosophically as well, liberalism has been sub-jected to trenchant critiques, including by Hegel, who has roundly deconstruct-ed the 'contract theory' of society as ontologically naïve. Hegel's apposite cri-tique — e.g. society cannot be regarded as an "atomistic *heap* of individuals" (atomistischer *Haufen* von Individuen, *RPh.* § 273 Note) or his socio-ontological insight that commonality is the crudest conception of the universal — even parallels to some extent Heidegger's deconstruction of subject-object dualism to show and insist that Dasein is always already being-in-the-world-with-others, albeit that the socio-ontological question concerning how Dasein and Dasein share the world in Mitsein remains underdeveloped in Heidegger's thinking.

These philosophical critiques of liberalism, however, do not by any means dispose of the free individual at the heart of liberal thinking, but merely situate it anew as a priori already in the social world. Hegel, in particular, does not negate "subjective freedom" — which would amount to abstractly rejecting the core of liberalism, whose essence is individual freedom — but seeks to integrate, i.e. sublate it into a reconciled totality. Despite the flaws that can be pointed out in Hegel's supposed dialectical reconciliation of individual freedom with uni-versality in a State that must be regarded as overbearing and even authoritarian (cf. Chapter 12), Hegel nevertheless remains true to the phenomenon of human freedom itself *insofar* as he acknowledges that the freedom of human being, like the truth of being, is, of its deepest nature, individualized, i.e. singularized, no matter to what bond an individual human being may commit itself.

Heidegger, by contrast, in his abstract negation of individual freedom from the 1930s on, proposes an authoritarian concept of 'authentic' individual freedom as submission and even self-sacrifice to a necessity, namely, that of a greater universal — the call and claim of being itself — which presumably motivated also his initial commitment to National Socialism. In the present study, the existential-ontologically resituated individual in its whoness is always already engaged in the mutually estimating power interplay through which it comes to be who it is, which includes committing itself *freely* and through its *own* thinking to others, to tasks and missions and even to larger, 'universal' causes, whilst never surrendering the moment of singularity at the core of human being. Moreover, these individuals *are such* only by virtue of the abstract, reified, individualizing relations of a society based on the medium of reified value and they are only tied back into society as a universal connection precisely *through* the ongoing interplay within these abstract, reified, universal sociating power plays, which is a basic form of modern ethical life.

If the socio-ontological critique of liberalism is tenable, then the free individual is always already in the world as Mitsein (Heidegger), i.e. as shared being-in-the-world, or, in Hegelian terms, the individual has already been raised willy-nilly to the level of reason with its objectifications in the forms of ethical life. This means that a kind of liberal We has always already been constituted; the social world can never be thought as derived from a multitude of individuals, for these individuals as somewhos are always already immersed and entangled in the sociating interplay, in order to even *be who* they are. Even the moralistically much maligned cell form of interplay in modern society, the contract, although constituted freely and capriciously by two or more individuals entering into it, already exceeds the sum of the two individual contractual parties, bringing about a form or 'look' of shared freedom with its own socio-ontological dignity that is irreducible to (the compromising sum of) two single wills.

The contract as a free, reciprocal giving of one's word raises the parties into a freely constituted We which is then *binding* on both parties and therefore *beyond* each party individually. Even though the incentive to enter a contract may be pure, arbitrary self-interest on each side, the contract as a form of free mutuality has already bound the self-interests into a We to which both parties are obligated, and that in complete correspondence with each of their particular free wills. Even though the individual parties are free to enter or not to enter a specific contract, and are insofar capricious free wills, their freely give commitment to a contractual We is itself a 'look' of (now sociated) freedom, and therefore corresponds to the being of free will as such, i.e. the contractual We is *true* in the Hegelian sense. Keeping one's word in a contract is therefore itself an issue and noble expression of freedom, for the individual parties are bound to their word given in a freely constituted We. They have freely constituted and subjected themselves to a common will which is more than merely common, but *an sich*, inherently universal, i.e. 'infinite' or 'absolute'.[228]

The contract is the abstract shell-form of intercourse in civil society based on private property, which is itself a face of freedom as the individual taking-possession of thingly beings in the world. As such, the contract-form is an abstractly universal shell open to receiving infinitely many different contents, and therefore can be concretized in countless different ways each representing a Gestalt of habitual, ethical life in its interplay. Furthermore, the contractual form is also the abstractly universal form of *movement*, of *metabolism* of civil society as a form of mutually mirroring interplay which, in the first place, is based on recognition of each other as abstractly free persons, independently of whether a contract is entered into or not. Civil society in its movement is therefore, in the first (socio-ontological) place, formally an abstract, mirroring interplay among free persons. Substantially, or rather with regard to the content that fills this shell of formally free and civil interplay, civil society's movement is able to take up all sorts of contents in myriad interchanges. Civil society therefore builds a bewilderingly complex network of metabolic interchanges which is civil social life itself. This bewilderingly diverse interplay itself is nothing other than an intermeshing, mutually estimating exercise of the individual freedom of the countless individuals involved who, in turn, are themselves bound by the

---

228 "Here [in contract ME] starting-point — *common will* — property has a contingency, externality — up to now only desire or some other external contingency whether I can have this or that — in nature —, or whether the contingent will of another wants to relinquish the thing to me [...] *Value* and *common, mutual* will, — both a contingent universality. The bound and binding factor — in the will of both — is this, that therein there is something *existing-in-itself* — *right-in-itself* — i.e. the existence of will as such — both have in the contract not only renounced their particular will, but also presupposed that the existence of the will *in general/in its universality* prevails — right in this matter — this is the essential inner *precondition* — breach of contract, non-performance is *against right in general/in its universality*, — i.e. not only against my particular will as *particular* will;" (Hier [beim Vertrag ME] Ausgangspunkt — *gemeinsamer Wille* — Eigentum hat eine Zufälligkeit, Äußerlichkeit — bisher nur Begierde oder sonst eine äußerliche Zufälligkeit, ob ich dies oder jenes haben kann — in der Natur —, oder ob der zufällige Wille eines Andern mir die Sache überlassen will [...] *Wert* und *gemeinschaftlicher* Wille, — beides eine zufällige Allgemeinheit. Das Gebundene und Bindende — im Willen beider — ist dies, daß darin ein *Ansichseiendes* ist — *das Recht an sich* — d. i. überhaupt das Dasein des Willens — beide haben im Vertrag nicht nur ihres besonderen Willens sich entäußert, sondern auch vorausgesetzt, daß gelte, das Dasein des Willens *überhaupt* — das Recht in dieser Sache — dies ist die innere wesentliche *Voraussetzung* — Vertragbrechen, Nicht-leisten ist *gegen das Recht überhaupt*, — d.h. nicht nur gegen meinen besonderen Willen als *besonderen*; Hegel *RPh*. § 81 handwritten addition) Hence, even the common will of the contract, according to Hegel, has already superseded the capricious freedom of two mere particular wills.

commitments they have freely entered. Hence, beyond the cell form of the contract that brings two parties into play with one another and binds them to a contractual We, there is the infinitely complex metabolism of the interplay of civil society itself, which, as a form of free interplay, also has the socio-ontological dignity of a free, civil, social We to which the participants are bound and committed. The players in the complex, universal interplay that emerges from the abstract, universal form of personhood lead their lives within this on-going interplay and find themselves as more or less highly estimated whos reflected within it. They belong to it, and so it is part of their mirrored identity as who they are, namely, estimated and estimating players in a freely constituted interplay of powers.

This interplay is itself recognized and honoured as a 'look' of freedom constituting the We of civil society. This We is still an abstract kind of We because it is an immediate, spontaneous outgrowth of the abstractly universal form of freedom residing in personhood. Nevertheless, the individuals are freely bound to this interplay, belong to it, find themselves and their selves as mirror reflections in it, and so affirm the interplay itself as realization of their own freedom. Civil society is therefore not merely abstract (because of its basis in abstract personhood), but is a concrete way of social living, a way in which the universal breaks down into endlessly complex, particular parts. Moreover, as a complex, concrete form of free interplay with its own socio-ontological dignity as a freely constituted, civil We, it is a form of ethical life with its own *ethos*. This ethos is that of *fair play*. The interplay in civil society can be either *fair* or *ugly*, and civil society is only truly free insofar as its ongoing interplay is fair in the double meaning of the word as both equitable and beautiful (cf. τὸ καλόν in Plato and Aristotle).

The acknowledgement of each free individual as being free to exercise its powers, first and foremost, its abilities of whatever kind, is at the core of the ethos of fair play. This means that the will to effective power over movement and change of all kinds of the traditional, metaphysical ontology of productive movement, becomes a will to mutually estimating interplay that cannot will one-sidedly any foreseen outcome, but only an outcome acknowledged by both sides as fair. The fairness of fair play depends upon each individual player being enabled to play to the best of its abilities under fair rules of play. These abilities are not necessarily of the economic kind, and can be related to all the numberless different forms of concrete ethical life that may be constelled on the basis of particular, concrete worldviews, but always *within* the abstract, universal forms of personhood that admit and can enable and sustain such concreteness. This being-within means that the freely and spontaneously arising concrete Gestalten of ethical life conform with individual freedom. In the first place, however, the fairness of fair play pertains to the fair rules of play under which the players in civil society earn their living, not merely in monetary terms, but also as the fulfilment of their particular, individual talents and abilities. Such talents and abilities are shown off in the interplay and are estimated and rewarded (or ignored or disparaged), and such showing-off and estimation in a contractual context enable the individual player to play, perhaps even fulfillingly and satisfyingly.[229]

It is no coincidence that the fundamental conception of justice inherited from Plato and Aristotle is that of *fairness* (ἰσότης, meaning also equitableness and equality). For the sociating interplay of civil society to be fair and just, each player must be on an equal footing with regard to the rules of play. The ethos of fair play thus infuses civil society with its own ethics which is abstract in the sense of admitting and enabling countlessly many different forms of concrete, historical, social life in different places and different times. The state governs in the spirit of this ethos of fair play insofar as it directs its superior, acknowledged and legitimated power toward attempting to achieve that balance in the rules of interplay that allow the power play to be called fair rather than ugly. This attempt to achieve the balance of fairness in the finite, concrete world, of course, is an infinite endeavour, albeit guided steadily by a view of fairness and fair play that must be interpreted anew in countless new playing situations that arise and in each newly arriving historical time.

The liberalism spurned and despised by Heidegger therefore contains nonetheless the germ of a civil society based on the (ethos of the) free and fair, competitive power interplay among individuals, reciprocally estimating and esteeming each other's powers and abilities, and interchanging their fruits for each other's mutual benefit. Such competitive interplay is how free individuals as power-centres come to cast their ownmost who-stands in the mirror of the world and is how the essence of human being as free concretizes itself in the world. Liberalism is thus — contra Heidegger — the very soil in which the grounding of human being as Dasein can properly gain root because Dasein and Mitsein, thought as a shared belonging together in the open 3D-temporal clearing of history that enables beings to be *what* they are and human beings to be *who* they are, corresponds to the interplay among human beings who are who they

---

229 "Every person, if possible, ought to enjoy the fruits of his labour, in a full possession of all the necessaries, and many of the conveniencies of life. No one can doubt, but such an equality is most suitable to human nature, and diminishes much less from the *happiness* of the rich than it adds to that of the poor." David Hume 'Of Commerce' 1752/1987 p. 265.

are only by virtue of this mutually mirroring and estimating interplay of their individual powers. Far from being substantial subjects in standing presence, the truth of human being as free is the competitively playful, self-interested, vieing among inhabitants who are able to bear the abstract freedom of personhood with its many degrees of freedom, taking advantage of them to shape their own existences. They concretize their lives in freely given commitments to others and within forms of ethical life to which they have become accustomed and affirm, whilst hovering over and affirming also the unfathomableness of the power interplay itself, fashioning their own singularity out of this fathomless interplay of powers, and enduring the irreconcilable tornness of the primal split between singularity and universality.

12 Government and the state

Deutschlandreise
Die freiheitliche demokratische Grund-Ordnung entlang,
Man fährt von Freiheit ab — und kommt in Ordnung an.

12.1 Recapitulation via Locke: The liberal conception of government, its critique and socio-ontological grounding in the power interplay of civil society

The ground covering the question of legitimate government has been turned many times since Plato and Aristotle. John Locke, for instance, one of the prime historical sources of liberal thinking, i.e. a liberal cast of world, makes one of the most famous contributions in his *Two Treatises of Government*, in which he argues for the natural rights of man and government only by "Agreement which every one has with the rest to incorporate, and act as one Body, and so be one distinct Commonwealth"[230] against the pretensions of absolute monarchy with its hereditary claim to legitimacy. The issue of political philosophy in the narrower sense always turns upon the government of men by men and whether this government is legitimate (and not merely lawful; cf. Chapter 10.3). The absoluteness of absolute monarchy is that the monarch rules autocratically without any relation to the concurring will of the subjects whom he rules.

We continue to live in the modern liberal age in the West with the conviction that only government by consent of those governed, no matter how this consent is institutionally arranged, can be justified and is therefore just and legitimate. Strictly speaking, it is best to distinguish legitimacy of government from justice, which latter concerns both the question of fair interplay in civil society and that of each individual member and each group in society having and enjoying its due share of the goods of life in the broadest sense, both tangible and intangible, positive (beneficial goods) and negative (deleterious bads; cf. Chapter 6.1f). This conviction of government only by consent corresponds to and springs from an historical casting of the sociating in the world within which society exists solely for the sake of its individual members and their ways of life who each must have some sort of say in how and by whom they are governed. Human beings in the modern age are social *subjects*, i.e. they underlie society as its ground in terms of which society and its governing institutions are rendered

---

230 John Locke *Second Treatise of Government* § 211.

https://doi.org/10.1515/9783110617504-012

their reason, their very raison d'être. This makes them also political subjects underlying government, and not merely subject to, i.e. literally, thrown under, the state.

The divine right of kings, by contrast, was grounded on the Christian God as the ultimate subject underlying the totality of beings, which in turn were God's created objects. The superiority of the Christian God already pre-empted any need to legitimize government specifically in terms of its good for those governed. In medieval times, in accordance with the metaphysical cast of the totality of beings, government was legitimized in terms of some sort of correspondence to the ultimate underlying subject, God, say, as the expression of His will through His chosen monarch. In the modern age, however, the Christian God as supreme being gradually has given way to humankind itself as the ultimate, underlying subject — an ostensible 'we'— that must render to all beings their reason. Government can now only be legitimized if it proceeds ultimately in some way from the collectivity of individual human subjects making up society and for their good.

In the modern age, each individual human subject is now experienced and cast as an ultimate, free ἀρχή and any higher ἀρχή (an ἀρχός, a ruler) now has to justify itself to the human subject members of society and be *estimated* as such by them. Not only is individual consciousness, the ego cogito, now the ultimate locus of self-certain truth where the world is represented in its truth, but the individual, free, fathomless will is now the ἀρχή for all actions in the world, even if this act be an act of consent to submit to a superior authority in society. The individual as ultimate subject has to consent to being governed and only freely gives this consent because of an insight into what is necessary and beneficial for its own well-being and no longer as an act of submission to superior, divine will, to a superior stratum of society, i.e. an aristocracy, or to paternal figures legitimated by traditional patriarchal and tribal social orders.

The individual subject *understands* (pre-ontologically) that it is necessarily sociated in society with other individuals in a unified "Body Politick" (*TTG.* p. 459) so that its own freedom and well-being can only be realized, furthered and secured as part of the general well-being of society at large. Locke states many times that men only enter into society to preserve and secure their "Estates, Liberties and Lives" (*TTG.* p. 452) as the precondition for any individual or social well-being. This major premise of Locke's treatise stands opposed to the divine right of an absolute monarch to rule, against which both of Locke's treatises are directed and by which, therefore, all his arguments are held in tension. Locke's treatises (and, before him, Hobbes' writings) signify a shift in Western understanding of the totality of beings in which the supremacy of the Christian

God gives way to humankind itself as the underlying subject of all that is. This recasting of world runs in parallel to Descartes' casting of the self-certain subject that first and foremost is conscious of, i.e. co-knows, itself. Locke's thinking also plays midwife to a world that is twisting free of subjection to a supreme being, i.e. a highest power and cause, acting through a divine representative, the absolute monarch, to ground instead individualized humankind itself as the ultimate subject and ground. An epoch of humanization of the world has begun.

Locke, of course, remains nominally Christian in his thinking, but he appeals fundamentally to man's putative God-given "Reason", which is synonymous with the "Law of Nature" (*TTG*. p. 311), a shift which effectively makes humankind and its insightful reasoning the ultimate subject of how society is to be. Locke's entire argument throughout both treatises is held in its orbit by the pull of the position asserting the legitimacy of absolute monarchy which he is opposing. He aims to demonstrate that there cannot be any legitimate *absolute* monarchy precisely because a monarch's legitimate power must be *relative* to the end of government, which is the preservation of the life, liberty and estate of the members of society. This end of government is posited. It is a metaphysical positing which posits groundlessly individualized humankind as the ultimate subject, in line with the ultimately *individualized* nature of freedom, albeit that the nature of this individualization *as* a mode of sociation via reified power interplay remains hidden. The posited metaphysical casting of individualized humankind can be called humanism. The way society is set up has now to justify itself to "Reason" (not just to understanding or mere opinion), i.e. to the insight of men considering the constitution of society as a unified, governing body politic in the light of their own nature as free beings, their interests (especially private property interests), welfare and well-being, in short, their "happiness", or at least the pursuit thereof.

The opposition between the two hermeneutic casts can also be stated in terms of the opposed theses on the opening pages of Locke's first treatise. These are: "Men are not born free, and therefore could never have the liberty to choose either Governors, or Forms of Government." (*1TG*. § 5) as opposed to the admission of "the Natural Liberty and Equality of Mankind". (*1TG*. § 4) Mankind is either subject *to* an absolute monarch who rules absolutely by divine right, or it is the subject *of* all social institutions and government, underlying and therefore providing their very reason for being, thus making all government relative to the ultimate, underlying individualized subjects. Freedom here does not mean the freedom to do arbitrarily what one wants and wills, but the freedom arising from insight (which is necessarily ultimately individual) into human being itself and thus (ultimately individual) consent to the way society is set up and governed. Freedom has to accord with the necessary "Law of Nature", which is "Reason". Reason, however, is, properly speaking, ontological, speculative insight into the being of beings.

Originally, in Locke's conception, a "State of Nature" prevails which is "a State of perfect Freedom [of men] to order their Actions, and dispose of their Possessions, and Persons as they think fit, within the bounds of the Law of Nature, without asking leave, or depending upon the Will of any other Man". (*2TG.* § 4) This "State of Nature", however, is not to be thought as an hypothetical prior state of humankind back in the mists of time, but as an a priori, groundless metaphysical positing and casting of human freedom as individual freedom, and of society as compatible with the realization, i.e. the interplay, of individual freedom (cf. Chapter 10.7). To posit that "all men are born free" is not to state any sort of fact, but to cast human being itself into freedom, which is a thoroughly two-edged gift/poison eventuating from the open truth of being's temporality. Accordingly, reason dictates also that society be governed by laws passed by an elected legislature (to maintain the underlying, ultimate subjectivity of the people and the free expression of its will) under which each member of society is treated equally as a formally, abstractly equal bearer of rights, i.e. a person, rather than being subjected to the arbitrary decision of a divinely empowered absolute monarch, even though this monarch may decide wisely, paternalistically and benevolently to further the good of his people. Such an elected legislature, which places *demands* and *obligations* on the citizens in the exercise of their individualized freedom of movement, is a concrete realization of reason in the sense that it is the way in which the idea of individual human freedom in its interplay gains objectivity as an institution, which is a Gestalt of ethical life in such a society based on individual freedom (and not on a promise of assured happiness conceived as material well-being).

Human being is still conceived by Locke along the traditional metaphysical lines of an Aristotle, with Christian admixtures: "God having made Man such a Creature, that, in his own Judgment, it was not good for him to be alone, put him under strong Obligations of Necessity, Convenience, and Inclination to drive him into Society, as well as fitted him with Understanding and Language to continue and enjoy it." (*2TG.* § 77) Human being for Locke, too, is *animal rationale*, ζῷον λόγον ἔχον, as articulated in Aristotle's *Politics* and wedded inextricably with that other essential determination of human being, viz. ζῷον πολιτικόν, and the way society is governed also has to be according to and accessible to reason, i.e. rational, and ultimately open to no-longer-metaphysical questioning and grounding in the light of truth as disclosed in the 3D-temporal clearing.

In both Plato's and Aristotle's thinking, society is originally engendered by the exigencies of satisfying need in some kind of division of labour (and not for the sake of the freedom of interplay itself). Society is set up to bring what is good and useful for living into presence and to keep what is bad and harmful for living at bay, in absence. The securing of a material way of life, both positively and negatively, thus stands at the focus of attention, a pragmatic concern. Humans' relations to beings as a whole are marked by the (use-)value or otherwise they have for leading a good life. What is positively valuable and good is desired; what is valuable in the negative sense, i.e. harmful and bad for living, is repelled and must be warded off. The securing of the things necessary for a good life, no matter what shape this good life assumes in its concrete usages in various places at different times, requires safe possession, which is one of the functions society has to fulfil: that of guardianship to protect its citizens' property against the incursions of others from within (theft, robbery, fraud, etc.) or without (war, confiscation, brigandage, freebooting, piracy, etc.). Such protection of private property, however, is necessary in the light of reason not for the sake of the good life, but ultimately for the sake of freedom itself in its exercise as freedom of movement in leading a life.

For Locke as a father of liberalism, individual insight into the need to protect individual freedoms and the private property rights associated with them is a ground for consent to be governed in society by a government. The privacy of private property arises in the first place from the individual's having the freedom to enjoy what it has fairly acquired through an expression of free will and is in its possession, i.e. within reach as immediately present, and to deprive others of access to these things. The individual's private sphere therefore represents a limit and injunction to what can be made a public, shared good, and is the correspondence in the practical sphere to the individualization of truth as discussed in Chapter 10.6. Classical liberalism emphasizes the freedom of the private individual, although it argues on the basis of "the Natural Liberty and Equality of Mankind" in general. There is an ambiguity between the human being as a free individual and humankind as generically free with the consequence that the ontological structure of the freedom of human beings in their *plurality* does not come to its concept. The sociation of individual freedom is dealt with as the intercourse of contract which, however, remains dependent upon the caprice of two individual wills, as if it proceeded from entirely dissociated individual wills, and as if it were a matter of capricious individual will, as an expression of individual freedom, whether sociation took place at all or not.

This leads inevitably to the liberal dilemmas of the individual versus society and the individual versus the state. But such dilemmas are spurious insofar as the private individual on its own is a merely imagined abstraction, just like the worldless subject of subjectivist epistemology, i.e. the private individual who withdraws from society is always *also* the social individual already sociated through the interplay with others, and it is the (abstract, reified) form of sociation through (money-mediated) exchange that historically enables the private individual as a sociated human being in the first place. The historical-metaphysical liberal casting of human being as individually free was only possible *at all* because the form (idea) of sociating through interchanges among individuals had historically gained visible contour as a way of sociating human being in the world, thus calling on thinking to think this look of being as a possibility of human social being in line with freedom.

One could say that humankind had become strong enough to claim its freedom. Freedom as sociated cannot be thought merely as a possibility of withdrawal into privacy, nor as the individual's being free to express its capricious will, but only as the freedom, or free-for-all, of the sociating interplay of powers itself, which involves a plurality of players embodying a plurality of wills which nevertheless find room for play with one another in interchanges of all kinds. Classical liberalism has neglected the ontological structure of the interplay of powers in the practical realm of a plurality of wills, and thus the ontological problematic of esteem, estimation, evaluation, validation, recognition, etc. among both human beings and things. In short, like its successor, non-speculative analytic philosophy, it is *blind to the ontological difference and to the ontology of whoness in particular*. Instead it has imagined the free individual as a subject without a social world, and then tried to derive society from a bunch of atomistic individuals. Human being, however, is always already being-in-the-world, and this means in the present socio-ontological context, that it is being-in-the-social-world through definite forms of sociation.

In the liberal conception, government exists only for the sake of the "life, liberty and estate" of the individual, free members of society; it has no raison d'être in itself nor in a collective entity called a people or a nation. The liberal conception, however, does not include the realization of individual liberty in an interplay of powers as essential to its casting of a "State of Nature". In doing so, it would have had to take into account that, on the basis of private property, economic interaction unfolds, which is marked essentially by the competitive, uncertain striving to earn a living in the gainful game (cf. Chapter 6.8). The free exchange of goods and services on competitive markets is tantamount to a state of anarchy, or rather, to a state of a polyarchic interplay among free, individual origins of power, which the state is not empowered to quell or interfere with, but only to enable and enhance in its fairness. Anarchy is to be understood here in the strict sense that economic exchange is not governed by a single, unified superior ἀρχή, but emerges from the interplay of self-interested movements of many ἀρχαί (cf. Chapter 5). The term 'polyarchy' (cf. Chapter 5.6) is therefore more apt and perhaps less misleading than 'anarchy' that is often equated with lawlessness. The 'anarchy' that arises from 'polyarchy' is not chaos, but a spontaneous 'playful' order that orders itself through corrective cybernetic feedback loops transmitted by a multitude of markets that tell the individual players whether their strivings for gain are being esteemed and enjoying success or not.

The state is only legitimately empowered to guarantee the proper forms of intercourse, or rules of play according to which this economic activity takes place and, at the most, to regulate the workings of the markets for the sake of untrammelled interplay for the sake of the economic participants' well-being by smoothing out its conflicts, frictions and anomalies; it has no legitimation in the liberal conception to set positive aims for itself, since it is regarded as only the facilitator and (negative) guarantor of the individual liberties of the members of society in motion as interplay, based as it is on "the principle that all supreme power must be confined to essentially negative tasks"(Hayek *LLL*3:149.), and these liberties must only be curtailed insofar as the individual liberties of others are infringed, that is, insofar as the vieing and rivalry of the interplay overstep the bounds of fairness, including endangering the playing of the gainful game itself, especially by undermining the very medium of reified value through which it is played (financial crisis).

The liberal state has no legitimate power to curtail the polyarchic play of a capitalist market economy, to interfere with its metabolism as it happens spontaneously through the individualized, unco-ordinated strivings of the members of civil society, for this would be to quell and constrain the play of individual freedom itself in favour of substantial ends posited by the state itself.[231] If hap-

---

231 Hegel assumes a middle position between the liberal and an absolutist conception of state. Although he recognizes the basis of social living in "abstract right", which is the right of personhood, private property and contractual interplay, this basis is to be "aufgehoben" (suspended and lifted to a higher plane) in the State. "But the State is not a contract at all, nor is the protection and securing of the life and property of the individuals as such so unconditionally its substantial essence; rather, the State is the higher instance which itself also makes a claim on this life and property and demands its sacrifice." (Allein der Staat ist überhaupt nicht ein Vertrag, noch ist der *Schutz* und die *Sicherung* des Lebens und Eigentums der Individuen als einzelner so unbedingt sein substantielles Wesen, vielmehr ist er das Höhere, welches dieses Leben und Eigentum selbst auch in Anspruch nimmt und die Aufopferung desselben fordert. *RPh*. § 100 Note). Hegel is right to point out that the state cannot be based on contract, because contract is based on the caprice, the individual will of the individuals entering into it.

piness is to be attained at all, it must be through the hap and chance of good fortune in the power interplay. This impotence of the state in the face of the play of competitive capitalist markets is felt to be inacceptable by many, including above all those in government, who call for the state to intervene positively to revise the outcome of the free play of exchange in favour of realizing something called the 'social good' or (redistributive) 'social justice' (cf. Chapter 6.4 and 6.5) that the state itself posits by will. Such a call for intervention amounts to clipping the wings of (the plural interplay of) individual freedom for the sake of a substantial good called 'social security', i.e. a secure state of affairs in actualized standing presence, that is achieved through the positings of State power, which is now written with a capital 'S' because it has arrogated to itself the status and the power to posit and impose what it thinks best for society, which are substantial aims with which individual citizens may be in agreement or not. As we shall see in Chapter 13, the citizen of a democracy will be free to engage in the political power struggle over what the State posits as its will for the general good. A state of secure welfare of society as a whole in standing presence is to be erected, and this is the aim of politics as opposed to allowing and enabling the fair play of individual freedom in sociating interplay.

The kind of interchange that Locke has in view is principally the contractual exchange of property, which takes place in the striving of individuals to earn a livelihood. We can add the interchanges of all kinds of mutual estimation in which individuals have intercourse with each other and affirm each other in their social standing at least formally as persons, as investigated in Chapter 5.6, and more concretely within the ethos of civility, and more concretely still in the interchanges in which individuals strive for the good of being esteemed by others. The superior power of government exists only[232] to ensure fair rules of inter-

---

Sociated living, however, is not at the disposal of the individual to decide whether it wants in or out. The state exists for the sake of the *freedom* of sociating interplay, which already exceeds individual freedom. But Hegel goes further and allows the State to become an end in itself which can demand its tribute from civil society (taxation) and even sacrifice the lives of its individual members for the sake of defending its existence (war). Ultimately, however, it is individuals who must decide whether to risk or sacrifice their lives for the sake of defending a people's way of living. Therefore Hegel's claim for the State as a higher instance must be reconciled with his equally strong assertion that "only in the will as subjective will can freedom or the will in itself be actual" (Nur im Willen, als subjektivem, kann die Freiheit oder der an sich seiende Wille wirklich sein. *RPh.* § 106).

232 "In all governments, there is a perpetual intestine struggle, open or secret, between AUTHORITY and LIBERTY; and neither of them can ever absolutely prevail in the contest. A great sacrifice of liberty must necessarily be made in every government; yet even the authority, which confines liberty, can never, and perhaps ought never, in any constitution, to become

play among individuals, namely, that their personhood be respected and their private property ownership not be infringed. Disputes over property and personal honour among free individuals require an adjudicator who must be equipped with a superior power to be able to arbitrate effectively and pronounce judgement.

The liberal conception of the state could arise historically only within an hermeneutic cast of human being itself as individually free that re-emerged in the modern age with major figures such as Hobbes, Locke and Descartes, but which harks back to Greek philosophy insofar as the *questioning and quest for truth in which philosophy engages is itself only possible through the exercise of individual freedom*. The casting of human being itself as individually free makes each individual human an ἀρχή, an origin or 'whence' (ὅτι) governing its own freedom of movement, a source of power among many, to be exercised freely in the interplay with other free sources of power. This casting of human being casts human beings *as* free individuals also back onto themselves, so that they have to answer for and rely on themselves through the exercise of their own powers in mutually estimating power plays with others. They can no longer rely on a superior authority to whom they can turn for answers or prescriptions how to live. They also have to care for themselves. The cast of individual freedom pits individuals in competitive, rivalrous play against each other and also allows them to appreciate each others powers, The exercise of individual freedom in power intplay also demands of them insight that they must acknowledge and respect each other as free sources of power, and that this acknowledgement and respect must be guaranteed by a superior adjudicating power, if the power interplay of individual freedom is not to be snuffed out in internecine destruction.

The hermeneutic casting of human being as the free individual is not the metaphysics of modern subjectivity per se, — which is rooted in the traditional ontology of productive movement — precisely because it is thought as a casting of *sociating* human being that has to think a *plurality* of free individuals fathomlessly in interplay with one another, which demands another ontology of movement. This goes entirely against the grain of the metaphysics of modern subjectivity with its will to gain certain effective control of all kinds of movement, including sociating movement, through the mathematizing reduction of all that is, both whats and whos (i.e. of whos conceived *as* whats). The modern individual subject is not of its own positing but is itself an historical, ontological destiny into which we in the West have been cast that has opened up not only

---

quite entire and uncontroulable." D. Hume 'Of the Origin of Government' Essay V, Part I 1752 p. 40.

through *questioning* who we are as human beings in our human mode of being, but also in historically practising the usages of free interchange of both goods and thoughts. Moreover, neither the individual human subject nor individual human subjects in a collectivity is the underlying instance in control, but is itself entwined in the uncontrollable, groundless power interplay among a *plurality* of free human individuals.

The metaphysics of subjectivity, with its still theological orientation toward a supreme principle of will to effective power over all kinds of movement, tacitly adopted by the liberal conception of society and government overlooks not only that the subject always already 'stands out' in the world in its ek-sistence, and is therefore embedded in the world and never merely an isolated ego-point, but also that it is always already in the world with others, entangled in the fathomless interplay of a plurality of many subjects, each of whom is (striving to be) somewho and striving for gain. Because the individual human being in *what* it has depends upon the uncertain, playful metabolism of value-exchanges and because it depends to its core as *who* it is, i.e. in its worth as somewho, upon mirroring interchanges of recognition and estimation, this takes away the ground from under the feet of the modern, knowing, self-conscious Cartesian subject as the purported bedrock for the metaphysics of modern subjectivity, which is still a variant of productionist metaphysics rather than a metaphysics of groundless interplay.

The problematic of how government can be justified at all and reconciled with the mutually estimative power play of (individual) freedom is a problem not only for a liberal thinking, tacitly rooted as it is in the modern metaphysics of subjectivity that proceeds from a worldless ego. It is a problem for *any* thinking that confronts itself with the historical possibility of human freedom *as* social freedom at all, and thus continues as a weighty concern for any genuine philosophical thinking today. Even an anti-liberal thinker such as Heidegger, who undertakes a thorough deconstruction of the metaphysics of subjectivity, can formulate the problem of shared, social being as a *problem of freedom*, at least in 1928: "Being-together in a genuine relationship of existence is only possible if each co-existing human being can be and is properly him or herself. This freedom of being together with one another, however, presupposes first of all the possibility of self-determination of a being of the character of Dasein, and *it is a problem* how Dasein as essentially free can exist in the freedom of factically bound togetherness." (Das Mitsein als eigentliches Existenzverhältnis ist nur so möglich, daß jeder Mitexistierende je eigentlich er selbst sein kann und ist. Diese Freiheit des Miteinander aber setzt die Möglichkeit der Selbstbestimmung eines Seienden vom Charakter des Daseins überhaupt voraus, und *es ist ein*

Problem, wie das Dasein als wesenhaft freies in der Freiheit des faktisch gebundenen Miteinanderseins existieren kann.²³³) The question of how power of one human being over another can be reconciled with human freedom to cast its own self (which is always an expression of power) remains a moving issue for us in the West for as long as we are not seduced by the yearning for an *unquestioning, secure* identity into submitting ourselves willingly and wilfully to something greater such as a State, a Nation, a Church, an Ideal, a God, etc.

12.2 The totalitarian state as a counter-casting to liberalism – The yearning for a totally controlled "organic construction" at the pinnacle of productionist metaphysics (Ernst Jünger)

One example of a voice opposed to bourgeois, individual freedoms and the associated polyarchic interplay of civil society and a capitalist market economy is provided by Ernst Jünger's *Der Arbeiter* (*The Worker* 1932)²³⁴ which has been described by some as "the bible of totalitarianism".²³⁵ It was published at a specific conjuncture in German history, at the turning-point from the collapse of the Weimar Republic to the rise of the National Socialist State, and many readings of Jünger concentrate on this vibrant, unsettled, turbulent historical context. Here, however, the interest is solely in what kind of thinking is contraposed to liberal thinking about society and its government. It is important to get the totalitarian flavour of this strange book. Hence a long quote to start with. According to Jünger, in the bourgeois, liberal conception of civil society,

> Gesellschaft ist der Staat, dessen Wesen sich in demselben Grade verwischt, in dem ihn die Gesellschaft ihren Maßen unterwirft. Dieser Angriff findet durch den Begriff der bürgerlichen Freiheit statt, dessen Aufgabe die Umwandlung aller verantwortlichen Bindungen in Vertragsverhältnisse auf Kündigung ist. Im engsten Verhältnis zur Gesellschaft steht endlich der Einzelne, jene wunderliche und abstrakte Figur des Menschen, die kostbarste Entdeckung der bürgerlichen Empfindsamkeit und zugleich der unerschöpfliche

233 Martin Heidegger *Metaphysische Anfangsgründe der Logik im Ausgang von Leibniz* Summer Semester 1928 *GA*26:175, my emphasis.
234 Cf. Michael E. Zimmerman *Heidegger's Confrontation with Modernity: Technology, Politics, Art* Indiana University Press, Bloomington 1990 Chapter 5 Heidegger's Appropriation of Jünger's Thought pp. 66–76.
235 Letter from Maurice Schneuwly to Ernst Jünger 7 July 1978 in which Schneuwly mentions this accusation levelled by others; published in *Der Arbeiter* 1982 edition Klett-Cotta, Stuttgart S. 314. Here cited by the abbreviation, *Arb.*

Gegenstand ihrer künstlerischen Bildungskraft. Wie die Menschheit der Kosmos dieser Vorstellung, so ist der Mensch ihr Atom. Praktisch allerdings sieht der Einzelne sich nicht der Menschheit gegenüber, sondern der Masse, seinem genauen Spiegelbilde in dieser höchst sonderbaren, höchst imaginären Welt. Denn die Masse und der Einzelne sind eins, und aus dieser Einheit ergibt sich das verblüffende Doppelbild von buntester, verwirrendster Anarchie und der nüchternen Geschäftsordnung der Demokratie, welches das Schauspiel eines Jahrhunderts war. Es gehört aber zu den Kennzeichen einer neuen Zeit, daß in ihr die bürgerliche Gesellschaft, gleichviel ob sie ihren Freiheitsbegriff in der Masse oder im Individuum zur Darstellung bringen möge, zum Tode verurteilt ist. (*Arb.* p. 23)

society is the state whose essence is blurred to the same degree in which society subjects the state to its yardsticks. This attack takes place through the concept of bourgeois/civil freedom whose task is the transformation of all ties of responsibility into contractual relations subject to termination at any time. In the closest of relations with society stands ultimately the individual, that strange, abstract human figure, the most precious discovery of bourgeois sensibility and at the same time the inexhaustible object of its artistic formative power. Just as humanity is the cosmos for this idea, the human individual is its atom. Practically, however, the individual is not confronted with humanity but with the masses, its precise mirror image in this highly strange, highly imaginary world, for the masses and the individual are one, and from this unity results the perplexing double image of the most motley, confusing anarchy and the sober standing orders of democracy which [double image] has been the theatrical spectacle of a century. But it is one of the hallmarks of a new age that in it, civil society, no matter whether it prefers to present its concept of freedom in the form of the masses or the individual, is condemned to death.

According to Jünger, this bourgeois or civil society is "condemned to death". By whose agency? Through the rise of "the Gestalt of the worker" (die Gestalt des Arbeiters, *Arb.* p. 89) which, as a Gestalt of "being" (Sein, *Arb.* p. 92) representing a "mastery of the world" (Meisterung der Welt, *Arb.* p. 89) through "the emergence of a new principle to be designated as *labour*" (das Auftreten eines neuen Prinzips, das als *Arbeit* bezeichnet werden soll, *Arb.* p. 89), is destined to shape the world anew in a "total mobilization" (Totale Mobilmachung, *Arb.* p. 40). "The total work character, however, is the way in which the Gestalt of the worker begins to permeate the world." (Der totale Arbeitscharakter aber ist die Art und Weise, in der die Gestalt des Arbeiters die Welt zu durchdringen beginnt. *Arb.* p. 103) Society will then be composed of workers from bottom to top.

The inevitable emergence of the Gestalt of the worker signifies for Jünger the rise of a "metaphysical power" (metaphysische Macht, *Arb.* p. 119) which "as technology, mobilizes matter" (die als Technik die Materie mobilisiert, *Arb.* p. 119). This metaphysically underpinned historical prediction is expressed in the form of a critique of the bourgeois individual and civil society according to which the bourgeois conception of the state attacks the latter's true essence by subjecting it to its own "yardsticks", namely, the form of contractual intercourse which can provide no basis for the state because the contractual form of inter-course purportedly lacks that binding tie of responsibility which the state needs. Jünger is proposing instead something solid and binding and also does not refrain from expressing some ironic contempt for "bourgeois sensibility". The abstractness of the "strange, abstract human figure" is due to the atomistic nature of civil society composed as it is of private individuals, each with their own individual interests and strivings which result in a "motley, confusing anarchy" (which elsewhere in this study I call the power interplay of free indi-viduals in civil society) that is apparently antipathetic for Jünger, lacking the unity of a single, superior state will that is truly in control. The bourgeois indi-vidual with its associations and parties, which is a merely "abstract figure" of the human, is to be replaced by workers inserted into "organic constructions" (organische Konstruktionen, *Arb.* p. 119) which presumably allow humans to become more concrete and rooted:

> Einer organischen Konstruktion gehört man nicht durch individuellen Willensentschluß, also durch Ausübung eines Aktes der bürgerlichen Freiheit, sondern durch eine tatsächli-che Verflechtung an, die der spezielle Arbeitscharakter bestimmt. So ist es, um ein bana-les Beispiel zu wählen, ebenso leicht, in eine Partei einzutreten oder aus ihr auszutreten, wie es schwierig ist, aus Verbandsarten auszutreten, denen man etwa als Empfänger von elektrischen Strom angehört. (*Arb.* p. 119f)

> One does not belong to an organic construction through an individual decision of will, that is, by exercising an act of civil freedom, but through a factual involvement which the particular work character determines. To take a banal example, it is just as easy to join or leave a party as it is difficult to leave those kinds of association to which one belongs, say, as the recipient of electricity.

The "banal example" is in fact telling, because the ease with which consumers can change their electricity supplier is in fact a basic feature of bourgeois, capi-talist market interplay, including a multiplicity of competing electricity suppli-ers. Jünger apparently wants individuals to be bound organically through re-sponsibility and objective ties into a larger, unified, controlled whole and to be unable to exercise their merely individual will. A larger, more encompassing, totalizing will and central power is obviously envisaged to which individual will can only submit. The totality is particularized, into its particular organs into which individual workers are inserted. The economy itself, Jünger predicts, will not remain untouched by the rise of the Gestalt of the worker:

> Der geheime Sinn jedes Wirtschaftskampfes unserer Zeit läuft darauf hinaus, die Wirt-schaft auch in ihrer Totalität in den Rang einer organischen Konstruktion zu erheben, als welche sie der Initiative sowohl des isolierten als auch des en masse auftretenden Indivi-

duums entzogen ist. Dies kann aber erst geschehen, wenn der Menschenschlag, der sich in anderen Formen als in diesen gar nicht begreifen kann, ausgestorben oder zum Aussterben gezwungen worden ist. (*Arb.* p. 120f)

The secret meaning of every economic struggle of our time amounts to elevating the economy even in its totality to the status of an organic construction which as such is withdrawn from the initiative not only of the isolated individual but also of individuals appearing en masse. But this can only happen once the human type or breed of humans who cannot conceive of themselves at all in anything but in these terms has become extinct or has been forced into extinction.

The elevation of the economy to "the status of an organic construction" is the same totalizing aim of history envisaged by revolutionary socialism in which individual initiative is to be extinguished in favour of total state economic control, the pinnacle of a productionist metaphysical conception in the sociopolitical realm. The bourgeois individual with its individual civil liberties and entwined in interplay is to be replaced by the "type" of the worker, which is the stamp which the metaphysical Gestalt of the worker imprints upon a new "race" or "breed of humans" or "human type" (Menschenschlag, *Arb.* p. 295), where race "has nothing to do with biological concepts of race" (mit biologischen Rassebegriffen nichts zu schaffen hat, p. 152). The forced "extinction" of the bourgeois individual and its individual freedom signals political repression and violence. The "type" of the worker is the "impression of the Gestalt" (Abdruck der Gestalt, *Arb.* p. 151) and "one must make an effort to see through the steely and human masks of the times to surmise the Gestalt, the metaphysics which moves them" (..., muß man sich allerdings bemühen, durch die stählernen und menschlichen Masken der Zeit hindurchzusehen, um die Gestalt, die Metaphysik, zu erraten, die sie bewegt. *Arb.* p. 130). In the transformation of all collectivity into "organic constructions" within a "genuine state" (im echten Staat, *Arb.* p. 264) lies the totalitarian streak in Jünger's conception, since "the type knows no dictatorship because for it freedom and obedience are identical" (Der Typus kennt keine Diktatur, weil Freiheit und Gehorsam für ihn identisch sind. *Arb.* p. 151).

In contrast to the liberal conception of freedom in which the bourgeois individual is guaranteed freedom *from* interference by others, including above all by the state, thus enabling the ongoing, fathomless power interplay that is civil society, the rise of the Gestalt of the worker signifies "another kind of conception of freedom, for which rule and service are synonymous, [and which ME] is to be melted down into the state as the most important and most comprehensive means of change" (...ein andersartiger Freiheitsbegriff, dem Herrschaft und Dienst gleichbedeutend sind, in den Staat als das wichtigste und umfassendste

Mittel der Veränderung eingeschmolzen werden soll. *Arb.* p. 247). Jünger's totalitarian conception of "freedom" does away with mere individual freedom, which is merely "bourgeois". In this totalitarian conception of "freedom" as synonymous with "obedience", the individual in its singularity is a priori welded or 'closed together' with the universality of the totality, i.e. singularity is eliminated through a sham identification that has extinguished all contradiction, all gainsaying. This is the kind of language familiar also from Marxism, Stalinism and Maoism. Freedom of the individual from the state is denounced as a sham and becomes freedom to serve and obey the state to which the worker belongs in a totalitarian identity as part of an "organic construction" that provides room for difference only through the controlled particularization of the totality. Unlike the bourgeois individual, which is said to be the product of "abstract reason" and "virtue", and who finds its place in the totality through playing in the competitive interplay, the worker as type is said to be the embodiment of "purely elementary currents" (rein elementaren Strömungen, *Arb.* p. 255) and "instinct" (Instinkt, *Arb.* p. 265, a Nietzschean term); indeed, in the case of the German people, it is said to "possess a sure instinct for command and obedience" (einen sicheren Instinkt für Befehl und Gehorsam besitzt, *Arb.* p. 263).

Another way of putting this is to say that the German people is the Western people most 'thoroughly' (gründlich) enamoured with productivist metaphysics' ideal of total control and a correlative abhorrence of free interplay of individual powers. The irony of Heidegger's critique of the Gestell (set-up) as the essence of modern technology is that the German people itself is the people par excellence of the set-up, even and especially to the extent of transferring the mathematico-technological way of thinking of the modern sciences to the setting-up of society itself as a Gestell for *caring for* and thus *ruling over* a people. This is so even and especially today in the much-applauded sozialstaatlichen Gestell, when the Germans are supposedly now become a free, democratic people. Heidegger's notorious remark that "agriculture is now motorized food industry, in its essence the same as the fabrication of corpses in gas chambers and extermination camps" (Ackerbau ist jetzt motorisierte Ernährungsindustrie, im Wesen das Selbe wie die Fabrikation von Leichen in Gaskammern und Vernichtungslagern, 'Das Ge-Stell' *GA*79:27) has a special significance for a people so lacking an historical instinct for freedom and whose estimated standing in historical time is indelibly sullied by its mass murdering in the gas chambers of the Second World War.

In 1932, Heidegger, who enthusiastically, energetically, but also critically, took up Jünger's book when it first appeared at that time, characterizes "liberalism" (in the form of Neo-Kantianism which "is tailored to liberalism") similarly as a way of thinking in which the "human essence was dissolved into a free-floating consciousness in general and this ultimately thinned into a universal logical world-reason", thus "deflecting the view from humans in their historical rootedness and the folk-bound tradition of their origins in soil and blood" (Das Wesen des Menschen wurde da [im Neukantianismus, der "dem Liberalismus auf den Leib zugeschnitten ist",] aufgelöst in ein freischwebendes Bewußtsein überhaupt und dieses schließlich verdünnt zu einer allgemein logischen Weltvernunft. Auf diesem Weg wurde unter scheinbar streng wissenschaftlicher philosophischer Begründung der Blick abgelenkt vom Menschen in seiner geschichtlichen Verwurzelung und in seiner volkhaften Überlieferung seiner Herkunft aus Boden und Blut.[236]). There is a swipe in this passage at modern philosophical thinking from Descartes through to Kant and even Hegel (Weltvernunft). Ironically, Hegel is here classified as a liberal. Let us return to *Der Arbeiter*.

There is a yearning in Jünger for an identity in totality, a longing for overcoming τὰ πολλά in τὸ ἕν, i.e. the many in the one, in which "bourgeois", individual will and freedom are suppressed and extirpated:

> Viele Anzeichen lassen erkennen, daß wir vor den Pforten eines Zeitalters stehen, in dem wieder von wirklicher Herrschaft, von Ordnung und Unterordnung, von Befehl und Gehorsam die Rede sein kann. Keines dieser Anzeichen spricht deutlicher als die freiwillige Zucht, der die Jugend sich zu unterwerfen beginnt, ihre Verachtung der Genüsse, ihr kriegerischer Sinn, ihr erwachendes Gefühl für männliche und unbedingte Wertungen. (*Arb.* p. 246)

> There are many signs indicating that we stand at the gateway of an age in which one can again speak of genuine domination, of order and subordination, of command and obedience. None of these signs speaks more plainly than the voluntary discipline to which the youth is beginning to subject itself, its contempt for enjoyment, its warlike intent, its growing sense for manly and absolute values.

What is interesting here is not Jünger's prediction (and whether it has been fulfilled), nor simply his political views, nor merely his authoritarian, militarist, masculinist language, nor even the fact that he "welcomes this work" (wir begrüßen diese Arbeit, *Arb.* p. 307) on the historical emergence on the Gestalt of the worker, but, firstly, the purported metaphysical underpinnings of the entire work, *Der Arbeiter*, and secondly, in what way *Der Arbeiter* is to be understood

---

236 Letter to Einhauser about the Neo-Kantian Hönigswald dated 25 June 1933 and signed "Heil Hitler!" in *GA*16:132 No. 65.

as a decisive, totalitarian answer to the bourgeois, liberal conception of freedom and the corresponding liberal conception of state.

As has been shown, the liberal conception of state is that government is based on the consent of the individual members of society to subject themselves to a superior power for the sake of protecting the individual's "life, liberty and estate" and hence the interplay of powers that is the metabolism of civil society enabled by the æther of fair play in the medium of reified value as investigated in previous chapters.

The metaphysical, i.e. onto-theological, Gestalt of the worker is not only an answer and retort to "that anarchic-individualist element which is characteristic of all the formations of liberalism" (jenes anarchisch-individualistische Element [...], das allen Bildungen des Liberalismus eigentümlich ist. *Arb.* p. 252), but is also the constitution of a unified totality in which the singularity of the individual is suppressed, extinguished, absorbed into and made congruent with the universal whole through relations of subservience and obedience that insert the individual into its particular slot in the organic totality. This figure of a diremption or disjunction between singularity and universality or the individual and the state as the governing instance of society, and the overcoming of this diremption, runs throughout the entire political philosophical thinking of the modern age. Jünger resolves it by pronouncing, in militaristic fashion, obedience to a totalitarian state to be freedom itself in a simple, non-dialectical identity. The final act of individual freedom is thus the individual's 'free' submission to total state rule, its binding commitment to a superior, authoritarian will.

What is the metaphysical origin of the diremption between the individual and the state? It lies in the essence of human sociation itself which, as laid out in detail in preceding chapters, resides ultimately in the mutually estimating power interplay among whos, and therefore requires an explicit socio-ontology of whoness to come into clear focus. Already the elementary form of practical sociation represented by exchange of goods (if we leave to one side the ontologically more fundamental interplay of estimation among individuals), as has been shown in the pivotal Chapter 5, depends on the concurrence of two governing starting-points, which may be considered as two individuals who are free in the sense that the exchange only takes place if the two individual wills concur. Exchange is an-archic in the sense that it does not have a single ἀρχή, but two, and is thus 'bi-archic'. A market economy has myriad initiating starting-points for economic action through exchange and is thus in the literal sense 'polyarchic' or 'multiarchic'.

A single ἀρχή in sociating interplay can only be achieved if one ἀρχή submits to the other, allowing it to command. The relation of command and obedience is the alternative elementary ontological paradigm for human sociation (cf. Hegel's dialectic of master and servant, Chapter 11.1) complementing the elementary ontological paradigm of exchange interplay of powers. Submission reinstitutes a single ἀρχή, for the one submitting is no longer a free starting-point of its own self-movement but only an extension of the other, commanding ἀρχή. This power relation results in social hierarchy in which there are those who wield power and those who submit to it and are therefore nominally 'powerless' (but in truth are only repressed). The word 'hierarchy' comes from Greek ἱεραρχία meaning 'the power to rule of a high priest', derived from ἱερός and ἀρχή, hence 'super-human, divine, wonderful, holy rule', but today the word has a completely secular signification. Hierarchy is a model, an ontological mode, of human sociation which allows a single ἀρχή to rule through a chain of command and obedience, and thus it engenders order and predictability as long as subordinates obey (or can be enticed or coerced to obey).

The liberal conception of society concedes that the form of sociating interplay represented by exchange is not sufficient for the constitution of society and that there is thus the necessity for government, which can be regarded as a kind of superior ἀρχή for the whole of society that is to guarantee and enforce only its *forms* of intercourse, its *formal* rules of competitive power interplay as fair rules of play. The driving motive of liberalism, however, is to keep the necessity for rule and all sorts of hierarchy to a minimum in order to preserve and enable as much as possible the many ἀρχαί of initiating individuals as the multiple, free, governing starting-points for social interplay. For this reason, in liberal thinking, individuals have to consent to and have insight into the necessity of being ruled, thus insofar relinquishing their individual freedom. This, however, does not amount to overcoming the diremption between singularity and universality, the individual and the state, but only their power-playful mediation. Rule is consented to only insofar as it preserves and ensures the forms of intercourse of exchange and the interplay of mutual estimation. Social freedom itself is only possible socio-ontologically as this interplay of powers.

At the other end of the spectrum, authoritarian thinkers such as Jünger and Heidegger make the case for or are inclined to the paradigm of hierarchy as the mode of sociation since hierarchy creates a consistent, orderly, precalculable social whole governed by a unified superior will, an admired 'strong hand', which is therefore, apparently, more capable of acting in a unified way. Individual consent to and insight into the necessity of being ruled is replaced by the call to subordination and obedience, to commitment and obligation, and freedom itself is seen to lie in the act of submission to a superior, commanding will, a 'necessity' spuriously opposed to the alleged 'mere caprice' of individual freedom. Authoritarian thinkers therefore invariably express admiration for organizations such as the military or the Roman Catholic Church which is a highly successful historical example of hierarchical sociation in a literal sense, since in this organization it is truly the 'high priests' who rule by virtue of embodying holy, divine, unified truth. The Pope's supposed infallibility with respect to the one, unified, revealed truth goes hand in hand with super-human, holy, divine rule by authority. For many, such unity and submission are seen as remedies to a splintering of truth whose tensions and contradictions are experienced as insufferable (cf. Chapter 10.6).

When Jünger claims that the Gestalt of the worker is emerging as a shaping metaphysical force, he is expressly delineating another hermeneutic cast of being, for otherwise the worker's Gestalt would not be metaphysical; it would not be a shape of "being" (Sein, *Arb.* p. 92). A cast of being is always totalizing, encompassing the totality of beings and how the world opens up, presenting itself in its truth within historical time. The singular individual, the germ of the bourgeois form of society and of civil liberty, is to be dissolved in this new cast of the beingness of beings, which is also a cast of mind, and absorbed into an authoritarian totality in which the state commands its people.

The bourgeois individual is a private individual, i.e. it is withdrawn from the realm of the state and maintains an independence and freedom which the bourgeois-liberal state cannot legitimately touch, and it practises a self-reliance and self-responsibility in competitive interplay, in which it exercises its powers, which the bourgeois-liberal state is bound to only encourage, support and facilitate with fair rules of play that the state is obliged to posit and enforce as law. In its legally guaranteed private sphere the bourgeois individual thus deprives the state of control, mastery and command which, however, Jünger predicts will give way to "the possibility of new, terrible invasions of the state into the private sphere which are afoot under the mask of hygienic and social care" (die Möglichkeit neuer, furchtbarer Einbrüche des Staates in die private Sphäre, die unter der Maske der hygienischen und sozialen Fürsorge im Anzuge sind. *Arb.* p. 107). Private property, which likewise essentially characterizes the bourgeois individual, also represents a limitation and deprivation of state control and command which, however, will no longer be respected. The thin end of the wedge in this process that erodes individual freedom and its private sphere, thus effectively dissolving liberalism, is the care which the state provides for its citizens in the name of public health, social welfare (including especially healthcare) and (redistributive) social justice. Private property will be subordinated to the exigencies and requirements of the total, organic work-plan.

> Es gehört zu den Kennzeichen des liberalen Denkstils, daß sowohl die Angriffe auf das Ei-
> gentum wie seine Rechtfertigungen sich auf einer ethischen Grundlage vollziehen. In der
> Arbeitswelt handelt es sich jedoch nicht darum, ob die Tatsache des Eigentums sittlich
> oder unsittlich ist, sondern lediglich darum, ob sie im Arbeitsplan unterzubringen ist.
> (*Arb.* p. 288)

> One of the hallmarks of the liberal style of thinking is that both attacks against and justifi-
> cations of property take place on an ethical foundation. In the work world, however, it is
> not a matter of whether the fact of property is ethical or unethical, but solely of whether it
> can be incorporated into the work-plan.

The total work-state regards private property in a purely functional way according to its appropriateness and efficiency for total mobilization. Ethical considerations of justice and the preservation of individual freedom are dispensed with
as lacking substance, as ontological figments. In this totalitarian cast of social
being, technical, functional, efficiency considerations of "objective connections" (sachliche Zusammenhänge, *Arb.* pp. 127, 147) under the totalizing command of the state gain predominance. The total, organic construction of the
state with its particularized functional organs and workers with their "rational
and technical masks" (den rationalen und technischen Masken, *Arb.* p. 127)
must work coldly and efficiently. Efficiency replaces individual freedom as criterion.

Somewhat paradoxically, the total control and calculability of the work-
plan which are to overcome and replace the anarchy of markets and competition are supposed to be compatible with establishing "a new relationship with
the elemental" (ein neues Verhältnis zum Elementaren, *Arb.* p. 48) which has
two faces: "the world, which is always dangerous" (die Welt, die immer gefähr-
lich ist, *Arb.* p. 52) and "the human heart, which longs for games and adven-
tures, for hate and love, for triumphs and falls, which feels a need just as much
for danger as for security" (im menschlichen Herzen, / das sich nach Spielen
und Abenteuern, nach Haß und Liebe, nach Triumphen und Abstürzen sehnt,
das sich der Gefahr ebenso bedürftig fühlt wie der Sicherheit, *Arb.* p. 52f). The
bourgeois individual, by contrast, is said to be incapable of these elemental
extremes and instead "acknowledges security as a highest value and determines
its way of living accordingly" (... der Bürger, [...] der die Sicherheit als einen
höchsten Wert erkennt und demgemäß seine Lebensführung bestimmt. *Arb.*
p. 50).

The bourgeois individual, Jünger claims, has no inner urge to risk danger,
i.e. to enter into uncertain power interplays. Instead, it endeavours to achieve
an "ideal state of security" through a "world dominion of bourgeois reason
which is supposed not only to diminish the sources of danger but ultimately to

dry them up" (Der ideale Zustand der Sicherheit [...] besteht in der Weltherrschaft der bürgerlichen Vernunft, die die Quellen des Gefährlichen nicht nur vermindern, sondern zuletzt auch zum Versiegen bringen soll. *Arb.* p. 51). This striving of bourgeois reason is said to be apparent in "the comprehensive set-up of an insurance system through which not only the risks of foreign and domestic politics, but also those of private life are to be evenly distributed and thus subordinated to reason, in strivings in which one tries to dissolve destiny by means of probability calculations" (im umfassenden Aufbau eines Versicherungssystems, durch das nicht nur das Risiko der äußeren und inneren Politik, sondern auch das des privaten Lebens gleichmäßig verteilt und damit der Vernunft unterstellt werden soll — in Bestrebungen, in denen man das Schicksal durch die Wahrscheinlichkeitsrechnung aufzulösen sucht. *Arb.* p. 51).

But precisely the longing and striving for social security, and perhaps also a secure, functional social identity, could be said to be a hallmark of the "totalitarian social welfare state" (totalitärer Sozialstaat, Otto Graf Lambsdorff) whether it be erected on a capitalist base or not. Jünger's "heroic realism" with its closeness to the elemental seeks out the challenge of danger and has nothing but contempt for the attempts of bourgeois reason to make risk and danger calculable for the bourgeois individual. Ironically, it is precisely the bourgeois individual, and especially the great or small entrepreneurial bourgeois individual, that is prepared to accept the risky challenges and tough competitive fights of the polyarchy of the markets and the dangers and incalculable risks of competition which, in ever-new and surprising constellations of play that recur at irregular intervals, can mean bankruptcy and financial ruin. Even the existence of insurance companies and probability calculations does not rid the capitalist economic system of risk and danger, but at most contains it, so much so, that the economic annihilation of participants in a capitalist economy, both individual and corporate, is a normal, recurring phenomenon of capitalism, often lamented and criticized as 'inhuman'. In being responsible for itself, the individual must seek its own way through the maze of market exchanges and power plays. The risk-averse bourgeois individual (who tends to seek shelter under the state's all-encompassing umbrella) is such precisely because the world is essentially risky in its individualized forms of the sociating interplay of powers.

Not even "bourgeois reason" is able to master this risk, even though it may delude itself that this is somehow possible, say, through the models of economic theory. Nor can it be mastered by technology, since the sociating movement of human beings brings the fathomless, unpredictable interplay of freedom into play. Nor can even the social welfare state provide the rock-solid social security it promises if it ignores the continually changing challenges of a world market

economy. Jünger does not see, or simply despises, the dangers that lie essentially within a way of life based on uncertain market exchanges and civil interchanges. Nor, at the other pole, does he consider the security of existence and
identity that resides in obeying and serving a totalitarian state. Instead, he remarks contemptuously that "the citizen has almost succeeded in persuading the
adventurous heart that danger does not exist at all and that an economic law
rules the world and its history" (Fast ist es dem Bürger gelungen, das abenteuer-
liche Herz davon zu überzeugen, daß das Gefährliche gar nicht vorhanden ist
und daß ein ökonomisches Gesetz die Welt und ihre Geschichte regiert. *Arb.*
p. 55). This is a curious, self-contradictory remark, considering that the "economic law" of capitalism is market "anarchy" which very well provides room for
an "adventurous heart" to risk danger, whereas the totalitarian state promises
the abolition of the uncertainties and incalculabilities arising from individual
freedoms and also the secure identification of the singular individual with its
function within the organic totalitarian whole.

In Jünger's cast of a world conforming to the metaphysical Gestalt of the
worker that overcomes the "lack of totality" (Mangel an Totalität, *Arb.* p. 156),
"the total work-character [...] is the way in which the Gestalt of the worker begins to permeate the world" (Der totale Arbeitscharakter aber ist die Art und
Weise, in der die Gestalt des Arbeiters die Welt zu durchdringen beginnt. *Arb.*
p. 103) and "technology is the way in which the Gestalt of the worker mobilizes
the world" (Die Technik ist die Art und Weise, in der die Gestalt des Arbeiters
die Welt mobilisiert. *Arb.* p. 156). The total work-character of the world and
technology as the means for total mobilization of the world thus go hand in
hand in Jünger's conception. What is removed is the *adventure of the free interplay of singular, individual human powers*.

Totalization is thought here as total control and calculability on the basis of
a total work-plan, and technology is regarded as the means par excellence for
exercising total control. But it is doubtful whether the totalization of the work-
character of human existence has to assume the form of total control and
whether technology is the appropriate ultimate means for total mobilization of
the world. For, the totalization of work as mode of living conforms to the way in
which the movement of capital itself in its striving for profit, as one major moment in the overall striving for gain, mobilizes the world in its totality without,
however, such totalization requiring or allowing total control and calculability,
since not only does capital's movement of self-augmentation always have to
contend essentially with the incalculability of interplay, but the very movement
of self-augmentation under entrepreneurial leadership is stimulated by incalculability in the guise of competitive struggle. Moreover, technology itself is only a

(productivity-enhancing) means for capital in its competitive, 'playful' striving to which the totalitarian state with its striving for total control is antithetical.

Can a totalitarian state do better than competitive capitalism in achieving efficiency in the deployment of technology? Capital employs technology as a means to increase productivity and thus enhance the *chances* of its self-augmentation. Each capital is particular and exposed to the uncertainties of the (world) market, so that the results achieved in the striving for profit feed back into the way the capital can and does act, finding and re-finding its niche in the totality. Moreover, each individual economic agent is motivated by the incentive of individual gain and is *mobilized* thus to form part of the power-playful totality of capitalist economic activity. Such total mobilization does not require the identification of the worker (now conceived as encompassing all the capitalist economic agents right up to chief executive officers) with the state in a total organic construction demanding subservience and obedience.

Rather, on the contrary, it can even be questioned whether obedience is an adequate, efficient form for total mobilization[237] since it requires that individuals deny and suppress their individuality (and individual initiative) and instead subjugate themselves to serving an explicitly authoritarian hierarchy, with all its inevitable inertia, friction and inefficiency, strangely called "work-democracy" (Arbeitsdemokratie, *Arb.* pp. 268, 270, 271) in which "the break-through from work as a kind of life to life-style takes place" (vollzieht sich der Durchbruch von der Arbeit als Lebensart zum Lebensstil. *Arb.* p. 270). Such self-denial and suppression of individual interest and initiative re-emerges surreptitiously in phenomena such as lassitude and corruption which are only the reverse side of the coin to obedience and the willingness to serve. Or does Jünger, like many other totalitarian thinkers on the left or right, envisage that the "new breed" of worker-humans will have overcome petty individuality? It can also be asked whether it is not precisely bourgeois capitalism within which work becomes a kind of "life-style".

Totalitarian thinking, exemplified here by Jünger, is characterized by a suppression and elimination of individual will and individual freedom in favour

---

237 There is the further question of what "total mobilization" can mean, i.e. whether it maintains its sinister Nietzschean ring of a "will to power" that permeates the world, setting all beings into motion, and culminating in what Heidegger calls the "will to will", a formula for some kind of senseless circular movement in which all things and human beings are caught up, or whether the term "total mobilization" could have a more benign meaning of a movement of life in the sense of everybody being taken up into a movement in which they can strive to develop, realize and valorize their individual abilities in mutually estimative, mutually beneficial, competitive interplay with one another.

of a total "organic" construction of command and obedience. This is a crude and violent 'solution' to how singularity could be mediated with universality. In Jünger's cast of the worker, there is still room for an elite of mandarins, a kind of latter-day aristocracy consisting of the 'best' who have the task not so much of obeying and serving, but of leading and commanding. Intellectuals proposing totalitarianism and enamoured with totalitarian solutions of social unity invariably count themselves among this commanding elite rather than on the side of the willingly subjugated.

12.2.1 Heidegger's anti-liberal interpretation of the German tradition in 1933 (W. v. Humboldt, Kant, Hegel)

Ernst Jünger's totalitarian thinking in *Der Arbeiter* and especially his metaphysics of the Gestalt of the worker had considerable influence on Martin Heidegger at the beginning of the 1930s,[238] when National Socialism came to power in Germany under the leadership of Adolf Hitler. At this time, Heidegger had placed his hopes in and engaged with the National Socialist movement, and in this context, shortly after he resigned as Rector of Freiburg University, gave two short speeches to foreign students at the university which are published as No. 155 *Die deutsche Universität, Zwei Vorträge in den Ausländerkursen der Freiburger Universität, 15. und 16. August 1934* (The German University: Two lectures given in the courses for foreign students at Freiburg University) in the *Gesamtausgabe* Band 16 pp. 285ff. It is an interesting, revealing piece, somewhat different in character from Heidegger's notorious speech on assuming the rectorship of Freiburg University in 1933, *Die Selbstbehauptung der deutschen Universität* (The Self-Assertion of the German University). No. 155 could be criticized on details, but that would be unfair because it is so short and aims only at giving foreign students an overview. So I will concentrate on the essentials. To say it straight out: Heidegger is under a massive delusion with regard to his hopes of reshaping and reasserting (Selbstbehauptung) the German university in a reconstitution of the German spirited mind. And this delusion does *not* concern primarily Heidegger having pinned his hopes on Adolf Hitler (*GA*16:302), but for deeper, essential *philosophical* reasons that have to be worked out right down into the ontological depths. Let me make a few prelimi-

---

238 Cf. e.g. 'The German student as worker' (Der Deutsche Student als Arbeiter), a speech Heidegger gave at the immatriculation ceremony on 25 November 1933 in *Gesamtausgabe* Bd. 16 ed. H. Heidegger, Klostermann, Frankfurt/M: No. 108 pp. 198ff.

nary points about No. 155 that may at least clear the way for assessing philosophically Heidegger's political stance and make my assertion plausible.

i) Heidegger's pedagogic effort with foreign students in these talks is directed at finding a way back to the task set in those days, the heyday of German philosophy and Dichtung, in the period up to 1830:

> Drei große Mächte haben dabei zusammengewirkt: 1. die neue deutsche Dichtung (Klopstock, Herder, Goethe, Schiller und die Romantik), 2. die neue deutsche Philosophie (Kant, Fichte, Schleiermacher, Schelling, Hegel), 3. der neue deutsche politische Wille der preußischen Staatsmänner und Soldaten (Freiherr von Stein, Hardenberg, Humboldt, Scharnhorst, Gneisenau und von Clausewitz). Dichter und Denker schufen eine neue geistige Welt, in der das Walten der Natur und die Mächte der Geschichte einheitlich im Wesen des Absoluten zusammengespannt und -gedacht wurden. (*GA*16:291)

> Three great powers worked together: 1) the new Germany poetry (Klopstock, Herder, Goethe, Schiller and Romanticism), 2) the new German philosophy (Kant, Fichte, Schleiermacher, Schelling, Hegel), 3) the new German political will of Prussian statesmen and soldiers (Freiherr von Stein, Hardenberg, Humboldt, Scharnhorst, Gneisenau und von Clausewitz). Poets and thinkers created a new spiritual/intellectual world in which the prevailing of nature and the powers of history were held together and thought together in a unified way in the essence of the Absolute.

We see immediately that the attempt to find a way back does not by any means entail that the tradition of German liberalism, as embodied in Kant or Humboldt is to be taken up again, but is rather a return to a world held together in the unity of the Absolute. Liberal elements such as the following are to be purged in this attempted return to the great tradition of German philosophy and poetry. Wilhelm von Humboldt wrote in 1792:

> Der Staat enthalte sich aller Sorgfalt für den positiven Wohlstand der Bürger, und gehe keinen Schritt weiter, als zu ihrer Sicherstellung gegen sich selbst und gegen auswärtige Feinde notwendig ist. Um für die Sicherheit der Bürger Sorge zu tragen, muß der Staat diejenigen, sich unmittelbar allein auf den Handelnden beziehenden Handlungen verbieten oder einschränken, deren Folge die Rechte anderer kränken, die ohne oder gegen die Einwilligung derselben ihre Freiheit oder ihren Besitz schmälern. Jede weitere oder aus anderen Gesichtspunkten gemachte Beschränkung der Privatfreiheit aber liegt außerhalb der Grenzen der Wirksamkeit des Staates.[239]

> The state should desist from all care for the positive well-being of its citizens and should not go any further than is necessary to secure them against themselves and foreign ene-

---

239 Wilhelm von Humboldt *Ideen zu einem Versuch, die Grenzen der Wirksamkeit des Staates zu bestimmen* 1792 Verlag Freies Geistesleben, Stuttgart 1962 S. 44f.

mies. To care for its citizens, the state must prohibit or restrict actions connected directly with the actors alone whose consequences offend the rights of others, and which without or against assent to these actions lessen their freedom or their property. Any further restriction of private freedom or restriction made from other perspectives, however, lies outside the limits of the state's effectivity.

The title of Humboldt's essay concerns the "limits" of the state. These limits constitute the private sphere of civil society, the realm of life of its citizens in which they are free as individuals to pursue their aims and in which the state is deprived of control. The state's role is only to ensure that the private citizens do not "offend" each other's rights. This is the classical liberal way of thinking that allows for the plural freedom of individuals in mutually estimating interplay with one another. Notice also Humboldt's use of the words "Sorgfalt für" (care for) and "Sorge" (care) and compare it with Heidegger's understanding of National Socialism as "care for the inner order of the people's community" (Sorge um die innere Ordnung der Gemeinschaft des Volkes. GA16:304). In Heidegger's conception, the state is to care for the German people in their unity rather than for the unifying rules of sociating intercourse among its private citizens.

Humboldt's liberal thinking is echoed by Kant when he insists on the "freedom", "equality" and "independence/self-reliance" (Selbständigkeit) of "every link/member of a common system/community" (jedes Glied eines gemeinen Wesens[240]) Kant understands freedom in this essay as:

> Niemand kann mich zwingen, auf seine Art [...] glücklich zu sein, sondern ein jeder darf seine Glückseligkeit auf dem Wege suchen, welcher ihm selbst gut dünkt, wenn er nur der Freiheit anderer, einem ähnlichen Zwecke nachzustreben, [...] nicht Abbruch tut. (WVI:145)

> No one can force me to be happy in his own way [...], but rather, each individual may seek his happiness in the way that seems best to him as long as he does not impair the freedom of others to strive for a similar purpose. (WVI:145)

This conception of freedom as individual, bourgeois, civil liberty is not taken up by Heidegger, but is here tacitly rejected and in other places treated with disdain. For Heidegger in 1934, freedom is "*freedom* as a binding to the law of the people's spirit" (*Freiheit* als Bindung an das Gesetz des Volksgeistes, GA16:295) and he claims that muddle-headedly it was only *after* 1830 that "the binding to

---

240 I. Kant *Über den Gemeinspruch: Das mag in der Theorie richtig sein, taugt aber nicht für die Praxis* II. Vom Verhältnis der Theorie zur Praxis im Staatsrecht *Werke* Bd. VI ed. Weischedel, Wiss. Buchgesell., Darmstadt 1964 S. 145.

the law of the people's spirit was turned upside down into the arbitrariness of views and individual opinion" (die Bindung an das Gesetz des Volksgeistes wurde in das Gegenteil verkehrt: Beliebigkeit der Ansichten und des Meinens des Einzelnen, *GA*16:295).

For Heidegger, like other anti-liberal thinkers, the multitude of differing views of individuals is something merely arbitrary, lacking in self-responsibility, which is to be overcome in a unified knowing that knows the "law of the people's spirit". How can such a unifying law be known? And how can a "binding" into this unity be attained? Heidegger's conception of freedom assumes that a single truth is possible that unifies a people, thus not only that a people shares an open time-clearing of historical truth in which it lives in historically given ways of life with their corresponding understandings (and hence truths), but that there is *a knowable* truth that unifies and binds the people together in a knowing, willed way, i.e. that the strife of truth among many individuals can be overcome in a unified, law-bound will of the people's spirit. Like Plato, who could only allow the universal in his republic, Heidegger, too, re-presses individual freedom, which he traduces as mere arbitrariness. Against this, commenting on Plato and the Greek polis, Hegel remarks:

> Dies macht nun die Grundlage der Platonischen Republik aus. Sie hat dies Wesentliche, daß das Prinzip der Einzelheit unterdrückt ist, und es scheint, daß die Idee dies erfordere, daß eben hierin der Gegensatz der Philosophie überhaupt gegen die Vorstellungsweise liegt, welche das Einzelne geltend macht und so auch im Staate, als dem realen Geiste, Eigentumsrecht, Schutz der Personen und des Eigentums sogar als die Basis alles Staats ansieht. Das ist die Grenze der Platonischen Idee; jenes nur die abstrakte Idee. Aber in der Tat ist die wahre Idee eben diese, daß jedes Moment sich vollkommen realisiert, verkörpert und selbständig macht und in seiner Selbständigkeit für den Geist doch ein Aufgehobenes ist. Hiernach muß nach dieser Idee die Einzelheit sich vollkommen realisieren, ihr Feld und Reich im Staate haben und doch in ihm aufgelöst sein.[241]

> This constitutes the foundation of the Platonic republic. It has this essential characteristic that the principle of individuality is suppressed, and it appears that the idea requires this, that precisely herein lies the antithesis of philosophy in general against the way of thinking which asserts individuality and, thus also in the state as the real spirited mind, regards property rights, the protection of persons and property even as the basis of any state. That is the limit of the Platonic idea; this [individuality] only the abstract idea. But in fact the true idea is precisely this, that every moment realizes and embodies itself completely, makes itself independent and in its independence is nevertheless something waived and simultaneously raised up for spirited mind. Therefore, according to this idea,

---

241 Hegel *Vorlesungen über die Geschichte der Philosophie II* Werke Band 19 S. 127f.

individuality must realize itself completely, have its space and realm in the state and nevertheless be dissolved in it.

Heidegger, Ernst Jünger and others seeking totalitarian political solutions follow in the tradition of the Platonic republic, reject liberalism and do not learn from Hegel's thinking, which, as we have seen briefly above in section 12.1, includes also a critique of liberal thinking, but nevertheless accepts that individual freedom has its right in the state, i.e. in the way in which a people lives together. Hegel's dialectical thinking, which we shall consider further in the next section, allows for contradictions among the moments of an ontological totality that are mediated with one another and can thus coexist in a higher whole.

ii) Overlooking the liberal thinking in Kant and W. von Humboldt that admits the interplay of individual freedom, Heidegger laments that after 1830, the unity of the German Geist fell apart into the individual sciences that became more and more independent of each other and of philosophy and "now even explicitly turned away from philosophy" (jetzt sogar die ausdrückliche Abkehr von der Philosophie, *GA*16:295). This is the rise of positivism that is still with us today. One science which he does not mention at all is the social science of political economy, which arose out of English and Scottish moral philosophy and became the social science of economics or Nationalökonomie during the course of the nineteenth century. He also does not mention that German philosophers, too, lost touch with the individual sciences, in particular, economics. Hegel still read Adam Smith and Ricardo. Heidegger himself did not read economists, although the German-speaking world still had some good thinkers in this area such as F. v. Gottl-Ottlilienfeldt, G. F. Knapp, A. Amonn, L. v. Mises, Schumpeter. As far as I know, we have no writings by Heidegger grappling with how Hegel's *Rechtsphilosophie* takes up essential thoughts of Adam Smith, Say and Ricardo (*RPh*. § 189ff) on bourgeois-liberal freedom and economic value. Heidegger's prejudice against liberal freedom and the business of its associated economic reality, which he regards merely as "the arbitrariness of views", etc. has significant consequences, for it means that:

iii) Heidegger misdiagnoses why the unity of the German spirited mind fell apart and fragmented after 1830. On the one hand, he recognizes that the very "flourishing of the sciences" still held together as "forms of appearance of absolute spirit" by (Hegelian) philosophy, which was the "inner centre of all sciences" before 1830 was itself a "danger" insofar as the individual sciences became more and more independent and the connection with other "areas of knowledge" (*GA*16:295) became opaque. On the other, he claims that "this individualization and uprooting of the sciences was reinforced by the rise of *tech-*

nology and technical thinking." (Diese Vereinzelung und Entwurzelung der Wissenschaften wurde verstärkt durch das Heraufkommen der *Technik* und des technischen Denkens. *GA*16:295)

> Die Technik förderte die Industrialisierung und die Entstehung des Proletariats und damit die Zerreißung des Volkes in Klassen und Parteien. Eine ursprüngliche und einheitliche verbindliche geistige Macht fehlte. Die Weltanschauung wurde Sache des Standpunkts des Einzelnen, der Gruppen und Parteien. (*GA*16:295)

> Technology promoted industrialization and the emergence of the proletariat and thus the tearing-apart of the people into classes and parties. An original and unified, binding spiritual/intellectual power was lacking. Weltanschauung became a matter of the standpoint of an individual, of groups and parties.

But can it in truth be said that technology, i.e. the technological way of knowing, "promoted industrialization" and thus "the emergence of the proletariat and thus the tearing-apart of the people into classes and parties"? Was it not rather the rise of the individual subject of knowledge, the loosening of the authority of the church and aristocracy, the unfolding of individualized liberties in the gainful business of life that promoted technology as an indispensable means in the striving for gain, and the particularization of society into struggling individuals and social groups? Was not a central, binding truth of society only held together by a social authority and power that kept the classes in their assigned places through often brutal and bloody repression? Did not the emergence of liberal freedoms allow the standpoints of individuals, groups and parties to emerge in the first place and to struggle against each other? Could it be said that the unity of the "absolute spirited mind" that held the sciences together was only a prelude to its dissemination and dissipation into the manifold truths of different segments of reality?

If this were the case, then the question of sociating power interplay and its relation to truth and social unity would itself have to become a question that unsettled and drove philosophical thinking. But Heidegger, with his single-minded fixation on the phenomenon of technology as the epitome and culmination of Western metaphysical thinking, has no appreciation of the social ontology of sociating interplay (above all, of bourgeois-capitalist society). The fragmentation of the social body into individuals and social groups and parties would have to be seen in connection with the fragmentation of historical truth itself that allowed the ultimate Protagorean individuality of truth to come to the fore and be lived in the ontological structure of mutually estimative, sociating power interplay itself.

Hegel's system of the Absolute as an ontological totality shows how, putatively, individual liberty is mediated (vermittelt) with the freedom of the whole, the state. He says e.g.

> Ferner ist es die im Systeme menschlicher Bedürfnisse [i.e. kapitalistische Wirtschaft eingebettet in der bürgerlichen Gesellschaft ME] und ihrer Bewegung immanente Vernunft, welche dasselbe zu einem *organischen Ganzen* von Unterschieden gliedert. (*RPh.* § 200 Note, my emphasis)

> Furthermore it is reason[242] immanent in the system of human needs [i.e. the capitalist economy embedded in civil society ME] and its movement which structures the system into an *organic whole* of differences. (*RPh.* § 200 Note, my emphasis)

and

> Diese [zweite Basis des Staats in der bürgerlichen Gesellschaft ME] ist dessentwillen so wichtig, weil die Privatpersonen, obgleich selbstsüchtig, die Notwendigkeit haben, nach anderen sich herauszuwenden. Hier ist also die Wurzel, durch die die Selbstsucht sich an das Allgemeine, an den Staat knüpft, dessen Sorge es sein muß, daß dieser Zusammenhang ein gediegener und fester sei. (*RPh.* § 201 Add.)

> This [second basis of the state in civil society ME] is so important because private persons, although self-seeking, have the necessity of turning outward [and orienting themselves] toward others. Here is thus the root through which self-seeking is linked to the universal, the state, whose care and concern it must be that this connection be a solid and firm one. (*RPh.* § 201 Add.)

Note that when Heidegger or Jünger think of an "organic whole", they do *not* think of a mediation between the particular (self-interest) and the universal (the state in its care for the universal connection) but of some kind of monolithic, authoritarian construct of command and obedience in which particular self-interests have been at best 'eliminated' or at least subordinated with an iron fist.

---

242 "Vernunft" (reason) in Hegel's philosophy is a code-word for philosophical, speculative-ontological knowing that has insight into and conceptually grasps the looks of being, i.e. the Idea in Plato's sense, so that reason is both 'subjective' and 'objective', or both form and content. This is what distinguishes reason from understanding (Verstand) and makes the former "speculative", whereas the latter is oblivious to being (seinsvergessen in Heidegger's sense). "[...]for the *form* in its most concrete meaning is reason as conceptualizing knowing, and the *content* is reason as the substantial essence of both ethical and natural actuality, the conscious identity of both is the philosophical idea" ([...] denn die *Form* in ihrer konkretesten Bedeutung ist die Vernunft als begreifendes Erkennen, und der *Inhalt* die Vernunft als das substantielle Wesen der sittlichen wie der natürlichen Wirklichkeit; die bewußte Identität von beidem ist die philosophische Idee. *RPh.* Vorwort S. 27).

For Hegel, by contrast, the immense strength of bourgeois society resides precisely in its allowing the freedom of particularity, i.e. liberal freedom, which is nevertheless, he claims, led back to and tied into the unity of the universal by an "invisible hand" (Adam Smith).

Like Plato's republic ("It has this essential feature that the principle of individuality is suppressed" – "Sie [die Platonische Republik] hat die Wesentliche, daß das Prinzip der Einzelheit unterdrückt ist"[243]), Heidegger's notion of freedom remains one-dimensional and authoritarian, so that he is unable to mediate particularity with the universal. In other words, for Heidegger, just us much as for Ernst Jünger, liberal freedom has to be eliminated in favour of individual self-surrender to the whole, the state, the Volksgeist.

iv) Instead of thinking freedom as a mediation between particularity and universality, in which the pursuit of self-interest has its essential, socio-ontological place, Heidegger conceives the freedom of the German people in its "National Socialist revolution" (nationalsozialistische Revolution, *GA*16:302), i.e. its "binding to the law of the people's spirit" (Bindung an das Gesetz des Volksgeistes, *GA*16:295), as being achievable only through "inner re-education of the entire people to the aim of willing its own consensus and unity" (die innere Umerziehung des ganzen Volkes zu dem Ziel, seine eigene Einigkeit und Einheit zu wollen, *GA*16:302) under the leadership of "Adolf Hitler" (*GA*16:302).

> Die Herrschaft dieses Staats ist die verantwortliche Durchsetzung jenes Führerwillens, zu dem das gefolgschaftliche Vertrauen des Volkes die Führung ermächtigt. [...] Der Staat bedeutet die lebendige, von wechselweisem Vertrauen und Verantwortung durchherrschte Ordnung, in der und durch die das Volk sein eigenes geschichtliches Dasein verwirklicht. (*GA*16:302)

> The rule of this state is the responsible assertion of that will of the leader to which the trust of the people as followers empowers the leadership. [...] The state signifies the living order permeated and ruled by mutual trust and responsibility in which and through which the people realizes its own historical existence.

In his dream of a 'new human being', Heidegger sees the possibility for this unity of the people as arising out of the "comradeship" (Kameradschaft, *GA*16:299) that was engendered on the front lines, in the trenches of World War I, so graphically depicted by Ernst Jünger. But this only shows that Heidegger, despite deeper insights into the Jemeinigkeit of Dasein, i.e. the individual my-ownness of each individual human being's existence, in *Sein und Zeit*, not only

---

243 G.W.F. Hegel, *Enz.* II *Werke* Band 19 S. 127.

ultimately denies the moments of particularity and singularity in the concept of freedom, but also misconceives the ontological "condition of possibility" of the unity of a people in a We (cf. Chapter 11.5).

A people temporarily suppresses its civil liberties and pulls itself together into a unified We in certain moments and in certain situations that may or may not be historically momentous. A situation of distress and emergency (such as World War I) allows a transitory unity to arise, but everyday life tends to dispersal into individual concerns, the pursuit of individual interests and the enjoyment of individual freedoms. The insight into the "indifference" and "opposition to the other" as the predominant modes of caring for the other in everyday life is a deep one (*Sein und Zeit* § 26). Each of us cares for his or her own self-world in the first place and cares for the other at first and for the most part only in the mutually beneficial exchange of a quid pro quo. Nevertheless, as has been shown in Chapter 9.2, in everyday life we willy-nilly also care for each other in such mutually beneficial, mutually estimating exchanges.

After the historical emergence of the individual subject during the course of the modern age, conjuring the unity of the people through steely, submissive dedication and self-surrendering commitment to a unified task within hierarchical structures of command and obedience is inviting historical disaster if this unity is to be regarded as an enduring state of affairs, i.e. as a state. Nevertheless, Heidegger insists on living a Fascist fantasy of unity when he proclaims that under the nascent National Socialist state, "work is any deliberate doing and acting out of care for the people with a willingness to serve the State's will" (Arbeit ist jedes wissentliche Tun und Handeln aus der Sorge für das Volk in der Bereitschaft zum Staatswillen. *GA*16:303). Such "willingness" is the will to be absorbed by the totality and as such is *arbitrarily* posited by Heidegger as his politically inspired but philosophically ill-founded opinion.

The strength of liberal thinking, by contrast, is that it sees that individual freedom must have room for play — even and especially in pursuing its self-interests in acquiring the goods of living. The suppression of self-interest in a totalitarian state leads only to its re-emerging illicitly, both through individual (sometimes hideous) abuses of official state power and through surreptitious, 'unofficial' furthering of one's self-interests (corruption of all kinds) — all the worse for a totalitarian social reality that does not realize the full idea of freedom, i.e. its socio-ontologically grounded 'look'. The mediation of particularity with universality — and not the merely authoritarian and ultimately ineffectual subsumption of particularity under universality — remains a philosophical question that has to be seriously posed as a key aspect of the question concerning the possibility of a free society. How can the self-interested, particular striving to earn a living and care for one's own particular life-world — an irrepressible striving — be mediated with care for the whole, which is today a planetary whole?

12.3 The forever contradictory, moving realization of freedom in civil society and state as power play (Hegel's *Rechtsphilosophie*)

12.3.1 Diremption of particularity from the universal in civil society and their mediation

It will have become apparent that Ernst Jünger's *Der Arbeiter*, although written as a kind of pamphlet in a highly particular historical conjuncture in Germany coinciding with the collapse of the Weimar Republic, can also be read more abstractly — and thus philosophically — as a totalitarian reply to the liberal conception of government and state fathered by Hobbes and Locke. The totalitarian response abstractly and bluntly negates the particularity of the bourgeois individual, the individual member of civil society, and posits instead a total, organic unity of will based on obedience and subordination of the individual. Hegel's treatment of the liberal conception of state in his *Rechtsphilosophie*, by contrast, is not so brutally one-dimensional, but indeed sophisticated. Indeed, as could be expected, the Hegelian conception of state is achieved through an Aufheben — a suspension, preservation and elevation, or a waiving, saving and raising — of the individual freedoms of civil society so dear to liberal thinking in which particular interests, at least initially, are given rein to unfold. Particular interests of the individual are not abstractly negated as in Jünger's *Arbeiter*, but instead the diremption of particularity from the universal is mediated, and assertedly resolved and reconciled in the state, which brings particular interests back to the universality of reason. In Hegel's usage, reason is a synonym for the idea as, in this context, the correspondence between the concept of freedom and social objectivity, i.e. "objektiver Geist". As we shall see, while Hegel does have a genuine and tenable critique of liberal thinking on the state, we shall also see that his Aufhebung of individual freedom amounts ultimately to its suppression by a paternalistic state.

The linch-pin or "the one principle of civil society" as it is thought through in Hegel's *Basic Outlines of the Philosophy of Right*[244] is the "concrete person who as a *particular* person is the aim and purpose, as a totality of needs and a mixture of natural necessity and arbitrary will" (Die konkrete Person, welche sich als *besonderer* Zweck ist, als ein Ganzes von Bedürfnissen und eine Vermischung von Naturnotwendigkeit und Willkür, ist das *eine Prinzip* der bürgerlichen Gesellschaft, *RPh*. § 182). This "one principle of civil society" is complemented by another, however, because the particular person is "essentially in *relation* to other such particular persons, so that each can only make its claim and be satisfied *mediated* through the other and at the same time, if at all, through the form of *universality, the other principle*" (wesentlich in *Bezeihung* auf andere solche Besonderheit, so daß jede durch die andere und zugleich schlechthin nur als durch die Form der *Allgemeinheit, das andere Prinzip, vermittelt* sich geltend macht und befriedigt, § 182).

Civil society, according to Hegel, is constituted basically and essentially by the satisfaction of the needs[245] of particular individuals who are mediated with each other by the exchange metabolism of the market-place. The system of needs and their satisfaction forms a complex, multifaceted, organic whole based on a division of labour within which each particular person pursues his or her own self-interest, but only mediated through the satisfaction of others' needs and whims. In this sense, particularity is always already tied back to and mediated through something universal or general, namely, the totality of social needs.[246] In the "satisfaction of its [particularity's] needs, its contingent, arbitrary will and subjective whim" (Befriedigung ihrer Bedürfnisse, zufälliger Willkür und subjektiven Beliebens, § 185), the *particular* individual has to take *part* in the universal *whole* of a market economy, through which it is again "restricted by the power of the universal" (von der Macht der Allgemeinheit beschränkt, § 185) where the universal in this instance is thought as a whole

---

244 G.W.F. Hegel *Grundlinien der Philosophie des Rechts, Werke* Bd. 7 Suhrkamp, Frankfurt/M. 1970, abbreviated as *RPh*.

245 Cf. however the critique of needs vis-à-vis usages in Chapter 4.5.

246 Cf. David Hume for an earlier formulation of this mediation: "[...] it is requisite to govern men by other passions [than a "passion for public good as to make every one willing to undergo the greatest hardships for the sake of the public" p. 262], and animate them with a spirit of avarice and industry, art and luxury. [...] The harmony of the whole is still supported; and the natural bent of the mind being more complied with, individuals, as well as the public [i.e. the state in Hume's usage; ME], find their account in the observance of those maxims." 'Of Commerce' 1752 p. 263. Hegel is *insofar* in firm agreement with a principal tenet and insight of liberal thinking.

economy. Hegel therefore describes civil society as "the system of ethical life lost in its extremes" (das System der in ihre Extreme verlorenen Sittlichkeit, § 184), albeit that it is nonetheless abstractly in conformity with the idea of freedom and albeit that the metabolism of civil society itself, willy-nilly and unconsciously, constitutes a mediation of the extremes named, particularity and universality.

In ascribing "contingent, arbitrary will and subjective whim" to particularity, Hegel does not give it its due. Individual freedom is not merely the individual's freedom to capriciously do what it likes with its private property within its own private sphere or to pursue only its own enjoyment. This is only the caricature of individual freedom as individualistic arbitrariness as formulated, in particular, in so-called critiques of 'consumerist society'. In a more literal sense, the freedom of particularity means the freedom to find one's part in the universal totality, one's niche in the organic whole. Moreover, individual freedom in its exercise, its ἐνέργεια, does not imply selfish, solipsistic retreat, but is itself *sociating*; it is in the first place the mundane freedom of economic mutually estimative exchange with others in which individual freedom is *reciprocally* exercised between and among free individuals, thus intertwining them in an interplay of powers with its resulting interdependency and even interresponsibility. The freedom to exchange is the freedom to earn a livelihood by hiring out your own abilities, whatever they may be, and also to acquire and enjoy the services of others, the exchange of finished goods being indirectly also the exchange of human abilities. Such ongoing exchange is not merely a matter of caprice, but of leading and responsibly shaping your individual life as shared with your loved ones.

A people affirms (individual, liberal) freedom by *practically* living within the usages of free interplay and by affirming them also in consciousness, i.e. in the mind. This amounts to living an *ethos of fairness and civility* in interchanges with one another, which is the *obligation* that goes along with the rights of individual freedom. Such an ethos goes beyond the formal, abstract, universal respect of the other as person (which in itself is not to be underestimated), counteracting particularity's merely rude self-interestedness in civil society and constituting something resembling a liberal We as a valued way of sharing the movement of life beneficially with one another (cf. Chapter 11.7). Civility includes the courtesy and politeness that makes interchanges in civil society fine and beautiful rather than ugly and mean, and such an ethos must be practised and cultivated in a people over centuries to become the life-blood of interplay with one another, i.e. in Hegelian language, a Gestalt of objective spirited mind.

These individual freedoms played out in civil society are also the obverse sides of *individual responsibilities* to earn a living and to *stand* as somewho in the social world. Personhood is the formal, abstract universal status or mask of the individual as somewho — the formal 'face' or εἶδος of human being — that is guaranteed by law. Such responsibility for oneself also contributes an element of *pride* and *self-esteem* to the ethos of civil society, for in earning your own livelihood, you have come to a stand and achieved an independence within interdependence.

With regard to the state as a universal instance as conceived in liberal political theory, Hegel remarks that:

> Wenn der Staat vorgestellt wird als eine Einheit verschiedener Personen, als eine Einheit, die nur Gemeinsamkeit ist, so ist damit nur die Bestimmung der bürgerlichen Gesellschaft gemeint. Viele der neueren Staatsrechtslehrer haben es zu keiner anderen Ansicht vom Staate bringen können. In der bürgerlichen Gesellschaft ist jeder sich Zweck, alles andere ist ihm nichts. Aber ohne Beziehung auf andere kann er den Umfang seiner Zwecke nicht erreichen; diese anderen sind daher Mittel zum Zweck des Besonderen. Aber der besondere Zweck gibt sich durch die Beziehung auf andere die Form der Allgemeinheit und befriedigt sich, indem er zugleich das Wohl des anderen mit befriedigt. Indem die Besonderheit an die Bedingung der Allgemeinheit gebunden ist, ist das Ganze der Boden der Vermittlung, wo alle Einzelheiten, alle Anlagen, alle Zufälligkeiten der Geburt und des Glücks sich frei machen, wo die Wellen aller Leidenschaften ausströmen, die nur durch die hineinscheinende Vernunft regiert werden. Die Besonderheit, beschränkt durch die Allgemeinheit, ist allein das Maß, wodurch jede Besonderheit ihr Wohl befördert. (*RPh.* § 182 Add.)

> When the state is imagined as a unity of various persons, as a unity which is only commonality, only the determination of civil society is intended. Many of the more recent teachers of the right of state have not been able to get any further than this view of the state. In civil society, each individual is aim and purpose for itself; everything else is nothing to it. But without a relation to others, the individual cannot attain the full extent of its aims; these others are therefore a means to particular ends. But the particular end, through its relation to others, gives itself the form of universality and is satisfied by at the same time satisfying the other's well-being. Through particularity being tied to the condition of universality, the whole is the ground of mediation where all singularities, all abilities, all the contingencies of birth and fortune are set free, where the waves of all passions stream out and are only governed by reason shining in. Particularity, restricted by universality, is the sole measure through which each particularity furthers its own well-being. (*RPh.* § 182 Add.)

Hegel does not want to allow that a conception of universality based on shared or common needs and arbitrary whims is adequate for a concept of state, and with this he rejects the liberal conception of state, which he calls "the *outer state*, the *state of understanding and need*" (den *äußeren Staat,* — *Not-* und

Verstandesstaat, § 183). The universal in civil society, however, is the *form* (look) of free intercourse and interplay in which the particular individuals acknowledge each other as free persons and through which they pursue their particular purposes. Such a universal as a form (of freedom as mutually estimating interplay) is already a Gestalt of the beingness of beings and insofar an actual-reality in conformity with speculative-ontological reason, hence already exceeding a finite understanding of the state as merely a "unity which is only commonality", i.e. as merely a pragmatic means for securing the mutual satisfaction of particular ends. The kind of state that affirms and secures the universal, market-place nexus for the satisfaction of needs, is accessible to understanding but is already *implicitly* or unknowingly in conformity with reason, because precisely such a (liberal, minimal) state is a realization of the concept of *freedom as sociating interplay*, and the members of civil society pursuing their particular self-interests also affirm such a 'look' of freedom, thus consciously affirming preontologically something infinite or ontological, beyond mere understanding.

But Hegel aims at thinking the state as an *explicitly* self-aware agent of the universal, positing through will its universal aims that are above particular self-interest, thereby elevating understanding to conscious, self-aware reason. At the same time, he concedes that the state as a "higher power" (höhere Macht, § 261) "against the spheres of private right and private well-being, of the family and civil society" (gegen die Sphären des Privatrechts und Privatwohls, der Familie und der bürgerlichen Gesellschaft, § 261) must not simply suppress the particularity of self-interests but, on the contrary, that the state "has its strength in the unity of its universal final purpose and the particular interests of individuals" (hat seine Stärke in der Einheit seines allgemeinen Endzwecks und des besonderen Interesses der Individuen, § 261). The moment of particularity in the concept of freedom must remain in play if the latter is to be actually realized, i.e. actually presence, in a society.

The customary usages making up an historical way of life and protected by the rule of law are, and must be, in conformity with the interplay of individual freedom if talk of freedom is to have any genuine sense. Hegel allows for this insofar as he concedes particularity its right. Insofar, Hegel is a liberal, albeit that he argues from a socio-ontological concept of freedom, rather than from some notion or other of social contract proceeding from pre-sociated individuals. In conceding particularity its right, he admits that a core freedom is the free power interplay that comes about through each member of society exercising its abstract rights as person. Through laws, regulations and the judicature, the state as "higher power" has the task of ensuring the fairness of the interplay in pursuit of self-interest. This interplay must be flanked by the state's providing infrastructure of all kinds, including educational infrastructure to develop each particular individual's potentials. The remaining moment of the concept of freedom, viz. *singularity, remains conspicuous by its absence* in Hegel's dialectic of civil society (and also, and even, in his treatment of the family, which is posited as the first pillar of ethical social life). The moment of the singularity of freedom will occupy us further below.

Reason for Hegel is "the substantial essence of both ethical and natural reality; the conscious identity of both is the philosophical idea" (das substantielle Wesen der sittlichen wie der natürlichen Wirklichkeit; die bewußte Identität von beidem ist die philosophische Idee; *RPh*. Vorrede W7:27) from which it follows that Hegelian reason is speculative insight (ἰδεῖν) into the 'looks' (εἶδος) of being as they show themselves presencing for the thinking mind. Being here is now thought in an Heideggerian way and is not such an impoverished concept as it is, strictly speaking, in Hegel's ontology as the immediacy of total indeterminacy. (Note that the "*conscious* identity" is related to the "*philosophical* idea", and, according to Hegel himself, it is necessary for neither the members of society nor the rulers to have philosophical insight; see the last subsection of section 12.3 below). A first step in raising understanding beyond particularity to universality (but hardly the universality of reason as speculative insight, ontological knowing), according to Hegel, is the education or cultivation (Bildung, § 187) which civil society's developed system of the totality of needs *itself* demands of the particular individuals. They are compelled to develop their understanding of ontic interconnections to perform the work required by the overall economy, thus gaining insight into their interdependence and overcoming the subjectivity of mere whim and individual interest. Hegel therefore calls education a "smoothing of particularity" (Glättung der Besonderheit, § 187 Add.) through which particularity becomes aware that it is *part* of the universal whole.

12.3.2 The police and civic corporation as supplements to the interplay of civil society

Whereas i) the system of needs forms the basis of civil society, this is not sufficient to determine its full concept, which, according to Hegel, has two further moments: ii) "the actuality of the universal moment of *freedom* included therein, the protection of property by the *judicature*" (Die Wirklichkeit des darin enthaltenen Allgemeinen der *Freiheit*, der Schutz des Eigentums durch die

Rechtspflege, § 188) and iii) "caring for the contingency remaining in these systems and taking care of particular interest as something in *common* through the *police* and *civic corporation*" (Die Vorsorge gegen die in jenen Systemen zurückbleibende Zufälligkeit und die Besorgung des besonderen Interesses als eines *Gemeinsamen*, durch die *Polizei* und *Korporation*, § 188).

The universal connection of a market economy — a katallaxy — through which particular needs and whims can be satisfied is based on the freedom of private property (which is "unendlich", "infinite" because in conformity with reason as "divine" insight into the ontological concept) which accordingly has to be realized, administered and secured by a state administration of justice. For Hegel, such administration of justice is still part of the outer state, whose justification and necessity can be comprehended and affirmed by understanding. The actuality — the perfect presence or ἐντελέχεια — of the abstract rights of property requires concrete, universal existence in laws under which particular cases in their endless empirical diversity are subsumed by the courts. Such administration of justice by the judiciary guarantees the formal, "infinite", free framework of civil society, its rules of power play for the pursuit of particular self-interest mediated by the universal connection of a market economy.

But, as Hegel notes, "for [abstract] right as such, well-being is something extrinsic" (dem Rechte als solchem ist das Wohl ein Äußerliches, § 229 Add.) being as it is dependent upon the ongoing outcome of interplay. This deficiency, he says, has to be ameliorated by the institutions securing society, "the police and civic corporation" which in Hegel's time were understood differently from how they are today. The police as "the securing power of the universal" (die sichernde Macht des Allgemeinen, § 231) comprises firstly the prevention and punishment of crime which violates the universal connection of civil society and its particular exercise as well as preventing particular acts of the exercise of property rights and private freedom which "infinitely" infringe the universal interplay of powers (in its ontological, not merely pre-ontologically understood dignity). Secondly, the police qua civil administration has to supervise and provide for businesses and organizations serving the community as a whole with daily needs. Thirdly, the police has to regulate the markets in the general interest and also provide what today we would call infrastructure such as "to take care of street lighting, bridge construction, taxation of daily needs as well as health" (für Straßenbeleuchtung, Brückenbau, Taxation der täglichen Bedürfnisse sowie für die Gesundheit Sorge zu tragen, § 236 Add.).

The further functions of the police concern the well-being of the individual who is exposed to the contingent vicissitudes of the economy and thus take on the problem of *poverty*. The market economy and therefore also the striving of individual members of civil society to earn their living in it in the pursuit of self-interest, being an interplay of powers, are of their essence contingent. The provision of education gives each individual a chance to establish itself in the economy as a player and earn a living. The rationale of providing for the poor who have slipped into distress is to prevent the emergence of a mob which has lost a "sensibility for law, lawfulness and honour" (zum Verluste des Gefühls des Rechts, der Rechtlichkeit und der Ehre, § 244), thus endangering civil society. The contradiction inherent in providing for the poor, however, as has been shown in Chapter 6.5, is that "the subsistence of the needy would be secured without being mediated by labour, which would go against the principle of civil society and the feeling of its individuals for their own independence/self-reliance and honour" (würde die Subsistenz der Bedürftigen gesichert, ohne durch die Arbeit vermittelt zu sein, was gegen das Prinzip der bürgerlichen Gesellschaft und des Gefühls ihrer Individuen von ihrer Selbständigkeit und Ehre wäre, § 245).

Nevertheless, and paradoxically, Hegel concedes *"particular well-being* as a *right* (das *besondere Wohl* als *Recht*, § 230, § 255) to be concretely realized by the police and especially the civic corporation. The particular individual as a member of a civic corporation is to have the *"securing"* of its *"subsistence"* (*Sicherung* der Subsistenz, § 230), which makes the individual dependent upon the corporation and therefore also obliged to accept its rules, i.e. in return for its material well-being, the individual is obliged to acknowledge the corporation as an instance with power over it. The same applies if the securing of individual welfare is transferred to a 'state apparatus', for the welfare recipient becomes dependent upon the welfare agency. A possible resolution of this contradiction between dependency and self-reliance lies in coupling an individual right to well-being with "the obligation of the individual to earn its livelihood" (die Verpflichtung des Einzelnen, seinen Erwerb zu schaffen, § 255 Add.). Then an individual member of society cannot claim its right to welfare support without at the same time demonstrably fulfilling its obligation to strive to be a self-reliant individual. Such a demonstration inevitably entails cumbersome and tedious subjection to the state welfare agencies' regulations which are themselves the rules of play of a lop-sided estimative power interplay between the particular individual and the welfare bureaucracy is played (or fought) out.

There is an essential contradiction in civil society between the security and insecurity of existence in the sense that the strivings to pursue and realize self-interest — as an interplay or groundless game of powers — are essentially uncertain, whereas civil society is the site where individuals are supposed to achieve their material well-being and thus attain and enjoy material security. The incentive to action in the market economy is particular self-interest that is essentially exposed to the risk and uncertainty of the sociating movement itself. If this incentive is lacking, the metabolism of civil society is impaired. Hegel recognizes the uncertainty of modern economic life in contrasting "family life", whose principle is "the earth, firm *ground* and *soil*", with "industry" whose "vitalizing, natural element is the *sea*" (Prinzip des Familienlebens die Erde, fester *Grund* und *Boden*, [...] Industrie das [...] belebende natürliche Element das *Meer*, § 247). The "craving to acquire" (Sucht des Erwerbs) drives industry to expose itself to the "danger" of the oceans "and mixes the fixation to the clod of earth and the limited circles of civil life, its enjoyments and desires, with the element of fluidity, danger and downfall" (und versetzt das Festwerden an der Erdscholle und den begrenzten Kreisen des bürgerlichen Lebens, seine Genüsse und Begierden, mit dem Elemente der Flüssigkeit, der Gefahr und des Untergangs, § 247). This "craving to acquire" drives civil society to reach beyond itself, to educate itself to develop its potentialy, and expose itself to the dangers of foreign lands and climes with their power interplays, "in which intercourse the greatest means of education is to be found and at the same time trade finds its world-historical significance" (in welchem Verkehr sich zugleich das größte Bildungsmittel und der Handel seine welthistorische Bedeutung findet, § 247).[247]

The (civic) corporation is an institution in civil society which raises the particularity of self-interest beyond itself to the general and universal, without however negating it. At first, "the *self-seeking* purpose directed at particular interest" (der auf sein Besonderes gerichtete, *selbstsüchtige* Zweck, § 251) is bundled together in the "co-operative" (Genossenschaft, § 251) or the "corporation" (Korporation, § 251) to become a universal purpose, albeit that "its [the corporation's, ME] universal purpose has [...] no greater extent than that inherent in the trade, in the characteristic business and interest" (deren allgemeiner Zweck [...] keinen weiteren Umfang hat, als der im Gewerbe, dem eigentümlichen Geschäfte und Interesse, liegt, § 251).

Today what Hegel calls a corporation would resemble a professional guild or industry association or even a labour union which also fulfils welfare functions for its members who are exposed to "particular contingencies" (die be-

---

247 Despite this assertion of the world-historical significance of trade, Hegel will not name a 'liberal Anglo-Saxon Reich' in his list of four world-historical Reiche that have embodied the Weltgeist but instead, as highest stage, a "germanisches Reich" (cf. *RPh.* § 353ff). It could well be said that the German people was entirely inept in educating itself through global trade, especially in the short period for which the German Reich was a colonial one of the most oppressive, authoritarian kind.

sonderen Zufälligkeiten, § 252) as well as providing education for them "as a second family" (als zweite Familie, § 252). By banding the members of civil society together, the corporation achieves a "*securing* of subsistence, a firm *asset-base* [a kind of reified value as social power ME]" (*Sicherung* der Subsistenz, ein festes *Vermögen*, § 253) thus liberating the individual "from its own opinion and contingency, from danger to itself and others, recognizing and securing it and at the same time elevating it to conscious activity for a common purpose" (von der eigenen Meinung und Zufälligkeit, der eigenen Gefahr wie der Gefahr für andere, befreit, anerkannt, gesichert und zugleich zur bewußten Tätigkeit für einen gemeinsamen Zweck erhoben wird, § 254). Here there is a communitarian resonance. In guiding particularity a few steps beyond itself toward the universal by banding it together in common interests, the corporation signals the "*return*", after ethical life having been lost in the extremes (§ 184), of "the *ethical element* as something immanent into civil society" (so *kehrt* das *Sittliche* als ein Immanentes in die bürgerliche Gesellschaft *zurück*, § 249), thus quelling the excesses of self-interested, arbitrary particularity.

12.3.3 A problematic transition from civil society to the state – 'Infinite', singular affirmation of the concept of freedom through an ethos of free and fair interplay – The chimæra of a final resolution of the power play

The corporation therefore also forms a transition to the state, whose aim is consciously universal: "The purpose of the corporation as restricted and finite has its truth [...] in the *universal purpose* in and for itself and its absolute actual-reality; the sphere of civil society therefore passes into the *state*" (Der Zweck der Korporation als beschränkter und endlicher hat seine Wahrheit [...] in dem an und für sich *allgemeinen Zwecke* und dessen absoluter Wirklichkeit; die Sphäre der bürgerlichen Gesellschaft geht daher in den *Staat* über. § 256). This state is now to be more than the merely "outer state" (§ 183). Since commonality of interests is not the same as the universal, as Hegel underscores, it is not easy to see how the corporation as an institution of civil society could form a transition to the state, which must surely be a critical issue in a philosophy of right. Hegel criticizes his predecessors such as Rousseau and Fichte, who, situated within the liberal tradition emanating from Locke, conceive the state as based on a collectivity of individual wills, thus overlooking the speculative-ontological aether of their togetherness. Hegel agrees that the state is the realization of free will, but he claims that this will is "substantial", "universal" will based on "reason" and as such a realization of spirited mind (Geist) with its speculative, ontological insight into the 'looks' of being, here, the look of freedom. From the theological side of Hegel's version of ontotheology, the state is said to owe its existence to "God walking in the world" (es ist der Gang Gottes in der Welt, daß der Staat ist, § 258 Add.) and "its ground is the power of reason realizing itself as will" (sein Grund ist die Gewalt der sich als Wille verwirklichenden Vernunft, § 258 Add.). He argues:

> Wenn der Staat mit der bürgerlichen Gesellschaft verwechselt und seine Bestimmung in die Sicherheit und den Schutz des Eigentums und der persönlichen Freiheit gesetzt wird, so ist *das Interesse der Einzelnen als solcher* der letzte Zweck, zu welchem sie vereinigt sind, und es folgt hieraus ebenso, daß es etwas Beliebiges ist, Mitglied des Staates zu sein. [...] Gegen das Prinzip des einzelnen Willens ist an den Grundbegriff zu erinnern, daß der objektive Wille das an sich in seinem *Begriffe* Vernünftige ist, ob es von Einzelnen erkannt und von ihrem Belieben gewollt werde oder nicht, — daß das Entgegengesetzte, die Subjektivität der Freiheit, das Wissen und Wollen, das in jenem Prinzip *allein* festgehalten ist, nur das *eine,* darum einseitige Moment der *Idee des vernünftigen* Willens enthält... (§ 258 Anmerkung)

> If the state is confused with civil society and its definition is posited in securing and protecting property and personal freedom, then *the interests of individuals as such* is the final purpose for which they are united, and it also follows from this that it is something arbitrary to be member of the state. The state, however, has a completely different relationship to the individual; in being objective thinking-spirit, the individual too only has objectivity, truth and ethical life in being a member of the state. [...] Against the principle of the individual will, the fundamental concept must be recalled that the objective will is what is reasonable in itself according to its *concept*, whether it is recognized by individuals and willed by their arbitrary will or not, that the opposed element, the subjectivity of freedom, the knowledge and willing which *alone* is held onto in this principle, contains only the one, and therefore one-sided moment of the *idea of the reason-imbued* will... (§ 258 Note)

First of all it should be noted that, although in the passage Hegel speaks of the "interests of the individuals as such" and "the principle of the individual will", this cannot be taken to mean that now he has brought singularity (Einzelheit) into speculative-dialectical play, because individual self-interest in civil society has already been determined as civil society's principle of *particularity* (§ 182), and not as a principle of singularity, which would call for another path of thinking.[248] Furthermore, to conceive the state as based on a "*contract*" of individuals makes "their caprice, opinion and arbitrary, express consent into the foundation" (*Vertrag*, der somit ihre Willkür, Meinung und beliebige, ausdrückliche

---

248 Cf. the digression Chapter 3.3.1, 'Dialectic of self and other – Wrestling with Plato, Hegel, Heidegger'.

Einwilligung zur Grundlage hat, § 258 Note) which destroys "the divine existing in and for itself and its absolute authority and majesty" (das an und für sich seiende Göttliche und dessen absolute Autorität und Majestät, § 258 Note). In other words, a state based on a so-called social contract as expression of a *general* will would not correspond to the concept of freedom itself as an absolute universal that — "infinitely" and in its Gestalt as a unifying, majestic instance — always already exceeds and encompasses the merely self-seeking or opining individual, existing, i.e. presencing in the world, as it does absolutely in and for itself. Hegel formulates this also in a moral way in claiming that it is the "highest duty" (höchste Pflicht, § 258) of individuals "to be members of the state" (Mitglieder des Staates zu sein, § 258) and nothing "arbitrary" (etwas Beliebiges, § 258 Note) dependent upon individual will, and it must be conceded that his insight is in accordance with "reason" insofar as human being is essentially sociated, shared, customary being and in this sense ethical or sittlich. But this shared ethical life in mutually estimating, fair power interplay with one another is essentially fathomless, uncertain in a way that cannot be ascribed to individual caprice or arbitrariness. This is something other than a divinely universal conceived as absolutely unrelated to this free interplay.

The standpoint of civil society based on the pursuit of individual self-interest and, at most, common interests, along with the insight of understanding into the necessity of the outer state for protecting and securing civil society and its metabolism, according to Hegel, thus has to make a great leap to the divine, to absolute, substantial spirited mind if the individual is to gain insight into the true ground of the state. But insofar as the individual members of civil society affirm not just the pursuit of their self-interests and insofar also the state as a means to that pursuit, but also the *forms of freedom*, i.e. the 'looks' of the mutually estimating power interplay, which enable such pursuit as a *way of life*, as well as having customary-ethical dignity *in and for themselves*, they are already affirming something universal and "infinite" in Hegel's sense of ontology, if not in his sense of ontotheology. Such affirmation must not be confused with the arbitrariness of entering into a contract or not, or with the calculating, pro-and-con understanding that sees the necessity of the state to protect the individual freedom and enjoyment of private property.

The universal is latent and effective in civil society itself as "objective will" to a degree that Hegel does not want to concede. Hegel is right to point out the fallacy in a contract theory of state, because the particular individuals of civil society always already share a world through power interplay in that world; it cannot be a question of whether a 'free particular individual' wills arbitrarily to belong to civil society or not. The issue is rather to conceive the state as necessary for the realization of freedom understood as the power interplay of civil society, which goes hand in hand with the members of civil society affirming themselves as players in the mutually estimating power interplay within the abstract form of freedom as person.

Civil society is dirempted into the two moments of the "idea of the state itself" (die Idee des Staates selbst, § 256 Note); it "splits" into "the particularity of need and enjoyment *reflected into itself* and the universality of *abstract* right" (zur *in sich reflektierten* Besonderheit des Bedürfnisses und Genusses und zur abstrakten rechtlichen Allgemeinheit entzweit, § 255). This split is to be overcome in "[t]he state [...] as the actual-reality of the ethical idea" ([d]er Staat [...] als die Wirklichkeit der sittlichen Idee, § 257), "the actual-reality of substantial *will*" as "absolute, unmoving end in itself in which freedom comes to its highest right" (Wirklichkeit des substantiellen *Willens*, absoluter unbewegter Selbstzweck, in welchem die Freiheit zu ihrem höchsten Recht kommt, § 258), and that in the shape of an "independent power" (selbständige Gewalt, § 258 Add.), the word "Gewalt" suggesting that the state has, in particular, the option of exercising physical violence. The "absolute, unmoving end in itself" is an echo of the "unmoved mover", the god in Aristotle's *Metaphysics*. Such a realization of the "ethical idea" in the god-like state, however, does not resolve the diremption in civil society between particular interests and abstractly universal personhood, but only shifts it to a split between civil society and the state which, as actually-real "will" and an "independent power", subjugates civil society to itself, leaving the individual members of civil society only the option of a mediation with the universal by knowing themselves as "merely moments" (nur Momente, § 258 Add.) of this "independent power" in the standing presence of its "absolute, unmoving end in itself".

The individual members of civil society thus have only the option of identifying with the state as the realization of their own freedom in submitting to its independent, occasionally violent power which it can exercise over its citizens in the name of substantially realized freedom and in accordance with its consciously posited universal will. But this is no adequate resolution of the contradiction between self-interested particularity and the universality of freedom because the member of society is then only cleaved by the contradiction between being, on the one hand, a self-seeking individual and, on the other, a citizen of the state which, in turn, remains aloof from civil society as the embodiment of the quasi-divine, absolute "substantial will" of freedom.

An alternative resolution to the contradiction of the diremption of civil society is the actual-reality of a practised ethos of civil society according to which the individual members have gained insight and identified themselves (their selves) with the universal forms of freedom upon which the sociating power interplay of civil society essentially depends. Such a practised ethos as a usage or habituated "second nature" (*RPh.* § 151) is also an actual realization, i.e. a presencing in the shared historical 3D-time-clearing, of the universal moment of the concept of freedom, or rather, and in truth, *only* in this way can the concept of freedom "step into actual reality" (tritt in Wirklichkeit, *LII* W6:299) in its moment of singularity (Einzelheit) which mediates between the moment of particularity understood as the freedom to pursue one's own self-interest, and the merely abstractly-universal moment of freedom in personhood. Such an ethos is that of *fair play* in the — albeit forever fathomlessly uncertain — interplay, discussed in Chapter 11.7, that constitutes the real, living, free metabolism and pith of civil society. Insofar, the "substantial will" of freedom is realized in the will, i.e. presences in the mind, of each singular individual, thus making each individual genuinely singular in the Hegelian sense of the term, singularity (Einzelheit), as a moment of realization of the concept, in the present context, the concept of freedom, through which the concept "posits itself as something *real*" (sich als *Reales* [...] setzt, W6:403).

Hegel himself obfuscates this possibility of mediating the contradiction inherent in the concept of freedom when he asserts, "With freedom one must not proceed from singularity/individuality, from the singular/individual self-consciousness, but only from the essence of self-consciousness, for a person may know it or not, this essence realizes itself as an independent power" (Bei der Freiheit muß man nicht von der Einzelheit, vom einzelnen Selbstbewußtsein ausgehen, sondern nur vom Wesen des Selbstbewußtseins, denn der Mensch mag es wissen oder nicht, dies Wesen realisiert sich als selbständige Gewalt, § 258 Add.), i.e. as the state. Hegel abuses the ambiguity inherent in the terms, "Einzelheit" and "einzeln", meaning both 'singular(ity)' and 'individual(ity)', and this ambiguity runs throughout the *Rechtsphilosophie*. One could say that 'at first and for the most part', the individual is not singular in the sense that it does not correspond to the concept of freedom as the moment of singularity of this concept through which it "steps into actual reality", but the individual does correspond to the concept of freedom and therefore embodies a unity of particularity and universality, becoming truly free as a *singular* individual, insofar as it knows and practises the ethics of — forever uncertain, unpredictable, unmasterable — fair play in its interplay with other members of society.

Freedom is thus singularized in the individual who identifies with the universal ethos of fair interplay.[249] As Hegel would have it, however, the singularization of the concept of freedom, where it becomes reality, would occur only with the state as real, institutionalized, objective will, which paves the way for thinking the singularity of freedom in its realization in the world as the monarch (cf. § § 275, 279f) and consequently in the individual citizen's identification with the state's, or the monarch's universal will as an empowered anchor for power *over* sociating live-movement. But even on this point Hegel seems to vacillate. Consider the following passage:

> Die Vernünftigkeit besteht, abstrakt betrachtet, überhaupt in der sich durchdringenden Einheit der Allgemeinheit und der Einzelheit und hier konkret dem Inhalte nach in der Einheit der objektiven Freiheit, d.i. des allgemeinen substantiellen Willens und der subjektiven Freiheit als des individuellen Wissens und seines besondere Zwecke suchenden Willens — und deswegen der Form nach in einem nach *gedachten, d.h. allgemeinen* Gesetzen und Grundsätzen sich bestimmenden Handeln. — Diese Idee ist das an und für sich ewige und notwendige Sein des Geistes. (§ 258 Note)

> Viewed abstractly, conformity with reason consists above all in the interpenetrating unity of universality and singularity and here, according to the concrete content, in the unity of objective freedom, i.e. of the universal, substantial will, and subjective freedom as individual knowing and its [this knowing's, ME] will pursuing particular purposes — and therefore, in its form, in an action that determines itself according to *thought, i.e. universal* laws and principles. — This idea is the being of spirited mind that is, in and for itself, eternal and necessary. (§ 258 Note)

Hegel has already uncovered that the particular individual, "in pursuit of its particular purposes" is nolens volens led back and tied back to the universal as an organic social totality through the interdependency of the members of civil society (*RPh*. § 189). Moreover, the individual as a free person is always already tied to and obliged to acknowledge and respect something infinite and far exceeding itself, namely, the abstract-universal, socio-ontological status of *free personhood* of all members of civil society. Now he wants to insist that the universal connection cannot assert itself only unknowingly and implicitly through the interdependent actions of free, contract-making persons, but must assert itself knowingly and explicitly in the conscious actions of individuals who act in accordance with "*thought, i.e. universal* laws and principles" thus constituting a

---

249 Such an identification does not resolve the issue of how this real, unique, individual human being can find itself mediated, more or less brokenly, with the world at all, but that is another issue. Cf. the digression Chapter 3.3.1, 'Dialectic of self and other – Wrestling with Plato, Hegel, Heidegger'.

unity, no longer of universality and particularity, as one would expect from the earlier formulation of the diremption of civil society into its extremes, but of "universality and singularity", albeit that this *singularity* is characterized as "individual knowing and its [this knowing's, ME] will pursuing *particular* purposes". The universal moment of the concept of freedom is no longer singularized in the "substantial will" of the state as an "independent power", but in the knowing individual itself!

The interconnections between reason, the idea and being are explicit in this passage. Reason and the idea are synonymous, and "being" is here a synonym for reality, i.e. realized presence. The idea of freedom consists now in the reality of the individual member of society "pursuing particular purposes" knowingly acting according to "*thought, i.e. universal* laws and principles". Such "*thought, i.e. universal* laws" cannot be merely the positive laws posited by the state as the real agent of the universal, for such laws cannot be thought as universal by the individual. To attain the "unity of universality and singularity", the singular individual must now *know* the universal. It is no longer sufficient that the interplay of civil society itself — in which the members of civil society "pursuing particular purposes" are willy-nilly entwined and which has always already exceeded the individual and its "arbitrary will" to enter or not to enter a social contract — prevail as the universal, free game "behind the backs" of the players in civil society. Rather, now this universal, groundless power interplay itself must be knowingly affirmed as the "objective freedom" in which the individuals are partaking, and this affirmation takes place through the individuals' determining their actions according to the "*universal* laws and principles" of such free interplay which are nothing other than the rules of fair play. Singularity thus affirms the riskiness of freedom itself.

If there is to be a "unity of objective freedom, i.e. of the universal, substantial will, and subjective freedom as individual knowing and its [this knowing's, ME] will pursuing particular purposes" at all, this unity must exist in the first place in the singular individual's fair play, i.e. in "action that determines itself according to *thought, i.e. universal* laws and principles". The interplay of civil society knowingly affirmed by its singular, individual members thus attains, as the ethos of fair play, the socio-ontological dignity of "eternal and necessary" "objective freedom", and the state only *accords* with this "objective freedom" by adjudicating and judiciously steering the interplay and securing the forms of freedom of this interplay. The positive law posited by the state is in accord with freedom only insofar as it is in conformity with the deeper-lying "*universal* laws and principles" of free and fair social interplay realized in real individuals as players in the interplay. But then it is hard to regard the state as owing its existence to anything so lofty as "God walking in the world" (§ 258 Add.), as Hegel formulates in the addition to the very same paragraph, that is, unless God is understood simply as the 'fair god'[250] of free interplay, i.e. as a definite historical constellation of being whose pith is individual freedom.

Furthermore, although he dialectically unfolds the state as the substantial realization of the concept of freedom in the world, Hegel immediately concedes that this "actual-reality" can be and is already tarnished and corrupted, standing as it does "in the world and thus in the sphere of arbitrary will, contingency and error." (in der Welt, somit in der Sphäre der Willkür, des Zufalls und des Irrtums § 258 Add.) "With the idea of the state, one must not have particular states in view, nor particular institutions, but rather, one must view for itself the idea, this actually-real god." (Bei der Idee des Staats muß man nicht besondere Staaten vor Augen haben, nicht besondere Institutionen, man muß vielmehr die Idee, diesen wirklichen Gott, für sich betrachten. § 258 Add.) But the idea, as a look of the beingness of beings seen by the speculating mind, is invariably overlooked, "because it is [...] easier to uncover defects than to grasp the affirmative element" ([w]eil es [...] leichter ist, Mängel aufzufinden, als das Affirmative zu begreifen, § 258 Add.).

Indeed, Hegel insists on the paradoxical standpoint that the state is the "actual reality of the ethical idea" (Wirklichkeit der sittlichen Idee, § 257), regardless of any shabby, contingent, corrupted, empirical reality of the state standing in the "sphere of arbitrary will, contingency and error" (§ 258 Add.). This sounds very much like the state ought to correspond to the universal, the concept of freedom, but, in the finite human world, it does not and cannot. The real state in the world is therefore untrue in Hegel's sense. And yet Hegel is often extremely scathing and sarcastic about those who insist on an ought, "especially in the political domain" (vornehmlich auch im politischen Felde, *EnzI* § 6 Note). He accuses their mere understanding "proud of its *Ought*, as if the world had waited on it to find out how it *ought to* be but is not" (auf das *Sollen* [...] eitel ist, als ob die Welt auf ihn gewartet hätte, um zu erfahren, wie sie sein *solle*, aber nicht sei, *Enz.* § 6 Note). But here Hegel himself seems to be reduced to the position of saying that the state ought to correspond to its concept as absolute, divine, effectively productive power and substantial end in itself, which is knowable through reason but in human reality does not live up to its concept.

Does Hegel's scathing mockery of moralists redound here on his own head? Is it merely an irony that the state *ought* to be the concrete realization of the infinite idea of freedom but in fact is subject to the finiteness of the world in-

---

250 Cf. Aristotle's god of the fair in my 'Absolutely Divine Everyday' 2008–2014.

cluding the limited understanding and power struggles of mere politicians and also to the vanity and vainglory of monarchs, presidents and other individual heads of states? Is the realization of freedom in the world the sociating power interplay itself that, because it can never be effectively mastered, can be both fair and unfair? Where Hegel quips that if reality does not correspond to its concept, then all the worse for reality, do we not have to retort in this case that the concept of the state as embodiment of the universal is a mere dream of reason, bereft of adhesion with the finite, mortal human world which even misrecognizes the nature of freedom itself? Is it not more appropriate and truer to philosophical reason with its ontological insight to concede the everlasting, unbridgeable gulf between the concept of freedom and its realization in a finite human world, inevitably and *essentially* riven by strife and constantly in the motion of power play? Or is it something about the very socio-ontological *concept* of freedom *itself* that prevents social reality from ever being imbued by reason as Hegel envisages it so that it is, in truth, *not* a matter of a shortfall of reality measured against the yardstick of the concept, but of thinking through the concept of freedom itself differently from Hegel? Let us examine these not merely rhetorical questions more closely.

Hegel's speculative dialectic seeks in the transition to the state as a "higher power" a reconciliation of the diremption between the moments of particularity and universality in civil society, i.e. their unity in singularity, and this in accord with the concept of freedom. The concept of freedom here is nothing other than a look of being, an ontological structure as a facet of an historical constellation of being's truth as a cast of the beingness of beings. Could it be that this concept or ontological structure itself is irremediably torn? If that were the case, then any attempt to heal the rip to attain a standing presence would be *essentially*, i.e. in the concept itself, Sisyphean, and not merely a result of the "infinite" concept becoming sullied by having to be realized finitely "in the sphere of arbitrary will, contingency and error". And this is indeed the socio-ontological truth of the matter: Freedom, of its inner nature, its essence, is individualized, with each individual human being acting in the world as an origin of its own powers and according to its own perspectival understanding of the world in any given situation into which it has been cast. It is not merely that human beings do not act according to their "reason", i.e. irrationally under the control of their 'emotions' or limited self-interests, nor that human beings fail to act according to a unified, universal concept of freedom, but that *all* understanding of the world in its *truth* is essentially splintered into countless individual perspectives (cf. Chapter 10.7), even when the individual is *not* acting according to (the particularity of) self-interest, and that the concept of freedom itself requires its self-splintering into individual perspectives and corresponding individual moves in an interplay. Each individual human being is and remains *essentially* a free power centre in sociating interplay, no matter how 'universal' and un-self-interested its intentions are, acting even "according to *thought, i.e. universal laws and principles*" (§ 258 Note).

The *power interplay* among human beings can never be raised irrevocably to an harmonious, resolved unity in which all power has been defused or oriented in a unified direction. Nor can there be an irrevocable, final submission to a universal will of state without perverting the very concept of freedom, which can never 'close together' its universal moment of a state as a "higher power" with its moment of singularity, which resides inevitably in a multitude of individual human beings sociating via fathomless power interplay. In the present context we will take *singularity* of freedom to mean the free human individual who wills the *universality* of laws and principles governing ethical life, i.e. of a shared freedom, and thus corresponds to the universal moment of the concept of freedom not through willed submission to a higher, "unmoving" power, but by *living an ethos*. This is in line with Hegel's ontological determination of the concept in his *Logik*. According to the paraphrase of the *Logik* in the *Enzyklopädie*, "[...] each of its [the concept's ME] moments can only be grasped immediately out of and with the others" ([...] kann jedes seiner [des Begriffs ME] Momente unmittelbar nur aus und mit den anderen gefaßt werden, *EnzI* § 164) so that, in particular, "[t]he singular-individual is the same as the actual-real, only that the former has come forth from the concept and is thus universal [...]" ([d]as Einzelne ist dasselbe, was das Wirkliche ist, nur daß jenes aus dem Begriffe hervorgegangen, somit als Allgemeines [...] ist, *Enz.* § 163 Note). Applied to the concept of freedom, this implies that the free human individual as the singularity of freedom has to be thought first of all in unity with the moment of the universality of freedom, and not yet as having succumbed to the diremption of the concept of freedom into its extremes of singularity as the private individual, on the one hand, and universality as the state thought as a superior, aloof power embodying the universality of freedom, on the other.

Even if the state as a "higher power" achieves a "unity of its universal final purpose and the particular interests of individuals" (§ 261), such a unity is only ever a balancing out of *particular* interests (in a compromise) which can never encompass the *singularity* of human freedom, but at most suppress it by demanding unquestioning obedience and submission to the state's posited laws, which indeed, today, a state demands in the name of democracy. Even when there is (ethical) concord in a society with regard to the "*universal* laws and principles" of active interplay that are in accord with freedom, there remain ongoing, ever new, contentious differences among singular, reason-imbued individuals over the interpretation of these laws and principles in any given situation, and therefore also a power interplay over which interpretation is to prevail.

Even if there were a shared ethos of fair interplay (which would amount to the realization of the concept of a liberal society in an ethos of social living it-self), not only would the interplay itself remain a power play of particular inter-ests, but there would also be an ongoing power play over the concrete interpre-tation of fairness in particular game-situations of interplay coming about unforeseeably and unexpectedly in countless new combinations. The very ethos of free and fair interplay *includes* strife and conflict, and the individual player's ethical duty is in the first place to this ethos, and only in the second place to the state as the powerful instance through which the interplay is mediated and adjudicated.

As we shall see below in Chapter 13, the power interplay over the interpreta-tion of the universal as concretely shared, sociating freedom extends beyond civil society into the state itself, so that it can never be thought as the universal instance that is above the fray but, on the contrary, as a focal centre of the pow-er interplay itself in which, among other things, conflicting conceptions of the universal good are fought out alongside compromise outcomes of struggles among particular self-interests. This means, in particular, that the free individ-ual is only *partially* secured in its freedom by the liberal-democratic state which secures individual rights. Because the multiple individuality of freedom in its singularity never finally closes together in the conclusion of a free, democratic, universal, state will, the free individual, who consciously and responsibly wills a singular conception of universal freedom, and does not seek merely its own idiosyncratic advantage under a camouflage of high-minded universal senti-ments, can exist *as* free only 'unclosed' in the interstices of the power interplay into which state power does not reach, that is, in a certain sense, *an-archically*.

12.3.4 The inner constitution of the state and the singularity that remains plural – The endlessly contentious issue of taxation – Never-ending controversy over concrete conceptions of the universal good – The two-way power-mediation between civil society and state - The media and freedom of speech

Although it *ought* to be the embodiment of the universal, the state remains per-meated by the particularity of finite human beings wielding power in endless, mutually estimating power plays, whether they are seeking their own advantage or not, and insofar the state itself is never entirely 'above' civil society. No matter whether it be a monarch, a president, a minister, a head of a civil service department, a party leader or some other influential politician, it is individual human beings who wield political power, and that never absolutely but always relatively in power interplays with other players. No matter how the bearers of political power 'should' be imbued with the aim of the universal well-being of a people or with upholding through law and venerable institutions the forms of freedom lived out in the ethical practices of society, there are always abuses and questionable stretchings of political power: "bad conduct can disfigure it [the state] in many respects" (übles Benehmen kann ihn [den Staat] nach vielen Seiten defigurieren, § 258 Add.). Such "bad behaviour" on the part of agents of the state high or low would be accordingly merely an instance of reality not living up to its concept, which would not impinge on the state as the universal instance of freedom. Hegel even provides for "[t]he securing of the state and the governed against abuse of power on the part of the authorities and its officials" ([d]ie Sicherung des Staats und der Regierten gegen den Mißbrauch der Gewalt von seiten der Behörden und ihrer Beamten, § 295), thus already implicitly conceding the necessity of a division of powers within the state.

However, it is not merely a matter of those wielding political power in some office of state inevitably acting badly and thus failing to live up to an Ought, but of the 'good', well-intentioned, contentious, never-ending power play *over* (the interpretation of) the universal of freedom itself and *within* the state as the concrete universal with its various, *particular* organs. Whether *this* power play corresponds to its concept or not depends upon whether it is *fair* or not within the constitutional rules of play, but the power play itself as sociating movement is an *essential* moment of the state as free, arising not merely from the disparity of various, particular self-interests that distort the universal nature of the state in its sublime superiority in the direction of mere self-interest, but from the singularity of freedom itself in individuals which defies the unification of such singularity in the person of a single, sovereign head of state.

Paradoxically, the singularity of freedom, despite all attempts to unify it in a single subject, remains plural, and such plurality of the singularity of freedom cannot be attributed merely to the capriciousness and arbitrariness of individual will, but belongs essentially to the concept of freedom itself, just as has been shown in an earlier chapter (Chapter 10.6) that truth itself splinters into individual perspectives. The singularity of freedom, as already mentioned, is to be understood in the present context as that individual will that wills (its correspondence with) the universality of the concept of freedom, thus willing its own elevation above the plane of mere, particular self-interest. Such an individual is the citizen rather than the private individual playing the power play for gain in civil society or withdrawn into the enjoyment of its own private sphere and without a concern for the universal matters of politics.

Hegel, however, grants the state an ontological dignity and majesty of existence in itself, conceding even that the liberty and property rights of individuals, the life-blood of civil society, may be sacrificed to the state's higher, universal purpose. The state is thus accorded its own, autonomous raison d'être, and the foundation of the state that was supposed to reside, in the first place, in guaranteeing the infinite dignity of personhood is not merely aufgehoben, but relativized, diluted, negated and sacrificed to a self-positing, higher instance. This is nowhere more apparent than with the endlessly contentious issue of *taxation* as a major way in which personhood is relativized and diluted through an incursion into private property rights in the name of the universal good. Taxation exercised the minds of many of the early moral and political philosophers of the modern age as a major topic, and that for good reason, for it is indeed civil society that produces the wealth that enables the state to exercise real power. Today, by contrast, taxation as a crucial socio-ontological phenomenon has entirely disappeared from the philosophical agenda, being regarded as a subject for taxation specialists within the social science of economics. It nonetheless still deserves philosophical attention as one of the principal hinges between civil society and the state and as a major sore point between the state and its subjects that has many times become a running sore of rebellion, uprising and even revolution.

On the one hand, the levying of taxation is necessary and legitimate insofar as the necessity of the state as a real institution is granted in accordance with the concept of freedom itself. The state must have disposal over a part of social wealth and income to function as a state; the members of civil society must contribute something of (the fruits of the exercise of) their abilities to the state in its universal status. Because the state is the universal instance standing above civil society, the contribution to its upkeep must also be universal, and this universal Vermögen (asset, capability, potential) is money as the universal reified value which, on the one hand, allows the state to "*buy* what it needs" (*kauft* der Staat, was er braucht, § 299 Add.) and, on the other, leaves the individual free to make its contribution to the state as "mediated through its arbitrary will" (durch seine Willkür vermittelt, § 299). "What is to be contributed, however, can only be determined in a just way by being reduced to *money* as the existing universal *value* of things and services" (Das zu Leistende aber kann nur, indem es auf Geld, als den existierenden allgemeinen Wert der Dinge und der Leistungen, reduziert wird, auf eine gerechte Weise [...] bestimmt werden, § 299)

Hence, the existence of universal value reified quantitatively in money enables both an individual equality and therefore justice understood as fairness (the individual taxpayer only has to contribute so-and-so many dollars laid down quantitatively in a fair way that requires transparency and simple principles rather than arbitrary positing) and individual freedom (the individual can exercise its abilities any way it wants to earn the money income of which a part is siphoned off as taxes). This is the favourable side of the abstract universality of reified value in correspondence with the abstract universality of personal freedom and the concrete universality of the state: individual freedom and reified universality are essentially linked, enabling a contribution to the state's universal task to be made without the suppression of individual freedom.

On the other hand, however, there is the unfavourable side of the state's power to raise taxes. There is no intrinsic measure to a level of just taxation or principled criteria for the kinds of levies, duties, tariffs, excise duties, sales taxes, value-added taxes, stamp duties, fees, etc. etc. that the state can impose arbitrarily through its formally legitimate procedures for passing taxation legislation, which is a part of the state's administrative legislation, as opposed to the legislation applicable to the power interplay in civil society itself. Taxation legislation has no inner principle, but is posited arbitrarily by the state's formally proclaimed will which justifies specific taxation measures on an ad hoc basis, employing supposed 'arguments' that seem pertinent at the time. Such arguments *ought* to formulate the state's will to do the universal good for society and the nation as a whole, but they often smack of political calculation (e.g. pandering to sectoral interests of the electorate, raising taxes only *after* being re-elected, etc.) and of sovereign caprice, especially in the state's assessment, via its taxation officials and intricate, arcane bureaucratic regulations, of a given citizen's tax burden.

The more the state appropriates universal tasks of substance to its own agency, the more taxation it needs, and such universal tasks (such as health, education, old age care, defence, culture, environmental protection, etc. etc.) depend crucially upon a *concrete conception of universal well-being* that the state posits of its own will through the government of the day. The more the state arrogates universal tasks to itself, including tasks that could be fulfilled indirectly through the self-interest-driven interplay of civil society, the more it must make incursions into the private lives and private property rights of its citizens. This contradiction, which at core is that between self-esteeming self-reliance and being cared for, between the freedom of sociating moves and movement, and subjugation to a higher power, is never finally resolved but, at least in democratic societies, remains a perpetual point of political tension in the constitutionally sanctioned forms of political struggle (election campaigns, parliamentary debate, public controversy in the media of public opinion, etc.) over concrete conceptions of universal well-being.

In democratic societies, it may just be possible for civil society to claw back some of the purportedly universal tasks and universal value (taxes) that the state has arrogated to itself, or there may a broad social consensus that certain tasks must be undertaken by (a part of) the state, or there may be a clamouring on the part of the people to be relieved of the risks of the interplay in civil society in the name of 'solidarity', but this all depends not only on the nature of the task as part of the public weal, but also on the consciousness of the populace at large, i.e. on constantly wavering public opinion and whether it tends toward wanting to care for itself or toward wanting to be cared for. Caring for the people is also a way in which the state exercises and consolidates its rule over the people. The members of society who come to enjoy the state's welfare benefits are exposed to the state's definition of caring-for as laid down in a labyrinth of regulations and as administered by its bureaucracy (cf. Chapter 6.5).

Apart from the never-ending controversy and conflict over conceptions of the universal good as part of the concrete, living movement of the realization of the concept of freedom, which in turn has oscillating effects on taxation levels, there is the *inherent tendency of state power to augment itself* insofar as it meets no resistance, thus encroaching on the free interplay of civil society. The politician embodies a will to political power (that remains always contested in political power plays), and, since an accretion of power is invariably preferred by any holder of political power as compared to a diminution, the politician — who also enjoys his or her own reflection in the mirror of wielding political power, quite apart from whether any *abuse* of political power is involved in such self-enjoyment — is the agency through which the state augments its own power, thus assuming more and more paternalistic characteristics. The tendency for political power to augment goes hand in hand with the tendency to increase taxation as the universal, real, reified means of financing such political power and rule. The tax burden imposed upon civil society tends to rise 'naturally', 'of itself', in a scarcely perceptible creep unless counteracted by a decisive counter-movement and opposition from civil society that comes to forceful expression in democratic debate. Such a debate is held in tension by the contradiction between self-estimative self-reliance and the desire to be securely and comfortably cared for by the state.

By affirming the state, above all in the individual sovereignty of a monarch (see below), as an ostensibly "divine" instance "infinitely" above civil society which is driven by the striving to realize merely particular interests, Hegel does not dialectically resolve, but perpetuates the rift between particularity and universality which is then to be bridged by a kind of paternalistic trustfulness. Against this it has to be kept in mind that the state itself, even as "the actual-reality of concrete freedom" (die Wirklichkeit der konkreten Freiheit, § 260), remains always a finite human reality in which the singularity of the concept of freedom, if it is to be realized at all, must be realized in human *individuals*, and that the rift between particularity and universality in its guise as the gulf between civil society and the state can only be bridged and mediated — in a plurality of singularities — if there are *two-way political institutions* that allow the state's power, in turn, to be surveilled and controlled by civil society in both a perpetual conflict over the most adequate concrete conception of the universal well-being of a people and also a continual surveillance and control over the organs of state power and over how *particular* individuals holding political power concretely exercise that power (including even the option of impeachment of the head of state). In this way, the individual members of civil society are truly raised into singular citizens with a genuine concern for the universal without, however, leaving their self-interests behind. It is merely impotent moralism to demand that the members of society *ought* to forget their so-called 'egoism' and become truly and solely interested in the universal good. Therefore it is necessary that those entrusted with universal tasks within the state are also surveilled and controlled for the endless aberrations of particularity from the universal good.

A major institution of mediation between the state and civil society are the *media* with the associated right of *freedom of speech*. They are fora for public debate in terms of average, everyday understanding over issues concerning the universal good and themselves *organs of power* insofar as they approve or disapprove, acknowledge or reject (aspects of) the government's formulated policy. Such average understanding is itself a confused mixture of particular self-interestedness and universal disinterestedness. The public opinion voiced in the media in turn shows how strong the government's grip on state power is, because a government cannot continue to rule in the long run against a people whose consensus conception, or rather opinion, of some major aspect of the public weal is against it. Therefore, in turn, the government attempts to rhetorically present its policies to the media in a persuasive light to retain or regain legitimacy. Like any other organ of social power, the media, too, are tinged or can be outright corrupted by particular interests, whether they be the political opinions of a media mogul or of a particular sector of civil society such as a labour union or an employers' association but, even without the admixture of particular interests, the media are just one pole of the power play over concrete conceptions of the universal good conceived mundanely in terms 'ordinary people' can understand. The media's unwritten directive is to serve this average understanding and its continual flux back and forth in public opinion, i.e. in the way such wavering opinion, continually buffeted by fickle moods, holds the world to be in a perpetual controversy.

The culmination of two-way political institutions mediating between civil society and the state is that of democracy (cf. Chapter 13), through which the former is able to choose its government, or at least remove a government from power. The democratic process itself is infused with a mixture of particular sectoral interests and worldviews on the best conception of the universal good for society. Singular political leaders in which a definite conception of the universal good, or a workable compromise of particular interests, is embodied become the rallying points for the ongoing power play precisely over which conception of the universal good is to prevail. Such political leaders have to be skilful manipulators of public opinion the media in a touch-and-go interplay of rhetorical powers. This power play is a major instance of the phenomenon of rhetorical power as investigated in Chapter 10.2 which shows the peculiar socio-ontological structure of political power as a power play among a plurality of inevitably and 'infinitely' free social players.

12.3.5 Division of powers within the state in accord with the concept of freedom – Hereditary monarchy "outside human freedom" true to the hermeneutic cast of productionist metaphysics – The concept of freedom does not come to a unified closure – The people's (mis-)trust of the state

Individualized human being in its truth (in Hegel's sense) remains an open, contradictory, loose and ragged unity of the concept of freedom, whose moments — universality, particularity, singular — can never 'close together' into a final, tranquil, uni-focal unity and standing presence. The "apodictic judgement" which serves as the transition in Hegel's *Logik* from the concept's primal split between singularity and universality in the judgement to its closing-together in the conclusion[251] cannot be transferred without further ado to the concept of freedom. That is, it is not true (to the ontological concept) that a singular, individual human being having particular qualities of such-and-such a kind (e.g. non-egoistic) is truly free in corresponding to the universal of freedom concretized in the state. Rather, the determination of the state's concretely organized will as the embodiment of the universality of freedom can only ever be in part, the provisional and revocable outcome of the ongoing strife among a plurality of singular versions of the universal good and in part, the surveillance of these debatable and debated conceptions for signs of deformity through particular self-interests of individuals and groups. This implies in particular that the perpetual, and constitutionally-institutionally sanctioned mistrust of the exercise of political power is not only a corollary of even Hegel's admission that the state, existing as it does in the finite world with its arbitrariness and contingency, or rather, being infected as it is by the particularity of self-interest, is not necessarily up to its philosophical concept, corrupted by the particular interests of mortal human beings, but is also a consequence of the socio-ontological circumstance that freedom, in order to be actually real, concrete freedom, has to be mediated by a *plurality* of finite, individual, singular human beings and a corresponding controversial plurality of conceptions of even the universal good itself. This plurality is only ever mediated by some sort of compromise or transitory consensus, but remains basically in power play. The constitutionally sanctioned *division of powers* within the state by virtue of which one organ of state provides a check on another therefore corresponds to the concept of concrete freedom as sociating power play rather than being, as Hegel claims, an unwarranted destruction of the unity of the state in a single (monarchical) will.

The power play that infuses *all* social power thus carries over also to the state itself. Hegel, however, insists on the unity of the state's will, i.e. that the state attain the moment of singularity in the individuality of the hereditary monarch (§ 281). The hereditary character of the monarch ostensibly removes the determination of the head of state from the realm of will and leaves it to nature (that is, for as long as a power struggle does not wipe a monarch or a dynasty from the stage of world history). Thus, Hegel claims, the head of state as "pure decision" and "moment of the idea" must be "rooted outside human freedom" (das unvermischte, reine Entscheiden [...] Als Moment der Idee [...] außerhalb der menschlichen Freiheit wurzelnd, § 279 Add.) as "fate" (Fatum, § 279 Add.) and that "the right of the monarch [is] based on divine authority"

---

251 Cf. the digression Chapter 3.3.1, 'Dialectic of self and other – Wrestling with Plato, Hegel, Heidegger'.

(das Recht des Monarchen als auf göttliche Autorität gegründet, § 279 Add.). Since the monarch remains an individual, finite human being, however, and despite Hegel's endeavours to remove the determination of the head of state from the realm of mere "contingency" (Zufälligkeit, § 279 Add.) and, remarkably, even from the realm of freedom itself, whether the monarch deserves the name of sovereign or succumbs to despotism to a greater or lesser degree, or is simply a poor, ungifted head of state, itself becomes a matter of the contingency of nature. The monarch then has the final and absolute power of decision and is the single point into which the power of state is ultimately gathered as the "groundless *self-determination* of the will" (grundlose *Selbstbestimmung* des Willens, § 279) in which the initially "abstract concept of will" comes finally to its "singularity" as "sovereignty" (§ 278 Add.).

Such a constitutional monarchy is conceived to *put an end to the interminable power play* (which, however, nonetheless corresponds to the 'divine' concept of freedom as a cast of the beingness of beings) within the given society, making of *sociating* polyarchic power interplay a monoarchic *productionist* power with a single ἀρχή, namely, the monarchical ruler, the ἄρχων, thus remaining true to the covertly ruling hermeneutic cast of productionist metaphysics' ontology of movement. That Hegel has to resort, ironically, to anchoring the singularity of state power "outside of human freedom" in contingent nature, instead of in Geist, in itself indicates the deep socio-ontological dilemma of human freedom which by virtue of its very essence as estimating interplay inevitably remains infused with a power play among a plurality of human beings. *That* is the ontological "fate" that overcomes human being as free.

Hegel therefore assigns to the monarch "the absolute [part ME] in the final decision" (den absoluten [Anteil ME] der schließlichen Entscheidung, *Enz*III § 544 Note) within the "legislative power" (gesetzgebende Gewalt, *Enz.* § 544 Note) and also claims that "to imagine the set-up of the state [...] as the mechanism of a balance of powers in its [the set-up's ME] interior that are external to one another goes against the basic idea of what a state is" ([d]ie Einrichtung des Staats [...] als den Mechanismus eines Gleichgewichts sich in ihrem Innern einander äußerlicher Mächte vorzustellen, geht gegen die Grundidee dessen, was ein Staat ist. *Enz.* § 544 Note). The conception of the state in its interior being constituted as an ongoing power play "goes against the basic idea of what a state is" only within the traditional metaphysical hermeneutic cast of all movement *as* effective movement which demands, in particular, that the concept of freedom, too, come to a unified mono-archic closure, even though freedom is a *social, sociating* concept that can never conform to the productionist cast without doing violence to the very phenomenon of human freedom in its socio-ontological truth.

Hence, once not only the shortfall of reality vis-à-vis the concept of freedom in its universality, but, more decisively, the contradictory disunity of the concept of freedom itself in its unity of moments in perpetual power interplay is seen, it can no longer be argued, as Hegel does, that the nature of the state as an organic, articulated whole demands that it must not be fettered by the disunity of a division of powers instituted to control how the state's power is factually exercised. The state itself is therefore truly, i.e. according to its concept, a power play, an ongoing *power struggle*, and the state's constitution must provide for this circumstance. This power struggle within the state itself and in its relation to civil society, as provided for by a true constitution with its stipulated rules of play for the power struggle, is not entirely the open-slather power struggle among particular interests, which may be provided for in restricted areas of the constitution such as democratic elections to parliament as the legislative body organized in a party-political way, but above all the constitutionally admissible and organized conflict over the determination of concretely realized freedom in which one organ of state can question another or individual citizens can question the state's concrete will as expressed, say, in a specific law or government decision. There is therefore a *constitutional ethos* for the ongoing power struggle within the state. Moreover, the power struggle among political parties cannot be regarded purely as a struggle among various interest groups in civil society, but also as a fight over genuinely different conceptions of the concrete universal good in which mere blatant self-interest is put to one side. The media themselves, as one set of players in the political power play, have an important role in monitoring the various political parties with a view to judging whether their policies cater too blatantly merely to the self-interests of particular sectors of the electorate, their 'client' voters.

It is not sufficient for the state to be unified in a monarchical will and the members of society to find their satisfaction in the "trust and confidence" (Zutrauen, *RPh.* § 268) they experience that the state secures the framework within which they lead their habitual daily lives without having to be concerned about their security. Such "patriotism" (§ 268) lies in the awareness "that my substantial and particular interest is preserved and included in the interest and purpose of another (here, the state) [...] and with this, this other is not an other for me and I am free in this consciousness" (daß mein substantielles und besonderes Interesse im Interesse und Zwecke eines Anderen (hier des Staats) [...] bewahrt und enthalten ist, womit eben dieser unmittelbar kein anderer für mich ist und Ich in diesem Bewußtsein frei bin. § 268).

This describes a relation of trust to a caring, paternal instance and not a relationship of freedom, as Hegel claims, but of grateful dependence associated with the feeling of being looked after. The state is not an "other for me", is not alien only through an identification with the state that cancels out the inviolability of individual sites of freedom. It may well be that people are entirely willing to subjugate themselves to a superior power that guarantees order, and Hegel indeed claims that "what keeps [the state ME] together is solely the basic feeling of order that everybody has" (das Haltende [am Staat ME] ist allein das Grundgefühl der Ordnung, das alle haben, § 268 Add.) The order upheld by the state with its superior power is not an end in itself, however, but is for the sake of the free interplay of the members of civil society, which certainly requires an order, but one that is inconspicuously in the background rather than overbearingly in the foreground.

A similar comment can be made about the trust the people are supposed to place in "the highest state officials [who] necessarily have deeper and more comprehensive insight into the nature of the institutions and needs of the state" (die höchsten Staatsbeamten[, die] notwendig tiefere und umfassendere Einsicht in die Natur der Einrichtungen und Bedürfnisse des Staats [haben], § 301 Note) and who are therefore allotted the task of knowing "what [...] reason wills, [...] the fruit of deep knowledge and insight which is precisely not a matter for the people" (was [...] die Vernunft will, [...] die Frucht tiefer Erkenntnis und Einsicht, welche eben nicht die Sache des Volks ist, § 301 Note). This is a truly patronizing remark on Hegel's part. Of course the "highest state officials" have superior insight into the workings of the state, but this has to do with the implementation of a concrete conception of the universal good, and it is the leaders who emerge from the ranks of the people who forge conceptions of the concrete universal which can never be authorized top down, but must arise from the ongoing conflict and struggle precisely over a people's historical, ethical life. That is, if the concept of freedom as sociating, mutually estimating power interplay is to be concretely realized, this is something other than an orderly conception of the concrete universal as thought out by a more or less well-meaning, patronizing bureau-technocracy imposed from above. It is not simply a matter of state bureaucrats possibly being themselves corrupt or overly self-interested, but of the concept of groundlessly sociating freedom per se, i.e. true freedom, being stifled in its presencing in an historical people.

12.3.6 The transition from civil society to state reconsidered: The power play over sociating estimation and identity in belonging to a political whole — Constitutional rules of play for the ongoing political power struggle

The concept of freedom itself demands that a power play remain in play even within the state. Such a power play is indissolubly also a process of sociating estimation in which the players estimate each other as possessing certain powers. In the transition from civil society to the state, these powers become expressly political powers associated with holding some office or other within the state, whether it be as parliamentarian, state official, minister or (elected or hereditary, empowered or titular) head of state. An individual holding public office does so only because and only so long as its status as office-holder is mirrored and affirmed by others.

Let us retrace our steps to Hegel's treatment of the civic corporation, which he claims forms the dialectical transition in thinking to the state in which the gulf between particularity and universality starts to be bridged. How far does this bridge carry us? There is one aspect of this transition which has not yet been discussed, namely, that the civic corporation is the social locus where the member of society as a member of an "authorized", "legally constituted and recognized" (berechtigt, [...] gesetzlich konstituiert und anerkannt, *RPh.* § 253 Note) corporation "has honour in its social status" (es hat so in seinem Stande seine Ehre, § 253). This is the aspect of *social estimation* through which an individual comes to stand in a *social status* as somebody more than merely a self-interested individual, as somewho with a sense of civic duty who has something resembling the social good in view. The other as mirror is essential to the phenomenon of estimation. The estimation of status as member of a civic corporation is the integration of the individual into an association, to which it then 'belongs', that raises the individual above and beyond its merely narrow, egoistic interests, giving it a social standing and *identity* as a socially concerned, civic-minded somewho.

This can only happen because even the so-called egoistic individual is 'always already', i.e. in essence, a sociated being belonging to an association, a community, in short, a social world for which it cares, and is therefore susceptible in its very self-identity to the social estimation of a social status as somewho reflected by the others. But even more than that: in truth, the individual is not merely susceptible to its estimation in the socio-ontological dimension of whoness; its very *being* as presencing in three-dimensional time is constituted by the mirror play of whoness. Social estimation is an interplay, a mutual exchange in which individuals come into their own *self*-standing as *social* members by identifying their selves in a "shining-back" from the world (cf. Chapter 3.3.1.4 and Chapter 11.2). The individual self is essentially also sociated, i.e. mediated by the sociating mirror-interplay of estimation which constitutes an identity of difference.

It would seem that Hegel chooses the civic corporation as the point of transition to the state precisely because it is the raising of the individual beyond its particularity to the universal not only of common, shared, aligned interests as a bundling of particularity, and not only by educating it beyond its limited horizon of understanding so that it gains an appreciation of the greater, interconnected whole, but also by raising it to *belonging to a universal social nexus* within which it finds its own identity, i.e. its being as self within the dimension of whoness. In being a estimated as member of a civic corporation which in turn is recognized by the state (as the agent of the universal will) in law as authorized, the individual itself is estimated in its stand within a universal, social nexus. Therefore, for Hegel, "the state is the actual-reality of the ethical idea" (Der Staat ist die Wirklichkeit der sittlichen Idee, § 257) and "*association* as such is itself the true content and purpose, and the determination of individuals is to lead a universal life" (Die *Vereinigung* als solche ist selbst der wahrhafte Inhalt und Zweck, und die Bestimmung der Individuen ist, ein allgemeines Leben zu führen, § 258 Note). As ob-jects 'thrown toward' the openness of the 3D-temporal clearing and claimed by it, individual human beings cannot escape the socio-ontological destiny of being sociated as social beings, and their social being has the "infinite" and "divine" socio-ontological status of whoness. To be a social outcast does not mean being outside whoness altogether, but amounts to non-existence, to death as somewho, i.e. to a deficient mode of whoness.

The status of person is an abstract form of whoness which the members of civil society mirror to each other in their interchanges with one another and which enables them to pursue their particular interests under the mantle of this state-guaranteed form of mutual estimation. Now, however, the satisfaction of being estimates as somewho becomes more concrete as estimation of one's standing on universal issues concerning the whole community, or even the entire society. The concern for political issues ranging from the local to the national and global arises itself within civil society, and the struggle over political issues is simultaneously a struggle over the who-standing of those engaged in those issues, and such a who-standing is then invariably reflected in the *political power* that an individual attains, which is always only possible as the ongoing outcome of a conflictual struggle also over social estimation.

Someone can only wield political power because it is mirrored, validated and thus legitimized by others. The power interplay of civil society over particular interests thus becomes a *political power play* over concrete conceptions of the universal good, more or less tinged by particular interests, but imbued also with the striving to be estimated as a worthy, civic-minded who. The power play that is an essential look of (the ontological structure of) sociated freedom spills over to and infuses the interior of the state as the instance whose task it is to wield power for the sake of the universal good. Civil society serves as a *recruiting ground* for the selection of politicians on all levels, those civic-minded individuals who engage in and commit themselves to issues with a narrower or wider social horizon.

Whereas in civil society it is the right of personhood and its concretization in state-posited laws that are to serve as the framework within which the power play of self-interests is played out fairly, now, within the state, it is the *constitution* that is to regulate the power struggle over offices of power within the state by laying down the rules of play for such an ongoing struggle. As we have seen above, it goes against the concept of freedom for the head of state to be an hereditary monarch, supposedly situated entirely above the power play and "outside human freedom" (§ 279 Add). Rather, the head of state, too, in whom the state attains the singularity of an individual, must be elected out of the contenders for that office if the never-attainable settled unity of social freedom, its irradicable plurality is to be respected, i.e. if actual social reality is to correspond to the concept of sociated freedom. The political parties, the politicians, the members of parliament, the ministers and the head of state must all vie for political power in various kinds of struggles of estimation of their status as worthy holders of certain powers.

The constitution that lays down the rules of play for such political struggle does not have the relative simplicity of guaranteeing the abstract equality of persons in fair struggles over particular interests in civil society, but nevertheless must accord with a conception of fairness for the political power play in which no one instance, such as the head of state or the military, is given too much power. If the inner state is in its essence a power play, such an interplay must be kept in play through a *balance of powers*, and not degenerate into a totalitarian set-up in which one power-centre dominates or even quashes the others. Each people has its own constitution with its own idiosyncrasies that has evolved out its own historical experience. A people's democratic constitution lays down the rules of play according to which it will acknowledge and honour the holders of political office, thus according them popularly legitimated political power. Only on the basis of constitutionally legitimated political power can a state rule its people peaceably because in such a state of affairs, the people lives in the consciousness that its state is in joint, and hence it itself is free.

12.3.7 The reality of freedom as the shared, ethical social living of a people and its fracturing, through which free societies remain in flux

In the above quotation, "the state is the actual-reality of the ethical idea" (Der Staat ist die Wirklichkeit der sittlichen Idee, § 257), the German "sittlich", one of whose standard translations is "moral", has been rendered as "ethical". 'Sitte' is 'custom', 'usage' and refers to a customary way of a shared social life and not merely to the subjective, conscience-regulated inwardness of morality. Hegel distinguishes between Sittlichkeit und Moralität, between ethical life and morality. Ethical life consists above all in a shared, practised way of life ruled by customary usages and, according to Hegel, as this universal it must be concretized and safeguarded by the state above all through posited law. Such a concretizing of ethical life can take the form, for instance, of a social consensus, based on genuine insight into the universal, regarding some aspect of social life (such as the education of children), which has to be binding on all members of society and therefore also enforced in law by a superior power as the agent of the universal. Social consensus inspired by an appreciation of the well-being of a free people and the legitimate rule of men over men necessarily go hand in hand.

The (speculative, ontological) insight of reason into the beingness of beings, however, consists first of all in seeing that human being itself is essentially, from the start, i.e. a priori, customary, social, ethical and can never be truncated to merely isolated, individual existence pursuing its particular self-interest. This means that the state has its actual-reality (Wirklichkeit, ἐντελέχεια) first and foremost not in institutions, laws or some such thing, but in knowing, insightful self-consciousness itself: "The state, as the actual-reality of substantial *will*, which it [the state] has in particular *self-consciousness* that has been raised to its universality, is *reason* in and for itself" (Der Staat ist als die Wirklicheit des substantiellen *Willens*, die er in dem zu seiner Allgemeinheit erhobenen besonderen *Selbstbewußtsein* hat, das an und für sich *Vernünftige*. § 258). Seen in this way, the state is first and foremost a 'state of mind', albeit a state of thinking, reason-imbued mind or Geist that sees that it is essentially universal, an idea, a cast shape of the beingness of beings, the presencing of occurrents. As this cast of being (Seinsentwurf), the state's perfect presence, its ἐντελέχεια or actuality, is achieved first of all in reason, since it is reason and being that fundamentally belong together in the idea (τὸ γὰρ αὐτό νοεῖν ἐστίν τε καὶ εἶναι Parmenides, Frag. 3).

Reason in this sense can be taken both subjectively and objectively: subjectively as the way of thinking of the members of society, and objectively as the ethical usages and institutions within which people customarily live their lives. It cannot be demanded, however, that every citizen be a philosopher; it suffices that the citizens appreciate and cherish the "infinite" forms of freedom they enjoy in a free society in which the forms of free power interplay among individuals are protected, or the way in which laws are made according to principles that enshrine civil liberties. In this way, they *inkle* pre-ontologically the speculative concept of freedom, living with a *feeling* for freedom within its realization, its presencing. A pre-ontological appreciation of freedom cannot be calculated by understanding in terms of its utilitarian usefulness, but arises by cherishing an established way of life.

The social practices and institutions that constitute an historical way of living of a people are the concrete reality of an idea of the state in the sense of a customarily practised and dearly valued way of sociated living. Society is never conceivable as an "atomistic *heap* of individuals" (atomistischer *Haufen* von Individuen, *RPh.* § 273 Note), nor as a set of Leibnizian monads as power centres interacting like billiard balls on a level billiard table, but only as an interplay among human beings regulated by both law and custom, but remaining a power play nonetheless. People are held to these customs not just by a respect for tradition, but in the first place by the mirror play of sociating estimation that censures conduct which violates customary practice. Any such conduct therefore has to justify itself if it is not to be dismissed as unruly, rebellious, asocial and unethical. The break with social usages, through which free societies remain in flux, therefore has to articulate itself rhetorically in such a way that shows that it is in conformity with freedom in a certain respect, whereas accepted customary practice *in truth* is shown to be in violation of freedom, i.e. that customary practice does *not* correspond to the concept of freedom. A public debate is thus ignited in which a more or less clearly understood concept of freedom is invoked rhetorically and serves as a touchstone. This is the way in which freedom remains ultimately forever *singular*, never allowing itself to be finally tied down once and for all in accepted, universal ethical usages. Singularity must seek a closing-together with the universality of ethical life if it is not to be mere caprice, and it can only do so by arguing in favour of a new play of freedom, i.e. another historically possible constellation of free interplay that now, through public debate, comes to appear in a socially fair and favourable light.

12.3.8 Hegel's critique of the liberal conception of state – Kant's "idea of the original contract"

Hegel fears and mistrusts nothing more than the "mob" (Pöbel, § 301 Note) and insists on placing the care of the universal in the hands of those with "deep knowledge and insight", above all, the monarch whose hereditary right to rule ostensibly places him above the fray of the conflicts in civil society. Hegel's *Philosophy of Right* thus cements the rift between particularity and universality, offering only the solace of a relationship of paternal trust, instead of building mediations whereby the people, including perhaps even parts of the so-called mob, could be drawn into, and elevated and cultivated in the concrete matters concerning the well-being of a people living its historically embedded way of life. Today, with the coming of everybody as member of the people, the mob no longer exists. The organs of public opinion, especially the mass media perpetually pandering to a sham democratic 'we', become vital in any concretely practised mediation between civil society with its bewildering conglomeration and friction of particular interests and views of the universal, on the one hand, and the state which, through its articulation into its particularized organs of power (the government, the head of government, the head of state, the legislative assemblies, the judiciary, the bureaucracy with its public servants, etc.) is dedicated to realizing a (perpetually disputed and changing) concrete conception of universal well-being, on the other.

The very conception of concrete, universal well-being remains in movement, driven by the ongoing debates in politics and civil society over universal issues as they inevitably arise in ever new situations and conjunctures. Such a movement of constant, conflictual debate conforms well with Hegel's conception of the Bildung, i.e. the cultivation and education, of civil society. The liberal way of thinking — for the lack of an alternative for finite mortals thrown together and sociated willy-nilly in a world they have to share — puts its trust in the concrete, institutionally secured, two-way mediation between civil society and state in a power play, despite all the drawbacks and human defects of such a democratic constitution, whereas Hegel wants to insulate the universal state organs against the clamouring of public debate and the fights among the myriad self-interested social groupings and instead calls on the people to put its trust in this constitutionally insulated, superior instance of the universal which thus assumes a paternalistic character. Hence Hegel's low regard for "English" liberalism and parliamentarianism.

The late Hegel had a mistrust of the individual whose freedom he tended to abhor as akin to the capricious freedom of the mob. In an article written in 1831, the year of his death, he clearly favours a paternalistic model of state rule that avoids the disorder of unruly democratic struggles through parliament: "As much as a centuries-long, quiet work of scientific [i.e. philosophical ME] education and cultivation, of wisdom and the love of justice on the part of princes has effected in Germany, the English nation has not achieved through its people's representation..." (Soviel als in Deutschland eine mehrhundertjährige stille Arbeit der wissenschaftlichen Bildung, der Weisheit und Gerechtigkeitsliebe der Fürsten bewirkt hat, hat die englische Nation von ihrer Volksrepräsentation nicht erlangt...[252]) Hence, although he allows for the rights of particularity in civil society, Hegel gives priority to the supposedly more insightful 'powers that be', who may dilute and override the rights of particularity as required by state-posited universal interests.

In his commentary on Aristotle in the *Vorlesungen über die Geschichte der Philosophie* (*Werke* Bd. 19), Hegel uses the opportunity to formulate once again his critique of the liberal conception of state, viewing the "modern principle" (dem modernen Prinzip, W19:226) of individuality through quasi-Greek eyes. After citing the famous Aristotelean definition of essence, according to which the human being is "a political animal that has reason" (ein politisches Tier, das Vernunft hat, W19:225), and Aristotle's claim that the "state" (properly speaking, πόλις) is conceptually prior to both the family and the individual, Hegel proceeds:

> Aristoteles macht nicht den Einzelnen und dessen Recht zum Ersten, sondern erkennt den Staat für das, was seinem Wesen nach höher ist als der Einzelne und die Familie und deren Substantialität ausmacht. Der Staat ist wesentliche Existenz in Ansehung des Guten, Gerechten. 'Denn das Ganze ist das Erste (Wesen) gegen den Teil. Wird das Ganze aufgehoben' (der ganze Mensch), 'so gibt es weder Fuß noch Hand außer dem Namen nach, wie eine steinerne Hand; denn eine vertilgte Hand ist eine steinerne' (ist der Mensch tot, so gehen alle Teile unter). 'Denn alles ist durch die Entelechie und die Möglichkeit bestimmt; so daß, wenn diese Entelechie nicht mehr vorhanden ist, nicht mehr zu sagen ist, etwas sei noch Dieses, sondern nur dem Namen nach. So ist der Staat Entelechie, das Wesen der Einzelnen; der Einzelne ist so wenig etwas an und für sich, getrennt vom Ganzen, als irgendein Teil vom Ganzen.' Dies ist gerade entgegengesetzt dem modernen Prinzip, was vom Einzelnen ausgeht; so daß jeder seine Stimme gibt und dadurch erst ein Gemeinwe-

---

252 G.W.F. Hegel 'Über die englische Reformbill' *Werke* Bd. 11 S. 103.

sen zustande kommt. Bei Aristoteles ist der Staat das Substantielle, die Hauptsache;... (W19:226)

Aristotle does not make the individual and its right into the primary moment, but recognizes the state as that which is, according to its essence, superior to the individual and the family and constitutes their substantiality. The state is essential existence in view of the good and the just. 'For the whole is primary (essence) as against the part. If the whole is annulled' (the entire human), 'then foot or hand continue to exist in name only like a stone hand because a destroyed hand is a stone hand' (if the person is dead, all the parts perish). 'For everything is determined by entelechy and possibility; so that if this entelechy no longer exists, it can no longer be said that something is still this, but only in name. Thus the state is entelechy [perfected presence ME], the essence of the individual; the individual is just as little something in and for itself separated from the whole as any organic part of the whole.' This is precisely opposed to the modern principle that proceeds from the individual; so that each individual gives its vote and only through this does a community come about. For Aristotle, the state is what is substantial, the main thing;...

The "state" as a rendering of πόλις is, to say the least, misleading because the πόλις refers precisely to the *whole* of a *society* in its way of life which includes its polity, its political institutions and social usages which, in the case of the ancient Greek city-state, included also each (free, male) citizen's involvement in the affairs of the polis. The (justified) objection against the modern way of conceiving the state is that the individual can only *be* an individual within the entelechy or actual, perfect presence of a whole political order. The individual *is* an individual only within an historical world in which the individuality of individuals has been cast as individual rights and freedoms along with the pursuit of individual self-interests through the exercise of such individual rights in mutually estimating power plays or, as Hegel puts it, such an historical world (our own liberal Western world) is "dirempted into the particularity of need and enjoyment *reflected into itself* and the universality of *abstract* right" (zur *in sich reflektierten* Besonderheit des Bedürfnisses und Genusses und zur *abstrakten* rechtlichen Allgemeinheit entzweit, *RPh.* § 255). We have seen that the free individual is first historically possible in a society sociated through abstract, reified value that enable sociation primarily through a bewildering variety of market interplay.

The individual of liberal natural right theory, however, is an abstract construction abstracted from such an historical world, i.e. from a whole, which provides the individual *as such* with its "substantiality", i.e. its οὐσία, its standing presence. The individual *is* such only as part of this dynamic whole in which the idea of "the good and the just" can exist in the state considered now as a concrete, stable state of affairs in which good living is possible and in joint, justice being nothing other than the state of affairs in which the goods of life are interchanged through a social interplay whose lawful fairness enables the whole metabolism of social living to be in joint. The whole of the state, or society, is an organism in the sense of a living whole in which each part has its specific function.

As we have seen, Hegel is right to point out that it is a fiction to suppose that the state could ever arise from individuals giving up their vote, for whence could an 'idea' of living together arise? Any such 'idea' can only be a shape of the beingness of beings that must be fore-seen by human understanding and must be concretized in the practised, habitual usages of an historical world. Thinking and the shaping-up of sociated being in a state conceived as a social whole form an inseparable unity and identity. This view of the whole as a Gestalt of being is prior (in thought and in reality) to any individual and, in particular, it is prior to any individual 'voting' on any such thing as a social contract. As Immanuel Kant puts out, what is important is the "idea of the original contract" (Idee des ursprünglichen Vertrags[253]), not some actual, historically, empirically concluded contract.

The import of liberal thinking on the state, properly understood, is only the demand that reason has the *individual* 'right' to insight into the state as an historical shape of shared, historical sociated being and that such a state is not to be accepted merely on authority, but rather must be demonstrably compatible with individual freedom in its exercise as ongoing power interplay and also with the formal equality of individuals before such a state. Such an insight is not merely a matter of pre-ontological understanding that could justify the existence of the state in terms of its necessary 'practical usefulness' for preserving life and liberty, peaceableness and order, but must go beyond such mere finite reasoning or understanding to the affirmative insight of reason into the state as a 'look' of free sociated being itself. Freely sociated being, however, is a living *movement*, an estimative power play, and the metabolism of society is a manifold of various kinds of social interplay that are simultaneously power plays.

12.3.9 Pre-ontological ethical 'second nature' and ontological insight into the political realm

What kind of knowledge with respect to the political is attainable? In the first place there is the pre-ontological plane. Aristotle writes with regard to knowledge of the political (ἡ πολιτική) as a realm of practical action:

---

253 I. Kant *Zum ewigen Frieden* BA 20 *Werke* Band VI ed. W. Weischedel 1964 S. 204.

Λέγοιτο δ' ἂν ἱκανῶς εἰ κατὰ ὑποκειμένην ὕλην διασαφηθείη· τὸ γὰρ ἀκριβὲς οὐχ ὁμοίως ἐν ἅπασι τοῖς λόγοις ἐπιζητητέον, ὥσπερ οὐδ' ἐν τοῖς δημιουργουμένοις. [...] ἀγαπητὸν οὖν [...] τύπῳ τἀληθὲς ἐνδείκνυσθαι, καὶ περὶ τῶν ὡς ἐπὶ τὸ πολὺ καὶ ἐκ τοιούτων λέγοντας τοιαῦτα καὶ συμπεραίνεσθαι. [...] πεπαιδευμένου γάρ ἐστιν ἐπὶ τοσοῦτον τἀκριβὲς ἐπιζητεῖν καθ' ἕκαστον γένος ἐφ' ὅσον ἡ τοῦ πράγματος φύσις ἐπιδέχεται·

One could say that it is sufficient if one clarifies in accordance with the underlying matter, for the same degree of precision is not to be demanded in all discourses, just as it is not to be demanded to the same degree in all crafts. [...] We must therefore be content if [...] we succeed in demonstrating the truth in broad types, and if when speaking about things which are thus for the most part and starting from things which are thus for the most part, we also bring about conclusions which hold also only for the most part. [...] For it is the mark of an educated person to demand that amount of precision corresponding to each genus which the nature of the thing admits. (*Eth. Nic.* I iii 1094b11–25)

If the underlying subject matter of ἡ πολιτική is "that which is thus for the most part" (τὸ ἐπὶ τὸ πολύ) in contradistinction to what does not admit being otherwise (οὐκ ἐνδεχόμενον ἄλλως ἔχειν), i.e. that which is necessarily so and always so (τὸ ἀεὶ ὄν), then it would be more appropriate to speak of an art of politics rather than a science of the political or political science (as standard English translations of Aristotle do). Science for Aristotle is that knowledge that can be deduced from first principles, and it is applicable only to those areas of phenomena, notably natural — and among those, celestial — phenomena, that cannot behave, i.e. presence and present themselves, in any other way. The realm of politics, by contrast, is the realm of human action, human practices, which depend on decisions based on human freedom to act. "...the final end [of politics ME] is not knowing, but practical action." (τὸ τέλος ἐστὶν οὐ γνῶσις ἀλλὰ πρᾶξις *Eth. Nic.* I iii. 1095a6)

Deliberations and interchanges may lead to one outcome or another for action, and we have investigated the deepest socio-ontological ground for this in Chapter 5, which at the same time provides the socio-ontological basis for making the usual traditional distinction between art and science. The political is also the realm in which practical experience of life counts, because life experience teaches "that which is thus for the most part" in all its endless and continually surprising diversity. For this reason Aristotle says that "a young man is not a suitable auditor for the subject of the art of politics" (τῆς πολιτικῆς οὐκ ἔστιν οἰκεῖος ἀκροατὴς ὁ νέος· 1095a3). The art of politics is concerned with how constitutions come about, institutions are set up, governments empowered, political struggles fought out and issues deliberated for the sake of the well-being of society and its members. The understanding of what constitutes a 'good life' in a given society is always finite, (what Hegel would call mere understanding operating in his oft-invoked realm of Willkür und Zufälligkeit, arbitrariness and contingency) and above all, it is contentious, and hardly has in view divine, absolute reason (understood here as theological insight into a supreme being or, more down to earth, ontological insight into the prevailing hermeneutic casts of the beingness of being) but studies how people practically lead their lives and what ends they pursue in doing so.

Reason, by contrast, has the task not of running or deliberating everyday political affairs or of guiding social action, but of bringing necessarily simple and abstract socio-ontological structures to light as 'looks' of the hermeneutic casts of beings as such. In the present context, this means that the political realm as an ontological structure has to 'come to its concept', namely, the concept of free will, which, in turn, and according to Hegel's conception of truth, is realized as idea in a correspondence of the concept with reality. This is the polity or the political structure of an historical way in which a people lives together, but only in mutually estimative power interplay.

The above-quoted Aristotelean description of what politics is about preontologically rightly points to the necessity of having life-experience to be able to understand it, and it is also true that politics is not a science that could be derived from first principles, because it deals only with phenomena that are so only "for the most part", and that, in turn, because they have no single, governing point of origin. But this still leaves open the question as to the socio-ontological ground for this 'inexact' nature of politics which is not to be regarded as a deficiency compared to some sort of ideal of exact science such as mathematics, but in its own right as the socio-ontological, fathomless complexity and richness of the political realm itself, whose fundamental socio-ontological structure per se, however, can be rigorously brought to its concept. Despite the 'messy' and bewilderingly diverse ontic-factual character of the political, it is nonetheless possible to attain deep, socio-ontological clarity about key political concepts such as freedom (ἐλευθερία), justice (τὰ δίκαια 1094b14) and what is good for living together (τἀγαθά 1094b18). As investigated in preceding chapters, there are traces in Aristotle's political-ethical thinking on, say, esteem and value, of deeper socio-ontological insights that have been taken up and further worked out.

In the present chapter section we have seen, first of all, that the state can be understood as arising from the diremption of particularity from universality in civil society, and such diremption results necessarily from both the concept and the reality of individual freedom as plural power play. The diremption has its socio-ontological roots ultimately in the sundering of spirited mind itself "into different selves who are completely free, independent, absolutely aloof, resistant in-and-for-themselves and for each other — and nevertheless at the same time identical with one another and thus not independent, not impenetrable, but, as it were, confluenced, flowed-together." (*Enz.* § 436 Add. as cited in Chapter 11.2) The individual is therefore essentially also *not* an individual, inevitably infected by dialectical negation, and therefore penetrable, divisible. Furthermore, we have seen that Hegel does not bring the moment of the singularity of freedom into play in making the dialectical transition from civil society to the state, and doing so makes for a never-resolved tension between civil society and state in a power play that is of the essence of politics. The singularity of the concept of freedom does not come to be embodied in the monarch, but remains plural in the plurality of singular conceptions of the universal good which engage in the ongoing political power struggle proper.

The socio-ontological reason for the nature of politics as an art rather than a science rests therefore ultimately upon the nature of social, sociating power itself. As has been shown in earlier chapters (Chapters 5 and 10), social power does not conform with the ontological structure of effective power (δύναμις) investigated by Aristotle in Book Theta of his *Metaphysics*, but rather has to be thought as a polyarchic power play that can never be unified into a single ἀρχή without perverting the concept of freedom itself. The power play of dynamic human togetherness has the character also of a mirror play of mutual estimation in which the players estimate each other *as* who they are. The realm of politics as a whole is a mirroring power struggle over standing within the ontological dimension of whoness, and this essential ontological character lends it its unpredictable, groundless, even capricious nature. In contrast to things, which have a relatively constant standing presence for the mind *as* what they are, human beings can only struggle and strive, in the power play of mutual estimation, for an always revocable standing presence as who they are.

A social world is a form of Sittlichkeit, of ethical life, of "objective spirited ming", of world-play which is played out within habituated social practices or ethical usages in which the individuals are 'always already' embedded as social beings sharing a world, and, at least in the liberal conception which demands, according to the very concept of freedom, that the state *justify* and *legitimate* its very existence and its superior power to individual insight, the *state's legitimation and highest function is to guarantee and preserve an historical way of living with its usages for the well-being of the members of society*. Such a legitimation of the state is a philosophical, ontological, speculative one which is not for everybody.

The usages, in the first and fundamental place, are the manifold forms of free exchange and interchange among people, which constitute the true, vital metabolism of society as an interplay. The affirmation of social usages is not merely a matter of common (or so-called 'intersubjective') agreement and convention but involves fundamental, universal issues of human freedom. Common agreement or common interests cannot decide or clarify what human freedom in society *is*, and human freedom itself is an issue that is not up for political debate or a matter for the expression of public opinion, even of widely shared opinion, but is implicitly always already presupposed by these practices. Rather, it is philosophy as social ontology that has the task of clarifying the nature of human freedom as something "infinite", i.e. as granted by the historical time-clearing as a 'look' of the beingness of beings, i.e. as an idea. Such an idea of freedom cannot be clarified merely against the background of a socio-historical context as scholarly endeavour in the history of ideas, for this amounts to historical relativism.

As has been shown, especially in Chapter 6, according to the concept of freedom, the ethos of social interplay is fairness. The power play that is sociating interplay must be fair in order to be just, and this justice is not simply a matter of laws being posited and enforced by the state, but of the usages practised by the members of society as ethical 'second nature', so that the interplay is fair when it is beautiful, i.e. when the players in the interplay themselves live up to and also enjoy a fairness in mutually beneficial intercourse with others. Such fairness applies not only to civil society, thus making it civil, but also to the political power struggles both within the state and in the state's relations to civil society. As such, *fairness of interplay as power play* is a fundamental concept of social ontology that, however, may come to serve preontologically as a lived ethical principle within society that is itself adopted unconsciously, unknowingly by its members as second nature.

12.3.10 The dispensability of the philosopher king and the precipitation of socio-ontological structures in historically lived, ethical usages

I now take up the question regarding the venerable notion of the philosopher king, which is related to the question concerning the difference between pre-ontological ethical "second nature" and ontological knowledge of the political dimension. First of all, it must be conceded that insight into the beingness of beings is not for everybody. Those dedicating themselves to the endeavour of philosophy, leading a way of life which Aristotle calls the theoretical, speculative or contemplative life — ὁ βίος θεωρητικός — are rarities. For the affairs of practical political life, philosophy is out of place and useless, and anyone proposing philosophical knowledge as the *unmediated* foundation for the state and the polity, starting with Plato, is misguided in demanding too much of both the art of politics and of philosophical thinking. Hegel indeed points out that "it is not necessary that those governing have the idea." (Es ist nicht nötig, daß die Regierenden die Idee haben.[254]), because the shapes or 'looks' of politico-social being made out explicitly by philosophical reason (in a co- and fore-casting of history, or in an aftermath at dusk when the owl spreads its wings, but in gliding out into the future) precipitate historically into ethical life through the actions of subjects pursuing their "particular purposes" (besondere Zwecke, W19:34) "not with any co-knowing awareness of the idea" (nicht mit dem Bewußtsein der Idee, W19:34):

> ... wenn Platon sagt, die Philosophen sollen regieren, [meint] er das Bestimmen des ganzen Zustandes durch allgemeine Prinzipien. Dies ist in den modernen Staaten viel mehr ausgeführt; es sind allgemeine Prinzipien wesentlich die Basen der modernen Staaten [...] es ist allgemein anerkannt, daß solche Prinzipien das Substantielle der Verwaltung, der Regierung ausmachen sollen. Die Forderung des Platon ist so der Sache nach vorhanden. Was *wir* Philosophie nennen, die Bewegung in reinen Gedanken, betrifft die Form, die etwas Eigentümliches ist; aber auf dieser Form allein beruht es nicht, daß nicht das Allgemeine, die Freiheit, das Recht in einem Staate zum Prinzip gemacht sei. [...] Die Philosophen sind die μύσται, die beim Ruck im innersten Heiligtum mit- und dabeigewesen; die anderen haben ihr besonderes Interesse: diese Herrschaft, diesen Reichtum, dies Mädchen. — Wozu der Weltgeist 100 und 1000 Jahre braucht, das machen wir schneller, weil wir den Vorteil haben, daß es eine Vergangenheit [ist] und in der Abstraktion geschieht. (W19:36, 489)

> ... when Plato says that the philosophers should rule he means the whole state of affairs being determined by universal principles. This has been carried out much more in modern states; universal principles are essentially the bases of modern states [...] it is generally recognized that such principles should constitute the substance of administration, of government. What *we* call philosophy, the movement in pure thoughts concerns the form, which is something peculiar; but that the universal, freedom, right is not made into a principle in a state rests not on this form alone. [...] The philosophers are the μύσται who went along and were present in the innermost sanctuary at the jolt; the others have their particular interests: this reign, these riches, this girl. — That for which the Weltgeist needs a hundred or a thousand years we do more quickly because we have the advantage that it is a past and takes place in abstraction.

Philosophical truth concerns the casting of the beingness of being, i.e. their presencing in presenting themselves in the time-clearing, the Gestalt in which an historical world comes into the open and takes shape. This is the same as

---

254 G.W.F. Hegel *Vorlesungen über die Geschichte der Philosophie* II, *Werke* Band 19 S. 34, W19:34.

what Hegel calls Weltgeist, the mind of the world in which individuals may participate. The peculiar element in which such truth of the beingness of beings comes to light *philosophically* is that of pure speculative thinking which sees past the empirically given in its bewildering ontic diversity and contingency to the simple, pure, abstract outlines of the beingness of beings, the simple ontological elements which make up the scaffolding of the world in its worldliness. The kind of disclosive truth possible in the realm of practical political affairs where people act in pursuit of their particular, finite interests, by contrast, is often self-serving, dissentious truth tied to specific, concrete issues having practical effects on how people live.

Even universal issues in politics are invariably coloured by self-interest or are at least, as singular perspectives on the universal good, eternally contentious in political struggles. Furthermore, political reasoning, being bound to concrete political situationsa and temporal conjunctures, cannot give room to the disinterested pursuit of socio-ontological reason that demands above all abstraction, i.e. a drawing-off or withdrawal from any particular, all-too-empirical, given situation. The politician or states(wo)man, as a singular, well-intentioned agent of the universal good, does not need speculative, theoretical insight but has to know how to provide leadership in line with firmly held political principles that are nothing other than the translation of abstract ontological structures or contours of the beingness of beings into actual social reality which is understood pre-ontologically. These political principles serve as a guideline for political action, so it has to be said, contra Hegel, that *insofar* political action is not merely a play of *particular* interests, but also has the *universal* as a shape of the beingness of beings in view in a form amenable to political understanding embodied by *singular* political players. In the power play that politics is, political leaders and states(wo)men have to use forceful rhetorical means to sway opinion and instil confidence in a proposed course of political action, presupposing in the background certain political principles, especially concerning notions of freedom and security, that serve as rhetorical cornerstones.

The abstractness of philosophical thinking, as practised by those few pursuing a contemplative life, has its place in history in playing midwife to (contentious) truths that trickle down quietly in history without those who ultimately adopt them as commonplaces, convictions, fixed prejudices or self-evident axioms (e.g. the idea of individual liberty or universal, inalienable human rights), without ever knowing whence they came. They have become unquestioned and seemingly unquestionable 'second nature'. When Hegel does philosophical battle with Kant, for instance, not only a matter of scholarly interest is at stake, but the very question of historical human being-in-the-world, which is,

more deeply, a presencing in the 3D-temporal clearing. As Nietzsche's Zarathustra proclaims, "It is the stillest words that bring the storm. Thoughts that come
on doves' feet steer the world" (Die stillsten Worte sind es, welche den Sturm
bringen. Gedanken, die mit Taubenfüssen kommen, lenken die Welt, Friedrich
Nietzsche *Also sprach Zarathustra 2. Die stillste Stunde*).

Philosophical thinking *as such* is out of place in the context of the struggles
of practical political life, only surreptitiously providing the fundamental ways of
thinking of an age, including its range of fundamental, contentious political
principles, and thus only setting the universal scene for an historical world to
gain shape, unbeknowns to and behind the backs of those caught up in it. Even
the philosophers themselves can scarcely inkle what concrete cast their
thoughts on the whatness of whats and the whoness of whos will take in a future historical everyday life. The historical truths that percolate down from
philosophical Geist take shape in the institutions, customs and habits and ways
of thinking of an historical way of living that hold a world open in which the
universal "constellation of being" (Heidegger) has assumed a concrete, lived
form. Even though the exceptional historical figure of a "philosophical king"
(philosophischer König, W19:36) like the Prussian Friedrich II instituted universal forms in that

> ... er einen ganz allgemeinen Zweck, das Wohl, das Beste seines Staates sich selbst in sei-
> nen Handlungen und in allen Einrichtungen zum Prinzip gemacht hatte, [...] wenn dann
> später so etwas zur Sitte, zur Gewohnheit geworden ist, so heißen die folgenden Fürsten
> nicht mehr Philosophen, wenn auch dasselbe Prinzip vorhanden ist, und die Regierung,
> die Institutionen vornehmlich, darauf gebaut sind. (*VGPII* W19:36)

> ... he made a completely universal purpose, the well-being, the best for his state into the
> principle for himself in all his actions and in all institutions, [...]. when later suchlike has
> become custom and habit, the following princes are no longer called philosophers, even
> though the same principle still exists and the government, especially the institutions, are
> built thereon.

The figurations of objectified, objective spirited mind take on a life of their own,
apart from individual human actions and intentions, thus constituting, without
the aid of a philosopher king, historical forms of a We:

> Man muß wissen, was Handeln ist: Handeln ist Treiben des Subjekts als solchen für be-
> sondere Zwecke. Alle diese Zwecke sind nur Mittel, die Idee hervorzubringen, weil *sie* die
> absolute Macht ist. (W19:34)

> One has to know what action is: action is the activities of the subject as such for particular
> purposes. All these purposes are only means for bringing forth the Idea because *it* is the
> absolute power.

Here Hegel repeats a figure of thought according to which particular, self-interested purposes are tied back to the universal contours of being behind the backs of the actors. Insofar, individuals are implicitly singularities realizing the universality of the concept. Despite Hegel's admiration for Friedrich II's achievements (which include winning wars), Hegel would concede that he was not historically necessary, but a convenient, contingent tool of the Weltgeist in instituting a post-medieval German state. Hegel's Idea is only another name for the ontological casting of an historical world in which beings as such show up and present themselves *as* what they are and human beings show themselves off to each other *as* who they are in customary forms of mutual estimation. In the present context, it is a matter of the idea of freedom, of the correspondence between the socio-ontological concept of freedom and social reality in the modern age. It is questionable whether Prussian military discipline corresponds to this concept.

The principles of the modern world — including, above all, individual freedom, private property, freedom of expression, etc. — were inaugurated at the beginning of the modern age and have long since been firmly established as the Western ethos. Such principles constitute the fundamental rules of play for sociating power interplay in the Western world. We have seen, following Hegel, that the interplay of particular interests is willy-nilly tied back to the universal connection of an economy by an "invisible hand" serving as the 'religion' (from L. religare, 'to tie back') of civil society, and also that, by extension, the interplay of politics itself is a power play fought out, not just among particular interests but among contesting singular conceptions of the universal, within the rules of play of a constitution that represents a concretization of the principles of the modern world.

The ethos of fair interplay in civil society in the pursuit of particular interests and also respect for the constitution that provides the framework for the political power struggle suffice to keep social and political interplay compatible with freedom, without the players needing to have philosophical insight into the speculative dialectic of freedom. In particular, the head of state does not have to be a 'philosopher king', nor would this be desirable. The ongoing political power struggles are partly a struggles within the rules of play laid down by the constitution, partly struggles over whether these constitutional rules of play are being abused by particular interests, and partly over the interpretation of the constitution itself. Since the state exists in the world, it can always fall short of its concept which nevertheless serves as its yardstick and is lived out implicitly in certain ethical usages.

The task of the philosophers themselves, by contrast, is to carry on the strife over the concept of freedom itself without having any pretension of 'applying' it to the 'real world'. The concept of freedom and its relation to other concepts such as fairness, justice, solidarity, security remain also philosophically contentious, whilst the criteria for carrying on such a philosophical debate are the 'abstract ideas' which ground socio-ontological thinking.

13 Democracy

13.1 Democracy, competitive electoral struggle and majority will vs. individual freedom

13.1.1 The political power struggle for estimation as a worthy politician – The government's power to enact concrete policy and its mirroring in democratic public debate – The infection of the universal good with particular interests – Protectionism

The liberal conception of government and the state being a minimal one, law at its pith is concerned with the commutative justice of exchanges and interchanges of all sorts between individuals, and the state is legitimate insofar as it upholds and enforces this core law of individual liberty in its energetic exercise, its ἐνέργεια, in the diverse power plays of daily life. The enforcement of this core of law as in accord with the concept of freedom is a universal interest of all members of society even when it is not a common interest shared by all, for otherwise there would be no interplay of freedom at all. Nevertheless, there is a sundering of particular interests from the universal interest insofar as the state, according to its liberal socio-ontological concept, has to be an unbiased power superior to civil society and its members, and the universal at its core concerns the sacrosanct forms of individual freedom in interplay without favour to particular persons with their particular interests.

Despite its higher, universal status, the state itself is nevertheless composed of individual office-holders, each of whom wields some power in the name of the state in accordance with the position he or she holds and each of whom has particular self-interests, including especially ambitions to be estimated as somewho with standing. The actualization of law requires, at the very minimum, a legislature (controlled by a government composed of politicians who may also be ministers or the head of government), to formulate and promulgate law, a judicature to judge what is right and interpret the law in the context of the particular cases that arise, and a police force to bring those who have done wrong to justice. Furthermore, to enforce law, the state requires resources to carry out its tasks and therefore must raise taxes, for which it, in turn, requires a bureaucratic taxation apparatus administered according to administrative laws.

The fundamental concept of *democracy* is that those who are ruled by such an organized apparatus of state in which there is a multitude of individuals wielding power in a hierarchy are, in turn, also able to exercise *political power*, in elections, over who concretely are empowered to hold office and wield state

https://doi.org/10.1515/9783110617504-013

power. The superior power of the state is thus to be returned to the people ruled by that state, so completing the circle of social power and insofar healing the diremption of the universal instance of society from the particularity of the many members of civil society through real, practised, constitutionally guaranteed, institutional mediation. The submission of the members of civil society to the state is to be complemented, compensated and mitigated by the governing, policy-making agents of the state (the politicians) intermittently having to submit themselves, in turn, to estimative validation by the people in a process of *electoral estimation* as to whether they are *worthy* to hold such an office. The ambitious politician's aim is to wield political power, but at the same time, also to be estimated and esteemed as somewho, and such esteemed who-status is enabled by the who in question presenting him- or herself *as* an embodiment of the universal and not merely of particular interests.

But in this returning of power from the universal instances to civil society in its rivalrous diversity of particular interests, particularity itself does not remain unaffected. The members of society as having a say in and therefore also partly *responsible* for the universal affairs of state, i.e. in politics, are *citizens*, each with his or her own singular view of the universal good in which view the mere particularity of self-interest that does not have the whole in view, is supposed to be stripped off by the mediation of singularity, thus raising it to universality. In this way, too, universality "climbs down" (heruntersteigt[255]) into reality, thus becoming embodied in real, living individuals. Such closing together of particular interests with the universal interest through the mediation of a singular perspective on the universal good corresponds formally to the schema of the con-clusion called the "second figure" in Hegel's *Logik*, Particularity–Singularity–Universality or P–S–U.

Hegel writes with respect to particularity in this schema of conclusion, "the particular is not the universal unmediatedly and in-and-for-itself, but rather, the negative unity [of singularity ME] strips off its [particularity's ME] determinacy and raises it thus into universality" ([...] ist das Besondere [...] nicht unmittelbar und an und für sich das Allgemeine, sondern die negative Einheit [der Einzelheit ME] streift ihm die Bestimmtheit ab und erhebt es dadurch in die Allgemeinheit, *LII* W6:366). Such singularity is indeed a closing together of the rift between particularity and universality, but it remains irremediably plural because the concept of freedom corresponds further, at least in its formal schema, to the "con-clusion of induction" in Hegel's *Logik* (*LII* W6:384), in which not only singularity as such mediates between the extremes of particularity and

---

255 G.W.F. Hegel *Logik* II *Werke* Bd. 6 S. 296, W6:296.

universality, but in this case, "all singularities" (alle Einzelnen, W6:385), or a countless plurality of more or less nuanced, singular conceptions of the universal good (a multiplicity of 'truth') remain in play as an estimative power interplay from which emerges only a provisional, temporary, singular version of universal well-being as a *compromise* — in a given *conjuncture* of a present at which the two temporal dimensions of absence, beenness (or yesterness) and future abut — among all the various players in the political power play, including citizens, politicians, political parties, heads of government and state, etc.

Democracy is rule of the people by the people in the sense that each citizen at least has the power to vote, i.e. to give his or her voice, in periodical elections that choose those who are to hold office in the superior, governing power. Insofar, the democratic form of government *corresponds* to the concept of freedom, being an extension of the power interplay of civil society into another dimension of social power, viz. the political power play over *who* is to hold and wield state-governing power. Just as each individual member of civil society is free to enter the fray in civil society, exercising its abilities to do well in the competitive interplay, so too, each individual citizen has the right to be a player in the political power struggle over who is to govern, either as a voter or as a candidate for election.

The politicians who vie for state power as democratically elected representatives exercise above all their *rhetorical powers* in the political power struggle. To be a successful politician, an individual must possess and wield rhetorical potency, not only to win election but also to exercise power in government, for all political interplay requires rhetorical competence in persuading and winning trust. Such rhetorical powers, no matter whether they be cheap or sophisticated, populist or soberly reasoned, demagogic or dialogic, are those of engendering trust in others, of winning people over by showing oneself off in a winning way, of gaining estimation by the electorate *as* someone worthy of holding public political office. That the political power play takes place especially in the medium of rhetorical power corresponds thoroughly with the concept of human freedom for, in rhetoric, it is a matter of winning people over with words, thus addressing them as *free* beings who are not merely manipulable things. This remains the case, despite the endless possibilities of employing bad, manipulative, 'populist' political rhetoric that appeals to the people's baser instincts and interests, its floating, inarticulate anxieties and resentments, flatters it or caters to its urge to rid itself of its freedom for the sake of security under the strong hand of a ruler.

As shown in Chapter 10.2, it is above all *who* is speaking that carries most weight in a rhetorical situation, persuading and winning people over with a charisma that transports mood-swaying rhetorical arguments. Conversely, however, as *who* a politician is regarded is always also who he or she is *held to be* in the mirror of opinionated estimation by the others, in this case, the electorate. A democratic politician's who-standing is thus the reflection back and forth between rhetorical powers and their estimation by the electorate, and a politician only becomes *who* she or he is through this ongoing mirroring process of estimation. The political power struggle thus assumes the phenomenal form of politicians' struggles to be estimated *as somewho* with the competence to govern for the universal good. This contrasts with the economic interplay in civil society in which it is individuals' abilities of all the countless kinds, and not especially rhetorical abilities, that are evaluated in the mirror process of valuation and which lend individuals their status as somewho. Neither do the players in the gainful game have to present themselves as embodiments of the universal, but only as particular, competent, successful players.

Because elected politicians are *validated* as holders of political power through a process of electoral estimation, this provides them also with affirming *legitimacy* since the political power they then wield is mirrored as legitimate by the electorate, including even by those who did not vote for them. Just as the economic and other social interplay in civil society must take place according to rules of fair play formulated in law, so too must the democratic political power struggle proceed according to *fair rules of political power play* as enshrined in the constitution, whether written or unwritten. The democratic form of government therefore has a very high degree of legitimacy because the politicians holding political power are validated as such through the mirroring process of electoral estimation and according to rules of play that are constitutionally secured and acknowledged by society as fair. The freedom of the individual in sociating power interplay is mediated, more or less circuitously through democratic institutions, with state political power, and this cannot be claimed for any other form of government. If citizens are to affirm being governed at all, they can affirm being governed by their freely and fairly elected representatives. At the same time, the power struggle of democratic government is never-ending, being as it is a constant, ongoing struggle, mediated especially through the public media, for validation by the electorate.

State power is never limited to realizing the rule of law in its core sense of upholding the rights of personhood, which is the minimal, liberal conception of state. The state as superior instance of social power governs also in the sense that it posits and pursues myriad concrete purposes that are conceived to be for the universal or general good, including laying down the rules of interplay that are considered fair, the conception of fairness, as an ethical practice, being

itself a component part of the universal good. Even though the state promul-
gates what it calls laws also to realize specific purposes it has posited, this has
nothing to do with law in its originary sense as upholding the fairness of power
interplay in civil society. Apart from administrative laws covering the running of
its own apparatuses in all their myriad detail, there are laws positing the state's
will to provide certain universal services to society (e.g. education, healthcare,
roads, water supply) or its will to pursue a certain policy in a matter concerning
society as a whole (e.g. immigration, support for the family as a social institution, economic development, energy, new technologies, war and peace). State
services provided to society as part of its indispensable infrastructure are nothing essential to the state's role but depend entirely on pragmatic considerations,
the main one being whether it is possible for the market economy to provide the
same service at all or more efficiently. State service-provision is mainly a matter
for corporations in the old sense of the term as corporate bodies, mostly on a
regional or local level, charged with efficiently providing services to citizens
such as street lighting, street cleaning, garbage disposal, electricity, communications infrastructure and mail delivery.

The ever-changing complexion of the market economy may make it pragmatically more feasible and more cost-efficient to allow private enterprise to
take over the task of providing services deemed to be essential, especially since
state-owned enterprises are invariably monopolies. There is nothing essentially
'state-like' about essential services, and the state needs to act like an efficient
enterprise in providing them, which is hindered when state enterprises are not
subjected to both the competitive discipline of the markets and the discipline of
fulfilling the fundamental condition of a circuit of capital, namely, that of augmenting, or at least not losing, value in its movement through its circuit. Because they are removed from the discipline of the competitive value-interplay
on markets, state enterprises 'naturally' tend at least toward inertia and invariably also toward a gross abuse of monopoly powers, and also inefficiency, and
it is difficult for the electorate, through multiple mediations, to wield any political power over them.

Government is usually meant to cover the state's will in acting concretely to
pursue certain policies claimed to be for the public good. Democracy accordingly also goes beyond determining by elections simply who is to wield state power
as the agency enforcing the rule of law to cover also, and most importantly,
choosing those who are to govern as policy-makers of concrete policies formulated in terms of the general social good. The citizens want to have a say in how
society is to be shaped in the name of the well-being of the social whole. Citizens have their say on public issues in the public sphere in which *communica-*

tion media for the expression of public opinion arise. What citizens of all kinds, from laypersons to professional political commentators, say in their exercise of *freedom of speech* is a major form of mirroring to the government its legitimacy or lack thereof as a holder and wielder of superior political power for the sake of the universal. As has been shown in Chapter 10, *all* social power, and especially political power, is a process of estimation. The media are media for circulating the public word and, more than ever, the public image that, above all, presents publicly influential whos as who they present themselves to be.

The democratic election of government therefore turns not so much upon the rule of law, which, at least in established Western democracies, is taken for granted as a basic given and protected by the constitution, but more upon how the state is to exercise its superior powers in realizing its concrete will in accordance with government policy, what Hayek calls "governmental measures" rather than "legislation". (Hayek *LLL*3:27) Election of government thus becomes a contest among different, concretely formulated conceptions of universal social well-being, this contest being organized in political parties, and also politicians as the 'personifications' of certain policies or kinds of policy. The citizens as voters are supposed to vote in accordance with their evaluation of the policies proposed for the well-being of society covering the gamut of political issues vibrant in a given conjuncture. This means that they must, or rather *ought* to (in order to correspond to the concept of citizen) raise themselves above the standpoints of their own merely particular self-interests to adopt a universal viewpoint on the good of society as a whole. 'Pork barrel' politics that play out by pandering to particular interests in sectors of electorate damage the legitimacy of democracy per se as a form of government.

The political debates in the media, therefore, to be taken seriously, must raise themselves to the level of a concern with the universal interest, and a political standpoint can be devalued by showing in debate that it is nothing more than a thinly veiled strategy to pursue naked, individual or collective self-interest. The citizen, the politician and the statesman, as singular embodiments of the universal, must be seen to be, i.e. estimated as, above mere particularity of interests, whether it be merely their own self-interests or the particular interests of a sector of society, if they are to be acknowledged as who they pretend to be. On the other hand, *any* concrete policy at all that is adopted, pursued and implemented by a government, no matter how 'purely' it has been conceived with a view to the universal good, unavoidably also has concrete effects, both favourable and unfavourable, on particular interests in society, and therefore the universal interest and particular interests inevitably commingle. This is the ground for political parties that cater to one part of the electorate rather than another and thus have their clientele. Such political parties, in turn, are then criticized for their clientele politics that are claimed to be clearly not for the universal good.

The diremption between particular interests and universal interests — which from one perspective could be regarded as a healthy separation of particularity from the universal — is thus, on the one hand, transported back into the democratic citizen-voter's way of thinking, and, on the other, the supposedly universal subject, the state, becomes re-infected with particularity; the election of government becomes a power struggle also among particular interests within civil society, and the work of government becomes a bargaining process of reaching 'workable' political compromises in which particular sectoral interests of society are either furthered or thwarted or appeased or kept in balance. The conception of the universal social good becomes the ongoing, provisional, muddled, patchwork result of the formation of majorities based on the partial satisfaction of particular sectoral interests and lobbies and 'pork barrel' politics, and not only on genuine, broad consensus in society on specific issues affecting the general well-being. Those who wield power and formulate the government's policy — the politicians — are themselves subject to the democratic election process and have to tailor policy and even their law-making to particular sectoral interests in a kind of political electoral calculus if they are to be re-elected. Legislated law itself thus become infected with particular interests and the political power struggle among particular sectoral interests. In this way, such legislated law itself is delegitimized.

A well-known, 'classical' instance of such infection with particular interests — there are countless others with scarcely imaginable variations — is the *protection* that the government provides to certain industries through legislated trade barriers and the concomitant establishment of monopolies or near-monopolies by law, thus systematically biasing the competitive economic interplay to favour certain sectoral interests. Against this Adam Smith advises, "The legislature, were it possible that its deliberations could be always directed, not by the clamorous importunity of partial interests [a way of saying 'lobbying' ME], but by an extensive view of the general good [the true function of government], ought upon this very account, perhaps, to be particularly careful neither to establish any new monopolies of this kind, nor to extend further those which are already established."[256] What is said here concerning monopolies applies equally well to all legislation that comes about through lobbying by vested interests, allowing them to become entrenched and ensconced behind established

---

256 Adam Smith *The Wealth of Nations* 1776 Bk. IV Ch. II 1776/2000 p. 502.

positive law. Only insofar as a lobby puts forward proposals that can truly be regarded as contributing to the universal good can it be regarded as having raised itself above its merely particular self-interests.

13.1.2 The tendential danger of the dissolution of freedom in merely democratically mediated, state-posited will – The erosion of the freedom of interplay through the sham universal of redistributive social justice – Constitutional law as a bulwark against merely positive law

The state's primary raison d'être — upholding the fair, mutually estimative power interplay of individual freedom through the rule of law — tends to be taken for granted, is 'forgotten' and fades into the background in favour of the struggle over the assertion especially of material interests of sections of society through the formation of majorities in the democratic electoral process. In over-stepping the bounds of preserving the abstract, formal freedoms of personhood, the state even becomes the battleground for fighting over differing conceptions of the *accepted mores* in society based upon the customary usages within which various sections of society live ethically. With this step, the state enters the hazardous domain of morality and its Ought, making incursions even into the private sphere which is private above all in the sense of being a refuge from society and its social pressures of public opinion to which 'people' are suscepti-ble and to which, more often than not, they cave in. Any politicized ethical issue concerns also a political power struggle over where the limits of the private sphere are to be inscribed, and where these limits are drawn at any time is a reflection of the evolving ethical usages within which a people lives.

Such ethical usages can only evolve because they are simultaneously lived ways of thinking in preontological preconceptions, and therefore always ex-posed potentially to the freedom of thoughtful questioning. The state as the superior power that stands above the many powers of self-interested individuals in estimative exchange and interchange with one another in order to uphold the rule of law, is no longer impartial and aloof, but itself acts and governs accord-ing to the power struggle among diverse particular sectoral interests and moral convictions about how 'people' ought to live into which, through electoral con-siderations of government, it is inevitably drawn. Not only does abstractly pri-vate, individual freedom of the person fade as the state's primary concern, but individual freedom itself is curtailed by the government's positive, concrete, substantive, social policy measures that are legitimated and enforced by laws passed by the legislature. These laws are not law in the originary sense, but *positive law* posited and enforced by state will. Legitimacy is no longer a matter of laws conforming to the originary, 'natural right' requirements of justice as fairness, i.e. the commutative justice of individuals in power interplay with one another, but is conferred by legislation being enacted and promulgated in accordance merely with formal democratic procedures. The democratically elected government is empowered and legitimated to pass legislation according to its posited conception of the general good and social 'values' as expressed in strongly held convictions, especially moral and religious convictions, about how 'people' should live.

Law thus becomes a matter not of justice as fair play, but of will — the government's will and, mediated through the democratic election process, the people's opinionated will. Freedom itself comes to be understood as government of the democratically mediated will of the people as posited by the democratically elected government, thus becoming arbitrary, i.e. lacking inner criteria, since the people's will itself is only a moodfully shifting, vacillating, motley composite of majorities formed ad hoc through power struggles on various issues that also affect and are driven by particular sectoral interests and opinionated convictions. 'Just' and 'democratic' become synonyms, just as 'freedom' becomes synonymous with the formal procedures of the political electoral struggles of democracy as laid down by the constitution. 'Justice', 'freedom' and 'democracy' become interchangeable terms, with 'democracy', as a vague notion of the majority rule of the people's opinionated will encompassing its diverse moral and social opinions, enjoying the hegemonic position in this triangle.

Freedom is then equated with the 'people's will' as expressed through the democratic process, and thus becomes a matter of the contingency of changing majorities. The only protection against such contingency and arbitrariness is the *constitution* which, however, itself is partially exposed to merely posited will. Even the constitution itself becomes partly the object of democratic will and political power plays through referendums or qualified majorities in parliamentary votes. The constitution nonetheless serves as a bulwark against the arbitrariness and vacillations of politically posited will by enshrining those freedoms which a people holds dear and which have become ethical second nature for it. The constitution can only continue to serve as a shrine for freedom for as long as a people genuinely does hold its freedom dear and has a preontological conception of it that accords with its deeper-lying socio-ontological structure as investigated throughout the present inquiry.

Furthermore, as investigated in Chapter 6.5 and Chapter 9.7ff, in 'progressive' Western societies, the very conception of universal well-being or the general good of society which is concretized in the state's concrete, willed policy of action increasingly becomes interchangeable with a notion of *social justice*, and the state's power and its role increasingly become that of positively redistributing the wealth created by society rather then ensuring merely its fair commutatio or interchange in power plays of all kinds. The results of wealth creation and allocation that come about through the (often bruising) interplay of economic market competition (a 'value game') increasingly become revised by superior state power in the name of redistributive social justice, solidarity and social security. This does not by any means imply that self-interest in its particularity has been overcome in favour of a more 'universal', 'social' 'model', but merely that the power play that is competitive, economic interplay has shifted to the power play that is politics in which the terms of reference are conceptions of the social good intermingled with sectoral self-interests, especially those of the weaker players in the economic power play who exert their mass egoism in the name of (merely redistributive) social justice.

The market interplay mediated by reified value becomes progressively eroded, displaced or overridden by the medium of the political power game as the element through which social wealth is distributed and redistributed in the name of democratically formulated, concrete conceptions of the social good to be implemented through the government's empowered will. This means that the state's policies, the concrete, and therefore *particular*, policy aims it posits and pursues, have all the more impact on the *particular* self-interests of various groups in society and therefore, in turn, the democratically elected government itself increasingly becomes the target of lobbying activity of the *particular* interests of organized social groups. Any change at all in government policy will adversely affect vested interests of some sector or other of the populace, so that any policy change at all, because it is particular rather than universal, will carry with it a political risk for the elected government of the day, namely, a risk of losing votes at the next election. Government policies nominally for the *universal* good become increasingly infected by considerations of the political power game of staying in office by catering to *particular* interests. Policies introduced in the name of solidarity and social justice (with its sham 'universal' status) become entrenched by having sectoral, vested self-interests ensconced behind them, resulting often in the immovability of a *political gridlock*, which is the price paid for ensuring social security vis-à-vis the demands of having to adapt to the rough-and-tumble of competitive power interplay in civil society's gainful game in which agility is called for. The gainful game, however, nevertheless makes itself felt despite a protective wall of social security because its own competitivity is impaired, resulting, above all, in unemployement.

Individual freedoms in their sociating interplay can only be preserved if a part of law — namely, the constitution — enshrines individual rights and puts a constitutional limit upon what the government can posit as positive law. This possibility — that a law posited by the state in legislative procedure can be deemed to be unconstitutional and therefore unlawful — indicates that law and justice cannot be identified with positive law and the expression of the state's (or, more precisely, the democratically elected government's) will. A part of the state — namely, the constitutional or supreme court — must be given independence to decide whether the state's own posited law contravenes constitutionally guaranteed individual rights. This court has power that overrides the elected government's power to posit law by will. The superior universal subject is thus once again itself divided in its power, and this is in accordance with the concept of freedom itself, which, due to its inherent plurality, abhors oneness.

Furthermore, an attempt to undo the commingling of universal and particular interests in the administration of justice is made by separating the state's legislative organ from the judiciary. The division of state powers becomes a crucial means of weakening absolute state power in favour of preserving the core rule of law, whose task is to protect individual citizens in who they are and what they have and also the mutually estimating interchange-metabolism of civil society. *Absolutist democracy*, conceived as the (compromising) will of majorities formed in competitive electoral procedures, is clipped and held in check by constitutional guarantees of individual freedom conceived as the wedding of the moments of singularity and universality in the socio-ontological concept of freedom as a kind of social movement sui generis. These constitutional guarantees of individual freedom, however, only remain effective for as long as there really are free individuals who are prepared to struggle for the preservation of the power play of individual freedom, because the erosion of freedom resides as an inexorable tendency within the concept of will itself, namely, the will to assert oneself against the other in the incessant power play that is social living. Such a will can seek security rather than facing the challenges of free interplay.

With the advent of representative democracy as a way of completing the circle of power between the governing state and its governed people by giving the people the power to elect those who are to hold office in the state and govern, the state itself more than ever loses its status as a universal instance standing above civil society and itself becomes sorely infected with the particularity of self-interests which are not just those of its office-holders, but, above all, of sectors of the population with their mass will, their own particular self-interests and singular (social, moral, religious, etc.) opinionated convictions who exercise influence on government through the democratic vote. This degeneration could rightly be regarded, in part, as a moral failing of 'human nature' to raise itself above mere self-interest and idiosyncratic opinion to adopt the genuinely universal political standpoint of the well-being of society as a whole, but it has also a deeper, socio-ontological ground. The unity of the universal good has the inherent tendency to break down into the particularity of self-interests and *also* to splinter into a plurality of firmly held, singular views on ethical life that jostle against one another in the political power play. The more fundamental problem of democracy as a form government is that it tends to become understood merely as the freedom of the empirical will as formed in the ongoing power struggles over majorities, and not as freedom in its deeper socio-ontological dignity, according to which, in a basic, inviolable sense, that the free individual in fair, mutually estimative power interplay can never be 'outvoted' by a majority of whatever kind.

13.1.3 Schumpeter's competition theory of democracy – The democratic We not merely a summation of individual wills – The legitimacy of democratically elected government – The vacillating vagaries of democratic electoral power struggles – The necessary universality of the democratic vote

At the other end of the spectrum to Hegel's sublime characterization of the state as owing its existence to "God walking in the world" (der Gang Gottes in der Welt, *RPh.* § 258 Add.), which is insofar truly a universal instance, we can also learn something from Joseph A. Schumpeter's theory of democracy in his *Capitalism, Socialism and Democracy* (1975; cf. Chapter 6.3.2). At least in part it could be described as a pragmatic, realistic and down-to-earth, explanatory account with a touch of worldly-wise cynicism. As such, Schumpeter, although lacking speculative, socio-ontological insight, fulfils Aristotle's criterion of being experienced in life as a precondition for having something worth hearing to say about the political realm.

Here the focus is on a particular form of government, namely, modern, representative democracy, which is also proclaimed by many to be the freest form of government on the basis of some pre-ontological conception of freedom or other. Schumpeter takes issue in Chapter XXI *The Classical Doctrine of Democracy* with the eighteenth century Enlightenment notion of "the democratic method" as "that institutional arrangement for arriving at political decisions which realizes the common good by making the people itself decide issues through the election of individuals who are to assemble in order to carry out its will" (*CSD*. p. 250). Schumpeter questions the very notion of the "common good" and a "common will of the people":

> There is [...] no such thing as a uniquely determined common good that all people could agree on or be made to agree on by the force of rational argument. [...] [T]o different individuals and groups the common good is bound to mean different things. This fact [...] will introduce rifts on questions of principle which cannot be reconciled by rational argument because ultimate values [...] are beyond the range of mere logic. / [...] [T]hough a common will or public opinion of some sort may still be said to emerge from the infinitely complex jumble of individual and group-wise situations, volitions, influences, actions and reactions of the 'democratic process', the result lacks not only rational unity but also rational sanction. [...] In particular, we still remain under the practical necessity of attributing to the will of the *individual* an independence and a rational quality that are altogether unrealistic. (*CSD*. p. 251, 253)

The above selection of quotes, with its emphasis on so-called rationality, does not pretend to amount to a comprehensive retelling of all of Schumpeter's objections to what he regards as the classical Enlightenment theory of democracy that rests on rationalist assumptions, but it does provide the flavour of Schumpeter's qualms. He cannot discover the "common good" and the "will of the people" in "the democratic method", no matter how these entities are conceived, whether it be in a utilitarian way or otherwise. This agrees with my observation above that "the people's will itself is only a motley composite of majorities formed through power struggles on various issues that also affect and are driven by particular, sectoral interests".

Schumpeter's critique, however, is weakened by its assumption that the "common good" and the "will of the people" are rational entities that have to be known and willed by rational and independent individual minds attaining agreement. One should note first of all that Schumpeter's use of the word "rational" has nothing to do with Hegel's use of the term "reason". Hegel would call Schumpeter's rationality "Räsonieren", i.e. mere understanding or mere pro-and-con, expatiating reasoning (freed of 'irrational' emotion), for it has no speculative, i.e. socio-ontological insight whatever into freedom as a kind (εἶδος, 'look') of movement sui generis. We will have to consider the alternative that these peculiar collective entities, the "common good" and the "will of the people", are not collective at all and come about indirectly (vermittelt) behind the backs of individuals' striving and willing, i.e. that a 'we' is constituted (cf. Chapter 11 and the previous section) by way of mediation (Vermittlung) through the democratic procedure that is not merely a summation of wills, just as in civil society a 'we' is constituted in contract that is an elevating Aufheben of two merely individual wills to a contractual will that is neither the one will nor the other nor their 'rational' sum.

Moreover, if reason is thought in its ontological depth, the realization of reason then lies precisely in the affirmation of *freedom as power interplay* that is immanent in the democratic procedure. For the moment I shall concentrate on the simple, stripped-down, alternative understanding of democratic government which Schumpeter offers. He proceeds to investigate democratic government in Chapter XXII *Another Theory of Democracy* by restricting himself to a definition of "democratic method" as

> that institutional arrangement for arriving at political decisions in which individuals acquire the power to decide by means of a competitive struggle for the people's vote. (*CSD.* p. 269)

This is paraphrased also as democracy's being a system for "the elector's vote [...] to produce government" (*CSD:* 273) including "evicting it" (*CSD:*272), thus bringing about "acceptance of leadership" (*CSD:*272). Democracy is a "competitive struggle for power and office" (*CSD:*282), a "competitive struggle for political power" (*CSD:*283), a "competitive struggle for political leadership" (*CSD:*293), "free competition among would-be leaders for the vote of the electorate" (*CSD:*285). This definition presupposes that democratic governments are elected governments but, as already stated, it aims to avoid the pitfalls of the so-called classical doctrine of democracy, which purportedly asserts that the government must be a rational, collective expression of the will of the people, by restricting the people's power and role to simply electing those leaders who will wield government power for a certain term. Schumpeter does not hesitate to set this definition of the democratic method into relation with "the concept of competition in the economic sphere, with which it may be usefully compared" (*CSD:*271) — and which, we may add, in adhering to the rules of market interplay, results in the (abstract-universal) reified *value* of goods and services and thus, indirectly, the mutually estimative *valuing* of people's abilities. The competitive struggle for political power is above all among candidates for leadership of government as whos with a certain estimated standing, and the people elects, either directly or indirectly, the leader who is to lead the government (and hence the state) rather than a representative of the will of the people which, Schumpeter argues, cannot be said to come to expression in elections based on majorities, no matter whether the electoral system is designed along the lines of simple majorities or of some more elaborate scheme such as proportional representation that is supposed to better reflect the profile of what sections of the population want.

The outcome of a democratic election as an estimating power interplay among various candidates for office can be regarded as a will of the electorate, but not as a collective will, i.e. the aggregated will of a heap of individual voters. Rather, the electorate itself is constituted already beforehand as a kind of we by the rules of power play for the election, so that the majority election outcome is per se the will of the electorate, i.e. an electoral We.

Such a theory of democratic government as exemplified by Schumpeter's theory of a competition for power to rule the country shows that it is based on the viewpoints, convictions and interests of an electorate composed of human beings with finite understanding and preconceptions, and not infinite, speculative reason with its insight into the ontological concept, nor even necessarily with a sound appreciation of the universal interests of society, its general good. However, as I have cited above, just as Hegel claims that "it is not necessary that those governing have the idea." (Es ist nicht nötig, daß die Regierenden die Idee haben. G.W.F. Hegel *VGPII* W19:34), it also holds true that the voters do not have to have speculative, ontological insight. We also have to consider whether or in what way or to what extent it is necessary for the voters to raise themselves above their merely "particular purposes" (besondere Zwecke, W19:34). The standpoints adopted by individual voters are not necessarily merely aligned narrowly with self-interest, but they are based also on 'universal' opinions of how individuals firmly hold the world to be in its truth, or, above all, how it *ought* to be.

Schumpeter is at pains to emphasize that i) these opinions are open to being swayed by "psycho-technics" (*CSD*:264) akin to "advertising and other methods of persuasion" (*CSD*:257) so that "what we are confronted with in the analysis of political processes is largely not a genuine but a manufactured will" (*CSD*:263), and ii) in political issues of moment, the individual lacks a "pungent sense of reality" (William James, cited *CSD*:261) and most often "expends less disciplined effort on mastering a political problem than [...] on a game of bridge." (*CSD*:261) The individual's opined truth concerns not only the individual's self-interest, but usually also what the individual holds to be the best course for the general well-being of society, including the preservation of the valued ways of living practised in that society, in short, its 'values' or basic convictions about how to live ethically. The view held about the general well-being of society — and how voters accordingly act in elections — is, of course, not entirely divorced from or incongruent with self-interest, but it nevertheless exceeds the horizon of narrow self-interest.

Even if, especially after Heidegger's questioning of the ontotheological structure of metaphysical thinking and his insistence on the finitude of human being itself, the state cannot be regarded as owing its existence to "God walking in the world" (der Gang Gottes in der Welt, *RPh.* § 258 Add.) — a view which Schumpeter would dismiss contemptuously as metaphysical make-believe —, the following thought of Hegel's deserves further pondering with a view to a possible secular, metaphysical translation: "Actions are undertaken according to general/universal thoughts on what is lawful, ethical, pleasing to God; the idea is realized thus, but by mixing thoughts, concepts with immediate particular purposes." (Es wird nach allgemeinen Gedanken des Rechts, Sittlichen, Gottgefälligen gehandelt; die Idee wird so verwirklicht, aber durch Vermischung von Gedanken, Begriffen mit unmittelbaren partikulären Zwecken. Hegel *VGPII* W19:34) The Hegelian Idea is nothing other than another name for the 'look' of the beingness of beings, thought by Plato as the ἰδέα that is seen (ἰδεῖν) by the speculative eye.

People do not act with an (explicit) insight into the beingness of beings, even though they are intimately acquainted with and (implicitly) always already understand the beingness of beings, including the freedom of human being as a kind of freedom of movement in power interplay. Hegel's terms for explicit and implicit are für sich (καθ᾽ αὐτό) and an sich, respectively. Philosophical thinking is the endeavour to raise the implicit, pre-ontological understanding of the beingness of beings, without which a human could not be a human being, to explicit ontological insight or reason. The beingness of beings itself, however, takes shape nonetheless in history mediated also through the actions of people being led mainly by their restricted particular interests but within certain accepted ethical usages that, in the present context, are customary rules of power play. Beings show up and take shape in a world *as* what (and who) they are not through directly intentional human agency, but human individuals undertake their actions and shape their lives according also to what they glean in their preconceptions of how the beingness of beings is shaping up in an historical world. What does this realization of the idea, i.e. the coming to presence of a Gestalt, a cast of the beingness of beings, in history have to do with the democratically governed state and electoral struggle?

The democratic procedure provides for the opinions held by eligible voters determining by way of majorities of votes cast who is to gain legitimate power to govern for a given term. The institutional, constitutional set-up within which the competitive democratic procedure takes place as an estimative power struggle is itself accepted and validated a priori as a given ethical form of social movement that lends legitimacy to the outcome of the struggle. That is, the people accepts the government it has elected if constitutionally proper, fair democratic procedure is adhered to, and the election is regarded as being an expression of the will of the people precisely because free and fair elections are a *mode and rite of freedom* itself in its ontological dignity as a social power interplay.

The constitutionally enshrined rules of power play for the democratic election of government is a Gestalt of the We of a people. The issues on which an election is fought are those concerning both particular interests and general or 'universal' issues affecting the whole of the community or nation, including what the electorate holds dear as the nation's heritage, customary societal values and what role the nation is to play on the world stage. What becomes an election issue depends to a large extent on what those fighting to be elected through a kind of "process of estimation" choose to make into an issue, but also on what moves and concerns the electorate at a given time, in conjunction with what the mass media generate by way of issues, along with contingent events in the world that impact the electorate's fickle mood and can be taken up rhetorically by candidates to influence (including manipulate) voters. The election issues are presented and debated within the terms and horizon of eligible voters, i.e. within a sphere of finite understanding of largely practical issues, issues concerned with proposed courses of action to be formulated as government policy by the victorious political party, the bigness of government as expressed through taxation levels, social services, etc. etc.

The outcome of an election depends in part on the momentary mood of the electorate, especially of undecided or 'swing' voters, even on election day itself, which ultimately determines the majorities in the various electorates. This is analogous to how a product offered for sale fares on the markets and it is no coincidence that — as Schumpeter does — political elections are often compared with the purchase of products, where the dollars spent by individual consumers are regarded as the equivalent of votes cast by individual eligible voters. Schumpeter even condones and underscores this analogy between votes and the prices paid for commercial commodities when he approvingly cites a politician who remains anonymous, "What businessmen do not understand is that exactly as they are dealing in oil so I am dealing in votes." (*CSD*. p. 285) The democratic political struggle for power in the state is a struggle of politicians to be estimated and validated in their who-status as worthy representatives of the people, where individual votes of the electors function like dollars in the market-place which estimate the value of products offered for sale.

Like the market-place, therefore, democratic elections are very much exposed to contingency (after all, it is a fathomless power interplay), especially in the guise of the voters' arbitrary whims and opinions, and how these can be rhetorically influenced, swayed, wooed and manipulated by election campaigners through the various mass media which do not refrain from stooping to every possible tactic for flattering or scaring the electoral masses. And the analogy does not end there. Just as market-place interplay continually brings about value as an ongoing, ever-changing result, something that exceeds anything individuals as such can 'subjectively' posit, so too do democratic elections as an ethical practice bring about a will of the people as a Gestalt of the universal We that is more than a mere quantitative majority of votes dependent upon all sorts of contingent factors, including even the weather. The result of the democratic electoral process is a universal with its own dignity that is neither merely the sum of individual votes nor an outcome of mass individual rationality, but the culmination of an ethical, i.e. customary, practice sanctioned and legitimated and thus accepted as being in accord with freedom, just as the final score in a football match has its own status as a kind of universal acknowledged as such as long as it has been arrived at according to fair rules of play.

Already Plato, in discussing democracy in his *Republic*, points out that the democratic polity (πολιτεία) takes the question of the origins, ambitions and particular qualities of someone standing for election too lightly, "but instead esteems someone already when they merely say that they mean well with the people" (ἀλλὰ τιμᾷ, ἐὰν φῇ μόνον εὔνους εἶναι τῷ πλήθει; *Rep.* 558c). This characteristic of democracy of being easily swayable and exposed to all kinds of rhetorical flattery (and scare-tactics, a kind of negative flattery) is echoed down through Western history to modern times when, for instance, Schumpeter writes in the twentieth century with regard to the "classical doctrine of democracy" that "politicians appreciate a phraseology that flatters the masses and offers an excellent opportunity not only for evading responsibility but also for crushing opponents in the name of the people". (Schumpeter *CSD*. p. 268)

And Herbert Spencer writes in the nineteenth century with regard to politicians, "Each seeks popularity by promising more than his opponent has promised. [...] [W]hoever seeks their votes must at least refrain from exposing their [mass voters who "nurture sanguine anticipations of benefits to be obtained"] mistaken beliefs; [...] [S]uch hopes [of benefits provided by the state] are ministered to by candidates for public choice, to augment their chances of success" and, with regard to "journalists, always chary of saying that which is distasteful to their readers", he writes that "journalism, ever responsive to popular opinion, daily strengthens it by giving it voice; while counter-opinion, more and more discouraged, finds little utterance."[257] Today, the same could be said in

---

257 Herbert Spencer 'The Coming Slavery' in *The Man versus the State* (1884, 1892) ed. Donald Macrae, Penguin, Harmondsworth 1969 pp. 97, 98, 99.

general of the mass media which invariably frame all questions concerning all the 'burning issues' of the day in terms of how 'we' — the constantly invoked fake we that the media are chary to offend — are to deal with them, what 'we think', what 'we want', etc. The "promising more" addressed by Spencer conforms precisely with the endless striving to have more (πλεονεξία) discussed in Chapter 4.1 which accounts also for the state's finances being perpetually stretched to the limit and the state's tendency to mount up public debt to satisfy the electorate's endless desire for more.

"Meaning well with the people" is another way of saying that those vieing for political power must flatter the electorate in an attempt to sway how it exercises its voting power on election day. Democracy is accordingly for Plato "a pleasant, anarchic, motley polity, distributing a certain equality to those who are equal and those who are unequal alike" (ἡδεῖα πολιτεία καὶ ἄναρχος καὶ ποικίλη, ἰσότητά τινα ὁμοίως ἴσοις τε καὶ ἀνίσοις διανέμουσα; *Rep.* 558c). In a democracy, every adult is given a vote without prejudging and sifting out those who deserve a vote from those who do not deserve one. To make such a distinction would presuppose a criterion of 'just desert' and also a power superior to the people — perhaps an elite section of the population — empowered with selecting an eligible electorate. But such a preselecting power is intolerable for democracy, which has to be an open slather, market-place competition for gaining political power to govern a people without already allotting beforehand a preselecting power to some kind of elite that will inevitably select in its *own* interests.

The formal equality of all voters in a democracy corresponds to the deeper equality residing in the *abstract* character of free, formal personhood that does not tolerate the inscription of any concrete determination into personhood. Good governance and leadership of a country, if they are to emerge at all, have to emerge from the people holus-bolus, without distinguishing rank or social status, and despite the employment of more or less cheap rhetorical tricks to flatter, frighten or otherwise mislead the masses. Schumpeter says that all this, "the psycho-technics of party management and party advertising, slogans and marching tunes, are not accessories. They are of the essence of politics." (*CSD.* p. 283) Given Schumpeter's hostility to metaphysics and philosophy ("if we wish to understand and not to philosophize...", *CSD.* p. 271), his use of the venerable metaphysical term "essence" here is telling. We should give back this term its full ontological weight and consider whether his definition of the democratic method as a competition for the political power to govern a people by means of elections, does indeed capture its essence, i.e. *what* democracy *is*, its *whatness*.

The whatness of what democratic politics *are* presents itself to the socio-ontologically speculating mind *as* political power interplay.

13.1.4 The socio-ontological isomorphism between the competitive gainful game and the competitive democratic struggle for political power more closely considered – The democratic constitution of a people as We with its customary way of life – Democracy's wavering course between an appetite for freedom and a craving for security

Schumpeter is rightly comfortable with the notion that there is a strong analogy between competition on the markets and the competition for political power in the democratic procedure for electing government without, however, having the proper socio-ontological insight. One visible, pre-ontological basis for this analogy is that market competition and the democratic struggle for political power are both partly *rhetorical* undertakings in the sense that both depend on swaying and persuading people's opinions and therefore both are engaged in a rhetorical interplay with free human beings. The rhetoric of the market-place is advertising of all kinds, just as democratic politics must be continually concerned with rhetorically persuading (a majority of) the electorate of the rightness of policy. Furthermore, just as a market economy is driven by the private striving for monetary gain but results, on the whole and behind the backs of the economic players, in the production of goods and services catering to the wants of millions of people, so too is democratic government motivated by a competitive struggle for political power which nevertheless results in society being governed under the rule of law and more or less for (a particular conception of) its well-being. That such an analogy can plausibly work is due to a deeper, underlying socio-ontological congruence which needs to be uncovered, as we have done. Schumpeter, who, given his anti-metaphysical, positivist bent, is concerned with developing a theory of democratic government which fits the observable "facts", disdains digging too deeply into philosophical, "speculative" questions, so its falls to us to do so.

It is crucial to hold onto the insight that competitive struggle on the markets and for political power represent two different forms of *power play* in society relying on two different sociating media, namely, reified value and political power, respectively. The abstractly universal, quantitative medium of reified value, its role as mediator in exchange, arises through the social practice of commodity exchange itself and becomes, through use, a usage in leading a customary life. Money-mediated exchange becomes established historically in a society or between societies; it becomes "a custom, a habit" (zur Sitte, zur Ge-wohnheit, *VGPII* W19:36), an institution, a shared Gestalt of "objective spirited mind", an ontologically constituted, ethical We. As an established usage, com-modity exchange requires that certain rules of play are adhered to for it to take place at all. The economic players involved in exchange transactions must re-spect and estimate each other as commodity owners and carry out transactions according to accepted usage regarding delivery of goods, performance of ser-vices, promptness of payment, guarantee of quality, etc.

Moreover, what the countless goods and services are good for, their value for human living, becomes a reified, purely quantitative fact in monetary price. 'We' recognize and validate monetary value as the legitimate value of what is good for living as it comes about behind our backs through the ongoing practice of market exchange. The monetary value of goods becomes part of our shared values. In acknowledging money as the measure of value for goods and ser-vices, we carry on habitual — and in this sense, ethical — sociating interchange with one another. We are players in a game of interchange whose rules we re-spect and through which we become and are affirmed as a kind of economic or katallactic We. None of us, either individually or collectively, is able to revoke the monetary value-formation of goods and services because their value is root-ed in an habitual, ethical usage, a Gestalt of the being of beings that is under-stood and practised. Reified monetary value is a way in which beings that are good for living (material goods as well as services) show up and present them-selves *as* what they are. This reified Gestalt of the being of beings, monetary value — in Hegelian terminology, a "subject-object" (Subjekt-Objekt, *RPh.* § 214) — comes to shape our social lives insofar as we engage in economic inter-change and competition in the pursuit of monetary gain.

The 'ethical institution' of money (or more strictly: reified value) as medium of reciprocal exchange allows our particular self-interests in gain to be pursued according to certain rules of the game. Although each of us is interested pri-marily in personal gain, not just selfishly, egoistically, but to support a life-world shared with others and also in a mutual give-and-take nolens volens be-yond mere egoism, what we bring about through our reciprocating interplay is a functioning market economy that caters to the wants and desires of millions of participants, no matter how much critics of market economy bemoan the more or less effective rhetorical manipulation of these millions of consumers through advertising or the tacky consumerism thus practised to the detriment of alleged-ly 'higher' values. The 'abstract universal', i.e. reified value, thus enables an entire, shared way of life, gathering together the motley strivings for individual gain. Because this universal is abstract, by enabling multiple degrees of freedom through power interplay, it also allows for a bewildering diversity of concrete ways of livings, of life styles. The only prescription of the abstract universal of reified value on life style flows from its *quantitative* determination.

We are now in a position to better understand the deeper socio-ontological isomorphism between economic competition for gain and the competitive democratic struggle for political power. The struggle for political power is a kind of power interplay according to certain rules of play, just as the competitive struggle for monetary gain is, where reified value itself must be regarded as a kind of power (cf. Chapter 10.1). The democratic procedure for electing those who are to legitimately hold public office and govern constitutes a set of rules, an ethical usage that is institutionally anchored and constitutionally enshrined. The individual politician or would-be politician has to strive to be elected via voters' estimation to gain political power that is exercised preferably by sitting in government or at least by sitting in parliament. The leader of government, the government and the parliament, in that order, have the say in how the country is to be concretely governed through the organs of state. As representatives of the people elected according to the institutionally established democratic rules of play, they wield legitimate political power estimated as such by the people. The constitution (πολιτεία) lays down the structure of political power and the rules for the political power game for a society by setting up the political institutions and guaranteeing basic individual freedoms as rights under the rule of law. Thus, although "the incessant competitive struggle to get into office or to stay in it imparts to every consideration of policies and measures the bias so admirably expressed by the phrase about 'dealing in votes'" (*CSD.* p. 287), and although the power play of politics employs all the "psycho-technics" available to rhetorically influence and manipulate the electorate, and although "politicians appreciate a [democratic] phraseology that flatters the masses" (*CSD.* p. 268), the customary institutional arrangements of democratic government — despite the politicians' ambitions for gaining and wielding power — serve to raise the governing of a country above the oft phrenetic fray of the competition for political power itself.

The linch-pin in democratic institutions is the constitution itself that lays down limits to state power, the rules for the political power play and also divides its powers to keep the state's power in check (for any finitely human, social power can never be entirely trusted and has the tendency to augment itself, a kind of πλεονεξία sui generis often observed). Although Schumpeter asserts that "the democratic method cannot work smoothly unless all the groups that count in a nation are willing to accept any legislative measure as long as it is on the statute book and all executive orders issued by legally competent authorities" (*CSD*. p. 294), there is an important caveat. Those holding government power cannot put just any legislation on the statute books by force of numbers in parliament, even to please, or even at the risk of displeasing, sections of voters. The constitution must have such a definite form that it serves as a clear Gestalt for articulating, determining and protecting the *metabolism of freedom in civil society under the rule of law*. Individual freedom must have gained the form and fixity of a firm popular prejudice and second nature underpinned by certain institutional usages that represent red lines for the exercise of political power by those in power, beyond which government loses legitimacy.

Institutional safeguards, such as a supreme or constitutional court that serves to protect constitutionally rooted individual freedoms, democratic electoral procedure and the constitutional division of state power that serves to form a system of checks and balances, along with firmly held ethical convictions among the population at large, such as freedom from the state's prying into its citizens' affairs without very good reason and due process of law, together constitute an ethical shape of the beingness of beings, viz. the freedom of human being solidified in both 'subjective' and 'objective' Geist, and act as a bulwark against the unfettered accretion of state power.

The constitutional checks and balances of a division of state powers are one important feature of democratic government that takes account of the (human-)natural perversions of political power, but there is an impediment to democratic government that cannot be remedied by constitutional design. This impediment lies in the idea of democratic government itself as the attempt to create a 'feedback loop' of political power from the state itself to the people who are ruled. Since all social power tends to self-augmentation and thus, in the political realm, to overstep its proper bounds, those holding political office, too, tend to bend the limits of their legitimate power and to accumulate and extend political power. Not only is there the possibility of political corruption of all kinds (against which the constitutional system of checks and balances is wisely designed to serve as a safeguard), but of the more subtle reinterpretation of political powers which can go so far as to encroach upon and endanger constitutionally secured individual freedoms in sociating power play, the very basis of a free, democratic society.

Freedom of speech and the freedom of the media are in this connection crucial in maintaining vigilance over how the state, especially the politicians, concretely exercise or aggrandize their political power. All instances of political power within the state require oversight. But freedom of speech and the media, in turn, must be backed up by a vigilance of the people itself which holds its freedom of free and fair power play dear. People themselves must be concerned and engaged with political issues and prepared to take vocal political action against abuses of political power. The counter-tendency to this is the oft-lamented voter apathy that results 'naturally' from individuals being involved in their own private lives and the felt impotence about being able to influence how politicians and state officials concretely rule the populace and twist the rules of political rule. Such apathy and inertia reintroduce the rift between particularity and universality that democracy is intended to overcome. There is therefore a permanent tension in democracies between (the need for and exhortations to) vigilance on the part of citizens and the tendency toward apathy in which the citizens sink back into a passivity of allowing themselves to be ruled by those who occupy positions of political power.

The institutions and ways of thinking surrounding democracy are a way in which the historical We of a people is constituted socio-ontologically *as* customs. This does not exclude, of course, but rather includes the possibility that another Gestalt of human being, such as that based on the specious idea of redistributive social justice, may emerge and take shape to displace individual freedom in estimating interplay as essential to social human being. The hermeneuitc cast of human being as individually free, i.e. as each individual being the source of its own, self-chosen life-movements, along with the responsibility to care for one's own self-world that inevitably goes along with individual freedom, may fade historically in favour of a cast of human being as absorption into a total social whole within which the members are securely cared for, of course, at the price of being administered from above by increasingly totalizing social instances of power.

Regarding the democratic form of government as a Gestalt of the freedom of human being that assumes the form of well established institutions and usages allows us to see not only how state power in the hands of government and politicians can be curtailed, but also how the arbitrary power of the people (or, pejoratively, the 'rabble') itself in absolutist democracy can be held in check. Schumpeter is not the only one to point out how democratic government can descend into a state in which "political life all but resolve[s] itself into a struggle of pressure groups" (*CSD*. p. 298). The lament is old. It goes back to the ancients. "We find in general that at that time the Greeks were completely dissatisfied with, disinclined toward and damned the democratic constitution and the state of their times [...] All the philosophers declared themselves against the democracies of the Greek states — a constitution in which generals were punished, etc." (Wir finden im allgemeinen, daß damals die Griechen vollkommen unzufrieden gewesen sind, abgeneigt, verdammt haben die demokratische Verfassung und den Zustand ihrer Zeit [...] Alle Philosophen erklärten sich gegen die

Demokratien der griechischen Staaten, — eine Verfassung, wo die Bestrafung der Generale usf. geschah. Hegel *VGPII* W19:35)

This state of unfettered democratic caprice could only be corrected and pruned through the emergence of Gestalten of "objective spirited mind", i.e. shapes of an historically constituted We, in which "the lawful state, the state of the courts, of the constitution, of spirited mind is so firm within itself that only decisions for momentary situations have to be made" (der gesetzliche Zustand, Zustand der Gerichte, der Verfassung, des Geistes ist so fest in sich selbst, daß nur zu entscheiden bleibt für das Momentane; *VGPII* W19:35) The idea, a Gestalt of the beingness of beings, has to assert itself in history and assume firm, palpable shape in the mind-set, usages and institutions of a society, for democracy to become genuinely a noble institution of shared human freedom exceeding a merely capricious or cynical political power game, as it appears 'on the surface' of life as chronicled in the newspapers and other media. The mind-set, usages and institutions of a democratic society attain crystallized unity above all in the constitution as a firm framework for democratic political life, keeping its power struggles within bounds of fairness. The constitution is a core part of a people's ethical life in the sense of habituated usages in accord with the concept of freedom.

How is Schumpeter's assertion to be assessed that "the psycho-technics of party management and party advertising, slogans and marching tunes, are not accessories. They are of the essence of politics." (*CSD*. p. 283)? If the essence of politics is the competitive struggle for political power through the democratic procedure of popular elections, and the essence is exhausted in this struggle for power through winning votes, then of course the "psycho-technics" of manipulative rhetoric would also exhaust discussion of the democratic form of government. But we must consider also that when people act according to "particular purposes", but within established, accepted rules of economic and political interplay, they bring about something behind their backs that none of them intended. Whereas competition on the markets (this assumes neither so-called perfect competition nor a rational homo oeconomicus) enforces a discipline that the services offered and exchanged are provided efficiently and every effort is made to incessantly improve quality and efficiency, thus enforcing on the whole a highly productive economic metabolism of society in which demand for services, through the workings of an "invisible hand", is actually met, in the case of the competitive struggle to gain power by garnering electors' votes, one could doubt that this could lead to anything beneficial for the government of society.

Nonetheless, the political struggle does result in a selection of the personnel that is to govern the country, including the head of government, and this government is subject to dismissal by the voting population if it governs poorly. To be more precise, the government will be dismissed if it loses majority support of the voters, and whether it does so will depend on a multiplicity of public issues on which the voters decide to vote for one candidate rather than another. In ousting one governing party or coalition, there is no guarantee that the newly elected government will be any better, nor is it unambiguously clear what 'better' and 'worse' mean in the context of the exercise of power by a government, since the universal good always remains a contradictory, controversial, ever-changing unity. Voters will decide to withdraw their support for a given government in considering not only whether their self-interests have been furthered or hampered by the government, but also whether the government has performed well in serving (an estimated conception of) the general good, which in turn covers a gamut of issues from securing peaceable living in civil society through the provision of certain essential services and infrastructure, and preserving certain social values, usages and institutions, right up to foreign policy regulating relations with other states.

Because numerical majorities of votes will decide whether a government is re-elected or dismissed, by virtue of this practically workable quantitative reduction, in any particular election it will be impossible to say precisely what the electorate's vote means. This, of course, does not prevent pundits and party advisers from analyzing the election results interpretively and singling out the decisive issues on which a government was confirmed in power or defeated. This analysis is part of a disciplining, corrective cybernetic feedback loop, just like competition on the markets: if you have been unsuccessful, you must try to figure out why from what has factually come about in order to do better in future. This negative feedback loop, in weeding out bad governments that do not on the whole enhance the way a people lives, is how the evolution of government and the state proceeds and is cultivated over time as a cultural Gestalt of social life, where 'cultural' implies both 'venerating' and 'cultivating'. In fact, to win elections, political parties — a party being "a group whose members propose to act in concert in the competitive struggle for political power" (*CSD*. p. 283) — must strive to organize election campaigns around the issues which they surmise will be decisive for voters. It is a surmise because election campaigns, too, are a kind of polyarchic, rhetorical, social power interplay with an uncertain, unpredictable outcome. The election issues will be in part simply the interests of sectors of society such as sugar farmers or workers in the automobile industry or first-generation immigrants, and in part universal issues affecting the whole of society such as the education and healthcare system, taxation policy, or immigration policy.

These universal issues concern how the society as a whole is to live and how they are decided partly determines in the long run the particular national character of the way a people lives, even sedimenting to become part of its traditions and the customs of a people along with its characteristic mind-set or habitual way of understanding the world. Such a characteristic mind-set of a people is not a momentary affair but itself 'exists' in the 3D-temporal clearing of its history with its 'stretchedness' into both past (beenness, yesterness) and future. Above, who a people has been historically with its cultivated and cherished traditions pre-defines who it is today and in the future, including how certain decisive universal political issues are finally decided as outcomes of political power plays.

The democratic power struggle over who is to govern therefore does indeed bring about something that none of the participants, whether it be in the electorate or among the politicians, intended, and this is a shaping of a society's polity, i.e. how it lives together and also with other peoples. This way of living as a Gestalt of ethical life can be examined also socio-ontologically with regard to the concrete look which a people's freedom assumes historically and whether there is a shortfall measured against the yardstick of freedom. Just as the value of commodity goods and services as constituted through exchange interplay on the markets is beyond a judgement as to whether this value ought to be as it is, but rather comes about as the brute, reified fact of a given, quantitative market price, so, too, the way the democratic choice of government plays out and how this chosen government exercises its power, thus helping shape willy-nilly the shared historical way of life of a people, are beyond any simple extrinsic moral judgement. Rather, the traditions of democratic government themselves become part of a nation's identity, i.e. its understanding of itself and its values. 'Identity' here means that the people regard themselves, beyond and even against the mere particularity of their self-interests, as *belonging to* these democratic traditions that in part constitute *who* they are, and 'values' means that these traditional practices are held to be valuable to, i.e. good for, that people's historically established customary way of living.

Democratic government — pace Schumpeter — therefore goes far beyond or socio-ontologically deeper than the democratic method of an electoral competition for the power to govern in which voter-manipulative "psycho-technics" "are of the essence", being part of the very constitution of a people, where 'constitution' is taken in a double meaning as how a people is cast historically *as* a people, on the one hand, and how its government is organized in a constitutional structure or polity of the state, on the other. Only this constitution in the double sense can prevent democratic government from degenerating into an unscrupulous, cynical contest for political power in which voters' favour is 'bought' by a calculus of electoral favours to sectoral self-interests (thus reducing the electorate to mere *particularity* and ignoring its *singular* concerns also for the *universal* which come to expression in a *plurality* of contesting and contradictory conceptions of the universal good that only ever attain an ongoing, dynamic, ragged unity in a temporary *compromise* of political forces).

The traditionally established constitution in the double sense will also largely influence, in particular, whether a people tends to regard the state as the guarantor of its personal, individual liberty or rather is inclined to expect the state to secure and care for it. As shown in Chapter 9.10, this alternative corresponds to the distinction between two fundamental modes of caring for others. Where the government and the entire state care for the people by "leaping ahead", they *enable* and *encourage* personal liberty and private property intercourse as a mutually beneficial power interplay under which people can go about earning their livelihood in sometimes bruising competitive exchange and enjoying their lives in more or less fair and civil interchange with one another; they give the people secure room for play in which they can actively become themselves, learning in challenging interchanges who they are in casting their own selves.

Where, however, the government and the entire state care for the people by "leaping in", they relieve people of their cares of bearing the responsibility of having to take care of their own self-worlds and instead guarantee them a certain level of secure, material comfort, thus reinforcing their dependency, and consolidating and extending political power over them in myriad, often subtle ways, thus entangling the citizenry ever more in a web of minutely posited legislative will, bureaucratic regulations and control over the citizenry's every life movement. Whether this web of political rule is actually effective is not the crucial point, but rather whether an ethos of free and fair interplay within civil society is valued and practised as a counterweight to the ethos of the state's exercise of power for the sake of taking care of its people in the double-edged sense of 'taking caring of'.

The ongoing political metabolism of democratic government in so-called advanced Western countries post-WWII is incessantly charting a wavering course between these two alternative, contradictory conceptions of how a government and state are to care for the people: liberal democracy and social democracy. In some (Western) countries, or in certain periods and phases, the state will tend to become overbearingly paternalistic, bloating its power to the heights of social totalitarianism, with universality gobbling up particularity, even and especially to the people's applause, desiring as it does above all social security. In other places and at other times, a people will insist on its democratic, liberal constitutional traditions of self-reliance and being left to lead their own, private lives with minimal state interference, but at the price of bearing more personal risk. As already observed, what lies behind this wavering course of modern Western humanity are two different socio-ontological casts of human being, two *opposing* and therefore *contradictory* Gestalten of how human being itself, as ongoing socio-political power struggle, plays itself out and shapes up in history for a people as free and self-reliant, and also as craving the safe haven not only of security under the rule of law, but of material security under the watchful eye of a nominally caring state.

13.1.5 Carl Schmitt's critique of the "parliamentary law-making state"– The contradiction between formal law-making procedures and substantial rights – Direct plebiscitary democracy

It is instructive to note that there is a certain parallel between Schumpeter's proposed theory of democracy based upon the competitive struggle for political power and leadership, and Carl Schmitt's critical observations on the "parliamentary legislative state" (parlamentarischer Gesetzgebungsstaat[258]) in the particular Gestalt of the Weimar Republic, which is said to be necessarily based on the legitimizing principle of "equal opportunity for winning political power" (gleiche Chance politischer Machtgewinnung, *LuL.* p. 30) by means of gaining a majority in elections. "So everything depends on the principle of the equal opportunity to win power in domestic politics. If this principle is surrendered, the parliamentary legislative state surrenders itself, its justness and its legality." (So hängt alles an dem Prinzip der gleichen Chance innerpolitischer Machtgewinnung. Wird dieses Prinzip preisgegeben, so gibt der parlamentarische Gesetzgebungsstaat sich selber, seine Gerechtigkeit und seine Legalität preis. *LuL.* p. 36) In this democratic kind of thinking, legality and justice are reduced to a procedure for how governmental power is won through political power struggle, without considering the individual freedom exercised in estimative power interplay that needs protection by the rule of law and which is hardly of concern to Schmitt. After all, he is breathing the atmosphere and writing in a country whose historical struggles offers scant humus for any liberal ethos since it has known only rule from above, from an Obrigkeit, that was forged by a heavy

---

258 Carl Schmitt *Legalität und Legitimität* 1932, Duncker & Humblot, Berlin 2nd ed. 1968 p. 30; hereafter abbreviated as *LuL.*

Bismarckian hand into an authoritarian State in the second half of the nineteenth century.

In going along with the formal, ultimately procedural, democratic way of thinking for the sake of the argument, Schmitt is worried above all about the fragility of the principle, for "those holding the majority make the laws which are in force; moreover, they themselves validate the laws they make" (Wer die Mehrheit hat, macht die geltenden Gesetze; außerdem macht er die von ihm gemachten Gesetze selber geltend. *LuL.* p. 36). This implies that by controlling the legislature, the party in power can rig the rules of the power play to exclude or diminish the opportunity for its opponents to gain power, thus corrupting the democratic procedure and making a mockery of the electorate's power to elect, re-elect or dismiss government. The breakdown of fair play in the struggle for gaining power is said to be predestined in any "emergency situation" (Ausnahmezustand, *LuL.* p. 39) in which the party in legal possession of power, that enjoys a "large premium" (große Prämie, *LuL.* p. 39), acts to change the "rules for legal election to its advantage and to the disadvantage of its competitor in domestic politics" (die wahlgesetzlichen Regelungen zu ihrem Vorteil und zum Nachteil des innerpolitischen Konkurrenten treffen. *LuL.* p. 39). Doubtless Schmitt is pointing to a deficiency of democracy in general, for the governing party will do all it can to consolidate its hold on power, such as gerrymandering the boundaries of electorates. A democratic constitution must have safeguards against such corruption that are provided by a separation of powers within the state, so that citizens can call on the constitutional court to challenge the government's manipulation of the rules of play for democratic election. But this presupposes a democracy with roots in the soil of a liberal ethos, which the Weimar Republic is sorely lacking.

How does Schmitt come to this worrying assessment of the constitution of the Weimar Constitution? Is his critique to be understood as an attack on liberalism? Or does his critique miss the mark and only hit an already degenerate historical Gestalt of liberalism, namely, German legal positivism? Schmitt obscures the point. In one passage he brings "liberalism" (Liberalismus, *LuL.* p. 13) directly into connection with "the parliamentary law-making state with its ideal and system of a seamlessly closed legality of all state procedure" ([dem] parlamentarische[n] Gesetzgebungsstaat mit seinem Ideal und System einer lückenlos geschlossenen Legalität alles staatlichen Vorgehens, *LuL.* p. 14), treating them as synonymous. Already at the outset in his pamphlet, he connects the parliamentary law-making state with the "legal positivism handed down from the pre-war period" (aus der Vorkriegszeit überlieferten Rechtspositivismus, *LuL.* p. 7) and notes "the 'turn toward the total state' characteristic for the present moment [1932 ME] with its tendency toward the 'plan' (instead of toward 'freedom' as was the case a hundred years ago)" (die für den gegenwärtigen Moment charakteristische 'Wendung zum totalen Staat' mit ihrer unvermeidlichen Tendenz zum 'Plan' (statt, wie vor hundert Jahren, zur 'Freiheit'), *LuL.* p. 11).

It would seem therefore that the "parliamentary law-making state" as the target of Schmitt's attack is already the degenerate liberal state that has been undermined and hollowed out by nineteenth century German legal positivism and also infected by the idea of totalizing socialist planning. Such planning is the height of productionist metaphysics with its ontology of effective control of all social movement in the realm of politics. The "secure protection for freedom and property" (sicheren Schutz für Freiheit und Eigentum, *LuL.* p. 23) has become merely an example for "law in the material sense" (Gesetz im materiellen Sinne, *LuL.* p. 25) which, interestingly, is modified into an understanding of "law as '*interference* with the citizen's freedom and property'" (Gesetz als '*Eingriff* in Freiheit und Eigentum des Staatsbürgers', *LuL.* p. 25, my emphasis). From the liberal conception of the state as the necessary instance to protect the citizen's freedom and property, one has now degenerated, in German legal positivism, into a formal, legalistic understanding of the state's legitimacy as a "seamlessly closed" procedural system of law-making by parliament. Interference with individual freedom and private property is now legitimated if only the formal, rather than freedom-securing, rules of play of the parliamentary power struggle are adhered to.

The socio-ontological birth of the state in the liberal conception as the necessary power to protect the interchange of free individuals among each other in estimative power interplay is also the unfortunate hour of birth of its ugly twin, namely, the interference of state power with its citizens' freedom and property. This interference is immediately necessary for the state's very existence; the citizens' freedom must be restricted for the sake of the defence and security of the state which is charged not only with defending the country against invasion and outside interference but also with its subversion from within through undermining the state's institutions entrusted with upholding the society's way of life and its mode of government. Furthermore, and even more prosaically, interference with the citizens' property is immediately necessary to finance the state's very existence; the state is legitimately empowered to raise *taxation*, albeit with the democratic caveat of 'no taxation without representation'. Even a minimal state entrusted with the protection of individual liberty and private property has to interfere with private property to raise the taxation to finance the operation of its judiciary and police force. To this is added, at the very least, the taxation necessary for the armed forces and intelligence services. It is therefore not coincidental that from its inception, liberal thinking is concerned with the struggle of civil society against the government's overreach in levying taxes. Such scrutiny and struggle is a hallmark of a liberal society.

It is therefore consistent that Schmitt employs two quite different formulations for the state's core role: both "protection of" and "interference with" individual freedom and private property. This ambiguity lies at the essential core of the state as the instance of superior political power. It is the dilemma of sociated human being itself: human being can only be free if individual freedom in its power interplay is protected, but the very protection of individual freedom requires the individual's submission to a superior state power. Once an institution is legitimately endowed and entrusted with a superior social power, and given that any social power — including especially its bearers as ambitious whos seeking glory or at least some sort of who-radiance from their hold on power — tends toward a self-augmenting transgression of its limits, i.e. toward self-aggrandizement, the problem becomes how it can be controlled by a society composed of freely sociating individual citizens. How can it be trusted, when the essential tendency of all social power is to augment itself, if only by a creeping process of hardly noticeable encroachment?

The "Eingriff" to which Schmitt repeatedly refers can be rendered in English both as "interference" and "encroachment". "Law as '*encroachment* on the citizen's freedom and property" is a much more sinister and insidious affair than the state's legal "*interference* with the citizen's freedom and property", for the state's power has the inexorable tendency to grow and encroach upon individual liberty and private property, and that in the name of the universal good of society, especially in a society such as Germany with its long history of subjugation to rule from above. This encroachment is enabled by the above-mentioned essential ambiguity of the state. Such ambiguity can only be challenged in favour of protecting the rules of play for sociating interchanges when the *ethos of fairness* in such mutually estimating power play has taken root historically in a people, which was hardly the case in Germany. The ethos of fairness is the basis from which a people defends itself in struggles against incursions (another possible translation of "Eingriff") of state power.

Apart from the "citizen's freedom and property" degenerating to the status of merely an example for material law, according to Schmitt, German legal positivism understood "law in the material sense" alternatively as a "legal norm [...] 'that is supposed to be right for everyman'" (Rechtsnorm [...] 'was rechtens sein soll für jedermann, *LuL.* p. 25) which Schmitt paraphrases as "a universal, enduring rule" to be clearly distinguished from a "mere command or mere measure" (...das Gesetz etwa als eine allgemeine, dauernde Regel von bloßem Befehl oder bloßer Maßnahme deutlich abhob, *LuL.* p. 25). But this understanding of material law is itself formal and posited from above, i.e. by the Obrigkeit or higher authorities. It concerns only the formulation of law as universally applicable to the abstract citizen-person, guaranteeing abstract equality before the law and *insofar*, at least, rescuing the individual from an arbitrariness of state power directed against a particular person. Nevertheless, in legal positivism, the protection of individual freedom in the interplay of civil society, as the ultimate source of all freedom, has been lost (or was never present) as the inviolable content of law. Law has become its own Unwesen, its own degenerate essence.

Schmitt does not especially lament that individual freedom has been lost in the formalistic legal positivism embodied by the parliamentary law-making state. His aim is merely to coolly attack an "absolutely 'neutral', value- and quality-free, formalistic-functionalist idea of legality without content" (absolut 'neutral', wert- und qualitätsfreie, inhaltslos formalistisch-funktionalistische Legalitätsvorstellung, *LuL.* p. 27; case-endings modified ME) in favour of proposing the "recognition of substantial contents und powers of the German people" (Anerkennung substanzhafter Inhalte und Kräfte des deutschen Volkes, *LuL.* p. 97) to be revived by rethinking and strengthening the second, principal part of the Weimar Constitution. This renewed intervention (Eingriff) of the state he announces by proclaiming at the end of his pamphlet, "...thus the decision must be made in favour of the principle of the second constitution and its attempt at a substantial order", (...so muß die Entscheidung für das Prinzip der zweiten Verfassung und ihren Versuch einer substanzhaften Ordnung fallen. *LuL.* p. 98), although he concedes, aligning surprisingly for a final moment with German political liberalism, that "what lay [...] in Friedrich Naumann's intention [...] still had more of a connection with the essence of a German constitution than the value-neutrality of a functionalist majority system" (was [...] in der Absicht Friedrich Naumanns lag, [...] hatte doch noch mehr Beziehung zum Wesen einer deutschen Verfassung, als die Wertneutralität eines funktionalistischen Mehrheitssystems, *LuL.* p. 98).

Schmitt rightly points out that the formalistic parliamentary legality system "whose procedures and methods want to be open and accessible to various opinions, tendencies, movements and objectives" (dessen Verfahren und Methoden verschiedenen Meinungen, Richtungen, Bewegungen und Zielen offenstehen und zugänglich sein wollen, *LuL.* p. 29) tends toward a state encompassing "tasks of a state turning toward totality that becomes economic state, welfare state and much more besides" (Aufgaben des zur Totalität sich wendenden Staates, der Wirtschaftsstaat, Fürsorgestaat und vieles andere wird, *LuL.* p. 95). Without the kernel of individual freedom (exercised in free, civil, estimative power interplay) as a protected core of and inviolable *limit* to state power, signified by the word 'private', and enshrined in and protected by a constitution, the parliamentary democratic law-making state becomes total; it envelops the private sphere, intervenes in the economy and cares for its people according to generally applicable laws that are legitimate only insofar as they have been passed and promulgated according to the formal procedures and power play of a democratically elected parliament.

Any party winning a majority in parliamentary elections, thus voted into power by the electorate, becomes the government and is then in the position to 'legitimately' posit what it wills as law and even to override individual freedom and property rights in doing so. The total state encroaches on liberty under the 'legitimate' cloak of formalistic, procedural parliamentary-democratic legality and in the name of 'social justice' to secure the 'social fabric'. Such a total state is not merely a construction situated in the first part of the twentieth century, but is still with us, especially as a *way of political thinking* called social-democratic, i.e. as a way in which the constitution of a polity shapes up and presents itself to the mind.

Schmitt's critique of the Weimar Constitution aims above all at what he sees as an incongruity between its first and second parts. (Here it cannot be our aim to assess whether Schmitt's account of the Weimar Constitution in particular is adequate. We are interested only in his thinking on an adequate state and its constitution per se.) "The Weimar Constitution is literally split between the value-neutrality of its first main part and the value-fullness of its second main part." (Die Weimarer Verfassung ist zwischen der Wertneutralität ihres ersten und der Wertfülle ihres zweiten Hauptteils buchstäblich gespalten. *LuL.* p. 52) An attempt is made — unsuccessful in Schmitt's judgement — to paper over this crack by means of (mainly two-thirds) qualified majorities that are supposed to grant the second part of the constitution a higher status by modifying or 'super-charging' the formalistic, arithmetic voting procedures of simple majorities applicable to the first part.

The simple majority principle for gaining political power and making laws becomes more elaborate and restrictive in an attempt to protect 'higher' values, a rule of democratic play still widely esteemed and employed today. But for Schmitt, this more elaborate calculation of majorities does nothing to resolve the inherent contradiction. Any restriction to the principle of legality and legit-imacy through simple majorities in the legislature by securing, by means of qualified majorities, certain contents such as the institutions of "marriage", the "exercise of religion" or "private property" (*LuL.* p. 48) is said to represent a contradiction within the constitution and "gross and provocative breaches of the constitution" (grobe und aufreizende Verfassungswidrigkeiten, *LuL.* p. 51). It may indeed be conceded that a merely more complicated arithmetic of majorities for hindering alteration to certain material rights does not do justice to these ostensibly higher values. In Hegelian terms, something infinite is thus made merely finite, or the untouchable and inviolable ontological dimension of freedom is made ontically manipulable. The inviolability concerns the singularity of individual human freedom-in-interplay, which can never be subsumed beneath, or finally 'closed together' with, the universal without doing socio-ontological violence to it (cf. Chapter 12).

Why, however, cannot certain values of living together, constituting a cherished ethos, be placed directly on a higher constitutional plane than the laws that can be made by the party holding political power and protected by "higher instances and organizations superior to the ordinary law-maker" (höhere, dem ordentlichen Gesetzgeber übergeordnete Instanzen und Organisationen, *LuL.* p. 59) such as a constitutional court whose core task it is to protect the rules of play of the political power play in congruity with fundamental liberties of civil society, which are rules of play rather than substantial? Why should it be an insuperable problem that, to protect civil freedoms and thus guarantee the (socio-ontological) form of a free civil society and its content, viz. the metabolism of fair power interplay, "elements of a juridical state break in which become active in various ways, but mainly by judges examining the material legality of ordinary laws" (dringen Elemente eines Jurisdiktionsstaates, die sich auf verschiedene Weise, hauptsächlich durch richterliche Prüfung der materiellen Gesetzmäßigkeit von ordentlichen Gesetzen [...] betätigen, *LuL.* p. 62)? Why should the existence of a constitutional court as "an extraordinary, higher [...] law-maker" (einen außerordentlichen höheren [...] Gesetzgeber, *LuL.* p. 62) — which, as Schmitt notes, as element of a "juridical state", always has the "conservative tendency of any judiciary" (konservative Tendenz einer jeden Rechtsprechung, *LuL.* p. 12 case endings modified ME) as "the right means to preserve the social status quo" (das richtige Mittel zur Konservierung des sozialen status quo, *LuL.* p. 12) — to preserve core civil freedoms represent a "rift in the parliamentary law-making state" (Riß des parlamentarischen Gesetzgebungsstaates, *LuL.* p. 62)?

Surely it cannot be merely a matter of preserving the definition of a pure parliamentary law-making state vis-à-vis the pure typological definitions of the "juridical, governing and administrative states" (Jurisdiktions-, Regierungs- und Verwaltungsstaaten, *LuL.* p. 10). Perhaps it is the fact that the existence of a separate, higher instance for examining the legality of laws passed by parliament introduces a *separation of powers* that disturbs or destroys the state's organic unity. But the separation of powers and the so-called checks and balances of a liberal democratic state have long been essential parts of liberal thinking on how political power is to be divided and thus clipped in favour of preserving the citizens' sacrosanct private sphere and the individual freedoms exercised in the interplay of civil society. And, as we have already noted, Schmitt pleas at the conclusion of his pamphlet for the consistent strengthening and rethinking of the second part of the Weimar Constitution that contains substantial, 'higher', "inviolable" values that amount to incursions into the power plays of freedom in civil society.

At least with regard to the core "material rights" of individual freedoms, property rights and other civil rights (and apart from other substantial values such as "marriage" and the "freedom of religion"), Schmitt cites a reputed legal expert of the time, R. Thoma, who claims that "resolutions which suppress the freedom of conscience or 'do violence to any of the other principles of freedom and justice held sacrosanct by the entire civilized world today — with the exception of Fascism and Bolshevism —' can be unconstitutional despite having achieved a majority required to change the constitution" (Beschlüsse, welche die Gewissensfreiheit unterdrücken oder 'irgendeines der anderen Prinzipien der Freiheit und Gerechtigkeit unter die Füße treten, die in der ganzen heutigen Kulturwelt — mit Ausnahme des Faschismus und des Bolschewismus — heilig gehalten werden', trotz verfassungsändernder Mehrheit verfassungswidrig sein können, *LuL.* p. 50). Schmitt comments, "here at least, the civil legal system itself with its concept of law and freedom is still sacred; liberal value-neutrality is regarded as a value and the political enemy — Fascism and Bolshevism — is openly named" (Hier ist wenigstens noch das bürgerlich-rechtliche System selbst mit seinem Gesetzes- und seinem Freiheitsbegriff heilig, die liberale Wertneutralität wird als ein Wert angesehen und der politische Feind — Faschismus und Bolschewismus — offen genannt, *LuL.* p. 50).

If Schmitt opposes the arithmetic, procedural formalism of the democratic-parliamentary law-making state based on a competitive political power game of building majorities and pleas instead, as we have noted, for the constitutional "recognition of substantial contents und powers of the German people" (Anerkennung substanzhafter Inhalte und Kräfte des deutschen Volkes, *LuL.* p. 97), then it has to be considered whether the "liberal value-neutrality", whose essential tolerance allows a plurality that resists unification, is itself a value which, although abstractly universal, is nonetheless weighty enough for providing an anchor for the life of a people (not only the German people) that protects (the insubstantial power play of) civil society from state interventions and encroachments. In fact, Schmitt proposes "another distinction" (eine andere Unterscheidung, *LuL*. p. 60) "between states with a constitution restricted to organizational-procedural regulation and universal rights of freedom and other states whose constitution contains extensive material-legal stipulations and assurances" (von Staaten mit einer auf die organisatorisch-verfahrensmäßige Regelung und auf allgemeine Freiheitsrechte beschränkte Verfassung, und anderen Staaten, deren Verfassung umfangreiche materiell-rechtliche Festlegungen und Sicherungen enthält, *LuL*. p. 60) Constitutions of the first kind are further characterized as a "constitution that does not contain any material-legal regulation of substantial extent but a fundamental rights part that guarantees the civil sphere of freedom in general and as such is distinguished from an organizational part that regulates the procedure for how the state's will is formed" (Verfassung, die keine materiell-rechtliche Regelung wesentlichen Umfangs enthält, sondern einen Grundrechtsteil, der die bürgerliche Freiheitssphäre im allgemeinen gewährleistet und als solcher einem organisatorischen Teil, der das Verfahren staatlicher Willensbildung regelt, gegenübersteht, *LuL*. p. 59).

This is in line with Thoma's above-quoted claim which, however, Schmitt has criticized just a few pages before. Is it not possible for a (minimal, non-interfering) state to be based 'materially' on a constitution which in the first place protects the citizens' 'sacrosanct' private "sphere of freedom in general", leaving the putatively "substantial" shaping of social life to the interchanges and interplay of a civil society itself that is free, but not coerced, to value 'privately' the custom of marriage or certain religious beliefs, etc. and have them formally protected as aspects of civil freedoms for those particular individuals who cherish these ways of ethical life in marriage and religious belief? Individual freedoms would then be protected against the "contentless" formalism of parliamentary law-making with its power struggle focused on the calculation of majorities. They would even be protected against the state's "general reserved right to override a universal right to liberty" (allgemeinen Vorbehalt gegenüber einem allgemeinen Freiheitsrecht, *LuL*. p. 59 case endings modified ME) and to change the constitution "in favour of substantially defined particular interests and objects worthy of protection by fixing material rights and the properly acquired rights of particular groups [such as public servants, ME] under constitutional law" (zugunsten inhaltlich bestimmter, besonderer Interessen und Schutzobjekte, unter verfassungsgesetzlicher Fixierung materiellen Rechts und wohlerworbener Rechte besonderer Gruppen *LuL*. p. 59).

Why should the state have the right to override individual liberties? Only in emergency situations of extreme danger, and temporarily? Why should the state's servants, its Beamten ('Staatsdiener', state-servants as opposed to the Anglo-Saxon understanding of state employees as 'public' or 'civil servants') enjoy special privileges and protection from the vicissitudes of living? Why is it not enough for the interplay of civil society itself to bring about of itself the 'values', i.e. valued, customary practices and ethical ways of living, under the state's universal protection of the citizens' freedom? Why do 'material values' of a people have to be posited and *positively* instituted and enforced by state power, even at the cost of restricting and denying individual liberties, including free economic exchanges and shaping one's own private life, according to fair rules of play? Why should the state with its superior political power be needed as the site for nurturing and guarding the positive values of a people beyond its civil, individual freedoms if these positive values are not already rooted of themselves in the ethical usages of civil society itself? Why should the universal protection of civil freedoms as the state's chief role and raison d'être amount merely to a formula for nihilism lacking "substantial contents und powers" of a people?

The interplay of civil society itself in which the members of society vie with each other, showing off, acknowledging and estimating each other as who they are, especially in having their abilities monetarily valued, is a social metabolism that of itself brings about diverse customary ways of living that can gain dignity and be held dear by those living in and through them. It does not require the state to explicitly and positively value certain ethical ways of living (such as marriage) over others (e.g. companionships, gay and lesbian relationships), but rather, the state's role is only to guarantee the room for play that enables this metabolism of ethical life, which includes also controversial interchange in civil society over cultural issues of custom, to bring about its own, ever-changing outcomes.

Apart from pointing out that the Weimar Constitution contains a "second" or "counter-constitution" (Gegen-Verfassung, *LuL.* p. 81) in its second part that in effect brings into play a second, judicial law-maker next to the parliamentary law-maker with its "seamlessly closed" system of procedural legality, Schmitt also draws attention to two further candidates for a constitutional law-maker with a foothold in the Weimar Constitution, namely, a direct, *plebiscitary democracy* and an extraordinary *dictatorial law-maker* empowered to decree measures as laws. This makes the constitution a very messy, highly contradictory document in Schmitt's assessment. "As this constitution currently presents itself, it is full of contradictions." (So wie diese Verfassung vorliegt, ist sie voller Widersprüche, *LuL.* p. 98) The dictatorial powers given to the "extraordinary law-maker" (der [...] außerordentliche Gesetzgeber, *LuL.* p. 76f) under Article 48 of the Weimar Constitution allow this law-maker to suspend certain basic constitutional rights, "including in particular personal freedom (Art. 114) and property (Art. 153), the core of the bourgeois state based on the rule of law" (darunter insbesondere persönliche Freiheit (Art. 114) und Eigentum (Art. 153), der Kern des bürgerlichen Rechtsstaates, *LuL.* p. 75). "The ordinary law-maker can only interfere with fundamental rights by virtue of the privilege reserved for law, but he cannot suspend them. The extraordinary law-maker, by contrast, can do both and is [...] distinguished from the ordinary law-maker in a peculiar way and superior to him." (Der ordentliche Gesetzgeber kann nur vermöge des Gesetzesvorbehalts in die Grundrechte eingreifen, er kann sie aber nicht außer Kraft setzen. Der außerordentliche Gesetzgeber dagegen kann beides und ist [...] auf eigenartige Weise vor dem ordentlichen Gesetzgeber ausgezeichnet und ihm überlegen, *LuL.* p. 77) That the Weimar Constitution was shaky and not "safe from dictatorship" (diktaturfest, p. 79) was certainly a well-founded cause for alarm at the time, but this anomaly has to be compared with the other lawmaker, the sovereign people itself, envisaged by the constitution that at first glance seems to offer a very appealing, irresistible prospect.

It would seem to be the highest form of legitimacy of the state and its laws when the people itself presents itself as law-maker. Then it is the will of the people itself in a direct vote that lays down the law. Law becomes a product of will, the will of those themselves who are to be ruled by the law. In Hegelian terms, das Allgemeine (the universal) degenerates to that which is allen gemeinsam (common to all) in a common will, albeit a common will ascertained merely empirically by majority votes. Schmitt points out that the democratic plebiscitary elements of the Weimar Constitution clash with and contradict its primary, formally procedural, representative parliamentary law-making part. Be that as it may, here I consider only the thought or idea (ἰδέα, a 'look' of being) of direct plebiscitary democracy as the ultimate legitimate form of state for the government of a free people. The "legality system of the parliamentary lawmaking state" (das Legalitätssystem des parlamentarischen Gesetzgebungsstaates, *LuL.* p. 92) competes with "a plebiscitary-democratic *legitimacy*" (einer plebiszitär-demokratischen *Legitimität*, *LuL.* p. 92), and the latter can easily come out on top in the pre-ontological conceptions of a people regarding its freedom in which government is reconciled with freedom, thus legitimizing political power.

Even though representative, parliamentary democracy is well-established today as ethos in the West as *the* legitimate form of state and government, this by no means excludes ideas of direct democracy as enjoying high levels of legitimacy in everyday conceptions. The people is sovereign, and this sovereignty would seem 'obviously' to come to immediate presence in plebiscites, i.e. referendums, more perfectly than through democratic elections of parliamentary representatives. The people itself in "its quality as sovereign" (aus seiner Eigenschaft als Souverän, *LuL.* p. 63) is apparently the supreme instance, the "ratione supremitatis" (*LuL.* p. 63) for law-making. Today we could perhaps even still cite Schmitt's statement from 1932, "And yet plebiscitary legitimacy may be the only kind of justification of the state that today is universally recognized as valid." (Und doch ist die plebiszitäre Legitimität die einzige Art staatlicher Rechtfertigung, die heute allgemein als gültig anerkannt sein dürfte. *LuL.* p. 93) Today, as in 1932, democracy as a form of legitimacy of state power is regarded as the expression of the people's will, no matter what the issue, and the people's will exists in a referendum as the empirical expression "of the sovereign people immediately *present* and identical with itself" (des mit sich selbst identischen unmittelbar *präsenten* souveränen Volkes, *LuL.* p. 66), thus constituting a We that could also be aptly characterized as the 'tyranny of the majority'. This holds true as a mode of legitimacy in everyday conceptions of democracy (often adduced in the media) even when and precisely when referendums are not an institutionalized part of a state's constitution. Any expression of majority, collective will is then taken as somehow legitimate and binding.

There are many drawbacks in a plebiscitary democracy, and Schmitt draws attention to them. The main defect is that the questions for a referendum have to be formulated and presented to the people in a certain conjuncture whose timing is determined by the government or its leader, above all, according to the *momentary mood* of the electorate as assessed by the governing party's leader, who may well be a clever demagogue. Even if this defect is overcome by constitutionally allowing petitions from the people for a referendum, the referendum's issue cannot be deliberated upon adequately by a whole people and is borne more by swaying emotions and moods rather than by prudent deliberation, again leaving the door wide open to populist demagogy. The same objection can be made, of course, also against parliamentary elections and election campaigns in general, although with parliamentary representatives of the people, a certain mediation is inserted between the people's will and the state's. And the modern mass media do provide also a medium of deliberation of sorts, invariably shying away from any deeper questioning by invoking all the while the superficial, sham we of democracy with its average understanding supportive of the status quo. But even if these objections and the impracticability of government by plebiscite are regarded as surmountable, there is a deeper-lying, essential defect in delivering the final decision over state power and its exercise into the hands of the people's plebiscitary will.

Namely, the state with its superior legislative and governing power can only be justified if it is government under the rule of law, and law in the first and fundamental place — that is, according to its socio-ontological essence — is the law that protects the "life, liberty and estate" of its individual citizens in their estimative power interplay with one another in civil society. This law, which is higher than empirical will and rests upon a socio-ontological insight into human being itself as individually free-in-sociation (in all the senses developed in preceding chapters), must not be surrendered even to the people's sovereign will as it is expressed through majorities that come about in referendums, for this majority will is not per se in accord with (the socio-ontological concept of) freedom. If the people's plebiscitary will were to hold sway, there would be no limit at all to state power, and the state could legitimately, in the name of the will of the majority, interfere with and encroach upon the freedom of its individual citizens, say, by granting a demagogue leader even more constitutionally guaranteed power (as has happened more than once in the past century). The sovereign people's will would then lead inevitably to a total state based on the tyranny of the more or less whimsical and swayable majority, that knows no bounds and would be legitimately empowered to invade its citizens' privacy in the name of democratic freedom conceived as the brute will of the majority. Schmitt notes,

> Es ist sogar wahrscheinlich, daß ein großer Teil der heute zweifellos vorhandenen Tendenzen zum 'autoritären Staat' hier [in der plebiszitären Demokratie und ihrer Legitimität] eine Erklärung findet. [...] Von weitaus größerer Bedeutung ist die Erkenntnis, daß in der Demokratie die Ursache des heutigen 'totalen Staates', genauer der totalen Politisierung des gesamten menschlichen Daseins zu suchen ist, und daß es [...] einer stabilen Autorität bedarf, um die notwendigen Entpolitisierungen vorzunehmen und, aus dem totalen Staat heraus, wieder freie Sphären und Lebensgebiete zu gewinnen. (*LuL.* p. 93)

> It is even probable that a major part of the tendencies toward an 'authoritarian state' that today no doubt exist find an explanation here [in plebiscitary democracy and its legitimacy]. [...] Far more significant is the insight that the cause of today's 'total state' or, more precisely, of the total politicization of human existence in its entirety is to be sought in democracy and that it [...] requires a stable authority to undertake the necessary depoliticizations and, out of the total state, to regain free spheres and domains of living.

At this point, Schmitt is sounding, surprisingly, very much like a true liberal. Without doubt this passage has to be read in the specific historical conjuncture of 1932, in the period of degeneration of the Weimar Republic and the empowerment of the National Socialism under Hitler with its push to extend the German Volk's Lebensraum. But it also can be read from a suitable abstracting distance as a socio-ontological parable of the absolutization of the will of the sovereign people even against a higher concept of inviolable freedom of estimative power interplay among whos. The total politicization of all spheres of life amounts to the encroachment of the political power game into civil society with its mutually estimative social and economic power plays among the private members of civil society, including also incursion into the personal private sphere, with a resultant dissolution of private lives, in both senses, in the political sphere.

The abstract personhood of each individual member of civil society is an injunction against interference from others, especially from the state. Such an abstract injunction leaves a sphere of freedom of movement to be shaped by the individual's will in exercising his or her various powers according to abstract rules of play called abstract right. Any further concretion from above of how this private sphere is to be shaped amounts to an incursion into it. The only "stable authority" it requires to guarantee "free spheres and domains of living" is a genuinely liberal state for which individual rights and freedoms are sacrosanct and untouchable, including by any incursions of the people's plebiscitary will.

13.2 Democracy, freedom and justice: A recapitulation

Today in the West, democracy and freedom are generally (mis)conceived and (mis)treated as synonymous in popular discourse. The entire pathos of human freedom can be claimed and mobilized in any struggle for democratic rights. Yet, as we have seen, democracy is merely a form of government in which the citizens of a country are able to freely elect those who are to govern them from a selection of politicians currently available who are vieing for political office. The freedoms required for this are the right to free and fair, periodical elections and the right of free speech, including the right to free media of public opinion, able to criticize the government of the day and enable debate over who is best to govern. The issue of human freedom itself, however, goes much deeper than the question of how a people is to be governed and by what institutional arrangements; it concerns the question of human being itself, as investigated in depth in the present inquiry.

Democratic government does correspond to the concept of freedom itself, but only a facet of it. Freedom is not a mere concept, i.e. something thought up by human beings, philosophical or otherwise, but denotes rather the socio-ontological structure of human being itself as ineluctably free in its peculiar sociating movement of estimative power interplay among whos. The freedom of human being means that human beings are self-moving from a point of origin within themselves, where these movements are guided by an *understanding* of beings in their being and also *affected* by an attunement with the 3D-temporal clearing as a whole. Understanding and attunement are the two originary modes in which human being itself is exposed to the temporal openness of being, i.e. of presencing and absencing. Although each human being is always already cast into situations and circumstances not of his or her own making, to *be* a point of origin governing your own movements means that you are also a zero-point, a point of spontaneous nothingness in a conjuncture of yesterness and future whence you cast your own life-movements, in power play with others, according to how the world shapes up for you in your attuned understanding. To *be* a free point of origin and individual source of power implies therefore that freedom itself proceeds from this point of spontaneity that represents a hiatus between having already been cast and self-casting, so that, in particular, it is ultimately futile to attempt to *explain* human actions by 'blaming' them on temporally precedent causes. Rather, in casting yourself into the future from out of your own spontaneity of its presencing now, you are *responsible* for your self, i.e. for your own self-casting of your own life.[259]

---

259 Hegel: "...each person is the maker of his own happiness. This implies that each person only comes to enjoy himself. The opposite view is that we push the blame for what befalls us onto other people, onto the unfavourability of the situation or suchlike. This is in turn the standpoint of unfreedom and at the same time the source of dissatisfaction. By contrast, in that a person recognizes that what happens to him is only an evolution of himself and that he bears only his own blame, he conducts himself as a free person and has in everything he encounters the belief that no wrong happens to him. The person who lives outside peace with himself and his fate commits much that is mistaken and warped precisely because of the false opinion that wrong is done to him by others. Now, it is indeed the case that there is much that is contingent in what happens to us. This contingency, however, is grounded in the naturalness of the human being, but in that a human being otherwise has the consciousness of his freedom, the harmony of his soul, the peace of his heart will not be destroyed by the undesirable that befalls him. It is thus the view of necessity through which the satisfaction and dissatisfaction of people and thus their fate itself are determined." (...ein jeder ist seines eigenen Glückes Schmied. Hierin liegt, daß der Mensch überhaupt nur sich selbst zu genießen bekommt. Die entgegengesetzte Ansicht ist dann die, daß wir die Schuld von dem, was auf uns fällt, auf andere Menschen, auf die Ungunst der Verhältnisse und dergleichen schieben. Dies ist dann wieder der Standpunkt der Unfreiheit und zugleich die Quelle der Unzufriedenheit. Indem dagegen der Mensch anerkennt, daß, was ihm widerfährt, nur eine Evolution seiner selbst ist und daß er nur seine eigene Schuld trägt, so verhält er sich als ein Freier und hat in allem, was ihm begegnet, den Glauben, daß ihm kein Unrecht geschieht. Der Mensch, der in Unfrieden mit sich und seinem Geschick lebt, begeht gerade um der falschen Meinung willen, daß ihm von anderen Unrecht geschehe, viel Verkehrtes und Schiefes. Nun ist zwar in dem, was uns geschieht,

Moreover, each human being's understanding of the world to which it is exposed is both its own, *individualized* understanding and also an understanding which it inevitably *shares* with other human beings. It is individualized because understanding passes through each human being individually, and a world shapes up in general and in specific situations always according to an individual perspective on the world from an individual situation. The understanding of the world, however, is also ineluctably shared because the way a world shapes up for human understanding always comes about in 3D-historical time, by virtue of which we can sensibly talk of the understanding of a particular period or a particular age in particular parts of the globe. Individual understanding, which is how an individual holds the world to be, is then not entirely unique and an invention of that individual, but only a, perhaps highly idiosyncratic, combinatorial constellation of world-understanding in an age which is also attuned, within a certain range of attunements, with the mood of that age. There is no way in which an individual can escape its historical time. Within the understanding of an age in a certain part of the globe (and we have been inquiring into the conceptions underlying modern Western societies), the socio-ontological components of that understanding do not form an entirely consistent totality, but are also partly contrary to one another.

Thus, for example, as has been shown, there is contrareity in the very conceptions of human being itself which give rise to opposed factions of understanding among (groups of) human beings themselves which also assume the guise of opposed Weltanschauungen and political ideologies. There is a contradiction and tension in human being itself, known already to the Greeks, between an urge for freedom and a need for security, i.e. between a desire to stand on my own feet, taking care of myself and those close to me without outside interference and being the source of my own, freely determined life-movements, on the one hand. On the other, there is a willingness to gratefully submit to a stronger power for the sake of safety and of being led and cared for. Freedom and security thus partly go hand in hand, for there can be no individual free-

---

allerdings auch viel Zufälliges. Dies Zufällige ist indes in der Natürlichkeit des Menschen begründet. Indem der Mensch aber sonst das Bewußtsein seiner Freiheit hat, so wird durch das Mißliebige, was ihm begegnet, die Harmonie seiner Seele, der Friede seines Gemüts nicht zerstört. Es ist also die Ansicht von der Notwendigkeit, wodurch die Zufriedenheit und die Unzufriedenheit der Menschen und somit ihr Schicksal selbst bestimmt wird. *Enz. I* § 147 Zus.) If human being is necessarily splintered into a plurality of individual human beings in inexorable, estimative power play with one another and thus exposed to the contingency of this power interplay, then to be free and responsible for oneself means to accept one's status as player in this risky power play of whoness.

dom without protection of that freedom by a superior power, and partly they are diametrically opposed when freedom is exchanged for security in submitting to a superior will, whether it be that of a state or some other acknowledged authority.

Insofar as you accept your freedom as a point of spontaneous nothingness from which you cast your very own life movements, and do not seek shelter in merely obeying others or a superior instance, you are the source of your self-movement by exercising your *powers* of all kinds, including the power of reified value that you have acquired through interchanges. Your primary and elementary powers, however, are your *abilities*. Such abilities are expressed primarily by bringing about *changes* in things, which is productive activity in the broadest sense, and, in a derivative sense, by having them *estimated* and *valued* in *interchanges* with others in which your abilities are exercised for the benefit of another in exchange for something else of value.

The socio-ontologically originary *sociating, mutually estimating power-interchange* among human beings is their exercising, by agreement, their various abilities for each other's benefit. This must be regarded as the core of the sociating movement that constitutes *society* and also as the most elementary *expression of human freedom* as *social, sociating* freedom. Even the interchange of *speaking with one another* must be viewed in its elementary sociating function as always already embedded in pragmatic exchanges for each other's benefit. An individual exercises its freedom at first and for the most part in having its abilities esteemed and valued by others in ongoing, daily processes of estimation. Because abilities are powers, this process of estimation is a *power play* and society is constituted above all through the interchange of powers in ongoing processes of estimation and valuation. Because each of the participants in such interchanges is a free point of origin of its own actions, the sociating interplay itself is *groundless*, in contrast to the grounded nature of productive activity through the exercise of abilities in the primary sense for which a source of power exercises its power one-sidedly over an object.

Each individual only freely casts its own self out of spontaneity and comes to a stand in having its self reflected back estimatively from the world, and this takes place above all through having one's abilities valued and esteemed by others. My self-casting thus partly depends upon the validating reflections from others, and is partly independent of such validation insofar as I truly *have* ability as the source of my own able or excellent self-movements. I becomes *who* I am *essentially* through the mirror play of having my abilities, of whatever kind, estimated and valued, and my social status as somewho depends on the social estimation of my powers — for better or worse —, at whose core are my individual abilities and lack thereof. Because *whoness* is a social *interplay* of reflection in an ongoing mirror power play through which my spontaneity of individual freedom attains a more or less transient stand in the world that is constantly being regenerated and re-formed through the mirror play, it is not of the same essence as *whatness*, which consists in a *substantiality* of standing presence.

Such a sociating interplay of mutual estimation takes place on large scale through *markets* of all kinds and mediated by *reified value*, which serves both directly and indirectly as the sociating medium of abstract, quantitative estimation and valuation of individual abilities of all kinds. For the *products* of the exercise of human abilities of all kinds, money, as price, serves as the *value-mirror*. This is the *interplay of civil society*, which is the locus par excellence for the play of social freedom, and is also characterized by the *competitive vieing among powers*, both primary abilities and derived powers such as accumulated wealth and political influence. Civil society is therefore *as* the play of freedom simultaneously a *rivalrous power play*. In the power play, individuals strive both to *gain* the benefits from the exercise of others' abilities, which amounts to the enjoyment of what good living offers, and also to have one's own who-stand in society affirmed, esteemed and even also boosted. The power play is therefore a vieing and striving for *what* one gains and then *has*, and also for *who* one is estimated to be in the mirrors of social estimation. Hence it is twofold, but both are *value* interplays.

Because the interplay of civil society is a rivalrous power play both against and with one another, it gives rise continually to *rivalry* and *conflicts* and can also become *ugly* in countless different ways. The power play must be played out in such a way that each *player* is not disadvantaged by others' playing unfairly, for such *unfairness* detracts from gaining one's fair share in the twofold sense. *Fairness* is the pith of *justice* in the interplay of freedom that is civil society, and *injustice* is the ugliness of unfairness. What constitutes fair play becomes practised in civil society in habitual, customary *usages* which form the core of civil society's *ethos*. The ethical æther of civil society is fairness, which covers a gamut of phenomena such as civility, decency, uprightness, keeping one's word, reliability, etc. etc. In the atmosphere of an ethos of fairness, *trust* can be engendered, which is the life-blood of the civil society's metabolism. The ethos of fairness is a socio-ontological 'look' of freedom itself, now lived, practised and valued by a plurality of human beings sociating regularly with one another. It is both a way of understanding one's own and other's moves in the interplay, and also a universally, socially accepted way of interchange. Such fairness includes also *indifference* to others insofar as we have so far had no interplay with each other and leave each other also free to pursue one's own course in life on one's own responsibility.

The ethos of fairness of the power play in civil society, however, does not suffice to cope with and correct the numberless ways in which the interplay can become unfair and ugly. For this, a superior power, *government*, is necessary to adjudicate conflicts and remedy the abuse of individuals' powers. The government, too, is an habitual, practised form of social living *empowered* to regulate the power play of civil society to ensure fair play among free players. This is the core of liberal *political power*, and it is *legitimate* in being recognized and affirmed by the members of civil society, who readily *submit* to it, insofar as the exercise of this political power accords with, and is also for the sake of, the ethos of a fair play of powers. Not only is government recognized as legitimate, but it is truly in accord with freedom-in-power interplay insofar as its exercise of power is directed at securing and enhancing the fair play of civil society.

Although government requires also the construction of a *state apparatus* with various *organs*, along with resources from civil society in the form of *taxation*, its willed exercise of power for ends other than the securing of fair play, such as providing infrastructure, only remains in accord with freedom for as long as the interplay is not interfered with or, if it is interfered with, this interference is *justified* by political argument on the basis of it being necessary for the *good* of, and not directed against, civil society, unwarrantedly restricting its freedom of movement. Such justification must take place in *public debate* mediated by *media* in which civil society is also able to criticize government and the workings of the various organs of the state apparatus. Although government has, and must have, superior power to govern, and this is legitimated in the eyes of civil society, this power must remain open to the scrutiny, criticism and hence the influence of civil society if it is to still accord with freedom.

The superior political power of government is returned in a certain way to civil society itself to complete the circle of political power through the government itself being subject to periodical elections by the populace, which now, in relation to government and state, forms the *citizenry*, concerned not only about its *particular self-interests*, but also about *universal questions* concerning the social good as a whole and the preservation of individual freedom. The *democratic* form of government enables the *submission* of the people to government to be reconciled with freedom itself, which ultimately resides in each individual. The scrutiny of government is thus paired with the power of the electorate also to rid itself of those in government who abuse political power or exercise it in ways that fail to be justified to the electorate in political debate, perhaps because of sheer incompetence of individual politicians in office, especially government ministers. *Political debate* is an essential aspect of the political power play, also a variant of the mirror play of estimation, through which government justifies (or fails to justify) its actions and also legitimates (or fails to legitimate) itself to the opinions held in the electorate. Political debate is waged above all through the exercise of *rhetorical powers* of whatever kind, and such an interplay of rhetorical powers, both in *parliament* and in the various *public media*, is a paradigmatic expression of freedom, which also has the power to change government policy and even the government itself.

The media thus have only a limited role, for their discourse is inevitably that of average everyday understanding which is 'always already' preunderstood by readers, listeners and viewers. Political debates are therefore carried on in this kind of average discourse that understands via numerous clichés that are endlessly circulated in what 'people', and especially, what 'talking heads' in the media say. The status quo is thereby upheld since only certain kinds of 'comprehensible' discourse are admitted to the media, and also only certain topics and perspectives on topics that have already been selected by the media themselves as ruts of understanding along which discourse can run smoothly. Other topics and questions are excluded from the start simply because they are unfamiliar, therefore placing demands on the attentiveness of both media functionaries (journalists, editors, etc.) and media recipients (readers, listeners, viewers). This results inevitably in a blandness of the media that shores up the status quo, and also a censorship due to their subjecting all content to the criterion of being always-already-understood. This censorship is reinforced and effected via the filter of selecting those media persons (producers, editors, etc.), who, through the averagness of their own understanding, guarantee a pandering to the public's average understanding instead of widening or challenging it. Any 'singularity' in thinking is filtered out by averageness. Challenges to the ways 'people' think are invariably unwelcome in the media, and editors seek interlocutors from civil soceity (especially academics) who speak in terms 'people can understand' and therefore do not have much to say at all. All the phenomena addressed in media discourse are already precomprehended by widespread preconceptions through which media can ensure their successful acceptance by their respective audiences.

Government can only be reconciled with freedom if civil society itself is legitimately and *constitutionally* empowered to scrutinize government and the organs of state. The *division of powers* within the organization of the state itself, exercised in certain publicly visible, institutional usages, is a further means for preventing the absolutization of superior political power and for bringing it back under the surveillance and control of civil society. The constitution, rights of scrutiny, public debate over policy and legislation, and so forth, all become part of the habitual practices of the political life of a democratic society, and constitute together the *ethos of democratic government* which itself is in accord with freedom, but only so long as the ethos of fair play in civil society itself is respected and not encroached upon, clipped or stifled for the sake of other state-posited, 'substantial' aims. Even the electorate itself may be, and often is, tempted to truncate the free and fair power play of civil society for the sake of seeking security under the paternalistic care of the state's superior power. Instead of being overtaxed by the challenges of freedom, the individual then prefers to be overtaxed by the state, especially when stronger players pay more taxes. In doing so, human beings fail to live up to their own essential freedom, which is of its nature challenging. This is a contradiction in a democratic society which can never be finally resolved, and whose tension always remains in play in the ongoing political power play.

Freedom is movement, namely, at its core, the free and fair movement of the multifarious, rivalrous, mutually estimating power interplays of civil society itself. Justice consists fundamentally in the fairness of this metabolism of interchanges of all kinds which, itself, can only be approximated, but never finally attained in standing presence, through *unceasing conflict and political power struggle* over the *truth of issues of justice* which hover perennially between *disclosure* and *obscurity*, and split into rival perspectives. Already in a fragment from Heraclitus we read: εἰδέναι δὲ χρή τὸν πόλεμον ἐοντα ξυνόν, καὶ δίκην ἔριν, καὶ γινόμενα πάντα κατ' ἔριν καὶ χρεών. "It is necessary to know that fighting is common [to all] and justice is strife and conflict, and everything comes about by strife and conflict, and that in accordance with customary usage." (Fragment 80, Diels-Kranz) The cultivation of this usage of ongoing conflict, itself a power struggle, is the *ethos of justice*. Accordingly, justice, too, is a dynamic, perennial power play, above all among mutually estimating, persuasive rhetorical powers, which practice is the ethically valued usage through which the in-jointness of fair interplay continually comes about for a time as a defined, understood, sometimes beautiful contour, only to slip out of joint once again. Freedom itself never finally 'closes together' free, singular individuality with a universal state of affairs, but, for finite, mortal human beings, always remains in play as a controversial and conflict-ridden power play, both in civil society and politically, with ever new variations of play combinations arising from players' unforeseen moves. To be free, the individual has to *be* a player in these interplays of powers. In this way, freedom, at times even in its *singularity* under the protection of abstract rights, can be lived.

14 Global whoness and global power plays

Zum ewigen Frieden. Ob diese satirische Überschrift auf dem Schilde jenes holländischen Gastwirts, worauf ein Kirchhof gemalt war, die Menschen überhaupt, oder besonders die Staatsoberhäupter, die des Krieges nie satt werden können, oder wohl gar nur die Philosophen gelte, die jenen süßen Traum träumen, mag dahin gestellt sein.

To Everlasting Peace. Whether this satirical caption on the shield of that Dutch publican, on which a graveyard was painted, intended people in general, or especially heads of state who can never get enough of war, or perhaps only philosophers who dream that sweet dream, may be put to one side.

Kant Zum ewigen Frieden 1983 S. 195

14.1 Whoness of a people

What is the social-ontological task here? In what sense is it sensible to speak of global whoness and global power plays? Who are the players in such global power plays? The globe is here taken to mean the totality of beings on Earth, considered not as whats but as whos. Such whos are, in the first place, individual human beings and then all those associations of human beings — We's— formed by sociating estimative interplays, many of which have already appeared in previous chapters, such as families, enterprises, labour unions, industry associations up to governments and states. The last named are the 'biggest' We-whos so far considered who wield power over a people for the sake of that people's freedom of interplay. A people itself is formed through mutually estimating each other as sharing an historically shaped, cultural way of life with each other that is positively cultivated, treasured and thus esteemed. A people belongs together in some kind of cultural identity. This identity itself may contain tensions of not belonging when certain groups within the population distinguish themselves from each other by estimating each other only deficiently, as in the case of tensions and conflicts along lines of religious belief. Such differences may override a people's belonging together in a cultural identity through sharing a common history and cultural practices. Cultural identity itself consitutes a kind of We through which many individuals can feel a sense of belonging together despite obvious wide differences otherwise, such as two individual whos estimating each other as belonging together merely insofar as they recognize that they speak with the same accent.

Whos, therefore, can sociate estimatively in many different ways along very different lines of identification that abstract from other differences. Sharing a common descent, language, history, geography or customs provides bases for

https://doi.org/10.1515/9783110617504-014

estimating each other as belonging together in the one *nation*. The word 'nation' itself refers etymologically to a common birth from the same source. A shared geography where a cultivated culture is lived thereby becomes a *national territory*. Who you are become is decisively shaped by having been cast by your birth into a social milieu and environment with certain cultivated customary practices, especially speaking a language with a similar accent and lilt. In this social environment with its customary sociating practices with which you are intimately familiar from birth you feel at home. Through the course of your life you widen the horizon of the sociating environment to which you belong and with which you identify. One of these horizons is the nation that sociates many sharing a culture with each other. Such nations may coincide with being ruled by a unified government that overrides many regional differences otherwise, so that a people sociates under a *nation state*. In other cases, by dint of historical struggles to lead their lives, nations may be constituted as a We only within a region of a nation state. National territory thereby diverges from the territory governed by a state. This is also the case where a nation conceived as belonging together in a cultural We straddles the borders of territories governed by individual states. Belonging together as a nation therefore may conflict with belonging together under the rule of a state. Such conflict can go as far as rebellion by a culturally identified We against the state and civil war. Or it may restrict itself to frictions between different cultural We's that may or may not be located geographically, as in the case of religious antagonisms.

In all these cases, however, the various We's sociating people in an identity arise from mutually estimative interplays in which identity and difference are recognized and constituted. Where differences are ascertained in such estimative interplay, a difference between a We and a Them comes about which may or may not provide grounds for rivalry or even antagonism and hostility. The question as to the whoness of a people therefore has no clear-cut answer along the lines of a nation state with a sovereign territory over which it rules that coincides with the geographical region in which a unified We carries on its cultural life. The whoness of a nation may not be the We of a nation state. In other words, the We of a nation and the power of rule exercised by a state over a populace may be diremptred, thus rupturing any national we-ness of a people.

Belonging together in the We of a people coincident with a nation state may therefore be merely invocative in character, invoking the unity of a people under a nation state. If this is so, in what sense can we speak of global whoness, given that whoness itself is constituted through mutually estimative interplay between and among people marked by both identity and difference? A global We could only be invoked or evoked in summoning a togetherness in sharing the globe with which whos could identify themselves, as in 'we' all belong to-gether due to all of us being human beings and as such endowed with human rights, or due to our all sharing the same planet Earth, or, even more baldly and devoid of genuine whoness, our belonging to the same species of animal. Such an invoked we-ness is highly abstract and brittle, for there are also so many differences invoking far more narrowly circumscribed We's such as estimating each other *as* speaking the same language or sharing the same customs of eve-ryday life. This *as* signifies that all belonging-together in a We is always an hermeneutic performance and achievement of estimating each other *as* such-and-such, and this performance may well require also cutural rituals invoking a belonging-together such as the commemoration of decisive historic events through which a people defined itself as a people for itself and also toward the outside, for other people and peoples. Such a decisive event is often the victori-ous outcome of a power struggle such as establishing certain civil rights vis-à-vis a ruler, the outcome of a civil war or a foreign war. In commemorating, peo-ple together (co-) recall from memory an event, now absent, from the temporal dimension of yesterness (the 'past', Gewesenheit, beenness), thus invoking themselves hermeneutically *as* the We of a people.

The We of a people's cultural identity, by contrast, is lived more implicitly in belonging together by cultivating shared customs and practices which the people encompassed by that We value and esteem, such as the custom, or ra-ther cult, of ancestor worship. The culturally cultivated way(s) of life of a people may come to expression and even be established by literary works in the lan-guage of that people, including founding myths, which define who they are and with which they identify as facets of their selves to which they revert in under-standing themselves as the cultural We of a people. Such culturally significant works are themselves cultivated as part of a people's culture defining who they in their belonging-together.

Toward the outside there can be cultural exchange through which people from different cultures come to estimate and esteem each other's foreign cultur-al practices. Such estimative cultural interchange is furthered by learning for-eign languages to gain better access to another people's cultural way of life. There are also many deficient modes of such cultural interplay such as estimat-ing other cultures as inferior to one's own or simply 'cultivating' a disinterest in or narrow-minded ignorance of another culture. Migration between peoples with their distinctive cultures leads also to an intermixing of customs and a refashioning of a given people's own culture and ways of life. Cultures them-selves are permeable to each other in an estimative interplay sui generis. An hermetically sealed-off culture is the exception and, since the globalization of the 15th century initiated by European ships, and borne by the European thirst for trade, exploitation and colonies, anyway impossible. Intercultural interplay is the rule, not the exception; it softens the edges between self-defined cultures by engendering mutual appreciation of other ways of life and the works of foreign cultures. Whoness of peoples is thus a phenomenon of mutual estimative interplay that goes far beyond the trading of goods.

In the following I will consider only the interplay between nation states and peoples unified in nation states, thus assuming that a people is more or less itself united in a national identity and that this nation is governed by a single territorial state.

Throughout the present inquiry to this point, the focus has been on the individual, sociation of individuals and their power interplay amongst themselves and with government and state. On the level of the power interplays among nation states, now to be briefly discussed, the entire problematic repeats itself on a higher, extended plane with other phenomenal aspects. The core social ontology of whoness with its concepts of exchange, mutually estimative interchange, social power (as ontologically distinct from the effective power of traditional ontology of movement), are now played out among nation-state players on the global, geo-political stage carved up into sovereign state territories. This holds true even though empirically, the political world today is precisely not structured solely according to power interplays among nation states founded upon civil societies imbued with the rule of law. There are also numerous so-called 'asymmetric' power interplays with 'rebels' who revolt against any rules of play that have been established among nation states in international law intended to limit the means of violent force permissible in resolving conflicts among themselves. Such rebels, invariably labelled 'terrorists' by the nation states themselves, since they do not respect a state's sovereignty, do not respect any such rules, including the law of war, but employ all available means of violence without restriction, if only they seem advantageous in furthering their goals, including undermining a state's hold on power over its people by terrorizing the population at large. They need not have ambitions as global power players, but — fueled by regional, cultural grievances and long-standing historical antagonisms and struggles — may be revolting against a single nation state's power internally in an insurrection.

As already discussed, although the whoness of a people, as who it identifies itself mirrored in its lived world, may well be partially constituted by its belonging-together as a nation ruled by a state, thus constituting the unity of a nation state as an individual, sovereign, political player acting on the world stage of politics, there is no lack of deficient modes of existence of the nation state.

There are, for instance, failed states locked in quasi-civil war, and fragmented countries where belonging together in an identity is not constituted so much by nationality, but primarily by tribes and clans, or where religious, linguistic or regional differences divide a nominally national people into more or less latently antagonistic factions.

Furthermore, there are many nation states around the globe not based upon the rule of law for a civil society which regard such rule of law from the liberal tradition as alien to their own far more hierarchical or despotic cultures of political rule. In all these latter cases, the concept of the free individual and the abstract person under the rule of law, which is a Western, but nevertheless universal, conception of human being, has not been recognized throughout the entire world, and correspondingly, the state in question does not acknowledge that level of universality on which its citizens would be guaranteed and would enjoy the universal status of persons and therefore also the freedoms of free, mutually estimative power interplay among themselves. Nevertheless, the concept of the nation state based on rule of law with its core of liberal individual freedoms-in-interplay retains its status as the leading conception for organizing the world's peoples and countries, for the peoples of nation states do aspire, more or less, to the freedom of a people consisting of free individuals, their conceptions of living together having long since been infiltrated, if not subverted, by originally Western ideas of freedom. This is also documented in all the world's nation states having formally signed up to documents such as the Universal Declaration of Human Rights and also to membership in international bodies such as the United Nations. By paying lip service to universal human rights through becoming signatories to universal documents, even repressive nation states have committed themselves to at least playing a game of appearing to respect the core of free interplay among individual human beings, and so have to dissemble before global opinion that is overwhelmingly imbued with conceptions of human rights, no matter how confused, superficial, contradictory and vague such conceptions may be.

The major and essential difference between the power plays among nation states in world politics and the power interplays that go on within societies is the *lack* of an overarching world Leviathan that would keep all the individual states "in awe" for the sake of "comfortable, safe, and peaceable living one amongst another" (Hobbes), thus restricting the internal power interplays to the exercise of social powers *other* than physical force (cf. Chapter 10.1). The power plays among states are therefore in a perennial state of Ought-to-be. On this topic Hegel says, "that the *treaties* upon which the obligations among states rest ought *to be kept*." (daß die *Traktate*, als auf welchen die Verbindlicheiten der

Staaten gegeneinander beruhen, *gehalten werden* sollen. *RPh.* § 333, cf. § 330). A state breaking a treaty can lead to war with another state. Obligations among states, which are laid down in treaties of many kinds, are analogous to contracts among persons natural and otherwise in civil society, with the great difference in the rules of power interplay being that contracts can be enforced by the rule of law exercised by a state's judiciary, whereas treaties among states only *ought* to be kept under international law, whose bodies of enforcement are comparatively weak and often reduced to merely diplomatic interplay whose means of coercion reside mainly in trade sanctions imposed by a group of nation states acting in concert against a renegade nation state. A world body to watch over the obligations states have taken upon themselves in treaties of all kinds relies upon the *moral* power of an appeal to states' keeping their word combined with the inestimable value of *trust* in international interplay, whilst lacking an ultimate power of coercive enforcement.

A world community of states has arisen in the shape of the United Nations, with its own (highly deficient, highly deformed, because not universal) rules of play for the power plays among nation states, and specific treaties such as the World Trade Organization, which at least has the covenanted power to impose fines for infringements of international rules of trade. In cases of open international conflict, each individual nation state decides whether it is in its own sovereign self-interest to bow to the moral, ultimately *persuasive rhetorical power* as practised by diplomacy and the mass media, which have the power of moulding world opinion. As analyzed in Chapter 10, such 'soft' rhetorical power is certainly socio-ontologically different in kind from 'hard' physical force, but it is not entirely ineffective, if only because nation states profit reciprocally from bonds of trust that are so easily broken and difficult to re-establish once rent. In pursuing its calculated self-interest, a nation state, may well bend, over time, to the pressure of a world consensus derived from universal principles and rights serving as a moral world regulative. Let us listen further to Hegel on the global, estimative, power play among nation states.

14.2 The state as the universal that remains particular in the interplay among foreign powers

When dialectically unfolding the power interplay among states according to their concept in §§ 330ff (The Outer Right of State) in his *Rechtsphilosophie*, Hegel insists that the concept of an individual state striving for its own "well-being" (Wohl, § 336) is "particular" (besondere, § 340), not universal (allgemein). The diremption between particularity and universality is thus displaced from civil society, which was said to be "the system of ethical life lost in its extremes" (das System der in ihre Extreme verlorenen Sittlichkeit, § 184) (a contradiction only purportedly resolved by positing the state as the universal instance that substantially embodies freedom, as has been shown in Chapter 12), to a renewed, presumably irresolvable diremption between the particular, individual states in their "irritability" (Reizbarkeit, § 334) and the universal of "world history" (Weltgeschichte, § 342), which latter is claimed to be nothing other than "the interpretation and *realization of the universal spirited mind*" (die Auslegung und *Verwirklichung des allgemeinen Geistes*, § 342), i.e. nothing other than eine Gestalt of the hermeneutic As through which an age is cast ontologically behind the backs of those living in it.

The state itself, existing as it does in reality, is therefore ultimately, for Hegel himself, a *particular* state, and a truly *universal* state never comes to be realized as a state but remains hovering as Weltgeist, i.e. as world-mind, in which and for which the beingness of beings is cast in an historical age. The realization in world history for Hegel is an unfolding of universal Geist in a "transition to its next highest stage" (Übergang in seine nächste höhere Stufe, § 344) that can be understood as an historical constellation of being in the Heideggerian sense or as an hermeneutic cast, respectively. In this way, the realization of universal spirited mind as objektiver Geist, even according to Hegel himself, is constantly deferred, and the split between particularity and universality is retained on a higher plane beyond that of civil society and even beyond that of the nation state in the power interplay among nation states.

Hence Hegel himself concedes that the power interplay among states, "the outer right of states" (das äußere Staatsrecht, § 330), i.e. 'foreign relations', according even to its *philosophical, socio-ontological* concept, assumes merely "the form of *Ought*" (die Form des *Sollens*, § 330) because "the fact that it is real is based on *different sovereign wills*" (daß es wirklich ist, auf *unterschiedenen souveränen Willen* beruht, § 330); "...thus in this respect it must always remain a matter of Ought" (so muß es in dieser Beziehung immer beim Sollen bleiben, § 330 Add.). Furthermore, the vain, finite reality of "mutual, independent caprice" (der beiderseitigen selbständigen Willkür, § 332), personified as it is in heads of state, with their proclivity for arrogant, phallic hubris, is acknowledged by Hegel's philosophical thinking insofar as it pronounces, "the principle of *international law among peoples*" to be "the *universal* right that ought to prevail in and for itself among states" (Der Grundsatz des *Völkerrechts*, als des *allgemeinen*, an und für sich zwischen den Staaten gelten sollenden Rechts... § 333).

If the impotence of the universal concept in the realm of the power interplay among states is acknowledged insofar as its status as based on a 'mere Ought', and the particularity of capricious, hubristic, individual sovereign wills is conceded (and these sovereign wills do not have to be the wills of monarchs, but can equally well be the wills of, say, democratically elected heads of state, despots or other demagogues and autocratic rulers), then the "immediate reality" (unmittelbare Wirklichkeit, § 332) of the state as the instance that exercises real power inwardly over civil society and its cell unit, the family, must also be marked by the qualification that the state, in its inner reality too, is merely finite human beings, in their own striving for high who-estimation or gain, governing finite human beings. In particular, this implies that the speculative-dialectical τέλος of final reconciliation of reality with reason in the absolute idea remains beyond reach.

14.3 Brute international power interplays

The brute, physical force of military power is an option for a nation state to assert its self-interest, and the exercise of this option can lead to *war*. The *threat* of its exercise is also already a means of self-assertion of a state's power in global conflicts and plays a major role in global diplomacy (international persuasion, bargaining and arm-twisting) when it comes to a conjuncture when the outbreak of war is to be prevented. Even the territorial integrity guaranteed by international treaties outlawing territorial expansion or wars of aggression enjoy only the status of Ought which an aggressive nation state can infringe as part of its geo-political power strategy in an uncertain power game. The self-interest with the highest moral claim with respect to initiating military conflict is national self-defence, whereas economic national self-interest is asserted primarily through mutual interest, bargaining and mutual agreement, albeit that certain national economies with less economic power (mediated through the medium of reified value in all its forms through to foreign direct investment of capital) are generally disadvantaged in such agreements. Therefore there is a tendency to make multilateral trade agreements in which the economic weights of each national economy are somewhat evened out. Super-power states with potent economies may be inclined to bully other states to assert themselves.

The moral, rhetorical power of world opinion as shaped, manipulated and circulated through the world media, although a diffuse 'factor' in the power plays of world politics, nevertheless is the domain in which the legitimacy or otherwise of nation states' actions, especially their military actions leading to or threatening military hostility or outright war, is judged with palpable effects on a nation state's who-status in the world and therefore consequences, especially economic ones, for its interplay with other nation states. Today it is illegitimate for a nation state to wage war simply to assert its economic or similar interests. There are many, complexly interlinked levels in the power play among nation states, including the economic (e.g. free trade agreements), the cultural (e.g. fostering of cultural exchanges, of learning foreign languages), the diplomatic (e.g. formation of alliances, including cultural, economic, technological and military alliances) and, ultimately, war, which poses the greatest risk for a nation state, for its outcome and the surprising turn of events in armed conflict remain highly uncertain. Each level of this international power play can have infinite, unexpected twists and turns in how the power game is played out by heads of state, foreign ministers, diplomats, trade representatives, etc.

If war breaks out between states, the consequences quickly become incalculable, especially when it is taken into account that war between nation states also opens the opportunity for antagonisms within a nation state between sections of the population to erupt in civil war. To win a war, a nation state is prepared to deploy all means possible, including the most dastardly and unspeakably atrocious. International law concerning the conduct of war itself degenerates into mere words in the face of a warring nation state's determination to act ruthlessly and savagely, committing atrocities against the enemy's military and civilian population under the cover of propaganda, barefaced lies, deception, duplicity. The powerlessness or hesitation of a world Leviathan, or rather, a consensual world body like the United Nations, to intervene can make a bitter and cruel war with no holds barred the occasion for the world's nation states' performing a farce on the global diplomatic stage in open view of an impotent global audience.

Socio-ontologically, however, there are no new basic 'looks' of social power here (cf. Chapter 10.1), but nevertheless endless possible, even hitherto unheard-of, ontic variations of power plays to be played out in history. The main feature of interest is the above-mentioned *lack* of a world-state Leviathan. Such a power vacuum allows the moral, rhetorical powers of diplomacy and world opinion to have more sway, especially since the development of mass media supported by global communications networks. The mass media themselves report on geopolitical events from within their own preconceptions and cultural prejudices that have always already pre-formed the information to in-form, sway and pander to the mooded minds of their readers, listeners and viewers, invariably simultaneously invoking a fake We. Such rhetorical sway is also manipulable by individual nation states themselves via their own propagandistic media channels. Quite apart from any manipulative propragandistic intentions of individual media outlets or the government, the rhetoric of the media must be adapted to the cultural mind-set of a people for it to be understood and persuasive.

In particular, it makes a great difference whether and to what extent (originally Western) liberal conceptions of society and government with their core of free and fair interplay among all the players in civil society, the state and among nation states have taken cultural root in a people's mind. In the rhetorical exchanges between and among nation states a government will often revert to its own cultural traditions of hierarchical or despotic rule to deflect rhetorical incursions by universal conceptions of human freedom and human rights. In other cases, a despot will pay lip service to universal human rights in all respects while covertly trampling on them to cynically further political ends. The susceptibility of a people to demagoguery depends partly on the cultural mind-set that has itself been shaped through historical struggles.

14.4 Nationalism, protectionism and free, estimative power interplay among peoples

With regard to individual human beings, who are at the root of all interplay of freedom, if there is to be freedom at all, the formation of personal identity as a who through belonging to a certain people or a nation harbours the danger of *nationalism* which inscribes a difference among the world's peoples, asserting a superiority which goes against the grain of a universal fraternity of a multitude of peoples sharing the Earth. This is one of the side-effects of the constitution of a 'we the people' *as* a nation state. Whoness constituted through a national identity, when sharpened into political nationalism (based sometimes narrowly on ethnic birth rather than sharing customs in social living), can lead to dangerous frictions among, and also within nations. Such nationalism, in turn, is a *rhetorical* phenomenon which can be counteracted by rhetoric that makes the case for the *universal* status of human being (the dignity accorded to each and every individual through universal human rights) as against the *particularity* of national differences. There is an endless, ongoing struggle over asserting politically an *actuality* of the universal, inviolable dignity of the person against not only the crudities of bellicose, jingoistic nationalism (which is invariably linked also to ethnic, linguistic, religious or other particularities that become politically charged with potential and actual violence) but also the meanness of particular mass-egoistic self-interests. Such mass egoism has only been further inculcated by the idea of the social welfare state. Such meanness comes to the fore, shamelessly showing its ugly face, in all sorts of subtle variations of *protection-*

ism through which citizens in particular sectors and situations clamour for their nation state to protect them from the brunt of the world economic power play by putting other, foreign players at a disadvantage through wielding nation-state power. Since the striving for security (say, of jobs) competes with the striving for freedom, which is always risky and challenging, a people, or broad sections thereof, may suddenly 'discover' (or invent) its peculiar nationality as a good 'reason' to protect itself against foreign trade competition, quite apart from any considerations of fair trade-interplay.

If nationalism is an aggressive play against other peoples in the power interplay among nation states, and protection is a defensive play against other peoples, then there is another mode of power play in which peoples can be *for* each other in such international power plays by estimating appreciatively each other's powers in the mutual benefits they can bring through their exercise. This can be seen first of all on the economic level of international trade, and has long since (1817) been formulated in economics by David Ricardo[260] as the mutual benefit of *comparative advantage*. Already in Chapter 9.5 it was shown that there is no limit to what people can do for each other in exercising their powers and abilities in each other's favour. Such mutual benefit from estimative interplay, however, is not restricted to trade, but extends also and especially to cultural interchange and interplay in which two peoples can mutually benefit from getting to know each other's worlds, in particular in how they are set to work by the powers of creative individuals in works of art and literature. In this lies also the possibility of learning endlessly *from* each other in giving *to* each other. There are endless potentials for peoples to exercise their abilities for each other's benefit in interchanges and, in this sense, there are no limits to growth both economically and culturally. Such mutually appreciative power interplay is consonant with peoples' living peaceably with each other, whereas an aggressive or defensive stance *against* each other leads to tensions that ultimately do not enhance living with each other, but rather detract from its possibilities. Such tensions and antagonisms fanned by despots and demagogues can play into geopolitical strategies that include the threat of or actual unleashing of military forces in initiating incalculable hostilities.

Freedom **is** — that is, it presences in the world — only through mutually esteeming power interplays among people, including globally among peoples.

---

260 David Ricardo *On the Principles of Political Economy and Taxation* 1821/1996.

15 Bibliography

Alcott, Louisa May *Little Women* Folio Society, London 1966.

Aristotle *Metaphysics* in *Works in Twenty-Three Volumes* Vol. XVII and XVIII Loeb Classical Library, Harvard U.P. and W. Heinemann, London 1938ff.

Aristotle *Nicomachean Ethics* in *Works in Twenty-Three Volumes* Vol. XIX Loeb Classical Library, Harvard U.P. and W. Heinemann, London 1938ff.

Aristotle *Politics* in *Works in Twenty-Three Volumes* Loeb Classical Library, Vol. XXI Harvard U.P. and W. Heinemann, London 1938ff.

Arthur, Christopher J. *The New Dialectic and Marx's Capital* Brill, Leiden-Cologne-Boston, 2002.

Backhaus, Hans-Georg *Dialektik der Wertform: Untersuchungen zur marxschen Ökonomiekritik* Ça ira, Freiburg 1997.

Backhaus, Hans-Georg 'Über den Doppelsinn der Begriffe politische Ökonomie und Kritik bei Marx und in der Frankfurter Schule' in *Wolfgang Harich zum Gedächtnis* Band II Stefan Dornuf and Reinhard Mitsch (eds.), Müller & Nerding, Munich 2000.

Barker, Ernest *Greek Political Theory: Plato and His Predecessors* Methuen, London 1964.

Benseler, Gustav Eduard *Griechisch-Deutsches Wörterbuch* bearb. Adolf Kaegi, VEB Verlag Enzyklopädie, Leipzig 1931/1985.

Berman, Sheri *The Primacy of Politics: Social Democracy and the Making of Europe's Twentieth Century* Cambridge U.P. 2006.

Böhm-Bawerk, Eugen von 'Zum Abschluß des Marxschen Systems' in Friedrich Eberle (ed.) *Aspekte der Marxschen Theorie 1: Zur methodischen Bedeutung des 3. Bandes des 'Kapital'* Suhrkamp Verlag, Frankfurt/M. 1973.

Capurro, R., Eldred M., & Nagel D. *Digital Whoness: Identity, Privacy and Freedom in the Cyberworld* ontos/De Gruyter, Frankfurt/Berlin 2013.

Capurro, R & Holgate, J. (eds.) *Messages and Messengers. Angeletics as an Approach to the Phenomenology of Communication* Fink, Munich 2011.

D'Agostino, Fred superseded entry on 'Original Position' in the *Stanford Encyclopedia of Philosophy* at URL plato.stanford.edu/archives/fall2008/entries/original-position/ Accessed Dec. 2009.

Descartes, René *Regulae ad Directionem Ingenii* in *Philosophische Schriften* Meiner, Hamburg, 1996.

Descartes, René *Principia philosophiae* Oeuvres de Descartes Vol VIII, publ. par Charles Adam et Paul Tannery, Paris 1897–1910.

Destutt de Tracy, A.L.C. *A Treatise on Political Economy* Georgetown 1817.

Eldred, Michael 'Absolutely Divine Everyday: Tracing Heidegger's thinking on godliness' 2008–2014 URL www.arte-fact.org/untpltcl/absdvnev.html

Eldred, Michael 'Assessing How Heidegger Thinks Power Through the History of Being' URL www.arte-fact.org Ver. 2.0 2004.

Eldred, Michael *Critique of Competitive Freedom and the Bourgeois–Democratic State: Outline of a Form–Analytic Extension of Marx's Uncompleted System* with an appendix *A Value-Form Analytic Reconstruction of 'Capital'* co-authored with Marnie Hanlon, Lucia Kleiber & Mike Roth first published by Kurasje, Copenhagen 1984. Emended edition URL www.arte-fact.org 2010 with new foreword, published with CreateSpace, North Charleston 2015.

Eldred, Michael *Der Mann: Geschlechterontologischer Auslegungsversuch der phallologischen Ständigkeit* Haag + Herchen, Frankfurt/M. 1989.

https://doi.org/10.1515/9783110617504-015

Eldred, Michael *Entständigung* CreateSpace, North Charleston 2015.

Eldred, Michael 'Heidegger's Restricted Interpretation of the Greek Conception of the Political' URL www.arte-fact.org Ver. 1.0 2003, Ver. 2.0 2004.

Eldred, Michael 'Husserls Krisis: Fragen an die transzendentale Phänomenologie' 2017 URL www.arte-fact.org/untpltcl/hsrlkris.html

Eldred, Michael *Kapital und Technik: Marx und Heidegger* Verlag J.H. Röll, Dettelbach 2000. English version 'Capital and Technology: Marx and Heidegger' in: *Left Curve* No. 24 May, 2000 Oakland, California. Thoroughly revised in Ver. 3.0 2010 at URL www.arte-fact.org, and republished with CreateSpace, North Charleston 2015. Cited as Eldred 2000/2015.

Eldred, Michael *Phänomenologie der Männlichkeit: kaum ständig noch* Verlag Dr. Josef H. Röll, Dettelbach, 1999.

Eldred, Michael *A Question of Time: An alternative cast of mind* CreateSpace, North Charleston 2015.

Eldred, Michael 'Questioning the Earth's Value — Including a proposal for a capitalist carbon sink industry' URL www.arte-fact.org 2005/2006.

Eldred, Michael 'Technology, Technique, Interplay: Questioning *Die Frage nach der Technik*' first presented to the 41st North American Heidegger Conference, DePaul University, Chicago 3–5 May 2007 and published in the proceedings. Subsequently published in IEEE *Technology and Society* Vol. 32 No. 2 2013. Available also URL www.arte-fact.org

Eldred, Michael *The Digital Cast of Being: Metaphysics, Mathematics, Cartesianism, Cybernetics, Capitalism, Communication* ontos/De Gruyter, Frankfurt 2009. Emended, revised, extended, digitized Ver. 3.0, URL www.arte-fact.org 2011.

Eldred, Michael 'The Quivering of Propriation: A Parallel Way to Music' URL www.arte-fact.org Ver 1.0 1998, revised, emended and extended Ver. 3.0 2010. Also revised and extended as a book:

Eldred, Michael *Thinking of Music* CreateSpace, North Charleston 2015.

Eldred, Michael 'Vom Wesen der Polis und vom Unwesen des Beiläufigen' in *prima philosophia* Bd. 2 Heft 2 April 1989, included in *Entständigung: Philosophische Aufsätze* CreateSpace, North Charleston 2015.

Eldred, Michael 'Was heißt Männlichkeit' 2013–15 at URL www.arte-fact.org/untpltcl/wshstmnl.html

Eldred, Michael 'Why social justice is a specious idea' URL www.arte-fact.org Ver. 1.0 2005, Ver. 3.2 2010.

Eldred, Michael *Worldsharing and Encounter: Heidegger's Ontology and Lévinas' Ethics* URL www.arte-fact.org Ver. 1.0 1997, Ver. 3.0 2010.

Eliot, T.S. 'Burnt Norton I' *Four Quartets* Folio Society, London 1968.

Epstein, Brian 'A Framework for Social Ontology' *Philosophy of the Social Sciences* 2016, Vol. 46(2) pp. 147–167

Freeman, Samuel Entry on 'Original Position' in the *Stanford Encyclopedia of Philosophy* at URL plato.stanford.edu/entries/original-position/ Accessed Dec. 2009.

Georges, Karl Ernst *Ausführliches Lateinisch-Deutsches Handwörterbuch* Bde. I and II, Wissenschaftliche Buchgesellschaft, Darmstadt 1992.

Hayek, Friedrich A. *Law, Legislation and Liberty* Vol. 1 Rules and Order 1973; Vol. 2, The Mirage of Social Justice 1976; Vol. 3 The Political Order of a Free People 1979 Chicago U.P. cited in the form *LLL*1:22f, etc.

Hegel, G.W.F. *Enzyklopädie* in *Werke* Bde. 8, 9, 10 Suhrkamp, Frankfurt/M. 1971.

Hegel, G.W.F. *Grundlinien der Philosophie des Rechts* in *Werke* Bd. 7. Abbreviated *RPh*.

Hegel, G.W.F. *Logik* in *Werke* Bde. 5 and 6.

Hegel, G.W.F. *Phänomenologie des Geistes* in *Werke* Bd. 3.

Hegel, G.W.F. *Vorlesungen über die Geschichte der Philosophie* in *Werke* Bde. 18, 19, 20.

Hegel, G.W.F. 'Über die englische Reformbill' *Werke* Bd. 11.

Hegel, G.W.F. 'Über die wissenschaftlichen Behandlungsarten des Naturrechts, seine Stelle in der praktischen Philosophie und sein Verhältnis zu den positiven Rechtswissenschaften' (1802/03) in *Werke* Bd. 2.

Heidegger, Martin *Aristoteles, Metaphysik Theta 1–3: Von Wesen und Wirklichkeit der Kraft* Freiburger Vorlesung SS 1931, ed. Heinrich Hüni *Gesamtausgabe* Bd. 33 Klostermann, Frankfurt/M. 1981.

Heidegger, Martin *Einführung in die Metaphysik* Niemeyer, Tübingen 1953.

Heidegger, Martin 'Die Frage nach der Technik' in *Vorträge und Aufsätze* Neske, Pfullingen 1985.

Heidegger, Martin 'The German student as worker' (Der Deutsche Student als Arbeiter) in *Reden und andere Zeugnisse eines Lebensweges* ed. Hermann Heidegger *Gesamtausgabe* Bd. 16 Klostermann, Frankfurt/M. 2000.

Heidegger, Martin *Bremer und Freiburger Vorträge* ed. Petra Jaeger *Gesamtausgabe* Bd. 79 Klostermann, Frankfurt/M. 1994.

Heidegger, Martin *Grundbegriffe der Aristotelischen Philosophie* SS 1924 ed. Mark Michalski *Gesamtausgabe* Bd. 18 Klostermann, Frankfurt/M. 2002.

Heidegger, Martin *Prolegomena zur Geschichte des Zeitbegriffs* SS 1925 ed. Petra Jaeger *Gesamtausgabe* Bd. 20 Klostermann, Frankfurt/M. 1979, 3rd emended edition 1994.

Heidegger, Martin *Die Grundprobleme der Phänomenologie* Marburger Vorlesung SS 1927, ed. Friedrich-Wilhelm von Herrmann *Gesamtausgabe* Bd. 24 1975.

Heidegger, Martin *Logik als die Frage nach dem Wesen der Sprache* ed. Günter Seubold *Gesamtausgabe* Bd. 38 Klostermann, Frankfurt/M. 1998.

Heidegger, Martin *'Mein liebes Seelchen!' Briefe Martin Heideggers an seine Frau Elfride 1915–1970* ed. Gertrud Heidegger, dva Munich 2005.

Heidegger, Martin *Metaphysische Anfangsgründe der Logik im Ausgang von Leibniz* Summer Semester 1928 ed. Klaus Held *Gesamtausgabe* Bd. 26 Klostermann, Frankfurt/M. 1978, 2nd ed. 1990.

Heidegger, Martin 'Die onto-theo-logische Verfassung der Metaphysik' in *Identität und Differenz* Neske, Pfullingen 1957, abbreviated OTL.

Heidegger, Martin 'Phänomenologische Interpretationen zu Aristoteles (Anzeige der hermeneutischen Situation)' *Dilthey-Jahrbuch* Bd. 6 1989.

Heidegger, Martin *Phänomenologische Interpretationen zu Aristoteles: Einführung in die phänomenologische Forschung* Frühe Freiburger Vorlesung WS 1921/22 *Gesamtausgabe* Bd. 61, ed. Walter Bröcker and Käte Bröcker-Oltmanns, Klostermann, Frankfurt/M. 1985, 2nd ed. 1994.

Heidegger, Martin *Der Satz vom Grund* Neske, Pfullingen 1957.

Heidegger, Martin *Sein und Zeit* Niemeyer, Tübingen 1927, 15th ed. 1984.

Heidegger, Martin *Hegel 1. Die Negativität* (1938/39, 1941) *2.Erläuterung der 'Einleitung' zu Hegels 'Phänomenologie des Geistes'* (1942) ed. Ingrid Schüßler *Gesamtausgabe* Bd. 68 Klostermann, Frankfurt/M. 1993.

Heidegger, Martin 'Hegels Begriff der Erfahrung' (1942/43) in *Holzwege* Klostermann, Frankfurt/M. 1950, 6th corrected printing 1980.

Heidegger, Martin 'Der Spruch des Anaximander' (1946) in *Holzwege* Klostermann, Frankfurt/M. 1950, 6th corrected printing 1980.

Heidegger, Martin *Der Spruch des Anaximander*, the script of a lecture course that was not delivered and presumed written in summer/autumn 1942, *Gesamtausgabe* Bd. 78 ed. Ingeborg Schüßler, Klostermann, Frankfurt/M. 2010.

Heidegger, Martin 'Überwindung der Metaphysik' in *Vorträge und Aufsätze* 1985.

Heidegger, Martin *Vorträge und Aufsätze* Neske, Pfullingen 1985. Abbreviated V&A.

Heidegger, Martin 'Der Ursprung des Kunstwerkes' (1935/36) in *Holzwege* Klostermann, Frankfurt/Main 1950.

Heidegger, Martin *Vier Seminare* Klostermann, Frankfurt/M.1977.

Heidegger, Martin 'Der Weg zur Sprache' in *Unterwegs zur Sprache* Neske, Pfullingen 1959.

Heidegger, Martin 'Zeit und Sein' in *Zur Sache des Denkens* Niemeyer, Tübingen 1969.

Hobbes, Thomas *Elements of Law* in *Works* Vol. VII.

Hobbes, Thomas *Leviathan* (1651) eds. Richard E. Flathman and David Johnston, Norton, New York/London 1997.

Honoré, A.M. 'Social Justice' in R.S. Summers ed. *Essays in Legal Philosophy* Oxford 1968.

Humboldt, Wilhelm von *Ideen zu einem Versuch, die Grenzen der Wirksamkeit des Staates zu bestimmen* 1792 Verlag Freies Geistesleben, Stuttgart 1962.

Hume, David *An Enquiry Concerning the Principles of Morals* in *Works* Vol. IV.

Hume, David 'Of Commerce' Essay I in Part II *Essays Moral, Political, and Literary* (1752) ed. Eugene F. Miller, reprint Liberty Fund, Indianapolis 1985, 1987.

Hume, David 'Of National Characters' Essay XXI Part I in Hume 1752.

Hume, David 'Of the First Principles of Government' Essay IV, Part I in Hume 1752.

Hyde, Edward *A Brief View and Survey of the Dangerous and Pernicious Errors to Church and State in Mr. Hobbes's Book, Entitled Leviathan*, London 1676.

Jouvenel, Bertrand de *Sovereignty* London 1957.

Joyce, James *Ulysses* Penguin, Harmondsworth 1968.

Jünger, Ernst *Der Arbeiter* 1932 Klett-Cotta, Stuttgart 1982.

Kaltenborn, C. von *Die Vorläufer des Hugo Grotius* Leipzig 1848.

Kant, Immanuel *Der Streit der Fakultäten* 1798 in *Werke* Band VI ed. W. Weischedel Wissenschaftliche Buchgesellschaft, Darmstadt 1964.

Kant, Immanuel *Über den Gemeinspruch: Das mag in der Theorie richtig sein, taugt aber nicht für die Praxis* in *Werke* Bd. VI 1983.

Kant, Immanuel 'Was ist der Mensch?' *Logik* in *Werke* Band III 1983.

Kant, Immanuel *Zum ewigen Frieden* in *Werke* Band VI 1983.

Koshimura, Shinzaburo *Theory of Capital Reproduction and Accumulation* Jesse G. Schwartz (ed.), Toshihiro Ataka (transl.) DPG Publishing, Ontario 1975.

LaFollette, Hugh 'Why Libertarianism Is Mistaken' in *Justice and Economic Distribution* John Arthur and William Shaw (eds.), Prentice Hall, Englewood Cliffs 1979.
URL www.hughlafollette.com/papers/libertar.htm Accessed Dec. 2009.

Lamont, Julian and Favor, Christi Entry on 'Distributive Justice' in the *Stanford Encyclopedia of Philosophy* at URL plato.stanford.edu/entries/justice-distributive/ Accessed December 2009.

Lawrence, T.E. *Seven Pillars of Wisdom* Penguin Modern Classics, Harmondsworth 1962.

Leibniz, G.W. *Frühe Schriften zum Naturrecht* (ed.) Hubertus Busche, Meiner, Hamburg 2003.

Leibniz, G.W. *Monadologie* in *Werke* Bd. I Wissenschaftliche Buchgesellschaft, Darmstadt 1985.

Leibniz, G.W. *Principes de la Nature et de la Grace, Fondés en Raison* in *Werke* Bd. I.

Locke, John *Two Treatises of Government* with an introduction by Peter Laslett, Mentor Books, New York 1965.

Löwith, Karl *Das Individuum in der Rolle des Mitmenschen* (1928) reprinted in *Sämtliche Schriften* Bd. 1 ed. K. Stichweh, Metzler, Stuttgart 1981.

Marx, Karl *Grundrisse der Kritik der Politischen Ökonomie* Dietz, Ost-Berlin 1974.

Marx, Karl *Das Kapital* in *Marx Engels Werke* Bde. 23, 24, 25 Dietz, Ost-Berlin 1962 Abbreviated MEW.

Marx, Karl *Schriften, Manuskripte, Briefe bis 1844* (includes the Ökonomisch-philosophische Manuskripte) MEW Ergänzungsband (Erg. Bd. 1) Dietz, Ost-Berlin 1968.

Mises, Ludwig von *Human Action* Yale U.P. 1949.

Musil, Robert *Der Mann ohne Eigenschaften* Rowohlt, Hamburg 1987.

Nietzsche, Friedrich *Morgenröthe* in *Sämtliche Werke* Kritische Studienausgabe ed. Giorgio Colli and Mazzino Montinari, Bd. 3 dtv/de Gruyter, Berlin 1980. Abbreviated KSA.

Nietzsche, Friedrich *Nachgelassene Fragmente 1869–1889* in *Sämtliche Werke* Kritische Studienausgabe ed. Giorgio Colli and Mazzino Montinari, Bde. 10–13 dtv/de Gruyter, Berlin 1980.

Nozick, Robert *Anarchy, State, and Utopia* Oxford U.P. Blackwell 1974.

O'Neill, Martin 'Liberty, Equality, and Property-Owning Democracy' URL mora.rente.nhh.no/projects/EqualityExchange/Portals/0/articles/ONeill-2008.pdf Accessed Dec. 2009.

Patten, Simon N. *The Development of English Thought* New York 1899.

Plato *Gorgias, The Laws, Parmenides, Republic, The Sophist, Theaitetos* in *Werke* ed. Gunther Eigler, Wissenschaftliche Buchgesellschaft, Darmstadt 1988.

Pollock, Frederick *Oxford Lectures and Other Discourses* London 1890.

Radbruch, Gustav 'Vom individualistischen Recht zum sozialen Recht' (1930) reprinted in *Der Mensch im Recht* Göttingen 1957.

Rawls, John *A Theory of Justice* The Belknap Press of Harvard University Press first edition 1971; abbreviated TJ.

Reuten, Geert and Williams, Michael *The Value-Form Determination of Economic Policy: A dialectical theory of economy, society and state in the capitalist epoch* B.R. Grüner B.V., Amsterdam 1988.

Reuten, Geert and Williams, Michael *Value-Form and the State: The Tendencies of Accumulation and the Determination of Economic Policy in Capitalist Society* Routledge, London & New York 1989.

Ricardo, David *Principles of Political Economy and Taxation* 1821, Prometheus Books, New York 1996.

Ritter, Joachim and Gründer, K. (eds.) *Historisches Wörterbuch der Philosophie* Vol. 9 Wissenschaftliche Buchgesellschaft, Darmstadt 1995.

Rorty, Richard *Essays on Heidegger and Others* Cambridge U.P. 1991.

Rorty, Richard *Truth and Progress* Cambridge U.P. 1998.

Rothbard, Murray N. 'Robert Nozick and the Immaculate Conception of the State' in *Journal of Libertarian Studies* Vol. 1 No.1 1977. URL mises.org/journals/jls/1_1/1_1_6.pdf Accessed December 2009.

Sadurski, Wojciech 'Commutative, distributive and procedural justice – what does it mean, what does it matter?' in *Social Science Research Network Electronic Library.* URL ssrn.com/abstract=1471022 Accessed Dec. 2009.

Schmitt, Carl *Der Begriff des Politischen* (1932) Duncker & Humblot, Berlin 6th ed. 4th printing 1963.

Schmitt, Carl *Legalität und Legitimität* (1932) Duncker & Humblot, Berlin 2nd ed. 1968.

Schmitt, Carl *Politische Theologie* 1922.

Schopenhauer, Arthur *Aphorismen zur Lebensweisheit* Chapter IV 'Von dem, was einer vorstellt' ed. Rudolf Marx, Alfred Kröner Verlag, Stuttgart 1956.

Schumpeter, Joseph A. *Capitalism, Socialism and Democracy* Harper & Row, New York, 3rd edition 1950, paperback edition 1975.

Schumpeter, Joseph A. *Das Wesen des Geldes* Vandenhoeck & Ruprecht, Göttingen 1970.

Schumpeter, Joseph A. *Das Wesen und der Hauptinhalt der theoretischen Nationalökonomie* 2nd ed. Duncker & Humblot, Berlin 1970, unaltered reprint of the first edition from 1908.

Schweickart, David 'Property-Owning Democracy or Economic Democracy?' In Thad Williamson and Martin O'Neill *Property Owning Democracy: Rawls and Beyond* (Blackwell-Wiley, forthcoming) URL www.luc.edu/faculty/dschwei/articles.htm Accessed Dec. 2009.

Searle, John R. 'Social Ontology and Political Power' *Kadish Center for Morality, Law & Public Affairs* 2003. URL www.law.berkeley.edu/centers/kadish/searle.pdf Accessed Jan. 2010.

Smith, Adam *The Theory of Moral Sentiments* (1759) Prometheus Books, New York 2000.

Smith, Adam *The Wealth of Nations* 1776, edited with notes, marginal summary and enlarged index by Edwin Cannan, The Modern Library, New York 2000.

Spencer, Herbert 'The Coming Slavery' in *The Man versus the State* (1884, 1892) ed. Donald Macrae, Penguin, Harmondsworth 1969.

Strauss, Leo *Hobbes' politische Wissenschaft* Luchterhand, Neuwied 1965.

Strauss, Leo *Natural Right and History* Chicago U.P. 1953.

Taylor, Quentin P. 'Property in Rawls's Political Thought' in *The Independent Review* Vol. VIII No. 3 Winter 2004. URL www.independent.org/pdf/tir/tir_08_3_taylor.pdf Accessed Dec. 2009.

Theunissen, Michael *Der Andere: Studien zur Sozialontologie der Gegenwart* 2nd ed. W. de Gruyter, Berlin/New York 1977.

Theunissen, Michael *Sein und Schein: Die kritische Funktion der Hegelschen Logik* Suhrkamp, Frankfurt/M. 1980.

Trawny, Peter *Sokrates oder Die Geburt der Politischen Philosophie* Königshausen & Neumann, Würzburg 2007.

Vallentyne, Peter 'Robert Nozick, *Anarchy, State and Utopia*' in *The Twentieth Century: Quine and After* (Vol. 5 of *Central Works of Philosophy*) ed. John Shand, Acumen Publishing 2006. URL klinechair.missouri.edu/on-line%20papers/Nozick.doc Accessed Dec. 2009.

Vaughan, C.E. *Studies in the History of Political Philosophy Before and After Rousseau* Manchester 1925.

Walzer, Michael *Spheres of Justice: A Defense of Pluralism and Equality* Basic Books, New York 1983.

Weber, Max 'Freiheit und Zwang in der Rechtsgemeinschaft' in *Soziologie Universalgeschichtliche Analysen Politik* Kröner Verlag, Stuttgart 1973.

Weber, Max *Wirtschaft und Gesellschaft* J.C.B. Mohr, Tübingen, 5th. revised edition, 1980.

Whately, Richard *Introductory Lectures on Political Economy* London 1855.

Williams, Michael *Value, Social Form and the State* St. Martin's Press, New York 1988.

Williamson, Thad and O'Neill, Martin 'Property-Owning Democracy and the Demands of Justice' in *Living Reviews in Democracy* 2009. URL democracy.livingreviews.org/index.php/-lrd/article/viewArticle/lrd-2009-5/15 Accessed Dec. 2009.

Zimmerman, Michael E. *Heidegger's Confrontation with Modernity: Technology, Politics, Art* Indiana University Press, Bloomington 1990.

16 Index

ability/excellence 179, 216, 241, 455
advertising 138
Albertus Magnus 460
Alcott, Louisa M. 414
Anaximander 296, 299, 300, 301
Aristotle 3, 4, 5, 8, 15, **18**, 21, 23, 24, 29,
    32, 38, 39, 46, 50, 54, 66, 74, 79, 80,
    91, 92, 94, 96, 100, 106, 110, 111, 113,
    115, 116, 117, 118, 120, 122, 123, 126,
    129, 131, 139, 143, 147, 153, 163, 170,
    171, 173, 174, 178, 179, 181, 183, 185,
    186, 187, 188, 190, 192, 193, 194,
    215, 216, 219, 220, 223, 229, 272,
    277, 289, 295, 299, 346, 370, 372,
    382, 525, 535, 537, 540, **605**, 606,
    607, 608, 610, 611
– Aristotelean 22, 50, 91, 92, 97, 99, 105,
    117, 118, 132, 134, 142, 161, 180, 194,
    197, 205, 315, 317, 340, 605, 609
art of acquiring 126
Arthur, Christopher J. 151, 191, 313
attentiveness 87

Backhaus, Hans-Georg 387
Barker, Ernest 452
Berman, Sheri 330, 331, 332
Bernstein, Richard J. 2
Böhm-Bawerk, Eugen v. 187, 188, 189
Brandom, Robert 2

capitalism
– as gainful game 230
– earning a money income 231
– enterprises in gainful game 233
– labour power in gainful game 232
Cartesian cast of being 110
Clausewitz, Carl Philipp Gottlieb von 561
closing together
– of primal split 85
Commutative justice
– as fair interchanges 182
comparative advantage 676
conclusion
– closing together 68

consciousness 1
– call of conscience 38
– co-knowing 26
– co-knowing of self 39
– subjective 4, 25
cultural identity 668
cultural interchange
– estimative 668

D'Agostino, Fred 254, 255
das Man 79
– people 502
– selfhood 502
– the others 79
Dasein
– a priori being-in-the-world 76
– as free origin of own self-casting 79
– embedded in originary, three-
    dimensional temporality 76
– everyday involvement 75
– no inside and outside for 75
– Selbst des D. 75
– self as radiating back from things and
    others 79
Derrida, Jacques 157
Descartes 4, 26
Descartes, René 57, 105, 195, 285, 319,
    497, 545, 552
– Cartesian 78, 104, 105, 107, 132, 190,
    285, 316, 320, 329, 379, 514, 546
desire
– appetite 127
– derives from lack, absence 137
– for more 93
Destutt de Tracy, A.L.C. 153
Dewey, John 2
Donne, John 87, 223

Eliot, T.S. 16
energy
– at-work-ness 134
enpropriatedness 31
Epstein, Brian 5

equality 111, 112, 113, 179, 186, 205, 207,
        562
– abstract e. of persons 601
– abstract e. of persons before the law
        189
– and fairness 238
– arithmetical 181
– before the law 649
– formal 423, 607
– formal e. of voters 635
– geometrical 181
– individual 591
– material 338
– of being born potentially free 180
– of exchangers in power play 431
– of free, formal personhood 635
– of members of society 338
– of opportunity 208
– of outcome of fair power interplays 207
– of political liberties 257
– of potential to engage in competitive
        struggles 258
– of potentials 208
essence 27
esteem 33
– affirmative reflection 166
– and reputation 37
– and will to power 166
– electoral estimation 618
– estimation 36
– estimation of a special, creative
        individual 530
– honour and fame in social life 215
– human dignity 43
– love of 33
– misestimating 220
– mutual estimation 44
– mutual estimation in providing services
        347, 351
– mutually mirroring recognition and
        estimation 156
– openness and exposure to estimation
        by others 167
– reciprocal estimation 159
– rituals of public recognition 262
– social standing 33
– striving for 33

estimation
– of who-status 37
ethics
– habitual practice of usages in interplay
        172
exchange
– katallaxy 154
– polyarchy of 154
exchange-value
– as elementary socio-ontological
        concept of social power in accord
        with freedom 231
– as social change of position 140

fairness 535
– fair rules of political power play 620
Favor, Christi 237
Feuerbach, Ludwig 18
Fichte, Johann Gottlieb 561
Foucault, Michel 411
free birth 179, 180, 206, 207, 241, 455
– as criterion for distribution 242
freedom
– as spontaneity 164
– granted by the historical time-clearing
        611
– individual freedom hand in glove with
        reification of sociation 262
– moments of particularity and singularity
        in concept of f. 568
– of movement 160
– totalitarian conception of 551
Freeman, Samuel 256
gainful game
– among free individual players 233
– and capitalist employer 232
– and employees 232
– and labour unions 263
– and level playing field 263
– anomalies thereof 261
– as socio-ontological structure and
        movement 236
– incalculable, risky, groundless 234
– monopolies, oligopolies and cartels
        264

Georges, Karl Ernst 415

Gneisenau, August Wilhelm Antonius Graf
    Neidhardt von 561
Goethe, Johann Wolfgang von 561
government
– recognition as legitimate 439
– refusal of recognition as legitimate 442
– securing quotidian, customary way of
    life 267
– social democracy 330

Hardenberg, Karl August Freiherr von 561
Hayek, Friedrich A. 153, 164, 165, 170,
    207, 211, 213, 273, 318, 333, 354,
    363, 364, 407, 464, 543, 622
Hegel, G.W.F. 4, 8, 15, 18, 49, 50, 51, 52,
    53, 54, 55, 56, 57, 60, 64, 65, 68, 69,
    70, 71, 72, 73, 74, 80, 86, 145, 146,
    148, 150, 155, 174, 186, 188, 213,
    269, 271, 289, 290, 291, 292, 297,
    318, 342, 343, 400, 417, 442, 464,
    468, 484, 485, 488, 490, 492, 494,
    497, 498, 500, 526, 531, 533, 543,
    552, 561, 563, 564, 567, 569, 570,
    571, 572, 573, 574, 575, 576, 577,
    578, 579, 580, 582, 583, 585, 589,
    590, 593, 595, 596, 597, 598, 600,
    602, 604, 605, 606, 607, 608, 610,
    612, 613, 615, 618, 629, 631, 632,
    641, 659, 671, 672
– Hegelian 36, 49, 53, 66, 67, 74, 77, 88,
    145, 149, 150, 151, 270, 375, 492,
    525, 532, 564, 569, 574, 582, 632,
    637, 651, 655
Heidegger 459, 460
Heidegger, Martin 169
Heidegger, Martin 1, 15, 17, 23, 28, 33, 35,
    49, 52, 53, 54, 55, 66, 73, 74, 75, 76,
    77, 78, 79, 80, 121, 122, 127, 128,
    130, 143, 154, 274, 275, 287, 293,
    294, 295, 296, 297, 299, 317, 335,
    368, 376, 377, 378, 381, 382, 383,
    403, 464, 479, 494, 496, 497, 498,
    500, 501, 502, 503, 506, 507, 508,
    509, 510, 511, 512, 513, 514, 515, 516,
    517, 518, 520, 522, 526, 527, 528,
    529, 531, 532, 535, 546, 547, 551,
        554, 559, 560, 561, 562, 564, 565,
        566, 567, 568, 614
– Heideggerian 72, 369, 574, 672
Herder, Johann Gottfried von 561
hermeneutic cast
– beingness of beings hermeneutically
    cast 494
– of an age 434
Hitler, Adolf 560
Hobbes, Thomas 74, 173, 211, 353, 464,
    465, 466, 523, 531, 545
Humboldt, Wilhelm von 560, 561, 562
Hume, David 363, 366, 418, 535, 545, 570
Husserl, Edmund 1
Hyde, Edward 443

intentionality 1
interplay 36
– 'uncaring', reified sociating interplay
    347
– abstract simplicity of exchange 280
– abstract, reified exchange i. 351
– among foreign powers 671
– and caring-for 337
– and interchange 153
– and mutual caring-for 340
– competitive 178
– competitive struggle over wages 197
– configurations of mutually estimating
    power interplays 473
– contingency of 192
– engendering trust 162
– exchange and interchange among
    human beings 329
– fathomlessness of 133
– groundlessness thereof 192
– indifference in caring-for 337
– individual powers at work for each other
    156
– mirroring 37
– mutual estimation of individual powers
    156
– mutual recognition 37
– mutual self-interest and alienation 349
– mutually benefical 132
– of self-interests in civil society 283
– of social powers incalculable 162

– openness and exposure to estimation
   by others 167
– play of social powers 135
– power play 156
– reciprocal estimation 159
– social interchange 131
– sociating 133, 139
– sociating i. of civil society fair and just
   535

James, William 2
Jouvenel, Bertrand de 207
Joyce, James 48
judgement
– as primal split 68
Jünger, Ernst 547, 548, 549, 550, 551, 552,
   553, 554, 555, 556, 557, 558, 559,
   560, 564, 566, 567, 569
justice
– always considered in relation to others
   170
– and alien working conditions 203
– and alleviation of poverty 209
– and distribution of honour and fame in
   society 226
– and equity 113
– and fairness 113
– and welfare state 209
– as retaliation 181
– as retribution 181
– commutative 178
– corrective 178
– criterion of neediness 210
– disappearance of commutative justice
   236
– distributive 178, 206
– fair distribution 179
– four dimensions of personal worth 179
– judge as halver in commutative justice
   181
– of competitive struggle 208
– one's fair share 170
– ostensible injustice of capitalist wage-
   labour 198
– possible criteria for just distribution
   206
– redistributive social justice 209

– redistributive social justice a "mirage"
   211

Kaltenborn, C. von 170
Kant, Immanuel 4, 62, 164, 269, 270,
   289, 552, 561, 562, 607, 613, 666
– Kantian 34, 552
kindness 87
Klopstock, Friedrich Gottlieb 561
know-how
– art of acquiring 126
– commercial 127
knowledge
– axiomatic-mathematical casting of
   modern science 329
– guided by insight 138
– productive 110, 138
– productive know-how 126
Koshimura, Shinzaburo 313
Kuhn, Thomas 144

labour power 108, 334, 355, 356, 379,
   391, 401
LaFollette, Hugh 249, 250, 251, 252
Lamont, Julian 237
Lawrence, T.E. 131
Leibniz, G.W. 285, 286, 287, 288, 289,
   290, 291, 293, 319, 386
Lévinas, Emmanuel 78
liberal conception
– of civil society 547
– of division of powers 408
– of freedom 550
– of government 537
– of government and state 569
– of government and state minimal 617
– of right as fairness 302
– of social living 400
– of society 554
– of society and government 546, 675
– of state 572, 604
– of the state 545
liberalism
– abstractness of reified social forms 526
– and individual freedom 531
– blind to the ontological difference 542

- emphasizes freedom of the private individual 541
- neglected ontological problematic of esteem 542
- radical rethinking of 331
- so-called neo-liberalism 331
- socio-ontological critique of 530
Locke, John 190, 268, 523, 531, 537, 538, 539, 540, 541, 544, 569, 578
Löwith, Karl 17, 156, 496

Marx, Karl 92, 94, 100, 106, 109, 151, 183, 184, 185, 186, 187, 188, 190, 193, 198, 199, 201, 262, 280, 281, 286, 311, 312, 330, 347, 348, 349, 350, 352, 368, 369, 370, 371, 373, 374, 375, 378, 379, 380, 381, 387, 677
- Marxian 151, 187, 205, 369, 370, 374, 375
Marx, Rudolf 218
metaphysics 4
- onto-theological 4
- ontotheology 142
- productionist 154
- subject/object m. 4
Mill, J.S. 74, 366
Mill, James 281, 348
mind
- arranges the time-clearing 306
- can direct itself intentionally 306
- leaping in the time-clearung 306
- mind and the time-clearing are the same 308
- openness for time's presencing and absencing of occurrents 306
Mises, Ludwig v. 364, 564
money
- as a medium 111
- as middle term 182
- as store of exchange-value 125
More, Thomas 7
movement
- as presencing and absencing 32
- different ontologies of 130
- effective causal 7
- gainful social 232
- peculiarly social 154

- productive kinesis 7
Musil, Robert 36, 215, 459, 508, 511

nation 667
nation state
- concept of, based on rule of law 670
- sovereign 669
national territory 667
nationalism 675
need
- vs. usage 114
Newton, Isaac 195, 285, 312, 320, 386
- Newtonian 165, 190, 194, 196, 287, 311, 480
Nietzsche, Friedrich 4, 91, 213, 291, 292, 293, 297, 345, 378, 522, 614
nobility
- of birth 179, 207, 241, 455
Nozick, Robert 239, 244, 246, 247
- Nozickian 252
Nye, Joseph 413, 425

O'Neill, Martin 257, 259, 260
ontogenesis
- chronological priority 443
- historico-chronological emergence 245
- human society emerged chronologically, ontogenetically 22
- merely chronological historical origins 175
ontology 2
- apophantic as 2
- disjunction between ontology and ethics 39
- entrenched ontology of whatness 154
- essence 27
- form 128
- hermeneutic as 2
- idea 128
- keeping the ontological difference open 520
- look 128
- of intersubjectivity 1
- of mutually estimative sociating movement 154
- of whatness 2, 18, 157
- of whoness 18, 157

– ontological difference 2, 6
– ontological structure of exchange 154
– ontotheology 142
– quidditas 18
– quissity 18
– sight 128
– species 128
– subject/object split 209
– substance 27

particularity 151
– concrete 281
– p. and singularity of perspectives 467
Patten, Simon N. 354
Peirce, Charles Sanders 2
personhood
– abstractly formal recognition 167
phallocracy 43
Pindar 167
Plato 2, 4, 5, 13, 21, 23, 24, 29, 32, 33, 39,
    45, 46, 49, 50, 51, 56, 58, 70, 80, 92,
    94, 97, 106, 110, 111, 117, 142, 153,
    211, 212, 271, 277, 299, 330, 370,
    372, 460, 462, 468, 479, 498, 535,
    537, 563, 579, 583, 595, 612, 632,
    634, 635
– Platonic 49, 50, 53, 56, 88, 563, 564
plutocracy 257
– plutocratic control 260
– political 265
politeness 42
– formal mode of recognition 160
Pollock, Frederick 333
positivism 564
– formalistic legal 649
– German legal p. 407, 646, 647
– legal 649
– ontological difference closed off
    through p. 4
– sciences turn away from philosophy
    564
potential
– to exchange 124
power
– advertising as rhetorical power 138
– at-work-ness of 134
– brute, physical force of military p. 673

– complementary active and passive 136
– governing starting-point 124
– individual powers at work for each other
    156
– mutual estimation of individual powers
    156
– of freedom of movement 131
– of self-presentation to others 161
– opposed social powers 101
– power game 162
– power play 156
– power struggle over wages and working
    conditions 197
– powerlessness 471
– productive 124
– social power embodied in money-
    capital 93
– social power of exchange-value 135
– starting-point for an interchange 140
– to exchange 124
– useful abilities 155
– validation of individual powers 156
– wealthy more reified social power 209
power interplay
– among nation states 669
power play
– carries over to the state itself 595
powers
– interplay of 110
primal split
– between individual self and world 85
– between singularity and universality 84
principle
– governing starting-point 124
privacy
– garden of 262
proper name 495, 503
proposition
– as primal split 68
Protagoras 459, 460, 461, 464
protectionism 676
psyche
– as openness to the time-clearing 328

question of human being
– historically open toward the future 492
quidditas 18

quissity 18, 78

Radbruch, Gustav 407
Rawls, John 239, 242, 252, 253, 254, 255,
    256, 257, 258, 259, 260, 261, 265
– Rawlsian 237, 242, 243, 258, 259, 261
recognition
– between self-consciousnesses 18
relationship 501
reputation 38
reputational standing 37
Reuten, Geert 313
rhetoric
– as social power 131
Ricardo, David 183, 195, 321, 564, 676
Rickert, Heinrich 419
Rorty, Richard 2
Rothbard, Murray N. 246

Sadurski, Wojciech 238
Scharnhorst, Gerhard Johann David von
    561
Scheler, Max 17, 527
Schelling, Friedrich Wilhelm Joseph 561
Schiller, Friedrich 561
Schleiermacher, Friedrich Daniel Ernst
    561
Schmitt, Carl 267, 423, 645, 646, 648,
    649, 650, 651, 652, 653, 654, 655,
    656, 657
Schopenhauer, Arthur 218, 224, 225, 227,
    229
Schumpeter, Joseph A. 107, 108, 109, 110,
    195, 564, 628, 629, 630, 631, 632,
    633, 634, 635, 636, 638, 640, 643
Schweickart, David 260
Searle, John R. 418, 419
selfhood
– dialectic of self and other 49
– gaining of self 220
– mirror of self-recognition held in the
    hands of others 221
– recognition-mirror of the world 488
– self-comportment 166
– self-presentation of self 158
– self-understanding 158
self-reliance 562

Sextus Empiricus 460
singularity 81, 83, 84, 85, 151
– and medium of language 496
– and selfish particularity 490
– and universality were truly closed
    together 493
– broken mediation between s. and
    universality 487
– contradiction between singularity and
    universality 88
– contradictions among s., particularity
    and universality 491
– existential s. cannot be mediated,
    closed together 89
– exposure of s. to universality 505
– free 332
– gulf between particularity and s. 525
– moments of particularity and s. in the
    concept of freedom 568
– of a definite, singular, individual other
    86
– of freedom 583, 589
– of individual commodities 151
– of money 151
– of the individual suppressed 553
– of who I am 228
– offering s. its identity as self 492
– particularity and s. of perspectives 467
– particularity and universality 473
– problem of 496
– radical 474
– reconcilable with social living 332
– refractory, idiosyncratic 332
– remain always unreconciled 491
– requires mediation with the universal
    523
– selfish 487
– struggle to cast a facet of an other
    historical vista 491
– that remains plural 588
– under protection of abstract rights 665
– unique 281
Smith, Adam 22, 114, 164, 165, 182, 183,
    193, 313, 314, 315, 316, 321, 336,
    354, 359, 360, 364, 374, 385, 386,
    395, 405, 525, 564, 567, 623
social democracy

– tendency toward social totalitarianism 331
social interplay
– dangerous and risky 164
social ontology 18
– and social theory 330
– intersubjectivity 1
– of whoness 18
– supersedes ethics 154
social power
– does not conform with the ontological structure of effective power 610
– kinds of 425
– media as 593
– rhetoric 131
– various kinds of 234
Socrates 461
Spencer, Herbert 634
state
– all-caring social-democratic 211
– nation state 667
– paternalistic or 'nanny' state 406
– totalitarian 211, 512
– welfare state 270
state is legitimately taxation
– state legitimately empowered to raise t. 647
state of nature
– chronologically prior, asocial 466
Stein, Freiherr von 561
Strauss, Leo 172, 173, 174
substance 27
taxation 209, 261, 384
– as universal, real, reified means of financing political power and rule 592
– burden of 408
– bureaucratic t. apparatus 617
– democratic scrutiny of t. 408
– endlessly contentious issue of t. 588
– ever greater t. tribute 409
– intricacy of t. legislation 408
– just t. 591
– levying of t. necessary and legitimate 590
– no t.. without representation 647
– policy 325

– providing social welfare through t. 408
– redistributive t. policy 242
– resources from civil society 663
– tendentially asphyxiating 405
– voracious appetite for t. revenues 409

Taylor, Quentin P. 259, 260
Theunissen, Michael 18, 164
Thomas Aquinas 460
time
– 3D-temporal clearing 6, 38
– beenness 31, 169, 494
– chronological 306
– chronological sense of linear, successive time 172
– chronological, linear time of succession 307
– clock-time 189
– Da of the time-clearing 310
– discontinuous 306
– double temporal vision 137
– exposure of mind and psyche to the 3D-time-clearing 471
– futural horizon of the time-clearing 329
– future temporally withheld 137
– historical age 6
– historical time-clearing 230
– interplays of presencing and absencing 309
– linear 7, 305, 307
– linear succession 306
– mind and the time-clearing are the same 308
– moodful time-clearing 167
– mortal lifetime 307
– openness for presencing and absencing 38
– openness to the quivering time-clearing 327
– presencing and absencing in the 3D-time-clearing 116
– shared, universal-historical world in the 3D-time-clearing 473
– temporal clearing 31
– temporally triple vision 31
– three-dimensional temporal playground 135

- time-clearing 29, 30, 42, 47, 90, 117, 303, 309, 310
- time-clearing of history 513
- time-mind 219
- traditional 1D-linear conception of time lifted off movement 519
- two modes of absence 303
- yesterness 31, 169, 494, 505, 519, 619, 643, 668
- Zeitgeist 219
time-clearing
- people shares an open time-clearing of historical truth 563
tornness 89
totalitarian state
- as counter-casting to liberalism 547
- obedience thereto freedom itself 553
Trawny, Peter 45, 433
truth
- disclosive truth of markets 320
- disclosure in the time-clearing 323
- display of untruth 43
- limited by the horizon of the historical 3D-time-clearing 494

Universal Declaration of Human Rights 179, 670
universality 84, 151
- broken mediation between singularity and u. 487
- contradiction between singularity and universality 88
- singularity and u. never truly closed together 493
usage
- vs. need 114

Vallentyne, Peter 244, 247
value 39
- and income-sources 233
- and revenue-sources 233
- concept trivialized 108
- dividend form of value 232
- estimation 37
- exchange-value 106, 110
- exploitation of surplus value 184
- ground-rent form of value 232
- interest form of value 232
- labour theory of 104
- labour theory of value 183
- magnitude of 109
- money 93
- of commodities 108
- of goods or money relational 125
- of things and persons 180
- potency of money 125
- profit of enterprise form of value 232
- quantitative reification of a qualitative relation 109
- reified 104
- reified value and desire 134
- theory of surplus value 185
- untenability of labour theory of value 189
- untenability of theory of surplus value 196
- use-value 93, 110
- validation of enterprise's operations 283
- value equations 108
- value-form of capital 232
Vaughan, C.E. 451
veil of ignorance 254

Walzer, Michael 237, 239, 240, 241
We
- of a people 633, 640, 667
we ourselves
- in the time-clearing of history 511
Weber, Max 100, 101, 102, 103, 107, 198
welfare state
- contradicts principle of civil society 269
- totalitarian creep of bureaucratically administered state care 332
Western thinking
- radical turn in 32
Whately, Richard 364
whoness 27
- and hubris 222
- and reliability 164
- and self-inflation 222
- arrogance 43
- conceit 43

– flattery 44, 221
– of peoples 669
– ontological dimension of whoness 155
– polite comportment 44
– politeness 42
– proper name 38
– reciprocally showing off 158
– relational 27
– responsibility 38
– self-presentation masks 161
– social roles 44
– somewho 44
Williams, Michael 313
Williamson, Thad and O'Neill, Martin 259,
    260

world
– granting of w. itself 13
– hermeneutic As enables w. to show up
    13
– history 13
– quivering with the resonance of the
    time-clearing 507
world opinion
– moral, rhetorical power of 673

Yunus, Muhammad 177

Zimmerman, Michael E. 154, 317, 547

CPSIA information can be obtained
at www.ICGtesting.com
Printed in the USA
BVHW030941110921
616280BV00003B/186